TAJIKISTAN

Rafis Abazov

MARSHALL CAVENDISH BENCHMARK

NEW YORK

PICTURE CREDITS

Cover photo: © Ton Koene / Peter Arnold Inc.

AFP: 3, 17, 32, 34, 35, 38, 46, 49, 72, 83, 115, 116, 123 • Corbis, Inc.: 1, 9, 13, 14, 20, 22, 23, 27, 28, 29, 33, 37, 44, 48, 52, 53, 54, 55, 60, 66, 68, 69, 70, 78, 84, 88, 92, 96, 98, 100, 104, 107, 110, 111, 112, 118, 126 • Eye Ubiquitous / Hutchison Library: 76 • Peter Fryer / Panos Pictures: 120 • Getty Images: 19, 31, 43, 109 • HBL Network: 5 • R. Ian Llyod: 102 • Lonely Planet Images: 4, 6, 7, 10, 15, 21, 25, 50, 58, 63, 124 • Reuters: 36, 40, 42, 56, 59, 64, 67, 74, 77, 81, 82, 86, 90, 103, 108, 114, 117, 127, 128 • John Spaull / Panos Pictures: 94 • Stockfood / Klaus Arras: 130 • Stockfood / Michael Boyny: 131

PRECEDING PAGE

A group of traditionally dressed women in the region of the Tajikistani capital, Dushanbe.

Marshall Cavendish Benchmark
99 White Plains Road
Tarrytown, NY 10591
Website: www.marshallcavendish.us

© Marshall Cavendish International (Asia) Private Limited 2006
® "Cultures of the World" is a registered trademark of Marshall Cavendish Corporation.

Series concept and design by Times Editions
An imprint of Marshall Cavendish International (Asia) Private Limited
A member of Times Publishing Limited

Library of Congress Cataloging-in-Publication Data
Abazov, Rafis.
    Tajikistan / by Rafis Abazov. – 1st ed.
        p. cm. – (Cultures of the world)
    Summary: "A profile of the history, geography, government, culture, people, and economy
        of the former Soviet republic of Tajikistan" – Provided by publisher.
    Includes bibliographical references and index.
    ISBN 0-7614-2012-6
    1. Tajikistan – Juvenile literature. I. Title. II. Series.
    DK923.A2 2006
    958.6 — dc22   2005001166

Printed in China

7 6 5 4 3 2 1

CONTENTS

Tajik girls carry bundles of firewood home for use as cooking fuel.

The elderly hold a position of respect in Tajikistan.

INTRODUCTION

ONE OF THE MOST inaccessible countries on the Asian continent, Tajikistan has rarely made it into headline news. It has also attracted little attention from world powers or multinational corporations, since it is not rich in major natural resources such as oil or gas. Nevertheless, Tajikistan is fascinating. Historians and archaeologists trace its roots to early central Asian civilizations going back about 3,000 years and claim that the Tajik ancestors contributed greatly to the early Persian and Turkish empires. The Tajik ancestors were famous for their fine handicrafts and serviced trade caravans on the great Silk Road. Tajik writers produced fine poems and songs that became part of the classic literature of the Middle East and South Asia. Tajikistan is also known for its beautiful landscapes and is home to the world's third-highest mountain system, the Pamirs. Since independence from the Soviet Union in 1991, the Tajiks have struggled to keep their country united and to integrate it into the global economy.

GEOGRAPHY

THE REPUBLIC OF TAJIKISTAN is a landlocked mountainous country located in central Asia. It is a H-shaped nation with a land area of 55,252 square miles (143,103 square km), making it the smallest country in central Asia. The total area of Tajikistan is approximately the size of Greece or the state of Wisconsin.

Tajikistan stretches for about 218 miles (351 km) from north to south and about 435 miles (700 km) from east to west. It shares 749 miles (1,206 km) of its borders with Afghanistan in the south, 252 miles (406 km) with China in the east, 541 miles (871 km) with Kyrgyzstan in the northeast, and 721 miles (1,161 km) with Uzbekistan in the northwest and west.

Above: **Alalmeddin Lake in the Fann Mountains in Tajikistan.**

Opposite: **A view of the northern Gombezkol Valley from Gombezkol Pass near Murghab.**

The land that makes up present-day Tajikistan was part of various ancient central Asian states, including the empires founded by Alexander the Great, the Persians, the Mongol warriors, and Tamerlane, the Turko-Mongol conqueror who dominated western Asia in the 14th century. Tajikistan occupies the western slopes of the Pamir Mountains and the southern part of the fertile Fergana Valley. The rivers that begin in the glaciers of Tajikistan are important sources of water for drinking and irrigation not only in Tajikistan but also in neighboring Uzbekistan and Afghanistan.

GEOGRAPHIC REGIONS

Most of Tajikistan's fertile valleys are situated between the upper basins of two of central Asia's major rivers: the Amu Darya and the Syr Darya. The topography of the country is characterized by alternating small fertile valleys and mountain ranges that gradually gain altitude in the east. These mountains are home to the largest glaciers in central Asia and are the sources of many small and big rivers.

Most of the country lies above 10,000 feet (3,050 m). Tajikistan's lowest point is at Sirdar'inskiy in the Fergana Valley in the northern part of the country. The nation's highest point—Ismail Samani Peak (formerly Communism Peak), which is 24,590 feet (7,500 m) high—is located in the east, close to the border with Kyrgyzstan.

Tajikistan has four major regions that are quite distinct in terms of the landscape, climate, and soil found there.

THE NORTHERN REGION Northern Tajikistan straddles the Zeravshan River basin and the southern Fergana Valley, containing some of the most fertile land in central Asia. This is a moderately elevated area with few hills and few mountain ranges. The large flat swaths of land are divided by rows of poplars and mulberry trees into small well-cultivated plots. Completing the landscape are numerous human-made canals, which supply irrigation water from the Syr Darya, Zeravshan, and other rivers to the local cotton fields and apricot and apple orchards.

This is one of the most densely populated areas of the country, and thousands of villages (*kishlaks*) line the major roads. Most of the houses are built of mud bricks, painted in light colors, and usually have small gardens attached to them. This area is home to large Uzbek communities.

Towns and cities have existed in this area for centuries, but few of the region's historic monuments or buildings have survived until the present day. In fact, the city of Khudzhand, the second-largest and one of the oldest in Tajikistan, looks quite modern. Its red-brick and concrete houses, public buildings, and factories suggest a small town in eastern Europe, while the bazaars, or marketplaces, and several newly renovated and newly built mosques show more of a Turkish or Middle Eastern influence.

THE CENTRAL REGION With its relatively higher mountains and numerous smaller valleys, the countryside in central Tajikistan is more diverse than in the north. Several important rivers supply water to various human-made reservoirs or directly to the irrigated fields. High-altitude valleys and small canyons in the mountains are the sites of alpine forests and several national parks with picturesque landscapes. But other small valleys and hill groupings in central Tajikistan are dry and deserted, due to water shortages or deforestation.

The largest city and the capital of the country, Dushanbe, is located in central Tajikistan. It grew from a small trading center at the turn of the 20th century into one of the largest cities in central Asia by the beginning of the 21st century. However, rapid population growth in this part of the country brought about numerous environmental and social problems, which required significant attention from the national government as well as assistance from the international community.

Goatherds on horseback drive their animals across a river in the central Pamir Mountains.

A yurt in the Gombezkol Valley in Badakhshan.

THE SOUTHWESTERN REGION This region is also called Khatlon. It is the warmest part of the country, and its mild climate makes it ideal for growing cotton, vegetables, and other agricultural products. The Vakhsh and Panj river valleys are among the most productive lands in Tajikistan. These rivers begin as rushing streams high in the mountains and flow into the relatively low hills in the south. The banks and surrounding areas of these and other smaller rivers are famous for their *tugais*, dense forests made up of a variety of shrubs and trees.

The largest human-made reservoir, the Nurek, is located in this part of the country, preserving water for one of central Asia's major hydroelectric power stations.

THE EASTERN REGION This part of the country is also called Badakhshan or Kuhistoni Badakhshan. Tajikistan's frontier region, the east is known for its cold continental climate and often inhospitable environment. The nation's highest mountains are located in Badakhshan. Many ranges rise higher than 16,000 feet (4,880 m) above sea level. Glaciers and permafrost cover about 1,900 to 2,300 square miles (4,921 to 5,957 square km), and Tajik scientists claim that these glacier systems are among the 20 largest mountain glaciers in the world. Badakhshan makes up nearly half of the country, but it is sparsely populated since many parts of the region are inaccessible during winter and most of the small alpine valleys cannot sustain intensive agriculture. Badakhshan is home to one of the largest religious minority groups in central Asia—the Ismaili community, which has religious links with the Shiite Muslims of Iran.

CLIMATE

Tajikistan's central location and close proximity to several vast mountain ranges shape its climate. The unique feature of Tajikistan's annual temperatures is that their fluctuation depends on the area's elevation above sea level and not necessarily on the season or time of the year. Therefore some parts of northern Tajikistan are warmer than other areas to the south and east. In general, precipitation and temperatures vary widely both in summer and winter.

In the valleys of northern and central Tajikistan, the climate is relatively mild and dry. Temperatures range from 7°F (-14°C) to 45°F (7°C) in January, and the average daily temperature is between 79°F (26°C) and 95°F (35°C) in July. In most of the valleys of southern Tajikistan, the climate is subtropical, with slightly warmer average temperatures.

The weather in the mountains of eastern Tajikistan, however, is characterized by extremes. In the mountain ranges with low altitudes, the climate is drier, with temperatures ranging from 0°F (-18°C) to 41°F (5°C) in January and between 50°F (10°C) and 72°F (22°C) in July. The climate is more severe in the high Pamirs (13,120 feet, or 4,002 m, and higher), with temperatures dropping even lower. Rainfall varies between 7 inches (18 cm) in the northern and southern parts of the country and 40 to 50 inches (102 to 127 cm) in the central region. Tajikistan also possesses some of the most extensive water resources in central Asia, stored in numerous mountain lakes, glaciers, and reservoirs.

Tajikistan has been affected by global warming and the drying up of the Aral Sea, located in Uzbekistan and Kazakhstan. For several years in a row, a harsh drought plagued the Fergana Valley and vast areas of southern Tajikistan. In addition, summers were drier in central Tajikistan, and winters were much colder in the more mountainous parts of the republic. Deforestation of the mountain slopes has increased the risk of landslides across the nation as well. There were also alarming reports about the rapid shrinking of some of the glaciers in central and eastern Tajikistan. As the land is altered and as climate patterns change, even wiser management and monitoring of the nation's land and resources will be needed.

FLORA

Tajikistan is home to a diverse array of plants and trees, ranging from desert and steppe plants to alpine forests. Experts have identified more than 5,000 species of plants present in the nation.

Today the native flora of the valleys and steppes has been largely replaced by many domesticated plants. Often, rows of cotton spread for acres, leaving little space for wild vegetation. The land along the roads and canals and around the cities and towns is often reserved for grape arbors as well as apple, pear, and apricot trees. Land along the banks of some rivers is covered with poplars, reeds, and plum grass. Collectively, they form the *tugais*, impenetrable tangles of shrubs, swamp grass, and trees. During recent decades, however, the *tugais* have nearly disappeared since farmers have cut down vast tracts to use the land for cultivation and grazing.

On the slopes of low-altitude mountains and hills, different types of plant life abound. Grains, potatoes, vegetables, and fruit trees replace the rows of cotton. Pistachios, Bukhara almonds, hawthorns, junipers, walnuts, wild apples, cherries, plums, and other shrubs and trees find refuge along the mountain rivers and creeks forming small islands of natural habitat. Medieval chronologies report that about 1,000 years ago, large forests covered the slopes of numerous mountain ranges and hills.

However, the local population reclaimed the land to cultivate various cash crops and used the forest as a source of fuel and wood for both construction and industry. At present, forests occupy less than 4 percent of the country, and they continue to shrink due to the lack of funding for preservation and reforestation activities.

The natural habitat has been largely preserved in the alpine areas, especially in the eastern parts of the country. Junipers, barberries, pistachios, and some other trees can be found in these areas. The pastures and open fields of the alpine areas are rich with grass during summer and are used for fattening large herds of domesticated sheep, especially a local breed of fine-fleece sheep.

Tajikistan's highest mountains, such as the Pamirs, have sparse vegetation, usually the small bushes and grasses that can survive frigid winter temperatures.

Sparse vegetation grows on the shore of a high-altitude lake in the central Pamir Mountains.

Tajikistan's mountains are home to a variety of wildlife, including the ibex.

FAUNA

A wealth of animal life finds refuge in the valleys and forests and on the mountain slopes of Tajikistan. The nation's lowland hollows and dry steppes are home to many reptiles such as saw-scaled vipers, Egyptian sand boars, tortoises, and deadly central Asian cobras. Among mammals, it is still common to see porcupines, gerbils, and hamsters in open fields or on small hills. In the past these areas were inhabited by the famous central Asian gazelles, creatures that inspired many local poets and painters to use their images in famous works. However, the claiming of once wild land for agriculture and uncontrolled hunting contributed to the near disappearance of these gorgeous animals by the beginning of the 21st century.

The forests that blanket the mountain slopes and the banks of many rivers are populated by Bukhara deer, jackals, leopards, wild boars, bears, wolves, and ibex. At higher altitudes the alpine forest gives sanctuary to Siberian ibex, snow leopards, argalis, and numerous species of birds, including Himalayan and Tibetan snow cocks and golden eagles. In the nation's rockier regions it is still possible to see the world's largest wild sheep, the Marco Polo sheep, whose nearly 3-foot-long (0.9-m-long) outward-spreading horns were considered trophies prized by royalty and displayed in various palaces in Asia and Europe. Many central Asian historians reported that the local rulers (*begs* and khans) used these forests as hunting grounds. However, in the 19th and 20th centuries, the areas of wild forest shrank

THE GREAT SILK ROAD

This ancient network of trade routes connected China with western Europe. More than 3,700 miles (5,957 km) long, it started somewhere in what is now north-central China. One route passed through China's western provinces, the Tian Shan and Pamir *(below)* mountains, and Khotan, Yarkent, Balkh, Zemm, and Merv (territories of present-day Uzbekistan, Turkmenistan, and Afghanistan). The other route went through Turpan, Kashgar, Samarqand, Bukhara, Amol, and Merv, on to the eastern Mediterranean Sea and Byzantium and Rome. In the late Middle Ages, the major cities on the road served as important trade centers, linking India and Persia with the rising eastern European states. Merchants carried gold, silver, and weaponry eastward and brought carpets, silk, opium, spices, and luxury goods westward.

The earliest recorded references to the great Silk Road can be traced to the second and first centuries B.C. Life along the road was ever changing, calm when peace prevailed in the vast steppes of Eurasia and tumultuous when war gripped the region. Frequent military campaigns as well as changes in political conditions and the climate redrew the route over centuries. The Venetian adventurer Marco Polo (circa 1254–1324) traveled the road and reached the court of Kublai Khan (1215–94), the Mongol emperor and the grandson of Genghis Khan. Marco Polo became the first European to travel and describe the Silk Road.

The Silk Road passed through the land populated by the Tajiks in the medieval era. Numerous remains of caravanserais, or caravan inns, can still be found in present-day Tajikistan.

significantly, and many animals were threatened with extinction. The risk persists. Experts estimate that only between 120 and 300 snow leopards are left in the wild in Tajikistan.

Various types of freshwater fish, including trout, carp, and common marinka, can be found in the country's many rivers, creeks, and lakes. Tajikistanis like to fish both for recreation and for personal consumption, but a commercial fishing industry has yet to be fully developed in the country.

CITIES

Since ancient times many small trading centers and cities have sprung up in the territory that is present-day Tajikistan. However, due to the numerous devastating feuds and conflicts that have affected the central Asian region, few have survived until the modern era. The gradual decline in trade on the great Silk Road contributed to the further deterioration of urban centers.

By the time the Tajik Soviet Socialist Republic was established in September 1924, only about 10 percent of the nation's population lived in cities. The country, however, experienced rapid urbanization during the second half of the 20th century. By the beginning of the 21st century, nearly 30 percent of the population lived in cities and urban centers, contributing to the growth of Dushanbe, Khudzhand, Qurghonteppa, Kulob, and many other urban centers.

DUSHANBE Called Stalinabad between 1929 and 1961, Dushanbe is Tajikistan's capital and the largest metropolitan center in the country. It is located on the Varzob River about 3,000 feet (915 m) above sea level in the Hisor Valley.

Dushanbe was once a small village and an important trading post that grew increasingly famous for its Monday (which is the meaning of *Dushanbe* in Tajik) bazaar for caravans traveling between Samarqand and Bukhara—in what is today Uzbekistan—and Afghanistan. Initially the community had little political significance. In 1925 the Soviet authorities in Moscow chose Dushanbe as the capital of the newly created republic that was then a part of the Soviet state.

The population of the city grew rapidly—from about 6,000 in 1925 to 100,000 in 1941 to about 600,000 in 1991. The Tajik government invested heavily in city planning, as it wanted to avoid the congestion of the narrow and chaotic streets

An aerial view of the capital city, Dushanbe.

found in many older cities. A grid pattern was adopted, and almost all the streets were built along straight lines, dividing the city into square blocks. Four- to six-floor modern buildings made of brick or concrete reflect the European architectural style that dominates the central part of the city. Dushanbe has received a large influx of refugees and temporary workers since 1991. It is estimated that between 1 and 1.5 million people lived in Dushanbe (including its suburbs) in 2005. Many newcomers settled in the suburban districts, building small Eastern-style houses, *chaikhanas* (teahouses), restaurants, and shops.

The city is now home to the national government, several universities and colleges, the national library and museum, major theaters, world-class hotels, an international airport, and the headquarters of various national and international agencies and organizations. In the second half of the 20th century the city also became an important business center with several thriving industries, including textiles, silk, tobacco, and food products.

KHUDZHAND This city was known as Leninabad between 1936 and 1991. With a population of about 160,000 people, it is the second-largest city in Tajikistan and the center of the Leninabad region. It is located on the banks of the Syr Darya River in the northern Fergana Valley.

Tajik historians believe that Khudzhand is one of the oldest cities in central Asia. It is mentioned in ancient Greek chronicles. In 329 B.C. Alexander the Great stormed and captured the city, which was then an important trading and political center. For several centuries, the city continued to serve as a trading post in the area, experiencing its share of setbacks and successes.

Khudzhand faced one of its greatest challenges in the early 13th century when it was destroyed by the Mongols led by Genghis Khan. It was rebuilt a few decades later but was destroyed again several times during numerous intra-regional wars. No prominent ancient or medieval buildings or memorials survived the conflicts. However, a large collection of ancient and medieval artifacts in Khudzhand's historical museum, as well as the ruins of an old citadel and a medieval mausoleum, remind visitors of the past glories of the city.

In the mid-20th century, the Soviet government invested in establishing several large industrial enterprises, including one of the largest silk-processing plants in central Asia, as well as textile, metallurgy, and food-processing factories. Khudzhand's bazaars, mosques, and colorful shopping centers add a festive flavor to the city.

KULOB With about 80,000 people, Kulob is the third-largest city in Tajikistan. It is located in the southwest on the banks of the Yakhsu River.

Khudzhand was one of the central Asian cities that benefited immensely from trade along the great Silk Road, collecting taxes or providing military convoys to trade caravans. However, use of the road declined in the 18th and 19th centuries with the rise of cheaper maritime routes from Europe to India and China.

It is one of the oldest cities in the country, as mentioned in several ancient and medieval chronicles. Like Khudzhand, most of Kulob's historical buildings, found in the "old city," were destroyed in the medieval era or during the clashes of the 19th and 20th centuries.

Today Kulob is a prominent agricultural center that specializes in cotton, grain, and food processing. Although many industries and enterprises experienced difficulties and decline during the recession of the 1990s, Kulob is working hard to broaden and strengthen its economic base.

Tajiks trade at a bazaar in the northwestern part of the country.

QURGHONTEPPA The fourth-largest city in the country, Qurghonteppa has a population of about 65,000 people. It is located in the Vakhsh River valley in southwestern Tajikistan. A modern city, Qurghonteppa is one of the region's major industrial centers. There are several food- and cotton-processing plants, as well as businesses that specialize in the repair of machinery. Tajik archaeologists have discovered and studied the ruins of a large ancient settlement found near the city's present site. Some of the artifacts from that old community are displayed in the local museum.

KHOROG The capital of the Badakhshan Autonomous Province, Khorog is a city of about 30,000 people. Situated about 7,200 feet (2,196 m) above sea level, the city has one of the nation's highest elevations. Located on the banks of the Ghund River in eastern Tajikistan, Khorog is a city with a brisk economy, several small factories, a university, and a theater.

HISTORY

TAJIKISTAN, LIKE MOST other central Asian states, is a young nation. It achieved its independence in 1991 after the breakup of the Soviet Union. This land and its people have a long and fascinating history. The ancestors of the Tajiks lived for centuries in what is today Afghanistan, Kyrgyzstan, Tajikistan, and Uzbekistan, and their history is inseparable from that of the rest of central Asia.

The Tajiks contributed significantly to the development of ancient Bactria and Sogdiana, bravely fighting the armies of Alexander the Great, the Persians, the Arabs, and centuries later the hordes of Genghis Khan. Silk, handmade rugs, weaponry, jewelry, and many other products, made by the skillful local craftspeople, were prized not only across central Asia, but also in many parts of China, India, Persia, the Middle East, and the Byzantine empire.

Several factors contributed to the rise and fall of the central Asian civilizations. Fertile land, a mild climate, and an abundance of natural resources in the region provided local craftspeople with the necessary means of pursuing their trades. In addition, the people settled in towns and cities that were on or near the great Silk Road. The area became a melting pot of cultures, from the region's more established communities to the nomads who inhabited the Eurasian steppes.

Above: **The gates of Hisor Fort, built under Islamic rule in Tajikistan.**

Opposite: **A large hammer and sickle sculpture in Dushanbe serves as a powerful reminder of the decades the people of Tajikistan lived under Soviet rule.**

EARLY DAYS

Tajik, Russian, and Western archaeologists have conducted major excavations of cities and towns that flourished from the eighth to the fourth

A sculptor's portrayal of Alexander the Great. The people of central Asia strongly resisted Alexander's invasion, but after three years of onslaught he finally defeated them.

centuries B.C. in what is today Tajikistan. Piece by piece, they have uncovered the once mysterious histories of the legendary Bactrian and Sogdian empires. Even so, many pages of the histories of those states are still blank. People of this region most likely developed agriculture and industries in the eighth century B.C. and became actively involved in a trade network. They also acquired military and administrative skills.

When Alexander the Great led his Greek army into the region, he discovered prosperous cities, large and small, that had been integrated into the powerful Persian state and whose people followed the Zoroastrian religion. Alexander defeated local resistance and left behind a small Greek-influenced colony. The ancient Greeks who remained in the region interacted with local residents, and the cultures of the two groups blended. Numerous remnants of the art of this era can be seen in local museums and still fascinate scholars and the general public alike.

Bactria existed for nearly 200 years, but it was destroyed in devastating wars in the second and first centuries B.C. After decades of war and other turbulent events, the area became a part of another powerful state—the Kushan empire, which probably lasted until the late fourth or early fifth century A.D. During this era, local people developed art and culture and established their own writing system based on the Greek and Aramaic alphabets. They built numerous canals for irrigation and constructed many urban areas. Some ancient sources called Bactria "the country of a thousand cities." The people traded mostly with India, China, and the Roman empire, traveling

BACTRIA

Bactria was one of the oldest states in central Asia. It was the home of Persian-speaking people from about the eighth century B.C. and is thought to be the birthplace of Zoroaster, the founder of the ancient Persian religion, Zoroastrianism. Bactria was situated between the Hindu Kush Mountains and the Amu Darya River, in present-day Afghanistan, Tajikistan, and Uzbekistan. Its capital city, Bactra, was located in what is today northern Afghanistan. Since the 19th century the site has been no more than a village near the present-day city of Mazar-e Sharif.

Despite its rugged terrain of mountains and deserts, Bactria was strategically located on the great Silk Road. To control the lucrative trade and to try to subdue the troublesome nomads inhabiting Bactria, Cyrus the Great (circa 585–529 B.C.) incorporated Bactria and its nomadic people into the vast Persian empire that once stretched from Egypt to India. Alexander the Great (356–323 B.C.), during his conquest of the Persian empire, claimed Bactria in about 328 B.C. and ordered the execution of Bessus, who was then the ruler of the state.

Alexander left a small Greek garrison in Bactria and installed a Greek governor before continuing to India on his campaign. For the next half century, Bactria was a province of the Seleucid empire, ruled by Alexander's Macedonian Greek successors. During the reign of the ruler Diodotus I, however, Bactria revolted and became independent.

Despite its independence, Bactria remained an island of Greek culture in central Asia. During its zenith, Bactria controlled a significant part of what is today Afghanistan, Tajikistan, and Uzbekistan. In about 135 B.C., however, Sacae nomads from the steppes overran the country. Kushan nomads, from the eastern steppes, in turn conquered the Sacae and introduced their Buddhist religion to Bactria. By about 55 B.C., Bactria had disappeared as an independent political entity, and its territory became home to various nomadic groups.

The region of Bactria then became known as Balkh, and from the seventh century onward Islam began spreading through the area. Still to this day, though, the magnificent culture of Bactria continues to fascinate people, and artifacts of Bactrian culture, such as the large 20-stater gold coin with the profile of King Eucratides *(above)*, are displayed in major British, Russian, Tajikistani, and other museums.

to different parts of the world and bringing home new ideas and beliefs. Also during this period, Buddhist, Manichaean, and Christian (mainly the Nestorian Eastern Church) religions spread in central Asia, peacefully coexisting with Zoroastrian beliefs. In the fifth to the eighth centuries A.D., unrest generally prevailed when the region entered another wave of turbulent wars and conflicts with various Turkic-speaking tribes that had arrived from east-central Asia.

THE GOLDEN AGE

Between the sixth and eighth centuries A.D., central Asia underwent several fundamental changes. In the sixth century, probably even earlier, Turkic-speaking peoples began to arrive in the region in large numbers from their homelands in Siberia, Mongolia, and the northern steppes of China. Through both wars and peaceful agreements, Turkish peoples acquired control over the entire central Asian region, establishing vast but often unstable realms. These empires spread sometimes up to several million square miles. The nomads brought along not only their

ZOROASTER

Zoroaster was the legendary founder of the Zoroastrian religion, whose followers are often mistakenly believed to be worshipers of fire. Scholars still dispute the facts of his life and if he was even a real person at all. According to ancient sources, he was born in 628 B.C. and died in 551 B.C. He is considered to be one of the first to propose the notion of monotheism, the concept of worshiping one god. His teachings were reflected in the sacred book *Avesta* (also called *Zend-Avesta*). The original manuscript was lost in ancient times, probably destroyed during Alexander the Great's conquest of ancient Persia, but the loss did not prevent Zoroaster's teachings from influencing religious and philosophical thought in central Asia and the Middle East for many centuries to come.

Turkic language and culture, but also their superb military organization and skills in warfare. Often these newcomers settled close to central Asian cities and towns, adopting local traditions and cultures while their rulers indulged themselves in the luxuries of life. Gradually they lost their foothold in the region and were defeated by new conquerors. This political cycle would repeat itself time and again.

The second major change arrived from a very different direction and was in many ways more fundamental and profound. In the seventh and eighth centuries, the Muslim Arabs arrived in central Asia to spread Islam, a religious system taught by Prophet Muhammad. The Arabs conquered major cities in the region one by one and finally reached the western outskirts of the Chinese empire. In the decisive Battle of Talas in 751, the Arabs and the Chinese fought each other. Both armies suffered such huge losses that both were forced to retreat. Still, the conflict established a rough dividing line. For many centuries to come, the western outskirts of the Chinese empire became the boundary between the Islamic and Chinese worlds.

Initially the local population resisted the Arabs, but gradually, over many decades, they began accepting Islam. The caliphs, rulers of the Islamic world, encouraged the development of Islamic culture.

They tolerated other religions and cultures and supported numerous artists and scientists who arrived in the caliphate from around the world. Central Asia became one of the strongholds of Islamic civilization,

Opposite: **Genghis Khan was known for his vicious attacks, the mere threat of which often convinced his opponents to surrender rather than put up a fight.**

and central Asians contributed significantly to the great achievements of the time. Tajik scholars believe that many of the best examples of early Tajik culture come from this era. For example, the poet Rudaki produced beautiful and fascinating verse; Firdawsi wrote his monumental *Shahnameh* (*Book of Kings*), a poetic chronicle of the Persian world; and Ibn Sina (also known as Avicenna) wrote his encyclopedic works on medicine, astronomy, and philosophy.

Then, between the 10th and 12th centuries, central Asia began experiencing the first signs of decline. As the caliphate weakened and central Asian states and principalities became politically divided, central Asian rulers were increasingly involved in numerous internal wars as well as conflicts with the outside world. This further undermined their stability and unity, as new threats were rising from the east.

THE ERA OF DECLINE

Between 1219 and 1224 the Mongols, led by Genghis Khan, descended on the area, setting off the most devastating war in the region's history. These invaders conducted very different types of military campaigns. Not only did they crush armies and destroy fortresses that attempted any form of resistance, they also massacred the residents of entire cities, and even provinces, and destroyed irrigation systems and vital infrastructure. A number of cities were burned to ashes, and many irrigated fields, farms, wineries, and gardens were turned into barren wastes. The devastation was so complete that many areas would never be able to reclaim their former glories.

Despite the rapid decline these campaigns set off in the region, the huge Mongol empire—probably the largest in the medieval era—lasted only a few decades and experienced its own decline with the death of

Genghis Khan and the intense strife among his successors that followed.

Central Asia gradually found itself part of a blossoming economic network, though on several occasions local rulers such as Tamerlane tried to revive past glories by waging new wars and spending handsomely on new fortresses, palaces, public buildings, and monuments. By the 17th and 18th centuries, most international traders avoided central Asia, finding that sea routes from Europe to India and China were faster and safer. Meanwhile the central Asian economies continued to be threatened by internal wars and rivalries and increased bandit activity. Roving thieves and hoodlums raided trade caravans, or even small frontier cities and towns, capturing people who were then sold in slave bazaars across the region. In such an environment of chaos and turmoil, there was little technological innovation, since local economies remained significantly underdeveloped.

During this era new powerful khanates, or principalities, emerged in the region: Bukhara, Kokand, and Chorasmia. They vigorously competed for political dominance in various parts of the region, including the land populated by the Tajiks' ancestors. They invested seemingly boundless economic and human resources in a succession of brutal wars.

THE RUSSIAN EMPIRE

In the 19th century a new superpower emerged to the north of central Asia—the Russian empire. The Russian czars and their administrations made clear their interest in developing trade relations with central Asian khanates as well as in ending slave trade in the region. In addition, czarist military ministers were interested in establishing military and diplomatic control of the area, as they became increasingly alarmed by the aggressive British takeover of the Indian subcontinent, Afghanistan, and Persia. During that time, very little was known in Russia and Europe about the khanates. Their cultures remained a mystery, and their supposed wealth became the focal point of numerous legends. Tales of diamonds, rubies, and hoards of gold hidden in palaces and the ruins of ancient cities were repeated again and again.

In the second half of the 19th century the czarist army invaded central Asia and, after several decisive battles, asserted control over most of the region. Still, it took about 30 years for the Russians to establish dominance over what is today Tajikistan, since some communities mounted significant resistance to the invaders. In order to pacify the local

population, the czarist administration opted for diplomatic and military control over the region, and all middle- and high-level decisions were exclusively reserved for members of the vast colonial administration. But the local administration was left intact, and some degree of political power remained in the hands of the area's original central Asian inhabitants. The judiciary system at the community level was also left in the hands of local judges (*qadis*) who dispensed justice according to Islamic law (Shariah).

On the economic front, the colonial administration introduced few restrictions and actively promoted trade between Russia and its central Asian colonies. New railroad lines were built to Tashkent and Samarqand. This significantly increased trade volume in the region, and new small factories sprang up in major urban areas, especially those that processed

Above: **A gathering of Bolshevik honor guards in Petrograd, Russia.**

Opposite: **Nicholas II was the last czar of the Russian empire.**

THE GREAT GAME

This term is widely used to describe the bitter 19th-century Anglo-Russian rivalry for influence in central Asia. British and Russian strategists, mainly young military officers, saw the need for greater control over central Asia. They argued that before the 19th century most military campaigns against the Indian subcontinent were launched from central Asia, which at the time included Afghanistan and the eastern part of Iran. Thus, to the British, a strong foothold in central Asia was pivotal for defending their interests in India against Russian advances. In the meantime, it was crucial for Russia to defend its communications lines with Siberia and the Russian Far East by controlling central Asia, or what the then British prime minister Winston Churchill called the "soft underbelly" of the Russian empire.

The British and Russians initiated a number of spying and counterspying operations and highly adventurous geographic expeditions in search of local allies and routes for troops. These activities were recounted and glorified by such famous writers as Rudyard Kipling. The Russians conducted their first expedition to Khiva in 1839–40, but the campaign was unsuccessful, and they lost a number of soldiers and officers. Meanwhile the British lost their entire expedition army in a disastrous defeat in Afghanistan in 1842. Two British officers, Colonel Charles Stuart and Captain Arthur Connolly, were captured and hanged in Bukhara in 1842. Over time, fortune changed for these foreign powers, and the Russians defeated the Kokand khanate's army, capturing Tashkent, an important economic outpost of the khanate, in 1865; Khudzhand in 1866; and Kokand in 1875. The Russians also established their influence over the Bukhara khanate (in 1868), advancing all the way to the borders of Afghanistan, the last political barrier before India. Perceiving this advance as a direct threat to British interests in India, the British pushed on to the northwest, and after two Anglo-Afghan Wars (1838–42 and 1878–80), they established control over Afghanistan.

The strategic importance of central Asia was highlighted again in the early 20th century by Sir Halford John Mackinder, a British political geographer. He produced a simple geopolitical formula: "Who rules the Heartland [which included central Asia] commands the World-Island [the Eurasian continent]. Who rules the World-Island commands the World."

Since the Soviet Union was dissolved in 1991, a new competition for political influence and a share in the central Asian market—especially its natural resources—has emerged among various new powers. This competition has often been described in terms of establishing influence over the newly independent central Asian republics in a manner strategically similar to the campaigns and initiatives of Britain and Russia in the 19th century.

cotton, one of the main export commodities of the region. Nevertheless, many parts of central Asia experienced little social or cultural change and remained isolated from the outside world.

THE BOLSHEVIKS AND THE SOVIET SYSTEM

The Bolsheviks, a political group that overthrew the ruling Soviet regime in 1917, were locked in a bitter civil war for nearly five years. During this period, many parts of central Asia regained a significant degree of autonomy, or self-rule, from the Russian authorities. Only in 1921–22 did the Bolsheviks re-establish their control over most of central Asia, but this control was often limited, especially in the Pamir Mountains and parts of the Fergana Valley.

In order to win political support from the populace, the Bolshevik government entrusted many positions in the local and regional administration to the native intelligentsia and professionals. After a few years of consultations and planning, the Tajik Soviet Socialist Republic was established in 1924, its borders officially set by communist party officials in Moscow. In 1929 it was granted the status of a union republic, becoming a main part of the USSR, and was granted control of the territory that makes up Leninabad province. The Communist Party of Tajikistan came to power and remained the single ruling party for the next 70 years.

This was the first time in the history of the Tajik people that they were recognized as a nation-state and were able to develop their own distinct and defined economy, education system, culture, language, and art. However, this development came at a price. Soviet authorities established firm control over the political,

A statue of Vladimir Lenin stands outside a building in Dushanbe. Lenin was the leader of the Bolsheviks.

military, and diplomatic affairs of the republic. Bolshevik officials also endorsed a one-party political system and introduced heightened state control over economic development and the centralized five-year planning system.

In addition, Russian leaders banned private ownership of land and free entrepreneurship, while nationalizing most of the industries and banks. Thousands of individuals who resisted the Soviet system were imprisoned, exiled to Siberia, or executed. All political and religious organizations, except the Bolshevik party (eventually renamed the Communist Party) and its youth wing (called Komsomol), were banned. A Tajik government was in place, but it had little say in policy making, since it was obliged to get approval from the Soviet politburo for practically all national political and economic decisions. No free discussions and no criticism of the Soviet system or of the Communist Party were permitted.

Mikhail Gorbachev was secretary-general of the Soviet Union's Communist Party from 1985 to 1991. His years in power were marked by greater political freedom in the Soviet Union and its territories.

Only in the mid-1980s did the situation begin to change, as liberal-minded Soviet leader Mikhail Gorbachev came to power and launched a program of greater freedom and openness called perestroika. The Tajik political leaders and intelligentsia seized the opportunity and began criticizing many aspects of the Soviet social and political system and its totalitarian control of Tajikistan. Gradually, some groups in Tajikistan began demanding full independence.

INDEPENDENCE

The year 1991 became an important benchmark in the history of the Soviet state and of Tajikistan in particular. Several republics of the Soviet Union seized the opportunity to declare independence from the Soviet state, which, under pressure from various political groups, disbanded in December 1991.

Tajikistan declared its independence three months earlier in September 1991. The Tajik authorities immediately introduced many changes.

They established control over the banking and financial systems of the republic and nationalized many industrial enterprises that had been under the control of Moscow in the past. They also established their own military and security forces.

CIVIL WAR AND RECONCILIATION

A short time later, in 1992–93, the political situation in the republic became increasingly unstable. This was due to the growing confrontation between the conservative Tajik government, dominated by former communists, and members of the opposition front that included members of the liberal intelligentsia, democratic organizations, and Islamic groups. As in many developing nations, the struggle for power and reform was complicated by regional rivalries that existed among several political clans. Soon the political confrontation escalated into a devastating civil war, as both sides turned to violence, destroying property and kidnapping and killing opponents. According to some estimates, as many as 100,000 people were killed in the fighting, and about 200,000 refugees escaped to neighboring states.

PEACE ACCORD

It took several years before the rival factions were brought to a negotiating table under pressure from the United Nations, the United States, and Russia, the largest and most powerful state to emerge after the breakup of the Soviet Union. The intensive negotiations between the government, led by President Imomali Rakhmonov, and the United Tajik Opposition (UTO), led by Said Abdullo Nuri, continued throughout 1996 and 1997. In 1997 a peace accord was signed and an agreement to share power was finally achieved. A percentage of the positions in the government, army, police, and local administration was reserved for each of the opposition groups. In exchange, all parties agreed to end hostilities and dismantle local militia and armed paramilitary units. They also took part in the elections and established a reconciled and united governmental front.

Left: **Tajik president Imomali Rakhmonov** *(left)* **and UTO leader Said Abdullo Nuri** *(right)* **shake hands after signing the peace agreement in Moscow to end the civil war. United Nations Secretary-General Gerd Dietrich Meriam** *(center)* **looks on.**

Opposite: **A man in Dushanbe buys as many loaves of bread as he can carry, after fighting in the country caused food distribution problems.**

GOVERNMENT

ALTHOUGH THERE WERE a number of peculiarities rooted in central Asian cultural traditions, Tajikistan's modern governmental institutions and political culture were developed under the overwhelming influence of the Soviet Union's ideology and political system. The political changes that were brought about in the post-independence era significantly altered the ways in which the government functions today.

One of the most important features of Tajikistan's system of government is the concentration of enormous influence and executive power in the hands of the president and his administration. The other notable feature is the relative weakness of political parties and the sustained strength of groups built around regional political networks. Tajiks often support and vote for political leaders based on candidates' regional or local affiliation and rarely on their political views.

Above: **A building destroyed during the civil war in Tajikistan.**

Opposite: **A Tajik man casts his ballot during parliamentary elections in Dushanbe in 2000.**

After declaring independence, the conservative government resisted any kind of radical political and economic reforms and stuck to Soviet-era policies and views. In 1992 civil war, fuelled by a regional rivalry and growing Islamic radicalism, broke out in Tajikistan, leading to the removal of President Rakhman Nabiyev. After numerous clashes between the government and the opposition, a coalition of regional leaders installed Imomali Rakhmonov as the head of state.

In 1994 Rakhmonov won the presidential election. Then, in 1997, after signing the peace accord with the United Tajik Opposition (UTO), several government positions were filled with UTO supporters. In a bitterly contested presidential election in 1999, the UTO candidate lost to President Rakhmonov.

NATIONAL AND LOCAL GOVERNMENTS

Tajikistan is a presidential republic. The president is elected by popular vote for a seven-year term. (President Rakhmonov is in his second term.) According to the nation's constitution, the president has the power to appoint or dismiss regional government leaders, the prime minister and other ministers, and heads of state agencies. The president is also assigned the task of naming judges to the supreme court.

Tajikistan's constitution was introduced in 1994, replacing the Soviet constitution of 1978. According to the new document, Tajikistan is a unitary and secular state. It grants freedoms to independent media and various political organizations, and it prohibits the discrimination or persecution of women, ethnic minorities, and religious groups. Tajikistan's government organized several referenda that introduced some changes to the text of the constitution, but officials firmly rejected demands from some religious groups to declare Tajikistan an Islamic state or to introduce an Islamic legal system.

Tajikistan's constitution recognizes the division of powers among the judicial, executive, and legislative branches of government. In reality, however, this system of checks and balances is not really effective, since much of the power is concentrated disproportionately in the hands of the executive branch.

Tajikistan has a bicameral parliament. It is made up of two houses, or chambers, collectively called the Majlisi Oli. The lower chamber, or Majlisi Namoyondagon (Assembly of Representatives), is made up of 63 members elected for five-year terms. The upper chamber is the 33-seat Majlisi Milliy (National Assembly), whose members are also elected for five-year terms. Twenty-five of the National Assembly's legislators are selected by local deputies, while the remaining eight members are appointed by the president.

During the Soviet period, only the Communist Party was allowed to operate in the country, but since 1991 numerous political parties have emerged, ranging from liberal and democratic parties to Islamic groups. At least six political parties took part in the parliamentary elections of 2000, including the People's Democratic Party of Tajikistan, the Communist Party, the Islamic Resurgence Party, the Adolatkhoh Party, and the Socialist Party. Nonetheless, United Nations observers claimed that the elections did not meet minimum democratic standards for "equal, fair, free, secret, transparent, and accountable elections."

Administratively, Tajikistan is divided into two provinces (each called a *viloyat*) and one autonomous or independent province (called the *viloyati mukhtor*). The capital of the country also makes up its own administrative unit. Each province is headed by a governor, who is appointed by the president with the official approval of the parliament. Each province also has an elected council that makes the final decision on many issues, including the approval of the budget, annual spending plans, and other key directives.

Opposite: **Tajikistan's president Imomali Rakhmonov is greeted by his Iranian counterpart Muhammad Khatami in Tehran in 2000 when he made a state visit to Iran to discuss the civil war in Afghanistan.**

Tajikistani soldiers line up as part of a joint military exercise with Kyrgyzstan.

MILITARY FORCES

As in many developing countries that have experienced civil war, the military and security services play an important role in the political life of Tajikistan. The republic's military forces consist of an army, an air force, an air-defense force, the presidential national guard, and border guards. Due to the economic recession, these forces have experienced a significant shortage of funds and a lack of equipment in recent years.

At the start of the 21st century, the United States, the North Atlantic Treaty Organization (NATO), and the Russian Federation provided military equipment to Tajikistan and trained units in counterterrorism operations and in fighting illicit drug trafficking from neighboring Afghanistan.

COMMUNITY POLITICS

A *mahallya* (neighborhood community) plays an important role in Tajik society. The institution of the *mahallya* as the state's smallest administrative unit appeared most probably in the medieval period. It survived through the Soviet era and gained strength after the country's independence. The *mahallya* is usually formed by residents of a small village or a district in a town or city. It is usually run by a group of *aksakals* (elders). Traditionally, feasts (to mark weddings or funerals, for example), *hashars* (community projects, such as building mosques and repairing irrigation systems), and local charities are organized at the *mahallya* level.

WAR ON TERRORISM

Tajikistan faced significant difficulties after the civil war: transportation and communication networks were damaged during the war; many plants, factories, and mines could not resume operations because they lacked investments and equipment or lost foreign and regional markets; and many parts of the country remained unsafe for travel because bandits robbed travelers and businessmen. In addition, there was the ongoing threat of radical terrorist groups. According to the claims of Tajik officials, the Taliban regime of neighboring Afghanistan provided financial and other support to radical political groups in Tajikistan. Faced with an unexpected problem, Tajikistan's leaders struggled to attract international help.

The situation changed in 2001 after the terrorist attacks on various locations in the United States, most notably the World Trade Center in New York City. The U.S. government decided to wage an international war on terrorism and specifically the Taliban regime in Afghanistan. Tajikistan became an important U.S. ally in the region, condemning terrorism and agreeing to open its territory to U.S.-led coalition troops during the Afghan War in exchange for U.S. assistance in military training.

With greater political stability in Tajikistan, international donor organizations such as the World Bank and the Asian Development Bank began providing assistance in the hope of eliminating mass poverty and developing private business opportunities.

ECONOMY

SINCE ANCIENT TIMES, the Tajiks have been engaged in labor-intensive agriculture as well as various craft and service trades growing out of the commerce conducted along the great Silk Road. The people established flourishing city-states in central Asia and developed sophisticated architectural and irrigation skills. However, these city-states suffered considerable setbacks in the following centuries from wars, conquests, invasions, and general political chaos. Entering the 19th century, Tajikistan was still a feudal country with most of the population engaged in a subsistence economy, earning just enough to support itself.

Above: **A view from the railroad tracks of the once prosperous but now abandoned coal mine in Shorab in northwestern Tajikistan. The former Soviet Union is littered with towns like Shorab, which has been virtually deserted after the collapse of the regime.**

Opposite: **Two boys guide their donkey, laden with cornstalks, down a dusty village road near Dushanbe.**

Major economic and social changes swept through Tajik society after the Russian Revolution of 1917. The territory of Tajikistan was the last area in central Asia where the Bolsheviks had established their control, after they suppressed local resistance known as the *basmachi* movement. In the 1920s the Soviet government began enforcing total state control over all aspects of economic development.

Then, in the mid-1980s, Gorbachev's perestroika policy attempted to stimulate economic growth. However, certain policies and programs were inconsistently implemented. Competition among various groups within the ruling party for control of major resources created deep rivalries, ultimately leading to popular unrest in Dushanbe in 1990. Although the Communist Party won parliamentary elections in 1990, and its representative, Rakhman Nabiyev, won the presidential election, opponents refused to recognize the results. On the eve of its independence, Tajikistan was sliding into a civil war.

AGRICULTURE

Until the 1920s the agricultural industry was dominated by small subsistence farms that grew mostly grains, vegetables, fruit, and cotton. The Soviet government reformed the agricultural sector, claiming that such changes would help update and modernize the national economy. In the late 1920s the government limited private entrepreneurship and established tight state control over most economic activities. Officials

Soviet leader Joseph Stalin autographs documents for 11-year-old Mamlakat Nakhangova *(left of Stalin)* and Ene Geldiyeva *(right)*, members of a farming collective in Tajikistan.

also introduced central economic planning and control, dictating the course that certain regions and areas would take. In the 1930s the government forced all farmers to join *kolkhozes*, large state-controlled cooperatives, which specialized in making silk and cultivating cotton and other crops. This system dominated the republic's agricultural operations for the next 60 years.

LAND REFORMS

Land reforms totally altered agriculture in Tajikistan in the 20th century, taking farmers from one extreme to another. The first change came with the Soviet policy of collectivization that was introduced in the late 1920s and 1930s. Its aim was to create *kolkhozes* and *sovkhozes*, large agricultural enterprises capable of producing crops on a large scale. Initially the land and all the property of wealthy farmers, called *bais* and *kulaks*, were confiscated. The government also banned the private ownership of land. Some *bais* and wealthy individuals were deported to Siberia or executed, while others escaped to neighboring Afghanistan and Iran. As many as 100,000 individuals perished during the campaign, and 200,000 more moved to other countries. On a positive note, the Soviet government invested heavily in developing rural economies, producing modern machinery, and implementing more efficient farming techniques. Altogether these efforts significantly improved living standards among the rural population.

In the 1990s the government made a U-turn and reintroduced private entrepreneurship in the agricultural sector, allowing farmers to leave the *kolkhozes*. At the same time, however, officials no longer funded agricultural ventures. Despite this change, between 1992 and 2005, about 30,000 families decided to leave the *kolkhozes* and establish their own private farms.

Young Tajik women haul cotton, the nation's only significant cash crop, home from the fields. It is common in Tajikistan for children and youths to work in the fields.

MONOCULTURE OF COTTON

The climate and soil of Tajikistan are suitable for the cultivation of cotton, a highly valued cash crop. Tajik farmers have produced cotton for several centuries. However, it was the industrial revolution of the 20th century in Russia that generated a huge market for this crop. Many individual families, even whole villages and districts, were encouraged or forced to abandon other crops in favor of cotton.

By the mid-20th century, Tajikistan became the second-largest cotton producer in the USSR and among the top 10 producers in the world. What is called the monoculture of cotton—focusing on this single crop at the expense of all other agricultural products—led to several negative consequences. Farmers became extremely dependent on the decisions of the state institutions that controlled agricultural policies and funding.

This reliance made farmers extremely vulnerable to external shocks. It also rapidly increased the use of freshwater for irrigation, leading to the depletion of water reserves not only in Tajikistan but throughout central Asia. In addition, excessive irrigation led to the salinization and the depletion of soil in many places, reducing productivity or making land unusable for commercial agriculture. In the 1990s many farmers experienced great losses, since the government hastily cut off most of its agricultural funding at the same time a collapse in cotton prices gripped the international market.

MANUFACTURING

Until the 1930s and 1940s, there were few manufacturing plants in the country. During World War II, the Soviet government relocated a number of factories from Nazi-occupied territories to Tajikistan. The move helped establish new industries, including defense manufacturing, the production of agricultural and industrial machinery, food processing, textile and garment manufacturing, and the mining of nonferrous metals. Significant investments were channeled into the construction of huge hydroelectric power stations, one of the most expensive schemes the USSR undertook. According to official statistics, Tajikistan's economy grew 21-fold between 1940 and 1984. In the late 1970s and 1980s, economic growth slowed considerably due to pollution and the increased availability of foreign products.

The state-controlled development of the manufacturing sector led to several problems. First, state-owned enterprises were often inefficient and not competitive in the international market. Second, the aggressive development of land for industrial use led to severe environmental problems including the erosion of the fragile soil found in mountainous

A woman operates one of the machines at the Dushanbinsky Silk Factory in Dushanbe.

oases and valleys. Thus, many industrial enterprises, unable to compete with foreign goods after the opening of the national market in the 1990s, were closed or experienced significant losses.

RECENT DEVELOPMENT

Since 1997 the Tajik government has followed a program of postwar economic reconstruction, focusing on restoring major sectors of the economy as well as achieving self-sufficient food production. The government welcomes private initiatives and has opened up the national economy to international investment. It was among the last of the former Soviet states to introduce its national currency, the *somoni* (in October 2000). According to the World Bank, Tajikistan's economy declined at an average annual rate of 10 percent between 1990 and 2000, due to the devastating effect of the civil war. The country increasingly relies on exporting raw materials to the international market, especially aluminum, cotton, and fruit. Still, Tajikistan needs additional foreign direct investments and international assistance to modernize its existing technologies and to bring about major economic changes.

Agriculture, industry, and services are the three main pillars of the modern Tajik economy, contributing 19.4, 25.7, and 54.9 percent respectively to the gross domestic product (GDP). The country depends heavily on imported machinery, fuel, consumer goods, and food products. In 1999 and 2000 the national government appealed to the international community for food assistance because its population faced hunger and starvation from a devastating drought. The nation's total external debt reached $922 million in 2001, and it is expected to grow even more in the coming years.

Due to the civil war and the difficulties of the postwar reconciliation, there was a steady decline in the living standards of all population groups, especially women and children. The country remains the poorest nation to emerge from the former Soviet Union, with average monthly wages equaling about $12 to $15 and with more than 60 percent of the population living below the poverty line. At least 50,000 people leave annually in search of better jobs and a higher standard of living in other countries. In 2001 the United Nations Development Program's Human Development Index (HDI) ranked Tajikistan 103rd out of 162 nations, below all the other former Soviet republics.

A Tajik woman sells vegetables at a street market. Tajiks have been trading since ancient times, taking particular advantage of the country's strategic location on the Silk Road.

ENVIRONMENT

PEOPLE HAVE LIVED in Tajikistan for thousands of years, finding ways to eke a living out of the land. The situation has changed, though, during the last 200 years. The population of the country grew nearly sixfold within the last 100 years, dramatically increasing demands for water, arable land, and other resources.

In addition, the development of industry and widespread farming, especially in the 20th century, brought pollution and damage to the natural environment in many parts of the country, especially in the densely populated valleys and districts around the largest cities.

Recently, industrial pollution and global warming have led to the shrinking and eventual disappearance of some mountain glaciers, thereby decreasing freshwater reserves. The presence of humans continues to negatively affect the wildlife in many parts of the country as well as the delicate environmental balance of the nation's various habitats.

Tajikistan's government understands the urgent need to deal with the environmental issues at hand and to reduce the negative impact of people on the natural world. However, as a developing nation, Tajikistan has few resources for dealing with its various ecological problems. In addition, most Tajikistanis live in rural areas. In times of economic hardship or drought, the rural population often exploits and overly stresses natural resources to supplement its daily needs.

In recent decades the government of Tajikistan, along with international organizations and nongovernmental organizations (NGOs), introduced various projects aimed at preserving the nation's natural resources. For example, officials work intensively with farmers, hunters, herders, and many others to educate them about the importance of responsibly using and maintaining Tajikistan's valuable natural resources.

Opposite: **Kuli Kalon Lake in the Fann Mountains. While some areas of the country remain untouched, Tajikistan has not escaped its share of environmental damage.**

Snow melts on a hillside above a lake in the Pamir Mountains.

FRAGILE MOUNTAIN ECOSYSTEM

About 93 percent of Tajikistan is covered with mountains. In fact, very high mountains—more than 3,000 feet (915 m) above sea level—occupy more than 70 percent of the country. Tajikistan is home to many small and large valleys, canyons, and mountain slopes with unique landscapes and distinctive ecosystems.

The mountain ecosystem is very fragile, and damage done by humans often takes a long time to heal. In some cases the effects are irreversible. For example, due to the harsh climate of the mountains, many types of trees and shrubs grow slowly, and it sometimes takes several decades before they reach their full growth. But they could easily be wiped out in a matter of a few hours by accidental fires, by floods, or by local farmers who cut them for fuel or building materials.

Tajikistan possesses nearly 70 percent of central Asia's glaciers and about 40 percent of its clean water reserves. The glaciers have been affected not only by global warming but, to a large extent, by people as well. Trash left behind by tourists and hikers often contains lead, mercury, and other harmful substances that pollute the mountains' water reserves.

As of now, the government of Tajikistan has yet to turn its attention to some of the nation's most pressing environmental concerns. Preserving wildlife, protecting the alpine forests and *tugais*, and ensuring that the nation has a clean and sustainable water supply are just a few of its top priorities.

DEFORESTATION AND WILDLIFE

One of Tajikistan's most serious environmental crises is the uncontrolled cutting of alpine forests for wood in order to heat homes in winter or to construct new houses. In addition, pistachio, Bukhara almond, hedge rose, and other trees have been overharvested, cut down for their nuts and berries. During the last 100 to 150 years, nearly 50 to 60 percent of the native forests have been lost, including magnificent groves of walnut, fig, and wild pomegranate.

In recent years poaching and commercial hunting have emerged as major threats, not only to the wildlife of Tajikistan but also to the delicate ecological balance in the alpine zones. For example, the number of gazelles living in the Tigrovaia Balka preserve has declined during the last decade. The threats to the populations of wildcats, foxes, wolves, and other animals cause disruptions in the food chain. These animals are key predators of the rats, mice, and birds that, uncontrolled, damage the woodland and agricultural crops.

To protect lemons from severe winter frosts, these Tajiks plant their trees in deep trenches lined with bricks.

WATER PROBLEMS

Irrigation and drinking water are key concerns in Tajikistan. There has been a sharp increase in water consumption in recent decades, combined with years of drought, which has compromised irrigation systems and reduced the supply of drinking water.

The conflicting needs of the agricultural and industrial sectors make water-use management all the more difficult. Hydroelectric power stations store millions of gallons of water in summer, releasing most of it in winter to generate additional power for heating purposes. On the other hand, farmers need water in summer for irrigation, especially on large cotton and rice plantations, and if too much water is released in winter, fields could be flooded and arable land eroded.

Erosion is another serious problem. Deforestation often results in the soil being easily washed away, not only during the rainy season but after

Vladimir Lenin's image hovers over the hydro-electric power station near Nurek. Tajikistan has several large hydro-electric power stations and plans to build more.

the snow melts as well. The problem is even graver in the more mountainous regions. It may take just a few days of heavy rain to strip hundreds of acres of land of its soil, while it takes decades or even centuries to restore the fertile topsoil in the alpine zones. In some areas, poor farmers burn vegetation on mountain slopes to prepare the land for planting cash crops. Too often, after a few rainy seasons, the soil is washed away and the newly cleared patches are deserted. In the end, the land undergoes major changes for very limited returns.

CONSERVATION

Tajik scientists and conservationists understood the importance of preserving the natural environment long ago. The national Academy of Sciences, with government funding, launched several projects to educate people and encourage environmentally conscious industrial and agricultural undertakings. The oldest initiatives, the Tigrovaia Balka and Ramit wildlife preserves, were set up in the mid-20th century. About a dozen other wildlife sanctuaries were set up in the country at around the same time. In addition, there are three botanical gardens that serve as important centers for studying biodiversity in Tajikistan and ways of preserving the nation's growing list of endangered species.

Since the 1990s, however, the country has had a severe shortage of funds and expertise because of years of civil war and economic recession. In 2003 the government issued its First National Report on Biodiversity Conservation in which it evaluated the nation's environmental practices and trends. Officials used the report to develop a plan for the future, one that will preserve the nation's irreplaceable natural resources.

The Tibetan snowcock is an endangered species. It can be found in some of Tajikistan's nature parks and preserves.

55

TAJIKISTANIS

FOR CENTURIES THE AREA that makes up present-day Tajikistan was populated by various ethnic and religious groups. The groups that played the largest role in forming modern Tajikistani culture spoke Persian and Turkic-based languages. The Persian-speaking peoples established their presence and developed their cities first. The Turkic-speaking peoples began arriving in large numbers from the fourth to sixth centuries A.D., probably even earlier.

In spite of religious, linguistic, and cultural differences, the various people who settled in the region cooperated with one another in times of foreign invasion or in the face of natural calamities such as earthquakes, floods, or droughts. There were significant cultural exchanges between the Persian- and Turkic-speaking communities, and intermarrying between the two groups became common. At the same time, some groups and communities competed fiercely with one another for political and economic influence or dominance. The area experienced its share of turbulent times, as a series of devastating wars slowed the consolidation of the Tajik nation and further weakened the people's abilities to resist foreign invaders.

By the late 19th century, the Russian empire controlled most of the central Asian region, but in many places its presence was minimal. In the 20th century, however, the Soviet authorities established tighter control over the social and cultural aspects of the people living in central Asia. Although the Tajik state was formed, many Tajik communities remained outside the country's official boundaries, mainly in the provinces of Bukhara and Samarqand in Uzbekistan. At that time, in the late 1920s, when the modern borders of Tajikistan were established, the population of the country was about 1.2 million. In 2004 the total population of the country was estimated to be about 7 million. Tajikistan is one of

Opposite: **Tajik children outside their house in a village near the Tajikistan-Afghanistan border.**

the least urbanized countries on the Asian continent, with around 72 percent of its people living in rural areas. Dushanbe is home to 550,000 people, or 8 percent of the population. Tajikistan has one of the fastest-growing populations of the former Soviet states, and it is estimated that its population could double within the next 20 to 25 years.

Tajikistan is the only Persian-speaking country in central Asia and is a part of the Persian-speaking world, which includes a significant number of people in Afghanistan, Iran, Iraq, and many other countries.

TAJIKS

Scholars still dispute the origins of the Tajik people, their cultural heritage, and even the origin of the word *Tajik*. Some scholars translate the word *Tajik* as "crown," while others believe that it was probably just the name

Tajik women in colorful traditional dress.

of a medieval tribe. Nevertheless, there is some consensus about the origin of the Tajik people.

Most Tajik scholars believe that the Tajik ancestors lived in what is now Afghanistan, Kyrgyzstan, Tajikistan, and Uzbekistan after about 2,000 B.C. The scholars claim that these predecessors had direct links to the populace of ancient Sogdiana and Bactria and the early Parthian states. The name *Tajik* did not emerge until much later, sometime around the 11th century.

Starting in ancient times, three different groups came together to form the Tajik nation. The first was the Persian-speaking population of the Pamir Mountains and the surrounding area. The second was a Turkic-speaking population grouped mostly in large and small cities and towns in the Syr Darya, Zeravshan, Vakhsh, and Panj river valleys. From medieval times

Tajik girls gather near a fence in the village of Hauzako. About 38 percent of Tajikistan's population consists of children aged 14 and younger.

on, the Persian-speaking population interacted closely with the Turkic-speaking people who arrived in the region in several small and large waves. By the 19th and 20th centuries, it was quite common for many families to be bilingual. They spoke Tajik, which is close to the dialect of Persian spoken in Iran, as well as various dialects of the Turkic languages. In the past the Tajiks adopted Arabic script and used it until the early 20th century. The contemporary Tajik alphabet is based on Cyrillic script.

Arabs made up the third group that formed the Tajik nation. In the seventh and eighth centuries A.D., the Arabs introduced Islam to the area, and gradually a majority of the population abandoned Zoroastrianism, Buddhism, and Manichaenism for the newly imported faith. Today most Tajiks belong to the Sunni school of Islamic thought, unlike the Iranians, who mostly belong to the other main branch of Islam, Shia.

According to government estimates, there are about 4.5 million ethnic Tajiks in the country. A significant number of Tajiks live outside Tajikistan. Various sources estimate that between 3 and 5 million Tajiks live in many parts of the world, including Afghanistan, Iran, Kyrgyzstan, and Russia.

UZBEKS

Uzbeks make up Tajikistan's largest ethnic minority. They live in all parts of the country west of Badakhshan, but the largest enclaves are in the Fergana Valley. The Uzbeks speak a language belonging to the Turkic language group; it is different from the Tajik language, though many Uzbeks speak both languages.

The Uzbeks trace their origin to the Turkic-speaking group that began forming its own distinct language and culture probably in the 15th and 16th centuries. The Uzbek tribal leaders led several wars to defend their land against the aggression of the Persian shahs and succeeded in establishing independent states. With the creation of the various Soviet republics in the 1920s, a majority of Uzbeks found themselves living in the newly established republic of Uzbekistan. But small communities of Uzbeks remained in all the other central Asian republics, including Tajikistan.

At the start of the 21st century, Uzbeks living in Tajikistan made up about 25 percent of the country's population, or about 1.75 million people. The Uzbeks maintain close relations within their communities, but they do not isolate themselves from the rest of the populace. They also play an important role in the political life of Tajikistan, since several ministerial positions in the national government are traditionally filled by ethnic Uzbeks. The Uzbeks did not participate actively in the civil war in the 1990s, but they did play a significant role in the reconciliation process.

RUSSIANS

Russians, whose language belongs to the Slavic language group, constitute the second-largest ethnic minority in the country, though their numbers have steadily declined since 1991. They first arrived in Tajik-

Opposite: **An Uzbek sells melons at a market in Dushanbe. There are sizeable Uzbek communities in Tajikistan.**

populated areas in the second half of the 19th century. Initially, most of them were Russian imperial troops stationed in strategic cities and towns throughout the region. On the eve of the 20th century, several thousand Russian peasant families arrived in central Asia in order to escape the poverty and economic hardship of life in Russia. After 1924 several large waves of Russian immigrants entered Tajikistan—mainly skilled workers, engineers, administrators, and managers, most of whom found jobs in the newly established industrial enterprises, mines, factories, and various educational institutions. During the 1970s and 1980s, the number of Russians in Tajikistan reached its peak of about 380,000 people.

A significant number of Russians left the country in the 1990s due to the economic recession, the closing of factories and businesses, the civil war, and the ensuing political instability. By 2005 only about 100,000 Russians remained in Tajikistan.

ISMAILIS

The Ismailis are the largest religious minority living in Tajikistan. Most live in the Badakhshan Autonomous Province, though there are several small Ismaili communities found in other parts of the country. They speak a dialect of the Tajik language and identify with the Shia branch of Islam. Their practice of Islam is quite different from that favored by the Sunni Tajiks. For example, only the Ismailis recognize the supreme authority of the Ismaili spiritual leader, Imam Aga Khan.

According to government estimates, there are about 250,000 to 300,000 Ismailis living in Tajikistan. A significantly larger number live in other parts of Asia, the Americas, Africa, and Europe. Those living outside central Asia provide significant financial, administrative, and technical assistance to the Ismailis and other communities in Tajikistan.

OTHER MINORITIES

Several smaller ethnic minority groups make their homes in Tajikistan. The Kyrgyzs live mostly in the mountainous areas in northern Tajikistan close to Kyrgyzstan and Uzbekistan. These people live mainly in small villages high in the mountains and make their livelihood by breeding animals—specifically yaks, horses, and prized breeds of sheep—and by commercial farming in the small valleys of northern Tajikistan.

There is also a small community of Yaghnobis, people who speak a dialect of Persian that is different from Tajik. The Yaghnobis trace their origins to a group of ancient people known as the Sogdians. In the past the Yaghnobis lived in the small, extremely isolated Yaghnob River valley, but authorities have moved them into the valleys of northern Tajikistan.

Other minorities found in Tajikistan include small numbers of Tatars, Turkmens, and Kazakhs.

A Tajik boy uses his donkey to transport containers of water.

SOCIAL SYSTEM

Traditionally, the Tajiks had no nobles, no privileged class that controlled power and wealth exclusively because of their birth. However, certain extended clans and family networks were able to amass significant power, wealth, and influence in the nation. By the late 19th century upward mobility was limited, and it was practically impossible for farmers and other workers to gain access to the realms of privilege.

The situation changed dramatically with the arrival of the Soviet system in the 1920s. Soviet authorities specifically targeted the members of rich families and of the former political and Islamic establishments for their alleged support of the old regime. The Soviet government declared universal equality and recognized only three social divisions: workers, peasants, and the intelligentsia. Most young and talented people were offered the chance to enter government service, to join the military, or to receive a good education, regardless of their social background or family income.

By the end of the 20th century, however, a new exclusive social group, the *nomenklatura*, emerged in the country. This group consisted of the members of the Communist Party and their relatives; and it received nearly exclusive access to the best educational opportunities, jobs, promotions, and a better lifestyle, at the expense of other Tajiks.

Since independence was declared in 1991, Tajikistan's social structures have changed again. The Communist Party lost its privileged position, thus ending the era of the political favoritism that the *nomenklatura* enjoyed. That privileged group gradually disappeared from the country's political arena altogether. Since the early 1990s Tajikistani society has branched off into three main divisions. The upper class consists of small groups of high-ranking government officials and their close associates, who have access to the most power and prime business opportunities. Professionals such as managers, military and security personnel, landlords, and businesspeople make up the country's small middle class. The lower class consists of large groups of farmers, industrial workers, and former professionals who had difficulties adapting to a new social and economic environment. According to World Bank estimates, more than 60 percent of the people in Tajikistan lived below the poverty line in 2004.

NATIONAL DRESS

During the last hundred years, there has been a dramatic change in the styles and types of clothing worn in Tajikistan. Until the 19th century, men usually wore colorful homemade traditional clothes, while women often wore special cloaks called *paranjas* that covered their whole body from head to ankle. Sometimes even women's faces were veiled with special semitransparent material. The Tajiks began adopting Western-style dress in the early 20th century. By the end of the 20th century most of the people wore Western-style formal clothes at their workplace or at public events and more casual Western-style clothes, such as jeans, T-shirts, or track suits, in their free time. During traditional festivals, family events, or visits to rural relatives, however, most Tajiks wear their traditional national costumes, often handmade by family members or bought in the bazaars. In more remote areas, this style of dress is more common, especially among the older generations.

This owner of a yurt in a desolate area of the western Pamir Mountains wears a quilted overcoat.

TRADITIONAL MEN'S CLOTHING Men's traditional clothes consist of quilted cotton robes or buttonless overcoats called *jomas*. They typically reach the ankles and vary in color and design depending on the region in which they were produced. Generally, however, it is considered more appropriate to choose modest colors for *jomas*, or sometimes just black. In the past the garments were handmade. They are secured by long scarves tied around the waist. Winter *jomas* are much heavier and thicker.

The traditional robe was complemented by a white or gray turban or a special black-and-white skullcap. Under a *joma* a man wears a buttonless shirt, though during the last few decades, men have begun to wear Western-style shirts, typically white or another light color. The traditional pants are baggy and wide and are often also without buttons. The outfit is completed by boots made of soft leather. In the past young men often carried small knives hidden in their boots.

TRADITIONAL WOMEN'S CLOTHING Women's traditional clothes consist of a long colorful dress made of cotton and sometimes silk. Women also wear *jomas* in bright colors and patterns, and colorful, baggy wide-cut pants under the dresses. Traditionally, women wear leather shoes or rubber boots that vary in design.

The women's traditional outfit is completed by a head covering that varies depending on age, marital status, regional affiliation, and the time of year. Married women usually cover their hair with long scarfs of different colors. In some cases, the scarf may just cover the hair, but in other cases it may cover not only the hair but also the neck and face, leaving only the eyes exposed. Girls and young unmarried women, however, can wear special handmade brightly colored skullcaps.

These Tajik women selling bread at a street market wear head coverings in various forms.

LIFESTYLE

THE LIFESTYLE OF CONTEMPORARY Tajikistanis is a complex mixture of national traditions and modern, often urban-influenced ways. There are several factors that determine the way of life of the ordinary people in the country. The most important is whether one lives in the country or in the city. City dwellers have much higher incomes, more modern values, and greater access to modern means of communication, such as television, radio, and the Internet. Another factor is what generation a person belongs to, since younger people often have greater access to international mass culture and tend to be more cosmopolitan in their tastes. Meanwhile it is expected that mature people act their age and be more devoted to their families, social duties, and traditions, and less interested in leisure activities. The third factor that determines lifestyle is social status.

It is difficult to generalize about any nation, but even more difficult for a society as culturally diverse and complex as Tajikistan's. Yet there are several features that are common to most everyone in the country.

Tajiks highly value their close-knit communities and the sense of belonging that they provide. Tajiks often share their achievements and difficulties with the members of their communities. They also highly value hospitality, and they usually celebrate important events with their extended families, friends, and neighbors. Often even a total stranger is invited to join a celebration of such pivotal events as a marriage or the birth of a child. There is also a very strong sense of mutual assistance, since it is expected that people will help and support

Above: **In Tajik culture the elderly are highly respected, and children are regarded as a source of happiness.**

Opposite: **A Tajik woman cooks noodles over a wood fire.**

69

one another in times of difficulty with any reasonable means. The Tajiks highly respect the older members of their communities, the *aksakals*, and often turn to them for advice, for social and political support, or for resolving existing disputes.

FAMILY LIFE

As in many central Asian and Middle Eastern countries, the extended family is the cornerstone of society in Tajikistan. It is considered to be a social obligation to know the names of all close and distant relatives, including all cousins, nephews, and nieces (sometimes more than 100 people altogether), and their birthdays and, if applicable, anniversaries.

In rural areas, it is common for Tajiks of different generations to live in the same house.

The first questions people ask one another when they meet center on the health and well-being of parents and other relatives. Traditionally families visit their relatives and invite them to their homes for various events.

It is quite common for several generations of relatives to live together in the same place or sometimes in the same housing complex. Often a traditional household consists of a married couple and their parents and grandparents. After marriage young people are obliged to ask for their parents' permission to move out and build or buy a house of their own. Often, young families stay in their parents' homes if they do not have the financial means to move out. In the past most young families remained within the same community and rarely moved to different cities or towns. If they did move, they typically maintained close relations with their extended family and former community, regularly attending important celebrations and assisting their relatives. During the past few decades, however, strong community ties and obligations have begun to play a lesser role in Tajik society.

Children are received with happiness in Tajikistan. Families with six, seven, and even 10 children are common. In the past some wealthy men practiced polygamy and had several wives. (Islamic law allows for up to four wives.) This practice was banned by the Soviet government and later by the government of independent Tajikistan, although polygamy has recently been revived in some areas.

Urbanization, which first gained force in Tajikistan in the 1950s and 1960s, significantly changed the lifestyle of the general populace. For the first time, urban families began having considerably fewer children. In addition, it became part of a new urban tradition for young people to buy or rent a property and to move away from their parents' home immediately after marriage, since most city houses and apartments could not accommodate large families.

MARRIAGE

Marriage is considered to be one of the most important events in the life of a Tajik. The rite changes the social status of young couples, since it signifies the beginning of adulthood and full maturity in the eyes of all community members. Marriage also symbolizes independence and gaining a voice in the extended family and the community. In addition, marriage is considered to be a personal achievement for the parents of the bride and groom, since it often seals a union or partnership between the two families and ensures the continuation of two honorable and respected lineages.

A mass wedding for hundreds of couples in Tajikistan in May 2005.

In light of this, choosing a marriage partner is critical. Traditionally, when young people have reached marrying age or express a desire to establish a family of their own, all close and distant relatives are put on alert. Family and community members, friends, and colleagues are given the task of finding an appropriate spouse. They regularly organize various events and often set up "accidental" meetings between prospective partners. Even professional matchmakers are regularly called for help.

Often, the search is a short one, since parents might arrange a marriage themselves, choosing a partner they consider to be the most appropriate for their child. Yet the young people usually have the final say and may accept the arranged marriage or introduce to their parents a person they prefer instead. Traditionally, it is expected that the family of the bridegroom pay a *kalym*, a dowry in the form of money or gifts, to the family of the bride. The size of the *kalym* can vary and can become a substantial burden to the family.

Young people who marry are expected to stay together for life. However, divorce is allowed by Tajikistani civil law, and either partner can file for divorce. Under the current legal system, children of divorced parents usually remain with their mother, and the father is obliged to provide financial support for them until they reach the age of 18. In general, divorced people can remarry, though it is sometimes easier in urban environments than in rural areas.

NATIONAL TRADITIONS AND SOCIAL BEHAVIOR

In the past traditional Tajik social relations had been built around the concept of social and political rank and the separation of the sexes. The economic and political developments of the 20th century, however, significantly changed these notions. This has led to a complex mixture of

Elders occupy a position of esteem in Tajik society.

past and present, a vibrant interchange between traditional Islamic and central Asian culture and modern Western models.

The urbanization and modernization that characterized much of the 20th century left their imprint on national traditions, making them less restrictive and more flexible. More recently, the opening up of the country after independence to the outside world and the explosion of an international mass-media culture have contributed to major cultural shifts in Tajikistan. Young people have more independence and freedom, although tradition remains an important means of binding society.

Elderly people are considered to be a source of wisdom. They exert a strong influence both in their families and in their local communities. It is considered polite to listen to elders; to invite them for discussions of various social, political, and community matters; and to ask for their opinions about a wide variety of issues. Young people still go to the elderly members of their extended families and of their communities to ask for approval of major undertakings, such as decisions to move to other places or to accept work in other countries. This approval and advice, however, is not binding and does not carry the same weight it did about a half century ago. Still elders often play a central role at the local level, and sometimes they are even entrusted to carry out justice in cases involving minor offences.

Until the 20th century Tajik tradition strongly endorsed separating the sexes in public and family life. It was widely accepted that girls should be taught to be housewives only and to be prepared exclusively to perform domestic duties. Many women remained uneducated, because there was a strong traditional perception that they did not need extensive schooling. Women could not take positions in government or public life and could not vote or participate in any discussion of development at the community level. Moreover, they were not allowed to go out of their homes alone, even for shopping, especially without being properly veiled and dressed. Most houses were divided into separate sections for males and females, and the sexes could not mix in public even during weddings and other major family events.

In the late 1920s the Soviet authorities introduced and fiercely enforced a policy of liberalization of women. They allowed women to abandon veiling in public. Women were encouraged to enroll in schools and universities and to serve in public positions. The government even established informal job quotas for women in universities, local and national governments, ministries, and the agencies that made up the Communist Party.

By the late 20th century this policy had resulted in the creation of a large class of professional women, who had their own independent incomes and a strong presence in public institutions and many levels of government. Segregation of men and women in public was completely abandoned, and young people could meet at restaurants, nightclubs, sports centers, and other public places without any social stigma.

The situation began to change after 1991, as the steep economic recession, the civil war, and increasing isolation from the outside world resulted in a high level of unemployment. Women were among the first to lose their jobs and their voices in public life. Some older, premodern traditions also have made a comeback in many parts of the country. Segregation of women and men in public, for example, has begun to slowly re-emerge during the last few decades.

At present, urban women still enjoy a large degree of freedom; they can decide on their own education, jobs, and lifestyles. Many young women often prefer to wear Western-style dress and enjoy Western-style entertainment. Meanwhile, many rural women are often strongly encouraged not to attend school beyond the primary or secondary level

Young Tajikistani women share a happy moment in their graduation sashes.

and to prepare themselves almost solely to be housewives. In some families, girls' opinions are not counted when their families choose their future husbands, and young women are not allowed to go out alone without guardians.

EDUCATION

Education is highly valued in Tajik society. In the past it was the only means of overcoming social barriers and climbing the social ladder. After the Bolshevik revolution and the civil war of 1917–22, a whole generation of policy makers, administrators, professionals, and artists rose to power and fame completely because of the personal abilities and talents they acquired and developed through good education. People in Tajikistan today undergo considerable hardships in order to provide their children

Tajik children begin their 11 years of compulsory education at age 7.

(Left to right) Tajikistan's president Imomali Rakhmonov, the Ismaili spiritual leader Imam Aga Khan, and Afghan vice president Negmatullo Shahroni officiate at the unveiling ceremony for the University of Central Asia in Khorog, Tajikistan.

with a good education at the best universities. It is quite common for an entire extended family to share the responsibility of raising the money needed to support their children studying at prestigious universities in the capital city or overseas.

The education system in Tajikistan has a strong Russian influence. During the Soviet era, a modern education system provided free schooling to all children, with an emphasis on the sciences, mathematics, and practical day-to-day skills. By the 1940s the government had eradicated mass illiteracy. According to official statistics, in 1989 more than 1.3 million students (approximately 23 percent of the population) attended 3,100 schools. In addition, 41,700 students attended 42 specialized secondary schools.

After 1991 schools in Tajikistan underwent two major changes. First, there was a greater emphasis on the use of the Tajik language as the medium of instruction. Second, as a consequence of the 1992–97 civil war, there was a considerable withdrawal of state funding normally intended for education. To this day, spending on education is not a top priority in the nation. In 2003 Tajikistan spent only 13.2 percent of its national budget on education.

The constitution of Tajikistan, adopted in 1994, states that general education is compulsory and free and that the state guarantees access to general, vocational, specialized, and higher education in state-controlled educational establishments. Tajik is the major language of instruction. At age 7, children begin an 11-year compulsory education program, consisting of four years of primary school and seven years of secondary school. According to official statistics, in 1998 more than 1.4 million students (approximately 20 percent of the population) attended 3,522 primary and secondary schools. In addition, there were 50 specialized secondary schools and 74 vocational and technical schools. Approximately 94 percent of those between the ages of 7 and 16 were enrolled in some form of educational institution, though the dropout rate tended to be high.

After completing secondary school, students are given the option of moving on to universities or institutes, which usually offer a five-year program. In 1999, 75,400 students attended one of these 24 so-called tertiary schools. Students may complete postgraduate studies at a three-year *aspirantura* program, which combines course work with a dissertation. After completing an *aspirantura*, students receive a degree of *kandidat nauk* (equivalent to a PhD) and can then study for a full doctorate degree.

Throughout the 1990s the quality and accessibility of the education system in Tajikistan declined due to severe economic recession, civil war, and, more critically, a chronic shortage of textbooks. According to the

United Nations Development Program, fewer female students entered the education system. The government of Tajikistan is trying to reform its education system by attracting private investment and international assistance in an attempt to keep up with the technological necessities and developments of the 21st century.

URBANIZATION AND MIGRATION

Urbanization was a relatively recent concept for Tajikistan, since most cities and industrial centers grew rapidly only between the 1940s and 1980s. High levels of economic growth contributed to the creation of a large number of jobs in urban areas. This provided incentives for many people to move to the cities not only from the Tajik *kishlaks* (villages), but also from other rural areas of the Soviet Union. The urban population grew from 10 percent in 1924 to 35 percent in the 1970s. The development of a modern school system contributed further to a significant influx of people, because most talented young students received state scholarships to study at universities in Dushanbe. Those attending the best universities in central Asia and Russia often returned to the nation's urban centers, after completing their course work, in search of jobs and professional success.

Generally throughout the Soviet era, however, the government heavily regulated the country's population movement, trying to avoid an uncontrolled influx of unskilled labor into the large cities. People could not move until they received special registration permits called *propiska*. Due to these restrictions and a lack of industrial skills, many Tajiks preferred to remain in their rural communities. The government also provided large subsidies to the agricultural industry in order to sustain the large rural population.

The situation changed abruptly after 1991. The government cut off the agricultural subsidies, and Tajik farmers lost their access to the Russian market. These and some other factors made farming unprofitable in many parts of the country. The civil war and the political instability that followed only aggravated the economic situation. Not only did many people lose their jobs and incomes, but their land and, in some extreme cases, all their property were lost as well. Tens of thousands of families moved to the metropolitan areas and even abroad to countries such as Kazakhstan, Iran, and Russia. According to various estimates, between 500,000 and 800,000 people, or between 12 and 18 percent of the population, moved from Tajikistan to other nations. It made Tajikistan one of the largest contributors of immigrants in all the republics that made up the former Soviet Union.

Tajiks in Dushanbe carry buckets to collect water from designated sites after torrential rains cut off water supplies in the city in July 2004.

RELIGION

TAJIKISTAN IS A PREDOMINANTLY Muslim country. About 90 percent of the population is Muslim. There are two major groups. Like most of the Muslims in the neighboring central Asian republics, most Tajik Muslims are Sunnis, who follow the school of Islamic thought and practice as taught by Abu al-Hanaffi. The smaller group of Tajik Muslims belong to the Ismaili sect of Islam. The Ismailis are similar in their teachings and some of their rituals to the Shiites who dominate Iran as well as parts of Afghanistan and Iraq.

In addition to Muslims, Tajikistan is home to small groups of Christians (predominantly Eastern Orthodox) and Jews. Most of the Russians belong to the Eastern Orthodox Christian Church, but their numbers have declined steeply in recent years due, in large part, to the mass emigration of the last decade.

In modern Tajikistan, popular opinion is divided over the role of Islam in political life. The government and a majority of the population believe that religion should be a private matter, separate from the state, and should not interfere with politics. A smaller group believes that Islam should be an integral part of the state and that the religion should play a much bigger role in the political system.

Above: **Russian president Vladimir Putin attends the Orthodox Easter service at Saint Nikolai Church in Dushanbe during a 2003 visit to Tajikistan.**

Opposite: **A Tajik man attends Friday prayers at a mosque.**

BELIEF SYSTEMS IN EARLY CENTRAL ASIA

For centuries, central Asia has been home to many religious systems: Zoroastrians, Buddhists, and later Christians and Muslims. The prosperity of

the region's cities and towns heavily depended on the trade and the commercial interchange among peoples of various backgrounds and faiths. People in these areas were more tolerant of a variety of religious practices.

In ancient times the people who lived in the land that makes up present-day Tajikistan followed various polytheistic systems, believing in numerous gods and spirits. Their religious beliefs were probably close to those of ancient Persia and India.

In the seventh and sixth centuries B.C., central Asian states such as Persia came under the influence of the teachings of the prophet Zoroaster (known in ancient Persian as Zarathushtra). Zoroaster claimed that he received spiritual revelations from the "Lord Wisdom" (called Ahura Mazda). He set down his teachings in the sacred scripture known as the *Avesta*. Persian priests in major urban and political centers of the Persian empire resisted his teaching. However, he found many followers among people who lived in the mountains of central Asia. Gradually the religion received greater recognition, and Persian king Darius I and his son Xerxes I formally acknowledged this system of beliefs.

Between the sixth and third centuries B.C., another school of thought began spreading throughout central Asia—Buddhism. This system was established by the Indian philosopher Siddhartha Gautama, also known as the Buddha, who lived and taught in what is now northern India and Pakistan. Numerous followers of the Buddha came to central Asia spreading his doctrine and establishing Buddhist communities, which peacefully coexisted with other religious communities. Buddhist frescoes can still be found in Tajikistan, including in Kalai-Kafirnigan and Ajina-tepe.

In the fourth century B.C., Alexander the Great brought the polytheistic religion of the ancient Greeks to central Asia. Greek culture flourished for more than a century, significantly influencing the culture of the region. However, the impact of this school of religious practice was limited, since it was most popular among the ruling class. It is not clear to what extent this system affected the religious beliefs of the nonelite people living in urban centers, and if it affected at all the vast population of the rural settlements. Gradually Zoroastrians regained their influence among central Asians.

In the fifth and sixth centuries A.D., Eastern Orthodox Christian missionaries, also known as Nestorians, arrived in the region. The Nestorians, who came into conflict with the Catholic Church in the mid-fifth century over differences in doctrine, were escaping persecution and settled in Persia, central Asia, and as far east as Mongolia.

It was, however, the arrival of Islam in the seventh century A.D. that most profoundly changed the religious development of central Asia for centuries.

RISE OF ISLAM

Islam, one of the world's major religions, was founded by Prophet Muhammad in Arabia at the beginning of the seventh century A.D. Soon

Opposite: **Zoroaster founded the religion that bears his name and was embraced by the Persians.**

the Islamic state—the caliphate—grew in strength and rivaled the most powerful states and empires of the era. The religion quickly spread throughout the Middle East and gradually penetrated central Asia.

In the early eighth century, the first Arab warriors and missionaries arrived in the central Asian region. Initially they met strong resistance from the population, and local rulers fought the Muslim armies intensely. For example, in 720–22 and again in 728, the local inhabitants overcame several Arab posts and re-established their control over significant areas of central Asia. In 776–78 the population waged yet another large revolt and fought the Arabs and their local supporters for several years. It took several decades before the major cities in the region came under the firm control of the caliphate, and local rulers became loyal to the Arabs.

By the late eighth and early ninth centuries, major uprisings in the region had been cut down, and peace was once again established in the region. This led to the significant cultural and political changes throughout central Asia that became integral parts of one of the largest and most powerful empires of that era—the Abbasid dynasty. By that time the rulers of all the major cities and provinces in central Asia had accepted Islam. They had also adopted Arabic script for state administrative purposes and ordered the construction of new, magnificent mosques throughout the region. The central Asian scholars traveled to the era's major centers of learning, including Baghdad. After returning, they helped establish new educational institutions in central Asia. Many scholars from central Asia contributed greatly to the achievements realized by Islamic civilization.

SUFI ORDERS

By the eighth and ninth centuries A.D., Islam had become one of the dominant religions in the major urban centers of central Asia. Yet according to the medieval chronicles, it coexisted with religious communities of Zoroastrians, Buddhists, Nestorians, and others that were still influential in some parts of the region. Sufi mystics, who belonged to various orders, played a major role in converting those communities to Islam.

Sufism is a mystical movement of Islam, and many scholars trace the beginning of Sufism to the seventh and eighth centuries A.D., though there are some disagreements over more precise dating. Sufism emphasizes the development of personal spirituality and individual understanding of divinity. Five centuries after its establishment, Sufism developed into several distinctive orders, or *tariqats*.

Members of these groups traveled to the most remote areas in central Asia, including the Pamir Mountains and the Zeravshan, Panj, and Vakhsh river valleys. Many Sufis settled in local communities, teaching people about Islamic spiritual values and doctrine. Over time, these spiritual leaders (*ishans* and *sheikhs*) recruited many local students (*murids*). Central Asian disciples of the Sufi teachers made a significant contribution to the development of new *tariqats*. Some of the most influential *tariqats* originated in central Asia, including Naqshbandi, Kubrawiya, and Yasawiya.

Opposite: **A Tajik elder reads the Koran outside a mosque.**

Imam Aga Khan *(in white)* arrives in Tajikistan in 1998 to meet Ismailis in the region.

Sufi sheikhs, *murids*, and dervishes (members of one Sufi order) played an important role in spreading Islam among settlers, nomads, and herders in central Asia.

SHIITES AND ISMAILIS

Although the early Muslim communities of the first caliphates were united, gradually differences emerged regarding politics and the interpretation of important doctrines. The most divisive issue involved who became the caliph. Muslims of the Sunni branch believed that the community has the right to choose the caliph. In contrast, the rival group, the Shiites, believed that Prophet Muhammad had designated Ali, his son-in-law, as his earthly and spiritual successor. Therefore, only Ali's descendants (by Fatima, Muhammad's daughter) could legitimately become caliphs. Over time,

THE FIVE PILLARS OF ISLAM

Islam emphasizes five fundamental principles that all devoted Muslims must follow throughout their lives. These principles are called the Five Pillars of Islam.

CREED All devoted Muslims must declare and accept without reservation the fundamental principle that "There is no God, but Allah, and Muhammad is the Messenger of Allah."

PRAYER Devoted Muslims must pray five times each day. In their prayer, they face Kaaba, the holy place in the Saudi Arabian city of Mecca. People are strongly encouraged to go to mosques to offer up their prayers or to gather together for prayer in any suitable house or place, although they can pray anywhere they happen to be during the call to prayer.

In Islam, Friday is a holy day reserved for a special prayer at noon. In many predominantly Muslim countries, people choose Friday, rather than Sunday, as a day of rest, though in Tajikistan the traditional end of the week is observed on Sunday.

CHARITY Regular charity, called *zakat*, is also an obligation of devoted Muslims. All Muslims are strongly encouraged to give money or other forms of support to poor members of their communities, especially at the end of Ramadan, the special month of fasting. Such generosity, it is believed, helps keep selfishness and greed away.

FASTING During one month each year, Muslims are expected to fast from sunrise to sunset, abstaining from food, drink, sexual relations, and any activities that might harm others. This self-denial is intended to help people better understand the life of the poor and hungry and is intended to teach discipline and compassion. Traditionally, young children, the elderly, the sick, and pregnant women are exempted from fasting.

PILGRIMAGE Devoted Muslims are expected to make a pilgrimage, called a hajj, to the holy city of Mecca at least once in their lifetime. The journey is made in order to be purified and cleansed of sin.

both groups experienced uneasy relations, though they usually coexisted peacefully. By the late medieval era, the division and order that prevails today had emerged—Persia became the land where Shiites formed the majority, and central Asia became mostly populated by Sunnis.

From the ninth through the 12th centuries, the Ismaili sect emerged from within the Shiite community. Initially the Ismailis disagreed with

the other Shiites over the succession of Jafar al-Sadiq, believed to be the sixth imam and the spiritual successor of Muhammad. One group of Shiites recognized Ismail, the eldest son of Jafar, as his legitimate successor. They claimed that Muhammad, the son of Ismail, was the seventh and last imam, who would return on Judgment Day. This group became the Ismailis. In contrast, most of the Shiite community believed in the 12 imams.

Some Ismaili groups became involved in radical political action, such as the assassinations of several political leaders in the Middle East, and they were persecuted by their opponents. In response, some members of the sect escaped from the major urban centers of the Islamic world to settle in the mountains of central Asia.

RECENT DEVELOPMENTS

During the 20th century, the government's attitudes toward Islam kept changing dramatically, often from one extreme to another. In the early 20th century, the Russian imperial authorities chose not to interfere in religious issues in central Asia and strictly adhered to that policy. In the early 1920s the Soviet authorities also generally tolerated the

Islamic creed but banned Islamic groups from political activities. In the late 1920s and 1930s the Soviet leader Joseph Stalin radically changed the state policy toward religion. Many mosques and madrassas (Islamic schools) were destroyed, and some mullahs (Islamic religious leaders) were executed or exiled to Siberia (in extreme eastern Russia), Afghanistan, Turkey, and Iran.

During World War II, the Soviet government once again altered its position, and Islamic practices were tolerated as far as they were private actions and did not interfere with public life. However, the Soviet authorities retained strict control over the registration of mosques and mullahs, thus limiting their numbers.

Tajikistan experienced a major resurgence of Islamic practice in the 1980s and 1990s—almost 700 mosques were built, and many people embraced the religion. Yet the constitution of independent Tajikistan declared that the republic was a secular state, and Islam was considered a separate institution.

Despite this, an influential group of political activists emerged in Tajikistan in the early 1990s stating the need for a return of Islam to public life and the introduction of some Islamic beliefs and practices into the legal and political systems. Several pro-government groups strongly disagreed. This growing conflict over the role of Islam in Tajikistan became one of the driving forces of the civil war in the 1990s.

A compromise was achieved between 1997 and 1999—the government abandoned its earlier position and allowed Islamic political parties to participate in national decision-making. Yet the Tajikistan government swiftly restricted the power held by radical political groups, especially those that it suspected of having links with Al Qaida and other international terrorist organizations.

Opposite: **A bodyguard of the Tajik opposition leader Said Abdullo Nuri prays in the doorway of a mosque.**

LANGUAGE

TAJIKISTAN'S OFFICIAL LANGUAGE is Tajik, a dialect of Persian that is very similar to Farsi, the official language of Iran. Other languages are evident in full force in Tajikistan. The Uzbeks, who live mainly in northern Tajikistan, speak Uzbek. Uzbek belongs to the Turkic language group and is very different from Tajik. Turkic languages are spoken mainly in central Asia, western China, Turkey, and some parts of Russia and Iran. Through centuries of cultural interaction, however, the language of Tajikistan's Uzbek population has absorbed many words of Tajik origin. There are also small communities of Kyrgyzs and Turkmens who speak their native languages, which also belong to the Turkic language group but are quite different from Uzbek. Russian-speaking people are also found in Tajikistan but in small numbers.

Many people in Tajikistan are bilingual or even trilingual. It is common to hear Tajiks speaking Uzbek and Russian, in addition to their native tongue. At the beginning of the 21st century, a new trend emerged in Dushanbe and other metropolitan areas as many young people began studying English. English has slowly and increasingly replaced Russian in the school and university curricula. In addition, during the last decade Arabic has gained popularity in many small towns and cities, especially among devoted Muslims.

TAJIK

Tajik is the language spoken by as many as 4.5 million people, mostly in Tajikistan, Uzbekistan, and Kyrgyzstan. Because of its close links to the main language of Iran, it is sometimes called Farsi. It may also be referred to as another related language, Dari, a similar dialect of Persian that is spoken mostly in Afghanistan.

Opposite: **A poster in the Tajik language on a collective farm near the town of Nurek promoting the 25th Congress of the Communist Party of the Soviet Union in 1976.**

Tajik scholars believe that their language was formed mostly between the ninth and 11th centuries. During that time it was written in Arabic script, and numerous fine literary works were written by authors from Bukhara, Herat, Samarqand, and other places. Scholars from present-day Tajikistan, Uzbekistan, and Iran cite these works among their countries' literary masterpieces. However, it is hard to say if they were written by native Tajik, Uzbek, or Iranian authors, since at that time there were no clear ethnic or national divisions among various central Asian ethnic groups. Although Tajik is related to Farsi, unlike the official language of Iran, Tajik absorbed fewer Arabic words and acquired more words from Turkic languages.

By the late 19th and early 20th centuries, Tajik had two distinctive forms: the high classical language of medieval and modern literature and poetry, with complex grammatical rules and linguistic forms; and the

A boy in Dushanbe presents the pages of a copy of the Koran that he is reading. The Koran is written in Arabic, a language that has gained in popularity among some Muslims in Tajikistan.

everyday language of the common people, which was less formal and had simplified grammatical rules. The emergence of the two branches sparked some debate among intellectuals of the era. Some demanded that all literary works be written in the classical form, while others called for creating a national literature in the language of the common people.

In the 1920s Tajik underwent its first major transformations. The government switched from Arabic to Latin script in the late 1920s and then to Cyrillic script (the basis of the Russian language) in 1940. During the 1940s Tajik absorbed many Russian words. At present Tajik is based on the Cyrillic alphabet and has 39 letters. Thirty-three letters were taken from the Russian alphabet, and six letters were created to reflect and capture specific Tajik sounds.

CONVERSATION ETIQUETTE

The Tajiks are quite informal when speaking with friends and family. They will also usually not refrain from striking up a conversation with a foreigner or stranger. Yet there are some basic rules that are expected to be followed by everyone.

When people meet, it is customary to ask about the well-being of the immediate family and distant relatives and to ask other, often personal, questions, even if they hardly know each other. Teasing and telling humorous stories are common among close friends, relatives, and business associates. Sometimes people poke fun at each other's quirks or habits or tell stories of personal experiences in hilarious or difficult situations. At large parties and traditional gatherings, one favorite tradition is to listen to stories about Afandi, a comic hero from traditional folklore. The stories about Afandi ridicule people's greed, ignorance, poor judgment, and silliness, and they particularly target the follies and foibles of the rich.

Two Tajik women with gold-capped teeth smile as they catch up with each other at the Sunday market in Dushanbe.

The elders, or *aksakals*, are highly respected, and they enjoy a special place in Tajik society. When they talk, it is considered rude to interrupt them. Tajiks are generally prepared to spend a considerable length of time politely and attentively listening to *aksakals*, even if the listeners have little interest in the topic of conversation.

In many rural communities, it is considered impolite for a stranger or tourist to give excessive attention to women. Some women might even refuse to talk to strangers at all, even if they are asked a simple question about directions or local places of interest. In some conservative families, women are expected to keep silent and not to join any conversations. In the past, women could not join any kinds of gatherings, even large family events, though today this practice has been dropped.

NAMES

Tajiks traditionally refer to one another by the first name, followed by the father's name. For example, Faruh Vafo is the equivalent of "Faruh, son of Vafo." In the past people often added the name of their family's place of origin to their first names, as in Rudaki Samarqandi, meaning "Rudaki from Samarqand." This practice ended quite a while ago, although in private conversations people sometimes still identify colleagues by their places of origin.

During the Soviet era, names underwent major changes when they were Russianized. There are no last names or traditional family names in Tajik culture. So the Soviets created a family name by taking the father's name and adding a Russian ending: *-ov* or *-ev* for males and *-ova* or *-eva* for females. This family name was then to be handed down to generations to come. In addition, Russian-style patronymics, which indicated the father's first name, were introduced. The patronymic usually ended with a Russianized *-vich* for males and *-ovna* for females. In formal settings, people called one another by their full names (name and patronymic); when talking informally, the first name was good enough.

In the post-Soviet era, some people decided to "de-Russify" their family names by dropping the Russian endings. Thus Rakhim Jalilov became Rakhim Jalil. Traditionally, Tajiks—like most of the peoples in central and southern Asia—have used various titles with their names (usually with their first names) and have often been sensitive to the use of proper titles. For example, a younger person is encouraged to refer to an older person as *ako*, while an older or senior person refers to a younger person as *uko*. In everyday life, people add the ending *-jon* to first names (as in Zamirajon) as a polite means of referring to one another. In the pre-Soviet era, titles such as *mirzo*, *bek*, *boi*, and *khon* were widely used in addressing nobility, landlords, and officers of the state administration. The title *khonum* (madam) was used to address female members of the upper class. During the last decade, the use of some of these pre-Soviet titles is being revived.

Following Soviet name rules, Parviz Rakhmon (or Parviz, son of Rakhmon) was changed to Parviz Rakhmonovich Rakhmonov (Parviz, son of Rakhmon of the Rakhmonov family); his daughter would hypothetically be called Dilafruz Parvizovna Rakhmonova (Dilafruz, daughter of Parviz of the Rakhmonov family), and his son would be called Hussein Parvizovich Rakhmonov (Hussein, son of Parviz of the Rakhmonov family).

A group of mothers poses with their offspring. Children are believed to be a blessing by many Tajiks and often become the focus of family life.

The Tajiks love their children and are very proud of them. Therefore they often try to choose the most poetic or historic names for their children. Many are based on names from classical Persian literature. Others have an Arabic origin. Typical names for Tajik girls are Tahmina (a heroine of the classic Persian work *Shahnameh* by Firdawsi), Zarina (meaning "golden"), Zebo ("beautiful"), and Dilafruz ("the one who awakens the heart"). Typical names for Tajik boys include Alisher (*sher* means "lion") and Ilhom ("inspiration").

MEDIA

Forms of mass media, such as newspapers, magazines, and radio, first arrived in Tajikistan in the late 1920s and 1930s. During the years of Soviet control, a comprehensive mass-media network was established in the country, targeting and addressing special professional, regional, cultural, and other interests. Heavily subsidized, these publications and broadcasts were made accessible and affordable to all. However, these various media were strictly censored, and all materials that criticized the political regime, economic and social policies, or the Communist Party ideology were banned. The government also restricted and often blocked foreign radio stations, such as the radio channels Voice of America or Radio Liberty/Radio Free Europe. In a similar vein, satellite dishes were not allowed for private use.

The situation changed radically in the 1990s after Tajikistan declared its independence. Most of the media lost their subsidies and were forced to raise revenue through commercial advertising or through other sources. Officially, censorship and most of the restrictions were removed. In reality, however, these freedoms are limited by several factors that force journalists and owners of independent media to impose some form of self-censorship. Most of the media refrain from criticizing the government, its policies, or the activities of big business, since the stations and publications depend heavily on advertising or other forms of support from those sources. In addition, conservative groups disapprove of advertising that shows individuals clad scantily or wearing bathing suits or underwear.

Due to the civil war and severe economic recession that followed, the population of the country has limited access to international media, since subscriptions to foreign newspapers and magazines are prohibitively expensive for most people and access to the Internet is still significantly limited in Tajikistan. On the positive side, the government has removed all restrictions on the ownership of satellite dishes, and many Tajiks now use them as a vital source of news and entertainment. Sometimes neighboring families, in order to reduce the financial burden, share a single satellite dish.

Traditionally, Tajiks received important news from conversations in the bazaars and teahouses or at large public gatherings, since there were practically no newspapers or magazines in the region's towns and cities until the 20th century. To this day it is still common for people to gather at teahouses to discuss the news in terms of common folk wisdom.

ARTS

THE ARTS IN TAJIKISTAN have enjoyed a long and prolific history. For centuries, local artists have amazed travelers, adventurers, and traders with their incredible skill and craftsmanship. The Tajik masters have long been known as excellent architects, potters, and weapon and jewelry makers. Wool and silk rugs and silk dresses and scarfs made by local women are in great demand in central Asia as well as in many distant countries.

Tajik scholars have traced the deep roots of contemporary Tajik arts to the nation's vibrant history and long-standing traditions. These experts find many similarities between Tajikistan's present-day artistic traditions and the many artifacts excavated from the sites of ancient and medieval cities both in Tajikistan and in neighboring lands.

EARLY HISTORY

Ancient and medieval chronologists claim that the region was a "land of a thousand cities." Old manuscripts and miniature paintings indicate that, hundreds of years ago, cities and towns in the area were well-planned with numerous magnificent public buildings, palaces, and places of worship. Ancient craftspeople became masters of design, producing vivid paintings and imposing sculptures. The pictures and statues of mystical animals from that era still capture people's imaginations.

Archaeological excavations have found evidence of flourishing artistic communities in the states of Bactria and Sogdiana. These communities absorbed the highest achievements of the ancient Greek, Persian, and Indian cultures and developed their own styles. Archaeologists have discovered many sculptures and mosaic fragments, produced by local artisans, that reflect the influence of the classical traditions of Persian and Greek art. The remains of palaces and fortresses with Hellenic (Greek) columns,

Opposite: **A potter fashions a clay vessel in his workshop.**

decorative and ritual sculptures, copper medallions, amphora-shaped pottery, and many other artifacts have been excavated and put on display in the Tajik Historical State Museum and in museums in Russia.

ISLAMIC ARTS

The establishment of the Islamic caliphate stretching from central Asia to North Africa secured peace in the region and made it safe to travel and trade in these vast areas. With greater wealth and stability, the arts flourished. Artistic communities were established through the generosity of rulers, princes, and wealthy individual patrons who sponsored writers, architects, and musicians.

Above: **Tajik women work together to weave a rug.**

Opposite: **A mosque in Dushanbe reveals an Arabian architectural style, a legacy of the golden era of Islamic rule in Tajikistan.**

Between the ninth and 12th centuries, the central Asian region experienced a tremendous cultural flowering, and many scholars call this era the Central Asian Renaissance. The surviving historical artifacts show a great outpouring of artistic expression during that time, featuring a continuation of old styles as well as the creation of new visual and literary forms.

ARCHITECTURE   Many architectural monuments were produced during the golden era of Islamic culture. Local architects displayed great versatility and ingenuity in creating architectural forms using simple local materials such as brick, wood, and clay. They demonstrated great skill in designing the era's tallest buildings that were able to withstand earthquakes, hurricanes, and other natural disasters. They also built the largest domes without the use of modern machines and technologies.

Famous architects and engineers from central Asian cities were invited to as far away as India and Egypt to help design and build palaces and mosques.

Another achievement was the development of the beautiful and colorful tiles and mosaics used to decorate the exterior and interior spaces of public buildings, palaces, and mosques. Sky-blue tiles covering domes and minarets were visible from miles away; and for centuries they withstood storms, fires, the hot sun, cold winds, and many other environmental influences without fading.

Today the ruins of many buildings of the era can be found throughout the country. Archaeologists have excavated old fortified palaces in such places as Kalai-Kakhkakha, Munchak-Tepe, Urta-Kurgan, Pendzhikent, Kalai-Mug, and Kargani-Khisor. Khodja-Nakhshran and Muhammad Bashshar are mausoleums that stand as excellent examples of medieval religious architecture.

LITERATURE During the Islamic golden age, many writers and poets produced works that gained wide acclaim in other parts of the world and have since become classics of Persian literature. Poems about love and

human passion are still popular among the people, and many classic verses became well-liked songs.

Tajik scholars trace the roots of their literature to as early as the ninth and 10th centuries A.D. They also claim that the mid-ninth-century poet and musician Abu Abdallah Jafar Rudaki contributed to the development of early classic Tajik poetry by creating ceremonial odes, satirical poems, and beautiful lyrical verses called *ghazals.*

Tajiks also highly respect another word-smith, Abu ol-Qasem Mansur (Firdawsi), whom they regard as the most influential poet of the era, not only in central Asia but also in the Middle East and southern Asia. Firdawsi authored the monumental poem *Shahnameh* (*Book of Kings*). In poetic verse, he described the personal lives, loves, glories, and achievements of many generations of central Asian rulers.

CALLIGRAPHY AND MINIATURE PAINTING

The rapidly developing literature of the time led to a significant creative offshoot in two related fields: calligraphy and miniature painting. Since there was no printing technology available during the era, all books were produced by hand. There was even an entire social group of specialized workers who mastered the art of fine handwriting called calligraphy. The Arabic letters that were used in writing were transformed into beautiful patterns and elegant lines that became works of art in their own right. Such calligraphic writing could be seen not only in books but also adorning the walls of mosques, old public buildings, and homemade oriental carpets.

Miniature painting had a long history in the region. Visual artists captured the beautiful landscapes, historic battles and events, and magnificent architectural monuments of the era. They depicted their subjects in great detail and a matchless style. Often these pictures are the only remaining evidence of past glories, since many of the area's cities, villages, and monuments have vanished or been destroyed in the wars and calamities that have gripped the region.

Islamic tradition forbids artists to draw humans and animals, to prevent people from worshiping them. Unable to paint large portraits or compositions of humans or animals, the central Asian artistic masters created miniatures instead. They also adopted the use of more abstract forms, including rich colors and sometimes simple lines in their art.

MUSIC Music has always accompanied everyday life in Tajikistan, especially important celebrations. Typical Tajik musical instruments include various forms of percussion instruments (*tablak, nagora, doira, zang,* and *kairok*), trumpets (*karnai, nai,* and *surnai*), the fiddle, and the lutelike *dutor.* They often accompanied armies and trade caravans. Musicians, including *mavrigikhons* (male singers), *makomists* and *usto-navozanda* (male instrumentalists), and *sozandas* (female singers and dancers), were always welcome and played before various audiences not

Opposite: **A page from the *Shahnameh* depicts a scene from the poem by Firdawsi.**

105

only in the palaces of the rich and powerful but also at the *chaikhanas* (teahouses) and the homes of ordinary citizens.

One of the people's favorite forms of recreation was storytelling accompanied by various musical instruments. In medieval times, when traders and the guards of camel and horse caravans stopped for the night, sometimes joined by their local friends and curious hosts, they remained sleepless, on the lookout for bands of marauders or robbers. They kept themselves awake by listening to adventurous tales of past glories, distant travels, and beautiful love stories or *garibi* songs (songs about the difficulties of life far from home).

Unfortunately, many cities and towns of the era—along with most of their libraries, palaces, and greatest cultural achievements—were destroyed during the Mongol invasion in the 13th century and in the following centuries of instability and war. What too often survived were legends and myths but few examples of the region's glory and achievements in the arts.

Opposite: **A knotted Tajik carpet presents the portrait of Leonid Brezhnev, a Soviet statesman and Communist Party official.**

HISTORICAL COLLECTIONS The Tajik Historical State Museum hosts one of the largest collections of ancient and medieval artifacts found in Tajikistan and its neighboring countries.

THE *DUTOR*

This traditional Tajik stringed instrument has a pear-shaped body and a long neck. The *dutor* resembles the two-string lute and is usually made of wood. The *dutor* is commonly used by a *dutorchy* (literally meaning "*dutor* player," similar to a national poet-singer) during various major events and family gatherings. Traditionally, a *dutorchy* was invited to sing the songs of heroes and to entertain during various public events.

Tajik archaeologists have excavated many sites from ancient and medieval times, and their rich collections of jewelry, sculpture, and miniature paintings have been added to the museum's permanent holdings. Still there are many parts of the past that remain unexplained, and scholars continue to argue about the fate of many ancient and medieval cities and events.

For example, there is a legend about the lost treasures of Alexander the Great, who decided to temporarily leave gold, diamonds, and many other prized possessions in a secret cave somewhere in the mountains of Tajikistan. According to the tale, he never came back to reclaim them. There is also a story about the treasures of the last emir of Bukhara, who tried to hide his kingdom's treasury and his most valued personal belongings from the advancing Red Army in 1920. Scholars are still addressing these historical puzzles, attempting to separate fact from fiction.

CONTEMPORARY ARTS

During the 20th century, culture and art in Tajikistan experienced significant changes. Several factors contributed to the acceleration of these changes. The government invested

Above: **A Tajik art specialist examines a statue of the Buddha in a Dushanbe museum. The statue is the largest in the world of a reclining Buddha.**

Opposite: **An outdoor installation of a modern sculpture.**

extensively in the development of the arts after the establishment of the Tajik Soviet Socialist Republic in the 1920s in order to promote a strong national identity within the newly established Tajik state. Both old and new art forms received support from the state and various state-funded agencies. Another factor was the Russian influence. Between the 1930s and 1990s leading Russian universities, conservatories, galleries, libraries, and archives opened their doors to the most talented Tajik students, scholars, and artists. Tajik students received not only free education but also scholarships, internships, and advanced training.

After returning home, these students brought new forms of artistic expression with them, such as European-style theater, ballet, opera, and oil painting on canvas. They established the Tajik theater, the Tajik Academy of Sciences, the Tajik National Library, various historical and art museums, and many new cultural institutions. The Tajik National Theater was set up in 1929, the Tajik National Theater of Opera and Ballet first opened in 1940, and the Tajik Philharmonic Society was founded in 1938. Artists at these and other smaller centers also experimented with the creation of a new sound by combining local musical and poetic traditions with different kinds of Western music and instrumental styles.

Contemporary Western-like pop culture arrived in full force in Tajikistan in the 1980s and 1990s and influenced the youth culture of major urban centers considerably. During the last decade, several popular bands were established that perform hard rock, rap, and jazz, adding a local flavor to prevailing Western musical forms.

Yet, in the face of change, thousands of people still keep national traditions and styles intact, creating various handmade artifacts at home or in small workshops. With the rise of national pride and the growing nationalism of the 1990s, there was an increasing interest in traditional Tajik art forms. Since 1991 more people have turned to traditional arts as a source of income. Visitors to the colorful rural bazaars find many popular items sold there, such as handmade silver jewelry and colorful traditional blankets, rugs, scarfs, shawls, silk dresses, and pottery.

LEISURE

PEOPLE IN TAJIKISTAN USUALLY center their leisure and entertainment around family and community (*mahallya*) life. Generally in rural areas most events are organized around the seasons—people celebrate the beginning of spring, the end of the harvest, and other important annual milestones. In large urban areas, people enjoy leisure and entertainment activities similar to those of residents in most metropolitan areas, such as eating out and attending sports events, the theater, and parades.

Yet, in both small villages and large cities, people tend to socialize with their families or relatives and close members of their communities. Some leisure activities draw on existing religious and national traditions going back hundreds of years. The other ways people spend their free time, usually in cities, closely resemble what people do in New York, Chicago, or Istanbul.

Left: **A Tajikistani man tries to solve a Rubik's cube.**

Opposite: **Tajikistanis engage in *buzkashi*, an equestrian sport requiring strength, courage, and horsemanship.**

Rural Tajiks gather to celebrate with song and dance.

TOIS

Tois are family celebrations that mark important events in the personal lives of people of all ages. All major occasions, such as marriages, the birth of a first child or grandchild, circumcision, or the building of a new home, are usually heartily enjoyed.

Tois are usually quite large. It is common to have 100 or even 200 people attending an event that might last anywhere from one to three days. People usually invite all their close and distant relatives, neighbors, colleagues, and friends.

The celebrations are organized in a grand manner, with music, dance, and plenty of food and drink. Such events need to be planned well in advance, and many people are involved in the organizational process. It is also expected that the guests will help with such events either by contributing small sums of money or lending furniture, providing transportation or food for the event, or just helping to set up and clean afterward.

The *tois* in Tajikistan are more than simple family celebrations. They are also opportunities to learn about the developments and achievements in the personal lives of friends and colleagues. They serve as excellent occasions for networking as well. These celebrations are regularly used by young people to meet potential partners, too, or by their parents for matchmaking. For young artists and musicians, *tois* are ideal venues to show off their talents and gain greater recognition and followings.

GAPS

In traditional Tajik society, people organize themselves into informal interest groups called *gaps* (meaning "talk" or "discussion"). A *gap* is a group of friends or neighbors who get together for entertainment or the discussion of various political or nonpolitical issues. Such gatherings help provide mutual support through consultation and the soliciting of advice. Usually there are two types of *gap*: those organized according to a personal or professional interest, such as music, sports, or hunting; and simple community-based groups usually made up of the people from the same neighborhood, village, or town. A *gap* traditionally consists of people of the same sex—a female *gap* and a male *gap* never mix.

Gaps resemble social clubs, to some degree. Unmarried Tajik women often form *gaps* to cook while discussing their life plans, education, or prospective partners or sharing their insights on how to deal with difficult situations. Married women discuss family issues, bringing up children, or family budget planning. Men, on the other hand, come together to discuss issues related to neighborhood life, community development, or business. Other groups discuss literature, poetry, or provide mutual help in gaining recognition or voicing opinions. Generally *gaps* are quite exclusive, and informal membership is usually for life, unless a member

For Westerners, it might seem unusual to invite a stranger to a family event, but that is not the case in Tajikistan. Whoever happens to be in the neighborhood is invited to join the tois, *including foreigners. Even former rivals come to the* tois, *since they provide an excellent opportunity for reconciliation.*

113

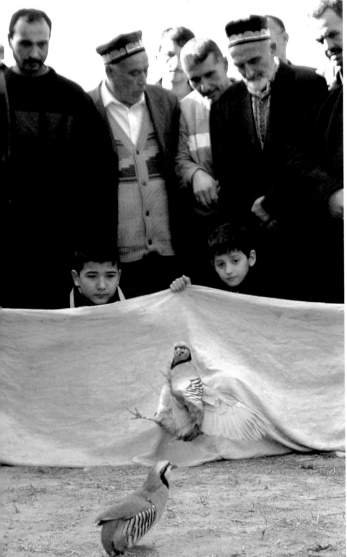

is excluded on account of misbehavior or any other wrongdoing.

BAZAARS

Many places in Tajikistan are famous for their specialized bazaars—marketplaces for selling animals, handicrafts, or consumer goods—where customers can find a variety of products in one place, from locally made silk shirts and teapots to imported electronics and children's toys.

People often go to bazaars to buy fresh and dried fruit and meat, exotic spices, and herbal teas, though these products are available at convenience shops. The bazaars often offer the freshest products at affordable prices for those who can bargain well. Bargaining is a ritual all its own, requiring skill, knowledge of the market tradition, and most of all an understanding of human psychology. In some instances, deals might be struck over a cup of green tea, while at other times the negotiations might turn out to be less peaceful affairs, with emotions running high and arguments erupting, depending of course on the size of the deal and the regional backgrounds of the buyers and sellers.

For people in Tajikistan, the bazaars are more than markets. They are places to socialize, meet friends and colleagues, show off wealth and success, or search for employees or a business partner. Often entire families dress up in their best clothes and spend all day at the bazaar, combining shopping, socializing, eating out, and business negotiations.

SPORTS

Sports have traditionally been a part of all major celebrations. Local strongmen (*palvans*) showed their strength by wrestling and lifting rocks; farmers raced their best horses; weapons makers displayed their skills as well as the quality of their wares in swordplay contests and exhibitions. Elite families often organized outdoor events such as hunting wild animals, sometimes with the use of birds of prey. These traditional sports are still quite popular and can be seen on display at large celebrations such as the spring festival of Nowruz.

During recent decades, however, modern sports have made their presence known in everyday life in Tajikistan. Soccer, for example, has become one of the most popular sports in the country. There are more than 900 soccer fields in Tajikistan and dozens of officially registered soccer clubs. Boys usually play soccer after school. Men of all ages often play soccer during the weekend on their local fields. Adults come together a few times each month to play formal and informal tournaments pitting one town or community against another. Tajikistan's soccer teams regularly play in central Asian regional tournaments and participate in several international tournaments within

Above: **Tajik Shamil Aliev** *(right)* **and German David Bichinashwili grapple as part of an Olympic free-style wrestling qualifying match in Sofia, Bulgaria, in 2004.**

Opposite: **Tajiks watch a partridge fight, a traditional bazaar attraction.**

the Commonwealth of Independent States and the Asian Soccer Confederation. Women's soccer, however, is not popular in the country, and there are no official organized women's soccer teams.

A new part of modern Tajikistani culture is sending children of school and university age to various sports clubs. The most popular ones focus on fencing, wrestling, and archery. The practice has paid off in the past, when Tajik athletes, competing for the former Soviet Union, won Olympic medals in fencing, archery, and gymnastics, as well as in other sports.

Tajikistan's Oev Dzhamolidin *(center)* vies with Oladi Meherdad *(right)* of Iran during the First Islamic Solidarity games in Jeddah, Saudi Arabia, in 2005.

TEAHOUSES

A *chaikhana* is a traditional teahouse. It is a common sight in rural areas and can be found in practically every city and town. People usually sit on a special elevated platform or around a low table. A *chaikhana* normally serves traditional drinks, such as tea, and traditional food, such as *pilov, sambusa, kurutob,* and *kichiri mastova.*

Naturally a *chaikhana* is more than just a place to eat and drink. It is an important institution in central Asia for socializing and networking. It serves as a kind of social club where some tables are reserved exclusively for those who gather on a regular basis. Over a cup of tea, people discuss community issues and developments at the local level as well as major political, social, and economic topics. Community leaders, especially in rural areas, regularly gather in teahouses to hear the opinions and gather the input of the *aksakals* in order to settle minor disputes or to organize a local charity event (*khashar*).

A *chaikhana* is a place where local public opinion can be formed or influenced, family and personal reputations established or ruined, and new businesses accepted or rejected. By and large it is a central place for many activities at a community level.

STORYTELLING

Storytelling is an important part of Tajik life and assumes various forms. At family events, *aksakals* tell stories of their adventures and travels or the battles in which they took part as well as relating the lives of legendary heroes of the past. In an informal and captivating way, they extract moral and personal lessons for their young listeners, whom they hope will make the tales and the art of storytelling part of their own family traditions.

In *chaikhanas*, storytelling is a part of the general entertainment, since there is always a skillful storyteller who remembers hundreds of stories about the life and adventures of one of the nation's favorite comic personalities—Afandi. Local heroes or the colorful personalities of the past and present are also the subjects of these vivid tales.

Sometimes friends and colleagues come together to listen to and discuss stories taken from the glorious pages of Tajik history, literature, and poetry. Others focus on tales about Islamic characters. Those gathered often invite local musicians, singers, or poets to present their creative works or to relate favorite legends in the form of songs.

A Tajik elder in a *chaikhana* in Dushanbe.

FESTIVALS

FOR DECADES, the communist government used most public festivals as a means of organizing people into public displays of support for the party's official policies. Many holidays were arranged on a grand scale, with sporting events, parades, and a military presence on display. The government tightly regulated such events. Until 1991 all Islamic religious celebrations were prohibited or were allowed to be celebrated only in private in small community or family gatherings. It was also forbidden to hold any anti-government rallies, to display antigovernment signs and slogans, or to have any unsanctioned demonstrations.

Since 1991 the situation has changed significantly. First, the government of independent Tajikistan has allowed the celebration of all Islamic festivals without any restrictions. It made those occasions as official public holidays, giving people an opportunity to take days off from their jobs. Second, the national government became less intrusive and less restrictive in organizing public celebrations. The organization of many events was delegated to community and local government leaders. Third, the economic recession of the 1990s contributed to the scaling down of public displays and to the near disappearance of government-subsidized parades and events.

In general, people are free to choose whether they want to celebrate secular or religious holidays or both. It is not uncommon to see families cheerfully celebrate Nowruz, Eid al-Fitr, as well as other holidays.

NOWRUZ

Nowruz is a spring festival that has been celebrated by Tajiks since pre-Islamic times. Nowruz starts on the first day of spring according to the solar calendar (in March), and people often call it the Spring Festival. Nowruz was not celebrated during the Soviet era, but it was reintroduced as a national holiday after 1991.

Opposite: **A group of Tajikistanis organizes a celebration for the arrival of Prince Karim Aga Khan, the Ismaili spiritual leader.**

One of the nation's most beloved festivals, Nowruz is traditionally celebrated in a grand way. Local communities and governments usually organize performances of various musical and dance groups in their town or city's major public parks or central squares. Merchants set up outdoor food stands and large bazaars. Families typically visit one another or attend major community events. The festival is also an opportunity for everyone to watch performances by local artists or to take part in them.

Many Tajiks believe that Nowruz unleashes good will and good luck that extends throughout the entire year. It is a special time of renewal when people tend to buy new clothes and make gifts for one another.

Women sell clothes at a bazaar in Khudzhand. Bazaars are a big attraction during festivals.

ISLAMIC FESTIVALS

Since 1991, once Islamic holidays were no longer outlawed, these religious observances have been firmly re-established in Tajik life. The Islamic festivals are celebrated according to the lunar calendar, which divides the year into 12 months, each lasting between 29 and 30 days. The lunar year is 10 or 11 days shorter than the Gregorian calendar year used in most Western countries. Therefore all events and festivals in the lunar calendar are moved forward 10 or 11 days every year.

RAMADAN Ramadan is the ninth month in the Islamic calendar, when all devoted Muslims are encouraged to fast from sunrise to sunset. Fasting is one of the Five Pillars of Islam and is considered to be an important duty for every Muslim.

According to Islamic teaching, it was during Ramadan that Prophet Muhammad began receiving messages from God. Fasting during Ramadan reminds people of the difficulties faced by the poor, teaches self-discipline, and helps them cleanse themselves of selfishness and open their hearts to the teachings of God. It is expected that all Muslims refrain from any wrongdoing, harming of others, or fighting with one another during the month. Islamic doctrine does allow for some exceptions. For example, pregnant or nursing women, travelers, or the sick are allowed to abstain from fasting during Ramadan. However, they are required to fast for the same number of days they missed later in the year.

While most Muslims fast during Ramadan, some restaurants, cafés, *chaikhanas* and food stores in Tajikistan are closed during the daytime and open in the evening. However, the nation is not as strict as other Muslim countries, particularly those in the Middle East. Many shops and food stores in Tajikistan remain open during Ramadan since there are communities of non-Muslims. Still, business and public work tend to slow down during this time.

People break their fasts after sunset. It is always done in a grand way, as many family members, friends, colleagues, and neighbors come together to share a prayer and then food. Children use this opportunity to visit other houses, where they receive small gifts from adults, usually in the form of candy and sweets. Rich and successful people are strongly encouraged to invite poor members of the community to their homes to share food after sunset.

EID AL-FITR This is one of the biggest holidays in the Islamic calendar. It signifies the end of the fasting that comes with the observance of Ramadan. Muslims celebrate Eid al-Fitr together and use this time to visit, since it is strongly encouraged that doors be opened to all members of the community and that everyone visit one another without special invitation. Traditionally, wealthy members of the community are expected to organize major feasts and to invite their relatives and neighbors to share their good fortune and success.

EID KURBAN People celebrate Eid Kurban in the 12th month of the lunar calendar, when Muslims commemorate the end of a hajj, a pilgrimage to the holy city of Mecca. As with all other Islamic festivals, the exact date that the holiday is observed shifts according to the year. The day is an opportunity to recognize all members of the family, to visit the graves of relatives, and to give food to the poor.

Traditionally, families buy a whole lamb for this festival and organize a big feast for their extended family and close friends. People are also encouraged to make donations to various charities or to poor members of the communities.

FAMILY CELEBRATIONS

Many people in Tajikistan have a strong sense of family, and they use every possible opportunity to meet with close and distant relatives and to bring extended families together. There is even an informal rule that all family members should take turns organizing feasts at their homes during the year, so a large extended family visits each of its members' homes at least once or twice a year. People believe that this way they keep strong ties among the various family members and provide the necessary support to one another in times of need or congratulations and best wishes in times of success.

Muslims pray in the central mosque of Dushanbe to celebrate Eid Kurban.

FOOD

THE NATIONAL CUISINE OF Tajikistan has been enriched through the years by the influences of many other cultures, most notably those from the Indian subcontinent, the Middle East, and the Eurasian steppes.

Within the country, there are several regional variations in the foods that are eaten and the ways they are prepared. The cuisine of the Pamir Mountains, for example, can be quite different from the dishes popular in metropolitan Dushanbe or northern Tajikistan. Rice, lamb, homemade noodles, homemade bread, various baked pies, and other dishes are popular across the nation. Traditionally, all Tajiks do not eat pork because it is not permitted by Islamic tradition. In contrast to the neighboring Kyrgyzs, they also do not eat horse meat.

Tajiks have a strong sense of hospitality. It is traditional to invite a guest or even a stranger who is visiting to share food with the host family. It is common to spend several hours at lunch and especially at dinner, since people often discuss family affairs, current events, or even business deals over elaborate meals. Hosts usually offer several courses and large quantities of food. They would be offended if their guests did not eat or ate only a little.

A TYPICAL MEAL

Tajik cuisine is rich and diverse because every region and even every district adds its own variations to typical recipes. Contemporary Tajik cuisine incorporates both Western and central Asian ingredients in various ways to make healthful everyday meals.

Traditional meals often start with a cup of green tea or a piece of homemade bread called *non* (sometimes referred to as the Russian *lipioshka*). This is followed by soup, usually made of meat and various

Opposite: **Melons for sale at the Panjshanbe Bazaar in Khudzhand.**

vegetables and often homemade noodles. Fish soup or vegetarian soups are quite rare, although they can be found in metropolitan Dushanbe. After the soup comes the main dish. Often the principal course is *pilov* (pilaf) made of spiced meat, rice, and thinly cut carrots. There are hundreds of versions of *pilov*, and some people claim that every city and town has at least one unique variation. Some cooks add herbs, apricots, raisins, garlic, nuts, quinces, or any number of other ingredients to *pilov*. The meal usually ends with fresh fruit in the form of apples, pears, grapes, watermelons, honeydew melons, or fresh or dried apricots. In addition, guests are always served plenty of tea, especially during the hot time of the year.

A traditional Tajik meal of bread, pomegranates, apples, raisins, milk, candies, and nougats.

A Tajik woman sells traditional bread at a market.

Meals are almost always prepared at home, with young children helping their parents, learning cooking skills from an early age. Often, in order to show particular respect to especially honored guests, male members of the family cook the meal themselves, though everyday food is traditionally cooked by the female members of the families.

Cooperation among family members is particularly important, because in many parts of Tajikistan modern kitchen appliances and facilities are uncommon. In many villages and small towns, people use natural gas, or if gas is not available, they cook using wood or coal.

DRINKS AND DESSERTS

Traditionally, Tajiks do not drink carbonated beverages or fruit juices, though in recent years the younger generations have increasingly embraced these kinds of drinks. Otherwise, the single most important and most popular drink is tea.

A woman waits with pomegranates neatly piled in pails for customers to survey and purchase.

People often prefer green tea because they believe that green tea is the best drink to overcome not only thirst but dehydration. Black, herbal, and fruit teas are also popular in more rural areas. Tajiks serve teas with various dried fruits, including apricots, raisins, dried honeydew melons, and various berries. In many parts of the country, people also add various nuts to their tea, including walnuts, pistachios, and almonds. Coffee and hot chocolate are the chosen drinks of sophisticated urbanites, but they are almost unseen in the rural areas.

Alcohol is served during some celebrations, although Islamic practice forbids its consumption. Locally made vodkas and sweet wines, along with various imported brandies and other strong liquors, can be found in all major stores and restaurants.

For dessert, Tajiks usually serve various types of pies, *halvah* (a sweet dessert typically made of nuts), or homemade bread and cookies topped with various homemade jams. In urban areas, ice cream has become an increasingly popular dessert.

TEA RITUALS

For centuries, central Asians have mastered the fine art of serving and consuming tea, developing complex rituals along the way. Table etiquette is very important in Tajikistan, since local tradition, social status, age, position in the family hierarchy, and many other factors are taken into consideration when serving tea.

People usually drink green tea served in small teapots. It is customary for the youngest person at the table to serve the others assembled. Alternatively, the host serves tea herself or himself in order to show great respect to the guests. Local etiquette often requires that all food and drink be received with the right hand. Traditionally, when the tea has been freshly made, people pour some into a teacup, then return it to the teapot, then repeat this twice to facilitate the brewing process. Certain positions around the table are reserved for the most respected person, usually an *aksakal*, who starts and ends the meal and generally leads the conversation.

ASH-KHANA

Tajiks love to dine out with their friends, colleagues, and business partners in national restaurants called *ash-khanas*. *Ash-khanas* serve traditional foods such as *kebab* and *pilov*. People are expected to linger over their meals and to spend hours enjoying conversation and the fine cuisine that is often specially prepared for each group of customers.

In contrast to Western-style restaurants, in an *ash-khana* people sit around traditional low tables on special rugs, cushions, or mats. In summer, food is often served in small and well-designed gardens or under coiling grape vines.

KABOBI ROKHATE

2 tablespoons oil
2 pounds thinly sliced lamb or beef
Salt, black pepper, and spices to taste
3–4 onions, thinly sliced
4 carrots, julienned
2 quinces, julienned
½ pumpkin (or turnip), julienned
1 bunch scallions (or dill), chopped

Heat the oil in a large frying pan or Dutch oven. Meanwhile, combine the meat pieces with salt, pepper, and spices. When the oil is heated, stir in the meat, followed by the sliced onions and the julienned carrots, quinces, and pumpkin (or turnip), and some of the scallions (or dill). Add more salt and spices to taste. Add just enough water to cover the meat. Cover with a lid, and let the meat and vegetables cook until ready.

PALAVI MURGDOR

3½ ounces oil
1 pound chicken, cut into small pieces
3 large onions, thinly sliced
4 carrots, julienned
Salt and spices to taste
⅔ pound rice
1 bunch scallions or dill, chopped

Heat the oil in a large Dutch oven. Stir in the chicken and onions, and fry until the onions are brown. Add the carrots, and fry for five minutes. Add the salt and spices. Add enough water to cover the meat, and cook for eight to 10 minutes. Add the rice, and cover with enough freshly boiled water. Cook on high heat until nearly all the water has evaporated, then on low heat until the rice is done. When serving, place the rice on a dish and garnish with the scallions or dill.

A   **B**   **C**   **D**   **E**

1

UZBEKISTAN

Sirdar'inskiy

Khudzhand

Syr Darya

Obanbori Qayroqqum

Fergana Valley

Langar

2

KYRGYZSTAN

Pendzhikent

Zeravshan

LENINABAD

R a n g e

A l a i

Surkhob

Ismail Samani
(24,591 ft / 7,495 m) ▲

P

Qa

3

Ramit

Hisor

DUSHANBE

Tursunzade

Nurek

Revolyutsiya
(22,882 ft / 6,974 m) ▲

e

Kuli Sarez

Kofarnihon

KUHIST

A

Yashilkul

4

Qurghonteppa

Kulob

KHATLON

Vakhsh

Panj

Khorog

Karl Marks
(22,068 ft / 6,726 m)
▲

Amu Darya

Panj

5

AFGHANISTAN

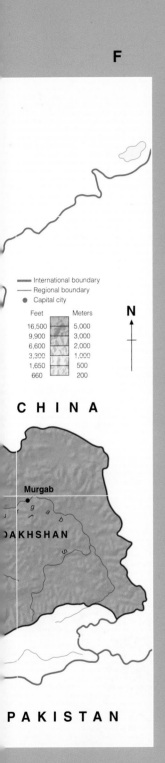

F

CHINA

Murgab

ʻAKHSHAN

PAKISTAN

N

MAP OF TAJIKISTAN

Afghanistan, A5, B4–B5, C3–C5, D5, E4–E5, F4–F5
Alai Range, C2–C3, D2, E2
Alichur (river), D4–F4
Amu Darya (river), A5, B4–B5

China, E2–E3, F1–F5

Dushanbe, B3

Fergana Valley, B2–C2

Hisor, A3

Ismail Samani, D3

Karl Marks, D5–E5
Khatlon, A3–A5, B3–B5, C3–C4
Khorog, D4
Khudzhand, B2
Kofamihon (river), A3–A5, B3
Kuhistoni Badakh-shan, C3–C4, D2–D5, E2–E5, F3–F4
Kuli Sarez, E3–E4
Kulob, B4
Kyrgyzstan, B2, C2, D1–D2, E1–E2, F1–F2

Langar, B2
Leninabad, A2, A3, B1–B3, C1, C2

Murgab, F4
Murgab (river), E3–E4, F4

Nurek, B3

Obanbori Qayroq-qum, B2, C1–C2

Pakistan, D5–F5
Pamirs, D3, E3–E4, F3–F4
Panj (river), D5–F5
Pendzhikent, A2

Qarokul, E3
Qurghonteppa, B4

Ramit, B3
Revolyutsiya, D3

Surkhob (river), B3–C3
Sirdar'inskiy, B2
Syr Darya (river), C1–D1

Tursunzade, A3

Uzbekistan, A1–A4, B1–B2, C1–C2, D1–D2, E1

Vakhsh (river), A4–A5, B3–B4

Yashilkul, E4

Zeravshan (river), A2

ECONOMIC TAJIKISTAN

ABOUT THE ECONOMY

OVERVIEW

Agriculture, industry, and services are the three main pillars of Tajikistan's economy, contributing 19.4, 25.7, and 54.9 percent respectively to the gross domestic product (GDP). The country's major export commodities are cotton, aluminum, silk, agricultural products, and textiles. Tajikistan depends heavily on imports of machinery, fuel, industrial and consumer goods, and food products. In the early 1990s the national economy was devastated by civil war and experienced a sharp recession. External debt reached $1.23 billion in 2003 and is expected to grow further.

GROSS DOMESTIC PRODUCT

$1.4 billion (2003)

GDP BY SECTOR

Agriculture 23.7 percent, industry 24.3 percent, services 52 percent (2004 estimate)

AGRICULTURAL PRODUCTS

Cotton, vegetables, fruit, tobacco, grain, silk

CURRENCY

1 Tajik somoni (TJS) = 100 dirhams
Notes: 1, 5, 10, 10, 50, and 100 somoni
Coins: 1, 2, 5, 10, and 50 dirhams
USD 1 = TJS 3.04 (February 2005)

INFLATION RATE

16 percent (2004)

WORKFORCE

2.2 million (2004)

WORKFORCE BY OCCUPATION

Agriculture 67.2 percent, industry 7.5 percent, services 25.3 percent (2000 estimate)

INDUSTRIAL PRODUCTS

Textiles, clothing, food products, aluminum, gold, silver

MAIN EXPORTS

Aluminum, cotton, agricultural products

MAIN IMPORTS

Food, fuel, machinery

TRADE PARTNERS

Kazakhstan, the Netherlands, Russia, Turkey, Uzbekistan

PORTS AND HARBORS

None. Tajikistan is landlocked.

INTERNATIONAL PARTICIPATION

Commonwealth of Independent States (CIS), International Monetary Fund (IMF), United Nations (UN), World Health Organization (WHO)

EXTERNAL DEBT

$1.23 billion (2003)

CULTURAL TAJIKISTAN

Petroglyphs
Rock carvings in caves above the town of Langar depict caravans and men riding horses.

Historical and Cultural Reserve
Hisor is home to the ruins of Hisor Fort and the 16th-century Sangin mosque and Makhdumi Azam mausoleum.

National Museum of Antiquities
This museum in Dushanbe features ancient Greek, Bactrian, and Persian sculptures, paintings, and jewelry.

Rudaki Museum
This museum named after the ninth-century poet Abu Abdallah Jafar Rudaki preserves artifacts from the ancient city of Pendzhikent. Excavations have also uncovered the ruins of homes and Zoroastrian temples in Pendzhikent.

Ajina-tepe
This ancient Buddhist monastery, 12km northeast of Qurghonteppa, includes a 12-m Buddha statue.

Amir Said Khamadoni Mausoleum
Kulob hosts the mausoleum of the great poet Amir Said Khamadoni.

ABOUT
THE CULTURE

OFFICIAL NAME
Republic of Tajikistan

NATIONAL FLAG
Three horizontal bands of red, white, and green. There is a stylized golden crown with seven golden stars in the center of the white band.

NATIONAL ANTHEM
A new national anthem was adopted in 1991. New words (by Gulnazar Keldi) replaced the Soviet-era Tajik anthem, but the music (by Suleiman Yudakov) remained the same.

CAPITAL
Dushanbe

OTHER MAJOR CITIES
Khorog, Khudzhand, Kulob, Qurghonteppa, Tursunzade

POPULATION
7.01 million (2004 estimate)

LIFE EXPECTANCY
64.47 years; male 61.53 years, female 67.55 years (2004)

ETHNIC GROUPS
Tajiks 64.9 percent, Uzbeks 25 percent, Russians 3.5 percent (declining because of emigration), Kyrgyz 0.1 percent, others 6.5 percent

RELIGIOUS GROUPS
Sunni Muslims 85 percent, Ismailis 5 percent, Christians 3.9 percent, others 6.1 percent

LANGUAGES
Tajik (official), Uzbek, Russian

LITERACY RATE
99 percent

INTERNET USERS
4,100 (2003)

ISLAMIC FESTIVALS
Eid al-Fitr, Eid Kurban

NATIONAL HOLIDAYS
New Year's Day (January 1), International Women's Day (March 8), Nowruz (March 21–22), International Labor Day (May 1), Victory Day in the Great Patriotic War (May 9), Independence Day (September 9), Constitution Day (November 6)

POLITICAL LEADERS
Rakhman Nabiyev—president (November 1991–September 1992)
Imomali Rakhmonov—chair of parliament and head of state (November 1992); elected president (November 1994)

TIME LINE

IN TAJIKISTAN	IN THE WORLD
First millennium B.C.	
The states of Khorezm and Margiana are mentioned in ancient chronicles.	**753** B.C.
	Rome is founded.
329 B.C.	
Alexander the Great conquers central Asia.	
Second century B.C.	**116–17** B.C.
The Great Silk Road starts to function.	The Roman Empire reaches its greatest extent, under Emperor Trajan (98–17).
Seventh to eighth centuries A.D.	**A.D. 600**
Arabs conquer central Asia.	Height of Mayan civilization
	1000
1221–22	The Chinese perfect gunpowder and begin to use it in warfare.
Genghis Khan conquers central Asia.	
1357	
Janibak Khan conquers Khorasan.	
1384	
Tamerlane (Timur) invades Khorasan.	
1500–12	
Sheibani Khan conquers central Asia.	**1530**
	Beginning of trans-Atlantic slave trade organized by the Portuguese in Africa.
1558	**1558–1603**
Briton Antony Jenkinson travels to Bukhara and Khiva.	Reign of Elizabeth I of England
	1620
1740	Pilgrims sail the *Mayflower* to America.
Nader Shah of Persia invades Bukhara and Khiva.	**1776**
	U.S. Declaration of Independence
	1789–99
1826–28	The French Revolution
Russian-Persian war, ending with signing of peace agreement in Turkmanchai	**1861**
	The U.S. Civil War begins.
	1869
1887	The Suez Canal is opened.
The borders of Russia's possessions in central Asia are formally established.	
1895	
Division of British and Russian spheres of influence in the Pamirs	**1914**
	World War I begins.

IN TAJIKISTAN	IN THE WORLD
1922	
Union of Soviet Socialist Republics (USSR) established, with its capital in Moscow	
1924	
Tajik Autonomous Soviet Socialist Republic established	
1929–31	
First of Stalinist purges; hundreds deported to Siberia. Mass collectivization programs begin; thousands of Tajiks escape to Afghanistan.	
1936–38	
Mass purges against Tajik intelligentsia and political leadership; thousands are sent to labor camps or executed.	
1937	
The constitution of the Tajik SSR is adopted.	
1939	**1939**
Census conducted in the Tajik SSR	World War II begins.
	1949
	The North Atlantic Treaty Organization (NATO) is formed.
	1957
	The Russians launch Sputnik.
	1966–69
1978	The Chinese Cultural Revolution
Tajik SSR adopts new constitution.	**1986**
	Nuclear power disaster at Chernobyl in Ukraine
1991	**1991**
Tajikistan joins the Commonwealth of Independent States (CIS).	Break-up of the Soviet Union
1992–97	**1997**
Civil war in Tajikistan	Hong Kong is returned to China.
2001	**2001**
Tajikistan's government agrees to open its airspace and airfields to U.S. allies in the U.S.-led international war against terrorism.	Terrorists crash planes in New York, Washington, D.C., and Pennsylvania.
	2003
	War in Iraq

GLOSSARY

aksakal
An elder; a respected older member of a local community.

ash-khana
A national restaurant where people are expected to linger and enjoy traditional foods that are often specially prepared for each group of diners.

chaikhana
A traditional teahouse in central Asia.

Eid al-Fitr
The Islamic festival that celebrates the end the monthlong fast of Ramadan.

Eid Kurban
The Islamic festival celebrated in remembrance of Abraham's nearly sacrificing his son Ishmael and God's sparing Ishmael's life in recognition of Abraham's faith.

gap
An informal interest group in traditional Tajik society. Members may be friends or neighbors, and topics range from personal to professional.

hajj
The pilgrimage to Mecca that is required of all Muslims who are able to make the journey.

Ismailis
An Islamic sect with close links to the teachings of Shia Islam.

kalym
A dowry in the form of money or gifts that is expected to be paid by the family of a bridegroom to the family of a bride.

Koran
The holy book of Islam. Muslims believe that it was dictated by Allah to Prophet Muhammad.

madrassa
An Islamic religious school.

mahallya
A neighborhood community in Tajikistan and other parts of central Asia.

mullah
An Islamic scholar or clergyman who leads Muslims in their daily prayers.

Nowruz
A spring festival in Tajikistan and other parts of central Asia.

Ramadan
The ninth month in the Islamic calendar; a time for fasting and the atonement of sins.

tois
Family celebrations marking important events in a person's life.

Zoroastrianism
An ancient religion originating in central Asia.

FURTHER INFORMATION

BOOKS

Abdullaev, Kamoloudin, and Shahram Akbarzadeh. *Historical Dictionary of Tajikistan*. Lanham, MD: Scarecrow Press, 2002.

Akiner, Shirin. *Tajikistan: Disintegration or Reconciliation (Central Asian and Caucasian Prospects)*. London: Royal Institute of International Affairs, 2002.

Bliss, Frank. *Social and Economic Change in the Pamirs, Tajikistan*. London/New York: Routledge Curzon, 2005.

Curtis, Glenn E. (editor). *Kazakhstan, Kyrgyzstan, Tajikistan, Turkmenistan, and Uzbekistan: Country Studies*. Washington, D.C.: Headquarters, Department of the Army, 1997.

Djalili, Mohammad-Reza, Frédéric Grare, and Shirin Akiner (editors). *Tajikistan: The Trials of Independence*. New York: St. Martin's Press, 1997.

Harris, Colette. *Control and Subversion: Gender Relations in Tajikistan* (Anthropology, Culture and Society). London: Pluto Press, 2004.

Landau, Jacob, and Barbara Kellner-Heinkele. *Politics of Language in the Ex-Soviet Muslim States: Azerbaijan, Uzbekistan, Kazakhstan, Kyrgyzstan, Turkmenistan, Tajikistan*. Ann Arbor: University of Michigan Press, 2001.

O'dea, Colleen. *Tajikistan (The Growth and Influence of Islam in the Nations of Asia and Central Asia)*. Broomall, PA: Mason Crest Publishers, 2005.

WEB SITES

Central Intelligence Agency World Factbook (select Tajikistan from the country list).
   www.cia.gov/cia/publications/factbook

Columbia University Internet resource page on central Asia and the Caucasus.
   www.columbia.edu/cu/sipa/REGIONAL/ECE/CACR

Embassy of the United States of America in Dushanbe, Tajikistan. http://dushanbe.usembassy.gov

Library of Congress Federal Research Division: Country Profiles (select Tajikistan from the country list).
   http://lcweb2.loc.gov/frd/cs/profiles.html

Lonely Planet World Guide: Destination Tajikistan.
   www.lonelyplanet.com/destinations/central_asia/tajikistan

News on central Asia and the Caucasus (select Tajikistan from the country list). www.eurasianet.org

Radio Free Europe/Radio Liberty (select Tajikistan from the country list). www.rferl.org

Tajikistan Development Gateway. www.tajik-gateway.org

U.S. Department of State International Information Programs (type "Tajikistan" in the search box).
   http://usinfo.state.gov

BIBLIOGRAPHY

Adle, Chahryar, and Irfan Habib, eds. *History of the Civilizations of Central Asia, Development in Contrast: from the Sixteenth to the Mid-Nineteenth Century.* vol. V. Paris: UNESCO, 2003.

Akiner, Shirin. *Tajikistan: Disintegration or Reconciliation (Central Asian and Caucasian Prospects).* London: Royal Institute of International Affairs, 2002.

Asimov, M.S. and C. E. Bosworth, eds. *History of the Civilizations of Central Asia. The Age of Achievement, A.D. 750 to the End of the Fifteenth Century.* vol. IV, part 2. Paris: UNESCO, 2000.

Frye, Richard. *The Cultural Heritage of Central Asia. From Antiquity to the Turkish Expansion.* Princeton, NJ: Markus Wiener, 1996.

Gleason, Gregory. *The Central Asian States: Discovering Independence.* Boulder, CO: West View Press, 1997.

Souchek, Svat. *A History of Inner Asia.* Cambridge: Cambridge University Press, 2000.

INDEX

THE IRWIN SERIES IN ECONOMICS

CONSULTING EDITOR

LLOYD G. REYNOLDS
YALE UNIVERSITY

BOOKS IN THE IRWIN SERIES IN ECONOMICS

INTERNATIONAL ECONOMICS

INTERNATIONAL ECONOMICS

BY

CHARLES P. KINDLEBERGER Ph.D.

PROFESSOR OF ECONOMICS

MASSACHUSETTS INSTITUTE OF TECHNOLOGY

REVISED EDITION

1958

RICHARD D. IRWIN, INC.

HOMEWOOD, ILLINOIS

REVISED EDITION

First Printing, April, 1958
Second Printing, June, 1959

PRINTED IN THE UNITED STATES OF AMERICA
Library of Congress Catalogue Card No. 58–9768

FOR AND IN SPITE OF C, D, S, AND R

PREFACE

This revision started out as an attempt to streamline the first edition, simplify it at a number of points, and correct some errors. Inevitably, however, the revising process has taken on a life of its own, and the book has grown in girth, rather than slimmed. The chapter on the theory of economic development has been dropped out, since there are now many books on the subject which were not available in 1953. Another chapter on the European Recovery Program has gone. But, like the heads of the mythical Hydra, two chapters have grown for each one eliminated. Chapter 7 takes the theory of international trade from the static world of fixed tastes, fixed factors, and a given state of the arts into the world of comparative statics where tastes, factor endowments, and technology may change. Chapter 9 on the price mechanism and Chapter 10 on income changes are now followed in Chapter 11 by a discussion of the international adjustment process when income and price both change. And a new Part V has been added to discuss international transfers, consisting of Chapter 22 on migration and Chapter 23 on intergovernmental economic assistance.

Despite the incorporation of this new material, the book is considerably easier than before. The emphasis is still on analysis, rather than description of institutions or history, but a number of the more complex notions, more appropriate for graduate than for undergraduate study, have been relegated to a series of appendices. These are gathered, out of the way of the undergraduate, at the back of the book.

A new theme has been incorporated in the revision. It is the fundamental importance of the distinction between partial-equilibrium analysis, where a single variable is treated subject to the condition that all other things are equal; and general-equilibrium analysis where other things are changed by the action taken in ways which return and have an effect on the outcome. The application of partial analysis to general-equilibrium problems—whether in discussion of tariffs or exchange depreciation—leads to serious mistakes. These are made not only by those much abused individuals—the man in the street, or the intelligent, lay newspaper editorialist—but also by the economics profession itself. Perhaps the outstanding case is the slogan produced by the (then) Chancellor of the Exchequer, R. A. Butler, calling for "Trade, not aid," which implies that an increase in trade as a consequence of a reduction in tariffs improves the balance of payments of the exporting country by that amount. The misconceptions are dealt with at length in the pages below.

The book continues to be written for a two-semester course, emphasizing international trade the first term, and international finance the second. The line of division comes after Chapter 16. For single-semester courses, it is recommended that Chapters 1–10 and 12 be retained from the first three parts, and 19–21, 23, 24, 28 and 29 chosen from the rest. The two-semester course would naturally include supplementary readings, on which bibliographical material is furnished at the end of each chapter, and possibly exercises. These would have to be rigorously circumscribed in a single-semester course.

I have benefited greatly in this revision by letters from a number of teachers on one or more points, large and small. Particularly helpful have been the extensive detailed comments of Professors T. W. Arndt, of University College, Canberra, Australia; William H. Baughn of the University of Texas; and Wolfgang F. Stolper of the University of Michigan. Raymond F. Malley of the Fletcher School of Law and Diplomacy was of great help in trying to clarify a number of the more difficult passages. Egon Sohmen went over the manuscript carefully to eliminate the egregious errors which marred the first printing. He and J. Vanek provided mathematical appendices on the Marshall-Lerner condition and the multiplier, respectively. Mrs. Frances Postma did the bulk of the typing. Miss Beatrice A. Rogers assisted importantly in the proofreading. To all of them, I am deeply grateful.

C. P. KINDLEBERGER

LINCOLN, MASSACHUSETTS
February, 1958

CONTENTS

LIST OF ILLUSTRATIONS

LIST OF TABLES

PART I

The Balance of Payments and the

Foreign-Exchange Market

Chapter

1

THE STUDY OF INTER-
NATIONAL ECONOMICS

International Trade and Economics

The student approaching international economics for the first time may well ask why it is a separate branch of economics. Money and banking, labor economics, and price theory are all reasonably distinct parts of the subject. International trade, however, seems to be merely general economics applied in a particular context. Why are not the over-all laws good enough?

This is a legitimate question, and it can be answered in a number of ways. International trade is treated as a distinct subject because of tradition, because of the urgent and important problems presented by international economic questions in the real world, because it follows different laws from domestic trade, and because its study illuminates and enriches our understanding of economics as a whole.

The International Trade Tradition

Many students will take issue with tradition as a reason for studying international trade. It may be satisfactory to segregate international trade in the history of economic thought and learn what Adam Smith, Ricardo, Mill, and Marshall thought about it. But if Bertil Ohlin, the modern Swedish economist, proved that there is no intrinsic difference between interregional and international trade, why not include international with interregional economics and be done with it?

The separation of international trade as a subject, however, is not based solely on theoretical discussions of the topic. Facts and figures are needed to convert economics from political philosophy into a social science. Data were originally available from two sources: from the separate markets of towns and villages and from the information collected by the king's custom. The market data could not be added up to get a complete picture because not all markets were covered. By aggregating the information collected at the separate ports of entry, how-

3

ever, one could form an over-all picture of foreign trade, correct except for errors due to smuggling. Foreign-trade statistics were thus the first source of material for empirical investigation into economics. And the study of the relations between economic entities must start at the level of the nation, the only unit for which we have adequate data.

International Economic Problems

But there are more, and more significant, reasons for studying international economics as a separate subject. Its details may not differ in kind, but they certainly differ in degree. Problems of money and banking, wages, and prices—to use the three separate branches of economics with which we began our comparison—are more difficult of solution in an international than in a national context.

In money and banking, the more difficult character of international economic problems is self-evident. Foreign-exchange crises in France, Turkey, India, Argentina; strong adverse pressure on the pound sterling at the time of the Suez crisis; the inconvertibility of most European currencies more than twelve years after the close of the war; and the continued necessity seen by the Executive Branch of the United States government for economic assistance to underdeveloped areas—all form an unfavorable contrast to payments within a country.

Interregional wage difficulties arise, but are of a different order of magnitude from those in international trade. Textile workers in New England, for example, are strong advocates of higher wages for textile workers in the Carolinas and other areas of southern competition. The regional differential narrowed from 10 cents an hour to 5 cents in the steel strike settlement of the summer of 1952. But these examples are rare within the United States. For the most part, the various trades are not particularly conscious of, or interested in, the return to competitors in other parts of the country. In international trade, on the other hand, we are continually hearing about the competition of "pauper labor" in foreign countries. In the European Coal and Steel Community and in the projected Common Market in Europe, much attention is being given to overcoming the resistance in a shortage area in one country to bringing in workers from surplus regions in other countries.

Interregional problems of price arise with more frequency. Farmers want parity; and city dwellers worry about the high cost of living. In periods of emergency, price controls are imposed to alter the operations of the price system. Internationally, however, the price seems seldom to be right. Underdeveloped countries complain about the low returns on the primary products which they sell and demand "fair and equitable" prices, whether for Brazilian coffee, Chilean copper, Malayan rubber and tin, and so on. A sharp rise in coffee prices, on the other hand, will bring a Senate investigation of gouging by foreigners; and an increase in the price of newsprint in Canada brings bitter protest from the United States Newspaper Association.

This is not a conclusive demonstration. There is, however, something of a presumption that international problems, especially those of payment, are different internationally and between regions in the same country.

These international problems are pressing, as well as difficult of solution. The most urgent is the payments issue, which has occupied a large part of the energy of the United States and other governments since the close of World War II. War debts and reparations were a major international issue in the interwar period. Dollar shortage and international capital for economic development are clearly major issues now. It is too much to say that the prospects for world peace turn on their solution. Not enough is known by social scientists of the causes of war or revolution to be able to make any such flat assertion. But it is clear that the prospects for world peace will be affected by the success or failure of efforts at their solution.

Interregional versus International Trade

What distinction between interregional trade and international trade can account for the differences in the character and intensity of the economic problems which arise in them? Why does international trade follow different laws of behavior from those of domestic trade?

Here it is possible to collect a number of different answers, no one of which necessarily implies a denial of the others. The classical economists found the difference in the behavior of the factors of production—land, labor, and capital. A few people appear to believe that the difference lies in the fact of different moneys and monetary systems. Modern liberal economists, using the word "liberal" in a special sense, believe that the crux of the matter is interference by the state. Political theory would ascribe the difference to national solidarity.

It is important, however, to underline one aspect of interregional and international trade which distinguishes them both from the rest of economics. In these subjects space becomes important. General-equilibrium theory normally appears to operate as if a national economy were located at a single point in space and as if national economies were separate points close beside one another. Goods and services then move in costless fashion. In interregional and international trade this is shown not to be so. For many purposes the assumption of cost-less transfer is borrowed from general-equilibrium theory. But for others, it is explicitly laid aside. In Chapter 8 we discuss the effects of space on prices, the movement of goods, and the location of industry.

Factor Mobility

In differentiating international from domestic trade, the classical economists stressed the behavior of the factors of production. Labor and capital were mobile within a country, they believed, but not inter-nationally. Even land was mobile within a country, if we mean occupa-tionally rather than physically. The same land, for example, could be used alternatively for growing wheat or raising dairy cattle, which gave it a restricted mobility.

The importance of this intranational mobility of the factors of production was that returns to factors tended to equality within, but not between, countries. The wages of Frenchmen of a given training and skill were expected to be more or less equal; but this level of wages bore no necessary relation to those of comparable Germans or Italians, Englishmen or Australians. If a weaver received higher wages in Lyons than in Paris, Parisian weavers would migrate to Lyons in sufficient numbers to bring down wages there and raise them in Paris, until equality had been restored. But no such forces are at work between Lyons and Milan, Dresden, Manchester, or New Bedford. The wages of weavers in these cities are independently determined and can fluctuate without affecting one another. The same equality of return within a country, but inequality internationally, was believed to be true of land and capital.

Today it is thought that this distinction of the classical economists has been made too rigorously. There is some mobility of factors interna-tionally: immigration has been important for the United States and is currently of great significance to the economic life of Australia, Ar-gentina, and Israel, to name but a few examples. Emigration has been a factor in the economic life of many European countries, but perhaps outstandingly of Ireland, now Eire, and Italy.

There is also some considerable degree of immobility within countries. The example used of Paris and Lyons is particularly unapt because the French do not typically move about. Migration within the United States takes place on a broad scale under the influence of major forces such as war. The invasion of Ohio, Michigan, and Illinois by the

South in and immediately following World War I was paralleled by a similar movement to California and Texas in World War II. But movement on this scale is not normal.

It may be accurate to say that there is a difference of degree in factor mobility interregionally and internationally and that in the usual case people will migrate within their own country more readily than they will emigrate abroad. Identity of language, customs, and tradition cannot be assumed between parts of the same country, but they are more likely than between countries.

Capital is also more mobile within than between countries. It is not, however, completely mobile within countries; and regional differences in interest rates do exist. At the same time, it is not completely immobile between countries. We shall see in Part IV what happens when capital moves from country to country.

To the extent that there are differences in factor mobility and equality of factor returns, internationally as compared with interregionally, international trade will follow different laws. If there is a shift in demand from New England pure woolens to southern synthetic woolen compounds, capital and labor will move from New England to the South. If, however, there is a shift in demand from French to Italian silk, no such movement of capital and labor to Italy takes place. Some other adjustment mechanism is needed.

Different Moneys

To the man in the street the principal difference between domestic and international trade is that the latter involves the use of different moneys. A dollar is accepted in California and in Maine. But the Swiss franc, which is the coin of the realm in Basel, must be converted into French francs or German Deutschemarks before it can be used to buy goods in Strasbourg in France or Freiburg in Germany, each but a few miles away.

With a little more sophistication, however, it is evident that the important fact is not the different moneys so much as the possibility of change in their relative value. When Switzerland, Belgium, and France belonged to the Latin Monetary Union and all three francs were convertible into each other on a one-for-one basis, an individual would be almost indifferent whether he held one franc or another, unless he were on the verge of making a purchase. For actual buying, it was necessary to have the unit acceptable to the seller; but if exchange rates were fixed, currencies convertible, and both were expected to remain so, one currency was as good as another.

This aspect of international trade is evidently linked to the mobility of capital. One of the reasons capital moves freely in the United States is that a dollar is a dollar from Florida to Minnesota (although not necessarily in purchasing power from 1945 to 1958). There are other reasons for the internal mobility of capital, such as the existence of a single law covering creditor and debtor, which makes debts more readily collectible; but the elimination of all currency risks and uncertainty is an outstanding one. If the exchange rate may move, the mobility of capital is likely to be affected. In some cases, capital movements will be increased: the prospect of appreciation of the Canadian against the United States dollar attracts United States capital. But the risk of a change in the value of foreign currencies on balance tends to make people keep their capital at home.

If all currencies of the world were on the gold standard at fixed and unchanging rates, then, as we shall see in greater detail later, exchange rates would be fixed. On this showing, it is the fact that different countries follow different foreign-exchange policies, rather than the existence of different national moneys, which distinguishes international from domestic trade.

Different National Policies

Foreign exchange, however, is only one of a number of areas in which countries can pursue separate ways. Closely associated with the exchange value of a currency is its internal value, which may be affected by policies in the field of money and banking, government-debt management, federal expenditure, and taxation. Tariff policy, action with respect to quotas, subsidies, and other controls of trade are also adopted by governments to interfere with the course of trade between nations.

This is not to assert that governments do not interfere in the economic life of regions. They do. The difference, however, is that for the most part this interference is based on general principles affecting individuals, and the geographic incidence of the effects is a matter of accident. In international trade, however, the liberal economist tells us, national policy is undertaken in order to achieve a geographic effect.

We may illustrate what we mean by the example of progressive taxation. If we tax incomes progressively within a country by legislating proportionately higher taxes on higher incomes, regional results will follow. The richer regions will pay a higher proportion of the yield of the tax, and the poorer regions less. But this is quite different from levying taxes by regions. The poorer man in the rich region pays only the same tax as a man of equal income in the poorer region, under the first of these two methods. If regions were taxed, on the other hand, he might pay more, the same amount, or less, depending upon how the burden of the tax was shared within regions. In international trade, independent national policies affect the separate national units as such, whereas within a country national policies affect the various regions incidentally in the course of legislating about individuals.

The liberal economist of a somewhat earlier day had the answer to this. If all national policies in the field of international economic relations were identical, then differences of incidence would be comparable to those which follow in a region. Governmental policy should be one of noninterference in the working of certain tried and true measures or rules of thumb, handed down by tradition. These measures were the gold standard, the balanced budget, and free trade. The policy of *laissez faire* or noninterference applied only to trade. Positive measures were called for in the monetary and fiscal areas. If these rules were obeyed, the state would not interfere, and trade would be conducted only among firms and consumers whose nationality did not matter. There would be no reason to think of the French market for wheat, since there would be no need to distinguish between French consumers and those of any other national group.

Separate Markets

Apart from purposeful state interference, however, national markets are frequently separate. On occasion, the reason for this separation will be interference by the state for national reasons. The British drive on the left. The French drive on the right. These traffic regulations are decreed by governments for national traffic safety. Since it is safer to sit close to the side of the car which passes the stream of traffic coming in the opposite direction, the British use right-hand drive cars, the French left-hand. The markets for automobiles are effectively separated.

But markets are also separated by language, custom, usage, habit, taste, and a host of other causes of difference. Standards differ. Some goods are designed in inches, feet, pounds, and short tons; some in metric measurements. Even within the nonmetric system, the Americans reckon oil in barrels per day, the British in short tons per year. Export and import trade must get outside of the culture of the domestic market to become acquainted with different goods, described in different words, using differing measurements, bought and sold on different terms, for different currency units.

Politically Different Units

These cultural distinctions between markets, important in the absence of different national measures, have led political scientists to take a look at the nature of countries. This brings us to perhaps the most significant distinction of all. A country organizes itself into a political unit, when it does so successfully, because its citizens and subjects have a sense of cohesion or belonging together. There may be more or less power applied from the top to repress deviations from the national pattern of behavior. But there must be some centripetal force, or the country falls to pieces. A *New York Times* editorial of a few years back underlined the point in reverse by discussing "Centrifugal Spain." Spain, rent by regional antagonism, class warfare, individual distrust, is economically the weakest country in Europe.

There may be regional pride. This is particularly noteworthy among Texans, Californians, and inhabitants of smaller areas in the United States. But if a country is flourishing, particularism is a subject for humor and sentiment rather than decision and action. Individuals belong to various groups of differing coverage—family, town, church, lodge, political party, profession, college, state, and region; but their primary loyalty runs to the nation, and every other geographical loyalty is secondary.

This cohesion of the national group helps to explain national differences in tastes and custom, which are dividers of national markets. It also explains the fact of national economic policies. Government has a responsibility to the national group, which transcends its responsibility, in the liberal formulas, to the nationals of other countries or to a world code. In the nineteenth century this was true to a lesser extent than it is today, with the increase of national sentiment and the breakdown of the old international community. It has frequently been said that members of the *haute bourgeoisie*—upper middle class—of widely different countries were closer spiritually to each other a hundred years ago than they were to the working class of their own community. Under these circumstances, an international code was possible. It would not be today. The difference between interregional and international trade is that trade between regions is trade among the same group, whereas trade between countries runs between different cohesive units. Friedrich List a hundred years ago expressed it: "Domestic trade is among us; international trade is between us and them."

This is one way of stating the difference, and a way which is suggestive of the links which run between international economics and international politics. But there are other ways, more positive and more hopeful. The task of international economics is to find, if it can, a basis for economic relationships which will be satisfactory among the various components of a peaceful world. This statement may be said to apply to the Western world alone, or to look beyond the cold war, as one chooses.

National Economic Life

The view of international economics as relating to the economic relations between national units of more or less internal political cohesion should not altogether neglect the valuable insights afforded into the changing character of the individual units themselves. This takes us back, in part, to the initial view that we have data for national units but not for constituent regions. But the point has more significance.

This is a world in which national independence has had a new lift in the years since World War II. Along with the political independence has grown a demand for economic self-reliance and self-esteem, expressed largely in plans and hopes for economic development. Increasing production, capital formation, and consumption are being sought in national units. A study of international trade has some purpose in enabling us to understand what is taking place, how development has occurred in other cases, and how other countries of the world are likely to be affected by the economic changes now burgeoning.

The interest of the United States in economic development is not confined to its indirect concern in the growing younger countries of the world. The developmental process extends to the final stages of decline and decay. In some quarters it may be regarded as indecent to contemplate the possibility of this country's ceasing to be the richest and most powerful nation in the world. But other countries have had to adjust their thinking in this regard. In particular, Britain and France after Suez are having to face an adjustment in their world economic and political position. It is unlikely that the laws of social, political, and economic development, which carry over into a stage of decline, will be set aside in the case of our country. The theory of international trade has lessons to offer on how a country makes the best adjustment to its position in the world.

At the same time that political and economic nationalism is growing in Asia, Latin America, the Middle East, and Africa, the old answers in terms of national interest have lost their validity for Europe.

This creates a new problem: how to put Humpty-Dumpty together again. Various alternative solutions have been proposed—customs and economic union, exemplified by the not-quite-accomplished efforts to form Benelux out of Belgium, the Netherlands, and Luxemburg; partial economic union, represented by the Schuman plan for a European community in coal and steel; EURATOM, an international authority to operate the peaceful uses of atomic energy among France, Germany, Italy, and the Benelux countries; the European Common Market Treaty, signed in March, 1957, which provides for a customs union among the same six countries of Europe and their African colonies, plus an investment program; and political union, to precede economic integration, on which the Council of Europe in Strasbourg represents a first step.

In a world of rising nationalism, rising internationalism, or both, international economics is a subject of importance.

Scheme of the Book

There is no established way to organize the subject of international trade. A look at the tables of contents of other texts will make this clear. Some books follow a historical thread. Others find a place to start and continue until the subject has been covered, with no necessary place to begin or end.

In this book, the arbitrary design is given by the balance of payments. Part I discusses the total balance of payments, the means of making payments, and, in elementary fashion, the processes of adjustment. Parts II and III then concentrate on the current account of the balance of payments, dealing with the theory of trade and commercial policy, respectively. Part IV turns to the capital account. A brief Part V touches on the movement of labor and intergovernmental assistance. Part VI concludes the book, apart from the series of appendices, with a discussion of equilibrium in the balance of payments as a whole, including the current and the capital account.

Summary

International economics, which is a traditional branch of the discipline, has a more solid basis for separate study than tradition. It differs from domestic or interregional trade in degree. Factor mobility is greater between regions than between countries; and equalization of factor prices is therefore greater. National markets also differ more widely than regional markets on grounds of tastes, customs, habits. But international trade can also be distinguished in kind from domestic trade. It runs between different political units, each with a sovereign government responsible for the well-being of the unit. This accounts for differences in national economic policies—in monetary, exchange, trade, wage, and similar areas.

Interregional and international trade are both concerned with problems of overcoming space. The relative abundance of records on the trade of nations, as contrasted with that of regions, makes the former a better subject for the study of the growth and decay of complex economic, political, and social entities.

BIBLIOGRAPHICAL NOTE

It is customary in textbooks in this field to append to each chapter, or possibly gather in the back of the book, lists or a list of additional reading. In my experience, these lists are seldom used. The average student is not accustomed to riffling through a series of books to find what he wants. If the various items on a list are undifferentiated, except by their titles, the lot remains undisturbed on the library shelf.

In the first edition, I attempted to suggest parallel readings in a number of textbooks for the purpose of offering the student another way of looking at the point of a chapter. Since 1952, however, a substantial number of new books has appeared, which makes it impossible to undertake the task without being subjective, arbitrary, and invidious. Accordingly, there will be only a few references to other textbooks, and these when one or another author has explored the subject at greater leisure and length than the present treatment. These readings will be grouped under a single paragraph of the selected readings, headed "Texts."

Some students may wish to go deeper into the subject of a given chapter, to learn more about it, or to meet the demands of a required paper. This may lead them into a treatise, in which the subject of the chapter is developed at length, or a monograph in which some major aspect of it is verified. The student should have brought to his attention the major articles in the development of the theory and the most significant treatments of the subject by authorities, as distinguished from the writers of texts. For convenience we may call this second category "Treatises, Etc."

A third section will deal with odds and ends of references where this and that point referred to in passing is set out, or where some empirical or historical treatment of an aspect of the problem can be found. This is a catchall category which gathers up what is left after texts and treatises have been disposed of. We shall call it simply "Points."

The chapter bibliographies will be annotated in some degree. References in the second category will be to a wide list of books and a still wider number of articles. The books will, none the less, include repeated references to modern classical presentations, among which will be found:

G. Haberler, *The Theory of International Trade* (London: Macmillan & Co., Ltd., 1937).

J. E. Meade, *The Theory of International Economic Policy,* Volume I, *The Balance of Payments* (New York: Oxford University Press, 1951).

J. E. Meade, *A Geometry of International Trade* (London: Allen & Unwin, 1952).

J. E. Meade, *The Theory of International Economic Policy,* Volume II, *Trade and Welfare* (New York: Oxford University Press, 1955).

J. Viner, *Studies in the Theory of International Trade* (New York: Harper & Bros., 1937).

These, together with the American Economic Association volume mentioned below, should form the core of the personal library of advanced student specialists. Meade's *Balance of Payments* and *Trade and Welfare,* the reader should be warned, make dry reading.

In the realm of articles, the American Economic Association has collected a series of outstanding contributions into a bound volume of *Readings in the Theory of International Trade* (Homewood, Ill.: Richard D. Irwin, Inc. [formerly Philadelphia: Blakiston Co.,], 1949). Other articles in the major professional journals will be referred to by abbreviations as follows:

AER—*American Economic Review*
EJ—*Economic Journal* (London)
Ec—*Economica* (London)
JPE—*Journal of Political Economy*
MS—*The Manchester School*
OEP—*Oxford Economic Papers*
QJE—*Quarterly Journal of Economics*
RES—*Review of Economic Studies* (London)
RE & S—*Review of Economics and Statistics*
SP—*Staff Papers* (of the International Monetary Fund)

Since many courses require term papers on international economic problems, it may be useful to list here the major international sources of statistical and other material. Domestic statistical yearbooks, annual economic reports (of the President or the Chancellor of the Exchequer), monthly and annual trade and financial statistics, etc., must of course be consulted for some problems.

The two major sources for current data are: International Monetary Fund (IMF), *International Financial Statistics* (monthly), which is organized by countries; and United Nations (UN), *Monthly Bulletin of Statistics* (monthly), where data for a wide number of countries are gathered by function.

For detailed international trade data, the UN's *Direction of World Trade* (monthly) and its *Yearbook of International Trade Statistics* may be consulted.

For current analysis, the outstanding international sources are:

UN, *World Economic Report* and Supplements on the Middle East and Africa.

UN Economic Commission for Europe (ECE), *Economic Bulletin for Europe* (Quarterly), and the masterly annual *Economic Survey of Europe in 195–,* which appears each spring referring to the previous year.

The UN Economic Commission for Asia and the Far East (ECAFE) also published an *Economic Bulletin for Asia and the Far East* (quarterly) and an *Economic Survey of Asia and the Far East* (annual). The Economic Commission for Latin America (ECLA) publishes only an annual survey, *Economic Survey of Latin America in 195–*.

The Bank for International Settlements has published an *Annual Report* on international financial questions since 1931.

The contracting parties to the General Agreement on Tariffs and Trade (GATT) put out an annual report entitled *International Trade,* followed by the appropriate year since 1952.

A highly useful reference book for the interpretation of statistics of international economic significance is R. D. G. Allen and J. S. Ely (eds.), *International Trade Statistics* (New York: John Wiley & Sons, Inc., 1953).

The two outstanding sources of information on world economic questions, of course, are *The New York Times* and *The Economist* (London weekly). It has frequently been remarked that the United States badly lacks the equivalent of the latter, an informed weekly magazine of opinion on international economic and political questions; but, like the weather, nobody has successfully done anything about it.

At this stage it is appropriate to call attention to some general bibliographical material in economics. The Department of Political Economy of Johns Hopkins University publishes *Economic Library Selections,* of which Series II, No. 1, dated December, 1954, is an annotated bibliography of books in international economics. A bibliography of articles, very thorough but now somewhat out of date, is contained in the American Economic Association, *Readings,* referred to above. Finally, the textbook by J. N. Behrman and W. E. Schmidt, *International Economics* (New York: Rinehart & Co., 1957), contains a series of excellent chapter bibliographies, carefully annotated.

SUGGESTED READING

TREATISES, ETC.

The major work on the subject is B. Ohlin's *Interregional and International Trade* (Cambridge, Mass.: Harvard University Press, 1933). This pioneering study advances the proposition that international trade differs but little from interregional as it attempts a complete revision of the theory of international trade.

Lionel Robbins, *Economic Planning and International Order* (London: Macmillan & Co., Ltd., 1937), is representative of the view that the difficulties in international trade come from state interference.

Penelope Hartland's article, "Interregional Payments Compared with International Payments," *QJE,* August, 1949, is a useful review of the subject for the advanced student which emphasizes the role of government payments within countries.

See also Haberler, chap. i; and Viner, Appendix A.

Chapter 2　　THE BALANCE OF PAYMENTS

Purposes

The balance of payments of a country is a systematic record of all economic transactions between the residents of the reporting country and residents of foreign countries during a given period of time. Such a record may be useful for a variety of reasons, large and small. The major purpose of keeping these records, which are becoming increasingly elaborate and detailed, is to inform governmental authorities of the international position of the country, to aid them in reaching decisions on monetary and fiscal policy, on the one hand, and trade and payments questions, on the other.

The distinction between monetary and fiscal policy and trade and payments emphasizes the twofold nature of the balance of payments. In its origin, it was essentially directed, as an accounting device, to the provision of information appropriate to a foreign-exchange budget. The authorities—officials of the central bank, national treasury, and subsequently of the stabilization fund—wanted to be assured that the country could go on buying foreign goods in foreign currencies and meeting its payments to foreign residents as they became due. More recently, with the development of national-income accounting and the depressed state of employment in the 1930's, the balance of payments has been directed to explaining the influence of foreign transactions on the national income. Happily, as explained below, the differences between the foreign-exchange-budget concept of the balance of payments and the national-income concept are limited.

In addition to these broad national purposes, the balance of payments is made to serve a host of other purposes, of varying degrees of importance. Like any accounting device, its purpose is informational and its detailed compilation may be changed in any direction, for any particular purpose, so long as the method of keeping the record is clear and consistent. For national-income purposes, it is important to

16

get more frequent information. Accordingly, the Department of Commerce in the United States is now compiling the balance of payments of this country on a quarterly basis. In connection with foreign-exchange problems, it is often significant to know the separate balances of payments of a country with particular countries, groups of countries, or currency areas. In consequence, a great many countries, and some international bodies, are constructing balances of payments in area and currency terms. But at the other extreme from the international economic position of the country, the balance of payments is used to gather detailed information and make it available to those who have an interest in it. The accounts must show, therefore, as much detail as is feasible of the transactions of a country in shipping, tourist travel, interest and dividends, as well as the breakdown of merchandise trade and financial transactions.

Definition

The balance of payments of a country is "a systematic record of all economic transactions between the residents of the reporting country and residents of foreign countries." This seems straightforward enough. But it also raises questions. For example, who is a resident? What is an economic transaction?

For purposes of the balance of payments, persons are considered residents of the country in which they normally reside. Tourists, for example, are residents of the country from which they come rather than the country they are visiting; the same is true of diplomatic and consular personnel, of traveling salesmen, and of students studying abroad. Military personnel are residents of the country whose uniform they wear. The transactions of American tourists, diplomatic and consular officials, traveling salesmen, students, and military personnel abroad are considered as foreign transactions of the United States; when an American military base in Japan buys food and fuel, or rents housing from the Japanese, these purchases are regarded as the equivalent of United States imports and Japanese exports.

The question of residence is less important than systematic coverage of all transactions. Suppose an American tourist brings $2,000 from the United States and spends it in a summer in Paris. If he is taken as a resident of the United States, because he is abroad for less than six months, his expenditure is an international transaction of the United States; if he is regarded as nonresident, because he is abroad more than the arbitrary six months, the international transaction is the payment of $2,000 to him. So long as he saves nothing, the two amount to the same thing. Saving (or, conversely, overspending out of borrowing in France) will add complications, but the principle is still the same.

This principle can be applied to more complicated problems of nonresident corporations. Typically, a foreign subsidiary of a corporation resident in another country is a resident of the country in which it is located; and an agency, which deals for the account of its parent company abroad, a nonresident. These distinctions are legal. Some nonresident companies, like the United Fruit Company operating in Central America or the oil companies in Venezuela, loom very large in the balance of payments of countries in which they do not "reside." It makes no real difference, however, whether United States corporations operate in Latin America through subsidiaries or agencies. If subsidiaries, their dealings with their head offices are foreign and those with Latin American suppliers of material and labor are internal, for the purposes of Latin American accounting. If branches, the dealings with head offices in the United States are domestic and those with Latin American suppliers and governments are international. Where the transactions of a given group of companies are large in relation to other totals, they are often given separately. Thus the Venezuelan and Chilean balances of payments for 1955, given by the International Monetary Fund, show separately foreign-owned oil companies and "large mining companies," respectively.

Note also that international organizations are nonresidents of the country in which they are located; their transactions with the country of their location are thus recorded as international. For example, subscriptions by residents of the United States to bonds of the International Bank for Reconstruction and Development sold in New York are recorded as foreign investment of the United States, even though the Bank is physically located in Washington. And loans extended abroad by the Bank are transactions of the Bank, not of the United States.

Economic Transactions

The final concept included in the definition of the balance of payments is that of economic transactions. An economic transaction is normally an act in which there is transfer of title to an economic good, the rendering of an economic service, or the transfer of title to assets from one party to another. An international economic transaction evidently involves such transfer of title or rendering of service from residents of one country to residents of another.

Normally an economic transaction will involve a payment and a receipt of money in exchange for the economic good, the service, or the asset. But it need not. In barter, goods are exchanged for goods, and in private compensation, assets against assets. Moreover, some goods are transferred to other ownership as a gift, without expectation of payment. In each case, there is an international economic transaction, and the necessity to make an entry in the balance of payments. But some entries are made where there is no international "transaction" in the sense of an international payment: the foreign subsidiary of an American corporation earns a profit in its foreign operations and reinvests it in the country where it operates, without paying a dividend to the parent company. There are those who insist that this should go into the balance of payments as a credit on current account, receipt of profits, and debit on capital account, new investment, even though no international payment takes place. Or a *contra* item may be required to offset some overstatement elsewhere in the balance of payments, as we shall see below in the treatment of the transport accounts. Here is the necessity for an entry even though the transaction may be purely domestic.

Balance-of-Payments Accounting

Let us now consider the mechanics of balance-of-payments accounting. In theory, the balance of payments is kept in standard, double-entry bookkeeping under which each international transaction undertaken by residents of a country will result in a credit and a debit entry of equal size. Let us suppose that a company in the United States exports $100 worth of goods to a customer in Britain. This will call for two entries in the balance of payments in each country. In the United States, exports will be credited $100:

BALANCE OF PAYMENTS OF THE UNITED STATES

	Credit	*Debit*
Exports	$100	

because transactions which give rise to receipts are recorded as credits. In Britain, the importation of $100 worth of merchandise will be recorded as a debit because transactions which give rise to payments to residents of foreign countries are debits:

BALANCE OF PAYMENTS OF THE UNITED KINGDOM

	Credit	*Debit*
Imports		$100

But there should be two entries for each transaction in each country, a credit and a debit. What the other entry is will depend upon how the transaction is financed. To take only the United States view of the matter, the other side of the transaction can be an increase in the American company's open-book account in Britain; a reduction in an old obligation to the British company; the accumulation of a sterling balance in a London bank; the acquisition of dollars from the sale of sterling to an American bank which holds it; the receipt of dollars from a reduction in the dollar balances of the British company; or a gift by the United States company to the British. In all but the gift, the debit entry is "Capital Outflow." If the goods are given to the British recipient, the debit entry is "Donation."

A capital outflow from the United States, which is a debit entry in its balance of payments, may consist in an increase in United States claims on foreigners or a reduction in United States liabilities to foreigners. The transaction which gives rise to the claim is a credit; the increase in claims (or the reduction in liabilities) itself is a debit. In ordinary, domestic bookkeeping, one credits Sales and debits Cash. In the balance of payments, one records a credit for Exports and a debit for the Capital Outflow.

The student will do well to pause here and make sure that he takes due note of this complex fact: An increase in claims on foreigners (foreign assets) or a reduction in liabilities to foreigners is a capital outflow and is a debit in the balance of payments; a decrease in claims on foreigners (foreign assets) or an increase in liabilities to foreigners is a capital inflow and is a credit in the balance of payments.

Let us suppose that there are two transactions: one an export of goods from the United States worth $100 against payment out of a British importer's account in New York; the other an import of goods valued at $100 by an American buyer from an English exporter, settled by a payment into the account of the latter in New York. The reduction in the English account in New York in the first transaction is a decrease in American liabilities to foreigners or a capital outflow or a debit. The increase in the English account in New York in the second transaction is an increase in American liabilities to foreigners or a capital inflow or a credit.

The balance of payments after the first transaction looks like this:

BALANCE OF PAYMENTS OF THE UNITED STATES

	Credit	*Debit*
Exports	$100	
Capital Outflow		$100

The balance of payments for the second transaction alone looks like this:

BALANCE OF PAYMENTS OF THE UNITED STATES

	Credit	Debit
Imports		$100
Capital Inflow	$100	

When both are added together, the capital transactions cancel out, and it is recorded that exports paid for imports:

BALANCE OF PAYMENTS OF THE UNITED STATES

	Credit	Debit
Exports	$100	
Imports		$100

This elementary exercise in balance-of-payments accounting indicates a fundamental point. In theory, the balance of payments is devised on the basis of double-entry bookkeeping. In practice, however, it is possible to collect data on only one side of a given transaction. Recorded exports and imports are easy enough: These go in as credits and debits. The claims and liabilities of the reporting country vis-à-vis foreigners are then examined, and the net change in the balance of claims or liabilities is taken as the capital movement. Through this net change in the balance have passed many entries, both credit and debit. To the extent that they cancel out, the physical side of the transactions (i.e., exports and imports) will offset each other in the balance of payments.

Some transactions, however, will not be fully reported in this way. Suppose that a gift of money is made by a resident of the United States to a foreign resident, who deposits it in his New York account (or that of his bank or central bank). American liabilities to foreigners have increased—a capital inflow, or a credit. What is the offsetting debit? It is the gift itself. In this case, however, there is no physical import to record as a debit. An estimate must be made of the amount of these gifts of money, and the sum entered in the balance of payments as a debit. Or suppose that an individual in the United States sends a CARE package to Korea. The export of goods is a credit. The other side of the transaction is not recorded anywhere else, so that the balance-of-payments estimators put in an offsetting debit entry.

The Balance of Payments Always Balances

The fact that the balance of payments is theoretically built on double-entry bookkeeping means that the balance of payments must always balance, i.e., that the total number of debits equals the total number of credits. If in the process of estimating individual items on a single-entry basis, estimators get totals for debits and credits which differ, they must add a balancing item entitled "Errors and Omissions."

Various reasons account for the failure of the estimators to get complete coverage. The valuation of exports and imports may be inaccurate. This will evidently lead to error unless the misvaluations cancel out. The capital accounts may be confused by changes in residence. Suppose an individual in Europe with funds in a bank in New York shifts his residence to New York. His account will be transferred from "Due to Residents of Foreign Countries" to "Due to Domestic Depositors" on the books of the bank. The reduction in liabilities to foreigners will appear to be a capital outflow (or debit), when actually no international transaction of any kind has taken place. If all other items in the balance of payments are accurately estimated, a balancing credit will be needed to offset the unreal "debit."

The fact that the balance of payments always balances in an accounting sense does not mean that a country never experiences balance-of-payments difficulties or that the demand for its exchange is equal to the supply of it available. This is far from the case. Equilibrium requires not the trivial and automatic balance between total credits and total debits but balance in certain categories of credit and debits. Or the current account need perhaps not balance if its imbalance is offset by the appropriate type of entry on capital account. But first we must discuss the current and capital accounts in the balance of payments.

The Current Account

While the balance of payments is divided vertically into credit and debits, horizontally it is generally broken up into a number of categories depending upon the broad nature of the transactions concerned. The criteria by which the choice of category is made are two: the relation of the transaction to the national economy, on the one hand, and the function of the transaction in the balance of payments, on the other.

The major breakdowns of the balance of payments in these senses are the current account, the capital account, the gold account, and errors and omissions.

The current account includes all transactions which give rise to or use up national income. We shall examine this notion further below and in Chapter 10.

The capital account contains, gross, all changes in claims on or of a country owned by or owed to other countries. The net of these changes, together with the net gold account, is partially reflected in the change in savings in the country. Fuller explanation of this last remark must again wait until Chapter 10.

The gold account is separated from merchandise which is in the current account, because it performs a special monetary function in the banking system of most countries and in the balance of payments.

Errors and omissions, as we have seen, are purely a balancing item.

The usual categories included in the current account are merchandise trade, or exports and imports of goods, and so-called "invisible" items—shipping, income on investments, rents, royalties, payments for insurance, and donations.

Of all the items in the current account, merchandise or visible trade is almost always the most important. The difference between credits and debits (exports and imports) is frequently called the balance of trade, and this is often regarded as "favorable" when exports exceed imports and "unfavorable" when imports exceed exports. For some purposes, the balance of trade has significance and furnishes a shorthand indication of the position of the current account as a whole. But in many countries its significance is limited, and use of the term may be misleading. In Norway, for example, in 1955, exports were little more than gross shipping earnings, and the unfavorable trade balance was three times as large as the deficit in the balance of payments on current account:

CURRENT ACCOUNT OF THE BALANCE OF PAYMENTS
OF NORWAY, 1955
(In Millions of Norwegian Kroner)

	Credit	Debit	Net
Merchandise (exports, f.o.b., imports, c.i.f.)	4,724	7,896	−3,172
Transportation	4,350	2,230	+2,120
Investment income (net)	..	134	− 134
Other goods and services (net)	164	..	+ 164
Current account			−1,022

In Venezuela, on the other hand, exports are practically double imports, but the balance of payments on current account is barely positive:

CURRENT ACCOUNT OF THE BALANCE OF PAYMENTS
OF VENEZUELA, 1955
(In Millions of United States Dollars)

	Credit	Debit	Net
Merchandise (f.o.b.)...............	1,904	1,007	897
Transport and insurance (net).......	..	120	−120
Investment income (net)............	..	571	−571
Other services (net)...............	..	135	−135
Current account...............			+71

These instances are exceptional. For the most part merchandise transactions cover between two thirds and four fifths of current-account credits and debits alike. Part II, devoted to a discussion of the theory of the current account, concerns itself almost exclusively with merchandise trade. Much of the theory, however, can be applied with little change to the analysis of invisible items.

Exports and imports must be valued on a consistent basis. It used to be the practice to record the value of goods in trade statistics as of the country's border. This meant that exports were valued f.o.b. (i.e., free on board), and imports c.i.f. (or including cost, insurance, and freight). This difference in valuation created the statistical difficulty that when the world's exports and imports were converted into a single currency and totaled, the value of imports exceeded that of the same goods as exports, by the amount of the insurance and freight. Today, following a procedure laid down by the International Monetary Fund, both exports and imports are valued on an f.o.b. or f.a.s. basis, which means free alongside. The difference between f.o.b. and f.a.s. is the cost of stevedoring or loading the merchandise into the carrier, whether ship, truck, or railroad car. Whichever system of valuation, however, the transportation account must be altered, as we shall see presently, to form a consistent over-all pattern.

Ascertaining the totals of a country's exports and imports is not so simple a problem as it might at first blush appear to be.

In the first place, there may be a question whether a given good which is shipped from a country's shores should properly be regarded as an export of that country, if, in fact, it was imported there from another country. Some countries ignore both imports for re-export and re-exports, and deal exclusively with exports of domestic produce and imports for consumption. In the reports of others, exports of domestic produce and re-exports are recorded along with imports for consumption and total imports, so that the user can adopt the figures which best suit his purpose. Imports into free ports or bonded warehouses are not included in the statistics, since legally these never enter the country at all. By the same token it is possible for a country to import goods from a bonded warehouse located within its physical borders.

The problem of estimating the value of exports and imports is getting more, instead of less, complex as the world network of communication increases. Statistics on foreign trade are among the oldest collected in most countries; they antedate by several hundred years the statistical revolution which gave rise to the widespread enumeration which began in the middle of the nineteenth century. Countries used merely to watch a few ports and border towns and make an estimate of smuggling which cheated the king of revenue. Today the problem is more complicated, with exports and imports conveyed not only by boat but also by rail, truck, airplane, transmission wire (electricity being a commodity rather than a service), and pipeline.

It is not enough to enumerate the physical volume of exports and imports. Unless they are valued consistently in terms of a single currency, they cannot be added together. Certain goods, such as parcel post and the household effects of migrants, which are partly non-market in character, do not lend themselves readily to valuation procedures. More difficult, however, are the problems presented by intercompany transactions, in which wholly arbitrary valuations may be placed upon the raw materials or semifinished goods. The existence of exchange control or of tariffs based on the value of merchandise may also give shippers in foreign trade an incentive to report some value other than the true one.

Finally, there are certain commodities which may not be commodities, or at least may not be commodity exports. Films shipped abroad are rented rather than sold, and the amount collected for them belongs under services rather than under exports. The same has been true under certain types of contracts to rent machinery rather than sell it. Silver is on the narrow border line between a raw-material import and money. Nonmonetary gold exported from South Africa is regarded as monetary gold when it gets to Britain. This last difference in the reporting methods of two countries gives rise to an inconsistency among the balances of payments of the world as a whole and makes world exports exceed world imports by the amount of newly mined gold exports.

Our list of difficulties and problems must not give the wrong impression. Estimating the balance of payments on merchandise account is relatively easy, certainly as contrasted with the invisible items in the current account or with the capital account. But it is not all plain sailing.

Services

The service items in the current account, sometimes called "invisible" exports and imports, include a number of things which are services pure and simple and some which are included under the rubric for convenience and for lack of anything better to call them. Insurance, which is generally net (or premiums less expenses and losses), banking, freight, film rentals, royalties (authors' and patent), and expenses of tourist travel are clearly payments tendered for services performed. Interest on investment is also properly regarded as a return for service rendered by the capital loaned; and profits may, with some stretching, be regarded as the return for the efforts of entrepreneurs.

There are other items, however, about which there is more doubt. Government transactions are frequently included in the current account as service items in their entirety, on analogy with the national-income device of including all governmental expenditures as part of national income, regardless of whether they are for final or intermediate product. Government payments to foreign countries for armaments or rent of air bases are clearly a proper item for inclusion in the current account, but government sales of surplus property, payments of reparations, and grants to foreign countries could be and frequently are classified otherwise. Sometimes governmental transactions are regarded as sufficiently important to be separated out from private transactions. But frequently they are divided between the current and capital accounts, or the current and a special governmental account, according to the nature of the transactions involved.

Private transfers of income, such as personal, immigrant, and other remittances, or institutional charitable donations, are typically but not always included in the current account. Much depends upon the purpose for which the balance of payments is drawn up. If the record is used mainly as a budget of foreign-exchange receipts and expenditures, the current account should include recurring receipts, and immigrants' remittances may belong there on that account. In pre–World War I Italy, for example, immigrant remittances were estimated at 500 million lire (or approximately $100 million) and, with an equivalent amount of tourist expenditure, offset the greater part of the gap between exports of 2,500 million lire and imports of 3,-600 million lire (to use the 1913 figures).

If the main purpose of the balance of payments is to relate it to the national-income accounts, however, these transfers are usually kept separately. This is because, although a credit in the receiving country, they are not income, nor are they consumption or other final expenditure in the paying countries, even though they are a debit in the balance of payments.

Government transfers such as reparation payments used to be included in the capital account; they were regarded as once-and-for-all transfers of purchasing power comparable to capital investments, in contrast to the recurring private transfers. Old-fashioned economists still think of reparations and governmental grants as capital items. The International Monetary Fund and the Department of Commerce, however, have abandoned this practice. Using a balance-of-payments concept which emphasizes the links to national income rather than the foreign-exchange-budget approach, they treat reparation payments and intergovernmental assistance in a special category of "transfers." These differ from capital movements since they are final payments, whereas a capital transaction properly gives rise to a claim or debt or extinguishes one.

Gathering information on the service account of a country is more difficult than for merchandise. By and large, the figures are approached by estimation rather than by enumeration. Income-tax returns of corporations and individuals are used to estimate interest and dividends; and these are supplemented by questionnaires for the largest corporations operating in the foreign field.

A sample of questionnaires made out on postcards constitutes the basis on the estimate of tourist expenditures per person. This is expanded to a total figure through multiplication by the numbers of people crossing the border under different types of visas and circumstances and for varying periods of time. Other items, such as insurance, film rentals, and royalties, are estimated from a number of sources, primarily the accurate records of a handful of the most important individuals and firms concerned, extrapolated by estimate to the entire body.

The shipping account may or may not include payments to the country's nationals for imports, depending upon the system of valuation for exports and imports. If imports are valued c.i.f., they already cover payments to foreigners for freight. Since they include a debit for payments to nationals, too, an offsetting credit for freight earned on imports carried in the bottoms of the reporting country is needed in the shipping account to indicate the true position. Even where imports are valued f.o.b., however, it may be desirable, in order to have a complete record of the freight bill for imports, to record all freight as a debit, including freight on imports carried by the country's nationals, with an offsetting credit for the latter portion of it. If a country wants to keep a record of total freight on exports (a credit), there would have to be an offsetting debit for exports carried in foreign bottoms.

Almost all transactions involving physical movements are included in the current account. The exceptions to this are few and include mainly gold transactions. But the physical nature of the transaction is not the basis for putting it in the current account. The current account is that part of the balance of payments which can be related to national income. Goods and services recorded in it are almost entirely part of national income produced (exports or credits) or of national income consumed (imports or debits). Exceptions to this generalization exist. Transfer payments, which are not part of national income, are often included in the current account. This means both types of transfer payments, i.e., those which confer purchasing power on their recipients without a *quid pro quo* in the form of income produced, and those which represent payment against intermediate goods or goods already in existence. Immigrant remittances, charitable donations, reparations, for example, are not part of the national income produced in the recipient country (where they may constitute a credit in the balance of payments); nor do exports out of inventory or of antiques or old masters constitute part of national income.

Again, however, the exceptions are for the most part minor. The general rule is that the current account is concerned with physical transactions in the balance of payments and that these international transactions are part of national income produced or consumed.

Capital Account

The capital account records changes in the claims of residents of a country on residents of other countries, and changes in liabilities owed. For ease of exposition, it is handier to talk of claims of one country on the rest of the world, and vice versa, leaving out mention of the residents in both cases. This is permissible only if we remember that an accurate statement would require us to bring the residents back in.

The recording of movements in the capital account sometimes gives the student (and even the teacher) difficulty. It seems strange, for example, that a capital outflow should be a debit in the balance of payments when it makes the country a creditor. But such is the case, and the student must master it. An inflow is a credit, and a capital outflow a debit.

Some writers, and occasionally an official compiler of balances of payments, will try to make things easier by pointing out that a capital inflow involves the export of securities, bank deposit books, or IOU's. By analogy with an export of merchandise, an export of securities (bankbooks, IOU's) is a credit. And an import of securities (an export or outflow of capital) becomes a debit. This device, though cumbersome, may be helpful to remember.

Another way of keeping in mind that an export of capital is a debit, and inflow a credit, is to concentrate on the direction of payment. An export of capital gives rise to a payment to foreigners—just as does an import of merchandise. Both are debits. An inflow of capital, however, means that foreigners make payments to the reporting country and that the country is "collecting receipts" such as would be the case with an export of goods. It may be helpful to think more narrowly in terms of the exchange market: capital exports and goods imports add to the supply of a country's currency on the foreign-exchange market; capital imports and goods exports add to the demand.

A capital outflow or export is brought about by an increase in a country's net claims on foreigners or a decrease in foreign claims on its residents. A capital import, contrariwise, represents an increase in net foreign claims on a country or a decrease in net foreign assets of the country. Ignoring the question of what currency the claims may be in, a country normally both owes and is owed money internationally. If it is owed more than it owes, i.e., if it has net claims on foreigners, an increase in net claims is a capital outflow; a decrease, a capital inflow. An increase in net claims, of course, may come about through an increase in gross claims on foreigners or a reduction in foreign counterclaims. Similarly, an increase in net liabilities, which is a capital inflow, may be brought about either through an increase in foreigners' claims on the reporting country or through a decrease in the claims of the reporting country on the rest of the world.

The capital account is divided into debits and credits but also into various lesser categories. Usually, it is broken down into short- and long-term accounts, depending upon the nature of the credit instruments involved. We shall have occasion to examine this question and to qualify some of our present remarks in Part IV, dealing with the capital account. For the moment, however, we shall regard as short-term capital movements all those embodied in instruments of less than one year's maturity, i.e., bank deposits, both demand and time, drafts, acceptances, bills of exchange, open-book accounts, etc. Long-term capital, on the other hand, is that embodied in ownership instruments such as equity holdings of shares, enterprises, or real estate, or in credit instruments of more than a year's maturity, including term loans, mortgages, and especially bonds.

A peculiar short-term capital movement takes the form of shipments of currency. Exports of United States currency to Europe for hoarding, for example, are reported as a capital inflow to the United States, since they increase United States debts to Europe or European claims on the United States. The capital inflow is, of course, a credit. The capital inflow takes place at the moment the United States currency is purchased, but if the bills are held for a time in a safe-deposit box in New York, the fact of foreign ownership is not known. To the extent that changes in ownership differ from reported shipments, the capital movement through currency shipments is inaccurately recorded.

It is frequently useful to divide the capital account in other ways. One distinction separates private from official capital movements. Private capital movements are undertaken to make a profit or to minimize a loss. Governmental transactions, however, are for the most part induced responses to autonomous changes occurring elsewhere in the balance of payments. This is evident for official short-term capital movements, occurring through changes in central bank or Treasury foreign assets or liabilities. It is equally so for some other broad classes of governmental transactions like Lend-Lease or Marshall Plan credits and International Monetary Fund transactions. It may be true in the case of some intergovernmental loans like those of the Export-Import Bank and the International Bank for Reconstruction and Development. But it clearly is not the case of other governmental capital movements like reparations. The International Monetary Fund sometimes classifies governmental capital movements into compensatory, or balancing in character, which are lumped with monetary gold movements, and others. It is important to bear in mind that the capital account, like the balance of payments as a whole, may be arranged in any number of ways, depending upon the use to which the information is going to be put.

Monetary Gold Account

Nonmonetary gold is generally included among current-account items, frequently as merchandise. The gold account in the balance of payments deals then with monetary gold. The two are separated because their economic behavior is vastly different. Indeed, as we have mentioned, and as we shall later see in detail, it is sometimes difficult to distinguish gold movements from short-term capital, private, and especially official, in motive or effect.

Monetary gold exports are entered in the balance of payments as a credit; monetary gold imports as a debit. The rule is the same as for merchandise, and the opposite of that for capital. Included with gold movements are changes in title to gold at central banks, where the gold is not, in fact, physically transferred between countries. An increase in gold under earmark for foreign account in a country is the same as a gold export and is included as a credit, while a decrease is treated as a debit. Changes in titles to merchandise in a country are similarly included in the merchandise account as an adjustment item where it is possible to learn of them. When gold under earmark in a country is shipped to the country owning it, the export and import of gold in the two countries concerned must be kept out of the balance of payments, since no international transaction has, in fact, taken place.

Recent practice calls for making offsetting entries in the balance of payments in the case of newly mined gold which is bought by the central bank for its own monetary stock. The new production goes into the balance of payments as a merchandise export (in the current account), even though it is not in fact exported. The central-bank purchase of monetary gold is recorded as a debit, like a gold import. The two items offset one another in the balance of payments, as they should since no transactions have been undertaken with residents of foreign countries. If the gold is later actually exported, an entry of export of monetary gold (a credit) will offset the earlier debit entry recorded for the central-bank purchase and leave the original merchandise entry in the current account of nonmonetary gold. This device, designed to explain changes in the gold stock of gold-producing countries in a logical way, is still another example of a fictitious entry in the balance of international payments, i.e., an entry when no international transaction takes place, made for the purpose of making the balance of payments as informative as possible.

The Balance of Payments of the United States

It may be useful to illustrate the variety of ways in which the balance of payments can be set out by presenting some data on the balance of payments of the United States. In Table 2.1 the data for 1946 to 1952 are given in a form which shows the supply and use of United States dollars. The International Monetary Fund points

TABLE 2.1

BALANCE OF PAYMENTS OF THE UNITED STATES, 1946–52

(In Millions of Dollars)

	1946	1947	1948	1949	1950	1951	1952
A. U.S. expenditures, donations, and investment abroad:							
Private transactions	−7,269	−8,800	−10,282	−9,295	−12,534	−14,227	−14,082
Merchandise imports	−5,073	−5,979	−7,563	−6,879	−9,108	−11,202	−10,838
Services and donations	−1,475	−1,539	−1,751	−1,760	−1,860	−1,844	−2,020
Net payments to foreign carriers	12	76	−13	−36	−135	−112	−137
Travel	−457	−548	−600	−678	−727	−722	−811
Other services	−351	−403	−459	−523	−543	−599	−626
Donations (net)	−679	−664	−679	−523	−455	−411	−446
U.S. private and bank capital	−721	−1,282	−968	−656	−1,566	−1,181	−1,224
Direct investment abroad	−230	−749	−721	−660	−621	−528	−850
Other long-term capital, excluding redemption of securities	−181	−344	−131	−183	−796	−550	−280
Short-term capital	−310	−189	−116	187	−149	−103	−94
Government transactions	−5,646	−6,793	−6,182	−6,844	−4,871	−5,138	−5,235
Military expenditures	−493	−455	−799	−621	−576	−1,270	−1,957
Other services	−92	−240	−162	−369	−360	−372	−469
Nonmilitary grants (net)	−2,274	−1,897	−3,894	−4,997	−3,484	−3,035	−1,960
Long-term loans extended	−3,025	−4,088	−1,415	−684	−414	−458	−847
Short-term capital	238	−113	88	−173	−37	−3	−2
Total	−12,915	−15,593	−16,464	−16,139	−17,405	−19,365	−19,317

B. Foreign expenditures and investment in United States:							
Merchandise exports	11,707	16,015	13,193	12,149	10,117	14,123	13,319
Services	2,536	3,037	2,932	3,010	3,070	3,827	3,761
Net receipts by U.S. carriers	912	1,079	684	574	350	694	510
Travel	257	342	308	368	392	430	511
Investment income	772	1,102	1,340	1,395	1,593	1,882	1,828
Other services	595	514	600	673	735	821	912
Redemption of securities held in U.S.	308	295	62	103	301	113	66
Repayment of U.S. government loans	86	294	303	205	295	305	429
Long-term investments in U.S. (mainly private)	−97	−192	−185	64	53	182	141
Short-term capital	......	......	......	......	......	442	86
Total	14,540	19,449	16,305	15,531	13,836	18,992	17,802
C. Net errors and omissions	204	911	1,152	764	−33	472	509
D. Excess of U.S. (−) or foreign expenditures (A through C)	1,829	4,767	993	156	−3,602	99	−1,006
E. Change in foreign official and bank holdings of gold and U.S. dollars:							
U.S. government long-term securities	−250	94	13	55	941	−659	302
U.S. bank liabilities to foreign officials and banks	−633	−2,012	524	−47	918	613	1,083
Monetary gold	−946	−2,849	−1,530	−164	1,743	−53	−379
Total	−1,829	−4,767	−993	−156	3,602	−99	1,006

out that this way of looking at the data does some violence to reality by separating widely the parts of certain transactions, like barter or private compensation, which either involve no dollars at all or whose parts are inseparable. This table illustrates the foreign-exchange-budget approach.

Table 2.2 sets forth the regular balance of payments form of the International Monetary Fund, using the figures for 1953 to 1955, inclusive. This summarizes goods and service transactions, donations, capital and monetary gold, and finally errors and omissions. Credits and debits are intermingled rather than separated horizontally. This represents the national-income approach.

Table 2.3 sets out the balance of payments for the fiscal year, ending June 30, 1956, drawn up in a modified fashion by the Fair-less Committee, investigating foreign aid in behalf of the President of the United States. The purpose of this particular arrangement is to emphasize the role of governmental transactions and to give explicit detail on their composition. It is converted from a calendar to a fiscal-year basis to enable it to be related to the governmental budget accounts.

Finally, Table 2.4 gives an historical summary of the balance of payments by period averages, as compiled by the United Nations from Department of Commerce data. Here the arrangement is a com-promise between the foreign-exchange-budget approach and that which emphasizes the connections with national income. The student will want to observe the development of the various items in the United States balance of payments in all these tables. He should bear in mind that some of the growth is inflationary because of the decline in the value of the dollar.

The essential point which the tables reveal is that the balance of payments can be set out in any way at all, so long as it is meaningful for questions being asked about a country's international payments and consistent in its treatment of the data.

The Balance of Indebtedness

The balance of indebtedness of a country is a statement of the total claims of its residents on foreign countries and the total claims of residents of foreign countries on its residents. While the balance of payments covers a period of time, generally a year, but with increasing frequency a half- or quarter-year period, the balance of indebtedness relates to a given point in time, such as the end of a year. Table 2.5 presents Department of Commerce estimates of the United

TABLE 2.2

BALANCE OF PAYMENTS OF THE UNITED STATES, 1953–55
(In Millions of Dollars)

	1953	1954	1955
A. Goods and services..............................	296	1,721	1,851
1, 2. Merchandise and nonmonetary gold: exports f.a.s..................................	12,294	12,814	14,264
Merchandise and nonmonetary gold: imports. f.a.s.................................	−10,990	−10,354	−11,516
3. Foreign travel: credits.......................	574	584	645
Foreign travel: debits........................	−929	−1,009	−1,155
4. Transportation: credits......................	1,198	1,171	1,336
Transportation: debits.......................	−1,081	−1,026	−1,202
6. Investment income: credits..................	1,190	2,227	2,512
Direct investment.........................	*1,442*	*1,725*	*1,978*
Other.....................................	*468*	*502*	*534*
Investment income: debits...................	−450	−419	−512
7. Government, n.i.e.: credits.................	364	328	333
Government, n.i.e.: debits...................	−2,943	−2,980	−3,190
U.S. military expenditures................	*−2,535*	*−2,603*	*−2,804*
Other.....................................	*−408*	*−377*	*−386*
5, 8. Insurance and miscellaneous: credits.........	741	814	825
Insurance and miscellaneous: debits...........	−392	−429	−489
(Military goods and services transferred under aid)..............................	(4,254)	(3,161)	(2,134)
B. Donations......................................	−2,313	−2,133	−2,321
9. Private...................................	−476	−486	−456
10. Official...................................	−1,837	−1,647	−1,865
Total (1 through 9).......................	−180	1,235	1,395
Total (1 through 10)......................	−2,017	−412	−470
C. Capital and monetary gold......................	1,721	234	19
11, 15. Long-term liabilities.....................	124	252	873
U.S. government securities....................	*−82*	*8*	*529*
Other......................................	*206*	*244*	*344*
12, 16. Short-term liabilities....................	1,023	1,210	560
Bank liabilities to foreign official and banks....	*1,021*	*1,234*	*700*
Other......................................	*2*	*−24*	*−140*
13, 17. Long-term assets.........................	−765	−783	−918
U.S. direct investment abroad................	*−721*	*−664*	*−679*
Other private and banks.....................	*185*	*−320*	*−280*
U.S. government loans repaid.................	*487*	*507*	*416*
Other U.S. government......................	*−716*	*−306*	*−375*
14, 18. Short-term assets........................	178	−743	−537
Private and banks..........................	*167*	*−635*	*−194*
U.S. government...........................	*11*	*−108*	*−343*
19. Monetary gold............................	1,161	298	41
Net errors and omissions...........................	296	178	451

TABLE 2.3

ESTIMATED INTERNATIONAL TRANSACTIONS OF THE UNITED STATES
FISCAL YEAR 1956
(Revised Balance of Payments Basis)
UNITED STATES EXPENDITURES ABROAD

$ Billion

Private:
Commercial imports and United States expenditures on travel, transportation, and
  services abroad...15.4
Gross new private United States investments abroad (including investments from
  cash earnings abroad)... 3.7
Net personal and charitable remittances abroad............................... 0.5
Cash earnings of foreign investments in private sector of United States economy
  (net income plus depreciation and depletion charges)....................... 0.8

    Subtotal, private expenditures..   20.4
United States government
Mutual Security Programs (gross basis):
  Military grants... 3.9
  Nonmilitary grants... 0.5
  Nonmilitary loans.. 0.2

    Subtotal, Mutual Security Programs................................... 4.6
Other nonmilitary grants (e.g., from Public Law 480 proceeds).................0.3
Other nonmilitary loans and investments (e.g., from the Ex-Im Bank and Public
  Law 480 proceeds)... 0.3
Net increase in holdings of short-term claims against foreigners (principally
  Public Law 480 proceeds)... 0.4

    Subtotal, all foreign assistance programs............................ 5.6
Expenditures abroad by United States military forces (excluding counterpart)..... 2.1
Expenditures abroad by United States civilian agencies (excluding counterpart).... 0.2

    Subtotal, collective security expenditures abroad.......................... 7.9
Interest payments on public debt held by foreigners......................... 0.1
Pension and other transfer payments....................................... 0.1
Net gold purchases... 0.1

    Subtotal, United States government expenditures abroad...................   8.3

     Total, private and governmental expenditures abroad....................   28.7

UNITED STATES RECEIPTS FROM ABROAD

$ Billion

Private:
Commercial exports and foreigners' expenditures on travel, transportation, and
  services in United States... 18.6
New foreign investment in private sector of United States economy (including
  investments from cash earnings in the United States)....................... 1.1
Cash earnings of United States private investments abroad (net income plus
  depreciation and depletion charges).................................... 4.2

    Subtotal, private receipts...   23.9
United States government:
Net increase in foreign holdings of United States government securities........... 1.2
Loan repayments... 0.5
Income from loans and investments abroad................................... 0.3
Export of military goods and services...................................... 2.4
Export of nonmilitary services (e.g., the services of civilian experts).............. 0.3

    Subtotal, United States government receipts............................   4.7
Errors and omissions...   0.1

     Total, private and governmental receipts from abroad...................   28.7

TABLE 2.4
UNITED STATES BALANCE OF PAYMENTS, 1919–54
(Annual Averages, Millions of Dollars)

Item	1919–21	1922–29	1930–39	1946–49	1950–54
United States exports of goods and services	8,848.3	6,176.6	3,706.5	16,751.5	17,097.6
Goods	7,319.3	4,805.0	2,701.8	13,266.0	12,529.8
Investment income	590.0	917.1	591.0	1,152.3	1,880.0
Other services	939.0	454.5	413.7	2,333.2	2,687.8
United States imports of goods and services	5,345.0	5,099.2	3,139.5	8,175.0	13,242.2
Goods	3,983.7	4,048.4	2,261.1	6,373.5	10,481.2
Investment income	118.3	198.8	205.0	267.4	392.0
Other services	1,243.0	852.0	673.4	1,534.1	2,369.0
Balance of goods and services	3,503.3	1,077.4	567.0	8,576.5	3,855.4
Private capital and remittances	−1,075.7	−1,315.9	48.9	−1,351.0	−1,545.2
Direct investment	−119.7	−326.6	−43.5	−590.0	−696.4
Other long-term capital (new issues, redemptions, other)	−317.3	−512.7	130.9	−17.7	−238.6
Short-term capital	...	−131.6	−158.7	−107.0	−162.8
Government disbursements	−928.6	27.1	−5.1	−6,790.7	−4,433.8
Capital outflow	−824.3	42.5	10.0	−2,917.2	−171.8
Nonmilitary unilateral transfers	−104.3	−15.4	−15.1	−3,281.5	−2,483.2
Military expenditures	...	...	...	−592.0	−1,778.8
Foreign capital and gold	−332.7	344.6	−905.7	−1,192.5	1,887.8
Foreign capital	−165.7	422.8	173.9	−72.8	1,333.4
Gold	−167.0	−78.1	−1,079.6	−1,119.7	554.4
Errors and omissions	−1,166.3	−133.2	294.9	757.8	235.8

TABLE 2.5
INTERNATIONAL INVESTMENT POSITION OF THE UNITED STATES
IN SELECTED YEARS, 1914–55
(In Billions of Dollars)

	1914	1919	1930	1939	1946	1953	1955
United States investments abroad	3.5	7.0	17.2	11.4	18.7	39.6	44.9
Private	3.5	7.0	17.2	11.4	13.5	23.8	29.0
Long-term	3.5	6.5	15.2	10.8	12.3	22.2	26.6
Direct	2.6	3.9	8.0	7.0	7.2	16.3	19.2
Portfolio	0.9	2.6	7.2	3.8	5.1	6.0	7.4
Short-term	....	0.5	2.0	0.6	1.3	1.6	2.4
United States government	....	....	....	....	5.2	15.7	15.9
Long-term	....	....	....	....	5.0	15.4	15.2
Short-term	....	....	....	....	0.2	0.3	0.7
Foreign investments in the United States	7.2	4.0	8.4	9.6	15.9	23.6	29.6
Long-term	6.7	3.2	5.7	6.3	7.0	9.2	12.6
Direct	1.3	0.9	1.4	2.0	2.5	3.8	4.3
Portfolio	5.4	2.3	4.3	4.3	4.5	5.4	8.3
Short-term assets	0.5	0.8	2.7	3.3	8.9	14.4	17.0
United States net creditor position	−3.7	3.0	8.8	1.8	2.8	16.0	15.3
Net long-term	−3.2	3.3	9.5	4.5	10.3	28.5	29.2
Net short-term	−0.5	−0.3	−0.7	−2.7	−7.4	−12.5	−13.9

NOTE: Data for various years are not wholly comparable because of different sources and methods but are adequate to show trends.

States balance of indebtedness for selected dates since prior to World War I.

The balance of indebtedness is not a particularly useful tool in international economics, but one which we must discuss because it is so widely referred to. In the first place, it is difficult to estimate with accuracy. A good many claims and liabilities lie hidden from view, only occasionally being brought to light in such major surveys as those conducted by the United States Treasury Department during World War II under Foreign Funds Control legislation. Again, there is no check on accuracy, comparable to the knowledge for the balance of payments, because the books are kept on a double-entry basis, that total credits equal total debits. If the item "errors and omissions" is large, the estimators of the balance of payments know that they must search further. Assets are not equal to liabilities in balance sheet accounting, however, but to liabilities plus net worth. No running internal check on accuracy is available.

Even if one had all the facts, however, there would still be difficult problems to solve. One of the most serious is that of valuation: Should one take book (or historic) value, market value, or the amount which could be realized in liquidation under stress as the basis for calculating the monetary amounts of claims and liabilities? As anyone who contemplates what a house costs, what it can be sold for in six months, and what can be realized on it in a week will understand, these may be very different amounts. The exclusion of World War I loans from Table 2.5 illustrates the point further. Some of the "fuzzy" loans made under United States governmental assistance programs, in dollars and in local currencies, should perhaps also be excluded from the table.

Apart from what the figures for the balance of indebtedness are, there is a further serious question of what they mean. The concept is one which is very much misunderstood and frequently badly used. After World War II, for example, the United States could have been reckoned as a net debtor internationally because of the piling up of dollars, particularly by Latin American countries, which could not immediately be used. This position was quickly altered, however, when goods became available for export, and the balance of indebtedness shortly reversed itself. This negative balance of indebtedness had corrected itself by the end of 1946, and does not therefore appear in the table. A survey in India in 1950 observed that that country was a creditor in international account because of the reduction in long-term debt to Britain and the accumulation of sterling balances. At the same time, the report warned against regarding India as a creditor country for any practical purpose.

The student familiar with accounting may compare the balance of indebtedness with the corporate balance sheet and be tempted to go further and identify the balance of payments with the corporate income statement. The analogy is valid for timing. One pair of statements relates to a point in time; one to a period of time. But in other respects the analogy is misleading and dangerous.

An income statement includes all credits and debits which relate to a year's income; it excludes capital expenditures and borrowings. The balance of payments, on the other hand, covers all international payments, whether income or capital. It is the equivalent of the daily journal in which all transactions are recorded. It is equally, or perhaps more, wrong to compare the current account of the balance of payments with the income statement. Imports include goods purchased for capital construction, while expenditures in the income statement are limited to those which are chargeable against the year's current output.

Balance of Payments and Foreign-Exchange Market

The balance of payments comprehends all expenditures of a country to, and receipts from, abroad. As we have already seen, in some cases it goes further and includes payments to the country's own nationals. As an introduction to the theory of foreign exchange, which will be the subject of the next chapter, it may be useful to ask how the balance of payments of a country differs from an account of its foreign-exchange transactions. These differences will occur in coverage, valuation, and timing.

If the foreign-exchange market of a country is taken by itself, it will quickly be seen that the balance of payments includes many more transactions than pass through the foreign-exchange market. In the United States, for example, many exports are sold to foreigners for dollars. These enter into the balance of payments but involve no foreign-exchange transaction in the United States. In similar fashion, many importers buy goods abroad for dollars. These affect the balance of payments but not the record of foreign-exchange transactions in the United States.

So narrow a view of the foreign-exchange market, however, is inadmissible. The foreigner who buys from an American export house for dollars or the foreigner who is willing to receive dollars from an American importer acquires or sells, respectively, these dollars in the foreign-exchange market abroad. The foreign-exchange market for a currency is not limited to the country in which it is legal tender but includes every geographical market in the world where the currency is traded. On this showing, the balance of payments and a complete record of foreign-exchange transactions come more nearly into line in coverage.

The coverage of the two records never entirely matches, however. As we have indicated earlier, some transactions are included in the balance of payments involving international economic intercourse, but really take place in local currency between residents of the reporting country: e.g., the balance of payments may set out a record of all freight on imports, including that paid to domestically operated carriers. In addition, the balance of payments includes certain kinds of transactions in which there are no payments and hence no foreign-exchange transaction. These include donations (in kind), barter, and what is called "private compensation." The latter involves the matching of exports and imports outside the foreign-exchange market, in the case of a private company which exports for foreign currency and then uses the foreign currency to buy goods for importation into its own country. It also includes the sale of foreign exchange to another private firm without the intermediary of a bank or foreign-exchange dealer. In this case, the transaction would not be recorded in the list of deals of the foreign-exchange market as such; but it is clear that the transaction is one in foreign exchange, even if there is no way of taking note of it.

The difference in valuation between the balance of payments and a record of foreign-exchange transactions arises from the fact that the balance of payments is kept on a consistent basis, whereas the valuation used in foreign-exchange transactions depends upon the terms of the myriad separate deals. Exports and imports are now generally valued for balance of payments on an f.o.b. basis. In the real world, some exports are sold f.o.b., some f.a.s., some c.i.f. The goods may even be shipped for sale on consignment, in which case the exporter will bear not only all the foreign costs of the sale but also internal transport costs, such as shipment from New York to the market in Chicago. In this case the exporter originally has to buy foreign exchange to meet his local expenses; but ultimately—assuming that his operation was successful—he recoups and sells in the foreign-exchange market the c.i.f. value of the merchandise not to the border but to the internal point of sale.

Finally, the balance of payments and a foreign-exchange record may differ in timing. This is the respect in which balance-of-payments estimates are weakest. The method for estimating the balance of payments requires that exports and imports be listed at the time goods cross international borders. But payment may take place through the foreign-exchange market any time from years ahead to years afterward. Some goods are shipped on consignment. When sold, they may be sold for credit. In this case, payment will follow the recorded export and import by some months. At the other extreme, certain types of capital goods which take a long time to produce, such as ships, may be ordered years in advance, with a down payment made at the time of the order, and the remainder undertaken progressively and completed before delivery.

If the compilers of the record of international economic transactions could choose and were limited to one type of record, it is not certain whether it would be most useful to take down orders, production for export, payment, or deliveries. For some purposes, one would be the most desirable; for other purposes, another. Perhaps the most significant of all would be payments. But ease of computation limits the statisticians to the record of deliveries.

A small point: payment takes place simultaneously in two separate countries with telegraphic transfers. The export and import are entered in the balance of payments separately, the export sometimes a month or more before the import. This may be significant, especially when a large change takes place at a year end.

The main difficulty from the difference in timing between the balance of payments and the record of exchange transactions occurs when the terms of payment in foreign trade undergo alteration. Normally, the question is of no importance: payments lag or lead deliveries by a small and constant margin. But if, in any one year, the exports of a country which were sold on three-month credit shift to a cash basis, the country will receive fifteen months' payments in twelve months, and the balance of payments based upon export deliveries will convey an erroneous impression of actual payments. The same would be true of a shift from a cash to a credit basis. In this case the country would receive nine months' payments, while the balance of payments derived from customs-house records gave a tally of twelve.

The issue has great significance when the speculative view of a currency changes. If the foreign-exchange market decides that a currency is likely to be devalued, imports into that country will be accelerated, to build up stocks before the cost of imports rises; and its exporters will hold back, in the hope of getting higher prices in local currency for the foreign exchange earned by their sales abroad. Even if this effect on trade is small, however, payments for past imports will be sped, while the currency is still worth what it is and receipt of payment for exports will be postponed as long as possible in the hope of getting a more favorable rate for foreign exchange. This is partly what happened to the pound sterling in the summer of 1949, and in the Suez crisis beginning in July, 1956, and heightened the following October. Drives to prepay imports and to delay receipts from exports put heavy pressure on the foreign-exchange market, increasing the supply of sterling and limiting the demand, even without significant change in foreign trade.

Summary

The balance of payments of a country is a systematic record of all economic transactions between the residents of the reporting country and residents of all foreign countries. Certain problems must be settled in determining who is a resident and what is a transaction. But any consistent scheme of reporting is adequate for the purpose, so long as it is organized in such a way as to serve the uses to which it is put. The most important use of the balance of payments of most countries is to describe in a concise fashion the state of international economic relationships of the country as a guide to monetary, fiscal, exchange, and other policies. While the balance of payments was originally estimated to explain the sources and uses of foreign exchange, more recently emphasis has been on showing the impact of foreign transactions on national income.

The balance of payments is divided in a number of ways, generally into a current account, related to the income-producing and consuming items, such as merchandise trade, shipping, insurance, investment income, donations, etc.; a capital account, which shows changes in net assets and liabilities; and an account for monetary gold movements. A separate item for errors and omissions is required. The balance of payments is theoretically organized on the basis of double-entry bookkeeping, in which every transaction has a debit and a credit. In estimating the balance of payments, however, a single-entry system is used, which leaves room for imbalance.

The balance of indebtedness is a statement of assets and liabilities of a country. It is less accurate, and less informative even if accurate, than the balance of payments.

The balance of payments may differ from the record of foreign-exchange transactions in a currency (but not limited to a national market) in coverage, valuation, and timing.

SUGGESTED READING

TREATISES, ETC.

Haberler, chap. ii; Meade, *The Balance of Payments,* Part I.

The *Balance of Payments Yearbooks* of the International Monetary Fund are worth consulting, especially the initial volume for 1938, 1946, and 1947, which sets out detailed introductions on "Underlying Principles and Nature of the Statistics" and "The Concept of Compensatory Official Financing." The latter is attacked by F. Machlup in "Three Concepts of the Balance of Payments and the So-Called Dollar Shortage," *EJ,* March, 1950, to which we shall have occasion to refer later.

The International Monetary Fund also published a *Balance of Payments Manual* of instructions to countries compiling balance-of-payments statistics, which provides useful material on the treatment of separate items in their full complexity.

A valuable addition to the literature is the long article by D. G. Badger, "Balance of Payments—a Tool of Economic Analysis," *SP,* September, 1951, which summarizes a wide range of technical discussion.

POINTS

S. Enke, "Some Balance of Payments Pitfalls," *AER,* March, 1951, discusses whether the terminology "credits and debits" is superior to "receipts and payments." It is commented on by R. L. Sammons of the Department of Commerce in the *AER* for December, 1951.

Tables 2.1 and 2.2 are from Volume VII of the International Monetary Fund's, *Balance of Payments Yearbook,* release of February, 1957. Table 2.3 is from the *Report to the President* by the President's Citizen Advisers on the Mutual Security Program, B. F. Fairless, Co-ordinator. The report is published by the U.S. Government Printing Office on March 1, 1957. Table 2.4 comes from the United Nations, *World Economic Survey, 1955* (New York, 1956), p. 76, and rearranges Department of Commerce data. The balances of indebtedness in Table 2.5 are from Department of Commerce, *Survey of Current Business,* August, 1956.

Chapter 3 ┆ THE FOREIGN-EXCHANGE MARKET

Foreign Exchange

In the course of their business, exporters collect foreign currency which they cannot use and therefore must exchange for domestic funds. Importers who start with a supply of domestic currency seek to acquire foreign currency in order to buy goods abroad. The unacceptability of foreign money for exports and of local money for imports is the basis for a market in which foreign moneys are bought and sold. This is called the foreign-exchange market.

Different mint marks on coins and different engraving designs and colors on notes are not the sole reason for organizing and maintaining a foreign-exchange market. In a more fundamental sense the market transfers purchasing power. Transfers of purchasing power take place within a single national economy, as, for example, when checks against New York bank accounts paid to people in San Francisco are cleared against checks on San Francisco drawn in favor of New York payees through the Federal Reserve interdistrict clearing. Different names and units of money dramatize the process; the possibility of variation in the foreign-exchange rate adds a new element. Nonetheless, the primary function of the foreign-exchange market is to transfer purchasing power and clear transactions in opposite directions in essentially the same sort of way as do the Federal Reserve System, the separate Federal Reserve bank, local clearinghouses, or even the informal clearing which takes the form of swapping of checks between the clerks of banks in the same small town.

Foreign exchange appeals to many people as a mysterious, recondite subject which requires long and arduous study. Much of the difficulty is caused by the fact that one can look at a given transaction either way. In commodities, we think for the most part of the dollar price of wheat but not of the wheat price of dollars. (We do, however, occasionally quote soup or gasoline at so many cans or gallons to the dollar.) This sort of reciprocity is necessary in foreign exchange. Moreover, there is no single-standard way of calculating foreign-exchange rates. Most countries quote foreign currencies in terms of the number of units of local currency required to make one foreign unit. In the United States, for example, we say the pound sterling is worth $2.80 and the French franc $0.0028¾; in France, the pound is said to be worth roughly 1,000 francs and the dollar 350. But London, instead of regarding the dollar as worth 7 shillings 1¾ pence and the franc as roughly ⅖ of a penny, uses $2.80 and 1,000 francs to the pound. This gives the result that in London in September, 1949, the dollar went up from $4.03 (to the pound) to $2.80 (to the pound). Many students (and teachers) get confused because of the lack of a consistent way of describing foreign-exchange transactions and rates. With a little time and care, however, the mystery dissolves, and the subject can be handled by those of us with average intelligence.

The International Character of the Foreign-Exchange Market

The foreign-exchange market is not limited to a given country. The market for sterling, for example, covers transactions in pounds in New York, Montreal, Zurich, etc., and the London transactions in foreign exchange. One is continuously tempted to refer to the foreign-exchange market as if it were a geographic entity. This is wrong. It is the market for a currency. If the supply of sterling in New York exceeds the local demand, there need be no change in the exchange rate; the surplus can be used to buy dollars in London.

Functions of the Exchange Market

The three functions of the foreign-exchange market are to effect transfers of purchasing power, to provide credit for foreign trade, and to furnish facilities for hedging foreign-exchange risks. Of these by far the most important is the transfer of purchasing power—from one country to another and from one currency to another. The means of effecting these transfers is identical in broad outline with that used in domestic trade, through the clearing of payments in opposite directions.

Foreign-Exchange Instruments

At a superficial level of analysis, the transfer of purchasing power is carried out with the use of credit instruments. The main instrument for this purpose is the telegraphic transfer, or the cabled order by one bank (in country A) to its correspondent abroad (in country B) to pay B funds out of its deposit account to a designated account or order. The telegraphic transfer is nothing more than a check which is wired or radioed rather than mailed. Or bank drafts (a more usual type of check) can be used. Some considerable amount of payments is still effected through what used to be the primary instrument, the commercial bill of exchange or acceptance. This is more or less the opposite of a check. A check is an order on a bank to pay a stipulated sum of money to a given person. It is drawn by the buyer of the goods and requires the bank to which it is addressed (where he has a deposit) to pay the seller. A bill of exchange, on the other hand, is an order written by the seller of the goods directing the buyer to pay the seller or the party, bank, discount house, or other financial institution with whom he has discounted the bill.

There are many variations on the basic theme of the bill of exchange. The order to pay on sight is a sight bill or draft. More usually, however, the bill will stipulate that payment must be made so many days (typically ninety) after sight. This is a time bill or draft. The bill may be accepted, i.e., it may contain the signature of the draftee (person on whom the bill is drawn) across its face. This is an indication to anyone who may wish to buy the bill for investment that the buyer of the goods acknowledges that he owes the money specified in the draft. The buyer of the goods is encouraged to accept the draft and acknowledge his debt by refusal of the seller to release the bill of lading, which permits him to claim the goods from the shipping company, until he has so accepted. The bill of lading is attached to the original draft and is detached only upon acceptance.

A bill of exchange accepted by the importer is called a commercial acceptance. Frequently, however, terms of sale will call for the seller to draw not on the importer but on the importer's bank. The importer must arrange with his bank ahead of time to accept the draft. Sometimes the exporter will want to be assured that the importer, whose credit is unknown to him, has, in fact, the backing of a bank. In these circumstances, he will require an importer's letter of credit, and the draft on the importer's bank will specify the fact that it is drawn under a particular letter of credit. An importer's letter of credit is to be distinguished from a personal letter of credit. This latter instrument is issued by a traveler's bank specifying and guaranteeing that a certain sum has been set aside to his credit. Purchases of local currency may be made against the letter of credit in foreign banks, which will note on the letter that the original sum has been reduced by the amount of the sale. The personal letter of credit is much like a traveler's check, except that the latter is issued in a fixed amount which must be sold as a unit, whereas the letter of credit is flexible.

Finally, as just noted, the instrument most in use in foreign trade today is the telegraphic transfer or order. This is an instruction from one bank to its correspondent in a foreign country to pay a specific amount of local currency to a particular person, debiting to the bank's account carried with its correspondent. Telegraphic transfers may be telephoned by a corporation to its bank in the paying country, while the correspondent bank in the receiving country calls up the payee and asks how he wants to receive the funds.

The nature of the instrument used to effect international payments is largely governed by the credit aspect of foreign exchange. Much will turn, for example, on whether the exporter knows the importer and trusts him and whether the exporter is large and well equipped to deal directly with the details of foreign exchange or operates exclusively through the foreign department of his bank. In the nineteenth century the commercial bill of exchange was the primary instrument of foreign exchange, and later it was the bankers' acceptance. Today telegraphic transfers predominate, largely because the risk of variation in foreign-exchange rates limits the extension of short-term credit between nations. In addition to exchange risks, the fact that foreign trade is conducted by large corporations which are able to finance themselves without recourse to banks for separate transactions tends to keep it on a cash basis.

International Clearing

Purchasing a telegraphic transfer or a bank draft, or paying off a bill of exchange when it comes due, enables the importer to discharge his obligation for the goods he buys from a foreign supplier. But how does the exporter collect payment? Or if the exporter discounts the bill with his bank, how does the bank which has paid out B funds, and holds an obligation denominated in A funds, get even with the transaction? This is where clearing comes in, which is the essence of the process of transferring purchasing power.

In the final analysis, a country pays for its imports with its exports. But it is also true that the exporters in any given country receive payment in domestic currency from the country's importers, who are thereby enabled to pay domestic currency for their purchases from abroad. Goods and credit instruments move across the border, but payment in domestic currency takes place within the country as part of the clearing process. Figure 3.1 provides a highly stylized illustration of this basic proposition. The exporter in the United States ships goods to the importer in Britain; and the importer in the United States acquires goods from the exporter in Britain. The United States exporter is presumably paid by the British importer, and the British exporter by the United States importer. But in an ultimate sense the United States importer pays the United States exporter and the British importer the British exporter. The detailed way in which this is done will depend upon the way in which the transactions are organized.

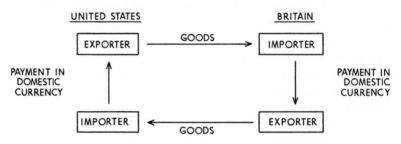

FIG. 3.1. International Clearing through the Foreign-Exchange Market

Suppose the British importer buys dollars to pay his obligation to the United States exporter. How are dollars produced in the London market? Evidently by British exports to the United States for dollars. Dollars paid by the United States importer to the British exporter are bought by the British importer and paid to the United States exporter.

Or the transaction can proceed in sterling through the medium of the New York exchange market. The United States exporter draws a sterling bill on his British customer and discounts it with his bank. The bank then sends it to London for rediscount, selling the resulting sterling to the United States importer who needs it to discharge his debts for goods bought in Britain.

The variety of possible combinations which will clear the market can be summarized as follows:

Foreign-Exchange Transaction	Payment by British Importer to United States Exporter	Payment by United States Importer to British Exporter
U.S. exporter sells £ in New York to U.S. importer.....	Payment in £	Payment in £
British exporter sells $ in London to British importer.................	Payment in $	Payment in $
U.S. exporter sells £ to (buys $ from) British exporter...	Payment in £	Payment in $
U.S. importer buys £ from (sells $ to) British importer.	Payment in $	Payment in £

The international character of the exchange market is evident from the fact that the third and fourth of these transactions between the two exporters or the two importers can take place in either London or New York.

This limited example in which one export is paid for by one import evidently requires that the separate transactions involve identical amounts of money. Clearing on a more substantial scale, such as is involved in domestic clearings and in the actual foreign-exchange market, occurs for instruments ranging over an almost infinite variety of amounts, with large sums on each side canceling out and leaving only small net balances to be settled. But the essence remains simple. Like any other clearing arrangement, the foreign-exchange market carries out payments, in this case internationally, by simultaneously clearing debts owed in both directions.

The clearing need not be bilateral. In fact, trade thrives best when the clearing takes place on a multilateral basis. Malaya earns dollars from its sales to the United States, which it pays to Britain for textiles, enabling Britain to pay dollars for its purchases of machinery in the United States. Or Canada, by means of the exchange market and multilateral clearing, exchanges wheat and bacon sold to Britain for automobiles and coal bought from the United States. The clearing function of the foreign-exchange market applied multilaterally enables countries to effect exchanges of goods far too intricate to negotiate without the use of the international means of payment provided by foreign exchange.

If a country's exports exceed its imports, then its claims on foreign countries will exceed its debts. Perhaps speculators will be willing to hold foreign exchange for a rise in the rate. In this case the exporters of those goods which may be arbitrarily chosen to represent the excess will receive payment in their own currency from the speculators. Or commercial banks may be willing to increase their deposits of foreign exchange and pay these exporters. Or perhaps, if neither speculators nor commercial banks are willing, the central bank will buy the foreign exchange and provide the exporters with the local currency they want.

If nobody is willing to hold the additional foreign exchange and there is no automatic mechanism, such as the gold standard, to convert it into domestic currency, then the supply of foreign exchange will exceed the demand for it, and the price will have to change. This price change will proceed until enough buyers are attracted into the market, or sellers driven out of it, to equate the supply of and the demand for exchange at the new price. The basic function of the foreign-exchange market, then, is to clear the demand and supply for foreign exchange and by so doing to effect payments into and out of a country.

Credit Function

In addition to its primary function of clearing payments, the foreign-exchange market is also called upon to provide credit. We do not propose to discuss this matter in great detail. This is more properly a subject belonging in books on the techniques of foreign trade, and involves detailed discussion of the credit instruments used in the foreign-exchange market. Here we propose merely to make clear that the credit function falls into two parts: the national and the international.

That international trade requires credit follows from the fact that all trade does. It takes time to move goods from seller to purchaser. Someone must finance the transaction for this period, and possibly for longer. In the normal case, credit will be needed as well by the exporting firm during the period required to manufacture the goods and by the importer for the time between his payment for the goods and his receipt of payment after selling them in their original or processed form. But if the exporter can finance manufacture and the importer can finance marketing, credit is necessary for the transit of the goods. If the importer pays cash, he may be said to finance the transaction. If the exporter holds the accepted bill of exchange for his own account or finances the export through an open-book credit to the importing house, the exporter undertakes the financing. In general, however, when the special credit facilities of the foreign-exchange market are used, the foreign department of a bank or the bill market of one country or the other will be called upon to extend the credit.

Whether a country's foreign trade will be financed at home or in part abroad depends upon a host of considerations, including particularly comparative rates of interest and willingness to run an exchange risk. If world trade were all financed by bills of exchange drawn in the buyer's currency, if discount rates were the same in all markets, and if no one were willing to run an exchange risk, importing countries would finance their imports, while exports get paid in cash. The sequence would be: The exporter discounts a bill drawn in foreign exchange with his bank, his bank simultaneously rediscounts the bill in the money market of the importing country (repatriating the proceeds), and the importer's money market would hold the bill until its collection at maturity. If exports and imports were equal in all countries, every foreign-exchange market would finance a portion of its foreign trade but none of any other country. If one country had an import surplus (and another an export surplus), the importing country might be said to extend credit internationally in a limited sense, but much less so than if it financed its imports and its exports as well.

Or with every country's exports and imports equal, each foreign-exchange market could finance its exports and still avoid exchange risks by exporters drawing bills in their own currency, discounting them in their own money market, which would hold them to maturity. With exports and imports equal, there would be domestic but no international extension of credit. Any country which had an export surplus could be said to be extending credit internationally in the same limited sense as in the previous paragraph.

Neither of these hypothetical pictures has any reality. Interest rates do differ, and frequently people have been willing to take exchange risks. These conditions have led to substantial international financing of foreign trade.

In the nineteenth century the world financed its trade in sterling. Exporters to London drew bills of exchange on London. The London discount rate was below that in other centers. Foreign banks therefore discounted their sterling bills and repatriated the proceeds to their own money markets. A New York bank, for example, which could earn 8 per cent on its money at home and only 4 per cent in London would be foolish to hold sterling bills. In discounting for its local exporter it had used the New York rate, but it rediscounted in London at the lower rate. This meant that a three-month bill for which it has paid 98 (8 per cent a year is 2 per cent for three months) could be rediscounted for 99. With the London rate typically lower than rates abroad, there was a strong incentive to draw bills in sterling and to discount them in London. In this way London financed its import trade.

London, however, also financed its export trade. London banks would have earned a higher return by encouraging their exporting customers to draw bills in foreign currencies which the banks would hold to maturity. But this would have involved taking an exchange risk which these banks were unwilling to undertake. During the period the bills ran, the foreign currencies might change in value. Accordingly, the London banks were resigned to earning the lower rate of interest available in their own market. British exporters drew their bills in sterling, and these were discounted and held to maturity in London. This involved an exchange risk for the foreign importers, who received goods for which they had to pay in foreign currency in three months. But since sterling provided the world's standard of value, exchange risks in sterling were taken unhesitatingly. In this manner,

London financed its imports and exports, representing a substantial part of the rest of the world's exports and imports, respectively. In addition, London financed a considerable amount of trade which did not touch British shores by discounting sterling bills drawn by exporters in second countries on importers in third.

The credit function of the foreign-exchange market has dwindled in importance today. Much more foreign trade is conducted by sight drafts and telegraphic transfer than by bills of exchange, as corporations finance themselves to a greater extent than formerly, and as willingness to take exchange risks has declined. On occasion, changes in credit terms are used by speculators as a means of opening up adverse speculative positions in a currency which is under attack: foreign exporters insist on early payment to avoid any chance of depreciation before receiving what they are owed, and foreign importers delay payment of their obligations in the currency in the hope of being able to buy it cheaper. This means that credit is extended not by the strong market with abundant resources and the lowest rates of discount but by the weak market, frequently with high discount rates, and one which has shown signs of weakness by losing foreign exchange. To the extent that international lending through the finance of foreign trade takes place today, it occasionally becomes perverse.

Hedging Function

With foreign-exchange rates fixed and assuming no exchange controls, it makes no difference whether a businessman has sterling or dollars. The one can be converted into the other and back again. When the dollar-sterling rate is subject to alteration, however, a firm with its major assets and liabilities in one currency is taking an "exchange risk" if it has net claims or net liabilities in a foreign currency. An excess of uncovered claims over liabilities in a foreign currency is called a "long position"; an excess of debts over assets, a "short position."

The foreign-exchange market provides facilities for hedging anticipated or actual claims or liabilities. This is the forward or futures market in exchange. A man who expects to receive £1,000 in the near future and is fearful of the risk of exchange can eliminate the risk by selling the £1,000 forward. He receives no money; he delivers no money. He merely enters into a contract to deliver £1,000 against, say, dollars at a given rate on a fixed date in the future. Whether the spot rate rises, falls, or remains unchanged by that date is of no consequence to him. The price at which he will sell his sterling, when it is received, is already settled by contract. A man expecting to need £1,000 at a stipulated date in the future may similarly buy sterling for forward delivery.

Forward contracts are normally for three months at a time, though special arrangements of a shorter or longer nature can be made through a bank. At the end of this three months, if the anticipated receipts have not come in, the man who has sold £1,000 forward and has to deliver on the contract can get the sterling he needs by "swapping." He sells more forward sterling and buys spot. For the spot sterling he has to pay the spot rate. The sale of forward sterling, like the previous one, is merely a contract to deliver sterling in future at a stipulated price. If he swaps sterling forward with the holder of the previous forward contract, the purchase and delivery of spot sterling may be omitted as unnecessary, and he pays or receives the difference between the old forward price and the new.

The ability to buy or sell forward exchange enables a firm which is not in the exchange business to hedge its exchange risks. It also permits banks, which are unlikely to run any considerable exchange position, to cover their commitments. A given bank whose customers want to sell a considerable amount of foreign exchange on balance, whether spot or forward, can buy the exchange from its customers and in turn sell exchange spot or forward, without running the risk of a change in exchange rate.

The existence of the forward market also makes it possible for speculators to establish positions in foreign exchange. If New York speculators think sterling is going up, they may buy it forward. If it does rise in price, they can resell at a new and higher rate the spot sterling which has been delivered to them at the old rate, and thus make a profit. Or they can swap the position forward again, if they believe that the rise is to continue, taking their profits on the portion of the anticipated rise which has already taken place.

Exchange positions have been discussed above in terms of money claims and liabilities. A firm with accounts receivable or accounts payable in a foreign currency should hedge them, unless it wishes to carry a position in foreign exchange. Inventories and other short-term assets present a more complicated problem. If goods are located in Britain but could be sold in dollars, there is no need to hedge them. If the pound sterling declines, the goods are likely to go up in price in sterling. Inventories of finished goods for the British market which cannot be sold in dollars except at a loss, however, are properly a subject for hedging.

The question of long-term money assets and fixed assets and equities is more straightforward. No investment in the former should be made unless an exchange position is entered into with eyes open, and the latter should not be hedged. An exchange contract due in three months is an inappropriate hedge for a ten-year bond. Only when the bond is in process of sale would the forward sale of the anticipated proceeds be appropriate. As for long-term assets or equities in property, these, like salable inventories, are normally expected to remain stable in value in foreign-exchange terms, though their prices may fluctuate for other reasons. To sell forward in an exchange market the net worth of a going concern is really to use the fact of ownership of foreign assets as an excuse to go short of a foreign currency.

The provision of hedging facilities is an important function of the foreign-exchange market, but it is not always in a position to perform it. Where capital movements are controlled, in particular, foreign-exchange rates may fluctuate in a wide range, without it being possible for given exchange positions to be hedged. It is sometimes thought that the existence of a forward-exchange market, by itself, provides automatically the hedging facilities needed on an inexpensive basis. Appendix A at the back of the book discusses this contention, which involves a fairly complex argument. The answer is negative. A forward-exchange market produces no fundamental enlargement in the capacity of a foreign-exchange market to fulfill its hedging function.

The Foreign-Exchange Rate

Money, the textbooks on the subject say, serves as a medium of exchange, a unit of account, and a store of value. Like money, foreign exchange is a medium of exchange. It differs from money in its internal functions by being less than fixed as a unit of account and store of value. The rate of foreign exchange, and with it the domestic value of a given amount of foreign money, can change. What brings it about that the pound is worth $4.00 in 1948 and $2.80 in 1950? Why does the market anticipate that the Deutschemark is likely to go up, despite the denials of the Economics Minister and the officials of the Deutsche Bundes bank?

The answer to these questions is demand and supply. The sterling exchange rate falls from $4.00 to $2.80 because the supply of sterling at $4.00 to the pound exceeded the demand at that price. This statement can be put the other way. The dollar rose from $4.00 to the pound to $2.80 because the demand for dollars at $4.00 to the pound exceeded the supply at that price.

Several things should be noted here. First, the supply of sterling arising from United States exports is the same as the demand arising from British imports, if we limit ourselves to the two-country example, and follows from the fact that the foreign-exchange market encompasses a currency, not a geographical area.

Second, it is generally true that the cheaper one can buy pounds sterling in New York, the larger will be the demand to buy sterling to purchase goods for import into the United States, and the smaller will be the supply of sterling arising from exports from the United States to Britain. The demand for foreign exchange for the purchase of goods will typically be downward sloping from left to right, and the supply upward sloping.

But exporters and importers are not the only participants in the market. Let us suppose in a given situation that an increase occurs in the United States demand for British goods at existing prices. This involves an upward shift in the United States demand for sterling (or in the British supply curve of dollars). Like any other schedule shift, it must be distinguished from a shift along a demand or supply curve. But the rise in the price of sterling (decline in dollars) may be halted by any one of a number of reactions, depending upon where the initiative is taken and the nature of the institutional arrangements in force.

Dollars may be purchased by the Bank of England or the British Treasury's Exchange Equalization Account in order to hold up the price of dollars. This is the equivalent of selling sterling to hold down its price.

Sterling may be sold by the Federal Reserve System or the United States Treasury's Stabilization Fund, in order to support the price of the dollar.

Gold may be bought by the Bank of England or the British exchange market in New York. To do this, the bank or the market would first have to buy dollars with sterling, which would tend to keep down the price of sterling.

Gold may be sold in London by the Federal Reserve Bank or the New York foreign-exchange market, the proceeds in sterling subsequently being used to buy dollars.

If the price of sterling actually does increase, any one or more of the foregoing means of enlarging the supply and halting the change in price may supervene after some price change. In addition, the price change may induce an increase in the supply of sterling or a reduction in the demand for it by other means:

Speculators in New York may be encouraged to reduce their long positions in sterling at the new high price, or to go short of sterling.

Speculators in London may be encouraged to reduce their short positions in the dollar or to enter into new or extended long positions.

In either of these cases, an additional supply of sterling and demand for dollars will ultimately restrain the change in price.

Importers in the United States may be discouraged from continuing their operations because of the high price of sterling, and reduce them, thereby limiting the demand for sterling.

United States exporters may be encouraged to expand their export operations because of the high price of sterling, thereby increasing the supply of sterling.

This list shows how demand and supply for foreign exchange may be balanced at a given price, equalized by the foreign-exchange authorities of a country, or brought into equilibrium at a price which the market settles upon without official support. Under the gold standard, the market clears itself without official support except beyond certain limits, when the authorities, or gold-dealers operating with the tacit approval of the authorities, act to halt the movement of the exchange rate. Intervention by the authorities may take place in a regular way by law or by custom; or the authorities may abstain from any action under the foreign-exchange policy in force. In the latter case the foreign-exchange market, excluding the authorities—i.e., the bankers, dealers, brokers, exporters, importers, and speculators—must find a price which clears the market and balances demand and supply.

The authorities must intervene in the market on an hourly, daily, weekly, or monthly basis if they want stability of the exchange rate over these periods of time and if the market is unable to provide it without their assistance. In these circumstances the authorities may intervene to iron out short-term fluctuations but not to eliminate long-term changes. The difficulty, of course, is one of distinguishing the long term from the short term as time unfolds from day to day.

Private speculation in the foreign-exchange market can be of two kinds. If bull speculators and importers buy less foreign exchange as the price goes up and exporters and bear speculators sell more, this means that their demand curve is negatively sloped and supply curve positively tilted. Under these circumstances, speculation is stabilizing. Speculators buy when the price declines because they expect the price to go up again; or sell when the price rises because they anticipate that the movement will be reversed. These expectations are called "inelastic"—that is, the market expects the price to return to its old level.

But expectations are not universally inelastic, nor speculation always stabilizing. Speculators may regard an increase in price as an indication that the price will go higher, or a decline as only the start of a movement to lower levels. These expectations are elastic. The market expects not a return to the *status quo ante* but more change in the same direction. With elastic expectations, a decline in price will lead to sales rather than to purchases; and a rise, to buying, not to selling. The demand curve will be positively sloped, as in Figure 3.2*b*, and the supply curve will run down from left to right.

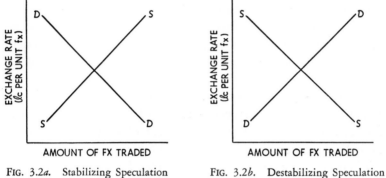

FIG. 3.2*a*. Stabilizing Speculation   FIG. 3.2*b*. Destabilizing Speculation

Figure 3.2*a* shows the position under conditions of stabilizing speculation. Any random change in the price tends to be corrected. Demand exceeds supply at lower prices than the equilibrium level, which drives the price up again; supply exceeds demand at higher prices, which tends to push the price down again. Under destabilizing speculation, as in Figure 3.2*b*, the position is different. Any change from the equilibrium position is self-reinforcing and cumulative— until the expectations of the market and with them the slopes of the demand and supply curves change. This will occur when the destabilizing speculators believe that a movement has run its course. Under these conditions of speculation, therefore, changes in the exchange rate will be exaggerated, rather than moderated as under stabilizing speculation.

While the market for foreign exchange is probably destabilizing on more occasions than scholars are prepared to admit, our discussions of the market will assume, unless specific mention is made to the contrary, that speculation operates to increase the demand at lower prices and the supply at higher.

Arbitrage

The force that keeps the market for a given currency unified all over the world is called "arbitrage." Suppose a change in demand for pounds occurs in New York. The increase in the dollar rate on pounds will be practically instantaneously communicated from New York to London by arbitrage. The rate for the pound cannot exist at $2.90 in New York with the rate for the dollar at $2.80 in London, because it would be profitable for arbitrageurs to buy pounds at $2.80 in London and sell them at $2.90 in New York. This would increase the demand for sterling in London and the supply in New York and would continue until the prices became the same or differed by no more than the cost of telegrams and interest. Arbitrageurs are not speculators. Except for a matter of moments, they have no open position in foreign currency. They make their profit from buying *and* selling foreign currencies, in the course of which they end in the same currency in which they started.

Two-point arbitrage is that in which the arbitrageur finds a spread in the price of his own currency in two markets, generally his own and one abroad. Three-point arbitrage would involve the purchase of francs in New York, their sale in Paris against pounds, and the sale of pounds for dollars in either London or New York. In this case it is assumed that the rates are identical for the franc in Paris and New York, and for the pound in London and New York, but not for the pound and franc in London and Paris. A three-point deal by an arbitrageur in New York would then accomplish simply what two-point arbitrage in francs and pounds would do from either London or Paris. Three-point arbitrage occurs only when exchange dealers in the local market are unaware of the opportunities or forbidden to take advantage of them. It is rare.

Arbitrage is the mechanism which makes two markets, physically separate, a single market in an economic sense. A single market is defined as the place where buyers and sellers of an article trade it at an identical price. In the same market only one price exists. Where the same price exists continuously for the same commodity, there is one market. Where there are two markets and the costs of buying in one and selling in the other are small, arbitrage will produce essentially one price and one market. Where arbitrage cannot take place for one reason or another—for lack of knowledge of the facts of the other prices, because of inadequate communication, or because of prohibitions—prices between markets will differ. In the last case, when arbitrage is prohibited, large price differences will encourage covert trading because the rewards for operating contrary to the law are great.

In the absence of exchange controls the foreign-exchange market for a currency, including all countries where it is traded and with which arbitrage takes place, is among the most nearly perfect markets of the world. This is because money is the most homogeneous of articles and because it can be transferred instantaneously. The wheat markets in Chicago and Liverpool were closely linked in normal times, but not so closely as foreign-exchange markets. The international gold market on the gold standard represented a series of markets separated within certain limits by the costs of transferring gold from one country to another. We shall have occasion to investigate this in the next chapter. But, for foreign exchange, the cost of the telegrams and the loss of interest on the money for the period of time it is tied up in arbitrage are very small in relation to the amounts of money which may be transferred. The time element is practically eliminated. Accordingly, the price of sterling in New York cannot differ by much or for long from the reciprocal of the price of the dollar in London. Arbitrage is the force which prevents the single market from separating into two markets.

Exchange Control

Demand and supply determine the value of foreign exchange in the market and under all institutional arrangements likely to be adopted by the exchange authorities, except one. The authorities may decide to equate demand and supply not by price or by interference with price involved in adding to the demand at low prices or to the supply at high. They may decide to maintain a fixed price and ration the limited supply among demanders. This is the method of exchange control.

In the next chapter, which completes the introduction needed before we can begin to study the current account intensively, we shall study the elements of the adjustment process in international economics to see how various disturbances, such as an increase in demand, are worked out. In particular, we shall pay attention to the gold standard, the exchange standard, and exchange control.

Summary

The foreign-exchange market is an international one. The market for a single currency, such as the pound sterling, is located in all the cities of the world where this currency is traded and in its own monetary capital, London.

The functions of the exchange market are three: to clear transactions, to provide credit, and to enable exchange risks to be hedged. The most important of these functions is that of clearing or enabling payments to be made at a distance in a foreign currency. The forward market, which trades in foreign exchange for future delivery, is useful for hedging exchange positions.

The foreign-exchange rate is maintained at a single price in all sections of the foreign-exchange market, under normal conditions, by arbitrage, or rapid buying and selling of exchange, without taking an exchange position except momentarily. The foreign-exchange rate is the rate which will clear the market. If the rate is to be kept stable, when the demand and supply for foreign exchange fluctuate, the foreign-exchange authorities must intervene to supply or bid for exchange, unless foreign-exchange speculation based on inelastic expectations buys foreign currencies when they decline in price and sells them when they rise. Speculation may also be destabilizing, within wide limits, i.e., selling currencies when they decline and buying them when they rise. Formal stability may be given to the rate by exchange control. By this method, the price is fixed, and the supply must be rationed among the demanders.

SUGGESTED READING

TEXTS

Two texts in foreign exchange are worth noting: F. A. Southard, *Foreign Exchange Practice and Policy* (New York: McGraw-Hill Book Co., Inc., 1940), especially chaps. ii and iii; and N. Crump, *The A B C of the Foreign Exchanges* (12th ed.; London: Macmillan & Co., Ltd., 1955), especially chaps. ix through xiii (all short).

For the student interested in foreign-trade techniques with special reference to bills of exchange, acceptances, and discounts, the textbook by M. S. Rosenthal, *Techniques of International Trade* (New York: McGraw-Hill Book Co., Inc., 1950), is recommended, especially Part VI.

TREATISES, ETC.

No major monographic literature exists in the field. The advanced student is warned away from J. Robinson's and F. Machlup's excellent articles, "The Foreign Exchanges" and "The Theory of the Foreign Exchanges," American Economic Association, *Readings,* Nos. 4 and 5, until a later stage in his progress.

Citations on exchange control will be held in reserve until Chapter 13.

ELEMENTS IN THE ADJUST-
MENT PROCESS

The Need for Adjustment

The British government can print pounds sterling any time it chooses (or create them through the banking system); it cannot, however, create United States dollars. If the supply of dollars coming into British hands falls short of the dollars that British residents want to use, at the existing exchange rate for dollars in terms of pounds, something must give. The problem of international adjustment is that of reconciling these differences between the demand for, and the supply of, a given foreign exchange at a given price. The reason why demand and supply may not remain equal at a fixed price is perhaps not obvious. But in international economic relations, as in all life, the only fixed point is the inevitability of change. Changes may be large or small, random or systematic, natural or man-made. One can only be certain that they will occur. Classical economists illustrated the adjustment mechanism with bumper crops and harvest failures. This cause of balance-of-payments disturbance is still fresh and up to date, as Turkish, Argentine, French, and Spanish experience of the 1950's demonstrates. Particularly in dry countries is there great variability in harvest yields. But adjustment is called for by many more causes than variability in the bounty of nature. Pure inflation, the business cycle, war, the introduction of new products, new ways of making old products, and a host of other disturbances put the machinery of international adjustment to the test.

Three Systems

Broadly speaking, there are three systems of international adjustment, each related to a system for regulating the foreign-exchange market. Two of these are international in nature; one is highly nationalistic. For many purposes the terms "gold standard," "paper standard," and "exchange control" suffice to indicate the three. On a more general level, however, we shall call them the "fixed exchange rate," the "fluctuating exchange rate," and "exchange control."

In essence, the fixed exchange rate system keeps foreign-exchange rates steady and expects other internal elements in the system—the quantity of money, national income, level of prices, and banking and fiscal policy—to keep the national economy in some sort of international balance. On the fluctuating exchange standard, more or less the reverse is called for: national income, the domestic price level, monetary, banking policy, and fiscal operations are presumed to be left where they are, and international adjustment is brought about through changes in exchange rates. Exchange control combines elements of both systems, leaving unchanged, in the first instance, national income, the quantity of money, etc., and maintaining a stable exchange rate. To achieve this, it restricts imports directly to the level of exports, brings exports up to the level of imports, or a little of both.

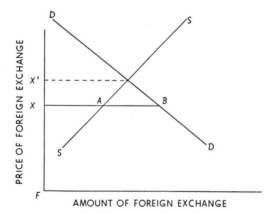

FIG. 4.1. Adjustment under Fixed Exchange Rate, Fluctuating Exchanges, and Exchange Control

A crude illustration of the differences among these three systems is furnished by the usual demand and supply curves. In Figure 4.1 the demand for foreign exchange (*D–D*) exceeds the supply (*S–S*) at the existing exchange rate *FX* by an amount *A–B*. Under a fixed exchange system, national policies would be altered so that the demand and supply for foreign exchange created by imports and exports would come into equilibrium with each other at the price *FX*. With a fluctuating exchange standard, the exchange rate would be allowed to change, say to *FX'*. With exchange control, the supply of foreign exchange, *XA,* would be rationed among users demanding *XB*.

Fixed Exchange Rate

The best-known standard under which exchange rates are unchanged is the gold standard. On this system, countries maintain the value of their currencies in a fixed relationship to the value of gold by standing ready to buy and sell gold at constant prices. Things equal to the same thing are equal to each other. If the currencies of the world each have a stable relationship to gold, they have a fixed relationship to each other. At least this would be true if the buying and selling prices were identical in each country and if gold were costless to move between countries.

It may not be clear to everyone why foreign-exchange rates are fixed when each country has a single buying and selling price for gold and gold movements are costless. But suppose the buying and selling price of gold is $35 an ounce in the United States and 175 shillings an ounce in London. The exchange rate between dollars and the pound sterling will be fixed at $4.00 to the pound, since

$$\frac{175}{35} = 5 \text{ shillings per dollar, or } \$4.00 \text{ per pound (20 shillings).}$$

The reason that the rate cannot depart from this figure is that no one in the United States would be willing to pay more than $4.00 a pound. At any higher rate for the pound, it is cheaper to buy four thirty-fifths of an ounce of gold in New York, which costs only $4.00, and exchange it in London for £1. At any lower rate, it pays those with pounds for sale to buy four thirty-fifths of an ounce of gold with each pound in London and sell them for $4.00 in New York.

The fact of the matter, of course, is that central banks and treasuries charge a spread between buying and selling prices. It is also expensive to move gold between markets because of commissions, freight, insurance, and the loss of interest. In consequence, the price for the pound in New York can depart from the ratio of the gold prices of the two currencies, which is called the "mint parity," by the amount of these costs.

A man buying pounds will be willing to pay anything above the mint parity that he has to but not more than the cost of buying gold in New York and shipping it to London. These costs establish the gold-export point beyond which the value of the pound cannot rise. Conversely, a man selling pounds will be willing to accept anything below the mint parity that he has to but not less than the cost of using his pounds to buy gold in London and shipping it to New York, where he can sell it for the dollars he wants. These costs establish the gold-import point.

A change in the price of gold in either market will change the mint parity and, with it, the exchange rate. If the London price of gold were to increase from 175*s.* to 250*s.* per ounce (troy), with the New York price unchanged at $35, the mint par of exchange would be altered to $2.80 per pound sterling (if 250*s.* = $35, 20*s.* = $2.80). If the price of gold were to remain unchanged in London, but the mint par of exchange were altered to $2.80 from $4.00, this could come about only through a reduction in the gold price in New York from $35 to $24.50 (175*s.* : $x = 20*s.* : $2.80).

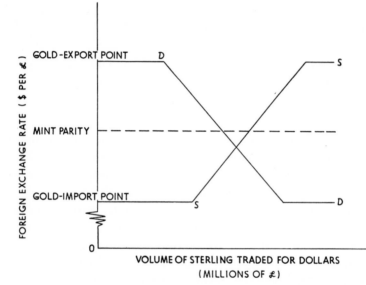

Fig. 4.2. Establishing an Exchange Rate between the Gold Points under the Gold Standard

Between the gold points, the price of exchange is set by demand and supply, as suggested in Figure 4.2. This diagram, it will be observed, shows the position under conditions of stabilizing speculation, since the demand curve is negatively sloped and the supply curve positively. There is no pull of the exchange rate toward the mint parity, which serves only as a basis for the calculation of the gold points. The actual rate of exchange is shown in Figure 4.2 below the mint parity, but it could be anywhere within the range set by the gold-export and the gold-import points.

At the gold-import point, the demand for pounds sterling becomes infinitely great, since sterling can be converted into dollars through gold shipments at this rate. Similarly, at the gold-export point, the supply of pounds becomes infinitely great, since at this high price for sterling it pays to obtain sterling by means of gold exports.

Under stable gold-standard conditions, the movement of the foreign-exchange rate between the gold points used to have significance, at least between distant money markets where costs of shipping gold kept the gold points fairly separate. Some of these movements were regular and were taken advantage of by stabilizing speculation. Prior to World War I, for example, the dollar was weak in the spring, when imports were high, and strong in the fall, when the harvest in cotton and wheat was exported. In consequence, it tended to hover near the gold-export point in the spring and to advance toward the gold-import point in the fall. Speculators felt safe in buying dollars with sterling in the spring and selling them in the fall. This stabilizing speculation had the effect of preventing the dollar from going all the way to the gold points.

Lord Keynes once suggested that it would be useful to widen the area in which stabilizing speculation could work by separating the gold points further. The addition of a handling charge of $\frac{1}{4}$ per cent on purchases and sales when the Treasury gold price was changed from $20.67 to $35 an ounce in 1933 and 1934 had the effect of widening the gold points, though the distance involved was small. The farther apart the gold points, of course, the more nearly the system resembles a fluctuating paper standard rather than a fixed exchange rate standard.

When a wide change occurs in the demand for, or supply of, foreign exchange, the movement of gold generated by the change in the exchange rate will balance the demand and supply for foreign exchange in the short run. When the demand for sterling exceeds the supply forthcoming at prices between the gold points, the demand will be partly satisfied by gold exports which convert dollars into sterling. In Figure 4.3a, for example, a shift in the demand for sterling from

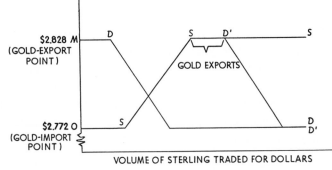

VOLUME OF STERLING TRADED FOR DOLLARS

Fig. 4.3a. Demand for Foreign Exchange Partially Satisfied by Gold Exports

$D–D$ to $D'–D'$, brings it to the right of $S–S$. Demand and supply will be balanced, none the less, at point D', which lies on the gold-export point of $2.828. The amount $M–S$ of the total demand $M–D'$ will be satisfied by the supply of sterling generated, say, by exports of goods and services. The amount $S–D'$ of the demand will be satisfied by gold exports.

In Figure 4.3*b*, on the other hand, a shift to the right of the supply schedule for pounds from $S–S$ to $S'–S'$, created perhaps by an increase in

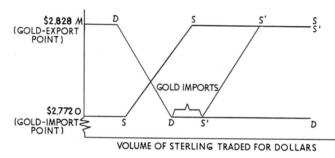

FIG. 4.3*b*. Supply of Foreign Exchange (Demand for Local Currency) Partially Satisfied by Gold Imports

the demand for United States exports, will lower the exchange rate to the gold-import point. The amount $O–D$ will be disposed of to importers of goods and services, and $D–S'$ to gold arbitrageurs, who use it to arrange gold imports.

Price-Specie-Flow Mechanism

While gold flows produce a short-run balancing of the supply of and the demand for foreign exchange, they evidently cannot be continued indefinitely. A country cannot sustain gold exports forever without running out of its gold stock. Gold imports can go on somewhat longer perhaps, but eventually a country's trading partners will exhaust their supplies of gold. What longer-run mechanism of adjustment is involved in the gold standard?

One answer was given to this question by the classical economists, such as David Hume, Adam Smith, John Stuart Mill, and Alfred Marshall, writing from about 1750 to 1914; and another has been given by modern economists since their time. The classical economists worked out the so-called price-specie-flow mechanism, in which price changes induced by gold flows were supposed to bring about the adjustment. Modern economists do not exclude the effects of price changes but are inclined to think that the major burden of adjustment on the gold standard is carried by changes in income.

The price-specie-flow mechanism works like this. An excess of merchandise imports leads to gold exports in the short run. This loss of gold, however, reduces the amount of money in the country, since either gold is money or the banking system keeps the supply of money adjusted to the quantity of gold reserves. A decrease in the money supply of the country will lead to a decline in goods prices, according to the quantity theory of money, which holds that, with less money, people spend less, and less spending with unchanged output requires lower prices. This reduction in prices as a result of the gold outflow is the key to the long-run adjustment mechanism.

Lower prices for goods will increase exports, as foreigners find the country a cheaper place in which to buy. This will shift the supply schedule in Figure 4.1 to the right: i.e., with lower goods prices, more foreign exchange will be forthcoming at every foreign-exchange rate. Lower prices will also reduce imports, since domestic consumers find it advantageous to turn from the now comparatively expensive foreign sources to cheaper domestic supplies. This shifts the demand for foreign exchange in Figure 4.1 to the left and downward. With lower domestic prices, less foreign exchange is demanded at each rate of foreign exchange. In this way, the flow of specie or gold was believed to bring about adjustment in the international position of a country as well as narrowly in the foreign-exchange market.

At the time it was first developed by David Hume in the eighteenth century, this was a revolutionary notion. It helped destroy, at least in England, the mercantilist view that an increase in exports was desirable because it led to gold imports and gold was valuable per se. Hume insisted that gold inflows would reverse themselves, as the rise in prices induced by the enlarged supply of money increased imports and reduced exports. It followed that mercantilist policies were useless.

Criticism of the Price-Specie-Flow Mechanism

The simple price-specie-flow mechanism, however, has been unable to stand the test of time as a general explanation of the adjustment process under fixed exchange rates. As economists learned more about the workings of the banking system, they undertook to elaborate the description of how gold flows affected the long-run demand and supply of foreign exchange. Changes and qualifications were inserted, dealing with the effects of gold movements on the supply of money, the effects of changes in the supply of money on prices, the role of the rate of interest, the importance of central-bank policy, etc. We have not the space to deal fully with all these criticisms and qualifications, but one example may suffice.

In the second half of the nineteenth century it became apparent that the link between gold movements and prices was complex and involved. In particular, men like Walter Bagehot observed that the policy of the Bank of England, which was an important aspect of "the rules of gold-standard game," was critical to the process. (Mr. Leon Frazer, former president of the Bank for International Settlements and of the First National Bank of New York, once observed that everybody talked about the rules of the gold-standard game but no one ever produced a copy of them.) In a fractional-reserve banking system, in which the commercial banks are required to hold reserves with the central bank equal to a stated fraction of their deposit liabilities, and central banks maintain reserves of gold which are only a portion of their note and deposit liabilities, a change in gold reserves can have a large impact on the money supply if the central bank is willing to permit it. If the Bank of England reacts to a gold outflow by raising its discount rate, for example, the contraction of money will be more certain. Commercial banks will raise their charges, call loans to dealers, who will be forced to sell goods, which will lower prices. If, on the other hand, rediscounts are permitted freely at the old rate, the loss of gold in the banking system's reserves will be offset by borrowed reserves. The importance of the role of central-bank policy made it clear that the price-specie-flow mechanism was no automatic balancing wheel.

More recently, however, economists have begun to doubt that the gold standard worked significantly through prices at all. In the first place, a re-examination of nineteenth-century experience suggested that gold flows were ultimately reversed in England not so much by changes in the prices of goods as by short-term capital movements which were evoked by changes in the Bank of England's discount rate. When interest rates in London declined relative to the rest of the world, in response to a gold inflow, short-term capital moved abroad, which halted the gold inflow and furnished the debit to balance the credit of increased exports. Conversely, when short-term rates increased, capital flowed in. The inflow of capital was sufficient to cut off a loss of gold. If the increase in the interest rate was substantial, it might, in fact, produce a capital inflow in excess of the unfavorable balance and lead to a gold inflow.

Secondly, and more important, it was found that the classical economists had neglected an important element in the adjustment process—the role of changes in spending and income.

Income Changes under Fixed Exchange Rates

A rise in exports creates additional income in the hands of exporters. This extra income is in turn spent—on wages, salaries, supplies, and consumption goods—or saved. Generally, most of it will be spent. That part which is spent will become income of the suppliers of services and goods, which they in turn will spend (or save). The part spent will go on increasing the national income.

The increase in income, however, will proceed only so long as the income is spent on domestic goods and services. If it is spent on imports, the chain of spending breaks down (with exports remaining unchanged). Exports create income; imports extinguish it. If no part of the increased income is saved, as we shall see in Chapter 10, the increase in income initiated by the additional exports will continue until an equal additional amount is being spent on imports.

The change in income can be brought about by a change in exports or in imports. Suppose, for example, that the British pay less for imports because they are suddenly cheaper. This leaves them with extra unspent income on hand, in the first instance, which is available for spending on additional domestic goods and services or imports or savings. That part spent on domestic goods and services will increase national income, and if no part of the increased income is saved, this will continue until sufficient new imports are purchased to offset the original decline in imports. If some (but not all) of the funds not spent on old imports are saved, the increase in income will be less, and the rise in new imports insufficient to balance exports and total imports. But income changes play an important role in the adjustment process with or without the necessity for changes in relative prices.

Exchange Standards

The gold standard permits exchange fluctuations within the limits set by the gold points. More truly a fixed exchange standard is the gold-exchange standard, under which a country stands ready to buy or sell a particular foreign exchange which is convertible into gold, without itself buying and selling gold; or the pure exchange standard, in which a country buys and sells a stipulated foreign exchange at a fixed rate. This assumes that the spread between the buying and selling prices is narrower than the spread between the gold points.

The gold-exchange standard was adopted by a number of countries after World War I to conserve gold, which was believed by experts to be in short supply. A country with an excess of exports over imports could gain foreign exchange convertible into gold, which would increase its reserves, without actually drawing gold out of the other country or depleting its reserves. The system was inflationary over-all, i.e., it added to world reserves on balance, and was regarded by some as a departure from the rules of the gold-standard game.

The fixed exchange standard, irrespective of whether the currency into which convertibility is maintained is itself convertible into gold, was a product of the depression. Countries with strong trading ties to another currency found it more important to maintain stability in terms of this currency than in terms of gold. On this account, for example, the rupee is pegged to the pound sterling, whatever the relationship between the pound sterling and gold. It is possible, of course, for a country on a fixed exchange standard to change the rate at which its convertibility is maintained. New Zealand depreciated its pound in terms of the pound sterling in 1928 and appreciated it again in 1948. Similarly Pakistan kept its old parity to the dollar when sterling was depreciated in 1949, and got back into line with sterling in 1955. The sterling area is, by and large, on the fixed exchange standard, although the fact that the degree of convertibility into dollars and Swiss francs is limited may cause some economists to classify the sterling area as an example of exchange control.

Under the gold-exchange standard or the fixed exchange standard, the process of adjustment is the same as if gold were in use. A gain in foreign-exchange reserves is practically equivalent to a gain in gold. The increase in income in the economy will be the same in either event.

Fluctuating Exchange Rates

If there is no automatic or official mechanism for clearing the foreign-exchange market, as that under the gold standard or a fixed exchange standard operating without exchange restrictions, adjustment in the balance of payments is brought about through changes in prices. These do not come from changes in the quantity of money or from the impact of changes in spending under conditions of full employment. They are produced directly by a change in the exchange rate.

Here also operate short-run and long-run mechanisms of adjustment. In the short run, the demand and supply of foreign exchange are brought into an equilibrium by a change in price which clears the market. If the demand for foreign exchange exceeded its supply at the existing price, as in Figure 4.1, the price would rise until a new supply and greater (on the same curve) was elicited and a portion of the existing demand was curtailed.

But this change in the exchange rate, if it is enough to be significant, has more important effects. It changes the relationship between the prices of internationally traded goods—goods exported and imported, and goods produced domestically which are close competitors of imports—and the prices of domestic goods which do not enter into international trade. An increase in the prices of internationally traded goods will expand the production of exports and of import-competing goods which are now more profitable, and will curtail expenditure on imports. A decrease in the prices of internationally traded goods, relative to domestic goods, on the other hand, would increase imports and lead to a contraction of exports.

Depreciation of a currency will increase the domestic price of internationally traded goods if we assume that world prices are unchanged. Suppose that the world prices of cotton textiles and wheat are represented by their New York prices and stand at 30 cents a yard and $2.00 a bushel, respectively. Leaving out of consideration costs of transportation, with sterling at $4.00 per pound, the London prices of these commodities will be 1s. 6d. per yard for cotton textiles and 10s. per bushel for wheat. If the value of the pound sterling is changed by the foreign-exchange market, still assuming world prices unchanged, the sterling prices of these commodities will be affected. A depreciation of the pound to $2.80 will raise the price of cotton textiles to 2s. 2d. per yard and that of wheat to 14s. 4d. (approximately). Cotton textile manufacturers will be disposed to expand their production and sales abroad, which increases exports; domestic producers will raise more wheat at the higher price, which will enable millers to limit imports.

An appreciation of the pound from $4.00 to $5.00, however, would lower the prices of textiles and wheat to 1s. 2d. and 8s., respectively, which would discourage exports and encourage imports.

Even if we abandon the assumption that the world price remains unchanged, the first effects of depreciation will be to encourage exports and discourage imports, while the converse will be true of appreciation. Suppose that sterling depreciates from $4.00 to $2.80 but that instead of the sterling prices of cotton textiles and wheat rising to 2s. 2d. and 14s. 4d., respectively, the world prices fall in New York to 21 cents and $1.40. In London, the price of cotton textiles is still

1*s*. 6*d*. and of wheat 10*s*. There may be no incentive to alter foreign trade in Britain, with prices unchanged; but there will be in the rest of the world. It is less profitable to produce wheat for export to Britain at the lower price, so that British imports will decline; and since the goods bought from England are cheaper than before, it pays to buy more. British exports will increase.

A change in the exchange rate alters the relationship between prices of internationally traded goods in two countries. At one limit and the other, the price change will occur all in one country, while the price in the other remains unaffected. In the normal case with only two countries, prices will change somewhat in both and will alter the relationship of internationally traded to domestic goods in both countries.

There will be secondary effects operating through income, if only those which are brought about by the initial repercussions on foreign trade. These will work in the opposite direction from the foreign-exchange rate change. A depreciation of the exchange rate, for example, will expand exports and reduce imports. But both the expansion of exports and the reduction of imports will increase national income, and this will tend to decrease exports and expand imports. These secondary effects may be offset through action of the monetary or fiscal system; or they may be exaggerated through policy decisions or mistaken action. Price is then not the whole story in adjustments brought about through exchange rates. But it bears the initial impact.

Freely Fluctuating versus Occasionally Changed Rates

We have indicated that a country need not be on the gold standard to have fixed exchange rates. It may be on a "paper" standard, in which its currency is inconvertible into precious metal, and may adopt a variety of exchange policies: a fixed rate in terms of another currency; a freely fluctuating rate in which the authorities never intervene; a flexible rate with no fixed par but in which short-run variations are smoothed out by official operations; or a rate which is stable most of the time but altered occasionally.

A freely fluctuating exchange rate in which the authorities never intervene is hardly usual. Apart from exchange controls, the central bank or Treasury is likely to find some occasions when it buys foreign exchange to prevent the domestic currency from rising, or sells foreign exchange to prevent the domestic currency from falling. To this extent, the exchange standard functions like a fixed standard.

The need for official intervention in the market arises in practice from the unlikelihood that the market can clear itself each hour, day, week, month, or year with exchange fluctuations limited in a narrow range. If all foreign-exchange speculation were stabilizing, this would in fact be the case. Speculators would take positions on the short side when the foreign exchange rose, and on the long side when they declined. In these circumstances, the exchange rates would fluctuate around the long-term level by no more than the minimum movement necessary to compensate the speculators for their balancing operations.

If the outlook for the exchange market is not stable, however, but one beset with uncertainty, the exchange rate is likely to gyrate in the absence of official intervention. Speculation may then be destabilizing, and short-run failures of demand and supply for foreign exchange to match each other will lead to exaggerated changes in rate. If the exchange rate careened about, first advancing and then declining, it would be disruptive of foreign trade. Exporters and importers must be able to calculate the returns from exports and imports in advance. The case is strong for intervention in the exchange market in the short run, to achieve some degree of stability, whatever the usefulness of long-run changes. This short-run stabilization, however, should not run counter to a trend, for this would encourage destabilizing speculation.

There are some economists who advocate leaving the exchange market to clear itself without official intervention. They argue that the governmental authorities have no better idea than anyone else what the long-run equilibrium rate may be; that these authorities are likely too long to defend an indefensible position and hold the rate too high or too low for equilibrium, thereby encouraging destabilizing speculation; and that the best way to encourage stabilizing speculation which makes money by buying low and selling high is to leave the market alone. We are not yet in position to judge these intricate issues, to which we shall recur in Part VI, but it may be well to alert the student at this early stage to their controversial nature.

Purchasing-Power-Parity Theory

A fixed exchange standard requires that national incomes in the countries involved be brought into a relationship which brings about the desired balance between imports and exports and makes the rate effective. Under fluctuating exchange rates, what factors should be brought into an appropriate relationship when an old rate has proved inadequate to the task of balancing trade and a new rate is needed? This problem was first posed after World War I. During the war, trade had been disrupted between allies and halted between enemies. With the resumption of trade, a choice of exchange rates was required. A tendency to return to prewar rates made itself felt; but, among countries with differing degrees of inflation, this was evidently inappropriate. The countries with more inflation would import more and sell less, i.e., run up big import surpluses on current account; the countries with less inflation would be drained of goods as exports exceeded imports.

The Swedish economist, Gustav Cassel, suggested that the new exchange rate should reflect relative changes in prices in any two countries. Working from a base period o, and dealing with two countries A and B, the exchange rate (R) in period 1 should reflect the change in relative prices since the base period:

$$R_o : R_1 = \frac{P_{ao}}{P_{bo}} : \frac{P_{a1}}{P_{b1}}.$$

This formula assumed that the relationship between the two countries was more or less appropriate in the base period and that no major changes in the structure of foreign trade, i.e., in the demand or supply for any basic commodities entering into the trade between the countries, had taken place without offsetting changes elsewhere.

On the basis of this formula, the exchange rate between A and B should be halved if the price level in B is now twice as high, relative to the base period, as that in A. If, on the other hand, A's price level has doubled and B's trebled, the rate of exchange on B in the market of A should fall from 100 to 66, for

$$100 : 66 = \frac{100}{100} : \frac{200}{300}.$$

In theory, the purchasing-power-parity doctrine emphasizes that the price relationships which once produced balance-of-payments adjustment will again produce equilibrium provided no far-reaching changes in the economic relationships between the two countries have taken place. If the price level in A has doubled while that in B has trebled, an exchange rate of only four fifths the original one will leave B's currency overvalued. B-goods will be overpriced in A's markets, and A's goods underpriced in B, with the result that B's exports will decline and her imports rise to distort her balance of payments. With the same price levels, however, and a rate of 50 per cent of the base-period quotation, B's exchange rate will be undervalued (the exchange rate has fallen more than prices have gone up relative to A's prices) and A's balance of payments will tend to become adverse.

If A and B buy and sell identical goods in markets which have no transport costs, then these must sell at the same price in both markets (after conversion at the existing exchange rate) because of the law of one price. Only one price can exist in one market. The possibility of prices rising higher in B than in A cannot apply to internationally traded goods but must be limited to domestic goods, which do not move in international trade, or to costs of production, including wages, interest, etc. This will still have the same effect, however. If costs rise farther in B, relative to the new exchange rate, than in A, it will be less profitable to sell goods from B to A at A's prices, and more profitable to buy A's goods in B at A's prices. Exports will decline and imports will rise, under an overvalued rate, whether the law of one price holds or not.

Some writers have regarded the purchasing-power-parity doctrine as an absolute rather than a relative matter and taken it to signify that the same goods will cost the same amount of money, after conversion of the exchange rate, in every country. But this would be true only if all goods were international goods, without transport costs, and behaved according to the law of one price. The fact of the matter is, as we shall see in greater detail in subsequent chapters, that only a small portion of goods and services are traded internationally, that these traded goods are cheaper in the exporting than in the importing country, because of costs of transport, and that there is no tendency to equalize prices of purely domestic goods. It has been suggested, for example, that there is a very different purchasing power of the pound in Britain in terms of dollars for every substantial change in income. For the first £1,000 of income, largely spent on rent and basic foodstuffs, the pound is worth $5.00 or $6.00; for the next £1,000, $3.00 or $4.00, and for the third and fourth £1,000 of income, the implicit rate approaches £1 = $1.00. A careful study by Gilbert and Kravis of real incomes in the United States, the United Kingdom, France, Germany, and Italy reveals the widely different implicit purchasing power of European currencies in terms of dollars for various types of goods. As Table 4.1 shows, the 1950 absolute purchasing power of the European currencies in terms of local-currency units per dollars ranged from a high of 380 per cent of the exchange value in terms of foodstuffs and household and personal services to a low of 62 per cent of the exchange value for purchases of transport equipment in Germany. The table is given in European weights; somewhat different results would be obtained in measuring the United States standard of living at European prices instead of the European standard of living at United States prices. But the broad conclusion is unchanged:

The purchasing power of European currencies is different in different classes of goods.

Even after we abandon the absolute version of the purchasing-power-parity theory, which is clearly invalid as shown by Table 4.1,

TABLE 4.1

PURCHASING-POWER EQUIVALENTS BY PRODUCT GROUPS, 1950
European Currency Units per United States Dollar
European Quantity Weights

	United Kingdom (Pounds)	France (Francs)	Germany (Marks)	Italy (Lire)
Household and personal services........	0.166	140	1.42	165
Government......................	0.154	181	1.92	174
Food............................	0.220	228	2.43	392
Gross national product...............	0.212	229	2.48	333
Consumption......................	0.217	228	2.58	342
Foreign-exchange rate................	0.357	350	4.20	625
Clothing and textiles................	0.303	369	4.42	654
Household goods....................	0.370	559	4.32	1,062
Transport equipment................	0.455	448	6.76	1,054
Equipment and appliances............	0.384	489	4.75	1,055

the relative version poses a number of difficult problems. What index numbers should be used to measure the price level: sensitive whole-sale, sluggish wholesale, retail, cost of living, or costs of production? If we assume that the law of one price dominates sensitive wholesale prices, comparison is required of the prices of those goods and services which do not normally come into foreign trade. This is because trade will be balanced between countries in the appropriate measure when the relationship between prices of domestic and international goods in the subsequent period is roughly the same as it was in the period of previous balance. But, in fact, none of the standard indexes measures this relationship.

The foregoing assumes that no fundamental changes have taken place in the basic circumstances of trade between the two countries. Suppose that consumers in Latin America have experienced a decline in demand for Europe's products. During the period of disruption of trade, for example, they were obliged to get along without these com-modities and found satisfactory domestic substitutes, which they now prefer. To achieve a new equilibrium, Europe's prices must now be lower relative to Latin America's, in order to produce new exports from Europe or to discourage old imports from Latin America and balance debits and credits under the new conditions. Or suppose that Britain had been lending capital to the Commonwealth in the base period but that the growth of domestic requirements for savings now means that she no longer has capital available for export. With capital exports taking place, Britain had an export surplus in the base period; now a simple balance of current payments is sufficient. Accordingly, a somewhat higher level of prices for Britain relative to the Commonwealth is suitable. If, further, Britain had a great deal of unemployment in the base period and an export surplus, the validity of the purchasing-power-parity doctrine diminishes toward the vanishing point. Only under conditions of relatively full employment, when changes in money income produce changes in prices, can the doctrine serve usefully. It was valid in 1919, when it was originated, since between 1913 and 1919 there was full employment. Finally, the theory is rendered useless by any change in methods of trading, and particularly in the imposition of exchange controls which cut world markets into segments and detach prices in one country from those in another. This is what happened in the course of World War II. It has been necessary on this account to abandon the purchasing-power-parity doctrine except as the roughest possible guide to exchange rates.

Exchange Control

A number of countries lack gold, have had unhappy experiences with exchange depreciation (due to offsetting inflation in national money income), and have turned to exchange control to regulate their international payments. Here the task is to restrict imports to the level of exports directly or to impose more comprehensive exchange control if it is necessary to limit expenditure on foreign services and restrict the movement of capital as well.

In the process of controlling imports, prices and incomes are unlikely to remain unaffected. A restriction of imports will raise prices in the market which has reduced supplies and will lower them in the export market, where they become redundant. Since there are two prices, there must be two markets, though they are partly linked through such trade as remains. A restriction of imports also affects national income, as expenditure which used to pour over a country's borders to be spent on imports is now diverted to home expenditure. But the essence of exchange control is rationing.

In rationing, some nonmarket choices must be made as to which goods shall continue to be imported and which not. Generally, the authorities attempt to set some social standard and to restrict "luxuries" while continuing to permit the import of "essential commodities." These are not likely to be the goods which would continue to be bought after a reduction in imports of the same over-all amount brought about through deflation of income or a depreciation of the exchange rate. Exchange control is selective (or arbitrary). Its value, however, is that its effects on the balance of payments in the short run are certain.

Systems of Exchange Control

Some exchange controls discriminate by currency, some by commodity, some by both. All discriminate. It is discriminatory, in economic terms, when a purchaser is required to buy at a price dearer than another cheaper price or when a seller is required to sell at a price cheaper than another dearer price or when a seller is not allowed to sell or a buyer with purchasing power to buy at any price.

Exchange control which discriminates by currency is most widely represented by clearing systems. Here an importer may or may not be allowed to buy abroad, depending upon what currency he plans to use. If Argentina has a surplus in its clearing with western Germany, it permits the purchase of imports from that country, but not the same goods if they have to be paid for in, say, dollars.

Under a clearing system, the proceeds of imports into Germany from Argentina are paid into an account in Frankfurt while the earnings of German exporters to Argentina are paid out of this account. A comparable account is created in Buenos Aires. The purpose is to bring about a balance of exports and imports between sets of countries clearing with one another. If German imports from Argentina exceed German exports to Argentina, Deutschemarks will pile up in Frankfurt in favor of Argentina. In Buenos Aires, exporters will have to wait for payment, or the central bank or Treasury may have to advance them funds because importers have not yet paid in enough. In either event, pressure will be brought to bear to achieve balance. German exporters will be urged to sell more to Argentina; German importers to buy less. Argentine exporters will be urged to sell less to Germany; Argentine importers to buy more.

A number of exchange controls discriminate by commodities. The most usual method is to prohibit or limit the import of goods which are regarded as nonessential. Brazil may refuse to issue permits for consumers' durable goods like refrigerators, for example, or Britain to allow tourists to take more than £20 of British money with them in their trips abroad.

Exchange control may discriminate both by commodity and by currency. Normally imports of a given commodity are allowed, but only from certain countries. Thus British may be favored over United States movies, or sterling oil (oil sold for sterling) over dollar oil.

All these systems of exchange control have been described in bare outline as if their purpose was to balance imports against exports at a fixed exchange rate. This was, in fact, their original aim. After exchange control had been developed, however, it was found that balance in some cases could be achieved more readily if exchange-rate fluctuation were allowed in parts of the system. This led to multiple exchange-rate systems.

A multiple exchange-rate system, like the simpler system of foreign-exchange control at a fixed rate, can discriminate by commodities, by countries, or both. In a simple two-rate system discriminating by commodities, there is likely to be an official exchange rate, at a relatively high level, at which those export products most in demand abroad are sold and essential imports are bought. There may be a spread between the official buying and selling rates for foreign exchange, which is a source of income for the operating government. The free rate, which is likely to be much lower than the official, is left to handle all other transactions—imports of luxuries and exports for which markets abroad have not been fully developed. The partial depreciation of the free market acts as a deterrent to luxury imports and as a stimulant to marginal exports and helps to balance the over-all accounts.

Multiple exchange-rate discrimination by countries is rare, since arbitrageurs who can slip between the loopholes of the law are prepared to take advantage of it. It simply means letting rates of foreign exchange be found in separate clearings of a country, without regard to the relative cross-rates which develop between currencies and their relation to the exchange rates in the rest of the world. If the free sol is quoted in Peru at 6.65 cents and the pound in New York at $2.80, the cross-rate ought to work out so that the sol is 42 to the pound in the free market. In actuality, Peru may have a surplus of pounds sterling in its clearing which it is anxious to work off and may be prepared to sell them at 35 sols to encourage imports from the sterling area. In this case the exchange-control system discriminates by countries and uses multiple exchange practices.

Summary

The most widely known international standard is the gold standard, which operates to fix exchange rates within fairly narrow limits or gold points. It used to be thought that adjustment under the gold standard was brought about by the price-specie-flow mechanism. It is now recognized that while changes in the level of prices may sometimes play a role, the largest factor in adjustment is changes in income.

Under a freely fluctuating exchange system, the exchange market is cleared by altering the exchange rate. This has long-run effects in changing the relations between the prices of domestic and internationally traded goods. The purchasing-power-parity theory is an attempt to explain the level of exchange rates under a system of pegged rates, operating without restrictions when exchange is inconvertible into gold.

Exchange control clears the exchange market by rationing the supply of exchange among the demanders. This rationing is necessarily discriminatory. The system of discrimination may operate by country, by commodity, or by a mixture of the two. It may also incorporate elements of exchange-rate fluctuation.

SUGGESTED READING

TREATISES, ETC.

The definitive work on the gold standard is W. A. Brown, Jr., *The Gold Standard Re-interpreted 1914–34* (2 vols.; New York: National Bureau of Economic Research, 1934). More concise presentations are found in T. E. Gregory, *The Gold Standard and Its Future* (3d ed.; New York: E. P. Dutton & Co., 1935); and R. G. Hawtrey, *The Gold Standard in Theory and Practice* (5th ed.; London: Longmans, Green & Co., 1947). Walter Bagehot, *Lombard Street* (London: Macmillan & Co., Ltd., 1873), describes monetary practice at the heyday of the gold standard. W. E. Beach undermines the price-specie-flow mechanism as a description of what took place under the gold standard in his *British International Gold Movements and Banking Policy, 1881–1913* (Cambridge, Mass.: Harvard University Press, 1935). For references on the role of income, turn to Suggested Reading, Chapter 10, or wait until we reach it.

On the gold-exchange standard, see G. F. Luthringer, *The Gold-Exchange Standard in the Philippines* (Princeton: Princeton University Press, 1934); and E. W. Kemmerer, "The Gold Exchange Standard" in *Economic Essays in Honour of Gustav Cassel* (London: Allen & Unwin, 1933).

The purchasing-power-parity theory, originated by Cassel, is discussed in his *Money and Foreign Exchange after 1914* (New York: Macmillan Co., 1923). The best criticism of it is contained in L. A. Metzler, "Exchange Rates and the International Monetary Fund," in *International Monetary Policies* (Washington, D.C.: Federal Reserve System, October, 1947).

A somewhat different attempt to classify exchange controls than that given here is contained in the International Monetary Fund's *First Annual Report on Exchange Restrictions* (Washington, D.C., 1950). For further references, see Suggested Reading, Chapter 15.

POINTS

Lord Keynes's suggestion for widening the gold points on the gold standard is found in *The Treatise on Money* (New York: Harcourt, Brace & Co., Inc., 1930), Vol. II, chap. xxxvi, sec. 3.

Table 4.1 on the purchasing-power equivalents of Western European currencies in different types of goods has been taken from M. Gilbert and I. B. Kravis, *An International Comparison of National Products and the Purchasing Power of Currencies* (Paris: Organization for European Economic Cooperation, 1954), Table 14, p. 41, and p. 158.

Part II

The Current Account in the Balance

of Payments:

Trade Theory

Chapter 5	THE PURE THEORY OF INTERNATIONAL TRADE: SUPPLY

Basic Questions

Part I is an introductory survey defining and describing the balance of payments, the foreign-exchange market, and the methods of adjustment in international trade. In Part II we must get down to cases and see what lies behind the current account in the balance of payments—in particular, what underlies merchandise trade: exports and imports.

The classical economists asked three questions about foreign trade:

1. What goods does a country buy and sell in foreign trade?
2. On what terms are these goods bought and sold, i.e., what determines the prices at which exports and imports are exchanged in international trade? Another way of putting this question is to ask what is the gain from trade and how is it divided among the trading countries.
3. What happens to bring about adjustment when the pattern of trade is disturbed?

The third question has already been touched upon in Chapter 4 and will be addressed again in Chapters 9, 10, and 11 and again in Part VI. For the present we shall concentrate on the first two questions. Their answers form the subject of this and the following chapter on the pure theory of trade.

Law of Comparative Advantage

The classical economists asked what goods would be traded between countries because they believed that the answer for international trade differed from that for trade between regions within a country.

Within a country a region produces the goods which it can make cheaper than other regions. The value of a commodity within a country, moreover, is determined by its labor content. If the product of a certain industry can be sold for more than the value of the labor it contains,

85

additional labor will transfer into that industry from other occupations. Supply will expand until the price is brought down to the value of the labor it contained. Similarly, if a commodity sells for less than the worth of its labor, labor will move into other lines until the gap is closed. The tendency of wages toward equality within a country results in prices of goods equal to their labor such as to equalize the return to labor in all occupations and regions. If wages are higher in Ohio than in Massachusetts, labor will migrate to Ohio. This will lower wages in Ohio and raise them in Massachusetts, and the movement will continue until the return to labor is equated in the two regions.

The labor theory of value considered valid in trade within a country cannot be applied between nations, the classical economists thought, since factors of production are immobile internationally. If wages are higher in the United States than in Britain, they stay higher for migration cannot take place on a scale sufficient to eliminate discrepancies. Under these circumstances, the classical economists asked, what will the United States sell to Britain and Britain to the United States?

Let us assume two countries and two commodities. If each country can produce one good cheaper, i.e., with less labor, than it can be produced in the other, each will have an advantage in the production of one commodity and a disadvantage in the production of the other. Each country will then be able to export the commodity in which it has an advantage and import the commodity in which it has a disadvantage. The position is suggested in the following table, where wheat can be produced more cheaply in the United States and cloth more cheaply in Britain. The United States has an absolute advantage in wheat and an absolute disadvantage in cloth. It will export wheat and import cloth, which, with the numerical values given, may be assumed to exchange one for the other at the rate of one yard of cloth for one bushel of wheat:

PRODUCTION OF ONE MAN IN ONE WEEK

Product	In United States	In United Kingdom
Wheat......................	6 bushels	3 bushels
Cloth......................	3 yards	6 yards

But suppose that the labor content of both wheat and cloth is less in the United States than in Britain. Suppose that instead of only 3 yards of cloth per week a man in the United States can produce 10. The position is then as follows:

PRODUCTION OF ONE MAN IN ONE WEEK

Product	In United States	In United Kingdom
Wheat.....................	6 bushels	2 bushels
Cloth.....................	10 yards	6 yards

It is evident that labor is more efficient in the United States than in the United Kingdom, and wages in the United States will be higher on that account. But migration will not take place to equalize wage rates.

Trade cannot now be regulated by absolute advantage, and a new principle is needed to take its place. This was developed by David Ricardo, one hundred and fifty years ago, in the law of comparative advantage. Ricardo observed that in cases similar to ours, while the United States had an absolute advantage over Britain in both wheat and cloth, it had a greater advantage in wheat than in cloth. He concluded that a country would export the product in which it had the greater advantage, or a comparative advantage, and import the commodity in which its advantage was less, or in which it had a comparative disadvantage. In this example the United States would export wheat and import cloth, even though it could produce cloth more efficiently than Britain.

The reasoning underlying this conclusion may be demonstrated arithmetically. In the United States, without international trade, wheat and cloth will exchange for each other at their labor content. Ten yards of cloth will exchange for 6 bushels of wheat. In Britain, by the same token, 6 bushels of wheat—i.e., three weeks of labor—will exchange for 18 yards of cloth. If the United States can get more than 10 yards of cloth for 6 bushels of wheat by selling wheat to Britain, it will evidently gain by exporting wheat in exchange for cloth. Conversely, if Britain can get any more than $3\frac{1}{3}$ bushels of wheat for 10 yards of cloth, it will gain by giving up cloth for wheat in international trade.

The price ratios may be quoted the same way. At any price for cloth cheaper than 6:10, the United States will find it profitable to sell wheat for cloth, because in this way it can get more cloth (or give up less wheat) than at 6:10. Conversely, Britain will find it profitable to sell cloth for wheat at any price for cloth more expensive than 6:18. If the United States and Britain can agree on some intermediate price, such as 6:14, each country will be better off. Cloth will be cheaper in the United States, and wheat will be cheaper in Britain. Both countries will gain from specialization and trade.

The classical economists concluded on the basis of this type of demonstration that international trade does not require offsetting absolute advantages but is possible where a comparative advantage exists. It goes without saying, but must be said, as it is frequently forgotten, that a comparative advantage is always and by definition accompanied by a comparative disadvantage.

Production-Possibilities Curves

The labor theory of value on which this analysis rested was subsequently rejected as invalid. The tendency for the return to labor to be equal throughout a country was seen by observation to be weak and faltering. Labor is not homogeneous. If there is an increase in the demand for barrels, the wages of coopers will rise above those of smiths, with whom they are not interchangeable. It became recognized that there is not one great class of labor with a single wage but a series of noncompeting groups between which the tendency to equalization of wages, at least in the short run, is weak or nonexistent.

A more fundamental objection, however, which would apply to any labor theory of value, is that goods are not produced by labor alone but by various combinations of all the factors of production: land, labor, and capital. To compare the labor content of two commodities—say, gasoline and textiles, or meat and shoes—gives an erroneous view of relative values. Gasoline production requires far more capital than textiles, and meat output more land than shoes. Variable proportions of factors in the production of different commodities make it impossible to use the labor theory of value, however qualified.

An escape from this impasse has been provided by Professor Haberler in the theory of opportunity costs. The cost of wheat in the long run is how much cloth a country has to give up to get additional units of wheat. It makes little difference whether the factors which stop the production of cloth are all suited to the output of wheat or not. The question is simply how much of one commodity must be given up to get more of the other.

The notion of opportunity costs is illustrated in international-trade theory with production-possibilities or transformation curves. Instead of saying that a week's labor will produce either 6 bushels of wheat or 10 yards of cloth, one says that all the factors of production can produce either 6 bushels of wheat or 10 yards of cloth, or some intermediate combination of them. In Figure 5.1, where the vertical axis represents wheat and the horizontal axis cloth, the production-possibilities curves of the United States and the United Kingdom can be drawn with the same data. The United States curve means that the resources of the

United States, in the absence of foreign trade, can be used to produce entirely wheat, in which case 6 bushels (per capita per week) can be produced, 10 yards of cloth, or some appropriate intermediate combination, such as 3 bushels of wheat and 5 yards of cloth. The production-possibilities curve cannot tell what will in fact be produced. More information is needed for this purpose, on the side of demand. It merely sets out what the possibilities are.

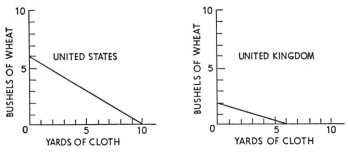

FIG. 5.1. Production-Possibilities Curves, Constant Costs

Constant Costs

A straight-line production-possibilities curve, such as those in Figure 5.1, is indicative of constant costs. At the limits in the United States, all resources can produce either 6 bushels of wheat or 10 yards of cloth. If any resources shift out of cloth into wheat or vice versa, they can always produce wheat or cloth in the constant proportions of 6:10, no matter whether all or only a small proportion of total resources are shifted.

A straight-line possibilities curve represents more than constant costs. It is a straight line, the slope of which can be taken as a price. Wheat and cloth will exchange in this economy for 6:10. Any higher price for cloth—say, 7:10—will shift resources out of wheat into cloth. The supply of wheat will decline, that of cloth increase, until the price ratio of 6:10 is restored. Any lower price for cloth will similarly shift resources in the other direction until the 6:10 ratio is re-established.

Let us now take a look at what happens when trade opens up between the United States and Britain. Figure 5.2 shows the two production-possibilities curves superimposed upon each other and reduced to the same scale. Instead of showing the two curves of the wheat/cloth scale with wheat at 6 and cloth at 10 and 18 in the two countries, respectively, the scales are enlarged and equated at the cloth end. Without trade, 60 yards of cloth will exchange for 36 bushels of wheat in the United States. In Britain, 60 yards of cloth will exchange for only 20 bushels of wheat.

If the United Kingdom had been consuming 10 bushels of wheat and 30 yards of cloth (at point *C* on Fig. 5.2) on its production-possibilities and price line, it would be better off if it could consume on a higher price line than 60:20. If it could trade at the United States price, for example, it could move from point *C* to point *C'*, where it could consume 40 of cloth and 12 of wheat—a clear gain of both cloth and wheat. It could do this, it may be observed, if it produced only cloth and exchanged 20 of its total output of 60 for 12 bushels of wheat of the United States. Its production is indicated by the arrow in Figure 5.2, consumption by *C'*, and exports and im-

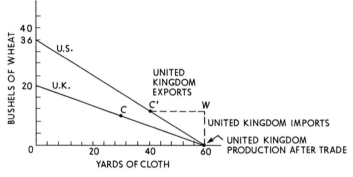

FIG. 5.2. International Trade under Constant Costs, 1

ports by the dotted lines converging at *W*. The horizontal dotted line represents exports of cloth, which, subtracted from total production, leave the amount consumed domestically. The vertical dotted line represents wheat imports. The ratio at which exports and imports exchange for each other—i.e., the slope of the hypotenuse of the right-angle triangle formed by them—is the price line of the United States. In this case the United States has not benefited from foreign trade, exchanging wheat for cloth at 6:10 before and after trade. Production has changed. Twelve additional bushels of wheat are produced and 20 yards less of cloth.

The price after trade may be the same as the price before trade for one of the parties. This cannot be the case for both. The new price may, however, land somewhere between the two prices before trade. It may, for example, settle at 60 yards of cloth for 28 bushels of wheat, as indicated in Figure 5.3. In this case, both parties will gain. The United Kingdom will not gain as much as in the previous example, but the

United States will share the gains from foreign trade. To demonstrate the fact of the United States gain diagrammatically, it is necessary to shift the wheat and cloth axes, or to quote both prices with a common point on the wheat axis, in order to show the United States production-possibilities curve lying inside the British. It is clear enough without an additional diagram, however, that if the United States can trade wheat for cloth at 60 cloth for 28 wheat instead of 60 cloth for 36 wheat, the country has gained in trade. It can take the gain by increasing its consumption of wheat (giving less wheat for the same amount of cloth), or of cloth (giving the same amount of wheat for more cloth), or, in lesser degree, both. But, so long as it can obtain from trade a higher price for wheat in terms of cloth, it gains.

Under conditions of constant costs, with straight-line production-possibilities curves, specialization after trade is complete. Before trade

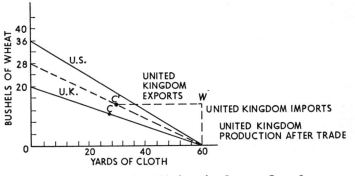

Fig. 5.3. International Trade under Constant Costs, 2

took place, a country produced some of one good and some of another. To maximize the gain from trading at a higher price, however, it is desirable to sell as much as possible, consonant with the satisfaction of domestic demand for the export article. Thus production will move from a central point on the curve before trade (Fig. 5.2) to one of the limits. It does not pay the United Kingdom, for example, to produce any wheat with resources which can produce either 6 yards of cloth or 2 bushels of wheat, if the price at which it trades is anything more than 2 bushels of wheat for 6 yards of cloth.

Increasing Costs

Our production-possibilities curves thus far have been those in which costs were constant and the ratio between commodity costs equal to price. But the notion that all resources can equally well produce either of two commodities involves an assumption as extreme as the discarded labor theory of value. If all resources are not equally at home in the production of wheat or cloth, but some, like land and out-of-doors men, are better at wheat, and others, like spindles, looms, and city folk, are better at cloth, we may have a situation of increasing costs. Some resources are equally adaptable to wheat or cloth production, but not all are.

The production-possibilities curve, under increasing costs, is concave to the origin at *O*. In Figure 5.4*a*, for example, where a production-possibilities curve *A–B* is shown, wheat and cloth are fairly substitutable for one another between points *r* and *t* on the curve. To the left of *r*, however, one can get only a small increase in wheat by giving up cloth, primarily because the resources taken out of the production of cloth are not suitable for the production of wheat. Possibly there will be no land with which to combine the labor previously in the textile industry. Similarly, to the right of *t*, a country can get only a little bit more of cloth by giving up a large amount of wheat.

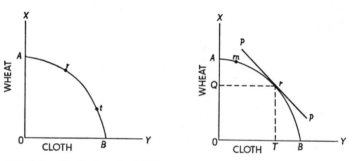

FIG. 5.4*a*. Production Possibilities under Increasing Costs

FIG. 5.4*b*. Production with Increasing Costs

Under increasing costs, the production-possibilities curve is not identical with a price curve, as in the case of constant costs. The price at which wheat will exchange for cloth cannot be determined by the production-possibilities curve by itself, but can be found only with the assistance of data on demand. The complex of problems presented by demand will be taken up later in the following chapter. At the moment, however, it may be noted that price is indicated by a straight line between the *X* and *Y* axes, the slope of which represents the ratio at which cloth will exchange for wheat, and that production, under a transformation curve representing increasing costs, will take place at the point on the curve tangent to the price in the market. In Figure 5.4*b*, production will take place at *r*, on the production-possibilities curve, *AB,* whenever the price is *P–P.* At *r,* production will consist of *O–Q* units of wheat and *O–T* units of cloth. If the economy produced cloth and wheat at point *m* on the production-possibilities curve, the price *P–P* could not be sustained. At this price there would be too much wheat in relation to cloth or too little cloth in relation to wheat. The unsold quantity of wheat and the unsatisfied demand for cloth would require a change in price to maintain production at *m.*

If demand keeps the price at *P–P,* however, it will be possible to earn a higher return in cloth than in wheat, and resources will shift out of wheat into cloth, moving production from *m* toward *r.* This shift of resources will continue until, given the price *P–P* and the production-possibilities curve *A–B,* an optimum allocation of resources is reached at point *r.*

Foreign trade will take place under increasing costs in broadly the same way as under constant costs, except that complete specialization of a country in a single commodity is not so likely. Figure 5.5

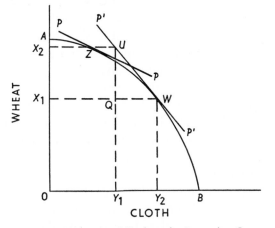

FIG. 5.5. International Trade under Increasing Costs

shows such a case. Before trade the United Kingdom price of wheat in terms of cloth is *P–P,* with production at *Z.* Omitting several steps discussed in the next chapter, by which the price ratio between wheat and cloth after trade is determined, the opening up of trade is assumed to raise the price of cloth in terms of wheat to *P'–P'.* Here *P'–P'* is a higher price for cloth than *P–P* (and a lower one for wheat) because more wheat is obtained for a given amount of cloth.

It now pays the United Kingdom to shift resources from the production of wheat into cloth, moving the point of production from *Z* to *W,* and exchanging cloth for wheat in foreign trade. The higher the price for cloth, the more resources should be taken out of wheat and put into cloth. Production will settle at that point where the new price is tangent to the production-possibilities curve.

Exactly how much cloth is exchanged for wheat is again indeterminate with the analytical tools we have developed. Consumption will take place somewhere along the price line, $P'-P'$, to the left of W—say, at U. The United Kingdom will then produce $O-Y_2$ of cloth and $O-X_1$ of wheat at point W; export Y_1-Y_2 of cloth and import X_1-X_2 of wheat; and consume $O-X_2$ of wheat and $O-Y_1$ of cloth. The quantities Y_1-Y_2 and X_1-X_2 are equal to $Q-W$ and $Q-U$, which, by simple geometry, are exchangeable for one another at the price ratio $P'-P'$. Through trade, Britain will have been enabled to consume more wheat and cloth than it could produce for itself with its own production possibilities.

The failure of specialization to become complete, of course, is due to the fact that some factors not suited to the production of cloth can continue to produce wheat after the price change. They are worse off after the change in the price of wheat from $P-P$ to $P'-P'$, but not so badly off as they would be if they tried to shift into cloth making.

Deprived of the labor theory of value and expressed in terms of opportunity costs, the law of comparative advantage is still valid. If a country is better at two things than another country, it profits by concentrating on the product in which it has a greater or comparative advantage and buying the good in which it has a comparative disadvantage. The basic criterion is that with trade it gets a higher price for its specialty or pays a lower price for the commodity in which it is relatively not so productive.

The law of comparative advantage has general validity. Billy Rose is a columnist, an impressario, and a world champion typist. It pays him to employ secretaries, however. While he may have an absolute advantage over his secretaries at typing, his advantage here is narrow compared with that in other occupations. It pays him and them to specialize.

More generally speaking, if the price of X in terms of Y is lower abroad than at home, it will pay a country to shift resources out of X and into Y, trading Y for X until the prices of X and Y (abstracting from transport costs) are equal at home and abroad. But in these terms the law of comparative costs comes closer to being a law of comparative prices. This would be the case if there were nothing economists could say further about it.

In answer to the question put by the classical economists, the law of comparative costs says that a country exports those products which are comparatively cheap in price at home, and imports those which are comparatively expensive. But economics can say more than this.

Factor Proportions

If international trade is based on differences in comparative costs, the curious student will proceed to the next question: What makes for differences in comparative costs? Why do the transformation curves of various countries differ?

The answer given to this question by the Swedish economist, Bertil Ohlin, is twofold: Different goods, he stated, require different factor inputs; and different countries have different factor endowments. If wheat is technologically best produced with lots of land relative to labor and capital, countries which have an abundance of land will be able to produce wheat cheaply. This is why Australia, Argentina, Canada, Minnesota, and the Ukraine export wheat. On the other hand, if cloth requires much labor relative to capital and land, countries which have an abundance of labor—Britain, Japan, India—will have a comparative advantage in cloth manufacture and be able to export it.

In Appendix B we show how transformation curves are derived from production functions for commodities. It is noted there that there may be some ambiguity about the technological factor proportions involved in producing a given commodity. Where these factor proportions are technically unalterable, we can agree that one commodity is more labor-intensive than another. Oil refining is more capital-intensive than cabinet making, and hydroelectric power generation unambiguously requires land, in the form of specialized waterpower sites. But in the production of many commodities, there is a range within which one factor can be substituted for another. Eggs can be produced by chickens roaming the range, using land, or cooped up in batteries of nests, in which capital substitutes for land and labor. It is impossible to say that one of these commodities is more capital-intensive or labor-intensive than another until we know more about the possibilities of factor substitution and the factor availabilities.

The factor-endowments explanation for trade further rests on the assumption that each country has the same technological possibilities of producing a given good, i.e., that the production functions are the same in both countries. This assumption will be modified in Chapter 7 where we explore the existence of trade based on technological differences between countries.

Finally, there is some difficulty in defining factors for the purpose of using this explanation. To define factors broadly, as land, labor, and capital, is to overlook the point that these factors are not homogeneous for many purposes but divided into noncompeting groups. It is not enough to have land to raise sheep, but one must have grazing land; nor can minerals be produced by land in general, but only by certain ore-bearing types. If one tries to multiply numbers of factors, however, to include all noncompeting groups as separate factors, it turns out that much trade is based upon absolute advantage, the existence of one factor in one country but not in another. One can keep comparative advantage and overlook noncompeting groups, or define factors narrowly and put comparative advantage to the side.

Despite these difficulties, the great majority of economists regards Ohlin's explanation of the basis of comparative advantage as broadly true. The United States is thought to be well endowed with capital and to export capital-intensive goods. Foreign countries are more favorably situated with respect to labor and sell labor-intensive products to the United States. A recent study by Professor Leontief, however, greatly disturbed the serenity in which these conclusions were held by purporting to demonstrate statistically that the labor content of United States exports was higher than that of this country's imports, and that the capital content of imports exceeded that of exports. These findings are still being debated. The debate has been highly useful in producing a thorough examination of the underlying basis of the Ohlin doctrine. For the purpose of what follows in this book, the Leontief claim is taken as not proven and the Ohlin explanation of United States trade, modified for technology as in Chapter 7, as presumptively true.

Trade and Factor Efficiency

What about trade between two countries with the same factor proportions and different factor efficiencies? Suppose we have two countries, Britain and Japan, with the same proportions of land, labor, and capital, but with these factors of production more efficient in Britain than in Japan. Let us assume that labor is not more efficient in Britain than in Japan because it is combined with more capital and land; it merely works harder in every industry. And British land is richer, let us assume, than Japanese; and British machinery more highly developed. Can trade take place then?

The answer is "No." Japanese factors of production will receive less income than British because of their reduced effectiveness in production; but this will not help trade, because all factors receive proportionately less. The production-possibilities curves of the two countries will resemble those set forth in Figure 5.6, the Japanese capable of producing less than the British. But if tastes are the same in the two countries, the prices of wheat in terms of cloth and cloth in terms of wheat—to restrict ourselves to our two familiar commodities—will be the same. When the Japanese production-possibilities curve is adjusted to a common point with the British, as must be done following the technique of this chapter, it will be seen that the shape of the two curves is identical. This clinches the point that trade is impossible.

It follows from this that it is not the efficiency of factors as a whole which creates a basis for trade but the existence of factor differences, or of differences in factor efficiency which are not the same for all commodities and which are not offset by differences in tastes. If Japanese people were more efficient in cloth, because they had a

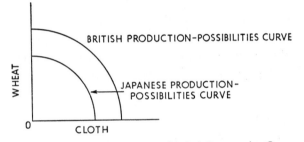

FIG. 5.6.   Different Real Costs; Identical Comparative Costs

predilection for city life, and less efficient in agriculture, the basis for a difference in relative prices and for trade would exist.

Equalization of Factor Prices

Trade takes place when relative prices differ between countries, and continues until these relative differences—aside from transportation costs—have been eliminated. In the absence of transportation costs, in fact, trade would equalize relative commodity prices. In a more roundabout way, it may be noted further, trade tends to bring about the equalization of factor prices.

The export of products of the abundant factor increases the demand for its services and makes them relatively less abundant. The import of products embodying large amounts of scarce factors makes those factors less scarce in the domestic market. Exports will raise the price of the abundant and cheap factor; imports will reduce the return to the scarce and expensive factor. For example, the export of farm products from the United States raises the income of agricultural land, and hence its value, while the import of precision instruments reduces the scarcity and hence the return to the type of skilled labor employed in this field.

Under certain limited conditions, this tendency toward factor-price equalization will be carried to the point where factor prices are fully equalized. The assumptions are highly restrictive. There must be as many or more commodities than factors; broadly similar tastes; identical production functions of a simple character and providing a limited degree of factor substitution; no transport costs or other barriers to trade to inhibit full commodity-price equalization; perfect competition; and something of every commodity produced in every country after trade. Appendix B contains a formal proof of the proposition with two commodities and two factors. But while full factor-price equalization may be an intellectual curiosity rather than a significant proposition for the real world, the tendency toward factor-price equalization is much more meaningful. Trade tends to raise the price of the abundant factor and weaken the price of the scarce factor, and where trade is based on differences in factor endowments, this repercussion of trade on factor prices is vastly important, politically as well as economically.

Increasing Returns

All this has been described in terms of general-equilibrium theory under conditions of perfect competition. One important exception to the competitive analysis must be considered. This is the case of decreasing costs, or increasing returns. Under competitive conditions, decreasing costs cannot be considered, except for the limited external economies, because any firm which has the possibility of increasing returns will gain by enlarging its production.

In the real world, however, increasing returns, including increasing returns due to internal economies of scale, are an important explanation of trade. In some cases, the increasing returns have resulted from imperfections of competition, such as inadequate knowledge, or barriers to entry, such as unavailability of technology or capital. Many of these cases of increasing returns are irreversible, and the economic theorist may call them historical downward shifts of the supply curve rather than increasing returns.

Increasing returns may be diagrammed in either of two ways. In Figure 5.7*a* the production-possibilities curve *AQB* is convex to the origin and shows decreasing costs of automobiles in terms of agri-

cultural machinery and of agricultural machinery in terms of automobiles, starting from the position Q where the price of automobiles
in terms of agricultural machinery is given as $P–P$. If the increasing
returns are due to internal economies, Q is an unstable equilibrium
which cannot exist under competitive conditions. Any slight disturbance, increasing the price of automobiles in terms of agricultural machinery, i.e., flattening the $P–P$ line, will make producers shift out
of agricultural machinery into automobiles. They will, however, be
unable to find a new equilibrium position until they have shifted all
their resources and arrive at A. If originally the price of agricultural
machinery had risen, i.e., if the $P–P$ line had become steeper, there
would have been a pull toward B which would have to continue until
B was reached.

Figure 5.7b shows the position where $A–B$ is the production-
possibilities curve on which a country is actually operating in ignorance

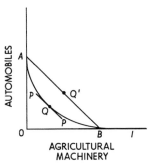

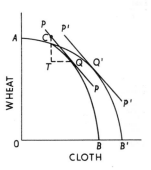

Fig. 5.7a. Increasing Returns, Two Commodities

Fig. 5.7b. Increasing Returns, One Commodity

of the fact that it could take advantage of increasing returns in cloth
(but not in wheat) and move out to another production-possibilities
curve $A–B'$. In this case, production is at Q, with the price $P–P$. Given
knowledge of the true curve, production could well be at Q', at the
same price ($P'–P'$ having the same slope as $P–P$), with much more
cloth produced. To be sure, the increased production of cloth would
probably occasion some reduction in the price of cloth, which would
change the point of production from Q', unless there were a parallel
shift in demand. The impact of increasing returns remains.

Under increasing costs there is no reason for relative prices in
two countries with roughly the same sort of resources and comparable
tastes to differ sufficiently to disclose comparative advantages which
will lead to trade. And yet it is known that trade takes place among

industrial countries with roughly the same factor proportions, such as Britain, Germany, Japan, and the United States, and that between countries with different factor proportions some trade takes place in like, but not quite identical, goods. Twenty per cent of Britain's imports consist of finished manufactured goods, and 20 per cent of the imports of the United States. This trade is of the sort based on specialization which springs from increasing returns.

While increasing returns may be inadmissible in the short run as largely incompatible with static equilibrium, their long-run historical validity makes Figures 5.7a and 5.7b an important explanation of the rise of trade. Differences in comparative costs come about not only because of differences in factor endowments but also through specialization in different commodities. To a degree the choice of whether the United States or Britain specializes in one kind of an automobile or another, or this tractor or that, may be determined by historical accident. The fact is that, with each specialized, a basis for trade exists, since each can produce one good cheaper than the other.

When increasing returns are due to internal economies of scale, Figure 5.7a represents the position only momentarily as the country in question is poised between specialization in automobiles or agricultural machinery. After a choice has been made, capital committed, and capacity built, the production-possibilities curve will no longer be convex to the origin but will resemble the more normal curves in previous diagrams.

The other half of the diagram—Figure 5.7b—illustrates a standard argument in behalf of tariffs. This fact will be merely noted here, since the subject of tariffs will not be addressed until Chapter 12. The country is engaged in trade, producing at point Q some cloth and much wheat, and consuming at point C, after exporting $T-Q$ of wheat in exchange for $T-C$ of cloth. The argument, however, is that if the price of cloth were higher, as it would be with less trade, the producers of cloth would discover the production-possibilities curve $A-B'$, which there was no means of finding with the price at $P-P$. To the extent that this is true and that the reduction of trade leads to the discovery of increasing-returns situations which would not otherwise be known, the argument is correct and less trade is better than more. But this case, we hasten to add, is a limited and special one. In general, increasing returns tend to widen comparative-cost differences and to open up opportunities for profitable trade, rather than narrow them and make it possible to dispense with existing commerce.

Summary

The basis for trade, so far as supply is concerned, is found in differences in comparative costs. One country may be more efficient than another, as measured by labor time, in the production of every possible commodity; but so long as it is not equally more efficient in every commodity, a basis for trade exists. It will pay the country to produce more of those goods in which it is relatively more efficient and to export these in return for goods in which its absolute advantage is least.

Differences in comparative costs arise because of the fact that different countries have different factor endowments and because different commodities are best produced with a predominance of one or another factor. Trade arises out of differences in relative factor prices but assists in narrowing them.

Differences in factor endowments explain that large portion of total trade which is represented by economic interchange between the temperate zones and the tropics, between densely populated industrial communities and sparsely settled agricultural lands in the temperate zone, not to mention mining communities, and other countries with specialized resources. But trade may also flourish between countries with similar factor endowments, particularly industrial areas, owing to differences in comparative costs produced by historically increasing returns.

Comparative costs thus furnish the basic ingredient of the answer to the classical question: What commodities will a country buy and sell in international trade? It is not the whole answer, since we have been concentrating on supply to the complete neglect of demand. But the subject of demand, as we shall see in the next chapter, can appropriately be covered in providing the answer to the second classical question: At what price will these goods be traded?

SUGGESTED READING

See Suggested Reading for Chapter 6 and Appendix B.

THE PURE THEORY OF INTERNATIONAL TRADE: DEMAND

The Law of Reciprocal Demand

There is a temptation to say that the law of comparative costs determines what commodities will be bought and sold in foreign trade, while the law of reciprocal demand sets the prices at which they will be traded. Some economic literature comes close to stating this. And many students learn the theory of foreign trade with some such generalization. But it is not quite true. In general-equilibrium theory, of course, both demand and supply together determine the quantities of goods bought and sold and their prices. In a famous analogy Alfred Marshall compared demand and supply to the upper and lower blades of a pair of scissors, neither of which can be said to do the cutting alone. For ease of exposition, however, we may follow the development of classical theory for a distance and approach something like an analytical separation of supply and demand.

Let us go back to our simple example of wheat and cloth produced in a man-week in the United States and Britain:

PRODUCTION OF ONE MAN IN ONE WEEK

	In United States	In United Kingdom
Wheat......................	6 bushels	2 bushels
Cloth......................	10 yards	6 yards

Before trade, wheat and cloth will exchange at 6:10 in the United States and 6:18 in the United Kingdom. These will be the limits beyond which the price after trade will not settle. Britain will be unwilling to pay more for 6 bushels of wheat than 18 yards of cloth; the United States to accept less than 10 yards for the same amount of wheat. The United States is indifferent to foreign trade at 6:10; it makes no difference whether it exports wheat for cloth or produces both at home. But at this price, when it gets all the gain,

102

Britain will be eager to trade. Conversely, Britain will be indifferent to trade, and the United States eager for it, at 6:18. Where, then, will the price settle?

There may be a tendency for the lazy theorist to split the difference and suggest 6 bushels of wheat for 14 yards of cloth. This was the rate we used, arbitrarily, in the last chapter. But the technique cannot be defended. John Stuart Mill found the answer to the difficulty. More information is needed to settle on a price. In addition to production costs, there must be data on demand. What counts is the strength of the United States demand for wheat and cloth and the reciprocal strength of British demand for the same products. The price at which foreign trade will take place is determined by what Mill called the "law of reciprocal demand."

The nature of the interacting demands can be illustrated by the device of stationing an auctioneer in mid-Atlantic. He has the task of finding a price to apply in both countries, where the exports of wheat which the United States is willing to ship against imports of cloth will match the exports of cloth which Britain is willing to sell for wheat. Too high a price for cloth in terms of wheat will call forth offers of cloth from Britain and demands for wheat, but inadequate offers of wheat or calls for cloth. Conversely, too high a price for wheat in terms of cloth will burden the auctioneer with unsought wheat from the United States and more bids than offers for cloth.

If the two countries are of unequal size, the reciprocal aspect of demand may not come into play at all. The price ratio of the larger country will prevail, and the smaller country can sell as much cloth or wheat to the other as it chooses at the established given price. This is the importance of being unimportant. The small country can reap large gains from trade. Guatemala, which cannot dream of manufacturing automobiles for years to come, can buy automobiles at the United States price and sell coffee at the price determined by Brazil and the United States. The case of trading at the price ratio existing in the larger country before trade, which is one limit of profitable trade, may be more frequent than the classical economists have suspected. But where demand and supply in one country or the other are not so large as to overwhelm demand and supply in the other, the law of reciprocal demand comes into play to settle price.

Marshall-Edgeworth Offer Curves

The theory behind Mill's law of reciprocal demand has been portrayed graphically by Edgeworth and then by Marshall with so-called "offer curves." These start out with a somewhat different geometrical perspective than production-possibilities curves. In Figure 6.1*a* we show a price ratio between X and Y, which is the same as the production-possibilities curve with constant costs. As a production-possibilities curve, we are concerned with the increase in the production of one

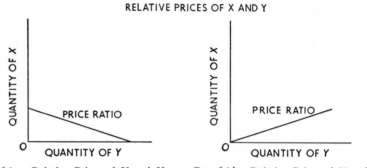

FIG. 6.1*a*. Relative Prices of X and Y   FIG. 6.1*b*. Relative Prices of X and Y

good as the other's production is decreased, i.e., in the absolute values of the curve. As a price, however, we are interested merely in the quantity of X which has the same value as a quantity of Y, i.e., in the slope of the line. In this case the negative slope, that is, the downward slope from left to right, has no significance, and we can draw the line X with a positive slope from the origin (O). In Figure 6.1*b* the price ratio between X and Y can be extended any distance to show what quantity of X will be exchanged for what quantity of Y.

The offer curve of a country, i.e., the amount of wheat it is willing to offer for cloth, may start out like this price curve. In any event, the price line is a limit beyond which the offer curve cannot go. This is obvious enough; no country will export products for less in the way of imports than it can produce in import-competing goods at home. For a small amount of imports, a country may be indifferent whether it produces at home or buys at the same price in foreign trade, so that the offer curve, as in Figure 6.2, may follow the price line in the absence of trade, from Figure 6.1*b*, for a distance.

Beyond this distance, however, the offer curve moves away from the price line. Figure 6.2 portrays the British offer curve, O–Z, which shows the amounts of cloth Britain will offer at various prices for given amounts of wheat. Line *a* is the ratio at which cloth and wheat exchange in the absence of trade (6 bushels against 18 yards). The offer curve, O–Z, is a series of amounts of cloth which Britain is willing to exchange for given amounts of wheat. The same thing may be expressed oppositely. The offer curve shows how much wheat Britain will buy at given prices for wheat in terms of cloth. The price ratios are the slopes of the lines *a, b, c,* and *d,* drawn from the origin *O* to the offer curve. The price ratios represent varying amounts of wheat exchanged against varying amounts of cloth. The offer curve, on the other hand, consists of definite amounts of cloth offered in exchange for stipulated amounts of wheat demanded.

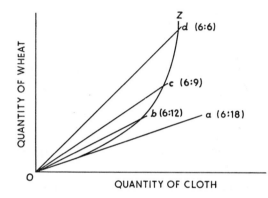

FIG. 6. 2. Britain's Offer Curve of Cloth (Demand for Wheat)

At the lower part of the curve, Britain may be willing, as we have indicated, to buy wheat, if only a small amount of it is available, at the high price which exists in her own country without trade. As more and more wheat is available, she will offer less and less cloth per unit of wheat. In part, this will be because she wants wheat less, and in part because cloth becomes more valuable as its supply is reduced. At some point, like *d,* Britain may be unwilling to give up any more cloth for additional wheat. At this point her demand for wheat in terms of cloth (or supply of cloth to be exchanged for wheat) is completely inelastic. Some distance beyond this point, moreover, the offer curve may bend backward. At this point Britain would be willing to accept more wheat only if she had to give up less cloth.

The offer curve should be distinguished from a demand curve. It is a demand curve, but only in the sense that it expresses the demand for one commodity in terms of the supply of another. Ordinary demand curves express the demand for varying amounts of a single commodity in terms of money. The money measure used, however, is price per unit, not total money spent. If the second commodity be regarded as money, which is possible, the offer curve would be a demand curve in terms of quantities of commodities against total amount of money. It would be a total-revenue curve, as opposed

to a demand curve, which represents average revenue per unit.
The British offer curve of cloth in exchange for wheat has been
given in Figure 6.2. The comparable United States curve of wheat
in exchange for cloth is given in Figure 6.3*a*. But if the *X* and *Y*
axes are set up on the basis used in Figure 6.2, the offer curve for the
United States (*O–V*) will curve in a horizontal direction, as in Figure
6.3*b*, rather than vertically, as in Figure 6.3*a*.

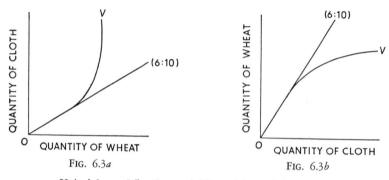

FIG. 6.3*a*   FIG. 6.3*b*

United States Offer Curve of Wheat (Demand for Cloth)

If the offer curves for the United States and Britain now be
taken on the same basis, they will cross. This point (*P* in Fig. 6.4)
will show where our auctioneer would get the same price for wheat

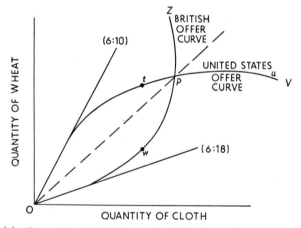

FIG. 6.4. Law of Reciprocal Demand: Intersection of Two Offer Curves

and cloth in both countries (*O–P*) and equal amounts of wheat and
cloth exported and imported by the United States and Britain. At any
other point than *P*—say, *t*—the United States would be willing to
pay almost as much wheat as at *P* for a good deal less cloth. But, for

this amount of cloth, Britain is willing to accept a great deal less wheat, as indicated by the point w. Neither t nor w can serve as a point of equilibrium. At the high price of wheat in terms of cloth represented by $O-w$, for example, the British would offer only a small amount of cloth, and the United States would want a great deal (see point u).

Graham's Attack

A modern theorist, the late Professor Frank B. Graham, has attacked the law of reciprocal demand on the ground that it pays too little attention to supply. It pays, he suggests, none. It appears to make the theory of international trade the theory of trade in a fixed quantity of production, such as antiques or oil paintings by Renaissance masters, rather than a theory of trade in goods which are produced and reproducible.

Graham's view is that the existence of many countries and many commodities makes it likely that trade will take place at the ratio in which some country would interchange them without trade, rather than at some "limbo" ratio in between.

Graham was wrong on the subject of supply. While it is true that many of the classical economists used the law of reciprocal demand as if it took no account of supply, this need not be the case. In Appendix C we demonstrate geometrically, for those who care to learn, how supply enters in with demand.

Given his assumption of constant cost, Graham was right that the introduction of more countries (or more commodities) would leave the terms of trade less at the mercy of the vagaries of demand. With constant costs and two countries of more or less equal size, each specializes completely in one commodity and the terms of trade are indeterminate without demand. With more countries and more commodities, the possibility is strong that some country will produce both the commodities after trade. Given constant costs, if one country produces both commodities, this determines the price ratio at which they all must trade.

If we abandon constant costs, however, and with it complete specialization, the fact that one or more countries produces two commodities after trade does not set the terms of trade. Every country may produce some of each commodity without this fact, making the terms of trade determinate. With increasing opportunity costs, which is certainly the only realistic assumption, there is room for the law of reciprocal demand. What lies behind demand? Unfortunately the answer to this question requires us to master still another geometrical technique—the indifference curve.

Indifference Curves

The indifference curve may be compared with a contour line. A single curve represents a single level of satisfaction, made up of varying combinations of two goods. Let us take our familiar (even tiresome?) products, wheat and cloth. The indifference curve *a–a* in

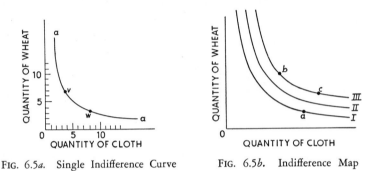

FIG. 6.5*a*. Single Indifference Curve   FIG. 6.5*b*. Indifference Map

Figure 6.5*a* shows an example in which a consumer is indifferent whether he has 7 bushels of wheat and 4 yards of cloth (*v*) or 3 bushels of wheat and 7 yards of cloth (*w*), or any other combination which may be read off the same curve. It will be observed that the single indifference curve is convex to the origin and flattens out to become asymptotic to the axes at each end. After a certain point, as in offer curves, a consumer is unwilling to give up any more wheat simply to get more cloth, of which he already has plenty, or, at the other end, to pay more scarce valuable cloth for redundant wheat.

The single indifference curve represents the combination in which a consumer with a given utility level would spend it between two goods as the price between them is varied. The notion of price here takes us back to the example we used in the previous chapter, which is demonstrated again in Figure 6.1*a*. This indifference curve is made up of a series of points designating quantities of wheat and cloth, respectively, which would be bought with a given income at an infinite series of prices ranging between infinity and zero for wheat in terms of cloth. The same thing may be said in still another way. At a given price, the consumer with a level of real income indicated by a given indifference curve will consume the quantity of the two commodities indicated by the point of tangency of the price to the indifference curve.

Like contour lines, indifference curves are arranged in maps in which the parallel lines indicate progress in the indicated direction from a lower degree of satisfaction (or altitude) to a higher. In Figure 6.5*b*, for example, point *b* on indifference curve *III* is taken to represent a higher level of satisfaction or welfare than point *a* on indifference curve *I*, even though it has more wheat and less cloth. The extra wheat is more than sufficient to compensate for the loss of cloth. Point *c*, where there is more of both, is clearly superior in satisfaction to point *a*, and the consumer is indifferent between *c* and *b*.

The higher branches of economic theory raise a difficult question about community indifference curves. It is agreed that the indifference map of an individual, if anyone is willing to make one up, is conceptually satisfactory. If an individual believes that he is better off than he was before with 5 more bushels of wheat and 2 less yards of cloth—substantially better off—there is no one who can gainsay him. But there may be objection, it is suggested, to the notion that the *community* is better off with an average of 5 bushels more and 2 yards less. Some members of the community lose the cloth, while others gain the wheat. Who can say that the increase in satisfaction of the one is greater than the decrease in satisfaction of the other? Or if the changes are evenly distributed, there is still a problem if there are some who vastly prefer cloth over wheat and others with opposite tastes. In this case it is impossible to say that the gain of the wheat devotees outweighs the loss in satisfaction of the cloth addicts. Levels of satisfaction or welfare cannot be compared from one person to another.

These are real difficulties, as we shall see later in our discussion of commercial policy. If one group in the community is better off as a result of some action, but others worse, it is impossible to say how the welfare of the community as a whole has been affected. Despite these difficulties, however, we continue to use indifference curves— although with caution. One basis for so doing is the simplifying assumptions that the tastes of the community can be described by the tastes of an individual, that these are consistent from one period to another, and that there is no change in income distribution. These assumptions are clearly contrary to realism. Another justification used by welfare economists has been the "compensation principle": If it is clear that the beneficiaries of a change in price have enough additional income to compensate (or bribe) the losers for their loss, and some left over, the new position represents an improvement. If the wheat addicts can afford to underwrite the losses of the cloth addicts to obtain the change, the change is one for the better, whether in fact compensation takes place or not.

However unrealistic, the community indifference curve is schematically a neat device. In the first place, it provides us with the answer to the price at which wheat and cloth will be traded in the two communities with decreasing returns and in the absence of trade. The price which will prevail in a single market is that which is tangent both to the production-possibilities curve (*AB*) and to the highest possible indifference curve (in this case curve *II*). Production and consumption will both take place, in the absence of trade, at this point of tangency. This is shown by point *Q* in Figure 6.6. At any other point on a higher indifference curve—say, *t*—the quantities of wheat and cloth involved are beyond the capacity of the economy to produce. At any point on a lower indifference curve, satisfaction can be increased by shifting production toward wheat away from cloth, or vice versa. Point *r*, for example, represents the quantities of wheat and cloth which consumers would take at a price for wheat and cloth in terms of each other tangent to indifference curve *I* at *r*.

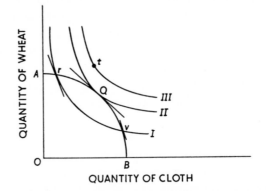

FIG. 6.6. Indifference Curves, Production-Possibilities Curve without Trade

But, at this price, maximum production would require output at *v*. Let the student who has doubts refer back to Figure 5.4*b* and the discussion it brought on. The price of cloth is so high in terms of wheat that resources will be shifted from wheat to cloth. But this production cannot be sold at these prices. There is far too much cloth and far too little wheat to satisfy consumers, who at this price would consume more wheat and less cloth. In order to get rid of output, the price of wheat will have to be raised and that of cloth lowered. This means another shift of production from *v*. And so it would oscillate, first consumers and then producers dissatisfied with the combinations of wheat and cloth until a stable equilibrium is found at the point where the production-possibilities curve is tangent to the highest possible indifference curve.

There will always be such a point. While there is only one production-possibilities curve, there are an infinite number of indifference curves which can be drawn representing infinitesimally small increases in real income. If these indifference curves do not intersect, as we shall assume they do not, any production-possibilities curve must be tangent to one indifference curve.

At the point of tangency, producers have a price—the line of tangency—in which they are in equilibrium as between wheat and cloth, and consumers are in equilibrium in consumption of wheat and cloth. Production, consumption, and price, therefore, will all be in equilibrium here.

The Terms of Trade

The indifference-curve analysis can now be applied in a wider scope to indicate a solution to quantities of goods bought and sold, and the prices at which they are exchanged in international trade— though the diagrams get somewhat complex. Let us assume that the United States and Britain have different production-possibilities curves (increasing costs) but the same set of indifference curves. In the absence of foreign trade, production (and consumption) will take place at the points of tangency to the production-possibilities curves which are also tangent to the highest possible indifference curves. In Figure 6.7, these points are *c* in the United States and *d* in Britain.

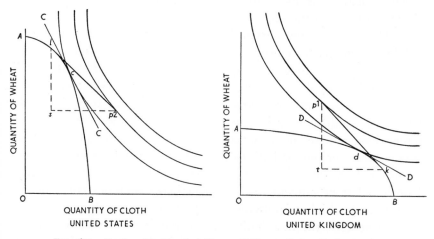

FIG. 6.7.   Trade with Identical Tastes, Different Factor Endowments

The tangents themselves, $C-C$ and $D-D$, represent the prices at which wheat and cloth are traded in terms of each other in the United States and Britain before trade has been opened.

With the opening of trade, the amounts of wheat and cloth exported and imported in the two countries and the price at which they will be exchanged will be determined by parallel lines of equal length tangent to the respective production-possibilities curves and tangent to a higher indifference curve. These lines, $l-p^2$ in the United States and $k-p^1$ in Britain, run in opposite directions from the production-possibilities curves in order to reach higher indifference curves. The requirement that the lines must be parallel, or of the same slope, fulfills the condition that the prices in the two countries must be the same after trade is open, if transport costs be disregarded. The requirement that they be of equal length, as well as of the same slope, is in satisfaction of the necessary condition that exports of one country shall be equal to imports of the other. It should be observed that Britain's exports of cloth $(t-k)$ are equal to the United States' imports $(s-p^2)$, while the United States' exports of wheat $(s-l)$ are equal to imports by Britain $(t-p^1)$.

The effects of trade with different production-possibilities curves and identical indifference curves are to make each country more specialized in production and less specialized in consumption. In both cases production slides farther along the production-possibilities curve toward the output of the commodity for which the factors are most effective. Consumption, however, given the shape of the curves portrayed in Figure 6.7, tends to move in the other direction—more toward equality, as the scarce commodity in each country becomes cheaper after importation.

The shape of the curves drawn in Figure 6.7 has no necessary validity. Tastes (and hence indifference curves) may differ, as well as supply conditions. Indeed, as we shall see presently, trade is possible with identical supply conditions and different tastes. Whatever may be the indifference maps or supply conditions, however, trade is possible when the equilibrium prices in two countries without trade are different. Under these circumstances, there will be a new price at which it is possible for one or both to gain from exchange. In mathematical terms, trade is possible when the two countries find lines of equal length and slope tangent to the production-possibilities curve of each country and a higher indifference curve in one or both.

In general, the new indifference curve attained will be a higher one for both countries than that reached in the absence of trade. The student may, however, enjoy working out for himself a case in which a big country trading with a smaller one receives none of the gain from trade. The price in the larger country does not change, and without a price change no move to a higher indifference curve is possible. The country consumes what it consumed before but produces more of one product, now exported, and less of another (the new import). This means, of course, that the production-possibilities curve must be a straight line over the relevant part of the curve with a slope equal to the international terms of trade.

The geometrical technique set out in Appendix C shows the production-possibilities curves and the indifference curves of both countries on the same diagram, along with their offer curves. While it takes a little work to master, it is worth it.

Different Tastes

The possibility of trade between countries with the same factor endowment and different tastes has already been mentioned. Two countries can produce wheat or rice equally well but, as consumers, rank them differently. Figure 6.8 illustrates this case. In the absence

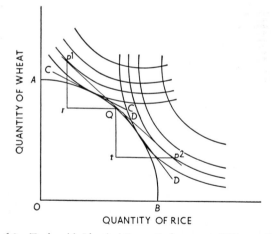

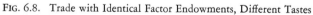

FIG. 6.8. Trade with Identical Factor Endowments, Different Tastes

of trade, wheat is more expensive than rice in the country which prefers wheat to rice, and rice more expensive than wheat in the other. The opening of trade equalizes prices in the two countries and enables each country to move its consumption to a higher indifference curve by exchanging wheat for rice or the opposite. In this instance— the converse of the more usual case, in which tastes are the same and factors differ—trade permits each country to specialize less in production and more in consumption. The explanation is that, prior to trade, each country had used for the favored commodity resources more suited to the product it did not prefer. In the bread-eating country, for example, land suited to rice production was used, in the absence of trade, to grow wheat. With trade possible, this land can yield a higher return in terms of satisfaction by growing rice, which is now exchanged for wheat.

Identical Factors—Identical Tastes

The basis for trade between countries with identical factors under increasing returns was set forth in the last chapter. Here it is necessary only to add the indifference curves which portray the demand side of the position. This is done in Figure 6.9. Identical tastes were implicitly assumed in the discussion in Chapter 5, so that no further explanation is required. In the absence of trade, production is at point P in both countries. After trade begins and after producers in

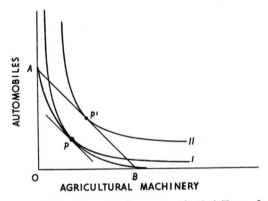

FIG. 6.9. Trade with Identical Factor Endowments, Identical Tastes, Increasing Returns

both countries have become aware of the possibility of economies of scale, production in one country will shift to the limit of the production-possibilities curve, at either A or B, and the other country will be likely to shift to the other extreme. Under these circumstances, trade takes place to shift consumption in both countries to a higher indifference curve, i.e., to point P' on indifference curve *II*.

General Equilibrium

In its most general form, the answer to the first two questions raised by the classical economists reduces to the statement that what goods will be produced and the prices at which they will be traded will be determined by supply and demand and that the supply and demand for goods will both determine and be determined by the supply and demand for factors of production. The system of equilibrium is an interacting one.

The analysis of this chapter has been limited to two countries and to two goods. There are a number of economists who believe that the analysis is fundamentally altered if it is broadened to include more countries and more commodities. The majority, however, do not accept this view, believing that the two-country, two-commodity analysis is capable of extension, by means of a variety of techniques, to the more intricate and more realistic models.

Given, say, five commodities produced in each of two countries, these can be ranged in order of comparative advantage in each country. Initially one can say only that a country will export the commodity in which it has the largest advantage, and import the commodity in which its disadvantage is greatest. The question of whether it will export or import the three commodities between these limits will then depend upon the balance of trade. If the demand for imports of the commodity offering a large disadvantage is very great, it may have to export all four of the other commodities, given the nature of the foreign demand for them, to balance its accounts.

Using what is left of the theory of comparative advantage and the law of reciprocal demand, the theory of general equilibrium deals with the classical questions raised about international trade as if transportation were costless. On the cost side, the entire discussion turns on production costs, or what students of the theory of location (which we discuss in a following chapter) call "processing costs." When transport costs are admitted into the analysis, the requirement that the price ratios shall be equal in the two countries after trade must be dropped. The price ratios may differ within the limits allowed by transportation costs. If the cost of transportation is very large in relation to the value of a product, the ratio between it and other prices in two countries can vary widely. Under these circumstances, it is not sufficient to say that a country will export those goods which can be produced efficiently by the factors which it has in abundance and which are therefore cheap. To this must be added, as we shall see in Chapter 8, the proviso that this is true so long as the differences in price per unit are greater than unit costs of transport.

Summary

Ricardo answered the question of what commodities are exported and imported by stating that this will be determined by the law of comparative cost; Mill answered the question of what prices will rule in international trade by stating that this would be determined by the law of reciprocal demand. It was necessary to find a price which would exchange all the goods that one country had to sell for all that the other wanted to offer. Marshall and Edgeworth developed intersecting offer curves to show how this law operated.

But this analysis tended to submerge the effect of changes in supply. A diagrammatic analysis has been developed which combines production-possibilities curves for supply with community indifference maps for demand. There are some difficulties posed by the community indifference maps, but they are used nonetheless. In the absence of trade, production and consumption will both take place at the tangent between the production-possibilities curve and the highest indifference curve. With trade, it is possible to effect gains which carry each country beyond its production-possibilities curve. Trade will take place at a price the same in each country, tangent to the production-possibilities curve and a higher (for at least one country) indifference curve of the same length. This price line is then the hypotenuse of a right-angle triangle in which the other legs measure exports and imports.

The theory of trade is shown to belong to general-equilibrium theoretical analysis in which goods are mobile but factors are not. One price reigns in one market—the terms of trade.

SUGGESTED READING

TREATISES, ETC.

No brief paragraph can do justice to the bibliographical material on the subject. What follows, therefore, is highly selective.

Haberler, chaps. ix–xii; Viner, chaps. viii and ix; and the articles of Leontief on the indifference curve, Samuelson on the gains from trade, and Williams on increasing returns in the American Economic Association, *Readings* Nos. 10, 11, and 12, respectively. The Scitovszky article in the *Readings* is one of the pioneering works in the field using the indifference curve, but treats of a subject matter with which we deal in Chapters 12 and 16.

Ohlin gives the best statement of the general-equilibrium position in his chapters v–vii and xiii. This theory is presented mathematically by J. L. Mosak, *General Equilibrium Theory in International Trade* (Bloomington, Ind.: Principia Press, 1944).

Haberler's article, "Some Problems in the Pure Theory of International Trade," in *EJ*, June, 1950, uses the production-possibilities, indifference-curve technique to tackle some more difficult problems.

A useful popular presentation is to be found in Professor Viner's recent lectures at the National University of Brazil, published by the Free Press as

International Trade and Economic Development (Glencoe, Ill., 1952), especially chaps. i–iii.

F. D. Graham's *The Theory of International Values* (Princeton: Princeton University Press, 1948), offers sharp criticism of the main lines of the classical theory. The point is more briefly made in American Economic Association, *Readings,* No. 14.

The teacher who wants to illustrate the theory of comparative advantage in practice is referred to G. D. A. MacDougall's "Some Practical Illustrations and Applications of the Theory of Comparative Advantage," *EJ,* December, 1951.

POINTS

J. B. Condliffe, *The Commerce of Nations* (New York: W. W. Norton & Co., Inc., 1950), gives an excellent account of the development of *laissez faire* in the nineteenth century which makes useful supplementary reading. See especially chapters vi–viii and xiii.

THE DYNAMIC BASIS OF TRADE: CHANGES IN TASTES, TECHNOLOGY, FACTOR ENDOWMENTS

Chapter 7

The Static Nature of Comparative Advantage

The basis for international trade discussed thus far rests essentially on static assumptions: with given tastes, given production functions, fixed factor endowments, etc., a case for specialization and exchange can be made. We reserve for somewhat later in the book a thorough statement of the objection to free trade raised by developing countries. This is largely built on dynamic arguments. But it is well at this stage to relax some of our static assumptions for the purpose of explaining part of existing trade, and indicating the nature of changes in the trade pattern even of fully developed countries. In particular we choose to depart from the initial assumptions of fixed tastes, identical production functions between trading countries, and fixed supplies of land, labor, and capital.

Fixed Tastes

We need not spend much time with tastes. It is sufficient to point out that the analysis based on opening up trade between two countries which had never traded before predicates a gain from trade on the existence of fixed tastes unchanged by the fact of newly opened trade. This of course is highly unrealistic. Trade has many origins—the exchange of gifts between primitive tribes; the plundering of the Middle East by Europeans during the Crusades, or of Europe by Scandinavian pirates; the opening of the western hemisphere by Spanish, Portuguese, and English explorers. In most of these historical means by which trade began, the initial exchanges involved the creation of new wants, as well as their satisfaction. Tastes change with trade rather than trade satisfying existing wants more fully.

The point has significance beyond recalling the origin of cotton, muslin, sugar, and even tariffs, as Arabic words, or the introduction of tobacco, rum, and the potato from North America to Europe.

Ragnar Nurkse has pointed to the "demonstration effect" under which underdeveloped countries have learned about the existence of goods in developed nations which will lighten their burdens, satisfy their physical appetites, and titivate their innate sense of self-expression or exhibitionism. When modern methods of production are introduced into some particularly primitive societies, it is necessary to introduce modern methods of consumption. With the initiation of plantation cultivation of fruit, sugar, rubber, tea, and the like, there must come a change in the diet of native laborers and the replacement of the varied native subsistence fare by staple imported foodstuffs. With the alteration in the pattern of living, there may be a worsening in the nutritional level of the diet and dietary deficiencies.

When the price of exports rises with trade, or that of imports falls, with all tastes and means of production unchanged, trade may be said to result in an unambiguous gain for a country as a whole, leaving aside the distribution of the gain within the country, and the difficulties inherent in measuring the extent of the gain. But when the improvement in the terms of trade is accompanied by an increase in the demand for imports, the case is not so clear. One can say that there is an improvement, as compared with the hypothetical case of increasing the demand for imports without satisfying it. A new want coming into existence along with trade to fill it, however, involves a departure from the classical assumptions and raises doubt as to the classical conclusion of gain.

There is some basis for thinking that the demonstration effect is stronger today than, say, before World War I. To take what may seem to be a trivial example, but one of some importance for international trade, international exchanges grew far in the nineteenth century without bringing about any substantial homogeneity of taste in dress, diet, consumers' goods, or cultural pursuit. Such is less and less true. Trade in Europe in the nineteenth century continued side by side with different styles of national diet and cooking: The British was distinct from the Continental breakfast, and on the Continent itself Italian, French, German, and Scandinavian cooking all differed. Today the Indo-Chinese complain that the native Asian breakfast is giving way to European eggs, bacon, and coffee; in Japan, rice is increasingly abandoned in favor of wheat; and Coca-Cola is a trademark known round the world. Demonstration effect is more significant for underdeveloped countries which frequently want to import—Swiss watches, British bicycles, and United States fountain pens at the most primitive level—before they have earned or arranged to borrow the necessary exchange. This possible source of disequilibrium will concern us in Part VI. But even between developed countries these changes in taste which come with the introduction of new goods are significant. The former editor of the *Economist* has said that American high-speed printing machinery and construction equipment are so efficient that Europeans have to have them. In this case, the change in taste is responsive to a change in technology.

Changes in Technology

When technological change occurred slowly, and not very often, it was appropriate for classical economists to ignore it and to rely on the assumption of a single and universal technology open to all countries. Taussig called it a "given state of the arts." The more rapid pace of technological change today and the frequent concentration of technological change in a few countries make this assumption less supportable.

It is difficult to construct a realistic model of trade based on technological differences. It may nonetheless be worth attempting a highly simplified one. Figures 7.1*a* and 7.1*b* show two countries,

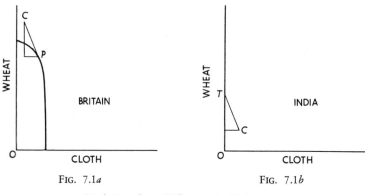

FIG. 7.1*a*   FIG. 7.1*b*

Trade Based on Difference in Technology

Britain and India, only the former of which has the technical capacity to make textiles on a commercial scale. Indian production possibilities in Figure 7.1*b* are the straight line *OT;* it can produce wheat in varying amounts, up to a limit of *OT,* but lacks the technology to produce textiles. Accordingly, it produces at *T* and exchanges wheat for textiles. Consumption takes place at *C.*

Figures 7.2*a* and 7.2*b* show the position after the technique for making textiles has spread to India. The Indian production-possibilities curve has changed from *OT* to *TW,* since the labor used in making labor-intensive textiles exists in abundance in India. In the first stage, trade was based not on factor endowments but on differences in technology. When the difference in technology was wiped out by the spread of knowledge, the trade pattern reversed itself. India exported cloth and imported wheat, rather than the reverse. Note that Britain gains as well from the change. Its factors, in the diagram, were always better suited for wheat than cloth and only produced cloth for export because the price was so high. When the price of wheat rises in relation to cloth, it becomes economic to switch from exporting cloth to buying it abroad.

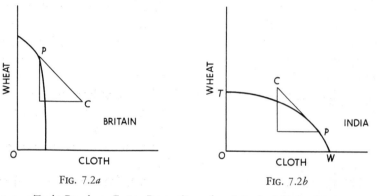

FIG. 7.2*a*   FIG. 7.2*b*

Trade Based on Factor Proportions after Spread of Technology

There is an element of realism in the example chosen, not perhaps in Britain as an exporter of wheat but in the history of textile exports. As the pioneer in the Industrial Revolution, Britain built an enormous export trade in textiles, which is regarded today as labor-intensive. The rise of Japan in the textile world came when Britain lost its monopoly in the relatively simple technology of textiles, and Japan with cheap labor found its comparative advantage in the same line. More recently, since World War II, Japan is itself losing out on the highly competitive world textile market, as new producers with still cheaper labor, like India, move into the export market, and other developing countries cut their development teeth on this elementary manufacturing industry.

Examples are by no means confined to textiles, or to other simple manufacturing products such as matches, salt, shoes, and similar industries in which developing countries get their manufacturing start. The Committee for Economic Development has pointed out:

> U.S. industries may be at a competitive disadvantage with foreign producers in lines where the American producer has no special advantage in raw ma-

terial costs or volume of output and where production techniques are about the same here and abroad. This could be true, for example, of products which are manufactured both here and abroad by much the same kind of machinery, and with about the same input of labor for each unit of production. In these cases American products are subject to foreign competition resulting in large part from lower wages prevailing abroad. Competition would be increased if tariffs were lowered. Products which appear to fall into this category include heavy electrical equipment, watches, woolen and worsted textiles, flat glass, rayon staple fiber, bicycles, some chemicals and some machine tools.

This statement contains an analytical omission. The list must be limited to goods which are relatively labor-intensive. In capital-intensive commodities where the same kinds of machinery are used and labor productivity is similar, the United States may have a comparative advantage over other countries "resulting in large part from lower *capital* costs prevailing in the United States." There is also some question whether the production functions are identical in Europe and the United States for bicycles and watches,[1] or whether in fact the two areas specialize on rather different products. But by and large the point is well taken. And the loss of a monopoly in a technology can result in the loss of a comparative advantage when factor endowments take over the determination of the direction of trade.

Heavy electrical generating equipment, for example, used to be exported from the United States to Europe, based primarily on the technological supremacy of the American companies. After a time, technological change in the United States slowed down; competitors abroad caught up; and with cheaper supplies of the highly skilled labor required, competitors were able to outsell United States companies on government contracts on which they were encouraged to bid, even with "Buy American" preference.

Radios were an export product of the United States when the rate of innovational change in this country was rapid, despite the labor-intensive character of many of the manufacturing operations, such as assembly, which called primarily for the dextrous hands of quickly trained women, available in abundance in practically every country. United States radio exports were replaced by assembly operations abroad, and German, Dutch, British, and Japanese imports were beginning to find their way into the United States market. Then came another innovation in production—the printed circuit—which elim-

---

[1] The writer understands that one United States watch manufacturer with facilities in this country and abroad produces in the United States those styles which are saleable in very large numbers and other styles with short runs in Switzerland. This would suggest that production functions are not identical.

inated a great deal of the handwork in wiring, and United States manufacturers gained back much of their lost ground.

The story is told of a General Electric salesman who visited Japan on two occasions ten years apart. On the second he sold no item which had been included in the first order, and many of these—light bulbs, household switches, etc.—were being made in Japan and exported to the United States. But since technology had not stood still in the United States, and since trade is based on differences in technology and new goods, his order the second time was larger than the first. The loss of a monopoly of the technology to make a given article need not be seriously adverse to a country's export trade if in fact it keeps developing new products and new ways of making old.

In some cases it is difficult to determine the basis for trade. The United States used to have a monopoly of the world exports in automobiles. Since World War II, the United States share of the world market has declined sharply, and European automobiles are beginning to find their way in increasing numbers into the North American market. Studies are being made, but have thus far no clear result, to determine whether the change in the world trade pattern in automobiles is based on (1) a change in tastes, in favor of the European sports cars and small cars, such as the Volkswagen; or (2) a loss in the United States technological monopoly, and the fact that the automobile is basically labor-intensive rather than capital-intensive. A British economist has suggested that automobiles may turn out to be the textiles of tomorrow—which any country can make. At the moment, however, it is interesting to observe that the Japanese have been unable to produce a car which can sell cheaply abroad, and not for lack of trying.

Sir Dennis Robertson has suggested that there is a real drawback to international trade if innovations are systematically concentrated in one or a few countries, and if the rest of the world is continuously finding itself displaced out of the market by innovations which undermine the value of their resources. He uses an analogy of a man who undertakes to work as a servant for a scientist who then proceeds to invent a machine to cook his dinner:

> The simple fellow who, to the advantage of both, has been earning a living by cooking the dinner for a busy and prosperous scientist wakes up one day to find that his master has invented a completely automatic cooker, and that if he wants to remain a member of the household he must turn shoeblack. He acquires a kit and learns the technique, only to find that his master has invented a dust-repelling shoe, but would nevertheless be graciously willing

for him to remain on and empty the trash-bins. Would he not do better to remove himself from the orbit of the great man, and cultivate his own back garden? And if he can find some other simple fellows in the same case with whom to gang up and practise the division of labour on a less bewildering basis, so much the better for him. Such, it is urged, has become the position of the rest of the free world vis-a-vis the United States.

This may overstate the case as applied to the United States, especially as many of the new products to come on the market—innovations in automobiles, trains, electrical generating equipment, etc.—are European rather than United States in origin. Nor do all innovations like synthetic nitrates, nylon, atabrine, and detergents replace the imported saltpeter, silk, quinine, and fats and oils with the product of domestic factors available in abundance. Some innovations—outstandingly the pneumatic tire and atomic fission—create a substantial demand for foreign goods.

It is nonetheless true, though the classical economists paid it little heed, that much trade is based not on differences in factor endowments, given identical production functions, but differences in technology, whatever the factor position.

What new products are replacing heavy electrical equipment, radios, automobiles, etc., in United States exports? One is air-conditioning equipment which reached $60,000,000 in 1956, after climbing at the rate of 35 per cent per year for a couple of years, and is regarded as capable of a fourfold expansion in five years to bring it to $300,000,000 by 1961. A wide range of electronic equipment comprises others. Another "new" export is coal, where the price of labor has risen with great rapidity and resulted in an equally rapid substitution for labor of capital equipment using new technology. The consequence was an increase in output per man from 3 to 4 tons per day at the end of the war to more than 17 tons in the most mechanized mines and a national average in 1956 of more than 10 tons. This enables the industry, despite a heavy burden of transport costs, to export to Europe where the output per worker is little more than a ton per man day.

Changes in Technology and the Terms of Trade

A change in technology can be neutral with respect to trade, export biased or import biased, depending upon its nature. A neutral innovation, for present purposes, is one which increases the productivity of existing factors equally in export- and import-competing goods. The production-possibilities curve retains the same shape; it only moves out further. The two production-possibilities curves in Figure 7.3 represent a neutral change in technology.[2] An export-biased innovation evidently increases productivity in the export good; an import-biased one reduces the cost of import-competing products. These are shown in Figures 7.4*a* and 7.4*b*.

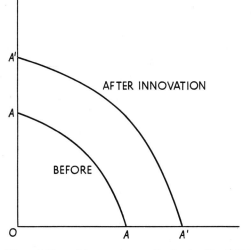

FIG. 7.3. Effect of Neutral Innovation on Production-Possibilities Curve

Export-biased innovation evidently reduces the terms of trade. The product was cheap without trade and before the innovation. It is now cheaper. The prime example is that of Britain whose terms of

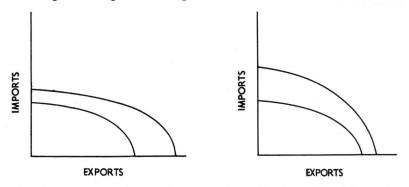

FIG. 7.4*a*. Export-Biased Innovation   FIG. 7.4*b*. Import-Biased Innovation

trade worsened from 1750 to 1850 because of her success in producing textiles more cheaply. Another is the reduction in the price of wheat exported by the United States after the completion of the transport

[2] Neutral in this case means neutral with respect to foreign trade. The term is sometimes used with respect to whether an innovation is labor-saving or capital-saving and denotes the intermediate position.

network across the Alleghanies and the settlement of the wheatlands north and west of Chicago after the Civil War.

Import-biased innovations tend to improve the terms of trade. The invention of synthetics in the United States has lessened its dependence upon foreign sources of supply and reduced the prices at which such sources can sell in the country, if at all. There have been times in the short run when the price of natural rubber has deviated from the synthetic price, because of the full utilization of synthetic capacity; and the price of wool in the short run can ignore that of the synthetics while productive capacity is still expanding. There can be little doubt, however, that import-biased innovation improves the terms of trade.

It should be noted, however, that even neutral innovation worsens the terms of trade, assuming that the offer curve of the other country has some elasticity. Figure 7.5 shows the effect of a neutral innovation

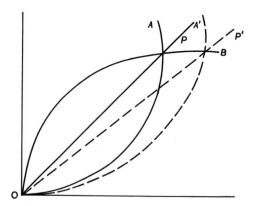

FIG. 7.5. The Effect of Neutral Innovation on the Terms of Trade

on the offer curve of a country. It is displaced from A to A' and the terms of trade worsened from OP to OP', because it can produce more of the export good for trading.[3] Only if demand conditions strongly favored the export good would this not be the case.

Thus not only export-biased innovations but even neutral increases in general productivity are shared throughout the world through international trade.

Changes in Factor Endowments

Another element in comparative advantage which will not stand still is factor endowment. The economics of growth deal with capital ac-

[3] In the language of Appendix C, the offer curve is displaced to the right because A's trade-indifference curves are flatter after the innovation.

cumulation. With annual savings, land and labor assumed fixed, comparative advantage would change toward more capital-intensive goods and away from more labor- and land-intensive goods. If labor also grows, but at a slower rate than capital, so that the capital/labor ratio is increasing, this will still hold true of capital-intensive goods, but comparative disadvantage may increase in land-intensive goods, at the expense both of labor- and capital-intensive products.

The question of capital accumulation can become quite complex when different countries are both accumulating capital, though at different rates. For present purposes it is enough to suggest that if only one country is accumulating capital, its comparative advantage in capital-intensive products will increase, and its comparative disadvantage, if one existed, narrow. Thus capital accumulation will act as an export-biased innovation in a country with a comparative advantage in capital-intensive goods, and as an import-biased innovation in a country with a comparative disadvantage in this line of commodities.

Land is perhaps more complex. In a given state of the arts, land can be increased by discovery or reduced by depletion, or, simultaneously, both. But the factor resource, land, as indeed every factor, can only be defined in terms of a technological process. An innovation will expand or contract the amount of land viewed as an economic agent. Land bearing low-grade taconite ores became an economic resource only after the taconite-refining process was discovered.

It is hard to know whether, in the economic history of the United States since the Civil War, land has been an expanding, fixed, or a contracting factor. For some purposes, such as oil production, land was enormously abundant and is now relatively scarce. In other minerals, depletion has exhausted the richest deposits. But discoveries and improvements in technology continue. Drilling for oil takes place in the Continental shelf in the Gulf of Mexico; improvements in refinery techniques have just about reached the point where it will pay to extract oil from the abundant shales of the Rocky Mountain area. Land, the fixed factor, is seen to be subject to all sorts of changes.

If we assume land fixed, for purposes of illustration, and capital and labor growing together at a steady pace, the nature of comparative advantage may be seen to change. The United States used to be an exporter of a wide variety of metals and minerals. Now it is a net importer of all but two—coal and molybdenum. Copper, zinc, lead, iron, and especially oil which we used to export are now on a net import basis. Figure 7.6 shows a stereotyped representation of the nature of the change. The vertical axis measures land-intensive goods; the horizontal axis, on the other hand, represents the goods embodying prima-rily labor and capital. The inner production-possibilities curve, marked 1870, shows a strong specialization in land-intensive production, which is in part exchanged for labor/capital-intensive goods. With the passage of time, the shape of the production-possibilities curve changes. Land is fixed, and capital and labor grow. Production possibilities in the land-intensive product increase somewhat, as more capital and labor will produce more land-intensive products even with land unchanged.

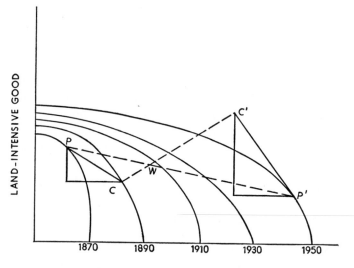

FIG. 7.6. A Schematic Representation of the Change in United States Comparative Advantage in Land-Intensive Commodities to Comparative Disadvantage

But the production-possibilities curve grows mainly to the right. By 1900, as the figure is drawn, the production-possibilities curve is fairly balanced on the scales shown. By 1950, it is skewed in favor of labor/capital-intensive products in place of its original skewness in the op-posite direction.

The dotted line, *P–P′*, represents the locus of points of tangency to the production-possibilities curve, where production has taken place. *C–C′* signifies the path of consumption. To the left of the intersection, i.e., prior to about 1905 as shown on the figure, land-intensive products were exported and labor/capital-intensive products imported. After 1905, or thereabouts, when the curves intersect, the trade position was reversed. The United States exported labor/capital-intensive products and imported the products of land.

This representation is of course purely schematic. It departs from reality in a hundred ways—two goods, constant technology, a fixed factor, incomplete specialization, and so forth. Problems of defining land-intensive products make it impossible to pin down when the change from an export to an import basis occurred in minerals. It was probably nearer 1945 than 1905. Nonetheless, the demonstration has validity in a very broad sense and helps illustrate how comparative advantages change with factor growth.

Factor Growth and Technological Change

While factor growth and technological change can be analytically distinguished, they may occur simultaneously or quasi-simultaneously in the real world to maintain a comparative advantage in a given commodity.

During the interwar period, for example, the United States was losing its comparative advantage in agriculture. Agricultural products which had represented 47 per cent of United States exports in 1922–24 dwindled to 25 per cent by 1937–39. Farm policies, including price supports, played a role in this deterioration, but one which we ignore. To a considerable extent the deterioration was the result of an increase in the price of labor which made a number of these commodities unable to compete in price on the world market.

Shortly before and during the course of World War II, however, a quasi-revolution occurred in United States agriculture. Machinery and fertilizer, plus new techniques of dry farming in wheat and irrigation in cotton, raised yields and especially labor productivity. A number of farm products which had been exported on the basis of land-intensive comparative advantage could now be exported once more because they were capital-intensive in a capital-intensive country. Others, such as rice, linseed, soy beans, and Turkish tobacco which had been imported changed over to an export basis.

The position was possibly even more striking in coal. Successive changes in technology developed successively larger steam shovels for open-pit mining until the present 2,400-ton size capable of removing 80 tons of overburden in one bite. The cost of development of mechanized mines has gone up substantially compared to those with hand-loading facilities—from $2.00 per ton of output per year to $7.00 to $10.00—but the labor cost as a percentage of the price of coal has declined from 70 per cent in the 1930's to 50 per cent in 1956. The depletion of land has been more than offset by the improvement in technology with the result that coal has become an export product.

Speeding Up the Rate of Change

A bright journalist, Samuel Lubell, has suggested that "the ever-quickening technological and scientific revolution . . . is undercutting the advantages of international specialization, making our world more fiercely competitive, but without forging adequate mechanisms of adjustment." This is only one of a list of objections Lubell poses to American foreign economic policy. It echoes a view expressed twenty-five years ago by Lord (then J. M.) Keynes that modern technology was rapidly narrowing the differences in comparative costs between countries and reducing the gains from trade below the risks inherent in specialization.

These views are based in part on the assumption that most innovation (and imitation) and factor change is biased against imports. Such is clearly not the case. There is merit, however, in the view that the speed of change has increased, and that, as a consequence, the unhampered operation of the price system cannot always be relied upon, in the confident expectation that it will bring about the appropriate shifts of resources and restore equilibrium. But this raises policy questions which are left to be developed later.

Summary

Comparative advantage gives an answer to the question of what products will be exported and imported in a world of fixed tastes, fixed resources, and fixed production functions. This static world no longer exists, however, if it ever did. Tastes change, particularly as the demonstration effect impresses one country with the articles of consumption or means of production developed in another.

Technology is altered by innovation, which is likely to occur in a single country before the change spreads by imitation to others. A considerable volume of the trade of a few developed countries is based on a technological difference rather than factor proportions, and it is likely to be destroyed, or even the direction of trade reversed, if technological change should halt and the rest of the world catch up. When technological change consists not in the introduction of new goods but improvements in productivity of the old, it may expand or contract trade and worsen or improve the terms of trade, depending upon whether it is export- or import-biased. Neutral change which expands productivity equally in the export- and in the import-competing sectors will expand trade and worsen the terms of trade, unless offset by the development of demand, because of the inelasticity of the offer curve of the rest of the world when the innovating country offers to sell more and buy more at the old terms of trade.

Factor change raises a number of complex problems. Capital tends to grow faster than labor, and for that reason still faster than land, which is usually taken as fixed. Land is, however, subject to depletion and increased by discoveries, in a given state of the arts. Technological change may further change the quantity of land available as an economic input by finding new uses for previously waste resources or increasing the productivity of land already employed.

When technology and factors both change, the task of calculating comparative advantage is an ever-changing one. So long as all change is not biased against imports, however, there will be a new basis for trade if adjustment can be made in time.

SUGGESTED READING

TEXTS

None directly on changes in modern technology. J. B. Condliffe, *The Commerce of Nations,* adopts an historical approach to the discussion of comparative advantage which is useful for earlier periods.

TREATISES, ETC.

D. B. Bensusan-Butt has an interesting article showing the change in comparative advantage as capital accumulation proceeds. It is entitled "A Model of Trade and Accumulation," *AER,* September, 1954.

The present writer has discussed new goods and new ways of making old goods as they affect international trade in "Anciens et nouveaux produits en commerce international," *Economie Appliquée,* July–August, 1954. The emphasis, however, was mainly on the effects on the terms of trade. The notion of export- and import-bias in productivity changes was introduced into the discussion by Professor John R. Hicks, in "An Inaugural Lecture," *OEP,* June, 1953.

POINTS

The reference to the former editor of the *Economist* is to Sir Geoffry Crowther and his Leatherbee Lectures on *The Balances and Imbalances of Payments,* at the Harvard Business School, April, 1957. For the other quotations, see:

The Research and Development Committee of the Committee for Economic Development, *United States Tariff Policy,* November, 1954, pp. 5, 6; Sir Dennis Robertson, *Britain in the World Economy* (London: Allen & Unwin, 1954), pp. 58–59.

On the possibility that automobiles will become a ubiquitous manufacture like textiles, see Sir Donald MacDougall, "A Lecture on the Dollar Problem," *Econ,* August, 1954, p. 196.

The Lubell reference is to Samuel Lubell, *The Revolution in World Trade* (New York: Harper & Bros., 1955), p. 2.

Lord Keynes article was entitled, "National Self-Sufficiency," and published in the *Yale Review,* Summer, 1933.

Figure 7.6 was developed by J. Vanek in his unpublished thesis, "The Natural Resource Content of United States Foreign Trade, 1870–1955" (Massachusetts Institute of Technology, 1957).

Chapter 8

TRANSPORT COSTS AND LOCATION THEORY

Transport Costs and Price Equality

The introduction of transport costs into the analysis of international trade disturbs the conclusion that international trade equalizes the prices of traded goods in the trading countries. If, in the absence of transport costs, wheat and cloth would have exchanged on a one-to-one basis, the necessity to overcome costs of transport will make the import good more expensive in both countries and the export good less valuable. In the United States, for example, wheat might exchange for cloth at 8 bushels for 12 yards, while in Britain the ratio would be 8 yards for 12 bushels. The implications of this may be illustrated in diagrammatic form. In Figure 8.1, the British offer curve

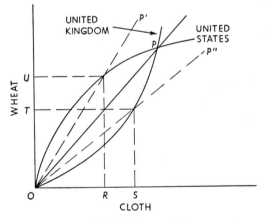

FIG. 8.1. General Equilibrium with Transport Costs

of cloth for wheat and the American offer curve of wheat against cloth cross at point P. But with transport costs, the price ratios in the two countries must differ, so that the line from O through P cannot be taken as the price in both countries. The effect of transport costs of both goods is represented by the angle formed by $O-P'$, the price in the United States, and $O-P''$, the price in Britain.

But these prices cannot solve the problem. At $O-P'$, the United States is willing to offer $O-U$ of wheat against $O-R$ of cloth. At P'', the United Kingdom is willing to offer $O-S$ of cloth for $O-T$ of wheat. Prices cannot differ and solve the equation of trade.

The difficulty, of course, lies in the fact that when transport costs are introduced, we really move to a three-commodity diagram, in which Britain offers cloth for wheat and transport and the United States offers wheat for cloth and transport. The difference between what the United States gets at the price $O-P'$ and what Britain is willing to offer in terms of cloth at the price prevailing in her country takes the form of transport. The offer-curve analysis can be used to illustrate propositions involving transport costs only when these costs are expressed in terms of the traded goods themselves. Examples of this sort can be made up: Transport costs of oil and coal can be expressed in terms of the proportion of the delivered commodity used up in transit—immediately after World War II Silesian coal was sold by Poland in France even though the train journey and return required burning up one third of the original trainload of fuel. Or one can hypothesize commodities like ice which arrive smaller than they start. In these cases, using the general equilibrium apparatus of offer curves or production-possibilities and indifference curves, transport costs will require the price lines in the two countries to differ in slope by an amount representing transport costs in terms of the two commodities.

We can show the effects of transport costs somewhat more readily, however, if we fall back on partial-equilibrium analysis. This shows the position before and after trade in one commodity only. The partial-equilibrium analysis, though incomplete, is useful for a variety of purposes. In particular, we shall find it invaluable in the analysis of exchange adjustments and tariffs later in Chapters 9 and 12. The analysis is partial because it suggests the impact of trade on the demand and supply of a single commodity, expressed in terms of money, without taking into account the repercussions on these demand and supply curves of changes in income, exchange rates, prices of other goods, or anything else, which may be affected. A demand curve can be drawn only with a knowledge of all other demand curves in the system, and it is valid only so long as all other demand curves in the system are presumed to be fixed. The Marshall-Edgeworth offer-curve analysis, as well as production-possibilities and indifference curves, all get away from considerations of money and income and represent a long-run equilibrium position. The partial-equilibrium analysis, on the other hand, deals only with the immediate position after trade is begun and abstracts from secondary effects, repercussions, and adjustments.

Transport Costs in Partial Equilibrium

Figures 8.2a and 8.2b give the demand and supply of cloth in the United Kingdom and in the United States before trade. Both demand and supply represent quantities of cloth sought and available, respec-

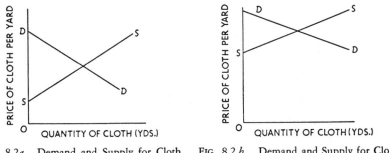

FIG. 8.2a. Demand and Supply for Cloth in the United Kingdom

FIG. 8.2.b. Demand and Supply for Cloth in the United States

tively, against a given price per yard. The price in the United States has been converted by means of the existing exchange rate to the English unit of account, or perhaps it is the other way; it does not matter. The price of cloth in the United States is much higher, in the absence of trade, than the price in Britain.

To indicate what will happen after trade is opened, it is necessary to get both figures on the same diagram. This can be done in either of two ways. It would be possible to construct a new curve from the quantities demanded in the United States and United Kingdom at various prices by simply adding the two demands at each price and drawing a single new curve. The same could be done for supply. The intersection of the two new curves would be the new price, after trade is begun, in the absence of transport costs (and, to issue the warning for the last time, as an initial response). This is done in Figure 8.3.

The other method is portrayed in Figure 8.4. Here the four curves are put on the same diagram with the same vertical axis. The horizontal axis, however, runs in two directions from the origin. For the United States it runs in normal fashion from left to right, and for Britain it starts from the same point as for the United States but goes from right to left. The United States demand and supply curves are exactly as in Figure 8.2b. The British curves, however, are now inverted. The demand curve is negatively sloped in proper manner, if one reads it from right to left. If one is not careful, however, it appears to be positively sloped, like a supply curve. The supply curve, on the other hand, now looks something like a demand curve, though in the latter incarnation it would have no vertical axis from which to start.

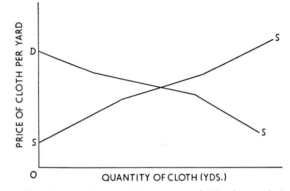

FIG. 8.3. Demand and Supply for Cloth in the United Kingdom and the United States

The new price after trade in the absence of transport costs is calculated by the horizontal price line common to both curves which will balance the excess of supply in the one country with the excess of demand in the other. In Figure 8.4 the price line *a–d* settles at that level

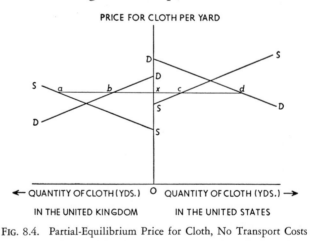

FIG. 8.4. Partial-Equilibrium Price for Cloth, No Transport Costs

where *a–b*, the excess of supply in Britain, is equal to *c–d*, the excess of demand in the United States. Of course, *a–b* then represents exports and *c–d* imports. In Britain home production amounts to *a–x*, while home consumption is only *b–x*. In the United States, on the other hand, only those producers within the range *x–c* are efficient enough to compete with imports. The rest of consumption is satisfied by imports.

The partial-equilibrium diagram is useful in showing how exports raise the price of a commodity above what would have been the case without trade and how imports lower the price. This is a truth worth emphasizing. When we put aside the fancy apparatus of production-possibilities and indifference curves, there is a tendency to remember merely that a good must be cheap before it can be exported from a country. This is true. But exports raise the price of the goods in which the country has a comparative advantage, as the partial-equilibrium analysis shows. The United States exports wheat because it is cheap; wheat is less cheap in the United States than it would be without exports. The selection of the example of wheat underlines an important assumption which the student should note: that of decreasing returns. With increasing returns or decreasing costs, of course, exports cheapen commodities.

Thus far the partial-equilibrium analysis has been like that of general equilibrium—in the absence of transport costs. But transport costs can readily be included. Prices in the importing country will be higher than in the exporting country by a determinate amount: by the unit costs of transport. The solution is the same as that in Figure 8.4, except that the price line must now be broken at the vertical axis and continued at a higher level. The equilibrium price is that which equalizes exports and imports and is higher in the United States than in Britain by the costs of transport. This is shown in Figure 8.5, where *a–b* equals *c–d,* and *w–t* represents the costs of transport.

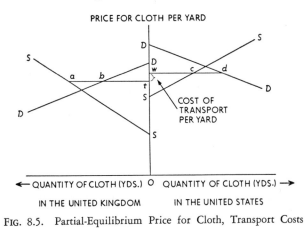

PRICE FOR CLOTH PER YARD

COST OF TRANSPORT PER YARD

←— QUANTITY OF CLOTH (YDS.)   O   QUANTITY OF CLOTH (YDS.) —→

IN THE UNITED KINGDOM   IN THE UNITED STATES

FIG. 8.5. Partial-Equilibrium Price for Cloth, Transport Costs

Costs of transport, the diagram shows, reduce trade below what it would otherwise be. No matter how frequently the theorist may abstract from them in his exercises, their existence means that prices in the exporting country are below what they would otherwise have been and that prices in the importing country are higher.

The notion of transport costs may be broadened to include all costs of transfer, mainly freight, but also insurance, handling, freight-forwarders' commissions, etc., and even tariffs. In the rest of the book we shall frequently mean transfer costs instead of transport costs, although transport is typically the most significant of these transfer costs and is always the inescapable one.

The Impact of Transport Costs

The existence of transport costs affects the theory of international trade in two ways. In the first place, it requires us to modify the answer given to the question of what goods are exported and imported. Price differences in two countries before trade must be wider than costs of transfer. In Figure 8.6, for example, transport costs, $w-t$, are wider

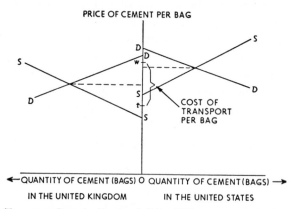

FIG. 8.6. Transport Costs in Excess of Price Differences in Partial Equilibrium

than the difference in price between the United States and Britain. The result is that international trade will not take place in this commodity, no matter what the factor endowments of the countries concerned or the factor requirements for its production. If transport costs did not exist, which means that all goods and services would be transportable in costless fashion, international trade would take place in every good and service. The existence of home goods has its origin in transport costs.

Some international trade then can be based primarily on transport costs and have nothing to do with factor proportions. This is particularly true of local trade which takes place across a long international boundary. With the reduction of trade barriers under the Schuman plan,

Germany now exports steel to France in the north and imports steel from France in the south. This economizes transport. Or, to take another example, Germany exports coal by rail and canal from the Ruhr but imports coal into Hamburg and Bremen because of the transport costs involved in internal shipments.

But transport costs do more than serve as a cause of some trade and a barrier to other. With the fact that processing involves changes in weight and bulk, a knowledge of transport costs can be developed into a generalized theory of the location of industry, whether internationally or between regions, to form the link between industrial economics and industrial engineering. Location theory is a new and growing branch of economics. Classical trade theory tended to think of each region as a point, and all regions so close to one another that transfer could take place in costless fashion. To the location economist, distance is either a cost to be met or an input, practically equivalent to a factor of production, along with land, labor, and capital. In this latter connection, of course, the input is distance with a negative sign—or rather nearness. Nearness to the market, like productive land, makes it possible to produce a commodity for sale more cheaply. Without nearness or productive land, there is a cost to be overcome.

The theory of location of industry has validity even though the principles of location have not always been understood explicitly and followed by business entrepreneurs. Location analyses are now being made by industrial engineers in accordance with these principles. But industry follows locational principles in Darwinian or evolutionary fashion. Industry which has been well located has survived and flourished. Industry which has been badly located has tended to die through perennially low profits and business failure.

Not all evolutionary location is due to transport costs, of course. A good deal of industrial location is related to economies external to the firm—particularly in the form of a supply of trained labor—which have their origin in accidental or random occurrences and grow by agglomeration. Fichtel and Sachs, a bicycle firm, happened to locate their plant in Schweinfurt and to prosper. Various workmen split off and formed separate competing firms, staying close by in the hope of attracting other trained workers. The old firm and the new trained more workers. The result of several generations of this kind of growth was the development of the ballbearing capital of the world. The location of the clock industry in Meriden, Waterbury, Derby, and Ansonia—a cluster of towns outside New Haven in Connecticut—is also due to accidental growth of this kind. With decreasing costs, an industry may evolve in a given location through an initial success, with the choice of location based on mere chance.

The Rationale of Transport Costs

It would be simple enough to take transport costs into account in the real world if they were proportional to weight and distance. But weight is by no means the only criterion relating to the goods shipped. Weight, bulk, and value are not all positively correlated. When a commodity is relatively valuable, it can bear a higher proportional charge to its weight than when it is relatively cheap. Orchids cost more to ship per pound than sand. This is a reflection of the fact that the market for transport services is not perfectly competitive as between different commodities. Transportation services have a large element of overhead cost in them which may be unequally assigned to different products carried. For cheap, bulky commodities, where transport costs are very large in relation to total value, on the other hand, the proportion of overhead charged must be kept low in order to make it possible to move the goods at all.

But there are many other aspects of transportation rates which indicate the imperfectly competitive nature of the market. Goods must move by fixed routes, and two different routes of different distance between the same points generally charge the same rate. So-called "back-haul" rates, or cheap rates given for cargoes on ships which would otherwise be returning in ballast to pick up a new cargo, are another indication of the same general phenomenon. The overhead costs are assigned mainly to the outward journey, and the back-haul rate can be kept cheaper because only direct costs must be met and any return in excess of these is clear profit. Examples of back-haul rates are to be found in the rate on coal from the lower lakes to Duluth, which is far cheaper per ton than the rate on iron ore from the head of the lakes to, say, Cleveland. Conversely, in export trade, the rate on coal from Hampton Roads to Norway is $12.00 a ton, while the back-haul rate on iron ore from Narvik to Sparrow's Point in Baltimore is $4.50.

Not only do rates differ per commodity, depending upon its value or the direction of movement. The ratio of overhead to total costs will also vary, depending upon the form of transport. Once a commodity is loaded upon a barge, for example, it makes little difference whether it is hauled ten or five hundred miles. The overhead element is less significant in railroads, but still important. In trucking, it is of almost no importance, but direct operating costs are high. The result is that truck rates are cheap for short hauls but become increasingly expensive as the distance is increased. Figure 8.7 shows the cost per 100 pounds for carload lots of commodities by railroad, barge, and truck in 1939 and 1940, to illustrate the point.

Implicit in the data in Figure 8.7 is the high cost of handling, as contrasted with simple haulage. This is seen especially when the fixed path by which goods must move causes their transshipment from one type of transport to another. In a few cases, transport by two types of

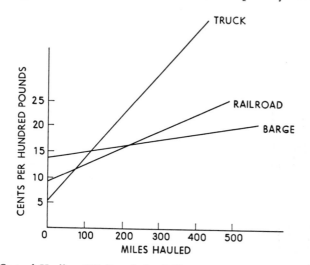

FIG. 8.7. Cost of Hauling 100 Pounds by Different Carriers for Different Distances (Adapted from E. M. Hoover, *The Location of Economic Activity* [New York: McGraw-Hill Book Co., Inc., 1948], p. 21.)

carriers is competitive with the use of a more expensive carrier for the entire journey. Part of the freight moving from Chicago to New York for export comes by rail the whole way, and part by barge to Buffalo and train (or by Erie Canal boat) thereafter. Frequently, however, transshipment from one means of transport to another involves such cost of handling that processing is undertaken at those places where transshipment is required.

Supply-Oriented Commodities

In terms of location theory, all commodities fall into one of three categories. They may be supply-oriented, market-oriented, or foot-loose.

Supply-oriented commodities are those in which the industrial processes tend to be located near the source of the major materials or fuel. These commodities are, for the most part, weight-losing or weight-saving in the course of processing or manufacture; or they may be products with heavy fuel consumption at a stage where the weight of the fuel (or its unique character) is important relative to the weight of the product; or they may be, particularly in agriculture, commodities which require preservation, grading, or standardization.

These industries or industrial processes will be located near the supply of the material or fuel in order to reduce procurement costs, which would otherwise include a large element for the transport of the materials. It is evidently sensible to concentrate ores near the mine, if the power or fuel can be found, in order to save on the bulk transport of waste material. It may, on the other hand, be necessary to move bauxite from Dutch Guiana to the Saguenay River in Canada, despite its bulk of unusable material, because the electric power necessary for the reduction of bauxite to alumina is unavailable in Dutch Guiana. (Atomic power may change this, and relocate all processes now strongly rooted to electric power.)

Cane crushing, the extraction of sugar from beets, the canning and freezing of vegetables and fish, and the grading of fruit are all supply-oriented industries. Frequently an industry will have a historic supply orientation which is no longer valid but will continue to remain where it is, more or less. Thus the textile industry in New England was originally attracted to water-power sites on the Merrimac, Taunton, and Blackstone rivers; the paper mills on the Connecticut River were originally constructed near a supply of pulp, long since cut over.

The iron and steel industry abundantly illustrates the intricacies of supply and fuel orientation. When charcoal was used to produce cast iron, the industry was located at the iron mines—in the Catskills, Berkshires, Adirondacks—where wood for fuel was abundant. With conversion to coal, the industry became coal-oriented, particularly as 17 tons of coal were originally required for 1 ton of iron ore. Improvements in technology and the substitution of scrap for iron ore gradually reduced these proportions, but only after the industry in the United States had a historic orientation in the Pittsburgh, Cleveland, and Gary areas. With the prospect of higher prices for Mesabi iron ore in the middle of the twentieth century, however, and imports of ore from Latin America and Labrador, mills are moving toward the East Coast. In part, this is supply orientation toward iron ore and recovery scrap. In part, it is market orientation, which was important for certain steel products like shipplate, but which now becomes stronger throughout the industry. Changes in technology produce changes in location pulls in industry and in international trade.

The completion of the St. Lawrence Seaway, scheduled for 1958, is expected to reverse some part of this movement to the East Coast by making Great Lake locations accessible to imported iron ore. All great innovations in transport—new means of locomotion such as the canal, steamship, railroad, pipeline, etc.—or enormous capital undertakings which shortened routes, such as the Suez and Panama Canals and prospectively the Seaway, have had wide repercussions on the size and character of international (and domestic) trade. Every reduction in transport costs thus brought about joins markets, opens trade opportunities, and connects to consuming centers hitherto inaccessible resources. Isard has expressed the view that of all innovations in economic life, those in transport have the most far-reaching consequences in stimulating economic growth.

This observation can be supported negatively by reference to the sensitivity of western Europe to the closing of the Suez Canal in 1956.

Market Orientation

Some commodities like bread have to be produced near the market because of their perishable nature (frozen bread, however, may eliminate the local bakery in the way that the automobile has led to the virtual demise of the corner grocery store). The product need not be perishable in physical terms. Other industries which are primarily service are pulled to the market where the service has to be rendered: gasoline stations, television repairs, plumbers, handymen.

Perhaps more significant for international trade is the fact that processes which add weight or bulk to the product are likely to be attracted to the market in order to minimize transport costs. Soft-drink bottling is a good example. The extract may be manufactured in a single location, but the process of dilution and bottling adds so much weight and bulk that it must take place as close as possible to the point of consumption. The point may be made more generally in terms of assembled and packaged products. Assembly adds bulk. Automobile fenders, chassis, and frames pack more neatly in knocked-down form and ship more readily than the equivalent number of finished automobiles. Accordingly, there is a strong pull of the assembly plant to the market, though parts manufacture may remain concentrated. And the same principle applies in all assembly operations, whether of radios, electrical equipment, tire making, bookbinding, or wine bottling.

In some lines of activity where the buyer is concerned to compare values and service, the market area attracts the bulk of the suppliers. This has been called the "coalescence of market areas." It is represented in a city by the department store, theater, garment, financial, and similar districts. A new firm starting an insurance business will be unlikely to seek a new location in New York City but will rather try to find office space in the Williams Street–Maiden Lane area, where other insurance firms and the insurance brokers swarm. In international trade, the same effect is obtained by insurance centers like New York, London, Munich (pre–World War II), and Zurich; style centers like Paris, New York, Vienna, and recently Hollywood; the fur market of Leipzig, etc. Coalescence of market areas is a phenomenon which occurs most frequently in service industries, where taste is likely to change.

In general, the early stages of production are likely to be supply-oriented and the later stages pulled to the market. To locate an industry at the early stages minimizes the costs of producing the article by keeping down the cost of transport of materials. At the same time, the establishment of an industry at the market will reduce costs of distribution of the product to the ultimate consumer. The transfer costs in procurement and distribution may be added, as in Figure 8.8, for dif-

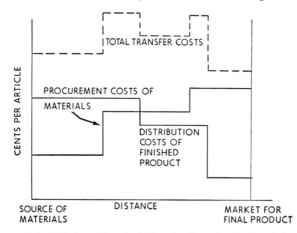

FIG. 8.8. Determining Minimum Level of Transfer Costs for Various Industrial Locations (Adapted from E. M. Hoover, *The Location of Economic Activity* [New York: McGraw-Hill Book Co., Inc., 1948], p. 31.)

ferent locations for an industry. The lowest point for the two types of costs will constitute the best location.

As the location of industry is moved from the source of material supply to the market, neither transfer costs of procurement nor those of distribution move in continuous fashion. Discontinuities occur for a variety of reasons but especially because of costs of handling due to the necessity for transshipment. Where transshipment is required both of materials on their way to processing and of finished products en route to market, there are likely to be sharp discontinuities in both curves, and a probable nodal point which will attract location. This is particularly true of ports, where a sea journey is transformed into a land journey. Ports as nodal points frequently attract supply-oriented industries dependent on imported materials and market-oriented industries which produce for export. Refining processes, whether of metals, oil, or sugar, are typically located at ports. Hamburg, Marseilles, and Southhampton all make soap and refine petroleum. Ports also attract automobile-assembly plants, whether in the export trade, like the Ford plant at Edgewater, or in imports, like the General Motors plant in Antwerp.

Where transport is performed on a single type of carrier, the economies of the long haul mean that processing is likely to be located at one end or the other, but not in between.

Foot-loose Industries

A number of industries have no strong locational pull either to supply or to market. The reason may be that costs of transfer are relatively unimportant; or the changes of weight and volume in the course of processing may be small. In these cases, following the proposition just enunciated, location is likely to be at either end of the transport chain, but not in between.

The textile industry has historically been loose-footed. Originally, cotton and woolen textiles had locational advantages either side of the Pennines in northern Britain. Cotton manufacture was concentrated in Lancashire, and especially in the city of Manchester, because of the moisture on the western side of the mountains which prevented cotton thread from breaking. Another locational attraction was the port of Liverpool, at which cotton was unloaded from the United States. Woolens, on the other hand, were mildly attracted to the supply of wool east of the Pennines and the Yorkshire coal fields which furnished fuel. But none of these forces was strong. An industry in which cotton can be bought in Syria for manufacture in Japan and the cloth resold in the Middle East is evidently one in which transfer costs are unimportant. The same verdict applies to the woolen industry, where produce from Australia and New Zealand, manufactured in Leeds and Bradford, is reexported to the Antipodes.

The refining of crude petroleum into various fractions involves little change in volume or weight. Accordingly, the question of whether a refinery is installed at tidewater near the wells or at the market depends on other considerations. Historically, some oil refineries have been located in Texas and some at the market, as in Bayonne and Edgewater, New Jersey, or Marcus Hook on the Delaware River in Pennsylvania. Europe used to import refined products from the Gulf, the Caribbean, and the Middle East. Since World War II, however, refining operations have tended more and more to concentrate in Europe. In part this has been the result of commercial policy and a response to fears of expropriation. In part, however, it has followed from the fact that European consumption of petroleum products ceased to be concentrated strongly in the light fractions, especially gasoline. It made sense, in the interwar period, to refine Venezuelan crude oil in the West Indies and to export gasoline to Europe and residual fuel oil to the United States. Now that Europe consumes a more balanced set of products—tending in fact to need a higher proportion of fuel oil to gasoline now than the United States—it is wasteful of transport to separate the products at a great distance from the market.

Since transfer costs are relatively unimportant in foot-loose industries, processing costs count for more. It is in these industries—textiles, matches, oil refining, etc.—that the theory of comparative costs in its undiluted form operates to determine what a country exports and imports in the absence of direct intervention by the state in the form of tariff policy. By the same token, as we shall see, it is in these foot-loose industries that commercial policy can be most effective in distorting the operation of the law of comparative cost. Tariffs can readily be used to attract a market-oriented industry to a market, or a loose-footed industry; they can do little with supply-oriented industry.

Location Economics

This short chapter, intended to make some amends for the unreality of international-trade discussion in abstracting from transport costs, should not be taken as a full-fledged introduction to location economics, to which it does much less than justice. This rapidly growing field requires detailed study of its own, and mastery of many more techniques than can be suggested in these pages.

Summary

The pure theory of trade has abstracted from a vital fact of life—the existence of transport costs. When this is reintroduced into the subject, it no longer follows that the price ratios between export and import goods are the same in the exporting and importing countries. Export goods must be lower in price to overcome transport costs; import goods higher. If transport costs are wider than price differentials in the absence of trade, trade cannot take place. This explains why many goods and services do not move in international trade.

The impact of transport costs can be illustrated with offer curves or in partial equilibrium.

Transport costs are not regular but vary according to the weight, bulk, value, perishability of the article, method of transport, and distance. Transport has to follow certain routes, and goods require handling in transport if the mode of travel changes. These characteristics make for complexity.

Three broad types of effects on the location of industry can be detected, emanating from transport costs. Supply-oriented industries are those in which weight and bulk of fuel or material are large in relation to value, and production involves weight-losing processes. These are generally the early stages of manufacture. The later stages of manufacture tend to be market-oriented, because assembly builds up bulk without adding weight. Goods which are valuable in relation to weight or in which weight and bulk do not change in process are likely to be loose-footed. Transport costs do less to determine their location than do the processing costs discussed in the theory of international trade.

SUGGESTED READING

TREATISES, ETC.

The classical work in international economics incorporating transport costs is Ohlin, especially Part III. From the side of location, reference may be made to three studies, and the literature discussed in them. August Lösch (translated by William Woglom with the assistance of Wolfgang Stolper), *The Economics of Location* (New Haven: Yale University Press, 1954), is a pioneering attempt to produce a general-equilibrium theory of economic location. It is uneven, brilliant in some passages and difficult in others. Walter Isard's *Location and Space-Economy* (New York: The Technology Press and John Wiley & Sons, Inc., 1956), provides the latest and most far-reaching statement of the state of the art. E. M. Hoover's, *The Location of Economic Activity* (New York: McGraw-Hill Book Co., Inc., 1948), constitutes the source of most of the diagrams in this chapter.

Chapter | THE PRICE MECHANISM
9 | IN INTERNATIONAL TRADE

The Classical Assumptions

After this investigation of the basis for trade, it is time to turn to the third question raised by the classical economists and discuss how adjustments take place to disturbances in the international economy. We start in this chapter with the classical position, in which price is all important. In the next we examine the income mechanism. The discussion concludes, in Chapter 11, with the little we can say about the adjustment mechanism when both income and price operate simultaneously.

The analysis evidently starts along partial-equilibrium lines. We discuss the price mechanism as if income were constant; and then we deal with changes in income as if prices were constant. This approach is pedagogically instructive, but it runs the danger of misleading the student who mistakes the analysis for a description of reality.

The classical economists devoted most of their attention to the price mechanism, largely ignoring changes in income, because of an underlying assumption of full employment. This assumption, which had its origin in Say's law of markets, that supply creates its own demand, was one of three classical assumptions which underlay the classical view of the efficacy of the price mechanism in international economic adjustment. The second is that there is a considerable amount of competition in markets, so that demand curves are elastic; the third is that within separate countries resources are highly mobile. In combination with further simplifying hypotheses, this assumption about mobility leads to the view that supply curves are relatively elastic. With full employment guaranteed, demand and supply elastic, the price system is ready to bring about international adjustment without difficulty.

Discussion of the full-employment assumption is reserved for later.

148

In this chapter, we must face the critical question of how elastic demand and supply in international trade really are.

Perfect Competition

Graham has said that it is wrong to think of a national demand curve and a national supply curve at all. In his view a household is a household and contributes to demand; a firm is a firm and contributes to supply—both regardless of nationality. Only the aggregate of the demands of all households in all countries has validity for demand; and the same for the supply curves of separate firms. It is not appropriate to add demand and supply by countries.

The point is not simply a verbal one. The student will recall that the demand curve for the product of the firm is sloped differently under competitive conditions from that for the industry. If there are in the industry many firms which compete with one another, the demand for the output of any one firm is perfectly elastic. At the going price, the firm can sell all it can produce profitably. It can sell nothing at a higher price. It is under no incentive to lower its price, because it already has an infinitely elastic demand at the going price. While the demand schedule for the industry may be negatively sloped, it is assumed that if any one firm sells more, either the increment is negligible or some one or more other firms will sell less.

For the industry as a whole, however, the effects of competition among the separate firms must be disregarded. The product of the industry will have a demand which is elastic or inelastic with respect to price, depending upon its character as a necessity, like wheat (inelastic), or luxury, like tourist travel (elastic), and upon the extent to which other products, partial or complete substitutes, are available and competitive in price.

If we cannot properly aggregate the demand curves for the firms in a single country into a national demand curve, then demand is necessarily fairly elastic, both for any one firm and for any group of firms which happen to belong to a single nation. In either case, demand is more elastic on a world than on a national basis because the number of firms is increased and hence the chances for substitution among single firms and groups of firms.

But it is not enough merely to assert that one cannot consider the national demand curve or the demand for a single commodity by a single country. One must demonstrate that the device is not legitimate. And the weight of the argument runs strongly in the opposite direction. Transportation costs which separate national (and regional) markets make it necessary to consider the national demand for some goods and services which do not move in international trade, either at all or at some level or range of customary prices (though they might be imported at much higher prices or exported at much lower). But transportation costs also make it necessary to consider the national demand for goods which are internationally traded.

Suppose the freight rate for wheat from Chicago to Liverpool is increased for any reason. This may change the price of wheat in Liverpool but not in Chicago. The effect on the British demand can be isolated. Transport costs require consideration of national demand curves.

A change in the relations between national markets, however, can be brought about through governmental intervention, as well as through a change in transport costs. A new tariff or exchange rate or the imposition of a quota or any other type of national action underlines the need for the concept of national demand and national supply.

If we move from world demand and supply for a commodity to national demand and supply, we necessarily acquire more inelasticity. This means that we depart further from the classical assumptions.

Inelasticity of Demand

The significance of these notions for demand is to be found in the realm of monopolistic competition. Much will depend on how inelastic the demand is between the limits of perfectly elastic (i.e., horizontal) and perfectly inelastic (completely vertical).[1] We shall come to this in a moment. If there is any negative slope to the demand curve, however, it means that there are some demanders who would be willing to pay more than others. In these circumstances, control over output, division of markets between nations, or other monopolistic manipulation or discrimination may earn a higher return for the monopolistic seller. Given perfect competition, on the other hand, or a completely elastic demand curve, each country as well as each firm can sell all it can at the existing price, and nothing at a higher price.

---

[1] We shall disregard goods subject to Giffen's paradox and, in the next chapter, inferior goods. In both cases demand is perverse. In Giffen's paradox, demand is positively sloped, i.e., it increases as price goes up and decreases as price declines. This is a comparatively common phenomenon in retail trade: viz., the lipstick which cannot be sold at 25 cents but which moves briskly at $1.00. We assume that it is rare in international trade. An inferior good is related to changes in income rather than price and is one in which consumption decreases as income increases. This is a more frequent phenomenon in international trade. The common example is potatoes in Ireland. When income increases, the Irish eat fewer potatoes and more bread. Rye grain for bread also elicited this response in Germany before World War I. In India in the early 1950's, imports as a whole were an inferior good: increases in income occurred through an increase in harvest yields which made it possible to reduce food imports from abroad.

With a perfectly elastic demand, a shift to the right in the supply schedule will lead to an increase in gross revenue, because it expands output at a constant price. With a perfectly inelastic demand which runs straight up and down, a shift of the supply curve to the right will lead to a reduction in gross revenue, since the same quantity will be sold at a lower price. Between these extremes, there is what we call unitary elasticity of demand, in which gross revenue remains unchanged, whether price is raised or lowered. At this point, the percentage change in price results in an equal percentage change in

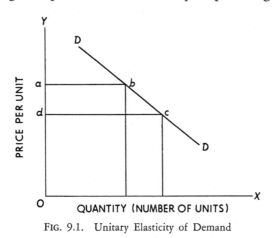

FIG. 9.1. Unitary Elasticity of Demand

quantity in the opposite direction, so that total revenue is unchanged. This is illustrated in Figure 9.1 between *b* and *c*. In algebraic terms, the elasticity may be expressed as

$$\frac{dQ/Q}{dP/P},$$

where *d* stands for change in the term it modifies. If the price elasticity of demand is greater than one, up to and including the case of perfectly elastic demand, where it is infinity, the quantity change will be greater than the price change; and total revenue will increase with price reductions and decline with price increases. If the elasticity is less than one, on the other hand, a reduction in price leads to a reduction in revenue, and an increase to an increase, since quantity changes less than price.

It makes a considerable difference, then, not only whether the demand curve is less than perfectly elastic but also whether its elasticity is less than unity. Another critical relationship, as we shall see later in the chapter, is whether the sum of the elasticities of demand, by a country for its imports and by the rest of the world for that country's exports, is greater than one.

Measurement of Elasticities

This discussion of the numerical coefficients of the elasticity of demand must be taken with a grain of salt. In the first place, there is considerable dispute among economists as to whether it is, in fact, possible to measure the elasticity of demand by one or more statistical devices in ways that are meaningful. In the second place, the elasticity of demand is likely to change over time and over various ranges of price. In this discussion it is frequently important to keep clear the distinction between "point elasticity," which is the elasticity of the demand curve at a given point, i.e., the relationship between the change in quantity and the change in price for infinitely small or very small changes in price, and the "arc elasticity" or elasticity of demand for a finite (and generally substantial) change in quantity and price. The point elasticity at a given point on the demand curve is constant, but the arc elasticity will differ for differing changes in price all of which start from the same point.

The only basis for measuring the elasticity of demand of a country is the historical record of the quantities of goods it has consumed at various prices. But a demand curve, as we have already had occasion to mention, is drawn on the assumption of other things being equal—and this, in recorded history, other things are notoriously not. A number of econometricians have nonetheless attempted to measure the elasticity of demand and have emerged with various results. By and large, these studies show low price elasticities not only on such articles of habitual consumption as coffee and tea but for almost everything else. Other statisticians, however, have challenged the methods as likely to include downward bias. It is possible to hazard the judgment that the price elasticity of demand is higher for automobiles than for wheat, and lower for work clothes than for fur coats. One can go further and adduce evidence in support of these propositions. But it is still something else to give an exact measurement for the elasticity of a country's demand for imported goods, or of the foreign demand for its goods, as the theory requires.

Elasticity and the Degree of Price Change

Further, any coefficient derived would have validity only for the range of observations studied. Look back at Figure 9.1. If the demand curve is a straight line, its elasticity will change as it approaches one co-ordinate or the other. Below point c the percentage change in price becomes large and that in quantity small as one approaches the X co-ordinate. The price elasticity of demand is declining. Above b, the percentage change in quantity becomes large and that in price small, as one approaches the Y co-ordinate. The elasticity of demand becomes larger. With a constant elasticity, such as unity, the demand curve must become nearly vertical close to the Y axis and nearly horizontal at the X axis. There is no reason to think that demand curves, if it were possible to determine them by some mass questionnaire technique, would conform rigorously to the one or the other of these patterns. It is probable that demand elasticity changes from one range of prices to another and differs between small changes in price and large. The elasticity of demand is likely to be greater for wide changes in price than for narrow, as consumers have an important inducement to overcome their inertia and the cost of shifting to substitutes.

Just where these changes will occur is of some interest, practically. The British government has progressively raised the tax on tobacco from 1938, in an effort to raise revenue to finance the war, until it amounted to 35s. 6d. per pound in 1947, and a package of twenty cigarettes cost 2s. 4d. (48 cents at the existing exchange rate of $4.00 per pound sterling). Over this range, the demand seems to have been inelastic, since expenditure on tobacco rose from £177 million in 1938 to £603 million, and consumption from 190 million pounds to 250 million pounds between 1938 and 1946. In 1947, however, the Labor government increased the duty by another 50 per cent to 54s. 10d. per pound, which raised the price of cigarettes to 3s. 4d., or 68 cents per package of twenty. Here the purpose was not to raise revenue but to decrease consumption in order to save dollars spent for Virginia tobacco. As it happened, however, some, but not many, people cut down or gave up. In 1947, total consumption fell by only 10 per cent from 250 million pounds to 225 million. Finally, in 1952, it was necessary to cut down expenditures for dollar tobacco with a quota.

Elasticities and Time

Finally, the short-term elasticity of demand is undoubtedly different from that in the long run—just as the short-run supply curve and the long-period curve differ. In the long run, demand curves are more elastic than in the short. A small price reduction may be insufficient at first to induce much change in consumption; over the longer period, as this differential persists, the advantages of changing from the slightly more expensive commodity to the slightly less become more compelling. This is true at least of partial elasticities, which assume that other things are equal. Whether it is equally true of complete elasticities, which measure the response of the quantity consumed to changes in price after all changes have occurred in substitution, shifts of resources, changes in wages, other prices, monetary and fiscal policy, cannot be predicted with any confidence.

Changing Elasticities

It is likely that the elasticity of demand for goods entering into international trade has been changing over the last hundred and fifty years—first increasing and then perhaps declining. A number of factors have brought about these changes. Foremost among them have been increased international specialization; the growing standardization of internationally traded goods up to World War I, and the growing product differentiation which has taken place since then.

The price elasticity of national demand evidently depends upon the number of countries which buy and sell on the world market and the relative size of each, as well as the character of the commodity. Coffee, for example, has over-all an inelastic demand. And the demand facing the Brazilian supply, which makes up some 55 per cent of the world's output, is also inelastic. But the demand for Costa Rican output (1 per cent) or Guatemalan ($3\frac{1}{2}$ per cent) is highly elastic, since an increase in their output will have an insignificant effect on consumption. And Colombia, at 18 per cent, falls in between.

Those countries which supply a considerable portion of the world's export—India in tea (49 per cent), Australia in wool (43 per cent), Cuba in sugar (49 per cent), the Philippines in copra (54 per cent), Malaya in tin and rubber (58 and 47 per cent, respectively), etc., face a demand curve as, or almost as, inelastic as the demand for the commodity as a whole, since national substitution cannot take place without repercussions.

Up to World War I, or perhaps only to 1900, the degree of standardization in international trade was increasing and with it the price elasticity of national demand. Native rubber, which is uneven in quality, was replaced by rubber produced on European-managed estates; the highly individualistic peasant butter in Denmark by the co-operative, trade-marked product; assorted wheat and coffee by the international standards which make it possible to specify Minneapolis Red No. 2 or Santos No. 7, respectively. The importance of standardization is that a buyer knows what he is getting without inspection. Standardization is also vital for manufacturing with mass-production methods, like milling wheat or combing cotton yarn. It is reported that the Shanghai wheat mills, for example, used to buy Canadian export wheat in preference to their domestic supply available from the Shantung peninsula in North China because the latter was not standard in quality and required continuous adjustment in the milling machinery.

The recent rise of international trade in manufactured goods of a differentiated character, however, has probably produced a decline in price elasticity of demand in international trade. Some manufactured goods, like cotton gray goods, are standardized. And standardization in others is increasing as defense departments adopt common specifications for rifles, tanks, airplane designs; as conventions are worked out by international conferences such as that which adopted a common pitch for screw threads in the United States and Britain. But the introduction of new differentiated goods increases. And even where there are practically standardized goods, as in cigarettes, beer, gasoline, and drugs, advertising campaigns by producers will attempt to convince buyers that they are different and increase the inelasticity of demand.

The degree of differentiation of manufactured goods will vary widely. Some goods, like the Ford and the Chevrolet, are close, if not perfect, substitutes for one another. In other cases, such as television sets, where American equipment operates on 60 cycles and European on 50, substitution is possible only by incurring a cost such as the purchase of a converter. A price reduction must be wide enough to cover the cost of the converter before it will induce a buyer in range of a 60-cycle transmitter to purchase a 50-cycle receiving set. Most electrical equipment, such as motors, vacuum cleaners, toasters, refrigerators, etc., operates on 110 volts in the United States and 220 in Europe. In international trade in manufactured goods, the problem faced in phonograph record competition in the United States with $33\frac{1}{3}$-, 45-, and 78-r.p.m. equipment is magnified many times.

The lesser substitutability of differentiated products for one another and the fact that a consumer committed to one has frequently an investment in clinging to it make the elasticity of demand with respect to price less for differentiated goods than for standardized articles. To the extent that international trade today deals more in differentiated commodities than a century ago, the elasticity of demand has declined.

While the elasticities of demand for a country's exports and of its demand for imports have probably declined and are still lower in the short run than in the long, and for small price changes as contrasted with large, economists still do not know what these elasticities are numerically.

Elasticity of Supply

The classical assumption of internal factor mobility, combined with roughly constant factor proportions, led to the notion that for many products the elasticity of supply was large. This is roughly an assumption of constant costs. In the short run, it was recognized that this elasticity might be limited; this was particularly the case in agricultural commodities after the planting season had passed. If surplus products had been held off the market, however, even short-term elasticities were high. With more time to allow for the next season's planting, supply was elastic, as well as demand.

The elasticity of supply today would appear to be a more complex matter. Differences exist between classes of commodities under differing conditions, depending upon the state of employment, the direction of the price change, and the length of time allowed for the response to take place. In manufacturing production, under conditions of less than full employment, supply may be highly elastic with respect to price increases and decreases; when capacity is reached, however, the supply schedule is likely to be kinked, i.e., elastic with respect to price decreases but inelastic, in the short run, for a price rise. Higher profits and wages are required to induce entrepreneurs to expand capacity and workers to shift into the industry from their occupations elsewhere.

In agricultural production it is still true that the elasticity of supply is likely to be low in the short run, except where stocks are held. For some commodities, moreover, where planting of bushes or trees takes place many years—five, ten, fifteen—before a crop is harvested, as in the case of apples, oranges, or cocoa, this elasticity may be low in the relevant period; a supply response to today's price change in either direction will be effective only after entirely new demand conditions have superseded those of today. But in other commodities, there is the phenomenon of too great a response—an overcompensation to the demand and price change. If potatoes are scarce and expensive this year, they may be plentiful and cheap next year, because too large a response of supply takes place. This so-called "cobweb" theorem—named after the pattern of lines connecting successive points on the demand and supply curves as the price first soars and then sinks—is a dynamic phenomenon which cannot be described in the shape of a single supply curve.[2]

[2] For those who have not been introduced to the cobweb theorem or who can remember its name but have forgotten its face, it may be well to append diagrams which show demand in one year and supply in the next (see Figs. 9.2a and 9.2b). At the initial supply, q_1, demand produces a price, p_1. But this price evokes in the following year a new

The cobweb theorem, however, describes the supply response in one farm product which is produced as one of a number of possible alternatives. For farm products as a whole and for mining, the long-run supply curve is generally thought to be inelastic for decreases in price because of the difficulty of shifting people in isolated communities, such

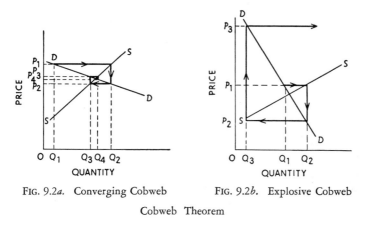

FIG. 9.2a. Converging Cobweb   FIG. 9.2b. Explosive Cobweb

Cobweb Theorem

as farming and mining require, into other occupations. These people must change residence, find new housing, pull up their social roots in a community and put down new ones. This can occur only under conditions of large price change or a drastic change in supply possibilities, such as those of the Oklahoma-Kansas dust bowl. Immobility of resources among occupations produces inelasticities of supply.

In most manufacturing industries there is more supply elasticity than in agriculture and mining. In the first place, there is likely to be some excess plant capacity, if only in the possibility of working overtime or on a third shift. This is not true in continuous-process industries, like chemicals, but has a general validity in the late stages of manufacture. In addition, an industry located in a city may draw upon the floating labor supply of other industries, if it is attempting to expand, or even upon workers in other industries who are already employed. There is little of this mobility in one-industry towns or regions: New Bedford, Lowell, and Lawrence in textiles, or Haverhill and Brockton in shoes. But, for the usual city with a more balanced group of industries, the elasticity of supply of each of them separately is made higher by the possibility of expansion at the expense of one another—only

---

supply, q_2, which leads to a new price, p_2. And so on. Note that if the curves are sloped one way, the oscillations get smaller; if another, they become more violent. In between, of course, the cobweb may consist of a single strand around which rectangles of prices and quantities move, as over a well-worn path.

possible, to be sure, when demand expands for a single industry, or at most two industries, at a time.

The foregoing remarks apply particularly to the response to decreases in price. When price rises, the possibility exists that agricultural supply is more elastic than manufacturing (or minerals). It is largely a question of ease of entry. In some manufacturing products, like cotton textiles, an abundance of world capacity and widespread knowledge of the technology make for ease of entry and elastic supply in the long run. But manufacturing products as a whole seem to be price-elastic in supply when price falls, and relatively inelastic for price increases, which is broadly the reverse of the position in agriculture.

Little or no attempt has been made to measure the elasticity of supply. In part, this has been the result of the more explicit recognition that long- and short-run supply curves were likely to differ in slope.

Interrelations between Demand and Supply

The elasticity of demand for imports is higher than the elasticity of demand for the product as a whole if there is any elasticity to the domestic supply schedule. Similarly, the elasticity of the supply of exports is higher than the elasticity of the supply curve as a whole if there is any domestic consumption of the export product and the domestic demand curve has elasticity greater than zero. These propositions may

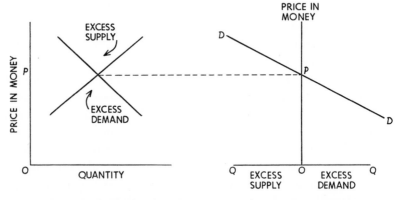

FIG. 9.3*a.* Domestic Demand and Supply in the Importing Country   FIG. 9.3*b.* Excess Demand for the Import Good

best be illustrated by the process of consolidating domestic demand and supply curves into a single curve representing excess demand or excess supply. It is this last excess-demand or excess-supply curve which is the operational schedule in international trade.

Figure 9.3*a* shows an ordinary set of curves representing the domestic demand and supply of a given commodity, say wheat, expressed in terms of money prices. Without international trade, the market would be in equilibrium at the price *P*. At a higher price, supply would exceed demand; at a lower price, demand would exceed supply. These amounts of excess supply and excess demand, derived by subtracting the demand curve from the supply curve at prices above *OP*, and the supply curve from the demand curve at prices below it, can be transferred in a single curve to another diagram, such as Figure 9.3*b*. This is a curve representing excess demand. Above the price *OP*, the excessive demand is negative (or excess supply). Note that the excess-demand curve has greater elasticity than the domestic-demand curve. If domestic production were nonexistent or had zero elasticity, i.e., were a fixed amount, the slopes of the two curves would be identical. If domestic production were infinitely elastic, the excess-demand curve would be infinitely elastic at the same price.

The position in the exporting country is shown in Figure 9.3*c*, and the excess supply, available to the importing country, derived in Figure 9.3*d*. Notice that this is calculated in the currency of the im-

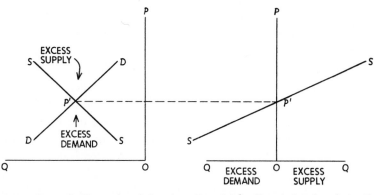

FIG. 9.3*c*. Domestic Demand and Supply in the Exporting Country FIG. 9.3*d*. Excess Supply of the Export Good

porting country. This means that the two curves can be put together on the same diagram and used to indicate the equilibrium of the international market in the single commodity, expressed in the currency of the importing country. This is done in Figure 9.3*e*. This is a simple variation on the partial-equilibrium diagram used in Figure 8.4 in Chapter 8, which, it will be remembered, is also expressed in a single currency.

Exchange Depreciation

We can use this partial-equilibrium diagram, or rather two of them, one for exports and one for imports, to indicate what happens when a foreign-exchange rate is depreciated, and the relevance of the

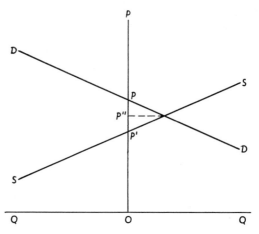

FIG. 9.3e. Partial-Equilibrium Representation of Trade in One Good with Excess-Demand and Excess-Supply Curves

elasticities of demand and supply to the outcome. Let me amend that statement. We need not two such diagrams but four: two for expressing the demand and supply of exports and imports in local currency, and two for translating these curves into foreign exchange. It is important to keep the distinction between the local currency and foreign exchange clear. For expositional purposes here, however, we use both.

Let us first pick a foreign-exchange rate of one, so that our initial, pre-depreciation demand and supply curves are identical in local currency and in foreign exchange. Figures 9.4a and 9.4b set out the curves for exports in the depreciating country, in local currency, and foreign exchange, respectively. If we assume only one export commodity, the horizontal axis measures the volume of that good, or exports as a whole. There is no need to draw any extension of the curves to the left of the vertical axis. Figures 9.4c and 9.4d represent the country's demand and supply for imports, also in local currency and foreign exchange, respectively.

What is the effect of a change in the exchange rate? Let us concentrate only on the local-currency diagrams. The impact of a depreciation, let us say, on exports is to shift upward the demand curve, which is fixed in foreign exchange. Every unit of foreign currency exchanges for more units of local currency, so that depreciation shifts the foreign demand curve upward, appreciation downward. The shift is not a parallel one, since it is a constant percentage. The dotted demand curve in Figure 9.4*a* represents the new demand curve for exports after a depreciation of 20 per cent.

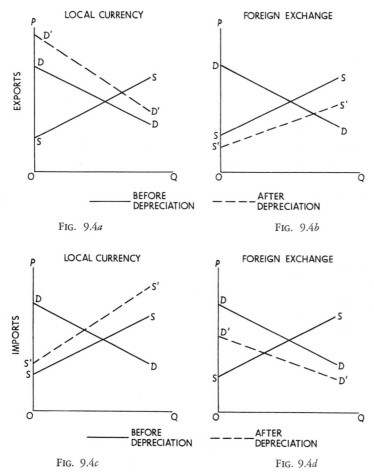

Fig. 9.4*c*   Fig. 9.4*d*

Excess Demand and Excess Supply of Exports and Imports, in Local Currency and in Foreign Exchange, before and after Foreign-Exchange Depreciation

The upward shift of the demand curve for exports, expressed in local currency, raises the local-currency value of exports. The value of exports is of course expressed in price times quantity (*PQ*) and is represented by the area under the intersection of the supply and demand curves. With exchange depreciation, the local-currency value of exports cannot fall. At the worst, if the demand curve is completely inelastic, i.e., straight up and down so that an upward shift could not be seen, the value of exports in local currency would remain unchanged.

Depreciation may, however, expand, reduce, or leave unchanged the local-currency value of imports. Depreciation involves an upward shift in the supply curve, which is fixed in foreign exchange as shown in Figure 9.4c. Whether the value of imports will rise, fall, or remain unchanged depends upon the elasticity of demand for imports. If this elasticity is unity, the value of imports will remain unchanged. If it is less than one, it will increase. If it is greater than one, it will fall.

The Marshall-Lerner Condition

These relationships have led to the development of the Marshall-Lerner condition which states, in effect, that depreciation will improve the balance of payments of a country and appreciation worsen it, if the sum of the elasticities of demand for a country's exports and of its demand for imports is greater than one. Take first the case where the demand for exports is zero. Exports in local currency are now no smaller than before. If the sum of the elasticities is greater than one, this must mean that the elasticity of demand for imports is greater than one, so that the value of imports falls. With no decline in the value of exports and a decline in the value of imports, the balance of payments has improved. At the other extreme, if the demand for imports has zero elasticity, the value of imports will rise in local currency by the full percentage of the depreciation; but if the demand for exports is greater than unity, as it must be if the sum of the elasticities of demand is going to be greater than one, the value of exports will expand by more than the percentage of depreciation and the balance of payments will be improved.

If each elasticity of demand is less than one, but the sum is greater than one, this will improve the balance of payments expressed in local currency because it means that expansion in exports in local currency exceeds the expansion in the value of imports.

These same relationships can also be found in the value of exports and imports worked out in foreign exchange. Here depreciation leaves the demand curve for exports unaffected, as in Figure 9.4b, since this is fixed in foreign exchange, but lowers the supply curve. For imports expressed in foreign exchange, depreciation of the "local currency" (appreciation of the foreign exchange) lowers the demand curve.

The Marshall-Lerner condition continues to operate. Depreciation can lower, leave unchanged, or raise the foreign-exchange value of exports as the foreign demand curve is less than, equal to, or greater than unity. At the limit, where its elasticity is zero, the foreign-exchange value of exports will decline by the full percentage of depreciation. The balance of payments will still be improved, however, if the sum of the elasticities is greater than one, since the demand for imports must now be greater than one. This means that the value of imports will be reduced by more than the percentage of depreciation. Depreciation can leave imports unchanged in foreign exchange or reduce them; it cannot serve to increase them. With zero elasticity of demand for imports, the foreign-exchange value of imports will be unchanged; but if the demand for exports has an elasticity greater than one, the foreign-exchange value of exports will rise and the balance of payments will be improved.

The Marshall-Lerner condition, which is derived algebraically in the appendix to this chapter, is broadly correct if supply elasticities are relatively large and if the balance of payments is in equilibrium to begin with. If the supply elasticities are low, as was the case for example in the supply of Scotch whiskey for export at the time of the British devaluation in 1949, the price will not fall in foreign exchange and the elasticity of the foreign demand curve can be lower and still improve the balance.

The condition that the imbalance of trade must not be large to begin with is grounded in the characteristics of percentages. If the sum of the elasticities is greater than one, the percentage increase in exports will always be greater than the percentage increase in imports, or the percentage decrease in foreign exchange will be smaller. But if imports are very large, relative to exports, the absolute increase in imports may be larger in local currency, or the absolute decrease in imports smaller in foreign exchange. This worsening of the arithmetic ($P_xQ_x - P_mQ_m$) balance of payments is accompanied by an improvement in the geometric balance $\left(\dfrac{P_xQ_x}{P_mQ_m}\right)$.

The Marshall-Lerner condition emphasizes the critical nature of unity for the sum of the elasticities. But for substantial improvement in the balance of payments from exchange depreciation, the sum should clearly be much higher, nearer four, or five, or six. The smaller the elasticities, the larger the price changes needed to effect a given balance-of-payments change. The larger the elasticities, on the other hand, the smaller the price change needed to obtain a given balance-of-payments improvement, or the larger the balance-of-payments effect from a given price change.

If the sum of the elasticities of demand is less than one, then the balance of trade of a country cannot be improved by depreciation. It can, however, be improved by appreciation. Because of the inelasticity of demand for the country's exports abroad, smaller exports will increase the value of exports, whereas increased exports would have lowered it. By the same token, cheaper imports will not greatly increase the volume of imports and will reduce the value. Some economists have used the unwillingness of many countries to try appreciation as a correction for balance-of-payments difficulties as a *reductio ad absurdum* of the position that elasticities are low in the real world. But, if demand and supply were inelastic in the short run and rather more elastic over time, the short-run advantage which could accrue from appreciation would melt away.

Terms of Trade

We are interested not only in the extent of the exchange depreciation needed to effect a given balance of payments adjustment but also the relative impact of adjustments on the prices of exports and imports. This relationship between the prices a country gets for its exports and imports, already referred to in Chapter 6, is the terms of trade. The nearest comparable concept in domestic trade is the notion of farm parity as a base for farm prices. Parity is that relation which prevailed in 1909–14 between the prices which farmers received for their produce and the prices which they were obliged to pay, both for producing those goods and services and for their own consumption. Farm prices today, or any particular agricultural price, may be compared with parity by ascertaining whether it has changed as much and in the same direction as have the prices of those things farmers buy. By the same token, the terms of trade of a country have improved or deteriorated relative to a base period if the price level of exports has increased or decreased, respectively, relative to the prices of imports.

The terms of trade in the Marshall-Edgeworth two-country–two-commodity example is the price line, *O–P*, in Figure 9.5. These terms of trade are neither favorable nor unfavorable, except perhaps in the sense that they are more favorable to both parties than the prices at which they enjoy the two commodities without trade. But a change in the terms of trade may be more or less favorable. A shift of the price line from *O–P* to *O–P'*, as might occur if the United Kingdom experienced a decrease in the demand for wheat, which shifted her offer curve from *O–B* to *O–B'*, would be a favorable shift in the terms of trade. A shift in the other direction, however, would be unfavorable.

It may be observed that the shift in the terms of trade takes place only because of the elasticity of the United States offer curve. If this were a straight line, like *O–C,* instead of *O–A,* the decrease in the British demand for wheat would leave the terms of trade unchanged.

The Marshall-Edgeworth diagram expresses the terms of trade under conditions of general equilibrium. Exports and imports are balanced in both cases. The terms of trade can therefore be expressed either as the price of cloth in terms of the price of wheat or the quantity

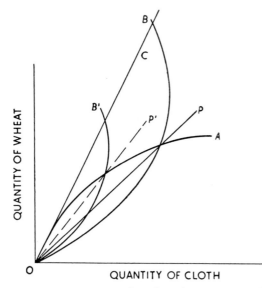

FIG. 9.5. The Terms of Trade under General Equilibrium

of cloth exchanged for a quantity of wheat. But in the real world of more than two commodities and more than two countries, exports and imports are not always balanced. Further, it is not known what prices would be in the absence of trade. Accordingly, it has been found desirable to develop several partial terms-of-trade concepts.

The ratio of export prices to import prices in a later, as compared with an earlier, period is called the "net barter terms of trade." In algebraic form it is expressed as

$$\frac{Px_1}{Pm_1} : \frac{Px_0}{Pm_0},$$

where P stands for price, x for exports, m for imports, and 0 and 1 for the base and subsequent periods, respectively. Suppose that prices of exports have doubled and prices of imports have trebled between the base period and the period of interest. Under these circumstances, the terms of trade will have fallen from 100 to 66,

$$\frac{200}{300} : \frac{100}{100} .$$

A decline below 100 is evidently unfavorable. If, on the other hand, export prices had trebled and import prices doubled, the terms of trade would have improved from 100 to 150.

The net barter terms of trade, however, say nothing of what has happened to the balance of payments. One cannot tell from the statement that the terms of trade improved from 100 to 150 whether exports and imports remained balanced, and less exports are being exchanged for the same amount of imports; whether $X = M$, as in the base period but more imports are being obtained for the same exports; or whether exports exceed imports and the surplus is being invested abroad. Indeed, there might be balance now and a deficit in the base period.

To make up for part of this deficiency, the gross barter terms of trade were devised (by Professor Taussig of Harvard) to relate the quantities of exports and imports exchanged for one another in a subsequent period as compared with a base period. Here again, in the many-commodity case, index numbers must be used. The quantity of exports and imports is sometimes expressed in tons in national statistics, but this is misleading except perhaps to people concerned with shipping, since a ton of gold and a ton of coal are not economically comparable. The gross barter terms of trade are expressed as follows:

$$\frac{Qx_1}{Qm_1} : \frac{Qx_0}{Qm_0} .$$

These quantities are derived, however, as index numbers by dividing index numbers of value (P times Q) by index numbers of price, P. If the balance of payments remains balanced when the net barter terms of trade have turned favorable from 100 to 150, then the gross barter terms of trade will have declined numerically from 100 to 66. This is a favorable movement, of course, since it means that a smaller quantity of exports is given for the same volume of imports or that a larger volume of imports is being obtained for the same amount of exports, or a little of both.

The meaning of the net and gross barter terms of trade is unambiguous only when the balance of payments remains balanced in the two periods concerned and when these periods are sufficiently close together to ignore large changes in productivity. Concepts which include productivity have been developed by Professor Viner and are called the "single factoral" terms of trade and the "double factoral" terms of trade. The single factoral terms of trade represent the price of imports relative to the price of exports adjusted for changes in the productivity of a country's factors in the production of exports. The double factoral terms of trade take into account as well the increase in efficiency of foreign factors in producing import goods.

The single factoral terms of trade have been called by Sir Dennis Robertson the most significant of all terms-of-trade concepts. It represents the rate at which the services of a country's factors are exchanged for goods from abroad. If export prices fall, relative to import prices, but productive efficiency increases more, a country is unambiguously better off in real terms. The net barter terms of trade are an inadequate measure of gains from trade under conditions of changing efficiency. This is a lesson which the farm population refuses to learn in its insistence on 1909–14 as a base for the calculation of parity.

Another problem is posed by possible hidden shifts in the quality of goods. An automobile cost $3,000 in 1913, let us say, and $1,500 in 1929. This is not an unfavorable shift in the terms of trade of manufacturers, because of the increase in productivity, which amounted, let us say, to ten times. But consumers must not get the idea that they are really being cheated because productive efficiency went up ten times while price fell only by two. One automobile (1929) is not equal to one automobile (1913), but more nearly four times or eight times or some other considerable multiple. This kind of difficulty can arise for single goods. It is met as the "index-number problem" when the composition of goods covered by an index changes radically, as well as the quality of the separate items. What meaning, for example, is carried by the statement that the quantity of United States exports in 1950 doubled compared to 1900, when a great number of the goods exported in 1950 had not even been invented in 1900?

When, however, a change in the net or gross barter terms of trade takes place without drastic changes in productive efficiency at home or abroad, or in the quality of foreign-trade goods or their composition, a change in real income has occurred. It is generally possible to say this with assurance only for short-run changes in the terms of trade. It can be said, for example, that the British terms of trade improved from 124 in 1924–32 (based on 1913 = 100) to 138 in 1933–37, as the decline in the world prices of its imports went much further than the fall in export prices. A more complicated issue is raised by European terms of trade before and after the war, which appear to have declined from 100 in 1938 to 83 in 1948.

Finally, the net barter terms of trade are sometimes modified by multiplying them by the quantity of exports. This gives $\dfrac{P_x Q_x}{P_m}$ expressed in index numbers, and represents the country's capacity to purchase imports. The net barter terms of trade, by themselves, may be misleading if the volume of exports has changed a great deal. An improvement in the terms of trade which comes about through a large decline in exports may leave a country worse, rather than better, off in command over foreign goods. This concept has been called the "income" terms of trade. It is also referred to as a country's "capacity to import"; if there is a strong pull toward equilibrium in the balance of payments (i.e., $P_x Q_x = P_m Q_m$), then $\dfrac{P_x Q_x}{P_m}$ determines Q_m. A country can buy more imports if any of three things happen:

The price of exports goes up;
The price of imports goes down;
The volume of exports goes up.

The Terms of Trade and Depreciation

What will happen to the terms of trade with depreciation? The temptation is to say that the terms of trade will decline, because export prices will fall and import prices rise. But export prices fall in foreign exchange, and import prices rise in domestic currency. In domestic currency, export prices rise, and in foreign exchange, import prices fall. The extent to which export and import prices fall abroad or rise at home will depend again upon the elasticities.

The classical position was that depreciation would turn the terms of trade against a country because increased exports would reduce the world prices of the goods that it sold, while reduced imports were unlikely to reduce the prices in foreign exchange at which it bought. This is the same thing as saying that the elasticities of demand and outside world supply of the goods that the country produced for export were likely to be lower than the elasticities of demand and supply of the products which the country bought. A country was regarded, so to speak, as likely to specialize in exports and generalize in imports.

This view can be illustrated with Figures 9.4*b* and 9.4*d*. If the foreign demand curve in Figure 9.4*b* is steeper than the foreign supply curve in 9.4*d,* depreciation lowers the export price in foreign exchange more than it lowers the import price.

There need be no change in the terms of trade from depreciation, however. One possibility which would achieve this result would occur if the foreign market on which the country sold had an infinite elasticity of demand for the country's product, over the relevant range, and if its supply schedule for imports were also infinitely elastic. In this case, prices of exports and imports would rise in the depreciating country by the full degree of depreciation, and the terms of trade would remain unchanged. The country in this case has no effect on world prices and is a price taker, in Metzler's expression, rather than a price maker.

Partial versus Complete Elasticities

The elasticity approach is based on a partial-equilibrium analysis. The demand for imports is linked not only to the supply of import-competing products, through the excess-demand summation, but to the demand for exports and for home goods. Each demand and supply curve is drawn on the assumption of other things equal—all other prices, income, productivity, etc. This is realistic when one deals with the demand or the supply of a very small product in a large world. But in exchange depreciation, we have quite a different position. Not only is the export price fairly certain to change, which requires a redrawing of the demand for imports, but if the balance of payments in fact is altered, national income must be adjusted, as the next chapter will indicate. This in turn requires a new statement of the demand for imports.

The elasticity optimists tend to minimize the difficulties with the partial-equilibrium nature of the price approach; and the elasticity pessimists to emphasize them. For the moment, and until Chapter 11, we will adhere to a neutral ground. But even assuming away the repercussions of changes due to elasticities derived from demand and supply curves back on these curves, there is room for difference of opinion as to whether the elasticities are high or low, and in which direction under what circumstances. The higher the elasticities, the more effectively will the price system function to bring about adjustments in international trade; the lower, the less.

The Efficacy of the Price System

The price system probably does not work as effectively in international trade as classical economists were wont to believe. But this is far from saying that it does not work. We know that demand and supply curves are less than completely elastic and that terms of trade change when exchange rates move or when a change in a demand or supply schedule occurs to disturb a previously existing equilibrium. We do not know that demand and supply curves are so inelastic that the system works perversely. In the short run, it would appear that in certain circumstances and for limited periods of time the elasticities are so low that the price system does not respond readily. Over the longer term, there is evidence that it does, in fact, operate in the right direction.

The conclusion that demand and supply are less than completely elastic means that competition is imperfect in the technical sense of that word and that factors are not so mobile that entry and exit to and from various industries are immediate in response to small changes. In short, the foreign trade of the world functions under imperfect competition. We shall have occasion in Chapters 12–15 to see some of the problems in commercial policy which this condition presents.

Summary

How effectively the price mechanism will work in international trade depends upon the elasticities of demand and supply. If these elasticities are high, as they would be if the classical assumptions of perfect competition, factor mobility, and constant factor proportions were realized, small price changes would produce large changes in exports and imports. This means that a deficit in the balance of payments could be corrected by a small price change or that the terms of trade would not have to move much.

Elasticities of demand and supply, however, are difficult to deal with in the real world. The elasticity for a given good will change through time and with different degrees of price change. In addition, methods of measurement leave much to be desired. Despite these handicaps to conclusive statements, it is probably true that elasticities in international trade are less now than they were fifty years ago.

The Marshall-Lerner condition requires that the sum of the elasticities of demand—the demand at home for a country's imports and the demand abroad for its exports—be greater than one if depreciation is to improve its balance of payments. This is true whether one deals in the foreign-currency or the domestic-currency balance. The condition assumes that supply elasticities are high and that the deficit in the balance of payments is not large. If the sum of the elasticities is less than one, currency appreciation will improve the balance.

A number of terms-of-trade concepts were discussed, and the classical presumption that the terms of trade of a country will deteriorate under depreciation explained.

Price changes cannot be isolated from income changes.

SUGGESTED READING

TEXTS

P. T. Ellsworth, *The International Economy* (New York: Macmillan Co., 1950). Chapter xix is good on the Lerner condition.

TREATISES

See Meade, *The Balance of Payments,* Part IV; and essays by Robinson and Machlup, American Economic Association, *Readings,* Nos. 4 and 5. See also G. Haberler's "The Market for Foreign Exchange and Stability of the Balance of Payments," *Kyklos* (Bern, 1949).

On the terms of trade, see Viner, pp. 558 ff., and my monograph, *The Terms of Trade* (New York: The Technology Press and John Wiley & Sons, Inc., 1956), and the literature there cited. Historical studies of the terms of trade worth noting include particularly the titles by Schlote and Imlah.

A. Marshall, *Money, Credit, and Commerce* (New York: Macmillan Co., 1924), Appendix J; and A. P. Lerner, *The Economics of Control* (New York: Macmillan Co., 1944), are the original references for the Marshall-Lerner condition. Modern citation may be made of L. A. Metzler, "The Theory of International Trade," in American Economic Association, *A Survey of Contemporary Economics* (Philadelphia: Blakiston Co., 1948); and A. O. Hirschman, "Devaluation and the Trade Balance," *RE & S,* February, 1949.

POINTS

Elasticity measurements have been made by T. C. Chang, *Cyclical Movements in the Balance of Payments* (Cambridge, Mass.: Cambridge University Press, 1951); by J. H. Adler, E. R. Schlesinger, and E. Van Westerburg in *The Pattern of United States Import Trade since 1923,* Federal Reserve Bank of New York, May, 1952, and in a number of studies produced by the research staff of the International Monetary Fund and circulated in mimeographed form or published in *SP.*

The case against these measurements is given by, among others, G. Orcutt, "Measurement of Price Elasticities in International Trade," *RE & S,* May, 1950.

Chapter
10
INCOME CHANGES AND INTERNATIONAL TRADE

The Assumptions

We now turn from the world in which prices changed and incomes were fixed to a world of constant prices and changing income. This is an analytically interesting world, but it may be no more realistic than the one we have left. And it behooves us, before we enter, to have clearly in mind the various assumptions under which it operates. A few of the major ones are set out here by way of introduction. Others, among them some no less important, will be encountered as we go along.

In the first place, if prices are constant, any change in money income is a change in real income and output. In the next chapter when income and prices both change, we shall have to worry whether imports should be related to real or to money income. The requirement that prices are constant implies that there are unused resources ready to be taken up into production with an increase in spending, or factors ready to withdraw from current employment if spending falls. Full employment is excluded by assumption.

The identity of net national product and national income with constant prices is worth noting. In a closed economy, product and income are identical. But in an open economy they can diverge if the terms of trade change. Suppose output is unchanged from period one to period two but the terms of trade fall due to a rise in import prices. Net national product is unchanged, but real income must fall. With constant prices, however, this distinction need not worry us. The terms of trade cannot change; and output and income are identical.

Second, we assume away time by using a simultaneous multiplier. Changes in income take time, and it is possible to divide time into spending periods and trace through who pays what to whom at each stage of the process. But the simultaneous multiplier shows the end result of a smoothly operating period analysis. It is neat in exposition. We use it.

172

Third, all balance-of-payments deficits and surpluses are assumed to be financed in some fashion or other by gold movements, short-term capital, or other means. At this stage the means do not interest us.

As we proceed, other important assumptions will be introduced and explained. A few may be listed here for convenience: functions are linear and constant; imports are for consumption or investment but not for re-export; exports are sold exclusively out of current production. There is no government expenditure nor any taxes.

The Import Function

The relationship between imports and national income is expressed in a variety of ways. One of these is the average propensity to import. This relation is simply the dollar value of imports as a percentage of total national income (M/Y) or the proportion of national income spent on imports. The average propensity to import may vary from low values of 2 or 3 per cent, as in the Soviet Union, to 20 to 40 per cent in small, highly specialized countries, such as Norway, Belgium, or New Zealand. Too much significance should not be attached to differences in average propensities to import; much will depend upon the size of a country as well as the degree of specialization. Each community in the United States may be as specialized as each community in, say, Britain; but if the United States includes within its borders areas as economically diverse as Maine, Texas, Florida, and Wyoming, the sum total of its communities will find it less necessary to import than those of Britain. Divide a country in two without disturbing trade patterns, for example, and you very much increase the average propensity of each part to import.

More important than the average propensity for many purposes is the marginal propensity to import. This is the *change* in imports associated with a given change in income. In algebraic terms it is dM/dY, where d stands for "the change in." If imports rise by $100 million, when income increases by $1 billion, then the marginal propensity to import will be 0.10.

The marginal propensity to import is likely to differ from the average propensity to import. Two typical cases may be cited. Brazil, for example, supplies most of its basic needs but has a standard of living close to the subsistence level. As the standard of living improves, it leads to the import of new types of goods not available at home. In this case the average propensity to import is low, but the marginal propensity may be high. Contrast with this the case of a country like Britain, which imports a number of necessities like wheat and tobacco (and movies?) and produces luxury products at home. In this case the average propensity to import is high, but the marginal propensity low.

The relation between the average propensity to import and the marginal propensity is expressed by the ratio called "income elasticity." This is more usually thought of as the percentage change in imports associated with a given percentage change in national income. If a 5 per cent increase in national income produces a 10 per cent increase in the value of imports, then the income elasticity of imports is relatively high—to be exact, 2. If, on the other hand, a 5 per cent increase in national income produces a change in imports of only $2\frac{1}{2}$ per cent, then imports are income-inelastic, or 0.5. When a given percentage change in income leads to an equal percentage change in imports, the income elasticity of demand for imports is unity, or 1.

Expressed in algebraic terms, income elasticity is measured by $(dM/M)/(dY/Y)$, which is the percentage change in imports associated with a given percentage change in national income. Since

$$\frac{dM/M}{dY/Y} = \frac{dM/dY}{M/Y},$$

income elasticity can be computed by dividing the marginal propensity to import by the average propensity. If these are the same value, the income elasticity of imports is unitary, or, in other words, a given percentage change in national income will produce a change of equal percentage in imports.

The average propensity to import at various levels of national income is the import schedule or propensity to import. This is shown in Figure 10.1, where $M(Y)$—in mathematical language, imports as a function of national income—is the propensity to import of the economy. It does not pass through the origin at 0, because at zero national income some imports may still be bought from abroad out of reserves. The marginal propensity to import is the slope of $M(Y)$. The assumption that $M(Y)$ is a straight line is, of course, an unreal simplifying aid to analysis.

The use of mathematic symbols to represent the various propensities and elasticities must not beguile the reader into thinking that the numerical values of these concepts for a country are constant under all conditions and circumstances. We shall assume that they are, but this is only for simplicity. In the real world, for example, the marginal propensity of a country to import may differ sharply between one year (1941 in the United States), in which the increase of national income occurs in the manufacturing sector of the economy, and another

(1947), when it occurs in the agricultural. Or the marginal propensity to import may differ for a country in depression and prosperity or in mild prosperity, with excess capacity available in domestic industry, as compared with an inflationary boom of full capacity, when additional purchases in the short run can only be made abroad.

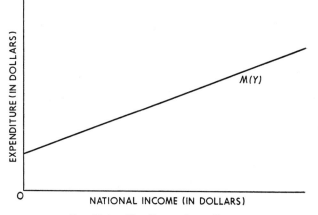

FIG. 10.1. The Propensity to Import

Still once more, the marginal propensity to import will differ between one period of prosperity in which the upswing in national income is generated by long-term investment in, say, housing, which in the United States uses little imported material, and another boom in which short-term investment in inventories is large, or one in which the autonomous change occurs in expenditure for durable consumers' goods. The marginal propensity to import has proved high in business cycles in which inventory investment was prominent, as in 1936–37 and 1949–50. We must not make the mistake (again) of those economists who, following Keynes, developed the marginal propensity to consume (dC/dY) and then assume it to be a constant regardless of liquid wealth, past abstinence or satiation, price anticipations, and a host of other variables. As those who predicted eight million unemployed in the United States in 1946 learned, this is a mistake. The import function is no more a constant than the consumption function, though for many purposes it is convenient to regard it so.

Propensities of the United States

The average propensity to import in the United States is now little more than 3 per cent. This means that 3 and a fraction per cent of national income is spent on imports. National income is currently $340 billion, and imports are $12.6 billion. This average propensity to import has been declining over the years. In the last century, about 1875, it was 10 per cent. By World War I it had fallen to 7 per cent. In the interwar period it slipped to 5 per cent. And after World War II it fell further, to 3. There are those who regard the decrease in the United States average propensity to import as the major problem facing international economics today. Others believe that this percentage is a product of deep-seated forces affecting tastes, innovation, size of country, etc., and that it cannot be manipulated readily. Still others believe that the depletion of minerals in the United States is certain to raise it from its postwar low of 2.8 in 1954 to 3.2–3.5 in 1975.

The marginal propensity to import in the United States has been about 0.04. That is, about 4 per cent of any change in income is reflected in a parallel change in imports. But this marginal propensity is variable, as we have pointed out, depending upon circumstances. In inventory cycles, it is higher; in other income changes, probably lower.

The income elasticity of imports in the United States is little more than one.

In what follows we assume that imports are entirely for consumption rather than investment or to hold as capital assets. This is an unreal but useful assumption and implies that imports are an alternative to domestic spending and extinguish income. The implications of relaxing this assumption will be explored subsequently.

Exports and National Income

As already noted, we assume that exports take place out of current production rather than from past production, such as disinvestment of inventories, or transfers of existing assets, such as antiques, rare paintings, etc. This means that exports increase income.

Exports, moreover, are assumed to be a constant at every level of national income rather than a positive or negative function of income. Figure 10.2 shows this relationship. Implicit in it is the assumption that the country exports commodities which it either does not consume at all or for which its demand is income-inelastic. This assumption is appropriate for a primary-producing country—Dutch Guiana exporting bauxite but consuming none of it, or Australia exporting wheat and wool. But it is unrealistic for those countries which export manufactured products, particularly consumers' goods.

In Britain, exports and consumption, and exports and investment are both competitive rather than independent as we show them. An increase in income under this circumstance will lower exports, and ex-

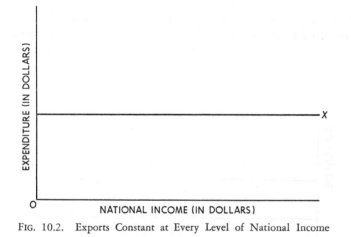

Fig. 10.2. Exports Constant at Every Level of National Income

ports may be taken as a falling function of income. In what follows, this complication is ignored.

The Multiplier in a Closed Economy

We propose to construct the foreign-trade multiplier by analogy with the domestic. This means representing the simplest kind of system in which there are savings and investment schedules (but no government expenditure, taxes, transfers, or similar complications). Savings are a rising function of national income with a negative vertical intercept (i.e., dissaving occurs at zero national income), as in Figure 10.3*a*. Investment is a constant at every level of national income,

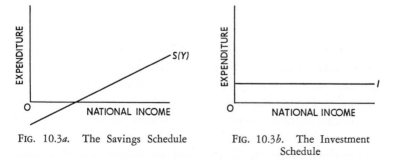

Fig. 10.3*a*. The Savings Schedule   Fig. 10.3*b*. The Investment Schedule

as in Figure 10.3*b*. The student whose income analysis was conducted in literary rather than diagrammatic terms is referred to the end of the chapter for a background reference.

Superimposing the investment on the savings schedule in Figure 10.3c gives us the equilibrium level of national income, Y, where

Income produced = income received.

Income produced is the sum of consumption goods and services and investment goods $(C + I)$; income received equals consumption

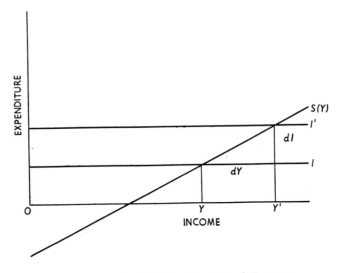

FIG. 10.3c. The Multiplier in a Closed Economy

plus savings $(C + S)$. We define investment goods to include any goods originally intended for consumption and not sold. On this definition the value of consumption goods produced equals the value of consumption goods consumed. From this,

$$C + I = C + S$$
$$C = C$$

Therefore $\qquad I = S$.

The equilibrium level of national income, therefore, is that level where the investment and the savings schedules intersect.

If now there is an autonomous change in the investment schedule, from I to I' in Figure 10.3c, national income is increased. The amount of the increase is determined by the increase in investment and the domestic multiplier. Using the symbol d for the change in, we want to find dY from dI. This is done either geometrically from the characteristics of the triangle combining them in Figure 10.3c, or by simple algebra. In Figure 10.3c dY is dI times the reciprocal of the slope of $S(Y)$. The slope of $S(Y)$ is $\dfrac{dS}{dY}$, so that the multiplier, by which we have to multiply dI to get dY, is $\dfrac{1}{\dfrac{dS}{dY}}$ or $\dfrac{1}{MPS}$, where MPS is the marginal propensity to save.

Algebraically, $I = S$ at equilibrium levels of national income. Therefore in equilibrium

$$dI = dS .$$

Dividing both sides into dY, we get

$$\frac{dY}{dI} = \frac{dY}{dS} \quad \text{or} \quad \frac{1}{\dfrac{dS}{dY}} \quad \text{or} \quad \frac{1}{MPS} .$$

This is the domestic multiplier in a closed economy. The change in income equals the change in investment times the multiplier,

$$dY = \frac{dI}{MPS} .$$

The question now presents itself, what is the foreign-trade multiplier? Assume a change in exports, dX, what is dY? Or $\dfrac{dY}{dX}$, the foreign-trade multiplier, equals what?

The Foreign-Trade Multiplier—No Savings, No Investment

In an open economy with foreign trade, goods produced (Y) plus imports (M) are equal to goods bought ($C + I$) plus goods exported (X). It is assumed, still, that there is no government. If there are no savings and no investment, all income is spent on consumption and Y must equal C.

Since $\quad Y + M = C + I + X$

and $\quad I = 0, Y = C$

∴ $\quad X = M$

and exports are equal to imports at every level of national income. Given the schedules of exports and imports, as in Figures 10.1 and 10.2, one can determine the level of national income. This is done in Figure 10.4, which combines the two early schedules exactly as Figure 10.3c combined 10.3a and 10.3b.

By comparable steps, we can derive the foreign-trade multiplier for this simple economy. If exports shift from X to X', the change in income, from Y to Y', is the change in exports multiplied by the reciprocal of the slope of the import schedule, or the reciprocal of the marginal propensity to import. In algebra

$$X = M$$

at equilibrium levels of national income.
Therefore in equilibrium

$$dX = dM .$$

Dividing both sides into dY we get

$$\frac{dY}{dX} = \frac{dY}{dM} \text{ or } \frac{1}{\frac{dM}{dY}} \text{ or } \frac{1}{MPM} .$$

Any continuing change in exports in an open economy without domestic savings or investment will raise the equilibrium level of national income to the point where it is matched by an equal increase

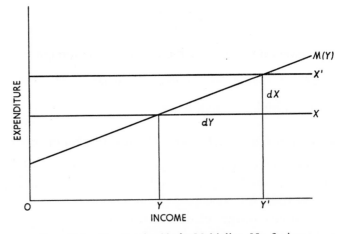

FIG. 10.4. The Foreign-Trade Multiplier, No Savings

in imports. With no savings, the increased spending injected into the system by the increased exports can be spent on consumption (which increases income) or spent on imports. In a period multiplier, at each round of spending current income is divided between consumption and imports, and every increase in income is also divided between them (though perhaps on a different basis if the marginal propensity differs from the average). Income will continue to grow because of increases in consumption until the cumulative increase in imports offsets the autonomous injection of new spending from exports.

A shift in the import schedule will also affect national income, as Figure 10.5 illustrates. Here exports remain unchanged, but imports are assumed to be reduced at each level of income from what they would have been. Such a shift in the import function may occur because of a change in tastes, or an internal shift in the distribution of income, or any one of a number of possible causes. It might have been caused by a rise in prices brought about by foreign inflation or by a tariff, except that we have excluded price changes from our

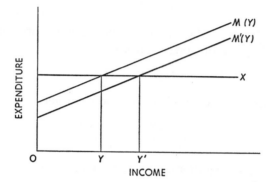

FIG. 10.5. The Foreign-Trade Multiplier, Shift in the Propensity to Import

analysis by assumption. It should be noted that the actual level of imports does not change. Under the conditions assumed, the reduction in the readiness to import at the old national income leads to such an increase in income that imports are built up again to their original level. The shift *of* the schedule, that is, is matched by a movement *along* the schedule. If the propensity to import were changed by an increase in tariffs, for example, the defenders of the tariff might argue that the tariff had no effect because the level of imports was unchanged. This would not be true. The balance-of-payments effect would not exist, because the income effect was so substantial.

Note that with no savings or investment, exports always equal imports. This is the world of David Hume, in which it made no sense to try to increase exports, since all increases in exports would be offset by increases in imports. Hume used the specie-flow analysis, relying on price rather than income. But it works more effectively through income, provided that there are no savings. Hume's law that exports equal imports is the foreign-trade equivalent of Say's law of markets that demand equals supply. And it is equally invalidated by the introduction of savings.

The Foreign-Trade Multiplier—Savings

With savings and investment present, the equilibrium condition of national income is still

$$I = S,$$

but investment (I) breaks down into two parts, domestic (I_d) and foreign (I_f).

$$I_d + I_f = S.$$

Foreign investment is the difference between exports of goods and services and imports of goods and services.

$$I_f = X - M.$$

Substituting this in the previous equation we get

$$I_d + X - M = S$$

or $$I_d + X = S + M,$$

which is the basic equilibrium condition of national income in an open economy.

This is readily diagrammed by adding the domestic investment schedule in Figure 10.3*b* and the export schedule in Figure 10.2, on the one hand, and the import and savings functions in Figure 10.1 and 10.3*a*, respectively, on the other. This is done in Figure 10.6.

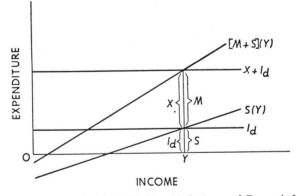

FIG. 10.6. The Foreign-Trade Multiplier with Savings and Domestic Investment

The multiplier is now the reciprocal of the slope of the sum of the two functions $M(Y)$ and $S(Y)$, and will be the same for an increase in exports or an increase in investment. To take the former only, in algebraic terms, with domestic investment constant at all levels of national income and

$$X + I_d = S + M ,$$

the change in exports must be equal to the change in savings plus the change in imports. Expressing this as

$$dX = dS + dM ,$$

we can divide both sides of the equation into dY and derive

$$\frac{dY}{dX} = \frac{dY}{dS + dM} ,$$

$\frac{dY}{dX}$ is k (the multiplier) ,

$$k = \frac{dY}{dS + dM} \quad \text{or} \quad \frac{1}{(dS/dY) + (dM/dY)} \quad \text{or} \quad \frac{1}{MPS + MPM} .$$

The diagram has been drawn in Figure 10.6 so that $I_d = S$ and $X = M$, at the equilibrium level of national income Y. This is not necessarily the case. If long-term lending takes place, X can exceed M, provided that S exceeds I_d by an equal amount sufficient to maintain the equation $I_d + X = S + M$. With a higher level of exports than X, say X' in Figure 10.7a, exports will exceed imports by the amount ab, the amount by which savings will exceed domestic investment. If exports were to fall to X' in Figure 10.7b, however, imports would exceed exports, and domestic investment would exceed savings. The

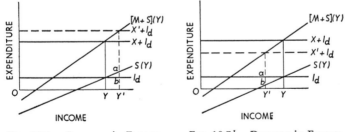

Fig. 10.7a. Increases in Exports   Fig. 10.7b. Decrease in Exports

The Foreign-Trade Multiplier with Changes in Exports

export surplus in the first case can be regarded as a deduction from savings; generally, however, it is thought of as positive foreign investment. In the second case the import surplus may be regarded either as a supplement to savings or as negative investment to be subtracted from I_d.

The new equilibrium of national income where savings differ

from domestic investment by the amount by which exports differ from imports, care being taken to get the signs right, emphasizes that we have been talking about national-income equilibrium, not balance-of-payments equilibrium. Any leakage, whether into imports or savings, is good enough to offset the factors tending to raise income. And the student will recall that we abstracted from balance-of-payments difficulties, at an early stage in this chapter, by assuming that any foreign-trade balance could be financed.

It will be appreciated that the leverage working to change national income at each stage is the change in consumption based on the increase in income in the previous period. On this basis, the analysis can be broadened to include other leakages, such as taxes, corporation profits, etc.

Income Changes and the Balance of Payments

Figures 10.7*a* and 10.7*b* are appropriate enough for illustrating the equilibrium condition for national income. They fail, however, to show very clearly the effect on the balance of payments. For this purpose it is useful to express the equilibrium condition of national income in another way. Instead of

$$X + I_d = S + M ,$$

we can transpose I_d and M, and get

$$X - M = S - I_d ,$$

which is to say that the balance of payments on current account equals the difference between savings and domestic investment. This can equally be diagrammed. It requires only that we subtract the import from the export schedule, on the one hand (Figs. 10.2 and 10.1), and the domestic investment from the saving schedule, on the other (Figs. 10.3*a* and 10.3*b*). This is done in Figure 10.8. The combined *X–M* schedule is downward sloping because the upward-sloping import schedule is subtracted from a constant level of exports. This indicates that the balance of payments is positive at low levels of national income and declines as income rises. The *S–I_d* schedule is upward sloping because savings increase with increasing income and have a positive sign, while investment is constant. The intersection of the two schedules gives the equilibrium level of national income and the balance-of-payments position. In Figure 10.8 as drawn, the two schedules intersect with zero balance of payments. But as already indicated at some length, this is not necessary.

This diagram is not well suited for showing the multiplier, but it can indicate what happens to the balance of payments, as well as to the national income, as a result of a change in any of the four schedules. An increase in domestic investment will displace the $S–I_d$ schedule downward to $S–I'_d$ because the negative term is increased. This will raise national income from Y to Y' and open up a balance-of-payments

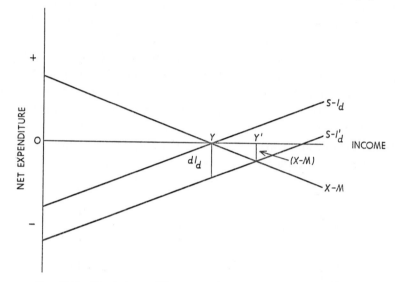

FIG. 10.8.   The Balance-of-Payments Effect of a Change in Investment

deficit. The deficit $(X–M)$ is less than the amount of the increase in investment (dI_d) because the movement along the schedule, represented by increased savings, partly offsets the shift of the schedule, represented by additional investment.

One can as readily explore the impact of changes in the other schedules—an increase or decrease in exports, which would move the $X–M$ schedule up or down, respectively; a change in the import schedule down or up, which would have the same effects on the $X–M$ as a whole; or a change in the propensity to save. Increases in exports, decreases in imports, decreases in investment, and increases in savings all help the balance of payments. And movements in the opposite direction hurt it.

We can see from this diagram what it would mean if exports declined with increased income because of the competition between exports and consumption or investment such as occurs in a number of countries selling manufactures, like Britain. The negative slope of the $X–M$ curve would be steeper; the balance-of-payments effect of a given shift in any of the schedules would be greater; and the income effect would be reduced.

The Foreign-Trade Accelerator

The diagrammatic analysis used in Figure 10.5 is inadequate to handle the business cycle, even after it has been elaborated to fit the economy described by the equation $C + I + G$ (government expenditure) $= Y$. It is essentially static analysis and fails to show that increases in income and consumption produced by changes in investment will, under certain conditions, become cumulative. When full capacity is reached, or nearly so, an increase in consumption will lead to an increase in investment, which, in turn, increases income. The cumulative path may be followed, with income ever-increasing until, for one reason or another, the cyclical downturn occurs. Thereafter, declines in national income and consumption brought about by a decline in investment lead to idle capacity and a new decline in investment.

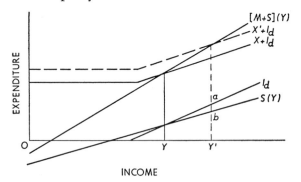

FIG. 10.9. The Foreign-Trade Accelerator, Increase in Exports Leading to Import Surplus

The multiplier, showing how every increase in investment leads to a limited increase in income as the injection into the system is siphoned off into savings, imports, taxes, etc., is vastly different from the accelerator. This latter shows why, on occasion, an increase in income leads to an increase in investment and a new increase in income by means of the multiplier.

The present diagrammatic analysis can be used to illustrate the domestic accelerator only to a limited degree. An increase in investment leads to an increase in consumption, which leads to a new displacement of the investment curve in the direction of increase, which, in turn, increases income once more. And so on, until the downturn begins for one reason or another. When there is no downturn, the increase in income leads on to full employment and then to hyperinflation.

In foreign trade there may on occasion be an effect comparable to the domestic accelerator. We may call it the "foreign-trade accelerator." An increase in exports leads through increases in investment to an import surplus. The increase in investment may take place in the export industries themselves: an increase in American tourist expenditure in London may lead to the construction of more hotels. Or the general prosperity created by expanded exports may lead to new investment in industries producing for home consumption.

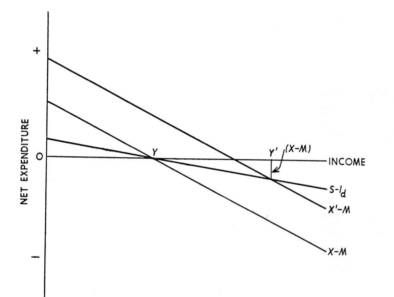

FIG. 10.10.   The Balance-of-Payments Effect of a Foreign-Trade Accelerator

This accelerator effect may be demonstrated in successive steps. In the first period there will be an increase in exports. This will raise national income and consumption in the second. The increase in exports and induced consumption requires an enlargement in capacity, so that the third period produces an increase in investment, which in turn stimulates income and consumption. And so on.

Or the accelerator can be approximated by the crude device of introducing a propensity to invest, which is positively sloped, and shows that investment expands with national income. This differs from the true accelerator, which associates the level of investment with changes in income, but it illustrates the point effectively. If the propensity to invest is sloped more steeply than the savings function, but less so than the combined curve representing the import and savings schedules, we may see the effect in simultaneous representation.

The investment schedule must have a greater slope than the savings schedule to get the paradoxical effect we are after (akin, to those who remember their Samuelson, to the paradox of thrift). But it must not be steeper than the combined curve. If it were, the system would be unstable, i.e., an increase in income from equilibrium would lead to further and further increases in investment and an explosive, uncontrolled inflation.

In Figure 10.9, with the curves as drawn, an increase in exports from a position of balanced trade leads to an import surplus by the amount by which investment, at the new level of income, exceeds savings. This is the amount ab. Figure 10.10 more clearly shows the effect of the foreign-trade accelerator on the balance of payments. The $S-I_d$ schedule is negatively sloped, because investment increases faster than savings. An increase in exports which displaces the $X-M$ schedule upward to $X'-M$ will therefore produce a balance-of-payments deficit shown at Y'.

Foreign Repercussion

Another complication may be introduced by the foreign repercussion, which is the effect of the change in exports and/or imports on national income abroad, and the backwash effect which this has on foreign trade and national income at home. If the country we are considering is small in relation to the outside world, the foreign repercussion can be neglected. An increase in such a country's imports will not stimulate income abroad by significant amounts. And even if there were a noticeable effect on income abroad, the repercussion may still be small if the marginal propensity of the countries affected to import from the original country is small. If an increase in the demand of Liechtenstein for Swiss chocolate is sufficiently large to raise national income in Switzerland, the effects are likely to be dissipated throughout the world and very little will return to affect so small a country as Liechtenstein.

With large countries, however, the foreign repercussion is significant. The United States accounts for half the money income in the world. An increase in United States imports raises incomes abroad, which increases imports in general and imports from the United States, which contributes an important share of total world trade and a more important share of income-elastic goods. From this example, it may be seen that national income in the United States is linked through United States exports to national incomes abroad. United States income therefore depends upon the marginal propensities to save and import abroad as well as upon the marginal propensities to save and import in the United States.

One way to set out the foreign repercussion diagrammatically would be to have two series of diagrams, one for each country in the analysis—"the United States" and the "rest of the world"—with each diagram in each series representing a different stage. In Figure 10.11*a*,

FIG. 10.11*a*. Stage 1 in the United States   FIG. 10.11*b*. Stage 1 in the Rest of the World

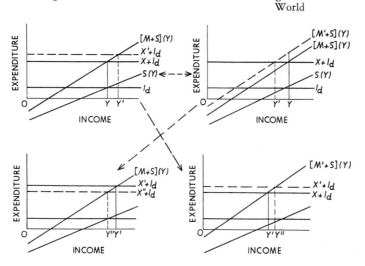

FIG. 10.11*c*. Stage 2 in the United States   FIG. 10.11*d*. Stage 2 in the Rest of the World

The Multiplier with Foreign Repercussion, by Stages

for example, the rest of the world has increased its imports from the United States, which raises exports, national income, and imports in the usual fashion. In Figure 10.11*b,* however, the autonomous increase in imports is shown to have reduced income in the rest of the world and induced a reduction in imports. Figures 10.11*c* and 10.11*d* show what happens at the next stage. The United States has a reduction in exports, partly offsetting the original increase. The rest of the world has an increase in exports (the induced increase in United States imports), which helps to sustain national income and imports (shown in the original Fig. 10.11*a*). Successive stages could be portrayed until the system came to rest.

A simultaneous geometric representation of the foreign repercussion has been worked out in which national income in each of two countries is expressed as a function of national income in the other. In Figure 10.12, for example, national income in A is expressed as a function of national income in B. Even if B's income is zero, A's income will be what it is from consumption, investment expenditure, and government expenditure in A, which is entirely independent of what is taking place in B. This independence is shown by the fact that the sum $Ca + Ida + Ga$ is a horizontal line, which means that it is constant at all levels of B's income.

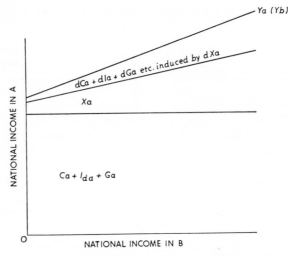

FIG. 10.12. Income in A as a Function of Income in B

Exports in A create income, however, whose size is not independent of the level of income in B. In Figure 10.12, B is assumed to import from A even at no income. This creates some income directly (Xa at the vertical axis) and, through the foreign-trade multiplier in A, induces some further increases in consumption (dCa). As B's income increases, A's exports increase and, with them, the induced increase in spending dependent on exports.

The total of the three lines indicates the level of income in A at various levels of national income in B.

A similar representation of income in B as a function of income in A can be drawn on the same diagram. This is done in Figure 10.13, where line A reflects income in A as a function of income in B, and line B, income in B as a function of A. If these two lines intersect in a stable system, the interaction between the national incomes of the two countries is indicated. Now, if national income in B rises because of a change of any sort—let us say, in this case, because of an increase in investment in B—the line representing B's income as a function of income of A will be displaced to the right, since B's national income will be higher even if national income in A is zero. In Figure 10.13, line B is displaced to B'. This will raise national income in A from Y to Y'. Notice that national income in B has increased by more than the displacement of income, i.e., that the distance between Y and Y' along the B axis is greater than the amount by which the B function was displaced. This is because the increase in investment

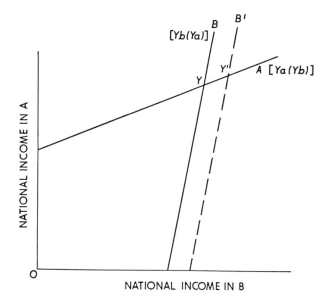

FIG. 10.13. Simultaneous Representation of the Foreign Repercussion

in B raised national income in B, imports from A, and hence national income in A, imports from B (or B's exports), and national income in B again.

This analysis can be used to demonstrate the interaction of national incomes in two countries (or in one country and the rest of the world taken as a whole) under a variety of circumstances. A change in the marginal propensities in B, whether to save, to import, to tax, or any other, will alter the slope of the curve of B's income as a function of income in A. This will produce a change in national income in both countries. A change in tastes in B which decreases domestic consumption in B and increases imports from A will displace both curves simultaneously but will lead to a unique new equilibrium, so long as the two curves continue to intersect. This diagrammatic analysis, which is needed where the foreign repercussion is important, is capable of handling all the various foreign-trade multipliers.

The derivation of one of these multipliers is given in an appendix to this chapter. Here it is sufficient to give a pair of formulas, one for a change in foreign trade and one for a change in domestic investment. The foreign-trade multipliers depend, of course, on the marginal propensities to save and import at home, which determine how much of the original increase in exports will be spent on consumption at home, in the first instance, and on the marginal propensities to save and spend abroad, which determine, first, how much of a change in income abroad is brought about by the original decrease in consumption and, second, how much of this is communicated through imports back again to A. The formula for the multiplier for an autonomous change in exports is

$$k = \frac{1}{MPSa + MPMa + MPMb\,(MPSa/MPSb)}.$$

This multiplier in A will be larger as

> the marginal propensity to import in A is smaller,
> the marginal propensity to save in A is smaller,
> the marginal propensity to import in B is smaller,

and   the marginal propensity to save in B is larger.

The first two propensities cut down the leakage of income in A and ensure that the first and successive doses of expenditure arising from the increase in exports will be larger than otherwise. The effect of a small marginal propensity to import in B is to increase the multiplier in A, since it limits the induced decline in A's exports resulting from any decline in income in B. Finally, the larger the marginal propensity to save in B, the smaller will be the decline in income and the smaller, in turn, the induced decline in A's exports.

All these relationships can be expressed inversely, of course, but we may limit ourselves to one. If the propensity to import abroad is large, the multiplier in A will be small because the decrease in income abroad will be quickly translated into decreased imports as an offset to the original increase in A's exports.

The multiplier for an autonomous change in home investment is

$$k = \frac{1 + (MPMb/MPSb)}{MPSa + MPMa + MPMb\,(MPSa/MPSb)}.$$

This value is larger than the multiplier for an autonomous change in exports, because the foreign repercussion is working in the same direction as the increase in domestic investment, rather than against it, as in the case of the change in exports.

One reminder may be useful before we leave the foreign-trade multiplier and the foreign repercussion. If the rest of the world (country B in our illustration) is large relative to country A and consists of many countries, the foreign repercussion can be neglected. Each country may have a large propensity to import over-all, but its marginal propensity to import from country A is likely to be small. The foreign repercussion is a negligible element, that is, in the foreign-trade multiplier for Guatemala and New Zealand and Egypt. It can, however, be neglected only with great peril in a discussion of the foreign trade of the United States or of western Europe.

The Sum of the Marginal Propensities to Import

In a two-country world, it makes a considerable difference for many problems whether the sum of the marginal propensities to import is greater than, equal to, or smaller than 1. Start from an increase in spending in A, matched by an equal decrease in B. If the sum of the marginal propensities to import is exactly one, national incomes will be unchanged in the two countries taken together and the balance of payments will turn against A and in favor of B by an amount equal to the change in spending. If the change in spending is 100, and the marginal propensities in each case are 0.5, the demonstration is easy. A's increase in spending is half on domestic goods and half on imports. Imports rise by 50. Similarly B's decrease in spending is half on domestic goods and half on imports. Its imports fall by 50. The decline of 50 in exports and increase of 50 in imports in A turns the balance of trade against it by 100, and this disinvestment offsets the original increase in expenditure to maintain national income. The converse holds in B.

If the values in A and B are somewhat altered but the sum of the marginal propensities to import still amounts to 1, the same results hold. If the marginal propensities to import are 0.4 in A and 0.6 in B, A's exports fall by 60, while imports rise by 40 to produce the identical outcome.

If the sum of the marginal propensities to import exceeds 1, the balance-of-payments change is greater than the original change in spending. Take *MPM*'s of 0.5 in A and 0.6 in B. The initial impact will be an increase in 50 of imports in A and a decline of 60 in imports. The disinvestment represented by the initial balance-of-payments deficit of 110 exceeds the original increase in spending in A, and A's income declines. Conversely, B's income will increase because the export surplus exceeds the decline in expenditure.

If the sum of the marginal propensities to import is less than 1, on the other hand, an increase in expenditure in A and a decrease in B will result in an increase in income in A, a decrease in income in B, and a balance-of-payments change which is less than the original changes in spending. This is generally regarded as the normal case. It is believed that countries spend more on home goods than on imports because of transport costs, which make it impossible for many heavy and perishable goods to move in trade at all. If A's *MPM* is 0.3 and B's is 0.2, an increase in spending of 100 in A matched by an equal decrease in B will produce an initial balance-of-payments deficit for A (surplus for B) of 50, and leave an extra 50 of domestic spending in A, and the contrary in B, to produce changes in national income in the directions indicated. What the final changes in the balance of payments and national income will be, however, cannot be told without knowledge of the *MPS*'s and the multipliers.

Summary

While Hume was concerned with price effects and our interest is in income, Hume's law that exports equal imports is valid only under conditions of no savings. In the absence of savings, an increase in exports will increase income to the point where sufficient additional imports are created to offset exports. The amount by which national income will increase is the increase in exports times a multiplier equal to $1/MPM$. But if savings take place, the increase in exports will be balanced by increases in imports and in savings, provided that investment is unchanged. In this case the multiplier is $1/(MPM + MPS)$. If an accelerator is at work so that an increase in income due to a rise in exports leads to an increase in investment, the increase in exports may produce a larger increase in imports and turn the balance of trade unfavorably.

The foreign-trade multiplier expresses the change in income caused by a change in exports or in investments in an open economy in which income spills over into imports.

If the effect of the change in imports on income abroad is significant and if the effect of income changes abroad on a country's exports is again appreciable, there is a foreign repercussion. More complex formulas are now necessary to express the relationships among savings and import propensities in the countries involved.

SUGGESTED READING

TEXTS

Marsh gives the most complete treatment of the multiplier in his *World Trade and Investment* (New York: Harcourt, Brace & Co., Inc., 1951), chaps. ix–xi and xvi–xviii. It is, however, complex and difficult.

A student who needs to brush up on the domestic simultaneous multiplier is referred to P. A. Samuelson, *Economics* (4th ed.; New York: McGraw-Hill Book Co., Inc., 1958), chap. xii.

TREATISES

Meade, *The Balance of Payments*, Parts II and III, gives a simultaneous analysis based on a generalized technique for solving problems. F. Machlup, *International Trade and the National Income Multiplier* (Philadelphia: Blakiston Co., 1943), is an early work but uses a period analysis. Some teachers swear by Lloyd A. Metzler, "Underemployment Equilibrium in International Trade," *Econometrica*, 1942. Among the pioneer writing, see J. M. Keynes, *The General Theory of Employment, Interest, and Money* (New York: Harcourt, Brace & Co., Inc., 1936), chap. xxi.

The refined treatment of the foreign repercussion used in the chapter is taken from R. Robinson's interesting "A Graphical Analysis of the Foreign Trade Multiplier," *EJ*, September, 1952.

POINTS

Some part of the notion of the foreign-trade accelerator emerged in the discussion of the multiplier by the writer and A. I. Bloomfield. See *AER*, March and September, 1949.

Measurements of import propensities are furnished by Chang in *Cyclical Movements of the Balance of Payments;* by J. H. Adler, "U.S. Import Demand during the Interwar Period," *AER*, June, 1945; and by I. de Vegh, "Imports and Income in the United States and Canada," *RE & S*, August, 1941.

The writer referred to above who expects the average propensity to import of the United States to rise is Henry G. Aubrey. See his *United States Imports and World Trade* (London: Oxford University Press, 1957).

Econometric models which attempt to set out the interrelations among incomes and trade in the various countries of the world (including some role for prices) are contained in H. Neisser and F. Modigliani, *National Incomes and Foreign Trade* (Urbana: University of Illinois Press, 1953); and J. J. Polak, *An International Economic System* (London: Allen & Unwin, 1954).

Chapter 11

INTERACTIONS OF INCOME AND PRICE

The Assumptions

We move now from the worlds of price changes with income constant and income changes with prices constant to a more realistic world in which income and price are both free to move. The difficulty with this world is that it is, so-to-speak, underdetermined. Anything can happen: there are too many unknowns and not enough equations. It is impossible to discuss international adjustment with this many degrees of freedom. We are obliged, therefore, to pose certain problems, and to see how the mechanism works under more narrowly specified conditions.

The mathematical language of that paragraph—"underdetermined," "number of unknowns and equations," etc.—should not distress the student lacking competence and/or confidence in mathematics above the high-school level. This is the sort of subject which lends itself to mathematical treatment, perhaps, but we shall remain in the highly simplified world of prose. The reasons lie not only in the possible fears of the reader but also in the competence of the writer.

Out of an almost infinite variety of possible cases, we will discuss six types. They are:

1. The alleged identity of the gold standard and flexible exchanges
2. Depreciation under full employment
3. Changes in spending with inelastic supplies
4. Flexible exchange rates and balanced trade
5. Changed productivity
6. Changes in income and price abroad

Gold Standard and Flexible Exchanges

In *The Balance of Payments,* Professor Meade asserts that there is little difference between the gold standard emphasizing income

196

movements, and flexible exchange rates, relying on price changes. In fact, they can be (are?) virtually identical. Starting from an adverse shift in demand which reduces a country's exports, and leads to an outflow of gold, he describes three effects which bring about balance-of-payments adjustment on the gold standard:

1. An increase in the rate of interest which attracts short-term capital and thus improves the balance of payments directly;
2. The response of business men in cutting down spending of borrowed funds because of the increased rate of interest, which reduces income, cuts imports and releases goods for export, thus improving the balance of payments a second time through improving the balance of trade;
3. The decline in prices as a result of the reduction in income, with supply curves inelastic, which makes the country a better place in which to buy and a poorer place to which to sell, improving the balance of trade and the balance of payments a third time.

In this example, he assumes, as the reader will recognize, that the sum of the marginal propensities to import is less than one, which makes income fall farther in the adjusting country than abroad; and that the sum of the elasticities of demand for imports is greater than one, which produces an improvement in the balance of trade from the price change. He takes these to be the normal state of affairs, as do we.

Under the flexible-exchange standard, with the same propensities and elasticities, Professor Meade insists that the effects are the same, even though their order may be altered. Depreciation first reduces the price of exports in foreign exchange and raises the price of imports in local currency, which brings about the first improvement in the balance of trade, equivalent to the third effect listed above. The increased demand for the country's products, and increased spending of income diverted from imports, lead the monetary authorities to raise interest rates, which in turn produces a decline in spending and an inflow of capital, the second and first of the effects under the gold standard.

Now it must be admitted that this could happen and that the income and price mechanisms could work out with identical results in comparable cases. But it does not seem likely, and it requires the introduction of strong policy steps. One normally thinks of exchange depreciation as an alternative to deflation. In this circumstance, it seems strange to postulate that the monetary authorities will take as vigorous steps to raise interest rates after having permitted depreciation as they would have done on a fixed rate. Moreover, the trigger mechanism is different. In the gold-standard case, the rate of interest was raised because of the adverse balance of payments. In the flexible-exchange instance, it was presumed raised because of the increase in domestic spending. If policy steps to raise interest rates and limit spending are in fact taken under the flexible-exchange-rate system, one would normally expect them to go no further than to prevent a rise in spending. If so, this constitutes a major difference between the two mechanisms: under the gold standard, incomes fall; under flexible exchanges, policy steps must be taken to prevent an increase in income.

There are, of course, other probable differences. Substantial income changes are likely to be required under the fixed exchange standard because supplies are elastic rather than inelastic, and prices do not move with changes in money income. If this is the case, as it seems to have been since World War I, the third effect is weak under the gold standard and strong under flexible exchanges.

One can then introduce enough assumptions to bring it about that the gold standard and flexible exchanges are similar. But these assumptions seem to be strong ones, departing substantially from what we know about the world.

Depreciation under Full Employment

At less than full employment, a change in the exchange rate which shifts the X–M schedule (as illustrated in Fig. 10.8)[1] upward will induce a change in income which will offset part of the initial balance-of-payments improvement. If the S–I_d schedule is upward sloping and unchanged by the exchange-rate adjustment, the net result is an improvement in the balance of payments: a shift in the X–M schedule partly offset by a movement along the S–I_d schedule. The improvement in the balance of payments is also represented by an increase in savings out of an enlarged real income.

Suppose, however, that there is full employment and output cannot be increased. How will the economy produce new net savings needed to offset the improvement in the balance of payments? What will bring about the reduction in consumption or investment, now that output cannot be increased?

It is useful here to remind ourselves that the net balance of payments represents the difference between output and domestic expenditure. Using our earlier notation (without government spending or taxes)

[1] Observe that we have to be careful in using the income diagram for cases where prices change. In this diagram, money and real income are identical, and since prices are constant under all circumstances, a change in the X–M schedule can be independent of changes in S–I_d. Not so when prices change. Strictly speaking we should stay away from the income diagram; but we propose to use it circumspectly.

$$Y = C + I_d + X - M,$$

which means that

$$X - M = Y - (C + I_d)$$

or that the balance of payments equals net national product less national expenditure. When the exchange rate is depreciated with less than full employment, the balance of payments can be improved as a result of increased output greater than increased expenditure. When output is limited by pre-existing full employment, however, the balance of payments can be improved only by a reduction in expenditure, or in what Professor Alexander has called "absorption." An increase in savings, with output constant, is the same as a decrease in "absorption." What is the mechanism by which exchange depreciation can increase savings or decrease absorption?

One possibility is "money illusion." Suppose savings are a positively rising function of money income rather than of real income. This implies "money illusion," i.e., that spending habits respond to money incomes without reference to the level of prices. Under exchange depreciation, people would reduce the proportion of income spent if money incomes rose despite the fact that prices were rising along with them and real incomes were constant. It would in fact leave us in the position indicated by Figure 10.8, provided the horizontal axis represented "money income" and not "real income" as well. An upward shift in the $X-M$ schedule would intercept the $S-I_d$ schedule at a higher money income and identical national output, but real savings would increase and the balance of payments would improve.

In the absence of money illusion, the $S-I_d$ schedule might remain constant above the level of full employment, as in Figure 11.1, or even decline. Without money illusion, therefore, or some other means of producing a shift in the savings schedule, depreciation shifts the $X-M$ schedule but fails to improve the balance of payments.

Another possibility is found in the so-called "Pigou-effect," named after the famous Cambridge economist. With a constant money supply, an increase in prices and money income may produce an increase in savings, Pigou thought, as consumers try to build back the real value of their cash balances which have depreciated in value because of the rise in prices. The standard question is put in terms of what would happen if all prices and incomes were doubled but money remained the same. There would clearly be an incentive to restore the old relationship of liquid and fixed-money assets to income, and the savings schedule would shift upward in relation to real income. This then is another possible avenue by which depreciation could lead to a decline in absorption and an improvement in the balance of payments. But it is unlikely to be a major force to be counted upon.

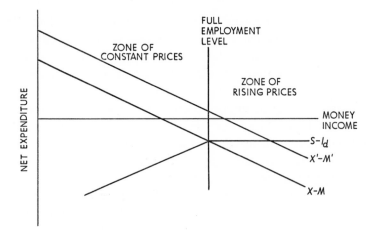

FIG. 11.1. Failure of Depreciation to Improve the Balance of Payments in Absence of "Money Illusion," Etc.

The main hope for improvement in the balance of payments with full employment probably lies in its effects on the distribution of income, which may affect absorption. If imports bulk large in ordinary consumption, depreciation raises the cost of living and reduces the real incomes of workers, civil servants, teachers, pensioners, etc., who have fairly fixed incomes. They will save less. But the rise in prices in the foreign-trade sector—exports and import-competing industry—will increase profits here, and this will, in the first instance at least, lead to new savings. Whether absorption will on balance decrease over the longer run depends in part on whether new investment is undertaken in the foreign-trade sector in response to the higher rate of profit, which would increase absorption again, or whether—a different response—the society is prepared to accept the major changes in income distribution without resisting them.

Much depends here on institutional forces: the political strength of labor, the readiness of various income groups to use every weapon at their command to resist any decrease in their share of the total income. Where wage rates are tied to the cost of living, as in the Scandinavian countries, there is almost no prospect of effecting substantial income redistribution, and increased savings, through depreciation. Or where, as in France, the separate income groups—peasants, workers, civil servants, veterans, industrialists, etc.—use every means, including strikes and violence, to prevent any reduction in the real income of the group, depreciation is unlikely to work in this way.

Unless one can count on income redistribution, money illusion, the Pigou effect, or some other means of increasing savings as a function of a given real income, exchange depreciation is unlikely by itself, with full employment, to improve the balance of payments. If real output cannot be expanded, there must be a decrease in absorption: a decline in consumption, or a decline in investment. If depreciation does not decrease absorption, prices will rise internally with depreciation, and the change in the exchange rate works like a change in dimensions from yards to feet, which alters the length of nothing.

The foregoing statement omits one possibility which may be significant in some circumstances. Assume that the deficit in the balance of payments had been limited before depreciation by import restrictions which distorted relative prices and resulted in mal-allocation of resources. It might be found, even with full employment, that depreciation and the freeing of the price system led to a substantial increase in real output out of which the increase in absorption could take place without the necessity for income redistribution, money illusion, or the Pigou-effect. But if relative prices have not been disturbed, full employment is equivalent to optimum production and the balance of payments can be improved only with an increase in absorption.

Changes in Spending with Inelastic Supplies

We turn from a case where the exchange rate changes with income free to move, to changes in spending at home where prices go up or down. In the former instance, the price effect and the income effect worked in opposite directions: the price effect through depreciation to improve the balance of payments (provided that the sum of the elasticities was greater than one); the income effect to worsen it. When spending changes at home with relatively inelastic supplies so that prices move, the price and income effects work in the same direction, provided that the elasticities and propensities are normal (i.e., provided that the sum of the price elasticities is greater than one and the sum of the marginal propensities less than one).

In these normal circumstances, an increase in spending at home raises income and increases the domestic price level. The increase in income works to produce a deficit in the balance of payments (or reduce a surplus); and so does the increase in prices. Or if domestic spending declines and prices fall, both price and income work together to expand exports and reduce the level of imports.

One assumption which underlies this conclusion is that the elasticity of supply abroad is no lower than in the country where the initial changes take place. This ensures that price changes abroad either don't take place or take place within identical or narrower limits. If the supply elasticity abroad were much smaller than at home, the income spilling over from increased spending at home could raise prices abroad more than those at home, which would worsen rather than improve the terms of trade and make the price effect work for rather than against the balance of payments of the spending country. But if foreign prices are unchanged, or change no more than those at home, price and incomes operate together.

This teamwork evidently depends crucially on the normal conditions of the elasticities and propensities. If the sum of the elasticities is less than one, the price rise at home from increased spending will improve the balance of payments rather than worsen it. Or if the sum of the marginal propensities to import is greater than one, the spending country will raise income abroad more than income at home, which will make the income effect work perversely to improve the balance of payments from an increase in domestic spending.

But with the normal conditions, we get an unambiguous result in the balance of payments from changes in domestic spending, whether prices move or whether they do not. If prices move, they help. If they do not move, they do not hinder. This contrasts with the antithetical behavior of the price and income effects under full employment when price changes take the lead through devaluation.

Flexible Exchange Rates with Balanced Trade

Another set of interrelationships between price and income changes can be explored with the help of a special assumption that flexible exchange rates keep exports always equal to imports. This requires a smoothly transforming society—one which reallocates resources from the foreign-trade to the domestic sector without friction in response to changes in world conditions. If the demand for exports falls off, the exchange rate depreciates to the point where either exports increase again in old or new lines, or imports decline, to restore balance automatically. If demand increases, the exchange rate appreciates to displace existing exports at the margin, or to stimulate new imports. The balance of payments is always in balance. The question is how will changes in the terms of trade, which are changes in the country's gain from trade, affect national income and expenditure?

In order to answer this question, we need to provide further assumptions about the economy. We need to know, in particular, how the rate of saving is related to changes in the terms of trade. A variety of such assumptions have been provided by a variety of economists.

Laursen and Metzler took as their assumption that savings are a function of real income, and that an improvement in real income from an improvement in the terms of trade will increase savings, a reduction reduce them. This led them to conclude that a favorable shift in the terms of trade will reduce national income by raising real income and increasing savings. An improvement in the terms of trade, they concluded, is deflationary. Conversely, a worsening of the terms of trade through depreciation was regarded as inflationary through its effect in increasing expenditure (reducing savings) because of a reduction in real income.

Stolper worked from import prices (rather than the terms of trade) directly to savings, using the assumption that savings and imports were competitors for the consumers' dollar. In this circumstance, an increase in import prices (worsening of the terms of trade) led to a reduction in spending on imports (elasticity greater than one) and an increase in savings. Total spending declined, and income fell. When imports were cheaper, on the other hand, savings were drawn down to buy more goods from abroad, which led to an expansion of spending. The reader will observe that no change in spending occurs in the domestic sector at home but that changes in spending on imports are transmitted back to domestic national income by the flexible-exchange-rate device. When imports rise as savings are drawn down, this requires an expansion of exports to keep trade in balance, and the flexible exchange rate is assumed to be able always to achieve this.

According to Laursen and Metzler then, an improvement in the terms of trade was deflationary; according to Stolper, inflationary; and vice versa for a worsening of the terms of trade.

The Laursen-Metzler assumptions can be criticized as highly limiting. A large change in the terms of trade—say 10 per cent—will produce a much smaller change in real income. If the average propensity to import is 20 per cent, this change in the terms of trade will affect real income by 2 per cent. Under no circumstance can a 2 per cent change in real income produce a very large shift in savings or expenditure.

More fundamental, an increase in real income arising from lower import prices cannot be very deflationary, since any considerable deflation would reduce real income and restore the level of real expenditure to its level before import prices fell. It seems likely, rather, on the Laursen-Metzler assumptions, that the country will end up with some small decline in money income but a small increase in real income and real expenditure.

The Stolper assumption, in its turn, has been criticized as unrealistic. There is less justification for assuming that imports and savings are alternatives than the opposite, i.e., assuming that cheaper imports mean more saving.

What will happen to imports, savings, and domestic expenditure as a result of changes in the price of imports depends on the structure of a country's trade. If price elasticity is high, the substitution effect will be substantial but the income effect will be small. There will be a substantial increase in imports; a necessity to shift the resources released from the import-competing sector into exports to balance trade; but very little change in over-all spending or saving. No substantial change in income arises from the model as it exists. Dynamic changes can occur, however, because of failure of adjustment to be that smooth. Thus, for example, the expansion in exports may require more investment in export industry than is provided by the savings released from the import-competing sector.

If the price elasticity of demand for imports is low, the substitution effect will be small but the income effect will be large. Some part of the increase in income will be saved, and money income may fall to some extent. But much will be spent. At higher real income, more is consumed as well as more saved. Resources will be released from the export sector and transferred to domestic occupations.

The classic example offered by the real world is that of Britain in the early 1930's, when a fall in the terms of trade increased real income substantially, because of the inelastic nature of the demand for foodstuffs and raw materials, and provided real income which spilled into domestic housebuilding (investment rather than consumption).

It is, in short, difficult to generalize about the interactions between the terms of trade and domestic spending. The nature of the income effect and the substitutability between imports and domestic goods will differ from country to country and circumstance to circumstance.

Productivity Change

Assume two countries, A and B, each producing one good and consuming two, i.e., each completely specialized in production but generalized in consumption. Now introduce a change in productivity in A. Whether this improves or worsens the balance of payments of A will depend upon the elasticities and the marginal propensities, and on whether the increased real output of A is reflected in higher money incomes, lower prices, or both.

To the extent that the increase in productivity takes the form of higher money incomes, the increase in output may worsen the balance of payments, assuming that imports are not an inferior good. More income means more spending on imports. Country B, with unchanged income and facing an unchanged price for its imports, experiences no initial reaction. The consequence of an increase in its exports is likely to include a rise in prices, an increase in imports through the multiplier, and a worsening of exports because of increased prices; but the net effect will be favorable in the absence of any perverse dynamic changes such as accelerators, since it starts with an increase in exports. And if B's balance of payments improves, A's worsens.

If the increase in productivity took place in the form of unchanged money income but lower export prices, the balance-of-payments effect will depend, in the first instance, on the sum of the price elasticities of demand. If these are greater than one, the balance-of-payments effect is favorable to A; if less than one, unfavorable. An income effect follows the balance-of-payments effect and offsets it in part, but only in part, assuming the sum of the marginal propensities to import less than one.

If the productivity change leads to a partial rise in income and a partial decline in price, the income and the price effects will move in opposite directions or together depending upon the relative size of the two movements and whether the sum of the price elasticities of demand for imports are greater or less than one.

This is a highly simplified model. All productivity changes are export biased if production is limited to one commodity; and competitive effects in third countries producing the same good are neglected. But the model is interesting in showing, from still another angle, how income and price changes may be related.

Changes in Income and Price Abroad

Our final case poses the question whether a country's balance of payments is more affected by price or by income when both change abroad in the same direction. We have by implication already dealt once with this question under our third case above, when spending at home changed prices, and the income and price effects operated in the same direction on the balance of payments with high elasticities. If one thinks of the rest of the world, in this instance, income and price effects must operate together on the balance of payments in the opposite sense to that in the spending country.

The income and price effects on a country's balance of payments of changes abroad may, however, be opposed. This is particularly true in the business cycle. In depression, incomes abroad fall, but so do import prices. If the price elasticity of the demand for imports is low, as it is likely to be in depression, these income and price effects work in opposite directions. The question is which is the stronger? Moreover, in prosperity, increased incomes make it easy to sell exports but imports are expensive. Which now is the more important, the price or the income effect?

The answer to this question, as to all those above, is that it depends on the circumstances. How elastic is the domestic demand for imports; how income-elastic is the demand abroad for your exports (their imports); how wide are the swings of income; how elastic is the supply of goods abroad which determine the amplitude of price fluctuation? So much is obvious.

What is not permitted, however, is for a country to complain of its lot in the world by pointing to one effect now and a different effect later. A European writer has suggested that industrial countries of western Europe suffer from the income effect in world depression and from the terms-of-trade effect in periods of boom. No reference is made to the income effect in boom, or to the terms-of-trade effect in depression.

Or a spokesman for underdeveloped countries bewailed the "fact" that these countries suffer from the terms of trade in depression, and tend to let inflation get out of hand in boom, so that their balance of payments is always in deficit.

If we look squarely at both the income and price effect when they thus operate in different directions because of price inelasticity, we can suggest that there may be different stages of boom and depression, with different income and price impacts. Take a country with substantial world trade like Britain which used to export income-inelastic and import price-inelastic products. Starting from some average normal level, such a country benefits from world depression and is hurt by world prosperity. In depression, prices of imports fall while demand for exports is sustained; in prosperity, the terms of trade become adverse, without any substantial expansion in export volume. The price effect outweighs the income effect.

If, on the other hand, the demand for imports is only slightly price-inelastic and the foreign demand for imports highly income-elastic, the country benefits from booms and is hurt by depression. The income effect outweighs the price effect.

It could happen that a country's demand for imports was price-inelastic, and the demand for its exports rather income-elastic, under conditions where prices rose only slightly during the early part of the boom and much more during the late stages after full employment was reached or closely approached. In these circumstances, the country might gain from world prosperity before full employment and price inflation, when the income effect prevailed over the price effect, but lose in the peak stages of the boom, when the positions were reversed.

The answer here then is that almost anything can happen, and that whether the income effect is more significant than the price effect when they work in opposite directions on a country's balance of payments depends upon the kind of country one is dealing with and the nature of the conditions which produce the price and income changes. In industrial countries which export income-elastic products and import price-inelastic, the income effect is likely to be more significant than price, except perhaps at the peaks of booms. But for some industrial countries whose exports are income-inelastic, like textiles, this may not hold, etc.

Elasticities versus Absorption

The quarrel between the elasticity-optimists, on the one hand, and the absorption school, on the other, is one which is rooted in the academic development of economics. In price analysis, we use partial-equilibrium elasticities, assuming other things, including income, equal. Similarly, in income analysis, we tend to use models which usually require an assumption of unchanged prices. When incomes and prices both change, we could use either general-equilibrium price elasticities—of the *mutatis mutandis* (changing those things which ought to be changed) type rather than *ceteris paribus* (other things equal)—and changing, among these other things, income; or we can use an absorption approach, in which the propensities to spend reflect not only consumers' response to changes in real income, with prices fixed, but also changes in relative prices. The elasticity approach is inadequate if it is partial. Ditto for the income approach. When the elasticities approach is generalized to include changes in spending, or the income approach to include changes in prices, they merge into one another.

It is wrong, as we have suggested, to regard the elasticities approach as appropriate for the impact of devaluation on the balance of payments, and the income approach as suitable to the analysis of changes in internal monetary and fiscal policy. As the song puts it, you can't have one without the other. The impact of devaluation on the balance of payments is indeterminate until one states what happens to income; ditto income changes . . . prices.

It is somewhat ironical that while price analysis was developed by the classical economists who assumed full employment, devaluation seems to work better under conditions of less than full employment. With full employment, the task is to cut down absorption. With less than full employment, some part of the improvement can come from increased output, whilst holding existing absorption constant (and preventing an increase in absorption parallel to the increase in output). In comparable fashion, a reduction of domestic spending is more effective in improving the balance of payments when it closes an inflationary gap than when it opens a deflationary gap, since in the former case output will not be reduced.

The upshot of this discussion is a warning to be careful. In discussing price, keep one eye on income, and vice versa. Bear in mind the assumptions being made and the assumptions appropriate to the case in question. When you specify the conditions under which price changes or income changes are to operate, make sure that you do not thus alter the problem from what was originally intended. And note that in moving from partial elasticities to general ones, the values change, just as the marginal propensity to absorb when prices are changing differs from the marginal propensity to spend at home at constant prices.

Summary

When price and income are both free to move, it is impossible to say how the system will operate unless one specifies the character of the problem posed.

The income mechanism is identical with the price mechanism only if some rather heroic assumptions are introduced. Changes in the exchange rate can produce a change in the balance of payments at full employment only if they result in a reduction in domestic expenditure, or "absorption." This may be induced through money illusion, a Pigou-effect, or, most probable, through the internal redistribution in income. Or it may be frustrated through resistance to such redistribution.

When the exchange rate is flexible and the balance of payments maintained in equilibrium by smoothly effected adjustments, some repercussion of changes in terms of trade on domestic spending is possible.

When the initial disturbance is a change in domestic spending, the balance of payments will be worsened by an increase in spending, helped by a decrease, with prices and incomes both operating in the same direction, provided that the sum of the price elasticities is greater than one and the sum of the marginal propensities to import less than one.

Productivity changes may have an impact on the balance of payments through income effects, price effects, or both. The income effect is adverse to the country experiencing improvement in productivity (in its export good); the price effect depends upon the sum of the price elasticities.

If incomes and price both change abroad, the net effect will depend upon price and income elasticities.

Finally, the elasticities approach can be broadened from partial-equilibrium analysis to include income changes; or the income approach can be broadened to include the effects of price changes in absorption. In either case, they become identical. But the price elasticities needed for a general approach differ from the partial elasticities normally calculated, and the marginal propensity to absorb differs from the marginal propensity to spend at home at constant prices.

SUGGESTED READING

TREATISES, ETC.

The absorption approach was introduced by S. S. Alexander in "Effect of a Devaluation on a Trade Balance," *SP*, April, 1952, and has been attacked by F. Machlup in "Relative Prices and Aggregate Spending in the Analysis of Devaluation," *AER*, June, 1955, and "The Terms-of-Trade Effects of Devaluation upon Real Income and the Balance of Trade," *Kyklos*, No. 4 (Bern), 1956.

One of the earliest attempts to incorporate income and price analysis into the same framework was A. C. Harberger's "Currency Depreciation, Income and the Balance of Trade," *JPE*, February, 1950. Only a few months behind were the papers by S. Laursen and L. A. Metzler, "Flexible Exchange Rates and the Theory of Employment," *RE & S*, November, 1950; and W. F. Stolper, "The Multiplier, Flexible Exchange Rates and International Equilibrium," *QJE*, November, 1950. The productivity case is discussed by H. G. Johnson, in "Increasing Productivity, Income-Price Trends and the Trade Balance," *EJ*, September, 1954.

Professor Meade's attempt at a demonstration of the identity of the gold standard and flexible exchanges is contained in *The Balance of Payments* and summarized in a diagram on page 192.

POINTS

For a discussion of the relatively greater importance of the income effect over the terms-of-trade effect, see R. Hinshaw, "American Prosperity and the British Balance-of-Payments Problem," *RE & S*, February, 1945; and R. Hinshaw and L. A. Metzler, "World Prosperity and the British Balance of Payments," *RE & S*, November, 1945.

Part III

The Current Account in the Balance

of Payments:

Commercial Policy

Chapter 12

COMMERCIAL POLICY—
TARIFFS

Seven Effects

Analysis of interferences with international trade—represented in this chapter by a tariff—can proceed through examination of various "effects" of its imposition. Our discussion is organized around seven such effects. They are:

1. The protective effect
2. The consumption effect
3. The revenue effect
4. The redistribution effect
5. The terms-of-trade effect
6. The employment effect
7. The balance-of-payments effect

Not all these aspects of the tariff refer to the same analytical viewpoint, and it is of the utmost importance to distinguish carefully at what level of interest the discussion runs. A tariff may be analyzed in terms of its impact on an industry, a region of a country, a factor of production, a country, or the world as a whole. An argument valid in terms of a given country will not be valid for the world, if the gain for the country is more than offset by losses of other countries, except under the particular circumstance that the international distribution of welfare can be improved by a redistribution of income in the indicated direction. A factor of production may gain from a tariff but only at the expense of other factors. Unless redistribution is required for welfare reasons (and is otherwise unobtainable), a tariff argument valid for a region is invalid for the country.

The Protective Effect

The protective effect can be illustrated in partial and general equilibrium, along with a number of other effects on the list. In Figure 12.1, $Q-Q_3$ represents imports at the price OP, prior to the imposition of a tariff. The tariff, $P-P'$, is presumed to have no effect on the foreign offer price, because of the infinite elasticity of the supply of imports at the price OP. The protective effect is shown by the increase in domestic production $Q-Q_1$. The consumption effect is the reduction in total consumption, Q_2-Q_3. The revenue effect is the money amount received by the government on the new level of imports, the rectangle b, and is derived from multiplying new imports, Q_1-Q_2, by

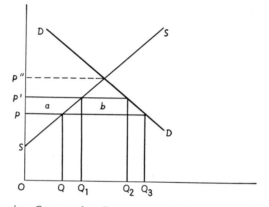

FIG. 12.1. Protective, Consumption, Revenue, and Redistribution Effects of a Tariff in Partial Equilibrium

the tariff, $P-P'$. The redistribution effect is the quadrilateral a, which is the additional economic rent paid to the pre-existing domestic producers, plus the rent paid to new producers above their supply price. In old-fashioned economic terms it is an addition to producers' surplus derived by subtraction from consumers' surplus.

The size of the protective effect, relative to a given tariff, is evidently determined by the elasticity of the supply curve. If the supply curve is highly elastic, the protective effect will be large; if inelastic, small. A tariff is prohibitive when the protective effect is sufficient to expand domestic production to the point where it will satisfy domestic demand without imports. In Figure 12.1 the minimum tariff which will keep out all imports is $P-P''$.

The protective effect can be shown in general equilibrium. In Figure 12.2, the tariff is represented by the difference in the price in the domestic market and in the foreign country. If we assume that the tariff did not change the world free-trade price, PC, the tariff is represented by the difference in slope between $P-C$ and $P'-C'$. In this case $P-P'$ is the protective effect, and $C-C'$ is the consumption effect.

Note that we have refrained from saying, in Figure 12.2, which product is subject to a tariff. It could either be an import tariff on wheat or an export tariff on cloth, or some appropriate mixture of the two. In the case of an import tariff on cloth, the protective effect is increased production of the protected article. If the diagram represents an export tax on cloth, the "protective" effect is misnamed and should be regarded as a "destructive" effect, reducing the profitability of production of the export good. The Constitution of the United States pro-

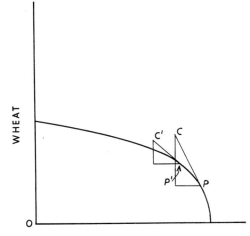

FIG. 12.2. The Protective and Consumption Effects in General Equilibrium

hibits export duties because the states in 1789 were unwilling to assign to the federal government this power to destroy export trades.

The protective effect of an import duty is always favorable for an industry or a region dominated by a single economic activity. The country as a whole may lose, but the particular industry which has its price raised benefits, at least in the short run. The resources engaged in an inefficient industry might do better in the long run to shift into occupations where they would be more productive. So long as they remain in the given industry, however, they gain from the tariff.

It follows that whenever a tariff is removed, an industry is hurt. This is by and large the case, and a number of attempts have been made to devise methods of offsetting the injury to an industry or the factory engaged in it from the removal of a tariff. But there will be times when an industry has gotten lazy and sluggish behind tariff protection, failing to take advantage of the opportunities for improving productivity by introducing new methods. In these cases, removal of the tariff may actually stimulate improvements in productivity through competition and help.

It further follows that a program of trade liberalization, like the Reciprocal Trade Agreements Act in the United States, which promises to reduce tariffs without hurting anybody, is based on misrepresentation or stupidity.

The Consumption Effect

The consumption effect is almost always adverse. When it is adverse, total consumption is reduced, by Q_2-Q_3 in Figure 12.1, or from C to C' in Figure 12.2; and the consumer pays more for each item he continues to purchase.

A region can be adversely affected by the consumption effect. Thus the South of the United States which sold its cotton on world markets was obliged by the northern tariffs on manufactures to buy its textiles and other manufactured products in a protected market at high prices.

The exception to the rule is the one argument for a tariff valid for the world as a whole: the infant-industry argument. This argument is based on external economies or an imperfect competition, due, in turn, to imperfect knowledge of difficulties of entry. A demonstration was made in Chapter 5 that increasing returns or decreasing costs invalidated the law of comparative costs. If a tariff imposed on a good attracts into its production entrepreneurs previously unaware of the opportunities available or induces them to accumulate capital (or labor or land) in the amount required to achieve the economical scale of operations, the tariff may be said to be justified. There may be other and more desirable methods of calling attention to these opportunities—such as a subsidy. This lowers the price to the consumer rather than raises it, and in this way helps to broaden the domestic market. But it must be recognized that the infant-industry argument, however much abused, is valid.

The infant-industry justification for a tariff is frequently abused. The world is full of industries with tariff protection which never have achieved sufficient economies to be able to dispense with protection. The test, of course, is whether the industry ultimately is able to function without tariff protection after the economies of scale have been achieved and the infant has "grown up." But occasionally an industry will grow up without actually removing the tariff. The removal of the tariff is not the only test. The pharmaceutical industry in the United States, for example, operates behind a wall of protection which is evidently not needed in many lines, since the industry is on an export basis. The tariffs which aided the industry in getting started, or rather helped it to stay alive after World War I, are retained through inertia or as a defense against possible dumping (discussed in Chapter 14). If a protected industry develops to the point where it can compete in world markets, as many have, it has grown up.

Typically, the infant-industry argument is used to justify the imposition of tariffs on an industry which had enjoyed the natural "protection" of trade disruption during war. This was the case of the famous "Corn Laws" imposed in Britain in 1819 to maintain the price of wheat at the levels reached during the Napoleonic Wars and so to prevent the collapse of grain production. The Corn Laws were not, in fact, removed until 1846, some twenty-seven years later, nor was farming seriously disturbed until the 1880's. The Embargo of 1807 in the United States gave the textile industry a start which the Tariff Act of 1816 was passed to defend. The same argument was used to justify the protection of machinery and chemicals in Britain after World War I and of chemicals and pharmaceuticals at the same time in the United States. The object was not the procreation of infants but the prevention of infanticide in the cold, cruel world of competition. In these cases the costs of entry had already been met: the question was whether, with time, increased efficiency could make the industry normally profitable without protection or subsidy.

No other argument for tariff protection based on efficiency is valid for the world as a whole. With decreasing returns, specialization based on comparative costs ensures maximum output. It is possible, perhaps, to create special cases in which the increase in income in one country, through an increase in tariffs, leads to a continuous increase in income through the action of the accelerator, while the decline in income in the original producing country is not cumulative. An employment argument could then be made for tariffs which would be valid for the world as a whole. But this case would need to be special rather than general.

Tariff Factories

While the infant-industry argument can be justified from a world point of view, great care must be taken, as pointed out, to apply it in individual cases. The theory of location may be helpful in this connection, as in the case of tariffs imposed on the finished product but not on parts or materials, to encourage foreign producers to establish tariff factories for final assembly or processing in the country in question. Pig iron and steel scrap may be duty-free in Italy, for example, while semifinished and finished steel were subjected to high duties (before the Schuman plan). Equal encouragement can be given to factories working up raw materials for export by the imposition of export taxes on material such as jute, while the manufactured product, in this case burlap, is exported without impost.

Tariff factories raise certain problems of capital movements. Briefly, doubt has been expressed whether this sort of tariff brings in capital which would not otherwise be attracted from abroad and, if it does, whether the gain of the capital-importing country is equal to, greater than, or less than the loss of the capital-exporting country. On the other hand, it has been argued that if trade substitutes for factor movements in producing goods- and factor-price equalization, factor movements can substitute for trade in the same fashion. If capital and/ or labor is free to move, a tariff which raises the return to one or the other of these factors may, under a number of highly restrictive assumptions, stimulate factor movements which equalize prices and eliminate trade. These issues cannot be resolved here. The point may be made, however, that a country hopeful of reaping the benefit of decreasing costs will do well to concentrate in market-oriented and foot-loose industries for import-tax protection and in supply-oriented or foot-loose industries for export-tax protection.

Much will depend upon whether the market is large enough—in the case of import taxes—to support an industry of the size necessary to achieve economies of scale. But it is clearly safer, other things being equal, to attempt to protect a market-oriented process, such as automobile assembly or flour milling, rather than an industry as a whole or a supply-oriented process; or to protect a foot-loose industry, such as textile manufacture or petroleum refining, rather than steel manufacture or another supply- or energy-oriented industry. Similarly with export taxes, the supply-oriented process can be protected more readily than can the market-oriented.

In the case of foot-loose industries, it makes little difference usually whether the process is located at the market or the source of supply, so long as it is not in between at a point which entails unnecessary handling. This leaves open the possibility that an importing country will tax gasoline and fuel oil, but not crude petroleum, in an effort to entice the refining process to its shores—as France did for national defense purposes in the interwar period—while the crude-petroleum-producing country will attempt to stimulate refining within its shores by an export tax on crude petroleum but not on refined products. The total effect would be a standoff, if the taxes were of equal magnitude, or a case of bilateral monopoly (a monopoly buyer facing a monopoly seller) in which the outcome is indeterminate. Only the consumer would lose.

These remarks are no warrant for taxing all exports of raw materials or imports of assembled products. Far from it. They should, however, convey the impression that this procedure makes more sense than putting export taxes on finished products and import taxes on raw materials and parts.

The Revenue Effect

Governments must raise revenue for a variety of public purposes, and from time immemorial foreign trade has been an object of taxation. In the United States 90–95 per cent of all federal revenues came from the tariff in the 1850's. The less developed the country, the more likely it is that a substantial proportion of governmental revenues comes from tariff duties. This is less a matter of equity in taxation than of administrative convenience. Goods are easier to tax than the intellectual abstraction which is "income." And the flow of goods is constricted at ports of entry so that foreign is more readily taxed than domestic trade.

A tariff for revenue only is one where the protective and redistributive effects are missing. The consumption effect will be eliminated only under the limiting assumption that prices abroad fall by the full amount of the tariff, so that the tax is in effect borne by the foreign producer. A tariff for revenue only can be on goods which are not produced at home at all; or one where an equal tax is imposed on domestic production to eliminate the protective and the redistribution effects. Some economists have included in the tariff for revenue only a flat percentage tax on all imports. This is an error: the protective and redistributive effects are arbitrary and random, depending upon the amount of the domestic price increases and the elasticity of the domestic supply curves. But they exist.

In levying excise taxes to support tariffs, one should tax domestic production (including exports) or domestic consumption (including imports). If the tax is on production and all supply curves in a country are equally elastic, a flat rate of tax does not distort production. If supply curves differ, the welfare disturbance is minimized by taxing more heavily the less elastic supply curves, since this results in less distortion of production. By the same token, if taxes are levied on consumption, the distortionary effects of raising a given amount of revenue are reduced by taking more heavily the less elastic demand curves since this minimizes the distortion of consumption.

There is a presumptive case, according to Professor Meade, for taxing domestic consumption at higher rates than imports. It will be remembered from Figures 9.3*a* and 9.3*d* that the excess supply curve of imports abroad is likely to be more elastic than the supply curve of domestic output; this is because of the elasticity of demand curves abroad, which must be added to the supply curve in calculating *excess* supply. If domestic output consumed at home is taxed at the same rate as imports, to raise revenue, the distortionary effect in imports is greater than that in domestic output. Ideally then, the rates on domestic output should be raised, and those on imports lowered, consonant with a fixed amount of revenue, until the distortion in the two cases is equalized.

The Redistribution Effect

The redistribution effect shown in Figure 12.1 represents a higher price, and higher profits, for existing producers. In the real world this may be much more important than the protective effect. The interests seeking tariff protection spend their time arguing the case of the marginal producer. The main drive for protection, however, is frequently the inframarginal supplier who will not be driven out of business by free trade but will make less money.

The partial-equilibrium diagram shows the redistribution effect as the transfer of consumers' surplus to producers in a single commodity. More fundamentally, tariffs will redistribute income among factors engaged in different proportions in producing different goods. Just as free trade raises the price of the abundant factor and lowers the price of the scarce, so a move away from free trade raises the price of the scarce factor and lowers the price of the abundant.[1]

In these terms, the tariff may represent an attempt by the scarce factor to reduce the trade which weakens its quasi-monopoly position. The drive to remove tariffs, on the contrary, can be equated with an attempt of the abundant factor to improve its position by widening its market. Under Hume's law, an increase in imports leads to an increase in exports, which raises export prices and the rate of return to the factor engaged intensively in export industry.

This analysis provides an insight into tariff history. The removal of the Corn Laws in 1846 is sometimes regarded as a response to the teaching of Adam Smith seventy years earlier. But the Corn Laws were imposed only after the Napoleonic Wars, already some forty years

---

[1] A geometric demonstration in general equilibrium can be provided by the Stolper-Samuelson box diagram set out in Figure B.6 in Appendix B. Here the tariff shifts production away from the factor-price-equalization points, *P* and *U,* and in the direction of the autarchic points, *S* and *T.* In so doing, it changes factor proportions and factor returns in both industries.

after *The Wealth of Nations* had appeared in 1776. And the removal of the Corn Laws was engineered after the rising industrial and commercial classes (enterprise plus capital) became plentiful. These groups asserted their political ascendance with the Reform Bill of 1832. Having achieved political power, they were able to increase their return, at the expense of the previously dominant agricultural classes who had engineered the tariff on wheat.

This same explanation in the United States setting ascribes the high tariff policies to capital in manufacturing attempting to maintain its scarcity value when land was plentiful and cotton and wheat would have benefited from free trade. This explanation does not fit nineteenth-century conditions well because of the greater importance of the infant-industry argument. At the present time, however, it makes much more sense. Labor-intensive types of manufacturing—shoes, textiles, pottery, hat bodies, etc.—are the strongest proponents of tariff protection. Large-scale manufacturing in mass-production industries, on the other hand, employs a predominance of the abundant factor, capital, and is identified with exports. As capital became more plentiful than land and as the role of agricultural products in exports shrank, large-scale manufacturing industry swung from protectionism to export-mindedness, and agriculture from free trade to protection. This explains much of the reversal in United States trade policy.

The Republican party, long the stronghold of high tariffs, lost a great deal of its protectionist drive as states like Michigan contemplated their interest in automobile exports and organizations like the Chamber of Commerce and National Foreign Trade Council responded to the foreign-trade views of farm machinery, business machinery, machine tools, and the oil industry. Some cultural lags remain: Southern states with a growing cotton textile industry clung for a long time to the free-trade position as if they still were predominantly exporting cotton. And Republicans from states like Ohio attempted to emasculate the reciprocal trade agreements in reverent memory of McKinley. But the factor argument means that business, especially big business, has an interest in low tariffs, not high.

Here the monopoly and the free-trade argument come into some conflict in the United States. It used to be the argument of the liberal (in the *laissez faire* rather than the left-wing sense) that free trade represented the general interest, while the tariff was the work of vested interests like big business. Today, the argument is found that since large companies with large volumes of capital are interested in freer trade—whether more exports which raise prices, like automobiles, or more imports which lower costs, like Middle East and Latin-American oil—free trade helps the monopolies while tariff protection favors the little fellow.

As regards big and little business, this may well be true. The economist must be neutral in this discussion, at least in his professional capacity, and simply point out what the relationships involved are in words as little loaded as possible. More specialization is more efficient, i.e., increases total product. More specialization, however, redistributes income in favor of capital and against labor. It accomplishes this by reducing the monopoly position of the scarce factor of production, which in this country is labor. Capital-intensive industry may be big business, and labor-intensive industry little. None the less, higher tariffs increase the return to labor by reducing the supply of labor-intensive goods, while freer trade increases the return to capital by increasing the demand for capital-intensive goods. Some noncompeting groups of labor, as, for example, those which make up the bulk of the membership of the CIO, may regard their interest as associated with capital-intensive industry rather than labor-intensive industry, and hence support freer trade. Conversely, small business is likely to side with labor-intensive industry rather than capital-intensive, even though it represents capital or entrepreneurship as a factor of production.

Under certain conditions, the factor argument has implications for employment of a sort, hinted at but not discussed above in the passages on the multiplier. If factor proportions in industry do not readily adjust to changed factor prices and if labor is the scarce factor, then, with a given national income, balanced trade at a high level will lead to unemployment of labor as contrasted with balanced trade at a low level. Moving from a low level of exports and imports, maintained by the operation of something akin to Hume's law and a high tariff wall, to freer trade, increased imports will displace labor, while increased exports will employ mainly capital. In the new position, capital may command a scarcity rent in these circumstances. But, unless factor proportions are adjustable or unless the increase in real income spills over into labor-intensive industries, labor will be unemployed. Here, of course, the remedy is not tariffs to maintain balanced trade at a low level but increased mobility of resources, which will shift factor proportions through all industry.

There is this much in the "cheap-labor" argument for tariffs, which, as normally put forward, is fallacious. If labor is the scarce factor, imports of labor-intensive commodities, which are those in which the country has a comparative disadvantage, will reduce the return to labor. But this is not much. The cheap-labor argument in its usual form is wrong, based on an erroneous labor theory of value and ignoring the obvious fact that countries with high wages are able nonetheless to export.

Noneconomic Arguments

When we leave the level of the industry and of the factor and move to national arguments for the tariff, we must recognize that there are some which are not economic and which are presumably excluded from the present discussion. In each case, the tariff involves a national loss which must be weighed against the gain in the other field.

Adam Smith admitted one such case, saying, "Defense is of much more importance than opulence." Clearly it is better for a country to continue as a going concern in the long run than to live at a higher standard in the short. But while the economist is prepared to admit the validity of this argument, he is forced by his common sense to suspect that many of the defense arguments put forward by special interests are rationalizations of positions which are really based on industrial interests. It is too much to say in this connection that "patriotism is the last refuge of a scoundrel," but it is easy for everyone concerned with the production of a given item to exaggerate its importance to the national interest, and easy for politicians who want to "do something" for a given area, to do so under the national defense label. In total war, everything is involved in defense. An inefficient watch firm, woolen manufacturers, the candle industry, and independent oil producers will all plead the need for tariffs in the national interest. The economist who has not thoroughly examined each case may nonetheless suspect special pleading.

One other noneconomic argument is concerned both with national defense and with sociology. Nineteenth-century German writers have argued for protection for agriculture to maintain the peasantry. In part this was to furnish a supply of soldiers for the army, since rural families were more reproductive than urban. In part, as recently in Britain, there has been a desire to maintain agriculture and the rural way of life—whether the life of the Junker baron or of the sturdy British yeoman. In France, protection against wheat imports provided in the 1880's and 1890's appears to have its origin in the urge to preserve the family and the family farm. The argument for maintaining the price of an import commodity in the face of a decline in price abroad—due to inelasticity of supply where factors cannot be shifted readily into other occupations—is both social and economic. We shall meet and discuss its counterpart in resources engaged in exporting which cannot be shifted into other occupations. This is the primary argument for intergovernmental commodity agreements in basic foodstuffs and raw materials, particularly minerals.

The Terms-of-Trade Effect

The static argument in favor of tariffs at the national level is that under the appropriate circumstances a tariff will enable the country to obtain its imports cheaper. In effect, the foreigner pays the duty, or some considerable part of it. This terms-of-trade argument in favor of a tariff may be demonstrated both with the partial-equilibrium analysis and, more completely, with Marshallian offer curves.

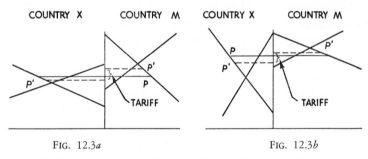

FIG. 12.3*a*   FIG. 12.3*b*

Tariffs to Improve the Terms of Trade—Partial Equilibrium

In the partial-equilibrium case, Figure 12.3*a* shows the effect of a tariff in widening the spread between prices in the exporting and importing countries. *P* is the price with trade, before the imposition of a tariff, assuming no transport costs. *P'* is the price in each market after the imposition of a tariff. In this case, where the elasticities of demand and supply are roughly the same in both countries, the tariff will partly raise the price in the importing country and partly lower the price in the exporting country. If the price in the exporting country is lowered at all, however, the country gets the product cheaper.

It is true that the consumer in the importing country has to pay a higher price. But this is offset, so far as imports are concerned, by the revenue effect. If the redistribution effect can be ignored, the revenue effect, which is the tariff times imports after the imposition of the tax, is levied partly on producers in the exporting country. If the supply is very inelastic in the exporting country, as in Figure 12.3*b*, and the demand fairly elastic in the importing country, the imposition of a tariff will have only a small protective effect, i.e., imports will not be much changed, but they will be obtained much more cheaply. The reader may be reminded that if the supply in the exporting country is very elastic, close to horizontal or constant costs, then the imposition of a tariff cannot improve the terms of trade at all. This is what the classical economists, for the most part, assumed.

A similar demonstration may be made more completely with Marshallian offer curves. Figure 12.4 shows a pair of offer curves of

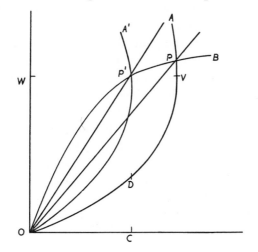

FIG. 12.4.   Tariff to Improve the Terms of Trade—General Equilibrium

Britain and the United States, *OA* and *OB,* respectively, which intersect at *P*. This gives a price *OP* between the two commodities, wheat and cloth. A tariff imposed by Britain on wheat from the United States may be represented by a new offer curve, *OA'*.

The tariff-distorted offer curve, *OA',* may represent either an import tax on wheat or an export tax on cloth. As an export tax, Britain is now prepared to offer less cloth for a given amount of wheat, collecting the export tax in cloth. For *OW* of wheat, for example, it used to offer *WV* of cloth but now offers only *WP'*, collecting *P'V* in taxes. Or it used to be prepared to offer *OC* of cloth for *DC* of wheat, whereas now it requires *P'C* in wheat, collecting *P'D* as tariff.

The shift of the offer curve from *A* to *A'* changes the terms of trade from *OP* to *OP'*. This is an improvement for Britain.

The improvement in the terms of trade may or may not make the country as a whole better off. In retailing, profit per item can be very high, but if sales fall way off, total profit is less than if the rate of profit had been more modest. Analogously, there is an optimum tariff at which any further gain from the improvement in the terms of trade would be more than offset by the related decline in volume. This optimum represents that tariff which cuts the opposing offer curve at the point where it is tangent to the levying country's highest indifference curve. Beyond this optimum, improvements in the terms of trade are still possible, but they are accompanied by a decline in the volume of trade which more than offsets the gain. Short of it, there is room for improvements in the terms of trade not completely offset by the shrinkage in trade quantities. Appendix F presents a geometric derivation of the optimum tariff.

Note here, too, that the gain in terms of trade from imposing a tariff depends on the elasticity of the foreign offer curve. If the foreign offer curve were completely elastic, a straight line from the origin with the slope of *OP,* the imposition of a tariff cuts down trade but leaves the terms of trade unchanged.

But two can play at this game. If Britain can improve her terms of trade by imposing a tariff, so can the United States. The original British gain will accrue only in the absence of retaliation. But if both parties retaliate, both certainly lose. Figure 12.5 shows such a case in which

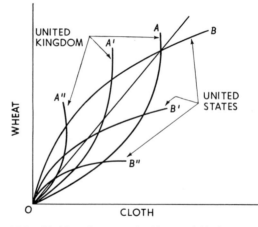

FIG. 12.5.   Tariff to Improve the Terms of Trade—Retaliation

tariffs imposed by Britain and the United States in retaliatory sequence *A, A', A'',* and *B, B', B'',* etc., leave the terms of trade unchanged at the end but greatly reduce the volume of trade. Each country would have been willing to buy and sell much more at these terms of trade if the price relationship in domestic trade were the same. The successive increases in British tariff on food and the United States duty on clothing, however, have resulted in a high price of the imported commodity after payment of duty in each country and the necessity to curtail consumption at these prices. The imposition of tariffs to improve the terms of trade, followed by retaliation, ensures that both countries lose. The reciprocal removal of tariffs, on the other hand, will enable both countries to gain. This is an explanation, or a rationalization, of the reciprocal nature of the Trade Agreements Program in the United States and the General Agreement on Tariffs and Trade.

The Income Effect

Our discussion in Chapter 10 has already touched on the way in which tariffs can increase income and reduce unemployment and reductions in tariffs reduce income and increase unemployment. The argument in brief is that a tariff will shift the import schedule downward by raising import prices.[2] On this account consumers shift their purchases to home-produced, import-competing goods. This will increase income by an amount which is a multiple of the decline in imports at the starting level of income. The change in national income is due not to any change in the trade balance; in Figure 12.6*a* there are no savings and no investment and hence no change in the trade balance, but nonetheless an increase in income and employment. Figure 12.6*b* shows the

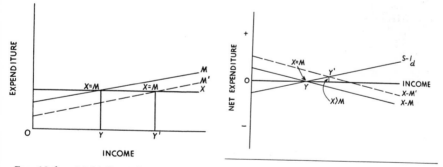

FIG. 12.6*a*. Multiplier Effects of a Tariff; No Savings, No Balance-of-Payments Effect

FIG. 12.6*b*. Income and Balance-of-Payments Effect of a Tariff with Savings

income effect (though not the multiplier) with the income-equilibrium condition $X - M = S - I_d$.

There can be no doubt that the employment argument for a tariff is valid for a country, provided that the initial assumptions of

[2] It will be recalled that we can use this income diagram when prices change, only by violating its original assumptions which call for constant prices and an identity of real and money income. One possible way out of this impasse is to assume that the demand for certain imports is almost perfectly elastic so that any tariff is prohibitive and imports fall without changing any prices. The price level has changed, however, if the composition of goods it measures is different in the two periods, even though some index numbers would not reveal it.

the analysis obtain, and provided further that foreign countries do not retaliate.

The gain in employment brought about by the increase in national money income in the tariff-imposing country, however, is achieved at the expense of a decline in national income and employment abroad, where exports are cut off. Since an opposite course of income abroad takes place and since the incentive of the rest of the world to increase tariffs is strong because of rising unemployment, it is not likely that an important country can get far in increasing employment by raising tariffs. For these countries the foreign repercussion is not negligible, nor can they count on the absence of retaliation.

While a shift in tariffs to promote an increase in national money income is a beggar-thy-neighbor type of policy, the alternative of an increase in domestic expenditure may lead to an import surplus on the multiplier technique. For this reason some countries with a high marginal propensity to import combine an increase in domestic expenditure (whether of business investment or government is immaterial for our purpose) with an increase in tariffs or a quota system. The increase in national income will not now be diverted into imports at the cost of the national gold reserves. This type of policy is preferable to an increase in tariffs by itself, since it may leave the value of imports as a whole unchanged—the movement along the import schedule balancing the shift of the schedule. It is not so desirable, however, as a policy of simultaneous expansion of expenditure in all countries concerned. This would make it possible to maintain balances of payments relatively the same (except for differences in marginal propensities to import not offset by differences in income expansion) and to preserve the benefits of free trade and equalization of prices.

It should be recognized, however, that in some countries where business investment cannot be readily stimulated, the inhibitions of the public regarding government spending may incline public officials to adopt a policy of tariff imposition, which is regarded as less undesirable than a budget deficit, since it appears to affect adversely only foreigners.

The strong reasons against raising tariffs as a means of expanding employment cannot unequivocally be turned the other way round to support a policy of reducing tariffs in depression. There is much to be said against putting on tariffs in depression, but it is a poor time to take them off. Additional imports in depression may lead to a shift of resources, not into domestic industry or export industry but into unemployment. The adoption of the Reciprocal Trade Agreements Act in 1934, in the midst of depression, is a tribute to the strength of the belief in the expansionary effects of increased exports and to the persuasive powers of Cordell Hull.

The removal of tariff barriers, however, is an ideal measure to restrain inflation, particularly when rising exports contribute significantly to the expansionary pressure. Germany has gone far since 1952 to lower duties unilaterally for this reason. Periods of buoyant business are appropriate periods for pursuance of a program of reduced trade barriers.

Discussion of the employment effects of tariffs has probably tended to overemphasize the multiplier and understate the price effects. The Smoot-Hawley Tariff Act, for example, is widely regarded as a beggar-thy-neighbor act, designed to increase employment through a reduced import surplus or positive excess of exports over imports. The widespread increase in trade restrictions which followed it, moreover, is regarded generally as retaliatory.

It is difficult in retrospect to sustain this view. The bill which culminated in the Act was introduced into the Congress in the spring of 1929, before the collapse of the stock market. Its concern was with the fall in the price of wheat, starting in Australia and spreading over the world. The oversupply in Australia threatened to lead to imports and to strand farm resources in the United States; more directly, it brought about a redistribution of real income in favor of consumers and adverse to farmers, which, in itself, had monetary repercussions because of the asymmetry between the responses of farmers and consumers. Farmers with reduced money income spent less; but consumers who were better off in real terms did not increase expenditure. The result was deflation.

Started to maintain the price of wheat, the Smoot-Hawley Tariff Act got out of hand as the log-rolling process developed. Hearings extended into 1930 after the bursting of the stock-market bubble. Most tariff increases, however, were sought for their price effects within separate industries rather than for their income effects on the country as a whole.

The Balance-of-Payments Effect

There has been some confusion about the effects of tariffs on the balance of trade. The curbstone, man-in-the-street opinion was that, of course, they improved it. Tariffs reduced imports—by an amount equal, in Figure 12.1, to the price $O–P$ times the protective effect $(Q–Q_1)$ plus the consumption effect $(Q_2–Q_3)^3$—but did not affect exports. Conversely, a reduction in tariffs worsened the balance of trade. This is the origin of (then) British Chancellor of the Exchequer R. A. Butler's slogan, "Trade not Aid," calling for a reduction in the United States tariff to remove the balance-of-payments surplus.

More sophisticated reasoning led to a modification of this view. The tariff diverted spending from foreign goods to domestic goods. This raised national income. While import prices were increased and the average propensity to import out of a given dollar of income therefore reduced, the increase in national income meant that there were more dollars of income. At the second stage of development it was thought that the balance of trade would be left unchanged.

We can now see that there is no simple answer to this question in a full-equilibrium situation, unless the assumptions are given. If there are no savings, no investment, and no foreign repercussion, as in Figure 12.6a, the balance of trade will be unaffected by the tariff. If the $S–I_d$ function is positively sloped, as in Figure 12.6b, a tariff which produces an upward shift in the $X–M$ schedule will improve the balance of payments, but by less than the initial gain in imports. So long as there is no accelerator and no foreign repercussion, an increase in tariffs will improve the trade balance; a decrease will cause it to deteriorate. This may be said to be generally the most acceptable position. If we introduce a foreign repercussion, the balance-of-payments effect is reduced. "Trade not aid" becomes less a means of correcting the European deficit if, in addition to a decline in income in the United States, the expansion of exports from Europe generates inflation there. If accelerators are introduced, moreover, any outcome is possible. A tariff which leads to a large-scale investment program, as, for example, in iron and steel in Australia, may so increase national income as to lead to an adverse balance. Or a reduction in the tariff of the United States may so expand foreign national incomes through the increase in exports and subsequent investment that it leads to a greater increase in exports than in imports. This is only a

[3] Figure 12.1, it will be remembered, assumed world prices unchanged. When there is some reduction in the world price, the initial change in the value of imports must also include that part of the revenue effect paid by foreigners. Thus at the limit, when the terms-of-trade effect is so large that it eliminates the protective and consumption effects because the world supply is completely inelastic, the initial change in the balance of payments (but not the ultimate balance-of-payments effect) is equal to the revenue effect.

possibility; it should be stated quickly and not regarded as an argument for higher United States tariffs.

The balance-of-trade argument for the imposition of tariffs again is beggar-thy-neighbor and holds only in the absence of retaliation. A recent illustration of the looseness of the connection between the balance of payments and tariffs is furnished by the German attempt to offset part of its balance-of-payments surplus since 1952 by reducing tariffs. Many duties and quotas except those needed to protect certain interests, largely agricultural, were removed, but the balance-of-payments surplus continued to grow. With its roots in the relation between output and absorption, the surplus in the current account was virtually impervious to tariff changes. German real income grew as a result of freer trade, but the balance of payments was hardly affected.

The Interaction of the Effects

The student must not get the impression that all seven effects of a tariff can operate with equal intensity at the same time. They are related to one another in many ways. The more the protective and consumption effects cut down imports, the less the revenue gained from a tariff. At the limit, of course, the tariff is prohibitive and yields no revenue. The more substantial the terms-of-trade effect in lowering prices abroad, rather than raising them at home, the less the protective and redistributive impacts.

While the balance-of-payments effect mainly depends upon the steepness of the slope of the $S-I_d$ curve, for a given schedule the greater the protective and consumption effects of a tariff change, the more the balance-of-payments effect. And so it goes on. The student (and even the instructor) may gain insights into the variety of the possible results of a tariff by relating the various effects to one another. If the revenue effect is very large, what does this mean for the balance of payments? The answer, it happens, turns out to depend upon what happens to the terms of trade.

Bargaining Tariffs

Adam Smith recognized two arguments for the tariff: national defense and bargaining. This latter is a question for the theory of games or strategy, more akin to poker playing than to economic theory of the usual sort. Two types of bargaining tariffs may be distinguished. The one is the antidumping tariff or countervailing duties to protect a country against predatory price cuts in an imperfectly competitive world. We shall save this topic for Chapter 14. The other case is essentially very simple: a country should have tariffs so that it will have something to give away in exchange for tariff reductions by foreign countries.

The Reciprocal Trade Agreements Act may be taken as indicative of what Adam Smith had in mind. Under this act, which reversed the trend of United States tariff history after World War I, reductions in United States tariffs were granted to foreign countries only in exchange for reductions in foreign tariffs on United States exports. The most-favored-nation clause extended the benefits of these mutual concessions to other countries. Part of the effect of the most-favored-nation clause was lost by reclassification: the limiting of concessions to new and narrow classes so defined as to exclude the products of competing countries.[4]

Is there an argument for reducing tariffs without the receipt of benefits in exchange? Such an argument can be made for a single factor of production. If the classical assumptions are valid, moreover, the case for unilateral tariff reduction is equally valid. Tariff reduction will not reduce the country's terms of trade, cause unemployment, or bring about an import surplus. The effects of removal will be to shift resources from import-competing industries, where they are relatively inefficient, into export industries (or, depending upon demand elasticities, domestic industries), where they are more efficient. If the classical assumptions are invalid, however, in the absence of retaliation, the imposition of a tariff will improve the terms of trade and increase employment. To this same extent, the reduction of tariffs without the benefit of "retaliatory" or reciprocal reductions would worsen the terms of trade and increase unemployment. There may nonetheless still be a valid basis for reducing tariffs without reciprocal concessions, if the purpose is to achieve redistribution of income from import-competing to export industry or simply to lower prices for consumers generally. The first of these effects would be greater if it were accompanied by concessions abroad.

Whether it is wise to raise tariffs prior to entering upon a tariff negotiation to exchange reductions belongs to poker rather than to economic theory. It is done.

---

[4] The classic example of reclassification is the concession on cattle imports granted by Germany to Switzerland in the agreement of 1902 extended by the most-favored-nation clause to all other exporters of cows to Germany. The reduction of the tariff was limited to "large dapple mountain cattle or brown cattle reared at a spot at least 300 meters above sea level and having at least one month's grazing each year at a spot at least 800 meters above sea level."

Alternatives to the Tariff

The presumptive case for free trade is hardly damaged by the demonstration in this chapter of the various effects which can be achieved by a tariff. This case, which we discuss again in Chapter 16, is essentially that free trade maximizes efficiency for any given distribution of income, allocating resources to their most efficient uses and distributing goods in such ways as to maximize consumer satisfaction. In addition, for any respect in which free trade falls short of the ideal, other and more efficient means than the tariff are on hand to correct the result.

Tariffs can, it is true, stimulate production subject to decreasing costs, raise revenue, redistribute income within and between countries, expand employment, and alter the balance of payments. But other and more equitable devices available for these purposes do not have the undesirable effects of distorting the allocation of resources and limiting consumption.

The valid case for interfering with the price system where increasing returns go unexploited is better tackled through subsidies. These stimulate output without restricting consumption. Producers resist subsidies, however, and prefer tariffs. Somehow the latter are regarded as perfectly compatible with the ethic of private enterprise while the former are not.

Direct taxes and transfers are superior to tariffs for redistributing income within a country. They achieve the desired result with less distortion in production and consumption.

In transferring income between countries, international transfers are superior to tariffs to improve the terms of trade.

Finally, employment and balance-of-payments objectives should be approached with monetary and fiscal policies.

If anything that the tariff can do, something else can do better, how do we explain the enthusiasm with which countries all over the world impose tariffs and the painfully slow way in which they take them off?

The movement for tariffs is strong because producer interests in particular are more politically powerful than producer and consumer interests in general. In fact, the free-trade movement in Britain was, and that in the United States is, essentially a producer movement, representing those industries embodying advanced technologies, on the one hand, or abundant factors, on the other. A representative of the protectionist interests once complained with a fair show of reason that he thought it unfair that the protectionists were always charged with being selfish (and frequently vested) interests, while the free-trade movement posed as public-spirited and above material considerations.

The Old-Fashioned, Genteel Tariff

The rapid development of a score of other devices for interfering in trade has left the tariff old-fashioned. A certain nostalgic attachment to it has developed. Some writers suggest that the tariff, respectable in comparison with quotas, trade discrimination, multiple currency practices, clearings, and the like, is respectable per se. This is nonsense. There is, however, this much to be said for the point. A tariff system introduces a change of price and still leaves to competition, or to such competition as exists, the choice of buyer and seller. Within the limits of the change in price, there is freedom to buy and sell at will. With quotas and other more direct interferences, or with discrimination, the choice of buyer or seller is not made solely on the basis of price. The buyer's or seller's currency or country may keep him out of a market in which discrimination is being practiced. Under a quota or exchange-control system, some buyers or sellers are chosen and some potential ones excluded. The beauty of the price system is that it operates with an invisible and impersonal hand. Tariffs are a major interference with the dictates of a free-trade pricing system. After the change, however, the choice of buyers and sellers is still handled impersonally.

Summary

The only valid argument for a tariff from the world point of view is the infant-industry argument. For a nation, a variety of valid cases can be made: a tariff may be needed for defense or other non-economic reason; to raise revenue, improve the terms of trade, expand income, improve the balance of payments. The last three of these are beggar-thy-neighbor in that the gain for the country creates problems or losses for foreign countries. Their success assumes no retaliation.

Redistribution of income within a country can result from a tariff between producers and consumers of a given product, between producing and consuming regions, between the scarce and the abundant factor of production.

Anything that a tariff can do, some other weapon of economic policy can do better.

SUGGESTED READING

TEXTS

L. W. Towle, *International Trade and Commercial Policy* (2d ed.; New York: Harper & Bros., 1956), Part V, chaps. xvii–xxiii, is highly institutional but excellent. A. Isaacs, *International Trade: Tariffs and Commercial Policies* (Homewood, Ill.: Richard D. Irwin, Inc., 1948), is almost exclusively devoted to tariffs and their history.

TREATISES

The classical statement of the free-trade case was that by Haberler, chaps. xiv–xvii. Recently Meade's, *Trade and Welfare*, Part I, has advanced the argument a number of stages in subtlety. The revenue discussion in this chapter was based on one of his second-best arguments for tariffs, chapter xii.

Apart from the optimum tariff, which is discussed in Appendix F, the modern developments in theory are found in Stolper and Samuelson, "Protection and Real Wages," which develops the factor argument; and Scitovsky, "A Reconsideration of the Theory of Tariffs," which discusses the terms-of-trade argument and retaliation. These are Nos. 15 and 16 in American Economic Association, *Readings*. See also N. Kaldor, "A Note on Tariffs and the Terms of Trade," *Economica*, November, 1940.

On recent tariff issues in the United States, see H. S. Piquet, *Aid, Trade and the Tariff* (New York: Thomas Y. Crowell Co., 1953); D. D. Humphrey, *American Imports* (New York: Twentieth Century Fund, Inc., 1955); and P. W. Bidwell, *What the Tariff Means to American Industries* (New York: Harper & Bros., 1956).

A useful description of tariff policies and procedures of the United States is contained in *Report to the Committee on Ways and Means on United States Customs, Tariff and Trade Agreement Laws and Their Administration* from the Subcommittee on Customs, Tariffs and Reciprocal Trade Agreements (Washington, D.C.: U.S. Government Printing Office, 1957). Also valuable is the statement in the Randall Commission on Foreign Economic Policy, *Report to the President and Congress* (Washington, D.C.: U.S. Government Printing Office, January, 1954); and by the same Commission, *Staff Papers* (Washington, D.C.: U.S. Government Printing Office, February, 1954), especially chaps. vi, vii, viii.

Some students of both human nature and economics enjoy reading *Hearings* before the House Ways and Means Committee and the Senate Finance Committee. They are replete with industrial detail and special pleading, chaotically organized. They should be searched or sampled, but not systematically read. In connection with the 1958 proposed renewal of the Reciprocal Trade Agreements Act, the Staff of the Subcommittee on Foreign Trade Policy of the Committee on Ways and Means collected a compendium of papers on United States Foreign Trade Policy entitled *Foreign Trade Policy* (Washington, D.C.: U.S. Government Printing Office, 1957).

Chapter
13

QUOTAS, COMMODITY
AGREEMENTS, STATE TRAD-
ING, ECONOMIC WARFARE

Effects of Quotas

If a country has a fair idea of the shape of the demand and supply curves involved in a particular commodity, and if these are not particularly inelastic, there is little difference whether it imposes a tariff or a quota. If the quota is set at the volume of imports which would result from the imposition of a given tariff, the protective effect will be the same in either case, and so will the consumption and the redistribution effects. In the partial-equilibrium diagram of Figure 13.1, for example, a tariff of 5 cents or a quota of 100,000

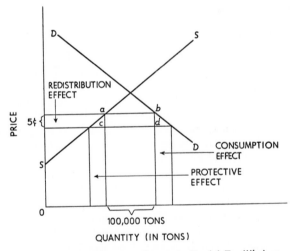

FIG. 13.1. Tariffs versus Quotas in Partial Equilibrium

tons would each have the same effect in raising the internal price, reducing over-all consumption, limiting imports, and encouraging domestic production.

There is, however, one considerable difference between a tariff
236

and a quota, even where conditions underlying the market are known. This is in the revenue effect. Under a tariff, the area *abcd* in Figure 13.1 would be collected as governmental revenue in the importing country. If a quota of 100,000 tons is laid down, the price of imports is greater than before. Who will capture this increase cannot be determined in advance. If the importers have a monopoly of the trade and exporters are unorganized, the importers may succeed in obtaining it. If the exporters are effectively organized and the importers not, the terms of trade may swing against the country as the foreign exporters hold up the price. Or the government of the importing country, by auctioning off import licenses, may succeed in obtaining for itself this increase in value due to scarcity, which economists sometimes call a "rent." This would make the quota the exact equivalent of the tariff, down to and including the revenue effect. The auction of import licenses is not used widely, however, so that the scarcity value inherent in the limited imports may accrue to either exporter or importer, depending upon the proximate conditions in the market. The greater likelihood is that importers will capture this rent.

In terms of offer curves, the situation can be set forth along the lines of Figure 13.2. If Britain, with the offer curve, *OA*, limits its

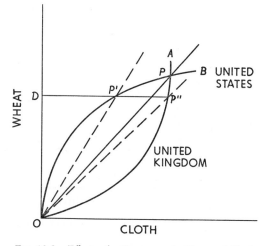

FIG. 13.2. Effects of a Quota on the Terms of Trade

imports of wheat to *OD*, the terms of trade between clothing and wheat may be *OP'* or *OP''* or any price between. Like the case of bilateral monopoly—with a monopoly buyer and a monopoly seller—the outcome is theoretically indeterminate. The new terms of trade, it will be observed, are either more or less favorable to the country imposing the quota. If the importers capture it, as has been suggested is likely, the terms of trade are improved by a quota, to the extent that the foreign offer curve is elastic.

Origins of Quotas

If the protective and redistribution effects are the same under tariffs and quotas, provided that elasticities are not zero, why did quotas come to supplant tariffs so widely in the 1930's? The question is a fair one, and the answer consists of three parts. In some commodities in which quotas were first imposed, the supply position abroad was almost completely inelastic. Under these circumstances, a tariff could not increase the price in the importing country or reduce the volume of imports. The only effect of the tariff was to improve the terms of trade and to gain revenue for the government by taxing the foreigner.

But while under ordinary circumstances a country is pleased to have its terms of trade improved and governmental revenue enlarged, these were beside the point. The French, who first developed quotas, were concerned in 1930 neither to get wheat cheaper from abroad nor to balance the budget. They wanted higher wheat prices for

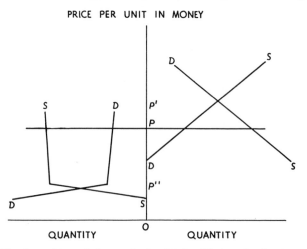

PRICE PER UNIT IN MONEY

FIG. 13.3. The Imposition of Quotas in Partial Equilibrium in the Face of Inelastic Supply

French peasants. When the increase in the United States tariff diverted the bumper 1929–30 Australian wheat crop to Europe, no simple tariff could keep it out. With an inelastic supply of imports, it was possible to raise or maintain the internal price only by setting a lower and fixed figure on the volume of permitted imports. Figure 13.3 shows such a case. Country M wants to raise the price of the import good to achieve a redistribution of income to producers. Any reasonable tariff will fail to do this, since the terms-of-trade effect will be large, given the inelastic character of excess supply in country X. A quota which halved imports, on the other hand, would clearly raise prices from OP to OP'. Note that if this quota is imposed and country X does nothing about it, the export price in X will fall to something like OP''. The imposition of a quota in M is therefore likely to be followed by some commodity-stabilization effort in X.

These inelastic offer curves are met particularly in agriculture; and it is in this field, so often subject to domestic policies to guarantee farmers or peasants a "fair return," that quotas abound. Where price-raising efforts, required for domestic political reasons, would be defeated by imports, they are often supported by quotas which eliminate imports or restrict them to some tolerable amount.

The more general consideration which gives rise to the wide use of quotas for protection and redistribution of income is that the shape of the excess-supply curve in exporting countries is unknown. How much of a tariff increase will prevent a price decline abroad from spreading to our country? It is difficult to answer this question if there is a single price abroad for domestic and export transactions. It may be impossible if foreign producers practice price discrimination and dump exports at prices lower than those in the home market. The possibility of such dumping, discussed in the next chapter, provides part of the inspiration for quotas.

Finally, there is a purely administrative reason which helps to explain the introduction of quotas. The use of tariffs had been so institutionalized in commercial agreements, with most-favored-nation clauses and other restrictions on independent action, that it was no longer possible to use tariffs as an emergency measure. Extreme circumstances called for extreme remedies, but the tariff was by this time a fair-weather device only.

The three reasons for the introduction of quotas, therefore, were inelasticity of foreign supply, certainty, and administrative flexibility. Of these, the most important was probably the certainty. This certainty, as we shall see, was gained at a considerable cost to world trade. Under some circumstances, however, a country will regard certainty as worth its share of this cost.

Quota Problems

Fixing the quantity of allowable imports in a class does not dispose of the problem. Which tons or casks or head will be allowed? If a single global quota is established, it is likely to invite a race among importers to see who can fill it first. The result is that the supply will come tumbling in during the early portion of the quota period and dry up at the end. In addition, nearby sources of supply will be favored over distant ones. If there are many ports of entry, there will be some difficulty in determining exactly the last barrel or hundredweight or gallon which may enter—a problem like that of, but more complex than, figuring out which is the first or 1,000,000th vehicle through a tunnel with two entrances. The result is overfulfillment.

These difficulties have usually led to the issuance of licenses or permits enabling importers to bring a specified volume of the restricted commodity into the country. Licenses can be issued either globally or for separate sources of supply; on a first-come, first-served basis, or on the basis of historic shares of the market; or licenses may be auctioned off by the government to importers. No system, however, is entirely or even quite satisfactory.

The establishment of national quotas tends to freeze the volume and direction of trade, regardless of changes in supply which might make one country ultimately a cheaper source than an older and established producer. One way to mitigate this difficulty is to leave some fairly considerable portion of the quota to "all other" unspecified countries. The tariff quota on oil imports into the United States—specifying a duty of $10\frac{1}{2}$ cents per barrel on imports up to 5 per cent of domestic production of the previous year and 21 cents per barrel after that— assigned large and fixed percentages of the quota to Venezuela and the Dutch West Indies (most refineries processing Venezuelan oil are in Aruba and Curaçao in Dutch Guiana), and left an open quota to be competed for among Canada, the Middle East, and any other potential source of supply, such as Indonesia. Quotas for oil imports by separate companies under the National Defense amendment to the Reciprocal Trade Agreements act produced vigorous protests in 1957 from all those companies which had newly begun to import or which had been about to do so to serve newly constructed coastal refineries.

In the 1930's, European countries went in heavily for bargaining about quotas, sometimes using the reassignment of unused quotas as a potential bargaining weapon. In some cases, quotas were established over imports where there was no serious intention of restricting purchases, simply to have quotas to be given away in bargaining. The draft charter of the International Trade Organization called for the ultimate removal of quotas and other quantitative interference in trade, but encouraged their reciprocal reduction in trade agreements en route to this end. Similarly, the Organization for European Economic Co-operation, established by the European recipients of Marshall Plan aid, obtained agreement of its members to reduce quotas on each others' imports (a form of regional discrimination) by stipulated percentages. This so-called liberalization took two forms: one, the elimination of quotas on intra-European trade; and, two, dollar liberalization or the elimination of quotas on imports from hard-currency areas. Percentages in this context are not very meaningful. Eighty per cent liberalization, for example, may cover only those products on which quotas are already large and have not been restrictive, leaving other quotas in effect which very much reduce trade.

Whether quotas are issued nationally or globally, the question remains of who may import. The restriction of imports raises the domestic price above the world price. Import licenses are accordingly valuable. In some countries, this has led to corruption and venality as import licenses were issued to friends or bribers of government officials. Even where these temptations are resisted, however, choice presents difficulties. To restrict the issuance of licenses to established importers has the disadvantage of preventing competition and new entry into the business. To reserve a portion of the quota for new business encourages fly-by-night speculators and middlemen in search of easy profits produced by the created scarcity rather than new economies of importing.

The suggestion has frequently been made, but seldom acted upon, that governments auction off import licenses to the highest bidder, thus recapturing for the people as a whole the scarcity value of the limit on imports. This would give quotas a revenue effect comparable to tariffs. The reasons that this idea has not been put into effect are partly theoretical: where there are many ports of entry, each with importing firms, there are, in effect, a number of import markets, and no single auction system would be appropriate. The main barrier to the introduction of this system, however, has been the insistent opposition of established importers. These believe that, on account of their overhead costs, they would be outbid by hole-in-the-wall newcomers, unless they were prepared to bid below cost. The result has been that this theoretically neat device has never been tried on a significant scale.

Quotas and the Balance of Payments

The certainty provided by quotas when countries seek to protect industries and redistribute income is even more urgently required in balance-of-payments issues. If we can use our $X-M = S-I_d$ diagram to illustrate the point, though it is inappropriate where prices change for any reason, quota restrictions, sometimes referred to as QR's, are frequently designed to alter the import schedule over the whole range of income. In Figure 13.4a $M(Y)$ shows the import schedule before QR's, and $M'(Y)$ afterwards. Figure 13.4b indicates how this

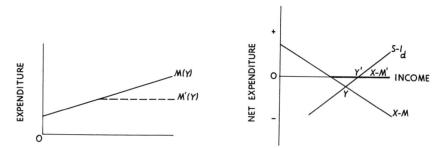

FIG. 13.4a.   Effect of Quota Restrictions   FIG. 13.4b.   Balance-of-Payments Effect of
on the Import Schedule   Quotas

affects the balance of payments, wiping out a deficit, and incidentally increasing national income (from Y to Y'). The new $X–M'$ schedule lies flat along the horizontal axis at zero balance-of-payments surplus or deficit.

The Income Effect of Quotas

The income effect of quota restrictions over the full range of imports is higher than that of an equivalent tariff. This is because the marginal propensity to import becomes zero (as in $M'(Y)$ in Fig. 13.4a) and this, by reducing the leakages, increases the multiplier. This greater expansive effect of quotas over a tariff is significant for underdeveloped countries which frequently run into balance-of-payments difficulties arising from inflation. Quota restrictions are a surer way of limiting imports than tariffs, if the inflation is not to be tackled at its seat in excess spending; but quotas pour fuel on the inflationary flames, while tariffs bring in revenue which removes inflammable material from the fire.

Quotas, Tariffs, and Monopoly

There is one further distinction between the effects of tariffs, on the one hand, and of QR's, on the other. If there is a potential domestic monopoly protected by a tariff, it can charge only the international price plus the tariff. If it tries to raise prices above this level, it will lose sales to additional imports.

To change a tariff into a quota, even without reducing the existing volume of imports, may convert a potential domestic monopoly into an actual one. The domestic monopolist or combine can now raise its price secure from the potential competition of imports. This difference, which is set out diagrammatically in Appendix G, is of greater importance for manufacturing than for agriculture, and in such situations as that of western Europe. Liberalization is a weapon against monopoly, even if the quota is replaced by an equivalent tariff.

Advantages and Disadvantages of Quotas

Most economists stress the disadvantages of quotas to the almost complete disregard of possible advantages. It is pointed out, correctly, that quotas tend to be too restrictive and administratively much more changeable and arbitrary, as contrasted with tariffs, which are altered less frequently. Under these circumstances, quotas are more expensive for consumers. They further tend to establish importers' monopolies or to reduce competition among foreign suppliers. Finally, quotas introduce a wholly arbitrary new dimension into international trade. Exports and imports are now determined not by the price system but by fiat. What goods may be imported and what exported are determined now not by impersonal forces working blindly at the direction of an invisible hand but by personal decision. The visible hand is more likely to evoke retaliation than market forces—although, if the quota be compared with the tariff, this must be admitted to be the work of a visible hand except in so far as it is impersonal with respect to what countries and what dealers may share in trade. The visible hand, moreover, is likely to be guided by considerations other than efficiency and maximization. Fairness, equity, justice may be used to decide what is bought, in what amounts, from what countries, and by whom. These considerations are not unambiguous in the same way that a price is, nor is it even likely that agreement can be obtained from different interests on what constitutes fairness. The use of quotas is a step backward toward the economics of the Middle Ages and the fair price.

These arguments are powerful. But we must give the devil his due. In the first place, quotas are being compared with international trade, not as it has been in the real world but with a model of an international trade system based on perfect competition and perhaps full employment. This is far superior to a system of quotas. In the interwar period, however, quotas had their uses, especially when a country was under serious deflationary pressure from abroad.

The London market in the nineteenth century, like the basement of Filene's department store in Boston, served as a place where distressed goods could be sold at some price. This was good for British consumers and for foreign producers. It may be argued that it was hard on British producers of import-competing goods and foreign consumers. But British producers of these goods had for the most part gone out of business, and factor mobility was sufficient to enable the resources concerned to shift into other lines. Under these circumstances, cheaper imports improved the terms of trade, and the distress sales of foreign producers were welcome to the British.

In a world of less factor mobility, less specialization, and with an important volume of resources engaged in domestic production of an imported article, distress sales from abroad are less tolerable. Resources cannot be shifted out of the domestic industry temporarily, later to be shifted back again. The tariff is a poor device to give temporary protection. The quota is, under these circumstances, the only feasible basis for defense of the domestic industry against a sudden and drastic decline in its income, which the society regards as "unfair."

This is not to say that the quota is not abused and brought into play in many circumstances when it is not appropriate. In some, domestic resources are uneconomically employed and should be moved. In others, what appears to be a temporary change due to a cyclical swing is really more basic and should evoke an adaptive response rather than a temporary cutting off of trade.

This is not to say, either, that a more fundamental attack on the problem is not superior to the use of the quota. Two such possibilities are evident: to prevent depression abroad and to increase the mobility of resources at home. Either or both of these courses of action should be undertaken too. Given a circumstance, however, where resources are relatively immobile and depression abroad occurs, the economist who would abjure all use of the quota fails to take account of the realities.

This defense of quotas as a measure to mitigate the effects of deflation abroad must not be extended to support for their use in the case of inflation at home. This is a horse of another color. Deflation abroad is outside the control of the country with the balance-of-payments deficit; domestic inflation is not. Quotas, as we have seen, are themselves inflationary. This is bearable in a world of deflation; it compounds the difficulties arising from domestic inflation. The dictum that quotas are less desirable than alternative lines of action is never more in point than in the case of quotas imposed to reduce the balance-of-payments effects of uncontrolled inflation at home.

Export Restriction

Restriction of exports, like restriction of imports, is a means of improving the terms of trade. In this case the terms of trade are of major concern. This is in contrast to the import quota, where principal interest generally attaches to the price effect for domestic producers or the balance-of-payments effect brought about by the reduction in the quantity of imports. The condition for successful gains from import quotas is inelasticity of local demand and inelastic foreign supply. Export restrictions flourish when domestic supply and foreign demand are inelastic. Only in the limiting case when demand is perfectly elastic is it impossible for a country to improve its terms of trade by restricting exports.

It is well to be clear on this point. It pays a country to burn its coffee, dump sugar in the sea, plow its cotton under, kill its pigs, or take supplies off the market through government purchase or loan when the demand curve facing the producers of that country is inelastic. That is, it pays producers. Consumers, whether in the country or abroad, and the world as a whole lose in real terms. In the case of overproduction and an inelastic demand, however, the redistribution of income from consumers to producers brought about by export restriction may act primarily to restore the position which existed before an increase in supply redistributed income in favor of the consumers and against the producers.

In most manufacturing lines, restriction of production automatically takes place before the consumers can gain at the expense of producers, i.e., producers reduce output when sales take place at a loss. In primary materials, where the bulk of the export-restriction schemes will be found, the opportunity to cut down production is generally limited either by the highly competitive character of production, as in agriculture, where a single producer can always improve his position by expanding output even though the industry as a whole loses in the process; or by lack of alternative opportunities for employment, as in highly specialized resources engaged in mining, plantation output, etc.

Given perfect knowledge of the slopes of demand and supply curves, an export tax would be as effective in improving the terms of trade as the restriction of production or export. To this extent, import and export restriction are identical. But export-restriction schemes fail, and export taxes defeat their own objectives more frequently than do tariffs and quotas on imports. The reasons are several. The inelasticity of demand is overestimated. The strength of potential competition abroad is underestimated. And, what is essentially the same as the first two reasons, differently expressed, the price sought is too high.

Demand is more elastic in the long run than in the short. Given time, substitutes can be found and other sources of supply developed. Since the demand involved is the demand abroad for the exports of a given country only, the monopoly must be airtight before export restriction can be counted a sure thing. The Stevenson rubber plan in Malaya encouraged production in Indonesia. The action of the United States in holding up world cotton prices in the 1930's developed alternative sources of supply in Egypt and Brazil. Perón's attempts to hoist the price of linseed oil to the United States encouraged the introduction of flaxseed production for oil in North Carolina and Minnesota. History is full of commodity-restriction schemes which failed because the new and high price held an umbrella over foreign producers and encouraged their expansion of production. Brazil's efforts to maintain the price of coffee have encouraged output in Colombia, Guatemala, Nicaragua, and lately in Ethiopia. The efforts of the West African Cocoa Marketing Board, combined with swollen-shoot disease, have in turn stimulated cocoa output in Brazil.

The economist must in humility confess that some of the burdensome stocks accumulated by control authorities turn out to be blessings in disguise, useful in different circumstances. The enormous supplies of wheat and cotton purchased by the Commodity Credit Corporation in the United States in the 1930's were highly valuable as reserves in World War II and immediately afterward. The wool accumulated during the war in Australia and New Zealand because of lack of shipping space prevented prices from going skyward at least until the brief splurge which followed the outbreak in Korea, after these stocks had been exhausted. In a highly changeable world, the price system does not always accurately forecast the long-run requirements for a commodity.

Export Restriction and Income

Export restriction seems at first sight symmetrically the opposite of import restriction. This is true of the protective and consumption effects. But both forms of restriction improve the terms of trade if the foreign offer curve has an elasticity less than infinity; both improve the balance of payments; and both expand national income. The reason that export restriction parallels import restriction in these latter respects is that the reduction in the quantity of exports involves an expansion of export by value; it is only undertaken when foreign demand is inelastic; and an expansion of the value of exports works on the balance of payments and national income in the same fashion as a contraction of the value of imports.

Export restrictions are sometimes imposed in order to prevent the loss of goods needed in the country. Recently, such export quotas existed in scrap steel, eagerly sought after by the Japanese and Schuman-plan industries, but also very much wanted by United States steel manufacturers. Here the effort of the United States government was not to raise the price abroad for balance-of-payments reasons. The demand, in fact, was elastic, and restriction reduced the value of exports. The object was rather to hold the price at home down in the interest of national defense.

Or restrictions can limit the export of machine tools needed for domestic investment. Despite elasticity of the foreign demand curve and a decline in the value of exports, this too raises national money income by permitting an increase in domestic investment.

Commodity Agreements

The history of international trade is replete with unsuccessful international commodity agreements. These agreements have their origin in the inelasticity of both demand and supply, in many of the commodities concerned, which results in large price changes for small shifts of demand or supply schedules. In addition, there is the claim of primary-producers that the long-run terms of trade run against them and give them less than "adequate, just, and equitable" prices, as a United Nations resolution backed by these producers put it, or less than a "fair share" of world income. But even when they start out to limit the range of price and income fluctuations, international commodity agreements end up trying to raise commodity prices. They all fail. The reason is that the elasticities are high in the long run, even though low in the short.

Price inelasticity of demand for primary products is due to many reasons. Some products, like wheat, rice, coffee, tea, and cocoa, have only a few major producers in international trade and demand for the commodity itself is price-inelastic. In others, the demand is derived, and all derived demands are less elastic than the demand for the products in which they are embodied. In still other products, inventory accumulation and decumulation bring about substantial shifts of demand from time to time but leave demand at all times price-inelastic.

The short-run elasticity of supply in agricultural products is determined by the nature of the production process and is low in the short run for annual crops and low over longer periods for crops produced from bushes or trees. Substantial shifts may occur as the bounty of nature varies. In minerals, there exists much higher short-run supply elasticity. Whatever the reason, primary products subject to short-run inelastic demand and supply vary widely in price. A United Nations study concludes that the average price of fifty primary products examined from 1900 to 1950 moved annually, on the average, 14 per cent. If the measure had run from monthly averages or between daily highs and lows, the range would have been extended.

Increased price stability has much to recommend it. The difficulty is how to achieve it. In some commodities where supply is variable because of crop failures and gluts, a certain amount of price variation is useful in stimulating expansion after short crops and contraction after long, but extreme fluctuations should be avoided. These commodities lend themselves to agreements which set maximum and minimum prices, with a range between, and minimum quantities to be imported by the consuming countries in abundant years, or to be exported by producing countries in periods of shortage. The International Wheat Agreement provides an example. Or if the main difficulty stems from the variability of speculative demand, stockpiling arrangements release additional supplies when demand is heavy and mop them up when demand is light. An example of this type of agreement is found in tin.

It evidently makes a substantial difference how wide the gap is between maximum and minimum prices and between the buying and selling price of the stockpiling authority, and whether the finance for stockpiling comes from the exporting or the importing countries. The wider the price range, the more instability, the higher the profits of the stabilizing agency, and the more the private price system is permitted or required to work. Whether finance is provided by exporters or importers affects balance-of-payments stability. Either arrangement equally affects income in the primary-producing country, but if stockpiling is financed by the exporting countries, their balances of payments get no benefit. In fact, the balance of payments may be more unstable than before. If the volume of exports fluctuates widely, foreign-exchange receipts will vary despite the added stability of price. To maintain imports in these circumstances by financing unsold exports through deficit financing will inevitably exaggerate the fluctuations in the trade balance.

There are other types of commodity agreements. In sugar, the need for an agreement is to deal with the small amount of production which is not already disposed of under preferential arrangements running between producing and consuming countries—largely Cuba and the Philippines with the United States, on the one hand, and the British West Indies with the United Kingdom, on the other. These preferential arrangements have narrowed demand and supply and increased the price instability in the "free" market.

The colonial marketing boards of the British Commonwealth attempt to stabilize the domestic price of primary products, but not the balance of payments, by buying at a fixed price from the domestic producer and selling at the world price. The West African Cocoa Marketing Board has denied that it attempts to raise the world price; it buys all that is offered and sells all it buys. But it has been attacked for this by economists who believe that in holding down the domestic price in periods of boom it has restricted output and thus raised the world price. Equally, if it holds the domestic price above the world level in depression, in stabilizing producers' incomes, it will contribute to a reduction in the world price by its encouragement to overproduction.

Similar stabilizing effects on domestic incomes and destabilizing effects on the balance of payments and world prices can be obtained from export taxes in periods of boom and subsidies in depression. There is, in fact, no difference of substance between an export tax and a policy of buying cheap at home and selling dear abroad. There will be (negative) protective effects, and effects on consumption, revenue, redistribution, terms of trade, balance of payments, and income.

Some economists object to paying too little at home and charging too much abroad. Many countries object to exactly the opposite course of action pursued by the United States Department of Agriculture and Commodity Credit Corporation, which hold prices above the long-run equilibrium level at home, encourage large crops, and then dump the surplus above domestic needs in foreign markets. The basis for the objection, however, differs in the two cases. In the first instance, the consumer objects but the competitive producer is grateful for higher prices. In the second, on the contrary, the consumer gains but the competitive producer is rendered unhappy. Surplus commodity agreements engaged in by the United States purport to make available free, at reduced prices, or for "fuzzy" loans to be repaid in local currency, only incremental supplies, over and above those normally bought through commercial channels. But Argentina and Australia in wheat, Denmark and New Zealand in butter, Canada in cheese, and Egypt,

Pakistan, and Brazil in cotton are difficult to convince. Moreover, the short-run benefits of higher prices for competitors and lower prices for consumers may not be sustained. Higher prices lead to expansion by competitors, and possibly to a cobweb overexpansion with a result-ant price collapse. Cocoa which reached a high point of close to 70 cents a pound in July, 1954, collapsed to 32 cents a year later. There seems little doubt that the action of the West African Marketing Board was destabilizing. Conversely, low prices which benefit the con-sumer in the short run may lead, over the intermediate period, to such discouragement of production that the price rides up again.

The draft charter of the defunct International Trade Organization restricted the use of international commodity agreements to transi-tional arrangements, employed to prevent the accumulation of burden-some surpluses while fundamental structural adjustments were carried forward under their protection. This is the view of the Department of State. It is not, however, the view of the primary-producers themselves. Their idea of the "adequate, just and equitable" price is the higher price and not the "long-run equilibrium price" that five international experts chosen by the United Nations believe it to be. But the higher price sooner or later brings trouble, overexpansion, discouragement on the part of the stockpilers, dumping of output on the world market, and price collapse.

The trouble with commodity agreements, in short, is that pro-ducers set the price too high. There is no way of determining the long-run equilibrium price, and even if there were, the strength of the producer interests, and their short-run profit motive, would leave it behind.

Unable to agree on a technique for handling commodity prob-lems, the United Nations experts suggested the appointment of a com-mission to keep commodity problems under continuous review. The United States turned down even this seemingly innocuous proposal. It feared, probably rightly, that the review commission would turn into a lobby for higher prices.

Bilateral Trade Agreements and Bulk Buying

The disruptions caused by the depression of the 1930's and of World War II have led to expanded use of international agreements to regulate trade. Some of these agreements have evolved from clearing arrangements required because of the exhaustion of internationally ac-ceptable reserves to settle trade surpluses. Others arose from the quest of a government for an outlet for a given surplus or access to a particular commodity which was scarce. Some countries, like Norway, embraced bulk buying and selling by governments as a means of protecting a domestic planning program against interference from uncertainties arising abroad.

The practice under bilateral trade agreements and bulk buying contracts will differ widely. In some socialist or quasi-socialist states, actual purchasing and selling is done for government account, whether or not production is undertaken in government-owned factories. In others, such as the trade agreements between Britain or Sweden, on the one hand, and the Eastern satellites, on the other, the western European governments have merely agreed in advance to issue export permits for a list of specified materials, without guaranteeing procurement of the goods in question or the prices at which they will be bought. These, then, are subsequently arranged between the Polish, Soviet, or other buying organization and the manufacturer.

The claim for bulk buying, to restrict ourselves to one sort of device, is that it gives certainty. Certainty for the consumer is regarded as desirable, since it enables him to know where he stands. Certainty for the seller is more significant because with an assured price he can plan his output more carefully and achieve economies of scale, which may be reflected in a lower price. It is argued, for example, that bulk buying should bring lower prices in the same fashion that private firms offer discounts for quantity because of the certainty they afford in production.

It may be noted, however, that assurance for the buyer is not at the same time assurance for the seller. In a buyers' market, where goods are in oversupply, a bulk contract provides a certain outlet for the seller but involves the buyer in paying more than the market price for his supplies. In a sellers' market, on the other hand, the buyer gets guaranteed access to supplies at reasonable prices, but the seller becomes restive in selling below the world market. If buyers' and sellers' markets alternate fairly rapidly and contracts are renewed in brief pauses between, the bulk-buying contracts may assist in the preservation of stability. If, on the other hand, the long-term contracts end in random fashion, sometimes in periods of low and sometimes in periods of high prices, the effect of bulk buying may merely be to shift prices discontinuously in a range almost as wide as the free market. Figure 13.5 suggests the two possible solutions mentioned, where contracts can give stability of price (A) or exaggerated long-run instability (B).

Bulk buying and selling can be designed or can operate without design to exploit competitive weakness. In a world of depression, a large market can use its monopsony power, or the monopoly power of a single buyer, to extract favorable terms of trade from its sellers. German trade with southeastern Europe in the 1930's provides perhaps the best example of this. Or in a sellers' market a producing country can exploit the need for its products to obtain favorable prices. Here the example of Argentina after World War II is illuminating. While the rest of the world operated within the framework of the Combined Boards of the United Nations, allocating scarce supplies and restraining

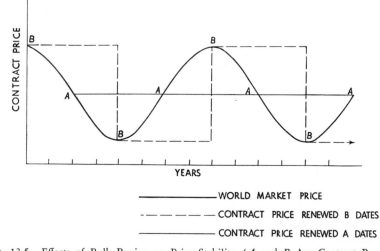

FIG. 13.5. Effects of Bulk Buying on Price Stability (*A* and *B* Are Contract Renewal Dates)

prices, Argentina kept aloof from co-operative efforts to solve shortages and, with the exception of one or two trades with countries like Spain and Italy with which she had a sentimental interest, charged the highest price the market would bear for marginal quantities. While Combined Board wheat sold for $3.00 to approved buyers in 1946, IAPI, the Argentine foreign sales organization, held out for $5.00 and $6.00 a bushel for quantities sold outside of international allocation.

Bulk buying can lead to bilateral monopoly and, on occasion, to stalemate. The classic example is the Argentine-British meat agreement, or the Andes pact. Protracted negotiations were required to reach an agreement in 1948, which lasted only a year. In February, 1949, negotiations began and dragged on for months. The talks were deadlocked on the price of meat, which was specified in the agreement, under a bulk-buying contract, although British exports of coal and oil to Argentina, fixed in amount, were traded at current prices. In

June, 1949, a new five-year agreement was reached under which meat prices were fixed for one year. Immediately after the new agreement had been concluded, however, there was dissatisfaction, first on the part of Britain because Argentine purchases were not carried forward at the agreed level; then, following the devaluation of the pound in September, 1949, on the part of Argentina because of the increase in the sterling price of oil. When the time came to extend the portions of the agreement relating to the price of meat, the British and Argentine negotiators were unable to reach agreement, and shipments of meat under the pact were suspended in July, 1950. Drought, low prices on the internal market, and high consumption kept supplies for export low and the Argentine bargaining position strong, while the British standard of living, dependent on meat imports, suffered. Finally, in February, 1951, the British agreed to a renewal of shipments under the agreement at the prices asked for by Argentina.

Since 1951 several things have happened, and British-Argentine trade in meat is expanding again. Bulk buying was abandoned in Britain by the conservative government, which came to power in 1951, and Argentine policies turned in favor of paying world prices to cattle producers, after the fall of Peron.

State Trading

It remains in this chapter to consider state trading as a protective device and as an instrument of international politics and war. Bulk buying probably forms the major kind of state trading after World War II. One more aspect of the subject—price discrimination—will be left for the next chapter. But state trading used to be regarded primarily as a means of giving protection to particular industries rather than stability to the economy as a whole; and during wartime, economic warfare requires large-scale state intervention in the trade process. Since these subjects are, for the most part, archaic or tangential in their interest for us, they will not detain us long.

The necessity of developing rules to regulate state trading, as in the draft charter of the International Trade Organization, for example, arose from the tariff issue. A number of countries had governmental monopolies in certain commodities—frequently in articles important for tax revenue, such as tobacco or alcohol. These monopolies were free of the obligation of paying duties, since they were governmental instruments, but they were frequently concerned with earning a return. They therefore bought abroad cheaply and sold in the domestic market at a high price. Thus far, there was no problem.

In some cases, however, it appeared that the monopoly used its position of concentrated purchasing power to effect other desired results. By paying more at home for brandy than it cost abroad, it was possible to give an indirect subsidy, equivalent to tariff protection, to domestic vintners. The possibility was regarded as particularly objectionable, since this sort of protection could be rendered arbitrarily, without notice and on a changing basis. To overcome this possibility, now for the most part academic in view of the more widespread effects of bulk buying and bilateral trading, the draft charter of the International Trade Organization included a provision which called, at basis, for states to conduct themselves in international trade as if they were guided by commercial principles, attempting to sell competitively and to buy competitively.

Economic Warfare

State interference in international trade may not necessarily be guided by the principles applicable to peaceful commerce under which a country is presumably interested in maximizing its economic well-being. A state, for example, may attempt to limit the output of another country, particularly of materials of war; or a state may attempt to depress markets in foreign countries for the sake of encouraging world revolution. This latter possibility has been cited in connection with the sale of wheat by the Soviet Union in 1932, when the world price broke to less than 50 cents a bushel, and again on September 26, 1936, when the Soviet Union sold £1,000,000 in the New York market on a Saturday morning at the beginning of a decline in sterling from $5.05 to $4.86. It may be pointed out, however, that the sale of wheat in 1932, which was accumulated only at the expense of starvation in the Soviet Union, may have been governed by necessity, while the sale of sterling at the time of the Tripartite Pact can be regarded as a shrewd move from a business standpoint. Nonetheless, while improbable, the possibility exists that one country could use its powers of purchase and sale in international markets to achieve nonmilitary political designs on another.

Economic warfare is unhappily a much more usual phenomenon. Here the entire purpose of trade changes. In economic warfare conducted parallel with military operations, such as that waged by the Allies against Germany and Japan during World War II, the weapons included blockade, preclusive buying, agreements with neutrals to cut off trade beyond the range of blockade. Preclusive buying is perhaps the most interesting, since here the purpose of state trading is not to acquire what a country wants but to prevent the enemy from getting access to it. In frequent cases, as in the rival attempts to buy tungsten and tungsten ore (wolfram) in Spain and Portugal, or chrome in Turkey prior to Turkey's entry into World War II, the effect of the rival preclusive buying is to divide supplies much as before, to raise the price many times above its original relative value, and to expand output. In some cases, like Swedish ball bearings, purchases were made to keep supplies away from the enemy; and the goods were mainly stored. Blockade-running British Mosquito aircraft could carry only a few tons of goods per trip in addition to their diplomatic traffic.

Short of "hot" economic warfare, there should perhaps be a stage of "cold" economic warfare. Here there is no military blockade imposed by force of arms, but one country will attempt to deny to its potential enemy those goods which are of extraordinary strategic interest to the latter's armament needs. The gain in slowing down the rate of armament of the potential enemy country, however, should be measured against its cost. Where no credit is extended, trade is a two-way balanced affair, and the restriction of exports involves a restriction of imports. Success in the denial of exports should therefore be weighed against the impact of the loss in imported goods.

It is important to calculate in sober fashion the effectiveness of economic warfare on specific industries and specific programs. The impact of the economic blockade of Germany in World War I was exaggerated by the German General Staff to excuse its own shortcomings. Even with aerial bombardment, the blockade of World War II had a supporting rather than a leading role in the defeat of the German armies. A modern industrial nation is capable of shifting and adapting resources among industries, substituting one material for another with only a limited loss of efficiency. In consequence, except in the relatively short run, the denial to an enemy or potential enemy of materials for a particular industry results in diversion of other resources to this industry. If the country is industrialized on a fairly broad front and moderately adaptable, economic warfare will deprive it of resources in general rather than final weapons in particular. Viewed in this light, it is particularly important, in hot or cold war, to weigh the potential gain in minimizing the position of the other country against the cost to one's own.

Where the country is not highly industrialized, such as the Soviet Union or even more Red China, a further consideration enters. To deprive these countries of industrial products in the short run stimulates them to increase their industrial capacity in the long. Much depends upon the most probable time of trouble. To an economist, it might even make sense to sell war material to a potential enemy, if trouble were far away, to reduce his incentive to develop his own weapons and to lull him, if this were possible, into obsolescence.

Summary

Quotas are like tariffs in their protective and redistributive effects. The revenue effect, however, is lost unless the state auctions off licenses. The quota, moreover, must be administered, and this creates a number of problems.

The advantage of a quota is its certainty in achieving the intended restriction of imports and sought-for price effects. The cutting off of expenditure on imports by quotas increases national income. Export restriction and export tariffs are related in the same way as import restriction by quota and import tariffs.

Commodity agreements have developed and spread in an attempt to overcome the difficulties faced in commodities with inelastic supply and demand. There is disagreement as to whether commodity agreements should be a transitional device, as provided in the draft International Trade Organization charter, during a period of adjustment of supply, or a permanent feature of international trade.

Bulk buying is intended to give stability of prices and output. Depending upon its timing, it may have this effect or may merely exaggerate instability. The difficulty with bulk buying is that there is no objective solution to the problem of bilateral monopoly in which the monopolist and the monopsonist bargain with each other.

State trading was originally regarded as a problem in protection. It is now considered to be more a problem in monopoly.

In economic warfare, it is important to weigh against the hurt to the "enemy" the cost of administering that hurt.

SUGGESTED READING

TEXTS

Towle, chaps. xxiv, xxviii. Yuan-Li-Wu, *Economic Warfare* (New York: Prentice-Hall, Inc., 1952).

TREATISES, ETC.

See M. S. Gordon, *Barriers to World Trade* (New York: Macmillan Co., 1941).

H. Heuser, *Control of International Trade* (London: Routledge, 1939), is excellent on quotas. See also F. A. Haight, *French Import Quotas* (London: King, 1935).

J. Viner, *Trade Relations between Free Market and Controlled Economies* (Geneva: League of Nations, 1943), explains itself. On the same subject see by the same author American Economic Association, *Readings*, No. 19.

The report of the international experts is entitled United Nations, *Commodity Trade and Economic Development* (New York, 1953).

Outstanding articles in this field are A. Henderson, "The Restriction of Foreign Trade, *MS*, January, 1949; S. S. Alexander, "Devaluation versus Import Restrictions as an Instrument for Improving the Trade Balance," *SP*, April, 1951; the United Nations study on the instability of primary products prices is *Instability of Export Markets of Under-developed Countries* (New York, 1952).

POINTS

The experience of the West African Cocoa Marketing Board is discussed in P. T. Bauer and F. W. Paish, "The Reduction of Fluctuations in the Incomes of Primary Producers," *EJ*, December, 1952. Articles are available in the scholarly journals on the wheat and sugar agreements. See H. C. Farnsworth, "International Wheat Agreements and Problems, 1949–56," *QJE*, May, 1956; and B. C. Swerling, "The International Sugar Agreement of 1953," *AER*, December, 1954.

For a special treatment of foreign-trade problems of United States agriculture, see D. G. Johnson, *Agriculture and Trade* (New York: John Wiley & Sons, Inc., 1951).

British bulk buying experience is reviewed in the Economic Commission for Europe, *Economic Bulletin for Europe*, last quarter, 1951. A history of the World War II blockade by Britain is contained in W. N. Medlicott, *Economic Blockade* (London: H. M. Stationery Office, 1951).

Chapter

14

PRICE DISCRIMINATION
AND CARTELS

Kinds of Competition

The previous chapter was concerned with over-all devices to modify or even to disregard the workings of the pattern of international prices on trade and the allocation of resources. Restriction of imports or exports can be calculated to give a monopoly or monopsony increased return, or, as in economic warfare, commodity agreements and much bilateral trading may spring from a feeling that the price system will produce an unsatisfactory answer and must be pushed aside in favor of quantitative controls and planning. The over-all measures dealt with were those employed by governments.

Price discrimination, on the other hand, does not involve disregard of the price system. It is instead a manifestation of the workings of the price system under particular conditions of monopoly, monopsony, and separation of related markets. Instead of over-all, we shall treat of differential techniques. For the most part we shall be dealing with the firm rather than with government. In order to understand how price discrimination operates and when, it is necessary to examine the question of competition.

The difficulty with the subject is that it uses everyday words which mean different things to different people. Competition, to an economist, means the process operating in an industry with a very large number of firms, where no producer and no purchaser can by his actions exert an influence over market price. Where the number of firms is smaller than this, so that an individual firm can control the price at which it sells or buys, competition is imperfect. Even in an industry which is imperfectly competitive, however, two types of price policy by the individual firm are possible. The firm can sell to all buyers at the same net price; this approaches the competitive solution. Or the firm can sell at different prices to different buyers; this is price discrimination.

The businessman has a hard time seeing what the economist is talking about in all this; to the extent that he does understand, he dislikes what he hears and dissents vigorously. In the first place, he objects to the words used. He is not certain that he is favorably disposed toward "competition," since it calls to mind "cutthroat competition," which he knows he dislikes. The words "imperfect" or "monopolistic" competition are clearly invidious and disagreeable. So is "price discrimination," which calls to mind racial, religious, or national discrimination, which is disapproved conduct rather than "a discriminating taste," which is held in esteem.

Most of all, however, the businessman and the economist fail to talk the same language and to understand one another. To a businessman, it is competition when two firms sell in the same market at the same price. To the economist, this is competitive if it is the only market in which the firms sell. But if either or both firms sell in other markets at prices which yield them a different return than in the market in question, it is evidence of less than perfect competition. Where so much confusion and misunderstanding abound, it is necessary to proceed warily. In what follows we shall employ the reasoning and terminology of the economist and shall hope that the reader used to thinking in the terms of businessmen will withhold judgment until he understands what is intended.

Monopolistic Competition

An industry is competitive when the demand curve facing the individual firm is infinitely elastic, i.e., when the producer can sell all he can make at the existing price. This is so, independently of the demand curve facing the industry as a whole, which may be inelastic. The demand for wheat is inelastic; the demand for the output of an individual wheat farmer is perfectly elastic. The resolution of this apparent paradox, of course, is found in the fact that there are great numbers of producers and all are engaged in production and sale of a homogeneous product.

When the individual producer has some control over the price at which he sells or when the individual buyer can exert an influence over the price at which he buys, this is regarded as evidence of imperfect competition. To limit ourselves to supply, there may be a considerable number of producers (the steel industry), a few, as in international oil (oligopoly), or only one, like the International Nickel Company (monopoly). Or products may be differentiated in type, like shoe machinery, or in location, like cement (monopolistic competition).

But, if some or all producers can exert an effect on price, the industry behaves differently than if they cannot.

When no producer can affect price, each maximizes his income by producing as much as he can at the market price. When any producer can affect price, on the other hand, the conditions under which he can maximize his income are radically altered. He must now take into account the effect of his output on price. This will make him aware, in addition to the total demand curve and his average costs, of his marginal-revenue curve and marginal costs. He is also likely to be aware of the extent to which the buyers to whom he sells are located in one or in different markets, with different demand curves.

A brief review of these concepts may be useful. For the student who has studied no imperfect competition in his elementary text, it will be insufficient. He must go back and acquire a little more background, directions for which will be found in the suggested readings. For the student who still retains a familiarity with the subject, it will be unnecessary. But for the student who has once mastered the subject and allowed it to slip, this review may prove of some help.

A demand curve represents the prices at which various amounts of a commodity can be sold. Since all units produced are sold at the same price in a single market—this constitutes the definition of a market—the demand curve can also be called an "average-revenue curve." It represents the average return for each unit sold at each quantity of units indicated. But the producer, if he is to maximize his return, must consider more than this. Unless the average-revenue curve is completely elastic or horizontal, as under perfect competition, the sale of additional quantities of the product may be regarded as lowering the price not only of the marginal unit but also of all other units, thus reducing the revenue which would otherwise have been received for these earlier units. A marginal-revenue curve may be drawn which indicates how the sale of additional units will affect total revenue. In Figure 14.1, AR is the average-revenue and MR the marginal-revenue curve.

Confronting the average- and marginal-revenue curves are average- and marginal-cost curves. The average-cost curve is the average cost per unit of production. In Figure 14.1 this is not drawn for very small quantities of output where total overhead costs must be included in the cost of only a few units. The existence of overhead costs—such as interest on the investment in a business, maintenance and depreciation on plant and equipment, and salaries of management and supervisory personnel—means that certain costs must be incurred even if no production takes place. As production expands, average cost per unit declines, since overhead costs can be spread over a wider number of units.

The marginal cost is the increased cost of producing an additional unit. This will decline in the early stages of production, as labor, materials, and selling costs can be utilized more efficiently. Beyond a given size for a plant, however, marginal costs will rise. The marginal-cost curve will cross the average-cost curve at the latter's lowest point.

The firm is making maximum profits when it equates marginal cost to marginal revenue. In our diagram this is at point *T*. The price

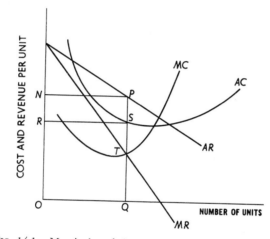

FIG. 14.1. Marginal- and Average- Cost and Revenue Curves

charged for this quantity will be read off the average-revenue curve and will equal *P*. Total cost is average cost times the quantity produced (*ORSQ*). Total revenue is the average revenue times quantity (*ONPQ*). Profit is the difference (*RNPS*). Increased output would reduce this profit, since the increment in cost (marginal cost of the additional unit) would be greater than the increment in revenue (*MR*). To produce less than this amount, on the other hand, would be to forego an opportunity for profit, since the income from additional output is greater than its cost.

Imperfect Competition with Two Markets

All this has been by way of review and has related to the imperfection of competition in a single market. In international trade the problem is one of more than one market, with different prices charged in each. Price discrimination of this sort is by no means limited to international trade: different admission prices are charged for first-run, second-run, and country movie houses; for professional services of doctors, lawyers, and others, depending on the patient's or client's income; and for the same article in the convenient corner store as opposed to the serve-yourself giant store at a shopping center some distance away from residential areas. In international trade, however, markets are differentiated at a minimum by space, and differences of custom, habit, language, etc., are likely to assist in this process, even though other factors common in the domestic market—like product advertising, snob appeal, or professional ethics—may not.

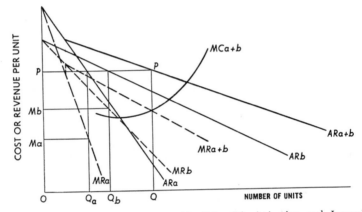

FIG. 14.2. Aggregated Demand Curves—No Price Discrimination and Inequality of Marginal Revenue

If a seller has access to two separate markets and can exercise some control over price in one or both, it will pay him to sell at different prices in the two markets if the elasticities of the demand curves differ. The general rule holds: profit will be maximized where marginal revenue equals marginal cost. But the marginal cost of his output will be identical for sales in all markets, since we abstract from transfer costs. (The price we are discussing is the price f.o.b. the factory. Transfer costs are eliminated from calculations of price, revenue, and cost.) The crux of the matter then becomes the difference in marginal revenue in the two markets.

The seller may ignore the difference between the two markets. In this case he will add the two average-revenue curves and the two marginal-revenue curves. Where the marginal-cost curve intersects the combined marginal-revenue curve will give the production point of maximum profit. In Figure 14.2, with average- and marginal-revenue curves added for markets A and B, the quantity OQ will be produced and sold in the two markets, at the same price, *OP*. The quantity *OQ* will be made up of *OQa* sold in market A and *OQb* sold in market B. But observe that the sale of *OQa* units in market A produces a marginal revenue of *OMa*, while *OQb* sold in market B gives a higher return, *OMb*. A policy of identical or flat pricing in two markets with different elasticities means that a higher marginal return is earned per unit sold in one market than in the other. The profit of the seller could be increased by shifting sales from the less elastic to the more elastic market.

Price Discrimination

This can be made clear by putting the two sets of revenue curves on different sides of the vertical axis, as is done in Figure 14.3. This

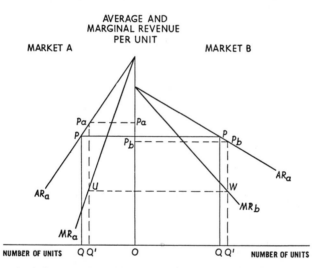

FIG. 14.3. Discriminatory Pricing by a Seller—Equating Marginal Revenue in Two Markets

diagram, which omits the marginal-cost curve, shows the same marginal and revenue curves in markets A and B, but not their total. The A curves are to the left of the vertical axis and run from right to left. The B curves perform in the usual manner. The quantity *QQ* is the same as *OQ* in Figure 14.2 and is also the same amount as *Q′Q′*. In this diagram, however, we can see that a shift of *QQ′* from market A to market B will equate marginal revenues (*Q′U = Q′W*). This will result in price discrimination, a higher price (*OP_a*) in A, the market with the less elastic demand, and a lower price (*OP_b*) in B, with the more elastic demand.

The fact that price discrimination can take place at all is due to the quasi-monopoly position of the seller and the fact that he can, whether because of monopoly, because the other few competitors in the business will follow his leadership, or because of a cartel agreement, fix his price.

It will be noticed that the higher price is charged by the discriminating seller in the market with the less elastic demand curve, and the lower where demand is more elastic. This underscores the monopolistic nature of discriminatory pricing. A maximum return is reached when the seller exploits to the full through price discrimination the inelasticity existing in each separate market. The limiting case is reached where the seller singles out in a separate market each potential buyer and charges him what he is willing to pay as a maximum for each unit. In these circumstances, the seller captures for himself the whole area under the demand curve. Under perfect competition the average-revenue curve is completely elastic, or horizontal, and marginal revenue equals average revenue. If one market is highly competitive, the discriminatory price solution comes to simply selling at a monopoly price in one market. In the other the discriminating seller has no power over price and has to sell at the market. The average and marginal revenue in this price are identical. Marginal revenue in the monopolized market will be equal to this price, since marginal revenues are being equated in the two markets.

Discriminating Monopsony

Not infrequent in international trade is the discriminating buyer, or monopsonist, who is sufficiently big to take account of the effect of his purchase on price (see Fig. 14.4). The monopsonist may be a big company, such as the de Beers syndicate which dominates the market for uncut diamonds, or a state trading organization, which goes in for bulk buying. It is an organization big enough to take account of the effect of its purchases in raising the prices it pays for goods. Accordingly, it will shift purchases from the less elastic source of supply to the more elastic and pay a lower price in the former than the latter, in order to reduce its over-all cost. It will equate the marginal cost of supplies in the two markets.

Note that the competitive buyer equalizes the delivered cost of his purchases, not the cost f.o.b. from different destinations, while the discriminating monopsonist equalizes marginal cost on a delivered basis. The return to the seller excludes the cost of transport, but the cost to the buyer most definitely includes it.

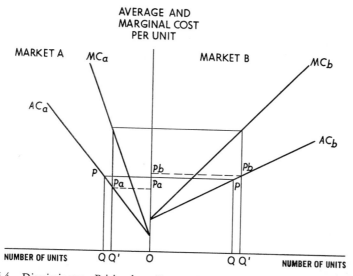

FIG. 14.4. Discriminatory Pricing by a Buyer—Equating Marginal Cost in Two Markets

Overhead Costs

It may be helpful to think of price discrimination in terms of overhead costs. After a company covers its overhead costs in one market, it is in a position to sell in another market at whatever that market will bring above marginal costs. This is implied when it is stated that marginal cost is the same in the two markets, but focusing attention on overhead costs helps to prevent exclusive attention on different elasticities of demand.

Opponents of price discrimination want overhead costs assigned to different markets in proportion to the units sold in each. This means that average costs, rather than marginal costs, should be the same in two markets. The difficulty of this position is underscored in questions of joint supply, where it is impossible to assign overhead costs to one item or another and price is determined by demand and marginal cost, with overhead costs covered where they can be. One of the best examples of this in international trade is petroleum products.

What is the average cost of crude oil, gasoline, aviation gasoline, diesel fuel, lubricants, fuel oil, and residual? Marginal costs can perhaps be computed, but how should overhead costs be allocated? The sellers, as all sellers do, allocate overhead costs to those products which can cover them in the market. Residual fuel oil has in the past sold for less than the value of its crude-oil content, in order to be sold at all in competition with coal. As the price of coal has risen, however, it has been possible to shift some part of the overhead costs of the production and refining of oil to the residual product. The day may not be far distant when the by-product which bore no share of overhead costs becomes a principal product which carries some or all of it. Examples of this shift are found in coking coal in the Ruhr. Prior to about 1929, coke for steel was the main product and coal-tar derivatives the by-product. The development of the German chemical and explosives industries in the interwar period, however, made coke the by-product and resulted in its sale as common fuel even to farmers. Overhead costs, which had been assigned mainly to coke, then became shifted to the coal-tar chemical products.

Price Discrimination and Policy

The fact of market control over price by buyers and sellers gives rise to certain dilemmas of public policy. It also poses troublesome issues for business enterprise. Under perfect competition, abstracting from transfer costs, the same price should be charged to every buyer. Under perfect competition, moreover, each firm is encouraged to maximize its profits. Public policy in free-enterprise societies embraces both objectives of policy: profit maximization and nondiscriminatory (flat) pricing. But when a firm is large enough to affect its prices, the two objectives are incompatible.

If profit maximization and flat pricing cannot be reconciled under imperfect competition, which should be favored? If the same price is charged net to all customers, the company foregoes some additional income. If different prices are charged to different customers, the latter complain of unequal access to materials, or competitors complain of unfair competition. If the same price is charged to all customers, the seller has to ration his sales in the more profitable market. At one time some United States automobile manufacturers charged the same price on sales at home and abroad and limited export sales to 6 per cent of domestic production. Somewhat analogously, a number of international oil companies operating both in the Middle East and in the United States find it currently more profitable to refine Middle East oil than domestic, but voluntarily limit imports, to sustain the United States crude oil price in behalf of the small domestic producer. This rationing of imports in the interest of price fixing for the industry is undertaken at the urging of the Texas Railroad Commission and under government quotas imposed federally in the name of national defense.

It is difficult, as a rule, to obtain data on private behavior in this area. Firms are naturally secretive about their pricing practices. A somewhat garbled story in the *Journal of Commerce* reported a survey of 138 manufacturing companies in the United States undertaken by the Export Managers Club of New York in 1953, which showed that:

70 of the group, or 50 per cent, maintained the same prices for both markets;

10 per cent quoted lower prices on foreign than on domestic sales;

a slightly higher proportion (than 10 per cent) charged higher prices on foreign sales;

a fairly large number (the remaining 30 per cent?) used a flexible pricing system, varying their prices according to the competitive situation abroad.

There is no way of telling how representative this sample is of exports of finished manufactures or of total exports, or whether those companies charging higher or lower prices did so persistently or merely found themselves in that position at the time of the survey and could be said typically to use a "flexible pricing system." But however accurate a reflection of the position as a whole, the survey suggests policy differences among the 138 private firms.

More research is needed in this area, but it is at least clear that there is frequently an arbitrary character to business policies with respect to foreign pricing. A company which operates largely in the domestic market and only occasionally sells abroad is likely to use a more "flexible" price policy on foreign sales. As the proportions of foreign and domestic business approach equality, there is a tendency to shift to flat pricing. If, however, the export market is very large in relation to the domestic, prices in the two markets may again be set independently. Further differences will turn on the absolute size of foreign sales, and on the practice of the industry, governmental policies, etc. It was observed in the British devaluation of 1949, for example, that some British companies thought of the prices of their products as determined in sterling and initially marked down dollar prices by the full amount of the devaluation. This was true of many manufactured products—lawnmowers, automobiles, bicycles. As costs rose, the sterling prices picked up and dollar prices started back toward their original level. In other instances, however, such as Scotch whiskey, it was recognized that the price was set in the foreign market, and the domestic price was raised, or not, depending upon whether flat or independent pricing existed.

The fact of equal prices in separate markets, whether for sales netted back or of purchases including transport, does not eliminate discrimination, though it makes it a mild sort which approaches the competitive solution. The competitive solution is identical prices *and* equality of marginal revenue and marginal costs. When costs in the two markets differ or demand curves have different slopes, equality of marginal revenue in the two markets (to limit our discussion to sales) will produce different prices, and equality of price will produce differential returns. Some discrimination is inevitable. The rationing of markets with flat pricing is generally the milder form of discrimination.

The objection to price discrimination is the objection to monopoly. The buyers in the country with the less elastic demand suffer. The Economic Cooperation Administration attacked the (European) practice of charging higher prices for steel in the export trade than those charged at home. The reasons for the practice were (1) the economic one of maximizing profit; (2) to hold down the level of home prices; and (3) to improve the competitive position of the steel-consuming industries at home. The effects of this pricing, however, were uneconomic utilization of resources in the selling country, which produced too little steel—the objection to all monopoly; the "unfair" imposition of higher costs on the foreign steel-consuming industries; and the incentive to develop new steel capacity in the importing countries, which was not economically justified.

While the United States government objected to dual pricing, through the Economic Cooperation Administration, no stand on the matter was taken by any country in the draft charter of the International Trade Organization. Governments were urged to act in a competitive fashion, but no such requirement was imposed on private enterprise. It could not be, because it is far from clear whether the firm should prefer, of the two horns of the dilemma, flat pricing or profit maximization.

Some large firms are beginning to act to maximize not short-run but long-run profit. This may favor flat pricing over price discrimination. Flat pricing offers no basis for retaliation or adverse action by foreign governments. It has a ring of fairness about it. Purchasers cannot complain of unequal treatment. Competitors are unable to argue unfairness. Even taxing authorities are confronted with an unambiguous position. This last point was raised by the action of Saudi Arabia government which objected to the discounts given by the Arabian-American Oil Company on oil sales to its owning companies on the ground that the company's profits, on which the government levied an income tax, were in reality being transferred abroad. Charging the same prices to all customers, all the time, may maximize long-run profits by earning good will even when short-run profits are less than their possible peak.

Dumping and Reverse Dumping

Charging different prices in different markets is called, in international trade, "dumping." The word is unfortunate. Its origin goes back to the case of the manufacturer with an unsold supply who "dumps" the excess abroad in a market in which he does not normally sell, in order not to break the price in his own market. By default, more than anything else, the practice of sale at different prices in two markets has become "dumping." The height of absurdity in nomenclature is reached when the manufacturer sells abroad at a higher price than at home. This is called "reverse dumping"—the notion existing that he is then dumping in the domestic market.

Dumping is simply price discrimination. It takes place when the demand abroad is more elastic than the demand at home. It arises only because of the monopolistic element in the home market. In reverse dumping, the demand abroad is less elastic than the home demand, whether because competition abroad is less keen than at home or for any other reason. In this case it is possible to exploit the inelasticity of demand of the foreign market by higher prices abroad than at home, balancing marginal revenue in the two markets.

In some cases, like the steel industry, foreign and domestic prices will go separate ways, and the United States industry dumps or reverse dumps as the occasion calls for. Prices outside the United States expressed in dollars tend to fluctuate in a wider range than prices in the United States. At times they are above those in the United States, and reverse dumping takes place; at times below, and market positions are maintained only by dumping.

Various kinds of dumping have been distinguished, including mainly sporadic, predatory, and persistent. Sporadic dumping is the sort which occurs when a company finds itself with distress goods on its hands which it wants to dispose of without harming its normal markets. It is engaged in by companies which typically stay clear of foreign markets and only occasionally find themselves with more inventory than they can hope to dispose of in orderly fashion through their normal outlets. For this company, the demand abroad is more elastic than the demand at home, where it wants to preserve its quasi-monopolistic position. Or it may regard the cost of the goods as already sunk (i.e., marginal costs ex transport costs as zero), and cut its losses abroad by selling the goods for anything that can be realized.

Predatory dumping is selling at a loss (as measured by average costs but not by marginal) in order to gain access to a market, to drive out competition, or for any other short-run cause. Predatory dumping is followed by an increase in prices after the market has been established or the competition overcome. Foreigners are frequently accused of this sort of price conduct by United States producers. It is difficult to establish cases. American textile producers after the removal of the embargo in 1814 charged that British exporters were dumping in the American market to drive them out of business. However valid, the argument was a powerful factor in the passage of the Tariff of 1816.

The reduction of sales price is only one way to get a product established in a foreign market. Another is to engage in extra costs, to advertise, to establish a distribution system, and to obtain an acceptance of the product in the new market. Increased selling costs—indulged in briefly—are almost exactly the same as predatory dumping, except that the harsh condemnation implicit in the adjective in public understanding does not apply.

Persistent dumping occurs when a producer consistently sells at a lower price in one market than in another. As a rule, this occurs when the firm regards two markets differently from the point of view of overhead costs. Suppose, for example, that marginal costs are low relative to total costs, and total costs can be covered in the domestic market. Additional sales at any price above marginal costs in the foreign market will increase the profits of the firm. It may then pay a firm to dump persistently. An example of this is the motion-picture industry, in which, prior to 1948, the cost of many motion pictures used to be covered in exhibition rentals in the United States, where marginal costs were low, especially if no new sound track was required, and where foreign sales at almost any price would increase profits. Overhead costs are not prorated between markets on the basis of quantity sold, and persistent dumping may be profitable to the firm. Most economists regard persistent dumping as beneficial to the importing country and harmful to the exporting country, in which consumers are charged a monopoly price. In the postwar period, however, it is reported that barely one in 75 or 100 motion pictures produced in the United States covers its costs from domestic rental revenue. The vast majority are dependent upon the foreign market as a whole, if not on any one particular foreign market. While this may not change the incentive of the producer to dump, it increases the capacity of the foreign market to insist upon a reduced price or, indeed, on any price policy it may lay down.

In the usual case, dumping and reverse dumping are thought of in relation to the foreign market as a whole, contrasted with the home market. Price discrimination operates on the side of exports much like the tariff with a most-favored-nation clause as regards imports. A tariff (or import subsidy) changes the relative price of imports at home as compared with those abroad. Price discrimination, which regards all foreign markets as one, brings about changes in relative prices at home and abroad.

Price discrimination, which takes advantage of different demand elasticities in different export markets, might be called differential dumping; it is more nearly akin to tariff discrimination, applying different rates of tariff to imports from different countries. To achieve equilibrium of the firm, marginal revenue should be equalized in each separate market, which means a variety of different prices. From the point of view of the markets, however, dumping, which makes a distinction only between the domestic and the foreign market, is less discriminatory than that which separates the various segments of the export market.

Most economists regard dumping as a vicious policy, much more to be condemned than tariffs. Unconsciously, these writers hold that while it is legitimate for a government to make distinctions between its citizens and foreigners (so long as it does not make invidious distinctions among foreigners), it is inadmissible for a firm to do so. The intervention of the government is charged with the general good—even though it may be used to advance a private interest. The producer in a position to discriminate, on the other hand, is a monopolist, in whole or in part, working for his own interest.

Dumping and Tariffs

There is a limit to the extent to which a foreign producer can sell abroad below the price in the domestic market. This limit is twice the cost of transport. If a product costs $100 in the domestic market and the transport costs in one direction are $10, the producer cannot sell the product below $80 net to him, or $90 in the foreign market. If he does sell below this level, it will pay foreign arbitrageurs to buy the product abroad and sell it in his market below his $100 price. A tariff on the export good in the exporting country will widen the cost of transfer in the reverse direction and widen the limits within which dumping can occur.[1]

Much more significant, however, is the question of tariffs to prevent dumping by others. When dumping does occur, especially predatory dumping, it is understandable that domestic producers may seek some sort of protection. This is likely to take the form of countervailing duties or quotas to eliminate the "unfair" competition. Many tariffs and import quotas are established for this purpose, frequently in export commodities in which one would normally expect no imports. Whether one approves or disapproves of countervailing duties against predatory dumping, however, there is little doubt that the admission of countervailing duties in principle and their application to sporadic and persistent dumping decrease the flexibility and elasticity of international markets and reduce the potential gain from trade. In addition, there is the considerable difficulty of differentiating between predatory and persistent dumping, which cannot be told apart until after the event.

The Basing-Point System

A special form of price discrimination which gives rise to much misunderstanding is that involved in the basing-point system and its variants. The economist, it will be remembered, is concerned with identical prices for different consumers at the point of production. The basing-point system, on the other hand, has been devised to ensure that prices paid by purchasers are identical on products delivered from separate points of production. To the economist, the "competitive" price is measured by identity of prices to different customers at each mill. To the businessman using the basing-point system in one of its forms, the essence of competition is the identity of price from different mills to each customer.

In a basing-point system, prices in a given market are calculated by taking the price at a given benchmark or "basing point" and adding freight from that point to ultimate destination, no matter where the goods are produced. If, in fact, the goods are delivered from farther away than the basing point, the company making the sale "absorbs freight," i.e., pays that part of the freight cost in excess of the cost from the basing point itself. If the goods are produced at a place nearer the consumer than the basing point, the customer is charged "phantom

---

[1] In the United States there is no tariff on goods of United States manufacture where these can be identified. An increase in the tariff in the dumping country would then be applicable only to standardized products where the national origin could not be ascertained, or to competitive products in the foreign country.

freight," i.e., freight costs which are not incurred. Most businessmen are prepared to recognize that charging phantom freight is somewhat less justifiable a practice than absorbing freight.

Frequently there will be no formal basing-point system but merely two or more points of production engaged in marketing a product in which freight costs are a significant portion of delivered cost. Here each producer will enjoy a monopoly position with respect to nearby customers and those who are located in the direction away from the other mill. Costs of the delivered product will be higher as customers are located farther away from each mill until one crosses over the watershed line dividing the two markets. The position is indicated in Fig-

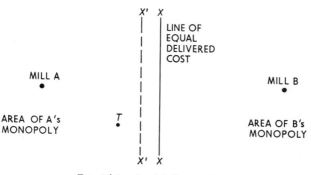

FIG. 14.5. Spatial Competition

ure 14.5, starting with prices at mill A and mill B, which may be assumed to be identical.

In this position, competition may take two forms. Mill B may sell to customers on A's side of the line X–X, say at point T, at the prices charged by A. Or B may lower prices to all its customers at once, which would move the line to the left, as indicated by X'–X', and undersell A in the intervening territory.

To the businessman, the first method is competitive because identical prices are being charged to the customer, whatever the origin of the goods. To the economist, the first method is discriminatory because it gives the customer at T a discount over the rest of B's customers, when prices are netted back to f.o.b. mill. The economist regards this pricing method as a prime example of the uneconomic character of price discrimination. It saves transport to serve point T from A. When goods move from B to T, there is crosshauling, which is prima-facie evidence of waste. Goods moving from east to west to T pass goods going from west to east to other customers of A located to the left of X–X.

The system of flat f.o.b. pricing, on the other hand, appears to the businessman as noncompetitive. Each mill has its own customers, to the west and east of the line X–X, and any extra production on the part of A or B cannot be sold, at competitive prices, in the territory of the other mill. The economist suggests, in reply, that the whole range of the watershed line X–X is an area of competition. If B has extra production or lowers his costs, the general good calls for this to be recognized in lowering the price at the mill, B. This will share the gain with all of B's existing customers and will shift from A to B some customers who now lie within the market sphere of B on an f.o.b. mill system. Carried to an extreme, where each customer becomes a separate base on which to fix prices, it would be possible for A to charge the same delivered price to all its customers, in disregard of real economies of transport, which should attract consuming industries to locations near the mill.

In international trade these basing-point or other spatial-monopoly competition examples have been found in oil, cement, steel, coal, and similar standardized bulky products. In oil, for example, the world price system used to be based on prices in the Gulf of Mexico and the Persian Gulf, with delivered prices calculated on the basis of these prices, plus freight. None the less, a number of anomalies persisted, as in the case of the flow of oil to Britain from the Persian-Gulf-plus-freight, because of the use of the United-States–Gulf-plus-freight price. The Economic Cooperation Administration objected to the prices paid for petroleum products for Italy and Greece, on the ground that they included phantom freight. The companies, on the other hand, disclaimed any charge of phantom freight to Mediterranean ports. They were prepared to admit to making freight discounts on sales to Britain from the Middle East, in order to meet the "competition" of prices from Venezuela. In the absence of underlying agreement as to what constitutes desirable public policy or appropriate conduct for a private company with duties to its stockholders and customers and the necessity to obey the law, the issue was initially settled by compromise to the extent that it was not avoided. This was done by shifting oil from ECA financing to a nonassistance basis. Later, in the summer of 1952, the Department of Justice brought a civil suit against the companies concerned to recover $67 million allegedly overcharged on sales to ECA and its successor MSA. The suit was won by the companies.

In this area of international trade, there is unhappily no consensus. While the economist can demonstrate to his own satisfaction that the basing-point system involves crosshauling and is therefore wasteful, he must admit that a firm is not in equilibrium where it is not exploiting the monopoly advantage it has and discriminating against those customers who have no access to other markets.

Even where the general rule calls for nondiscriminatory pricing f.o.b. mill or production point, a fundamental change in the trade pattern due to underlying alterations in supply or demand conditions may call for some transitional freight absorption before the outlines of the new pattern become stabilized. As Persian Gulf production grew, enormous profits were made at Gulf (of Mexico) plus. Then discounts were given, first to the United States Navy and later to further customers. Finally, a new basing point was established in the Persian Gulf with the watershed line of equal delivered cost fixed in Britain. This involved a reduction in the price of oil in the Persian Gulf from *Gulf-of-Mexico plus freight to the Persian Gulf* to *Gulf-of-Mexico plus freight to Britain minus freight to the Persian Gulf.* The discounts played a significant role in bringing about the adjustment to the new pattern. Similarly when the rising costs in Texas and Louisiana, on the one hand, and expanded production in the Persian Gulf, on the other, required a shift of the equal-cost line from Britain to the East Coast of the United States, freight absorption on crude sales from the Middle East to East Coast refiners provided a transitional link. Changes in the structure of trade under a geographic pattern of prices in which transport costs play a large part would bring about convulsive price changes if no discounts or freight absorption were allowed. This seems to be the reason that the European Coal and Steel Community, while it adheres in general to f.o.b. pricing, does not exclude freight absorption, or equal delivered prices, as an industrial practice.

Cartels

A cartel is a business agreement to restrict competition in matters of markets, price, terms of sale, conditions, etc. Whether this agreement is explicit and contractual or implicit and habitual is a matter of some semantic dispute but of little real economic interest. If businessmen understand one another's reactions to the same phenomena so well that they can act in the knowledge of the reactions of the others, there is no need for formal agreement. Legally, there may be no cartel; so far as the economics of the matter are concerned, the business agreement exists.

The content of cartel agreements, whether implicit or set out in formally negotiated documents, may differ. Some, like the electric light cartel, may be concerned with fixing prices; some, like the "as-is" agreement of 1928 in the petroleum industry with marketing arrangements (no company was to produce or market in any country in which it was not already established, i.e., everything stayed "as is"); some with patents, such as the arrangements between I. G. Farben in Germany and Du Pont and Standard Oil of New Jersey in the United States; some with conditions of sale, etc. But the essence of them all is that competition is limited by international business agreement.

These agreements occur in standardized products costly to transport, such as those mentioned in the discussion of the basing-point system; in raw materials and some primary products subject to inelastic demand and inelastic supply, such as those which form the subject of intergovernmental commodity agreements treated in the previous chapter; and in some highly differentiated goods, like pharmaceuticals, complex chemicals, such as rayon, nylon, synthetic rubber, dyes, etc., which operate within the sphere of patent control. In addition, shipping services themselves are likely to have their rates regulated by so-called shipping "conferences."

In most of the products covered by these areas, entry of new competitors is limited, and exit is unlikely. Entry may be limited because of a natural monopoly, as in mercury, nickel, sulphur, potash, etc.; because of the large amounts of capital needed to get started from scratch, as in oil, or aluminum; by government regulation, as in pepper, quinine, rubber, coffee; or by patent control, as in dyes, photographic supplies, optical instruments, electronic equipment. Exit is limited by the fact that large amounts of capital or the governments in question cannot afford to withdraw quietly from the business in case of losses. The result is that when price competition does occur, it is likely to be cutthroat in character and self-defeating.

Cutthroat competition is a phenomenon of oligopoly or a limited number of sellers. A price war may spread widely, in gasoline markets, by means of linkages between local markets. But essentially the problem arises because of competition among a limited number of competitors struggling for one another's business. The price is reduced below average cost, below marginal cost, and in some cases, such as in the famous railroad wars or a 1946 freight rate war on the east coast of India, below zero. Ten rupees, for example, may be given to the customer for each ton of cargo shipped between Madras and Calcutta. At this juncture the freight lines can profitably ship cargo of great weight and little value over their competitor's facilities. The self-defeating nature of this competition is evident. A predatory price cutter can sometimes force other concerns out of business if the firm's resources are much greater than those of its competitors. In this case, too, price competition is self-defeating. In the oligopolistic case, price cutting generally comes to a halt through agreement to maintain prices well before any firm has come to the end of its resources.

While the economist objects to cartels and to the elimination of price competition, he increasingly recognizes that healthy competition cannot exist in an oligopolistic industry. By "healthy competition" is meant, of course, that in which price cannot get too high because new entrants will be encouraged to come into the industry and may do so unhindered by capital costs, patent restrictions, lack of access to raw materials, or other barriers; and that in which price cannot get too low because existing firms will be encouraged to quit and to shift their efforts into other more profitable lines.

Cartel Policy

A number of interesting questions respecting cartels present themselves in international trade. It is argued by some that cartels cannot endure without government support; the case of the British governmental tariff action in behalf of the Iron and Steel Federation in its dispute with the European iron and steel cartel in the 1930's is cited. Some think that private cartels are superior to intergovernmental agreements or bulk-buying contracts because private cartels dissolve under the impact of diverse interests of individual producers. There is a body of American opinion which holds that international cartels are subversive of the national interest in self-preservation and that the member of a cartel somehow loses his patriotism—but this is difficult, if not impossible, to sustain.

What interests us primarily is the question of public policy toward international (and, if you like, national) cartels. Three possible lines of action present themselves: One may ignore them, attempt to break them up, or work out a way of living with them in which their worst features are softened or eliminated.

The policy of ignoring cartels attracts a wide body of conservative opinion. *Laissez faire,* a rule derived from competitive conditions with freedom of entry and exit, becomes perpetuated into a rule with validity after the underlying conditions which justified it have changed. There are those who are unable to make intermediate distinctions between monopoly and perfect competition. But the tenor of this chapter may have persuaded the reader that there are many shadings. If regulation is appropriate to monopolies like public utilities, then the principle of *laissez faire*—hands off business under any and all circumstances—has been breached.

The notion that it is possible to restore perfect competition by breaking up cartels, insisting upon the disintegration of combines and trusts, and enforcing arm's-length bargaining between separate stages of production in vertically integrated industries is perhaps more idealistic as a policy, but at the same time more naïve. Economies of large-scale production, especially in highly capitalized industries, may be in some part irreversible.

The third alternative has the drawback of being much less clear-cut than the other two. In part, it requires publicity for written agreements among firms and certain limitations on the content of such agreements, such as forbidding of division of markets and restriction on entry. In addition, it requires the instilling of restraint in pricing and of approximating, to the maximum degree consonant with the long-run interests of the owners of the business, the behavior of the trade under competition, including flat pricing. This involves restraint in the exercise of monopoly and oligopoly power. The difficulty with the pursuit of this line, however, is the absence of objective criteria. How high should profits be in oligopolistic industry? What is a fair price, a fair share, a fair profit?

In part, the basic difficulty occurs in the period of transition. Under perfect competition, with freedom of entry and exit, maximization of the short-run interest, i.e., of short-run profit, is a satisfactory rule and accords with the national interest. With its use, resources will be properly allocated among industries. Under imperfect competition, where a company is attentive to its long-run interest and long-run profit and is prepared to ignore short-run opportunities to increase profits, there may also be a satisfactory outcome. Companies will then abjure exploitation of monopoly positions because of fear of reprisal; will limit short-run profit maximization in favor of more security. The intermediate period is where the troubles press. Here companies have power but continue to exercise it in accordance with the rules applicable to the day of impotence of the private firm.

Summary

Perfect competition means that no individual buyer or seller has control over price, i.e., that the demand and supply curves facing the individual firm or consumer are infinitely elastic. In the real world of international trade, however, firms in many industries are of such a size that they can affect price.

When demand curves in different markets have different elasticities, a profit maximum is reached by charging discriminatory prices. The higher price is charged in the market with less elasticity. Or, looked at in different terms, a disproportionately high share of overhead costs may be allocated to the market with the less elastic demand curve.

Dumping is merely price discrimination. Sporadic, predatory, and persistent dumping have been distinguished in theory. While governmental action to prevent predatory dumping may be justified, when its existence is clearly established (a difficult matter), sporadic dumping performs a highly useful service for the seller, and persistent dumping is a benefit to the buyer.

Spatial price discrimination in international trade raises the question of basing points or stipulated places used for calculating price regardless of the place of production. The economist generally regards the basing-point system as less competitive than the system of identical prices for all buyers at the point of production, plus actual transport. The basing-point system requires freight absorption or phantom freight when production takes place elsewhere than at the basing point. This involves price discrimination.

Cartels are international business agreements to regulate price, division of markets, or other aspects of competition. They occur in industries with less than perfect competition. If the cartel is eliminated by some action, imperfect competition will still exist. This fact argues against the policies of either ignoring cartels or eliminating them by fiat, and in favor of a policy of regulation and publicity. In the present state of economic theory, however, no consensus exists as to how cartels should be regulated.

SUGGESTED READING

TEXTS

Marsh, chap. xxi, is excellent.

For a brief review of imperfect competition, see P. A. Samuelson, *Economics,* chaps. xxiv and xxv. More advanced treatments can be found in texts on intermediate economics by Boulding, Enke, etc.

TREATISES, ETC.

Haberler, chap. xviii.

E. S. Mason, *Controlling World Trade* (New York: McGraw-Hill Book Co., Inc., 1946), deals with cartels in Part I.

J. Viner's *Dumping* (Chicago: University of Chicago Press, 1923), is out of date in terms of examples but is still useful.

F. Machlup's *The Basing-Point System* (Philadelphia: Blakiston Co., 1951), is relevant, though it deals primarily with domestic cases.

Among the many interesting works on cartels, outstanding are G. W. Stocking and M. W. Watkins, *Cartels or Competition* (New York: Twentieth Century Fund, Inc., 1946); E. Hexner, *International Cartels* (Chapel Hill: University of North Carolina Press, 1945).

POINTS

For an impressive case study, see E. Hexner, *The International Steel Cartel* (Chapel Hill: University of North Carolina Press, 1943).

ECA comments on dual pricing are found in most quarterly reports, but especially in Nos. 7 and 8.

A 378-page report prepared by the Federal Trade Commission on the alleged activities of the international oil cartel was published by the Senate Small Business Committee's Subcommittee on Monopoly in August, 1952.

A useful source is United Nations, Economic and Social Council, *Restrictive Business Practices* (E/2379, and E/2380, including addenda), March and April, 1953, which includes texts of national legislation and governmental measures, an analysis of governmental measures, and a report of an *Ad Hoc* Committee which tried unsuccessfully to deal with cartels.

Chapter 15

EXCHANGE CONTROL

Origins

Parallel with the growth of quantitative restrictions on imports, and to a considerable extent an integral part of it, has been the development of foreign-exchange control. This depression product was born largely of necessity. A country found itself rapidly losing gold and approaching the end of its international reserves of gold and foreign exchange. The attempt to reduce national income through raising the discount rate and other deflationary measures did not usually elicit a rapid response. Depreciation was a possible resort in some cases but was excluded in a number of countries in Europe because of the painful memories of the concomitant inflation and depreciation after World War I. In other cases it was felt that depreciation would not work effectively because a new and lower exchange range would produce not increased exports but increased restrictions on imports in foreign countries. In any event, it was not clear that the depreciation would halt the outflow of capital. Accordingly, it was necessary to clamp down on purchases of foreign exchange and limit them to receipts. The usual device was to insist on receiving all foreign exchange resulting from exports and to dole it out to importers within the limits of the exchange available. From these crude beginnings in depression, foreign-exchange control developed into an elaborate world-wide institution with many forms and varieties.

The present chapter is limited to exchange control affecting the current account of the balance of payments. We shall not be concerned with controls over capital movements to restrain capital flight, although it is only fair to say, at this stage, that the separation of current and capital transactions made theoretically by economists has proved difficult for central banks and treasuries to effect in practice.

281

Kinds of Restrictions

As we have noted in Chapter 4, foreign-exchange restrictions may be divided into two basic types and a third mixed category. The first is quantitative, in which foreign exchange is rationed by amounts of currencies or types of imports. The second is cost, under which the foreign exchange used for certain purchases is limited by the necessity of effecting a clearing of demand and supply at a price reached by the market. The mixed system, which is perhaps the most usual, allows certain categories of transactions, quantitatively restricted by license or otherwise, to go forward at a fixed rate, while other types take place at rates determined by market forces. These systems of multiple exchange rates may involve as few as two and as many as ten or twenty different rates for the same foreign-currency unit.

Whatever the system of exchange control, price discrimination is involved—and not only discrimination between domestic and foreign producers but inevitably discrimination among different foreign buyers and sellers. Only by the most far-fetched coincidence could it happen that the system of foreign-exchange control would result in purchases of the same goods from all countries at equal prices delivered in the importing country. Only by the same impossible coincidence would export prices, realized from the sale of similar goods in different markets, result in the same rate of return netted back to the seller. When a country has a concern for the exchange gained or lost through an export or import, it is certain to depart from the nondiscriminatory, competitive rules of buying in the cheapest and selling in the dearest market, and buying and selling everywhere at the same prices. Exchange controls fragment international markets into many separate units.

Bilateral Clearing

One of the earliest forms of exchange control developed into a system of bilateral clearing. When a country had lost all reserves and was unwilling to change the nominal value of its exchange rate, foreign trade dwindled away to the point where it could be expanded through barter deals between governments. From this barter, there evolved a kind of clearing arrangement which eliminated the necessity of dealing in foreign exchange at all.

If Germany has a clearing arrangement with Yugoslavia, German exporters and importers can sell and buy to and from Yugoslav business concerns in marks. German importers pay these marks into an account at the Reichsbank or German treasury, where they are credited to the account of the Yugoslav clearing agency. German exporters are paid marks from this fund, which are debited to the Yugoslav account. In Belgrade, an opposite process is taking place. Yugoslav importers are making payments into the clearing account in dinars; exporters are receiving dinars from the account.

The rate at which marks and dinars are equated is fixed in advance when the clearing account is set up and remains unchanged except by negotiation. The prices at which goods move are established by the business concerns involved, with or without influence of a governmental character as the practice of the individual country determines. What goods may be sold and in what quantities is also a question for business decision, although this may be affected, in greater or less degree, by governmental intervention in the trade process by tariff or quota, export subsidy or tax.

So long as exports and imports between the two countries are bilaterally balanced, all is well. Clearing takes place between Yugoslavia and Germany; but, in fact, nothing in the way of payments moves between them. German importers in Berlin pay into the account marks which, in turn, are paid out to exporters. This is, of course, the way the foreign-exchange market operates when the balance of payments of a country is in equilibrium and the currencies of the countries to which it sells are convertible. In the clearing case, the process is more self-conscious and contrived and also—of the utmost importance—bilateral rather than multilateral.

When exports and imports deviate from each other, problems arise and require decision. Assume that in Germany imports from Yugoslavia exceed exports to that country. German importers will pay into the clearing account more than German exporters will be entitled to receive from it. This is a possible arrangement, since marks can be accumulated indefinitely in the account. It is evidently deflationary, unless offset by credit expansion elsewhere in the economy, as is any excess of imports over exports. The excess of inpayments over outpayments operates like the loss of foreign exchange or gold under a more normal fixed-rate standard of international payments.

More significant, however, is what takes place in Yugoslavia. Here outpayments of the clearing fund must exceed inpayments if exports are to exceed imports and the exporters are to be paid. But this cannot occur automatically without limit, since the dinars in the clearing are finite in number. Yugoslavia may decide to advance credit to the clearing account to enable it to pay the exporters. If the central bank does so—which is perhaps typical—excess payments to exporters serve to expand reserve credit and to provide a basis for a further expansion of bank credit. This operates exactly as if the excess of exports over imports had been paid in gold. The danger, of course, is that the rise in incomes generated by the net foreign investment (export surplus) is likely to spill over, via the marginal propensity to import, into imports from other countries, while the country has not general, but only particular, foreign purchasing power at its disposal.

Accordingly, some few countries would take a hard-boiled attitude toward the export excess and let the exporters wait for payment. They must wait, to take the case of Yugoslavia, until the clearing account favoring Germany has been built up again by importers making purchases in Germany. If exporters are paid in the order of the date of their sales, a waiting period—three months was not uncommon in the depressed 1930's, and six months not rare—will cool the ardor of exporters to sell to countries with which a deficit exists. In this case, the export surplus must be financed not by the central bank but by the exporters themselves, who pay out funds to produce the goods for export but are obliged to wait for payment.

During the 1930's, Germany, under the leadership of Dr. Clodius and Dr. Schacht, exploited this bilateral clearing system to borrow, in effect, from the poorer countries of southeastern Europe. Germany bought raw materials and foodstuffs from Yugoslavia, Rumania, Bulgaria, Hungary, etc., with an open hand, paying high prices in terms of dinars, lei, leva, and pengoes. The exporting interests, powerful in these countries, succeeded in getting the central bank to finance their export surpluses. Large claims on Germany were accumulated, but these could be used only as Germany reluctantly made goods available from its rearmament program, at prices dictated by Germany. This is the explanation of the fact that countries of southeastern Europe were flooded with aspirin and harmonicas, which were among those goods made most readily available by Germany to its creditors. The exploitation of its buyer's position stumbled upon by Germany was possible only in a world of depression, where other markets in western Europe —far away—offered lower prices, and a world in which Germany alone was fully employed. During the period of commodity shortages since 1946, the seller and not the buyer would have the advantage in bilateral clearing.

One should not feel too sorry for the countries of southeastern Europe at this period, nor criticize Germany too harshly for its trade policies. The Balkan countries were better off as a result of this trade than if it had not been available. In part, the benefits were of a multiplier variety. More rural purchasing power generated by exports helped to maintain urban employment. But insofar as they got any imports from Germany, they were better off than if they had gone without.

It used to be held that Germany improved her net barter terms of trade with southeastern Europe through this device, as well as the gross barter terms achieved through increased imports and reduced exports. It is clearly possible to achieve a terms-of-trade effect with a multiple-exchange rate system, but the data do not demonstrate this result in the German experience.

Payments Agreements

Clearing agreements are, by definition, those restricted to the matching of claims and debts arising from trade. The term "payments agreement" is wider in scope and covers bilateral accords which provide for settling a wider number of payments, particularly those on outstanding debts. When Switzerland had certain claims on Germany for outstanding bank credits or overdue bonds in default, it saw little advantage in agreeing to an arrangement for clearing merely current-trade payments; the need of Germany for trade made possible an extension of the arrangement so that, say, 10 per cent of all proceeds of Swiss imports from Germany would be set aside to pay outstanding claims of Swiss creditors. Or, if the Swiss market for German-made films was particularly important to the German industry, it could be agreed that half the proceeds from this particular export would be set aside to pay specified frozen credits.

Today payments agreements may modify exchange-control prohibitions against certain types of transactions. The sterling control, for example, divides nonresident sterling into a number of separate categories. Sterling-area accounts can be used freely for purchases and capital transactions within the sterling area. Transferable sterling is that owned by residents of countries with which the exchange authorities have concluded agreements or that arising out of trade with these countries. This may be paid to a resident account, a sterling-area account, or an account of the same country without limit; but it can be credited only under certain restrictions. Security sterling is contained in special nontransferable accounts—countries can be credited only from the sales of sterling securities, and debited only to buy such securities back. And credits to American accounts are the most restricted of all, because sterling in these is convertible into dollars.

Private Compensation

A system of private compensation grew up originally outside the system of payments agreements. Two firms in Germany might agree with two firms in Rumania to effectuate payments in each country outside the clearing in order to settle obligations arising out of shipments in opposite directions. The Rumanian importer would pay the Rumanian exporter; and the German exporter would receive payment from the German importer. This could occur only before the foreign-exchange control system had developed to the point where goods could not move across national boundaries without a certificate to indicate that the foreign-exchange control formalities had been compiled with, unless the offset were debts, or goods smuggled, or goods so unimportant that the foreign-exchange control did not apply to them. In one particular kind of private compensation, a firm, say, in America would sell goods to a country such as Italy, where foreign-exchange inconvertibility prevented it from selling lire for dollars, and then spend the lire on goods outside the controlled area of principal exports. These goods were then imported and sold in the United States. For the American firm to be allowed to buy normal exports would defeat the aim of exchange control, since it would divert the proceeds of basic exports to buying additional rather than basic imports. A number of companies which had previously considered themselves primarily exporters, found themselves in the importing business as well. Their ability to sell in amounts above the permitted minimum depended upon their success in assisting the country in expanding exports.

In the early days after World War II, a good deal of this private compensation took place between a firm or industry, on the one hand, and a government, on the other. The British exchange-control arrangements with the American motion-picture industry, for example, involved the collection of royalties due to Hollywood on movie exhibitions in the sterling area, with strict limits on their use. Under the 1950 agreement, $17,000,000 (about £6,100,000 at $2.80 to the pound) of earnings could be transferred without question. A further amount could be transferred depending upon the earnings of the British movie industry in the United States. Finally, the United States film companies were allowed to use the remaining sterling, of which there was originally a good deal, for certain specified purposes, such as the production of motion pictures in British studios, but not for other purposes, such as the purchase of theaters.

Similar arrangements were made between European exchange-control authorities and firms in other industries. Conspicuous among these was the oil industry. Oil companies had agreed to sell their products in Europe for a return partly in dollars and partly in inconvertible local currencies. This was necessary in order to compete with sterling oil. These local currencies were then used for a variety of purposes. Tankers could be purchased from foreign yards, even though delivery dates stretched years further into the future than those in the United States. Foreign crews were used to man tankers belonging to American companies, and repairs and maintenance were undertaken abroad. Administration of foreign operations was moved from New York into the field, in order to shift a portion of executive salaries and all clerical wages from dollars into foreign currency. Supplies for drilling, pipeline, refining, and distribution operations abroad were purchased abroad to the maximum extent possible with soft currencies, even though quoted prices were higher and delivery dates longer than those in the United States. While the quoted price was higher in dollars if local-currency prices were converted at the official rate, when the currencies were inconvertible the official rate was meaningless; and a subjective discount on the part of the company, of lesser or greater magnitude, was justified.

The full implications of this corporate compensation are not yet understood. There is naturally some confusion. This is illustrated by a statement of the representative of the Hollywood Film Council of the American Federation of Labor, quoted in the *New York Times:* "We are not objecting to the making of pictures abroad for the purpose of using up foreign assets or of obtaining authentic backgrounds. But we will try to stop the growing tendency here among Hollywood producers to do their shooting in foreign countries principally to cut costs." It is evident, however, that there is no ultimate difference between using up foreign assets and cutting costs. The value of blocked foreign currencies is below their nominal worth. One cuts costs by using them up at their subjective exchange valuation.

From the standpoint of the country involved, private compensation is comparable to currency depreciation which is limited to the single firm or industry. The firm with blocked assets will reduce its exports to the country and increase its imports, exactly as if the currency had been depreciated for its benefit.

The discriminatory features of these arrangements are obvious, as well as the uneconomic. In terms of quoted prices, purchases are made in the dearer rather than the cheaper market, and supplies are sold where they earn a lower return, at nominal exchange rates, than elsewhere. Trade settles into a strait jacket and follows narrowly bilateral lines. But the argument can be made that the system is more economic than the worse alternative of an overvalued currency and import restrictions. The currency is, in effect, devalued in a series of separate transactions with separate firms.

A vital objection to private compensation, however, is its highly administered character. It requires state interference with every aspect of foreign trade. The state must decide what a foreign firm can and cannot do with its balances. Quite apart from the theoretical distastefulness of this sort of interference, it is hardly likely to be done with great efficiency.

Multiple Rates

Foreign-exchange control based on cost essentially involves multiple exchange rates. Its origin is again German. When debts could not be paid in foreign exchange after the Hoover moratorium of 1931, the foreign owners were allowed to sell off the mark equivalent to other foreigners for designated purposes and at rates which would reduce the German obligations to foreigners at small cost in German resources. Gradually a wide number of different kinds of marks came to be distinguished, depending on their source, and with different limits on their use. Since the markets for these marks became separate, there was no necessity for them to sell at the same price. Accordingly, the Reichsbank established different rates for the Reisemark (travel mark), the Sperrmark (blocked mark), and the Askimark (the initial letters for *A*uslands-*S*onder-*K*onto für *I*nlandskredit—special foreign accounts for internal use, which referred to marks arising out of, and useful only for, trade with Latin America), etc. In some cases the rates were allowed to fend for themselves. In others, the Reichsbank intervened to affect the course of quotations. Some rates, such as those for Reichsmark currency notes in Amsterdam, Zurich, etc., were illegal from the point of view of Germany. They were fed by capital exports smuggled out in the form of notes. Demand was said to represent the requirements of foreign secret-service agents, but undoubtedly included primarily the inducement to illegal smuggling of notes offered by the large discount.

Foreign-exchange control in this complexity clearly made trade more difficult. Even tourists were affected. Most payments—hotel, restaurant, travel, etc.—were made with Reisemarks, which sold for about 25 cents. Certain prize German exports, however, such as expensive cameras, could not legally be purchased by tourists with Reisemarks. Stores selling those items were required to ascertain that the marks with which they were bought were official marks, which cost 40 cents. In those commodities in which Germany had a monopoly advantage, the highest rate of foreign exchange, and hence the highest price in terms of foreign currency, was the one which applied.

Multiple exchange-rate systems have flourished in the years since their origin in German necessity and ingenuity. Countries in all parts of the world have found them useful, but nowhere so much as in Latin America. In some countries there are merely two rates, the official and the free. The official rate is fixed at a high level to improve the terms of trade of a few staple exports in which the country has an outstanding position in world trade, and in those import necessities which the country must in any case purchase. Holding the value of the domestic currency high maintains the foreign-currency price of Brazilian coffee, Bolivian tin, or Chilean copper.

Outside the official market, which is supported by the central bank, all other imports and exports may be left to fend for themselves and to settle on a freely fluctuating rate in the process. Since the market must clear itself, the value of imports is limited to the value of exports. The rate of exchange must be that which will so encourage exports, other than the established ones which sell at the official rate, and so discourage imports, other than the favored necessities which may be purchased cheaply at official rates, that imports equal exports.

Under this system, and with only two rates, the task of the foreign-exchange authorities is to support the official rate, supplying foreign exchange to it when it is weak and buying foreign exchange when it is strong, and to ensure that the proceeds of exports due at the official rate are collected, while no additional imports not on the list are bought at this rate. Arbitrage pressure to unite the two markets will be strong, since exporters would make increased profits if they were allowed to convert the proceeds of prime exports at the depreciated free rate, and importers would make their purchases more cheaply with official exchange.

In some systems the official intervention goes further than these duties, however, and results in buying and selling exchange in the "free" market to peg its level and in forbidding the use of free exchange for certain types of transactions. In these cases a new "free" rate is likely to come into being outside the "official free" rate, as some rates have actually been called, with exporters reluctant to sell at the pegged rates and importers of certain products forbidden to buy. Such is the ingenuity of men with a "commodity" as small in bulk, as homogeneous, and as fungible, i.e., valuable in a wide number of uses, as money, that there is always some market in any foreign-exchange system which is not subject to official surveillance. When the authorities operate a complete system of foreign-exchange control, the uncontrolled market is a "black" one. The multiple-rate system in which one free market is open to any and all purchasers not specifically favored makes the free market legal.

In many systems a wide number of special exchange rates develops, dependent upon the market position in export commodities and the degree of necessity with which the country regards various imports. In some countries the matter is carried to such a degree that there appears to be a separate exchange rate for each commodity. In this limiting case the parallel between tariffs and exchange control becomes apparent.

A flat ad valorem tariff on all imports and an export subsidy of equal percentage on all exports would be exactly the equivalent of an exchange depreciation of an equal degree—except, of course, for transfers and capital movements. A multiple exchange-rate system, in which different export and import commodities are assigned separate exchange rates, is very much akin to a system of a single convertible exchange, in which each export and import commodity is assigned a distinct subsidy and tariff, respectively.

The analogy could be broadened to include import subsidies and export tariffs. An export duty would be much the same as the penalty now paid by those exports which must be sold at the highest exchange rates, say, the official rate; the export subsidy, the same as permission to sell at the free rate or at any rate below the average for all exports. The import subsidy would be accorded to those goods which are bought at exchange rates higher than the average, the highest being the official rate. Those imports which can be bought only with free exchange or at low rates are comparable to those which bear the highest rate of duty.

The analogy is widely applicable. Like tariffs, subsidies, quotas, and exchange-rate adjustments, foreign-exchange control has protective, consumption, revenue, redistribution, terms of trade, employment, and balance-of-payments effects. Its original purpose may have been the defense of the balance of payments. And income and consumption effects may remain incidental. But in different countries, under different circumstances, the multiple exchange-rate system may start out to correct the balance of payments and end up mainly or substantially retained for its protective, revenue, redistribution, or terms-of-trade effects.

The nature of the protective effect is evident. The redistribution effect involved in assigning necessities of consumption, like wheat, to the official market, and articles of luxury consumption to the free market, or vice versa, is also clear on reflection. The revenue effect, however, is a powerful influence in the perpetuation of the system of multiple rates, just as it was in the development of tariffs when administrative techniques made it easier for governments to collect taxes on goods than from persons.

Many countries introduce a spread between their buying and selling rates for exchange, which adds considerably to the national governmental revenue. This is especially the case when a country has jurisdiction over a profitable foreign investment engaged in exporting. In some cases the company will be required to turn over all the proceeds of its exports to the foreign-exchange control and to buy exchange, in remitting profits, at a low rate. In others the company will be permitted to keep the proceeds of foreign sales but will be charged a high rate for the local currency when it buys exchange with which to meet its expenses of production and transport. A considerable part of the revenue of the government and the country's foreign-exchange receipts, for example, accrued to Iran from its profit on exchange sales to the Anglo-Iranian Oil Company prior to its nationalization in 1951, to cover the company's expenses in the local currency, which is called the rial.

Some writers are inclined to attach predominant importance to the revenue aspect of multiple exchange rates and to regard the system as one of export and import taxes without subsidies. The monopoly-monopsony features must not be neglected, however. Few Latin-American countries are large enough purchasers to exert a monopsonistic influence in world commodity markets. This was a significant aspect of the multiple rate system in Germany in the 1930's. The monopoly element, on the other hand, has been of great importance in Latin America. A country will get improved terms of trade for the commodities it sells at overvalued rates, provided that the demand curve in the commodity is inelastic over the relevant portion. This means that the country has a monopoly, partial or complete, over the price range and within the time period.

At this overvalued rate, however, it may be impossible to sell in world markets certain products which are marginal to world supply. Some of these secondary products may even be excluded from world markets at an equilibrium exchange rate, and require depreciated levels of exchange before they can be sold. Such limited depreciation may be regarded as useful because of difficulty in using the resources in other occupations or because of anticipated increasing returns or for still other extra-economic reasons. A system of multiple exchange rates, effectively managed, will enable a country to maximize its terms of trade by exploiting its monopoly advantages and correcting for its competitive handicaps. To depreciate the exchange rate for the benefit of secondary products would be to give up a portion of the monopoly profit on the prime exports. To maintain an overvalued rate for the benefit of this monopoly profit would exclude secondary exports from world markets. Higher internal prices for the prime products and lower prices for the secondary could not be achieved, in the light of the structure of production and the degree of factor-price equalization, without the imposition of taxes on the former (to limit the return to factors) and subsidies on the latter (to increase the return). This, after all, is what the multiple exchange-rate system involves.

Multiple Cross-Rates

Discussion thus far has proceeded on the assumption of a multiple exchange system in one country vis-à-vis another single country or, what is the same thing, the whole world as a homogeneous unit. The real world is more complex. Quantitative exchange-control systems can balance trade in a limited number of commodities between one country and the world; in unlimited amounts of commodities, with bilateral balancing or clearing between countries; or in a mixture of the two—all at a single exchange rate. The cost principle in exchange control, or multiple rates, can be employed by a country in groups of commodities. It can also be used to clear trade between countries. Peru, for example, may try to balance her trade with the sterling area by allowing the sol-pound rate to find its own level, regardless of the sol-dollar rate and the cross-rate between the pound sterling and the dollar.

Multiple exchange rates which involve multiple cross-rates have been seriously objected to by a number of countries and by the International Monetary Fund. The basis for this objection is primarily because these rates encourage violations of foreign-exchange control and make the policing problem acute. A multiple rate system based on commodities and with fixed cross-rates presents a temptation to violation; but policing is relatively easy. If a firm was issued exchange to buy wheat, it is generally simple to ascertain whether it had, in fact, bought wheat. Suppose, however, that Peru offered sterling at a rate which would give a cross-rate of $2.00 between the pound and the dollar, instead of the actual rate of $2.80. This would encourage New York importers to buy their sterling in Lima at the depreciated rate. The sterling exchange authorities would prevent this through their payments agreement where they could. Sterling blocked for Peruvian account could be spent only for goods for shipment to Peru.

But there are many ways to get to Peru, and one is by way of the United States. Once the goods have left British shores and British jurisdiction, the destination can be altered to New York, as New York importers "buy" them from the original Peruvian "importers." The effect of this hypothetical transaction, of course, would be adverse to the British exchange position. Blocked sterling has declined. Exports to the United States have been unrequited, i.e., have been sold without payment in dollars. Peru has exchanged sterling for dollars at a depreciated rate. The New York importers have obtained their goods more cheaply.

Multiple exchange rates involving multiple cross-rates complicate the problem of surveillance by holding out to people, outside the control of the authorities of the depreciated currency, strong inducements to beat the system. Foreign-exchange controls are difficult to enforce at best. A good system with honest authorities is probably only 95 per cent effective when all cross-rates are at the levels of the official rates. A venal and corrupt bureaucracy, such as that of the Germans under Hitler, probably has little more than 85 per cent efficiency, i.e., 15 per cent of the foreign exchange which should accrue to the authorities is dissipated in one way or another, generally in capital flight. It was reported, for example, that the market system worked so effectively in Germany that refugees anxious to escape with as much of their capital as could be taken with them found the prices of obtaining bank notes for smuggling out and sale in Amsterdam, the cost of bribing Reichsbank officials, and the use of the examination-free facilities of foreign diplomats all roughly kept in line by supply and demand.

In these circumstances, it can be understood that foreign-exchange authorities are especially opposed to added inducements to evade foreign-exchange regulations given to persons outside their control.

Exchange Discrimination

Exchange controls are discriminatory because they depart from the general rule of nondiscrimination, which is to sell in the dearest and buy in the cheapest markets, charging or paying a single price on homogeneous commodities regardless of customer or supplier. But exchange controls are generally more explicitly discriminatory. Some of this discrimination operates against particular commodities and has already been discussed in Chapter 13. It makes little difference whether trade or exchange controls are used to keep luxuries out of a country.

In addition, however, exchange control is likely to discriminate against, or in favor of, particular currencies. Discrimination in favor of a particular currency is likely to take place when the currency is unduly abundant; discrimination against, when it is unduly scarce. Undue abundance of a currency is likely to occur when the country using it has a large import surplus over and above the capital requirements of foreign investors of that currency, and is unable to pay for its excess imports with gold, acceptable foreign exchange, or by borrowing.

The Inconvertible Surplus

In general, foreign-exchange control is an alternative to depreciation or deflation in a country which has a deficit and which is trying to avoid the effects of alternative lines of action. There is, however, another case of some importance: when a country has a surplus with one country and a deficit with another—and over-all balance—but when the currency in which the surplus is earned becomes inconvertible. With convertibility, balance. Convertibility removed, the deficit with one country is, in effect, a deficit over-all which must be met with loss of international reserves, or borrowing. General measures like depreciation or deflation may help to adjust the position vis-à-vis the deficit country or countries, but they make it worse elsewhere by increasing the inconvertible surplus. What is needed are measures which will reduce the inconvertible surplus at the same time that they decrease the hard-currency deficit.

The real world is full of nations which rely on surpluses with one country to pay for deficits with another. Europe used to have a surplus on current account with Southeast Asia, which produced the dollars to pay for the European import surplus from the Western Hemisphere. Within Europe, the Netherlands and Britain, especially, had import surpluses which were made good with dollars and sterling earned net overseas. The rest of Europe, on the other hand, especially Germany and to a lesser degree Scandinavia, France, and Italy, earned dollars and sterling from sales to the Netherlands and Britain to pay their net deficits with the dollar area and the overseas portion of the sterling area. Perhaps the most dramatic case is that of Canada, which sells nonferrous metals, lumber, and farm products like wheat, apples, and bacon to Britain, for which she was wont to receive dollars to help pay for imports of durable consumers' goods from the United States. When sterling became inconvertible, as early as 1941, Canada was obliged to devise means of attacking the deficit in dollars with the

United States which had previously been met with dollars obtained for her surplus with the United Kingdom.

When Britain depreciates sterling against the dollar, Canada has an opportunity to apply the appropriate medicine—appreciation against sterling, depreciation against the dollar. This course was followed in 1939 and again immediately after the British devaluation of 1949.

When the sterling rate is unaltered, however, the problem is more unyielding. If sterling were truly inconvertible, of course, it would be possible for the Canadian dollar to appreciate against sterling and depreciate against the United States dollar, if the authorities were reconciled to a cross-rate between the pound and the United States dollar which departed from the official rate in New York and London. With the pound at $4.00 in New York and the Canadian dollar at par, the latter could appreciate against the pound by 10 per cent and depreciate by 10 per cent against the United States dollar, if the cross-rate between the pound and the United States dollar were to go to $4.93+ ($4.40 ÷ 0.90). But this would encounter serious objection from the London exchange authorities, since the inconvertibility of sterling is not proof against the temptation to arbitrage, illegally or through commodity shunting, afforded by such a spread.

When sterling is inconvertible and cross-rates must be held at official levels, the Canadian position is more difficult. The Canadian government in these circumstances has imposed discriminatory quantitative import restrictions and exchange control. Imports from the United Kingdom are encouraged, those from the United States discouraged. If the discrimination extends to exports, which is less usual than discrimination in imports, it requires encouraging exports to the United States and discouraging those to the United Kingdom.

United States Treasury policy has been conscious of the difficulty faced by Canada. In 1941 President Roosevelt and Prime Minister King of Canada concluded the Hyde Park Agreement, under which additional goods sought by Canada in the United States for her armament program were made available to Britain under Lend-Lease, but delivered with her permission to Canada. It was understood that a considerable part of the Anglo-American Financial Agreement of $3¾ billion in 1946 would be spent by Britain in Canada and would finance in dollars the Canadian surplus with the United Kingdom. After this attempt to restore convertibility failed, another *ad hoc* arrangement was devised in the form of "offshore purchases," under the European

Recovery Program. Some aid furnished by the United States to Europe consisted of goods bought with United States dollars in Canada (and Latin America). This aided both Europe and Canada. With the 1949 depreciation of sterling, Canada was able more nearly to achieve balance in its separate trade with the dollar and sterling areas with diminishing reliance and finally abandonment of exchange control. Ultimately the discovery of oil in Alberta brought a substantial flow of capital from the United States, which, after the exchange rate had been freed, led to a premium for the Canadian dollar.

Discrimination against a Scarce Currency

Exchange controls are also applied in discriminatory fashion against a currency which is scarce. This is the most natural thing in the world. Suppose the United States dollar is in short supply, whether because the United States is experiencing a recession and has reduced its imports or because every other country in the world is experiencing an inflation, or for any other reason. In these circumstances, a nondiscriminatory reduction of imports on the part of, say, France would involve cutting out imports from Britain, Italy, and Scandinavia, as well as from the United States. But France may have enough pounds, lire, and kroner to maintain purchases. In this case she will be strongly tempted to cut down mainly imports from the United States and to maintain imports from her other trading partners. If Britain, Italy, and Scandinavia also cut down imports from the United States without reducing their purchases from one another and from France, according to a demonstration by Ragnar Frisch, this will reduce the volume of world trade in the process of achieving balance less than would proportional import restrictions.[1] This can be shown by a simple and somewhat arbitrary example, using a trade matrix.

In Matrix 1 the importing countries—A, B, and C—are listed in the row across the top, and the exporting countries—A, B, and C—in a column at the left. The squares in a diagonal line from left to right, top to bottom, are, of course, blank, since A, the importer (top row) does not buy from A, the exporter (left-hand column). The other squares of the matrix, however, are filled in with numerals which may be read either way, as imports by the column heading from the country indicated by the row heading, or vice versa. In the first matrix, for

---

[1] It should by this time be clear that proportionality is nondiscriminatory in the sense of equalizing marginal cost of imports from different sources of supply, only when all supply curves have the same elasticity. If differences in elasticity exist, import restrictions should be such as to maintain equality of marginal cost, not proportionality of reduction.

example, A exports goods worth 4 to B, or B imports goods worth 4 from A, whichever way you choose to regard it.

The first matrix shows the position in balance. B has an export surplus of 4 with A (imports of 4, exports of 8); but this is balanced by an import surplus of 4 with C (exports of 4, imports of 8). And so on for the other countries.

In the second matrix, A's imports have fallen in half, while B's and C's have been maintained. This gives A an export surplus of 6, and B and C import surpluses of 4 and 2, respectively.

MATRIX 1

Exporting	Importing A	B	C	Total Exports	Export Surplus
A...............	...	4	8	12	...
B...............	8	...	4	12	...
C...............	4	8	...	12	...
Total imports....	12	12	12	36	
Import surplus..	...	...	...		...

MATRIX 2

Exporting	Importing A	B	C	Total Exports	Export Surplus
A...............	...	4	8	12	+6
B...............	4	...	4	8	...
C...............	2	8	...	10	...
Total imports....	6	12	12	30	
Import surplus..	...	−4	−2		6

MATRIX 3

Exporting	Importing A	B	C	Total Exports	Export Surplus
A...............	...	2	4	6	...
B...............	4	...	2	6	...
C...............	2	4	...	6	...
Total imports....	6	6	6	18	
Import surplus..	...	...	...		...

MATRIX 4

Exporting	Importing A	B	C	Total Exports	Export Surplus
A...............	...	...	6	6	...
B...............	4	...	4	8	...
C...............	2	8	...	10	...
Total imports....	6	8	10	24	
Import surplus..	...	...	...		...

The third matrix demonstrates the position with proportional import restrictions. It will be observed that C had only half the import surplus that B had. But if it reduces its imports from both A and B, it makes B's position worse. And as B cuts its imports from A and C, it makes the latter's position, in turn, more difficult. The interaction of B and C on each other comes to a halt only when they have succeeded in matching the reduction in trade with which A initiated what the cliché regards as a vicious spiral. This cuts total trade in half. If, on the other hand, they discriminate against A in a co-ordinated fashion, B eliminating its trade with A altogether and C reducing its trade by one fourth, they will succeed in balancing all the accounts in the system with a smaller reduction in trade.

This demonstration has been criticized and evidently has its limitations. The matrix could be balanced from Matrix 2 with less reduction in trade if it were possible for either B or C to expand trade to A. The demonstration depends on the assumption, only sometimes valid —as, perhaps, if a depression were to strike in A—that this cannot be done.

Matrix 4, moreover, requires careful co-ordination between B and C, which cut their imports from A by widely different margins. The burden of the cuts from A falls heavily on B and relatively lightly on C. This may be difficult to arrange, if the income elasticity for A's goods is low—if, for example, they consist in wheat and coal, which are regarded as vital. While these and other objections may be raised against the general validity of the analysis, it nonetheless contains a kernel of force. This kernel is recognized in the "scarce-currency" provision of the International Monetary Fund, which permits countries to discriminate against imports from a country whose currency has been declared scarce by the Fund. The requirement of a declaration of "scarcity," of course, is to safeguard the provision and prevent its abuse.

Declining Trade Spiral

The matrix is becoming increasingly useful as a tool of analysis and demonstration in international trade. We may use the same figures, and the assumption that the demand for A's exports is highly income-

MATRIX 3a						MATRIX 4a				
Exporting	*Importing* A B C			*Total Ex- ports*	*Export Surplus*	*Exporting*	*Importing* A B C			*Total Ex- ports*	*Export Surplus*
A...............	... 4 8			12	+6	A...............	... 4 2			6	...
B............	4 ... 4			8	...	B............	4 ... 4			8	...
C............	2 4 ...			6	...	C............	2 4 ...			6	...
Total im-ports....	6 8 12			26		Total im-ports....	6 8 6			20	
Import surplus..	... ... −6				6	Import surplus..	... ...				...

inelastic downward, to demonstrate how fragile is the web of trade in a world of deficits and discriminatory trade controls.

B's initial concern with the position demonstrated by Matrix 2 is only mild. Its trade with A is balanced—exports of 4 and imports of 4.

Over-all, to be sure, it has an import surplus of 4, but this is recorded with C, and these goods are of less concern. C, on the other hand, takes a different view. Its over-all deficit is only 2. But this is made up of an import surplus of 6 from A, offset by an export surplus of 4 from B. If B fails to pay these 4, which are equal to B's total import surplus, then C must begin to worry, not about its over-all deficit of 2, but about the import surplus from A, three times this amount.

MATRIX 5

Exporting	Importing A	B	C	Total Exports	Export Surplus
A.............	...	4	6	10	+4
B.............	4	...	0	4	...
C.............	2	4	...	6	...
Total imports......	6	8	6	20	
Import surplus..	...	−4	...		4

MATRIX 6

Exporting	Importing A	B	C	Total Exports	Export Surplus
A.............	...	4	6	10	+4
B.............	4	...	0	4	...
C.............	2	0	...	2	...
Total imports....	6	4	6	16	
Import surplus..	...	−4			4

MATRIX 7

Exporting	Importing A	B	C	Total Exports	Export Surplus
A.............	...	4	2	6	...
B.............	4	...	0	4	...
C.............	2	0	...	2	...
Total imports....	6	4	2	12	
Import surplus.	...	...	...		...

A likely sequence of events is set out in the following series of matrices, which start from the position in Matrix 2. First (Matrix 3a), B cuts its imports 4 from C, to eliminate its export surplus and leave itself in a balanced position. This proves hard on C, which is saddled with all the A export surplus, viz., 6. If C can, it will reduce imports from A from 8 to 2, which would balance the matrix bilaterally, as in Matrix 4a. But if its demand for these goods is income-inelastic, it will try again to reduce imports from B or to expand exports to that country. If B is unable or unwilling to buy any further C-goods, C can balance its trade with the minimum decrease in A-goods by eliminating its imports from B altogether and cutting imports from A by 2. This is shown in Matrix 5. C is balanced, but only at the expense of B, which now has an over-all import surplus of 4, matching A's export balance.

The nature of B's reply is readily anticipated. It eliminates the remainder of its imports from C, in order to protect its precious wheat and coal from A. This is shown in Matrix 6, which leads inevitably into Matrix 7 and the reduction of total trade by the largest amount. Trade between B and C has been totally eliminated.

It is this condition—wherein B and C regard their trade with each other as much less important than their imports from A, with which both are in over-all deficit—in which Europe found itself in 1947 after the dollar reserves it had accumulated during the war had been used up. No country wanted to cut imports from the United States, whence vital supplies for sustenance and recovery could be bought. None was willing to pay dollars to buy less useful goods in Europe. The deficit with the United States was the cause of the difficulty. In a vain attempt to solve it with exchange control, trade within Europe was gradually cut and cut again in a spiral until it appeared likely to dry up. This exercise in the pathology of exchange control was finally brought to a halt only by the use of Marshall Plan aid, reshaped specifically to maintain and expand trade within Europe. But this account of the Intra-European Payments Scheme and its successor, the European Payments Union, must also wait for full discussion.

Exchange control, like import quotas, is certain to be discriminatory. Used in a consciously discriminatory way, it may, as in the Frisch case, limit the decline in trade which would otherwise be necessary. It may, on the other hand, merely create unnecessary difficulties and dry trade up more than would be the case with proportional restrictions or some other means to finance deficits. Whether quantitative or based on cost, exchange restrictions may be a necessity but never a virtue.

Summary

Exchange control has emerged from a necessity, used by countries which lacked international means of payment so that they could not run up trade deficits, to a means of trade manipulation in which monopoly and monopsony advantages have been gained. Bilateral clearing is superior to no trade, but it forces trade into a narrow channel and frequently enables one country to exploit the dependence on it of others. Bilateral clearing arrangements have evolved into payments agreements, which then emerge, in a number of countries, into compensation arrangements between corporations and countries. These require trade to balance at a narrow level and involve trade discrimination.

Some exchange-control systems clear the market by changes in price. Where the market is divided into subunits in each of which a separate price prevails, the system is one of multiple exchange rates. These multiple exchange-rate systems may discriminate among foreign currency units and involve multiple cross-rates.

All exchange-control systems involve discrimination. Control may discriminate against exports and in favor of imports relative to a country with which the currency has an inconvertible surplus. Or discrimination may be practiced against the hard currency with which a deficit is being run.

Trade discrimination, under certain circumstances, reduces total trade less than proportional trade reductions would reduce it. If the countries practicing trade discrimination have inelastic demands for imports from a hard-currency country, the practice of nondiscrimination may wipe out all other trade.

SUGGESTED READING

TEXTS

The fullest treatment at a fairly elementary level is contained in R. F. Mikesell, *Foreign Exchange in the Postwar World* (New York: Twentieth Century Fund, Inc., 1954).

TREATISES, ETC.

Meade, *The Balance of Payments,* Part V. For an account written early in the 1930's but combining theory with history, see H. S. Ellis, *Exchange Control in Central Europe* (Cambridge, Mass.: Harvard University Press, 1934). See also U.S. Tariff Commission, *Trade and Exchange Controls in Germany* (Report No. 150, second series; Washington, D.C.: U.S. Government Printing Office, 1942).

The principal monograph on clearing is P. N. Andersen, *Bilateral Exchange Clearing Policy* (Copenhagen: Einar Munksgaard, 1946).

The major work describing the multilateral pattern of world trade in 1928 and 1938 was performed by the late Folke Hilgerdt for the League of Nations. See League of Nations, *Europe's Trade* (Geneva: League of Nations, 1940); *The Network of World Trade* (Geneva: League of Nations, 1942). Annual matrices of world trade were published by the Economic Commission for Europe in its annual *Surveys,* but are currently published in the GATT Annual Report entitled *International Trade, 1956,* or appropriate year. Some interesting research on world matrices of trade and service payments is being performed by the National Bureau of Economic Research under the direction of Herbert Woolley.

The case for discrimination using the trade matrix was developed by R. Frisch in "On the Need for Forecasting a Multilateral Balance of Payments," *AER,* September, 1947. It has been widely criticized. See especially Polak (*AER,* March, 1948); Meier (*AER,* September, 1948); Hinshaw (*RE & S,*

November, 1948); Hirschman (*AER*, December, 1948); Holzman (*AER*, December, 1949); Koo (*RE & S*, February, 1952).

A substantial number of books have appeared on the sterling area, among them especially P. W. Bell, *The Sterling Area in the Postwar World* (London: Oxford University Press, 1956); J. Polk, *Sterling* (New York: Harper & Bros., 1956); and A. C. L. Day, *The Future of Sterling* (London: Oxford, 1954).

The annual volumes on exchange restrictions published by the International Monetary Fund should be referred to for both description and analysis.

POINTS

A useful description, especially of West German experience, is set out in M. Trued and R. F. Mikesell, *Postwar Bilateral Payments Agreements* (Princeton: Princeton University Press, 1955). For a discussion of multiple exchange rates which anticipates some problems of later chapters, see E. R. Schlesinger, *Multiple Exchange Rates and Economic Development* (Princeton: Princeton University Press, 1952). H. Mendershausen, "Dollar Shortage and Oil Surplus," *Essays in International Finance* (Princeton: Princeton University Press, November, 1950), is one of the few items in the literature which deal with private compensation between companies, on the one hand, and countries, on the other.

A useful reference which sets out the case against discrimination in luxuries is W. Roepke, "Austerity—the International Crusade against Luxuries," *Commercial and Financial Chronicle*, August 5, 1948.

Chapter 16 | THE CASE FOR FREE MULTI- LATERAL TRADE

The record of interference with the operation of international trade, set out in the last four chapters, makes a strong prima-facie case against free multilateral trade. If free trade is desirable, how does it happen that countries are so ready to interfere to prevent its results? If countries universally impose tariffs, quotas, and exchange controls and discriminate in their use of these and in pricing, what is there affirmatively to be said in favor of free trade? We have saved the positive general argument for free trade until now, in order to make it in the full awareness that the theory is more honored in the breach than in the observance.

Merits of the Price System

The case for free trade rests on the efficiency, but not necessarily on the equity of the price system, free of government interference. It is asserted that if trade is left alone and the invisible hand can do its work, the economy will achieve an optimum of output. Resources will be allocated among various lines of activity, and goods will be allocated among consumers, so as to produce the greatest possible amount of satisfaction. This requires that the price system work to equate goods prices everywhere (abstracting from costs of transport), which will eliminate any further gain from trading; equate the price (or value) of goods to the marginal cost of goods to ensure optimum production; and provide that factors earn the same return in every industry, apart from differences in productive capacity, which will ensure the optimum allocation of resources. If social marginal value is everywhere equal to social marginal cost, society has reached an optimum of efficiency in the allocation of resources and the production and distribution of goods. This may not be the optimum welfare position, because of differences in the significance of income for different income recipients.

For the moment, however, we will limit ourselves to the discussion of efficiency rather than equity.

The case for free trade rests upon the belief that free trade will provide the nearest possible approach to the efficiency optimum. This case is a powerful one. It assumes, however, that there is no marked divergence between social value and social cost, such as might occur if private value and cost in the market diverged from social value and cost. This it may do, and for a number of reasons. Among such reasons are economies and diseconomies external to the firm; lack of competition among firms for any reason; lack of competition among factors; and failure of the private-enterprise system to maintain full employment. While we have discussed most of these at some stage during the past few chapters, which touched on external economies in the infant-industry argument for the tariff, on cartels, and on increasing employment by beggar-thy-neighbor tactics, it may be well to recapitulate, and to add a word particularly on rigidities among factors.

Demerits of the Price System

When external economies or diseconomies exist, social marginal value diverges from the private marginal value given by the market. The private value may overstate social value, as in the infant-industry case: a tariff on imports, or better a subsidy on domestic production, is needed to develop for producers the new cost conditions which enable them to reduce costs and price to the lower social marginal value. Internal economies of scale, which may persist due to lack of competition arising from ignorance or lack of access to complementary factors such as land or capital, similarly produce a divergence between social and private value and reduce economic efficiency below the optimum.

External diseconomies receive less attention. These may exist where depletion enables private value to be higher than social value. Private costs which fail to take account of depletion of natural resources or pollution of air or water understate social costs, and production is excessive. Here the remedy is to require replaceable resources to be replaced (in farming or lumber), or steps to eliminate pollution. Where the resources are irreplaceable, as in mining, there is much to be said for taxation—not on imports but on domestic production, where the country is on an import basis, or on exports if the country sells abroad. The heavy taxes on oil profits in countries like Venezuela and Iraq have as their justification the replacement of wasting natural resources by man-made capital assets to maintain the productivity of the economy. (Note that as land is depleted and capital built up, the transformation schedule must change and with it comparative advantage.)

Where competition is imperfect, the results achieved by free trade again fall short of the efficiency optimum. Monopoly unduly restricts production and raises the private above social value. Monopsony unduly restricts consumption and holds private below social value. In goods markets, these results flow from the existence of market power, along with the existence of overhead costs. They can also stem from ignorance, habit, and tradition. Consumers purchase in the expensive rather than in the cheaper market for any of these reasons or because they lack the capital to act in economical fashion. Producers may fail to foresee how permanent a shift in demand is against their product.

It is not only firms which have overhead costs and which act with imperfect foresight. The same is true of factors. Factors may be badly allocated, keeping private above social cost (or private value below social value) in some lines of production and below in others, through lack of awareness of opportunities, inability to forecast their duration, or costs of moving. Labor has difficulty in transferring between occupations, except insofar as the alternative employments exist side by side in the same locality. There are costs of changing jobs—of selling one house and buying another in a different locality or of merely moving and starting a new home. Labor is mobile over a generation; young people hesitate to enter a shrinking industry unless family and local traditions are very strong; and the overhead costs of moving for young people fresh from schools and colleges are low or nonexistent. But the fact of depressed areas of highly specialized resources—the coal and textile industries in Britain in the 1930's; the shoe and textile industries in New England in the 1950's—attest to the immobility of labor.

Real, as opposed to financial, capital, of course, is even more immobile, although less so than land. Capital is completely mobile only over the long run as it wears out in one location and is replaced in another through the investment of depreciation allowances. This takes time, which may run as long as twenty years. In the short run, an individual may be able to move his capital, if he can sell his textile mill in New Hampshire, let us say. But this is not mobility of economic capital, since the buyer puts in what the seller takes out. In economic terms, the equipment may have some mobility, if it can be transported or sold as secondhand machinery or as salvage or scrap steel.

The building, however, is unlikely to be movable, and the capital it represents can be shifted only in the long run.

If firms and factors are frequently unresponsive to price signals in the market, and so fail to bring about equality of social and private value, they sometimes actively produce divergence by responding excessively to price change. The cobweb theorem mentioned in Chapter 9 is illustrative of this phenomenon. A higher price for potatoes this year produces too many next year, which leads to a low price then and a shortage the year after. Each rise in price elicits too large an increase in output to bring about equilibrium; each decline too large a decrease.

The cobweb effect arises because the expectations of producers and consumers are linked with one another rather than independent. If all producers are persuaded that a price rise means an upward shift in demand—as they may be if they read the same forecasts, meet in the same trade association, listen to the same commentators—they will tend to react in the same way. Consumers will equally tend to act together. The response of producers and consumers to price changes will then be destabilizing, like destabilizing speculation, which occurs when speculators' views are identical with those of the general public. The price system operates more effectively, as does speculation, when responses to price changes are independently made on the basis of separate, rather than mutually contagious, expectations.

Finally, there is the unusual case when the short-run response is too slight and the long-run too great. Perhaps the most dramatic illustration of this is found in such a crop as coffee, where it takes four years to get new plants to produce at all, and seven years before they reach full-scale output. An increase in demand will raise prices. This will ration existing output, but it can have no effect in increasing output beyond inducing producers to plant new bushes. The results of this planting, however, will not be felt for five to seven years, when the condition which gave rise to the increased price may long have vanished. They will, moreover, be sustained for forty years, the average life of a coffee bush. The high prices in coffee of the 1920's led to the overproduction of the 1930's. This lowered prices and discouraged planting, so that output declined during the 1950's, when demand increased. The high prices of 1949 to 1954 in turn produced new plantings which are just beginning to give rise to trouble, and Brazilian governmental intervention in the coffee market, as this is written.

How far the price system can serve as a guide to investment in new capacity remains a debated point. There are economists who attach great significance to the time lag which supervenes between the recognition of the need for new capacity—during which the supply of consumers' goods is inelastic with response to price increases—and the time when the new capacity is completed and goes into production. If this period is long, as it will be in capital-intensive processes, there is danger that the persistence of scarcity and high prices during the period of capital formation will lead to the establishment of what ultimately proves to be excess capacity. The inability of the price system adequately to guide investment decisions in this regard is charged with much of the responsibility for the business cycle.

Alternatives to the Price System

This book is concerned with international trade and not with comparative economic systems. It may nonetheless be worth mentioning that the possible weaknesses of the price system to which reference has been made do not imply that any alternative system—whether cartel or government planning or state ownership—is superior or, for that matter, worse. What appears to be important is the size of the decision-making unit and the scale on which decisions are taken. Monopoly industry, governmental planning, and competitive industry, in which all entrepreneurs are culturally identical and respond in the same way to the same stimuli, are likely to react in the same direction to a change in demand or supply. There may be differences in the speed with which they recognize errors of judgment—this is an advantage claimed for private enterprise. But both will differ from a situation in which tradition decrees what is produced and how, or in which production is carried on by a number of small firms whose views are arrived at independently.

It is probable that the price system works with more effective response, with less chance of excessive or erroneous response, when the economic society is composed of many firms, each actively trying to maximize its income but each with independent views on the course of events. The exact form of the alternative does not make much difference if it means either that the society ceases trying to maximize or that an industry responds as a unit.

This situation leads to the conclusion that the price system works with greater efficiency as one approaches the classical assumptions of perfect competition and constant costs, i.e., infinitely elastic demand and supply curves, with less efficiency as one departs from them. Viewed in this light, the change in the theory of international trade since its classical development has been a change in analysis only in limited degree. For the most part it has consisted in a revision of the underlying assumptions.

Efficiency and Welfare

The optimum in terms of efficiency would also be the optimum welfare position under either of two circumstances: first, that it made no difference what the distribution of income was, because a dollar of income produced the same amount of welfare no matter who received it; or, second, that the distribution of welfare did not change as one moved toward the efficiency optimum. Unfortunately neither of these assumptions is tenable. Accordingly, even if the price system worked well enough to produce an efficiency optimum, it is by no means certain that this would maximize world welfare.

The classical economists of course recognized that the marginal utility of income was different for rich and poor, so that it was inappropriate to assume that a dollar of income was a dollar of welfare for every income recipient; they also understood that a change toward freer trade redistributed income so that one cannot claim that free trade produces more welfare than protection even if free trade produces more goods at less cost than protection. They nonetheless held that free trade, like honesty, was the best policy.

Modern welfare economists have two hypotheses by which they attempt to say something about free trade and welfare. One device is to assign weights. If country A's income is worth one for every $1.00 of income, and country B's, one half, then it would be possible to calculate whether free trade produced more welfare than a given position of protection by deriving a weighted result. If free trade turned the terms of trade in B's favor, and lost A ten but gained eighteen for B, this would reduce welfare on the weights indicated: A's weighted loss of ten is greater than B's weighted gain of nine. But, on the basis of equal weights, free trade would produce gain for the world of A and B. If equal weights are assigned to income recipients in all countries, free trade produces an optimum of welfare. If A's weight is one and B's zero, on the other hand (a highly nationalist point of view), the welfare optimum is the optimum tariff which will improve A's terms of trade to the maximum possible without a counter balancing decrease in quantity.

The system of weights, which is one form of international social welfare function, should be extended to income recipients within each country. Free trade will distribute income in A against the scarce factor and in favor of the abundant one. If the abundant factor is rich, and the scarce poor, free trade may be a worse position in terms of welfare than the protected position. But of course it would be possible to adopt free trade and redistribute income through fiscal policy.

The other hypothesis is the so-called "compensation principle." Situation one is better in terms of welfare than situation two if the gainers in welfare in moving from two to one gain enough to be in position to compensate the losers, and still have something over. This reduces welfare comparisons to those in efficiency: any time there is an increase in the value of total output, it follows that the gross gainers would be in position to compensate the gross losers. But of course such compensation rarely occurs. The progressive income tax, and transfer payments to the needy who may become unemployed, go a short part of the way to provide compensation. But for the rest, the compensation principle remains a pure hypothesis.

Provided that the price system works efficiently to produce a material optimum, there is no doubt that free trade produces a welfare optimum, either with equal weights for countries and income recipients within countries or with the compensation principle, also between and within countries. This is like saying: "If we had some ham, we could have ham and eggs, if we had the eggs." Every country has rich and poor, and some countries are richer than others. From the free-trade position, then, it would be possible to impose tariff barriers and other interferences with trade which would improve welfare within and between countries. But this is far different from saying that any interference with free trade improves welfare. Some trade barriers transfer income from the poor in the protecting countries to the rich within their borders, and internationally from impoverished countries to wealthy. Unless one knows the distribution of income, there is just as much reason to believe that a movement away from free trade will worsen the welfare position as that it will improve it. Nay, there is more; and for two reasons.

First, the free-trade position tends to produce over-all more income. For any given distribution, more is better than less; for any random distribution, moreover, more is better than less. Since there is no presumption that free trade worsens the distribution, there is a presumption that the total welfare position is superior when efficiency is higher than when it is lower. Second, the rich are more likely to have political power and to exercise it than the poor. In consequence, tariffs are likely to favor the rich, and the removal of tariffs, the poor. If the internal welfare function calls for shifts of income from rich to poor, there is a second presumption in favor of freeing trade. The sum total of these two presumptions, however, is not sufficiently high to make an overwhelming case.

Part of the difficulty is that the price system both allocates resources and distributes income. It used to be thought that within an economy the price system and the tax system specialized and divided functions: the price system was used to create an efficiency optimum; the tax system to redistribute income and welfare. This is no longer true even within a closed economy; the existence of cartels, monopolies, price-parity formulas, cost-of-living clauses in wage contracts, etc., demonstrates the extent to which the price system has been used to affect the distribution of welfare. Perhaps the division of function never really existed except in the minds of economists. Internationally, however, no such division of function was possible, because the countries of the world were not bound together in a common budget and so were not linked through taxes. The price system is responsible both for efficiency in the allocation of resources and for the distribution of income and welfare internationally. The price system then tends to produce a maximum of efficiency, to the extent that it operates effectively, and achieves a distribution of income and welfare between countries. This welfare distribution is not necessarily the optimum. For the same distribution of welfare, however, free multilateral trade produces more welfare all round than autarchy.

One important feature of the price system when it operated with a considerable degree of competition was that its decisions were accepted as the impersonal judgments of a sort of fate. The market in a competitive society represents a collective judgment, different from the arbitrary or quixotic decisions of government, monopoly, or a foreign country. An adverse decision administered by the market gives less ground for retaliation through market forces or through extramarket action. Adam Smith regarded the market's actions as those of an "invisible hand." One of the strongest arguments for free multilateral trade with any considerable degree of competition is that it gives an objective basis for the allocation of resources and the distribution of income both nationally and internationally.

One possible qualification must be admitted. Free trade is both the optimum material position for all countries for a given distribution of welfare and the possible optimum for the abundant factor in the economically more advanced country. If all countries are of equal size and power, and income is distributed relatively evenly among them, the first consideration is relevant. If one country is more advanced technologically than the others and of greater economic (and political) power, then free trade may represent an optimum position for the existing distribution of income, but welfare may be capable of increase through a redistribution of income brought about by trade barriers.

The German School has consistently regarded free trade as the ideological weapon of the dominant country. A number of economists have considered the attempts of the United States to achieve a multilateral convertible world of lower tariffs in the same category. There can be no doubt that the distribution of income internationally will be different with trade barriers than with free trade, and the total material level lower. If the social welfare function or set of value judgments called for a shift of income from export interests to import-competing industry in the United States or if the terms of trade could be turned against the United States by tariffs abroad and the international social welfare function required a shift of income from the United States to other countries, the free-trade optimum position in material terms would not represent the desirable position in terms of welfare.

Theory of Retaliation

We have seen in Chapter 12 that a country can improve its terms of trade with a tariff but that this requires the other country to forbear from retaliation, despite the fact that it will gain a short-run advantage by imposing a tariff itself. The case is one which magnificently illustrates the fallacy of composition, which applies when the whole is not equal to the sum of its parts: each can gain at the expense of the other, but both lose.

To the extent that the international social welfare function calls for more rather than less equality of income between countries, other things equal, we may get a clue as to the proper view towards retaliation. If a rich country attempts to improve its terms of trade at the expense of a poor country, retaliation would seem to be well justified. The shift of the gains from trade in favor of the rich country and against the poor presumptively results in a decline in welfare, and the poor country can increase total welfare by gaining at the expense of the rich one. If, on the other hand, the poor country imposes a tariff or quantitative import restrictions or multiple exchange rates which enable it to gain at the expense of the rich country, world welfare may be said to be improved, other things being equal, and the rich country should not retaliate.

This is by no means an invitation for the rest of the world to impose trade controls against the United States. Other things are not always equal. Some export taxes or export restrictions or other interferences in trade are so flagrantly subversive of material efficiency that the shift in income implied by them is swamped. In these cases, the threat of retaliation, which means retaliation if necessary, should be used to stop them.

It may be maintained that international welfare comparisons are impossible and that one should favor free trade as the result of an objective distribution of welfare. This would be true if at least the major classical assumptions were fulfilled. More than this the economist perhaps has no business to recommend. But it may be important to say to students that if any interference in the free-trade position is allowed, that which redistributes income from the rich to the poor, à la Robin Hood, while not necessarily justified, is more likely to be justified than one which operates in the opposite direction.

But in these complex matters involving retaliation, it is important to say that economists have not reached final conclusions and probably, in the nature of the problem, never can.

The Case for Multilateral Trade

In a world of more than two countries the case for free trade becomes a case for multilateral trade and convertible currencies. If free trade takes place only between pairs of countries and, because of inconvertibility, each segment of paired trade must be in balance, the over-all criterion for a free-trade maximum of efficiency is breached. Goods will be bought in markets other than the cheapest and will be sold for less than the dearest price. This follows because of the necessity to balance. If a single pair of countries shows an export surplus for A and an import surplus for B, with all buyers and sellers maximizing their gain, balance will require the redirection of A purchases from a cheaper source to B, or a shift of A sales to a less profitable market than B.

Multilateralism requires convertibility. The export surplus earned by A in B's currency must be convertible into C's exchange to requite the gross deficit incurred by A in trade with C. The difficulty in a world of interconnected trade balances is that the maintenance of convertibility of a country's currency is not solely within its capacity. The currency of the countries with which it has export surpluses must be convertible if it is going to meet its gross deficits. In a system of interlocked export and import gross balances, convertibility requires that each country maintain over-all balance simultaneously or that any country with a net deficit have reserves which it is prepared to spend, in a medium of exchange acceptable to the country or countries with which it has gross deficits.

The International Trade Organization and GATT

The United States has taken the leadership during and after World War II in trying to achieve a nearer approximation of a convertible multilateral world. One approach to convertibility lay through the Bretton Woods institutions, the International Bank for Reconstruction and Development, and the International Monetary Fund. We shall recur to these in Part VI. The other lay in the construction of an International Trade Organization designed to eliminate quantitative restrictions, to reduce tariff barriers, and to establish the principle of nondiscrimination. The basis of the United States appeal for adherence to these rules lay in the paradox that while any one country might gain from trade restrictions, all gained from their elimination.

We cannot here examine the provisions of the draft charter of the International Trade Organization, as it evolved through successive stages of drafting at London, Geneva, and Havana. This has been well done by others. We should note, however, that the charter was not adopted by the United States or, in consequence, by any other powers. Other countries originally had misgivings that they were being required, through the forceful persuasion of the United States, to give up trade controls which were necessary to defend their balances of payments and standards of living. The United States Congress, on the other hand, took the view, through the persuasion of business groups, that other countries did not guarantee adherence to the rules with sufficient certainty to make it worthwhile for this country to commit itself. Both groups—the United States with its balance-of-payments surplus and other countries with their deficits—had avenues of retreat. The United States insisted on the escape clause by means of which it could cancel a tariff concession which caused or threatened serious injury to a national industry. Other countries, on the other hand, were permitted to relax the proscription of quantitative restrictions and discrimination if their balances of payments were seriously adverse, and under certain other circumstances. Both parties would have been willing to enact the charter if it had meant that the other countries would abide by the rules, while they were permitted to make use of the exceptions which favored their position. Neither, however, was ultimately disposed to take the chance that it would adhere to the rules while the other countries took advantage of the exceptions.

Much the same set of rules and a basis for reciprocal multilateral reductions of tariff barriers were obtained in the General Agreement on Tariffs and Trade (GATT), which was concluded among twenty-three nations in Geneva in 1947 as a parallel measure. While an executive agreement between governments has less force in international law than a charter ratified by legislatures and while the draft charter of the ITO created an organization to police its provisions with more powers than those of the small staff administering GATT, something of the principles of the charter were saved. An attempt has been made to regularize the position by drawing up the charter of a permanent agency, the Organization for Trade Cooperation, to administer the General Agreement on Tariffs and Trade, but the Congress of the United States has failed in two sessions to ratify the agreement. GATT has survived through the goodwill of the various signatory members, and despite a number of crises such as the admission of Japan, which would grant her access to further markets from which her textiles had been discriminatorily excluded; and the European Coal and Steel Community and the proposed Common Market, which called for organized discrimination against outside countries. A series of mutual tariff reductions has taken place regularly in 1947, 1949, 1951, and 1956, although balance-of-payments difficulties have made it impossible for a number of countries to put their concessions into effect. A small and capable staff has prepared annual analyses of world trade. The approach to the gradual elimination of trade discrimination has been unspectacular, free of dogma, empirical, persistent. But free trade and convertibility have not been legislated into existence.

The Regional Approach

If it is impossible to put Humpty-Dumpty together again all at once into a single free multilateral trade world, what about approaching it in stages through regional free trade or freer trade? In particular, what about customs union, partial or complete?

The ITO draft charter made a distinction between partial and complete discrimination. This was in line with the historical view of the most-favored-nation clause. Complete customs union is allowed between contiguous countries or countries in the same economic region as an exception to the most-favored-nation rule; a 99 per cent mutual reduction of tariffs between two countries is not. This rule has been attacked as illogical. But there are some concepts which are divisible and some which are not. The renunciation of use of all tariffs in the trade between two countries differs in kind from the reduction of tariffs to virtually nothing but their retention in principle.

The ITO draft charter also permitted a partial customs union in a particular commodity by countries embarked on programs of economic development. The two or more nations concerned could apply a common tariff in a commodity to the outside world, and none among themselves. Here again 100 per cent reduction was allowed, but not 99. Underdeveloped countries, led by the Arab League, fought for this concession in order to be able to start new industrial undertakings on a sufficiently large scale to achieve economical operation. In point of fact, however, only a Central American group has made much headway with this sort of functional customs union. The Arab League has recurred to the subject in time of political crisis. During the rest of the time, each country seems to be willing to accept the right to build a plant for the Arab League as a whole, but none is willing to give up such rights to other countries.

Customs unions do not necessarily mean an approach to freer trade. Paradoxically, they may mean a less economical use of resources. Much depends on the height of the tariff involved, and the nature of the economic relationship among the constituent parts. But first it may be well to discuss more generally the so-called "second-best argument" for tariff reduction.

The Second-Best Argument

If it be granted that complete free trade will result in an optimum position in which social (and private) marginal value equals social (and private) cost, it does not follow that any movement toward free trade improves an existing protected situation. If social value diverges from social cost throughout an economy, any tariff removal will improve the position if it, on balance, reduces the total divergence. This it may do. But it may not. The reduction of the tariff in one commodity may narrow the divergence in this commodity but give rise to an increase in trade in another commodity in which the divergence was larger. To determine whether a partial freeing of tariffs is good or bad, Professor Meade has devised a theoretical system of adding, algebraically, the weighted divergences of social marginal value from social marginal cost. A net reduction in divergences is an improvement; an increase is a setback.

Suppose Britain reduces the tariff on wine from France. This narrows the divergence between the social marginal value of wine and the social cost in Britain and increases its consumption. But many additional effects may occur. The increase in wine consumption in Britain may lead to increased consumption of a complementary product with a large divergence, or decreased production of a competitive product with a small or no divergence. Similar distortion may take place in the country expanding exports. If the tariff reduction is discriminatory, it is necessary to take into account the effect on, say Germany, which may or may not be able to sell its wine elsewhere, or to cease its production. Until one has a view of the total effects on consumption and production in all the affected countries, weighted in each case by the divergence between social value and social cost, one cannot really judge whether a given tariff reduction improves or worsens the welfare position. In some cases where free trade as a best solution is impossible, a second-best measure may be to impose a tariff on a single commodity. And, similarly, a partial step toward tariff reduction may not be a second-best solution.

This sounds somewhat overintellectualized, but it is easy to provide a simple demonstration. Suppose a country had a tariff of 10 per cent on all imports. To lower the tariff on raw materials without changing it on finished goods results in an increase in protection; not in an approach to freer trade. The reduction in the divergence between social marginal value and social cost in raw materials is more than offset by the increase in output of the protected manufactures where a large divergence exists.

Measuring the Height of a Tariff

The draft charter of the ITO required that a customs union adopt a tariff no higher than the average of those previously existing. This raises a difficult problem of measuring the height of a tariff. It is evidently a mistake to compare customs revenues with total imports, as is frequently done, because prohibitive tariffs eliminate all imports in given categories, and produce no revenue. One should compare the ad valorem rates of duty at two different points of time weighted by the trade of the lower tariff position, preferably by trade without any tariff at all. For comparison of the tariffs of two countries, one can either weight by free-trade values, which must be hypothetical since there is no free trade, or average ad valorem rates of tariff on an unweighted basis, which means assigning equal weights to each tariff category.

Trade Diversion through Customs Union

Putting aside the question of the height of the tariff, the question of whether a customs union increases or reduces efficiency can be approached on a number of levels. The first of these is concerned with a single commodity and raises the question whether the customs union creates or diverts trade. Trade creation through customs union, it is claimed, is indicative of increased efficiency; trade diversion of reduced.

For the student who thrives on abstract examples, assume that A and B form a customs union. Before union, A used to import its food from C which was a more efficient producer (i.e., enjoyed lower social marginal cost) than B. After union, A has a tariff on food and shifts its source of supply to B. Trade is diverted in the commodity food. The total efficiency of the world is reduced, and possibly its welfare.

This example is by no means a purely hypothetical one. In United States history the foremost example is the customs union between the plantation agriculture of the South and the nascent manufacturing of the North. These were not separate countries, but they were different regions in terms of factor proportions, factor prices, and comparative advantage. Before World War I, in fact, trade between the North and the South was conducted much like international trade and unlike internal trade. Little capital moved south or labor north. With factor immobility, factor prices failed to equalize, and it paid to employ different factor proportions. The South had a labor- and land-intensive agriculture; the North a capital-intensive manufacturing industry.

The inclusion of the agricultural South in the customs area of the North, which is what a common customs meant, required the South to buy in a protected market while it was selling in a free market. The price of its imports increased, and its terms of trade were reduced. It achieved less than an optimum of income or welfare because it had to buy in the dearer rather than in the cheaper market. This economic exploitation of the South by the North is generally regarded as a factor contributing to the War between the States.

A further example can be given from the history of Germany, in which Zollverein, or customs union, actually preceded political union by many years. The Zollverein was formed in 1834; Bismarck united Germany under the leadership of Prussia in 1870. In 1879 the first of the increases took place in the tariff on grain. This was combined with a tariff on steel; but Germany was in the business of exporting steel, so that the tariff was useful only in widening its scope for dumping. The tariff on rye, on the other hand, raised the cost of living of the worker in western Germany well above what it would have been, had Germany bought its grain on the world market. Customs union thus involved the exploitation of the working classes by the Prussian Junkers, who were both soldiers and managers of estates which grew rye.

Trade creation takes place when country A gives up production of some item which it then imports from B, and expands production in other lines, which it ships to B. In these single cases, trade is created.

Based on the analysis of single commodities, economists have concluded that customs unions which divert trade and are bad, are those between complementary economies, and while those which create trade and are good are those between competitive economies. This is a partial view, however, and one limited to a single commodity at a time.

If one attempts a general approach to customs union, it is clear that one has to see what happens to total trade, and to the total weighted divergence between social marginal value and social marginal cost. From this point of view, and using a number of countries, it is by no means clear that customs unions between competitive countries are good; those between complementary countries bad. If the competitive countries stop trading with outsiders in order to trade more with each other, this may reduce total world welfare; or if the complementary countries were already trading with each other, some increase in this trade is not highly diversionary. But it is necessary to examine the individual cases.

As a parenthesis, and apart from the main theme of this chapter, many economists stress the importance of customs union in breaking up local monopoly, operating with tariff, or better, quota protection. The primary benefits of the European Coal and Steel Community and of the proposed European Common Market have been realized and are being sought, respectively, less in the realization of economies of scale through wider markets than in the destruction of local monopoly.

Better than customs union is the approach to free trade on a wider basis. Most steps to remove or lower tariffs, to remove or reduce quotas, to separate trade from exchange or other restrictions, are worthwhile. These steps are particularly desirable if they are taken to eliminate discrimination between countries or to reduce barriers to trade in a nondiscriminatory fashion. Regional or discriminatory reductions are desirable, as a lesser evil to more restrictions. The economist is prepared to recognize the force of various objections on various levels, but he still concludes that the over-all efficiency, and probably the welfare, of the world are increased by a reduction in barriers to trade.

The difficulties faced by the real world in approaching, much less achieving, multilateral free trade do not constitute an argument against it as an ideal. The inability of countries with balance-of-payments difficulties to relax quotas and discriminatory exchange restrictions may be likened to the position of many consumers who are too poor (or regard themselves so) to act in economical fashion. It is, for example, an economy to buy good cloth in preference to sleazy, or well-made furniture rather than jerry-built. The man without resources, however, has little chance to take advantage of the long-run economies inherent in making a large short-run outlay. In the same fashion it may be good policy in the long run for all countries to forego maximizing their short-run return, in order to achieve a higher income over the long period. At the same time, it may be regarded as impossible for a country to afford to contribute to the achievement of the long-run optimum of itself and all other countries.

Summary

The case for free multilateral trade rests, at bottom, on the efficiency of the price system. The price system is not perfect: on occasion, demand or supply fails to respond to price changes because of rigidities. At other times a response will be excessive. The price system, too, may fail to discount the effects of dynamic changes. But the price system appears to be more efficient than any other system. Its efficiency would be improved if we could make business more competitive, factors more mobile, and eliminate or moderate the business cycle.

The efficiency optimum toward which the price system tends is not necessarily a welfare maximum. This is true only for a given distribution of income. A change in trade, however, involves a redistribution of income both within and between countries. This limits what we can say positively about trade and welfare.

From the case for freer trade, based on more efficiency, it follows that multilateral trade with wider markets is better than bilateral trade with narrower. The general rule for a maximum is the rule of non-discrimination, that consumers buy in the cheapest market and producers sell in the dearest.

The task of converting bilateral into multilateral trade has been attempted by the draft charter of the ITO (unsuccessfully) and, in a more limited way, through GATT. The regional approach through customs and economic unions runs the risk of being more disruptive of the world trading market than a world-wide approach.

SUGGESTED READINGS

TEXTS

The case for free trade and the ITO, GATT, and ITC are discussed in Towle, chap. xxxii; Behrman and Schmidt, chaps. iii, xxiii; L. Tarshis, *Introduction to International Trade and Finance* (New York: John Wiley & Sons, Inc., 1955), chaps. xi, xii, xxxviii, xxxix.

TREATISES, ETC.

The present version of this chapter is based to a large degree on the impressive work of Professor Meade, *Trade and Welfare*. Significant articles are those by Scitovsky, American Economic Association, *Readings,* chap. xvi; and M. Fleming, "On Making the Best of Balance of Payments Restrictions, *EJ,* March, 1951. See also P. A. Samuelson, "Welfare Economics and International Trade," *AER,* June, 1938; R. E. Baldwin, "The New Welfare Economics and Gains in International Trade," *QJE,* February, 1952. See also D. H. Robertson's essay, American Economic Association, *Readings,* chap. xxi; Haberler, chap. xiv.

On the draft ITO, see C. Wilcox, *A Charter for World Trade* (New York: Macmillan Co., 1949); W. A. Brown, Jr., *The United States and the Restoration of World Trade* (Washington, D.C.: Brookings Institution, 1950).

On customs unions, see Meade, above, and his several studies, *Problems of Economic Union* (Chicago: University of Chicago Press, 1953); *Negotiations for Benelux: An Annotated Chronicle, 1943–46,* Princeton Studies in International Finance (Princeton, 1957), etc. The classical treatment of trade diversion and trade creation is that of J. Viner, *The Customs Union Issue* (New York: Carnegie Endowment for International Peace, 1950), which contains an exhaustive bibliography of the early literature. It has been criticized in S. Ozga, "An Essay in the Theory of Tariffs," *JPE,* December, 1955; H. Makower and G. Morton, "A Contribution Towards a Theory of the Custom Union," *EJ,* March, 1953; and in a thesis at M.I.T. by G. A. Hay.

The flood of literature on the Schuman plan and the Common Market is impossible to summarize. See, however, William Diebold, *Trade and Payments in Western Europe* (New York: Harper & Bros., 1952), and the same author's forthcoming study on the Schuman plan. A strong regional emphasis is given to international economic policy in William Y. Elliott (ed.), *A Foreign Economic Policy for the United States* (New York: Henry Holt & Co., Inc., 1955).

POINTS

On the cost to western Germany of economic union with the east, see A. Gerschenkron, *Bread and Democracy in Germany* (Berkeley: University of California Press, 1943); and T. W. Schultz, "Effects of Trade and Industrial Output of Western Germany upon Agriculture," *AER,* May, 1950.

On measuring the height of a tariff, see Haberler, chap. xix, sec. 8. H. Liepmann, *Tariff Levels and the Economic Unity of Europe* (London: Allen & Unwin, 1938), makes a case for unweighted averages.

PART IV

The Capital Account in the Balance

of Payments

Chapter 17   SHORT-TERM CAPITAL MOVEMENTS

Types of Capital Movements

A number of attempts have been made to categorize capital movements. They have been divided into "induced and autonomous," "stabilizing and destabilizing," "real and equalizing," "abnormal and normal," "equilibrating, speculative, income and autonomous." The most usual division, however, is into short-term and long-term. Here there is an objective criterion on which to base the classification. A capital movement is short-term if it is embodied in a credit instrument of less than a year's maturity. If the instrument has a duration of more than a year or consists of a title to ownership, such as a share of stock or a deed to property, the capital movement is long-term.

While the distinction between short- and long-term capital movements is clear cut, it does not necessarily reveal what brought the movement about, what its effects in the balance of payments are likely to be, and whether it conforms to a desirable pattern. For these purposes we need to divide capital movements by motivation, by role in the balance of payments, or on the basis of normality. In terms of motivation, we will want to know whether a capital movement is equilibrating, speculative, undertaken in search of income, or autonomous. In the balance of payments, it may be induced or autonomous, stabilizing or destabilizing. And in pattern, it may be normal or abnormal. Since the causes and effects of short- and long-term capital movements differ, however, we must uncover these aspects of the subject as we go along.

Classification according to instrument, moreover, does not really indicate whether a capital movement is temporary or quasi-permanent. Many changes in foreign deposits take place slowly over long periods of time: an Argentine capitalist with deposits hidden away in Zurich is holding instruments payable on demand; in a more fundamental sense he has made a long-term capital movement from the standpoint of his country and of Switzerland. European speculation in the New York stock market in the 1920's and 1930's used the instruments of long-term investment—equity shares in companies—but demonstrated a high rate of turnover and only a brief loss of liquidity.

Since no ultimate basis of classification is good for all purposes, the short-term and long-term division, based on instrument, is taken as a point of departure.

Short-Term Credit Instruments

Iversen, a Danish economist, has described the possible kinds of short-term capital inflow classified by instrument. Converted to a United States setting, the list is as follows:

Inflow of capital through short-term loans and investments
  A. Transactions increasing United States foreign debt
    1. Increase in foreign deposits in United States banks
    2. Increase in overdrafts allowed United States banks by foreign correspondents
    3. Increase in foreign holdings of United States bills and acceptances
    4. Increase in foreign commercial debts of United States firms
    5. Increase in foreign holdings of United States "floating" (international) securities
    6. Increase in foreign holdings of United States bank notes and subsidiary coinage

  B. Transactions decreasing United States foreign assets
    1. Decrease of United States deposits in foreign banks
    2. Decrease in overdrafts allowed foreign banks by United States correspondents
    3. Decrease in United States holdings of foreign bills and acceptances
    4. Decrease in United States commercial debts of foreign firms
    5. Decrease in United States holdings of foreign "floating" (international) securities
    6. Decrease in United States holdings of foreign bank notes and subsidiary coinage

The list can be inverted to furnish a list of forms of short-term outflow.

Today the most important of these instruments is the bank deposit; in the nineteenth century it was the sterling bill. Our discussion will be limited primarily to these.

Short-Term Movements and Gold

On the gold standard, short-term capital movements, like gold, had two functions, one in the balance of payments and the other in the banking system.

In the balance of payments, short-term capital movements occasionally gave rise to movements of gold, but generally substituted for them. The short-term movement giving rise to a gold movement may occur, for example, when the current account is balanced. Exports of goods and services equal imports of goods and services, and there is no need for international payments on that score. In these circumstances, however, an outward short-term capital movement takes place: it may be an autonomous movement of capital in fear of taxation; a speculative movement which foresees an appreciation of a foreign currency; an income movement responding to an increase in the discount rate abroad or a reduction in the rate at home. If the current account is sluggish in reacting to the capital outflow, a gold outflow will occur. The short-term capital movement gives rise to a movement of gold.

In the more normal relationship, however, the short-term capital movement substitutes for gold in the balance of payments. A country has an export surplus. Instead of acquiring gold abroad, it adds to its foreign-exchange reserves. Thus the gold-exchange standard discussed in Chapter 4 grew out of the gold standard; the members of the sterling bloc use sterling rather than gold or dollars as their primary international reserves; and national monetary authorities outside of the United States and the Soviet Union have increased their holdings of gold from $11.4 billion in 1938 to $14.8 billion by the end of 1956, but their holdings of short-term dollar assets in the same years went from $474 million to $8,032 million.

When a short-term capital movement gives rise to a gold flow, the two items have opposite roles in the balance of payments. A capital outflow which produces a gold outflow is a balance-of-payments debit; the gold movement itself is a balance-of-payments credit.

When the short-term capital movement substitutes for a gold movement, however, they of course have the same sign. A capital outflow (debit) substitutes for a gold inflow (debit).

Gold and the Money Supply

Before setting out the impact of short-term capital movements on the money supply, it may be helpful briefly to review how gold movements produce monetary changes. Much depends upon the nature of the banking system and its ratios of central-bank reserves to central-bank liabilities, and member-bank reserves (deposit liabilities of the central bank) to member-bank deposits. Under the gold standard, an outflow of gold typically leads to a multiple contraction of money. The credit base is reduced, and member banks, because of traditional or legal requirements to maintain certain reserve ratios, are obliged to call loans and sell investments. If the central bank also operates on a reserve basis which is effective, there may be considerable leverage. The credit pyramid in the United States, operating at its maximum and neglecting any effect on note liabilities of the Federal Reserve Banks, would call for a contraction of $2.50 in Federal Reserve credit for every $1.00 loss in gold. This total shrinkage of $3.50 in member-bank reserves would produce, in turn, a decrease of $17.50 in member-bank deposits or money, assuming an over-all reserve ratio of 20 per cent. With a large margin of excess gold coverage of Federal Reserve liabilities, however, these ratios have no practical significance.

The British system, prior to the suspension of gold in 1931, operated somewhat differently. Here the liabilities of the central bank were not geared to gold in a simple multiple ratio, but above a certain minimum, called the "fiduciary issue," all liabilities of the Bank of England were matched one for one by gold. Incrementally, a change in gold holdings by the Bank of England produced a change of only the same amount in central-bank liabilities. Since the joint-stock banks maintained lower reserves with the Bank of England, however, at about 11 per cent, an outflow of a pound sterling in gold would lead to a shrinkage in the money in circulation of roughly £9.

On this showing, an outflow of gold under the gold standard leads to a multiple contraction of money in use. Conversely, an inflow of gold may result in multiple expansion.

Short-Term Movements and Money

An outflow of short-term capital may operate like an inflow of gold, by leading to multiple expansion in the money supply. Conversely, an inflow of capital may lead to multiple contraction.

These relationships are most readily demonstrated by reference to the gold-exchange standard, starting with an initial export surplus to be financed. Under the gold-exchange standard, an outflow of capital to offset the export surplus typically took the form of an increase in the foreign-exchange holdings of the central bank on a gold-standard country. This exchange, taken to be as good as gold, forms the basis for a possible expansion in central-bank credit. Even without this expansion, however, it provides the basis for an increase in member-bank reserves of the same amount, and hence for a multiple expansion in money. In response to a gain of 100 local-currency units' worth of foreign exchange, the balance sheet of the central bank would show the following changes:

CENTRAL BANK

Assets	Liabilities
Foreign exchange............+100	Member-bank reserves........+100

The balance sheets of member banks, in turn, would be changed as follows:

ALL MEMBER BANKS

Assets	Liabilities
Reserves with central bank.....+100	Exporters' deposits...........+100

The exporter who acquired the exchange which is sold to the central bank might just as well have acquired gold. The short-term capital outflow substitutes for a gold inflow, not only in the balance of payments but also in providing the basis for an expansion in the money supply.

Another form which the capital outflow may take is a reduction in liabilities to foreign banks. Suppose the export surplus which gives rise to the capital outflow is paid for through a reduction in foreign central-bank deposits with the central bank of the reporting country. The balance sheets will then read as follows:

CENTRAL BANK

Assets	Liabilities
No change	Member-bank deposits........+100
	Foreign central-bank deposits..−100

ALL MEMBER BANKS

Assets	Liabilities
Reserves with central bank.....+100	Exporters' deposits...........+100

The short-term outflow in this form has the same effect on the level of member-bank reserves as a gold inflow or an increase in central-bank reserves of foreign exchange. The effect at the central bank may be different, however. If the central bank regards its liabilities as all of equal importance insofar as they require it to maintain liquid assets, there is no effect on the credit policy of the central bank. If, however, the central bank typically worries about accumulations of liabilities to foreigners, because it regards them as subject to sudden withdrawal, but is not similarly concerned about liabilities to member banks, even this change on the asset side may produce a relaxation of credit policy. The reduction in quick liabilities to foreigners may induce the central bank to expand the credit base, just as an increase in foreign assets, whether gold or foreign exchange, would have done under our earlier examples. This form of short-term capital outflow may thus substitute fully for gold inflow. But this effect on the central bank is less certain than the effect in increasing member-bank reserve balances and leading thereby to multiple expansion.

It is this asymmetry between the expansionary effect of an increase in foreign-exchange assets and the contractive effect of an increase in liabilities to foreigners, which led the experts to conclude that the gold-exchange standard was on balance inflationary, as we mentioned in Chapter 4 (p. 70). Gold is money. Short-term capital is money when it represents an asset of a central bank, but not necessarily a subtraction from the money supply when it stands for a liability of a central bank. And as we shall see, some short-term capital movements brought about changes in near-money rather than in money, and some are not even close.

Here is an important reason for making a distinction between short-term and long-term movements of capital. The former may have a monetary function; the latter do not. In fact when we think of short-term capital we tend to think of capital in its financial manifestation: of credit, banks, deposits, and the like. When the question concerns long-term capital, it is frequently desirable to think of capital as physical assets rather than in financial terms. We must occasionally contemplate the physical aspects of short-term capital movements, to be sure, or the financial character of long. The bright economist is the one who knows when the general rule does not apply. For the most part short-term capital approaches money; long-term capital does not.

The accumulation of foreign dollar claims on New York, which *in toto* have risen from $4.8 billion at the end of 1947 to $13.4 billion at the end of 1956, has worried some observers. These writers note that foreign claims amount to more than half of the $22 billion of gold held by the United States, and if deducted from this amount, would leave less than the legal gold cover requirements of $12 billion. Other writers, however, insist that there is no need to deduct foreign claims from the gold reserves, since foreigners are most unlikely to withdraw the whole amount in gold. No bank is sufficiently liquid to meet all its deposits if they are suddenly and simultaneously withdrawn. Short-term capital assets can substitute for gold in the money supply of some countries without the necessity for subtracting an equal amount in the other countries which record the liabilities.

Primary and Secondary Changes in Money

The extent to which short-term capital movements substitute for gold in the money supply will depend upon where in the banking system the assets are held and where the liabilities are recorded. Much depends upon what we regard as money. Here it is defined to include all domestic demand deposits, but not the deposits of foreigners. This is somewhat arbitrary, and one could take the view that foreigners earn money (through their exports) and spend it (on their imports) so that their deposits should not be regarded as different from those of domestic residents. Nonetheless, the velocity of circulation of foreign deposits is probably very different from that of resident demand deposits, and money is generally defined to exclude them.

The changes in money supply brought about by short-term capital movements can be broken down into the primary, secondary, and tertiary. Note well that our concern is with changes in money, not income. We are dealing with multiple expansion and contraction of means of payments, not multiplier effects on income. The primary expansion or contraction in the money supply is that which results directly from the balance-of-payments surplus or deficit on current account. Exports exceed imports. This means that there is a net expansion of money in the hands of exporters. Imports exceed exports. This means that import transactions extinguish money over and above that amount of money created by export transactions. These are regarded as the primary expansion and contraction.

The secondary expansion and contraction in money are those which result from short-term capital movements which affect member-bank reserves. Suppose exports exceed imports, and these are paid for by a reduction of foreign monetary authorities' deposits with the central bank. Member-bank deposits increase; the offsetting increase in exporters' deposits is the primary expansion in money. But on the basis of the excess reserves thus created, it is possible to undertake new lending leading to a secondary expansion.

Conversely, an import surplus which resulted in a reduction in member-bank deposits and an increase in foreign central-bank deposits with the central bank would lead to secondary contraction through the loss of reserves. Secondary expansion and contraction assume, of course, that there are no excess reserves.

If the central bank operates on a reserve basis, and is prepared to expand its discount or open-market investment purchases when it gains reserves or reduces its foreign liabilities, or contract when it loses reserves or when its foreign liabilities increase, the resultant monetary change can be called the tertiary effect. But for most purposes the tertiary effect can be ignored, even though the balance sheet example we have just been through dwelt on it. The secondary change in the money supply then includes any and all changes in money resulting from the change in net claims on, or liabilities to, foreigners.

If the secondary change in money supply leads to a change in national income, through changes in liquidity, interest rates, and consequent changes in domestic investment, these must be distinguished from those which take place through the multiplier. The creation of income through net exports, or its extinction through net imports, is the multiplier change in income. If the primary and secondary changes in money accompanying the changes in income produce a further change in domestic spending and income, this may be regarded as the banking income change. And this banking income change is still different from any income change induced by a current-account surplus or deficit through the international accelerator. It is not necessary to give this change a designation, since we mention the accelerator so seldom that we can be explicit on each occasion.

Note this. A foreign central bank intent on its own interests may find itself conducting open-market operations in the United States. If it buys deposits at the Federal Reserve Bank with gold it expands our reserves. If it buys gold with deposits it contracts. But even when its dollar reserves are unchanged, it can affect the New York money market. To switch Federal Reserve deposits to a commercial bank or to use them to buy acceptances or government paper expands the money base; to build up deposits at the Federal Reserve through selling short-term paper or transferring deposits from commercial banks is contractive. A world banking center must learn to offset the meaningless changes in reserves arising from international transactions in the same way as it responds to seasonal and similar changes in the note circulation.

The Role of the Commercial Banks

But to return to short-term capital movements and the money supply. In the examples we have worked through, the change in assets or liabilities has taken place at the central bank. There is nothing which requires this. Suppose the short-term capital outflow took the form of an increase in commercial-bank holdings of foreign exchange, much as the Australian banks used to hold sterling directly as reserves, in addition to their deposits with the Commonwealth Bank. The primary expansion in money now takes place as the banks increase their holdings of foreign exchange and their liabilities to exporters. Whether secondary expansion will occur or not, however, is dependent upon whether the commercial banks are permitted to count foreign exchange as part of their reserves or, with reserves in excess of the legal limit, whether they feel safer with these added assets and therefore more in a mood to expand loans and investments. Some secondary expansion may therefore occur, though it is not so likely as in the case where the change in assets was located at the central bank.

The short-term capital outflow can take the form of a decrease in foreign deposits at the commercial banks. There will be no secondary expansion unless the banks have been worried about the size of their liabilities to foreigners and, relieved at the reduction of this potential drain, feel inclined to expand loans and investments. The banks must be in position legally to do so through the existence of excess reserves. These may be held because of lack of investment opportunities in a depression; they may reflect simply fear that foreign deposits are less "permanent" than domestic, so that more caution than that required by law is desirable.

The Money Market

As a third alternative, the short-term capital movement may be financed in the market rather than by the commercial or the central banks. In this case the secondary expansion of money is unlikely to take place, and even the primary expansion may be excluded. Suppose that the export surplus is financed by a speculative short-term capital outflow. As mentioned in Chapter 4, the seasonal surplus in the balance of payments of the United States was financed each autumn, prior to World War I, by speculators who bought sterling when it was cheap and planned to sell it later in the spring when it was dear (and the balance seasonally weak). Deposits of exporters would have increased, but those of speculators would have been drawn down. On balance, there has been no change in the money supply. But there is still a way to finance the increase in income. The expansion in balances in the hands of exporters is an expansion in what monetary economists call the "transactions circulation," i.e., those deposits which are used in the purchase of goods and services. The speculators, however, have paid them money, not from the transactions circulation, except in the unlikely event that the funds were newly saved, but from accumulated working funds pending investment. These belong to what is sometimes called the "financial circulation." In consequence, while the total supply of money is unchanged, the transactions circulation increases at the expense of the financial circulation, and the increase in national income due to the export surplus can be financed.

Finally, if the exporters financed the short-term capital outflow themselves, there would be no money change. Net exports take place. Assume that the exporters allow the foreign importers six months to pay. The export surplus is financed by an outflow of capital provided by the exporters. If the exporting house discounts bills or gets additional credit from its bank, then money is increased, whether the short-term capital is extended directly by the bank or indirectly through a bank loan to the export firm. If the exporter needs no additional financing, his deposits are drawn down, those of his suppliers of goods and services are built up, and the amount of money in circulation is unchanged. But the exporter cannot finance the shipment unless he had idle funds previously—in which case these may be regarded as having belonged to the financial circulation—or unless he is going out of business. In the latter circumstances a planned shift of funds from the transactions to the financial circulation does not take place, because the funds are moved abroad.

Varied Possibilities

This by no means exhausts the possibilities. Dealing with a capital outflow, we have not treated a reduction in liabilities to foreigners on the part of importing houses as a means of financing the export surplus, and what this may mean for the money supply. The indefatigable student and the enthusiastic one may work through these examples, as well as all the variations on the same theme associating a capital inflow with a contraction of the money supply. The essential points to retain, however, are these:

1. How does one define money for the purpose of this exercise? Are foreign deposits money? Is the financial circulation money? On the narrowest definition, an export surplus financed by short-term capital movements leads to a primary expansion of money, and an import surplus so financed to primary contraction. On a wider definition, the amount of money may remain unchanged, although significant changes take place within the over-all total.

2. The general rule governing the secondary change in the money supply resulting from short-term capital movements is that its certainty will vary with the distance of the movers of the funds from the central bank. If the short-term capital is moved on the books of the central bank itself, whether through assets or through liabilities, the second-

ary expansion can and will take place, unless excess reserves prevent. If the funds are moved by commercial banks, there is still some chance, but less. If the nonbanking market finances the movement, the secondary expansion is impossible.

Let us return to the short-term capital movement which gives rise to a gold movement, rather than one which substitutes for it. A short-term capital outflow takes place when the current account is balanced. The consequence is a loss of gold. The loss of gold leads to a primary and secondary contraction of the money supply. But the short-term capital outflow may lead to offsetting primary and secondary expansions. The result would be a standoff. The primary and secondary changes induced by the short-term capital outflow may be less certain than those resulting from the gold exports. In this case the net result might be a contraction of money, even though there was no decline in national income to be brought about because of an import surplus. We shall recur to this shortly in discussing the role of stabilization funds in ensuring that unwanted monetary changes do not result from the movement of hot money.

Short-Term Capital and the Rate of Interest

Under the nineteenth-century gold standard, the rate of interest moved short-term capital and played a considerable part in bringing about adjustment in the balance of payments. It should be observed that this requires that the various sections of the money market—dealers, banks, central banks—be willing to speculate, i.e., to take an exchange position. If no one was willing to take a speculative position in sterling, the only effect of increasing the discount rate in London would be to increase the forward discount on the currency (or reduce the premium). Any capital inflow in response to the change in the rate of interest would be hedged in the forward market, in order to avoid the exchange risk. Unless the increased sales of forward exchange, offsetting spot purchases, lead to speculative forward purchases, which, by assumption, they do not, the attempt to sell forward will fail to find buyers, and the rate will fall. When the forward discount is equal to the interest-rate differential, there is no advantage in moving funds to the high-interest-rate money market.

The use of the discount rate as a means of inducing short-term capital movements thus requires speculative capital movements in which the exchange risk is not covered. This condition prevailed in the nineteenth century. A foreign trader was, on the whole, indifferent as between assets in sterling or in his own currency and cared very little about which currencies his liabilities were denominated in. With the exception of the period from 1797 to 1816 during the Napoleonic Wars, the pound sterling had been immovable in terms of gold since 1717, while the value of the dollar, apart from a slight adjustment in 1834 and the suspension of specie payments from 1861 to 1879 because of the Civil War, had also been fixed in relation to gold since 1792. Expectations concerning exchange rates were inelastic, and speculation was stabilizing. Under these conditions, interest-rate changes induced movements of short-term capital.

The classical view of the role of the discount rate on the gold standard was that it operated through credit to alter prices, and thereby to affect exports and imports. In its most elaborate treatment by Hawtrey, the theory suggested that wholesalers operated in the London market on borrowed funds. A rise in the rediscount rate, by increasing the cost of carrying goods, would tend to make them sell. This would lower prices, encourage exports, discourage imports. A reduction in the discount rate, on the other hand, however, would induce them to expand their inventories. The impact of their buying on the market would drive prices up, discourage exports, encourage imports. In this way, the bank rate was believed to influence the balance of payments on the gold standard. An increase or decrease in the discount rate would attract or repel gold by encouraging and depressing exports and imports.

Recent investigation has suggested that short-term capital movements in a world of stable expectations short-circuited this roundabout process. An increase in the discount rate led to an inflow of gold into the London market through its effect in encouraging lending to London and discouraging borrowing from it. At a higher discount rate, borrowers would tend to pay off bills coming due in London, rather than renew them; and foreign banks would think twice before discounting bills drawn in sterling, preferring to hold them for their own account and earn the higher return. In either case, a capital flow toward London would be set in motion and lead to a gold inflow. Conversely, a decline in the rate of interest would lead to a capital outflow, which would have to be matched by a gold outflow, as more bills would be drawn on London and more bills would be discounted there.

So powerful was this short-circuit device that a gold flow resulting from the balance of payments on current account could be halted and reversed through opposing short-term capital movements. Through years of experience, the Bank of England learned that the remedy for a crisis, whether in domestic or in foreign payments, was to raise bank rate rapidly and to lend freely at the high rate. Liquidity was available to the market as a whole, but only upon payment of a penalty discount rate.

In the absence of speculation, however, a rise in the interest rate will merely change the forward rate.

On this account, the efficacy of interest rate changes in bringing about short-term capital flows today is very much open to doubt. Within the sterling area, where speculative positions are maintained—Australians being willing to hold pounds sterling, let us say, and Britishers Australian pounds—it may well be that changes in the Bank of England discount rate will attract or repel funds. And it may well be true that a rise in the rate of discount will pull back British funds from New York, Cologne, and Montreal by increasing the cost of maintaining a short position in sterling. But it is unlikely, in present circumstances, that United States, German, or Canadian funds would be attracted to London by an increase in the rate, as would have been the case prior to 1914 when the whole world was willing to hold sterling. On the other hand, a change in the New York rate structure is likely to bring about stabilizing short-term capital movements since the world is willing to take speculative long positions in dollars.

Destabilizing Movements

In a world of elastic expectations, however, the rules based on inelastic expectations do not apply. In many markets today, and at frequent intervals in monetary history since 1929, an increase in the discount rate not only failed to attract funds from abroad but actually led to capital outflows. The increase in the rate of interest is taken not as a sign of strength indicating the readiness of the authorities to protect the balance of payments but as a sign of weakness, and as a preliminary to eventual currency depreciation.

Under destabilizing speculation, an import surplus leads to capital outflow and increased loss of reserves rather than to the inflow which would finance the balance of payments on current account and render the reserve movement unnecessary. Conversely, an export surplus leads through a rising exchange rate and reduced rate of interest not to the offsetting capital outflow, which stabilizing speculation would produce, but to a capital inflow which brings about an embarrassing addition to gold and exchange reserves, excess banking reserves and monetary superabundance. Short-term capital movements came to be regarded in the interwar period as a menace to international stability rather than as an instrument in its achievement. An early step in the defense of a currency with a persistent disequilibrium was the forbidding of movements of capital.

If the current account is in rough balance, a destabilizing capital outflow will produce a gold outflow, and an inflow of capital a gold inflow. It may happen that the monetary effect of the capital movement offsets that of the gold movement. Such was the case, for example, when foreign central banks acquired dollars during the "gold scare" of 1937, in the expectation that the United States dollar was going to be appreciated through a reduction in the Treasury gold-buying price. Gold was exchanged for dollars. The Federal Reserve System acquired a new asset in the form of gold and a new liability, a deposit of a foreign central bank. So long as the increase in the gold ratio of the Federal Reserve System led to no change in reserve bank credit outstanding, the expansionary effect of the gold was offset in full by the contractive effect of the short-term capital inflow. But, as we have already suggested, this need not be the case. If the foreign balances are held in accounts not with the Federal Reserve Bank of New York but with a commercial bank, a net increase in member-bank reserves will have taken place, and a net secondary expansion of credit is possible.

There may be occasions when it is desirable to permit this net effect of the gold movement which overwhelms the opposite tendencies of the outflow of short-term funds. But, as a rule, countries prefer to have their monetary policy unaffected by destabilizing capital movements. The devices worked out to offset the net monetary impact of "hot money movements" were the exchange stabilization fund and gold sterilization.

Stabilization Funds

The first stabilization fund was the British Exchange Equalization Account, established in 1932 to moderate movements of the exchange rate after the abandonment of the gold standard by the British in September, 1931. Like so many other economic institutions, the uses of the Exchange Equalization Account were originally only dimly perceived. The primary focus of the authorities when it was established was upon variations in the exchange rate. In its actual operation, it did little stabilizing of exchange rates because it was unwilling to take exchange risks, converting rather the foreign exchange it bought each day into gold which it brought back to British shores.

Ultimately the Exchange Equalization Account came to be used less to affect the exchange rate than to protect the London money market from the excessive changes in liquidity which the movements of hot money would otherwise produce.

The Account was originally equipped with sterling bills. It was in a position to buy foreign exchange (and convert it into gold) to meet a capital inflow, but it would have been helpless before an outflow since it owned no gold or foreign exchange to supply to foreigners in exchange for sterling. But the EEA's bills—actually short-term government obligations—could be issued (or sold) in any amount. When a foreigner bought sterling, the EEA would sell sterling bills for the same amount and buy foreign exchange (ultimately gold). The foreigner was supplied with a sterling asset, and the sterling authorities acquired gold which they held outside the banking system. No secondary expansion of the money supply could occur as a result of a capital inflow.

Whether any primary expansion took place depended upon how one defined money and upon how the foreigner chose to hold sterling. If the foreigner held a deposit with a joint-stock bank, money had increased if foreign deposits are included in the definition of money, but otherwise not. In the latter case the joint-stock bank was likely to buy the bills sold by the Exchange Equalization Account:

BALANCE SHEET OF EEA

Assets	*Liabilities*
Gold.....................+£100	Bills.....................+£100

BALANCE SHEET OF JOINT STOCK BANKS

Bills.....................+£100	Due to foreigners..........+£100

If, on the other hand, the foreigner chose to hold bills directly himself, then there was no increase in money under any definition. The foreigner gave up foreign exchange convertible into gold for sterling bills, and the Exchange Equalization Account gave up bills for gold. The British government had to pay interest on these bills, which the foreigners earned. This was the price paid for permitting the capital movement, which it would have been costly to prevent without producing untoward effects.

The bright student may have observed that if the foreigner holds deposits and the joint-stock bank bills, the effect will be contractive in money terms. The liabilities of the banks have increased, but not their primary reserves. If their primary reserve ratio was just being met before the capital inflow, they now have a deficiency. The Bank of England frequently undertook open-market operations to rebuild the deposits with the Bank of the joint-stock banks and to prevent deflationary consequences from short-term capital inflows and expansive repercussions of outflows.

These so-called "trimming" operations called for small Bank of England purchases of bills in the face of a large capital inflow and large EEA sales of bills, to keep the monetary system on an even keel.

Later when foreigners withdrew funds placed in the London market, the entire process would be reversed. The Exchange Equalization Account would sell gold for foreign exchange, and in turn, sell the foreign exchange for sterling. The sterling would be used to retire treasury bills in the London market. Foreigners, on the other hand, would sell British Treasury bills for sterling (or sell sterling which would lead the joint-stock banks to sell Treasury bills) and buy foreign exchange which would lead their central banks to buy gold. The earlier transaction would have been reversed without an impact on the London money market, after a small trimming operation of the Bank of England. The Bank, in this connection, would sell bills to mop up primary reserves no longer needed by the joint-stock banks after their foreign deposits had contracted.

These stabilization-fund operations were successful, as already noted, because the Exchange Equalization Account was equipped with sterling and because the forces it was called upon to neutralize produced a capital inflow. If it had held gold or foreign exchange, it would not have been well placed to meet an inflow but could have coped with an outward movement. To meet an outflow, a stabilization fund needs gold; an inflow, domestic money or near money.

United States Stabilization Fund

The United States Stabilization Fund was originally established with part of the gold "profit" which came from the revaluation of the gold stock of the United States from $20.67 an ounce to $35.00 in 1934. With $2 billion of gold at the new value, the Fund was in an admirable position to finance a capital outflow. Confronted with a capital inflow, however, it was helpless. In order to provide dollars to foreigners, it had to obtain dollars. This it could do only by selling gold to the Federal Reserve Bank of New York. The first result of this transaction is as follows:

FEDERAL RESERVE BANK OF NEW YORK

Assets	*Liabilities*
Gold.....................+$100	Stabilization Fund deposit....+$100

When the Stabilization Fund now spends its dollars to buy foreign exchange offered to it by foreigners who seek refuge for their funds, the reduction in Stabilization Fund deposits results in an increase in deposits of member banks. This, of course, provides a basis for multiple expansion of money which the Fund was established to assist in preventing.

Gold Sterilization

Open-market operations are the means of preventing a capital inflow from affecting the credit base when the Stabilization Fund lacks power to borrow dollars. As gold increases in the balance sheet of the central bank, discounts and securities should be reduced, to leave the total volume of member-bank reserves unchanged. Assuming that the foreigners hold their funds in the form of deposits with the commercial banks, this policy requires no stabilization fund and is called simply "gold sterilization." The sterilization of a capital outflow which leads to a loss of gold calls for open-market purchases of securities by the central bank.

In 1936–37, the United States Treasury pursued a policy of gold sterilization without calling upon the Federal Reserve System to assist with open-market operations. Normally, when gold was sold to the Treasury by gold arbitrageurs, it would replenish its balances at the Federal Reserve Bank. In order to sterilize the imported gold, however, it chose to pay for gold with its balance, which it brought back to normal not from the deposit of gold certificates but from borrowing from the money market. The new borrowing needed to buy the gold acted as an offset to the increase in member-bank reserves in the same way as would a sale of government securities by the Federal Reserve System.

If the gold inflow takes place as a consequence of an export surplus on current account rather than a capital inflow, a policy of sterilization cannot prevent a shift of money from the investment circulation to the transactions circulation. This finances the multiplier expansion of income: money in the hands of exporters and their suppliers increases; money in the investment circulation declines as the Treasury or the Federal Reserve System sells government securities to the money market. Complete sterilization, which would smother the income as well as the monetary effects, would call for buying the gold with money raised through an increase in taxes. The government surplus (new savings) would then offset the export surplus (foreign investment). The increase in net taxation would take money out of the transactions circulation as fast as the export surplus put it in.

Central-Bank Dealings in Forward Exchange

We have stated that central banks cannot control short-term capital movements through changes in the discount rate so long as speculation is destabilizing. There is, however, one device which central banks have used—control or alteration of the forward exchange rate. This rather esoteric mechanism was once proposed by Keynes as a tool of central-bank manipulation. Although little is known about actual central-bank operations in forward exchange, these appear to have taken place primarily from necessity rather than from deliberate choice.

Toward the end of the 1930's, for example, large-scale movements of funds took place from London to New York as war appeared increasingly inevitable. Sales of gold by the Exchange Equalization Account and purchases by the Stabilization Fund and by gold arbitrageurs were not sufficient to hold sterling at the pegged rate of $4.68. For one thing, the flow of capital was so great that insurance companies balked at the marine risks they were being asked to assume and limited the amount of gold they were prepared to cover on a single liner. This tended to reduce the gold-import point into New York.

The insistent demand for dollars, however, could be satisfied either with spot or with forward dollars. If spot dollars obtained from gold shipments were insufficient to supply the demands of the market, the Bank of England could sell dollars forward. If the Bank of England sold enough forward dollars to drive the discount below the interest-rate differential, it would pay arbitrageurs, who needed to take no exchange position, to buy spot sterling and buy dollars forward. In this way pressure could be shifted from the spot to the forward market, when the former became unbearable.

The advocates of this device regard it as one for use during a short, sharp attack made against a currency with borrowed funds. If professional speculators are conducting a bear drive on a currency, there is some comfort for the defending authorities in the knowledge that ultimately the bears must repay their debts, cover their contracts, and turn the pressure in the other direction. If speculation is made costly through high discount rates and the authorities can hang on, ultimate cover will halt the outflow abruptly and lead to a return inflow. In 1938–39 this was not the case. The outflow from Britain represented not so much short-term speculative funds as capital owned by firms and individuals. The result was that the Bank of England was obliged to deliver dollars or swap the contracts still further forward when they came due. The device was useful in rearranging the pressure on spot sterling through time, but not in changing its volume.

Exchange Control

Experience with hot money in the 1930's led to the conclusion on all sides that the only effective means of coping with destabilizing short-term capital movements was exchange control. Supporting this conclusion was the large volume of liquid investment funds generated by monetary steps taken to assist in overcoming unemployment, and the cheap money policies of the period which made a wide number of assets, like government debt, close in character to money. It must be admitted that the problem is a difficult one in depression when liquidity is high. In a world of aggression, threats, taxes regarded as confiscatory, and civil war, capital outflow may take place suddenly, without warning, on a scale with which governmental authorities are incapable of dealing. In this case the argument for exchange control is very strong in equity. Citizens of a country subject to draft are not allowed to escape service by emigration in time of emergency. Why should capital be allowed to evade national service? Why should capital be allowed to get away, taking with it the national gold stock which may be needed in the defense of the country?

Whatever the merits of the argument in the abstract, the difficulty in the real world is to enforce control of capital movements. The proceeds of exports must all be collected; underinvoicing must be prevented. Stocks of foreign securities must be retained at home; and nationals must be prevented from taking the national currency abroad, and all foreigners and nationals from bringing it in. (The net sale of foreign currency abroad, of course, is a capital inflow, since it represents an increase in liabilities to foreigners. But it is necessary to cut off this capital inflow in order to prevent the reverse movement of sales of domestic currency for foreign and the use of this domestic currency by foreigners for purchases of goods and services.)

Apart from the difficulty of controlling purely financial transactions, it has been found since 1945 that large movements of short-term credit can take place through shifts in the financing of trade. When traders took a bearish view of sterling, everyone with payments to make in sterling delayed them as long as possible, while all those who anticipated receipts hurried them up. Exports to the sterling area picked up as traders with normal deliveries tried to obtain sterling and sell it for foreign currencies before depreciation took place. Concerns abroad which had every intention of buying British goods postponed purchase to the last minute, and payment still longer, in the hope of being able to pay with depreciated pounds. All this was legitimate business. Indeed, part of this bear selling was doubtless financed by British banks on the grounds that they normally financed imports. As was mentioned earlier, when twelve months of normal receipts are stretched out to fifteen, and twelve months of payments crowded into nine, a large short-term movement of capital takes place in the finance of normal trade. No system of foreign-exchange control which leaves considerable leeway for the exercise of private business judgment, normally in full sway in such questions as arranging credit, is likely to be able to prevent capital movements of this "leads-and-lags" variety at short term.

Capital Movements under the Paper Standard

Under the freely fluctuating paper standard, stabilizing capital movements may take place on short-term account and limit the extent of exchange-rate adjustment, or destabilizing movements may occur and widen it. History abounds with examples of both kinds. There is considerable difficulty, however, in forecasting which kind of speculation will take place.

Keynes once proposed that the distance between the gold points on the gold standard be enlarged—presumably by widening the gap between buying and selling prices of the central bank. The purpose of this proposal was to encourage short-term capital movements of the stabilizing variety by giving speculators more profit from foreign exchange bought just short of the gold-import point and sold close to the gold-export point. The proposal for permitting the foreign-exchange rate to fluctuate without official intervention had provision for forward rates which it was hoped would bring out stabilizing speculation. As we observe in Appendix A, however, the establishment of a forward market is no guarantee that speculation will be of the stabilizing variety. If it is, the foreign-exchange rate will move within a narrow range around the long-run equilibrium rate, much as an automatic pilot anticipates deviations from the course of the ship or airplane and makes adjustments in advance. If not, however, destabilizing speculation will exaggerate the deviations, like a servo-mechanism "hunting" in unstable oscillations, far each side of the norm.

If the foreign-exchange rate is not left to adjust to market conditions by itself, without assistance, but the authorities intervene to iron out daily, seasonal, or cyclical fluctuations, the authorities themselves will undertake short-term capital movements of a stabilizing variety. When the balance of payments is temporarily adverse, the authorities will supply the market with foreign exchange. This short-term capital inflow (reduction of foreign assets) may lead to primary and secondary contraction of the money supply in exactly the same way as if the currency had been on the gold standard. If there is a temporary surplus, on the other hand, the authorities will be called upon to absorb the redundant foreign exchange rather than permit an increase in the rate; and the capital outflow may act as an expansive force. To the extent that official short-term capital movements operate to steady the foreign-exchange rate, the country might just as well be on the gold standard, especially since the stabilizing capital movements are carried out by the central bank or other official body likely to be operating with central-bank funds or credit.

Short-term capital movements are like inventory fluctuations in national income. Production and consumption of all goods are not balanced each day, week, month, or year. Discrepancies between production and consumption are cared for by inventory changes. Over a long period of time, however, changes in inventories should cancel out, except for secular growth or shrinkage due to changes in the level of business or the manner of its conduct. In the same way, short-term capital movements should net to zero over a long period, except for growth or decline in working balances.

The analogy between inventory and short-term capital can be carried one or two steps further. Inventory changes can be stabilizing or destabilizing and voluntary or unintentional. A destabilizing inventory change occurs when business firms try to expand inventories at the same time that consumption is expanding. Destabilizing capital movements have already been discussed. An unintentional inventory increase occurs when production intended for sale cannot be disposed of in the market. And an unintentional short-term capital movement occurs when a country fails to meet its drafts under letters of credit, after the goods have already been released. Involuntary extensions of credit of this sort have taken place toward one and another country in Latin America when purchases of United States exports on short-term credit have exceeded the capacity of the country to meet payments.

Cyclical Role of Short-Term Capital Movements

This balancing role of short-term capital movements is never more important than during the temporary cyclical imbalances between exports and imports. We shall develop this topic in Chapter 25 when we discuss the International Monetary Fund. Here it is sufficient to indicate the nature of these imbalances. Suppose all the rest of the world is in continuous full-employment income equilibrium. If no long-term capital movements take place, an unstable country will have an import surplus in high prosperity, as the domestic investment multiplier increases imports, and an export surplus in depression. Stabilizing short-term capital movements can finance both and cancel out over the full cycle.

This is simply an introduction to the subject of short-term capital movements in the business cycle. These short-term capital movements have a balance-wheel role to play—daily, seasonally, and (of great importance) cyclically. If this role can be played by the money market, in a period of stabilizing speculation, well and good. If speculation is destabilizing, it may be possible to offset it and provide the necessary balance by movement of official funds. If official funds are insufficient to cope with the problem, it may be necessary to impose exchange control on movements of hot money and then use official funds to balance—or some other device, such as import restrictions.

Summary

Short-term capital movements are those embodied in instruments of less than a year's maturity. They can substitute for gold or give rise to a gold movement. When they substitute for gold, they have the same primary effects on the money supply and may, but are unlikely to, have the same secondary effects. They give rise to gold movements when the short-term capital movement is destabilizing.

A number of devices have been used or proposed to deal with short-term capital movements. In a period of stabilizing speculation, their course has been effectively controlled by changes in short-term interest rates. Stabilization funds and gold sterilization have been evolved to permit destabilizing movements, without experiencing their monetary and banking effects. Central-bank dealing in forward exchange has been proposed, but not widely used, as an offset to destabilizing movements. Finally, exchange control has lately come more and more to suppress them.

SUGGESTED READING

TREATISES, ETC.

See C. Iversen, *Some Aspects of the Theory of International Capital Movements* (Copenhagen: Einar Munksgaard, 1935), especially chap. ii, iii, and xiii; Bloomfield, *Capital Imports,* especially chaps. ii, v, and viii; and C. P. Kindleberger, *International Short-Term Capital Movements* (New York: Columbia University Press, 1937).

For detailed accounts of the working of the Exchange Equalization Account, see N. F. Hall, *The Exchange Equalization Account* (London: Macmillan & Co., Ltd., 1935); and L. Waight, *The History and Mechanism of the Exchange Equalization Account* (Cambridge, Mass.: Cambridge University Press, 1939). On the floating debt, see F. W. Paish, *The Postwar Financial Problem and Other Essays* (New York: Macmillan Co., 1950), especially "Twenty Years of the Floating Debt" and "British Floating Debt Policy." See also League of Nations (R. Nurkse), *International Currency Experience,* chap. vi.

POINTS

R. G. Hawtrey, *Currency and Credit* (London: Longmans, Green & Co., 1919), contains the exposition of the effect of short-term interest rates on the price level and the balance of trade. The evidence that the system did not work this way is furnished in W. E. Beach, *British International Gold Movements and Banking Policy, 1881–1913* (Cambridge, Mass.: Harvard University Press, 1935).

Keynes's proposal for central-bank dealings in the forward market is to be found in *Treatise on Money* (New York: Harcourt, Brace & Co., 1930), Vol. I, p. 531.

For an account of the gold scare of 1937, when destabilizing speculation took place in favor of the dollar in the belief that the price of gold would be reduced, see F. D. Graham and C. R. Whittlesey, *Golden Avalanche* (Princeton: Princeton University Press, 1939).

Advanced students interested in stabilization fund activities should consult a pair of articles by Harry C. Eastman and Stephen Stykolt in the *Canadian Journal of Economics and Political Science,* May, 1956, and August, 1957.

For an account and analysis of postwar autonomous capital movements, see A. I. Bloomfield, *Speculative and Flight Movements of Capital in Postwar International Finance* (Princeton: Princeton University Press, 1954).

Chapter
18

THE INTERNATIONAL
MOVEMENT OF LONG–TERM
CAPITAL: THE TRANSFER
PROCESS

Transfer and Adjustment

The study of long-term capital will occupy us not for one chapter, like short-term movements, but for three. This, the first, discusses the theory of capital transfer; in the two which follow we deal with separate forms of capital movement—bonds, bank loans, and direct investments and the problems to which they give rise.

The fact that the transfer process is basically an exercise in trade adjustment accounts for its prominence in the theory of international trade. Professor Taussig of Harvard and his students used international capital movements of Britain, Canada, Argentina, France, Australia, and other countries in an attempt to verify the classical theory of trade adjustment represented by the price-specie-flow mechanism. In debating the feasibility of German reparations payments after World War I, Keynes and Ohlin, along with most other prominent economists of Europe and the United States who joined in the controversy, assisted in developing the theory of international trade in important respects.

As an exercise in adjustment, the transfer discussion was not concerned with what happened after capital had been put in place, or who owned it and received the income from its marginal product. It was interested almost entirely in the manner in which physical capital was transferred between countries as a result of borrowing, or how payments which did not necessarily result in capital formation, such as reparations, produced a physical transfer of goods and services from one country to another. Reparations or tributes would not be regarded as capital movements today but as transfers of income. It is still appropriate for us, however, given our interest in the adjustment process, to treat reparations and voluntary international transfer payments, such as Lend-Lease and Marshall Plan aid, like capital movements. If we divide the balance of payments into categories along foreign-exchange budget lines rather than according to national-income categories, we arrive at the sensible division we need to study the adjustment process. Some transfers, like immigrant remittances, are recurring receipts and payments and can go in the current account; others, include reparations, tributes, and, let us hope, Lend-Lease and Marshall Plan aid, are nonrecurring items (even though they do not, like loans, have to be reversed) and are treated as capital.

The Transfer Process

Borrowers of long-term capital desire command in the short run over purchasing power. By and large, however, they desire goods. To get capital without saving, which is to invest or consume without producing, it is necessary to borrow or to liquidate past loans. A country gets capital from abroad in a real sense only when it gets goods or services, over and above the value of the goods it exports. A country lends abroad when it produces more than it consumes and invests at home, the difference representing the excess of exports over imports.

The goods and services borrowed or loaned need not be capital goods. The illustration most frequently used to drive this point home is that of a loan between two islands in, let us say, the South Pacific, each occupied by a tribe of natives. One island and tribe may be designated as A, the other as B. If B borrows from A to build a new hut for the B chief, the real movement of capital may take one of several forms: (1) net imports of building materials, together with assorted craftsmen to assemble it; (2) services of native field workers from A, who tend the coconuts in B while the B natives build the hut from indigenous materials; or (3) consumption goods—yams, coconuts, and other food—to enable B's population to work on the hut without the necessity of worrying about their subsistence.

When industry or government in one country borrows in another, it frequently is interested not in foreign but in domestic purchasing power. How the borrower gets purchasing power in his own country relates to the money transfer. But how this money transfer, in turn, leads to an import surplus, which is the only real way that capital can be loaned between countries, is called the "real transfer." The money and real transfers are interrelated, as we shall see. When one or the other or both offer difficulties, we may have a transfer problem.

The Classical Mechanism

Classical economic theory had one answer for the transfer problem under the gold standard and another under fluctuating exchange rates. In the former, the money borrowed in London, for example, was sold for dollars. This depressed the pound sterling to the gold-export point and led to a gold inflow to the borrower, which we shall call the United States. Prices declined in England as a result of the contraction of money resulting from the gold outflow. Conversely, prices rose in the United States because of the increase in means of payment. If bank rates were raised in England to halt the gold outflow by attracting short-term capital, the contractive process would still take place, though probably on a reduced scale. This would partly be the result of the increase in liabilities to foreigners, which, as explained in the previous chapter, has a contractive monetary effect. In part it would follow directly from the increase in interest rates. The reader can readily fill in the opposite picture in the United States from the barest outline: capital outflow; expansion of money or gain in the transactions circulation at the expense of the financial; stimulation of borrowing through lower interest rates: result—monetary expansion, higher prices.

The lower prices in England and higher prices in the United States would produce an export surplus in the former, import surplus in the latter. This involves the assumption that the sum of the price elasticities of demand is greater than one. And the resultant export surplus of Britain and import surplus of the United States was the real transfer.

The real transfer in goods reverses the original gold movement or subsequent short-term capital movement. As British exports exceed imports, gold returns to the Bank of England, or the London money market is enabled to repay the short-term capital borrowings from New York. When the entire capital movement has been transferred in goods, the gold or short-term capital movement has been reversed completely, and everything remains in balance if we ignore the effects of the interest payment and of the productivity of capital. The decline in export prices in Britain and the rise in prices in the United States will change the terms of trade in favor of the borrower and against the lending country during the process of transfer; but when real transfer has been completed, the terms of trade will revert to their original status.

The classical view of the transfer mechanism under the paper standard follows along familiar lines. The attempt by the borrower to sell pounds for dollars leads to a depreciation of the pound, in the absence of stabilizing short-term capital movements. The depreciation of sterling and the consequent appreciation of the dollar encourage the lender's exports and the borrower's imports and discourage the borrower's exports and the lender's imports. As Britain develops an export surplus, the original borrower buys the dollars he needs for expenditure in the United States. Money transfer and real transfer take place simultaneously. When all the funds (and capital) have been transferred from London to New York, the export surplus of Britain vanishes and the depreciation of sterling is corrected, as the demand for dollars is reduced and the export surplus of Britain creates a demand for sterling which can be satisfied only at a higher rate.

The addition of stabilizing short-term capital movements to the picture makes it more closely resemble the gold-standard mechanism. If in the beginning, as sterling begins to depreciate, speculators who believe it will remain at par over the long run buy it at a small discount, their offerings of dollars enable the original borrower to achieve the transfer of purchasing power. The expansive effect of the short-term capital outflow from the United States and the contractive effect of the short-term capital inflow into Britain will act like the gold movement, though with less certainty and force, to raise prices in the United States and to lower them in Britain. Whether short-term capital movements take place or not, the terms of trade normally turn against the lending country as a result of transfer.

Flaws in the Classical View

Objections to the foregoing analysis were directed mainly to the process under the gold standard. Three points were made: first, that some of the proceeds of the loan might be spent in Britain in the first place. This was readily conceded. To this extent, transfer took place automatically in real terms with no money transfer effected or required.

Second, it was argued that prices could not be raised in the United States and reduced in Britain, since a number of goods were traded in both, and the law of one price required that they be quoted at the same price in a single market. If wheat was $2.00 in Chicago and 10s. in Liverpool, it was impossible for the price to rise in one and decline in the other, since they were tied together. This objection, however, was in error. Wheat which was exported from the United States to Britain could be expected to rise in price in both markets; woolens which were exported from England to the United States, to fall in both. What the classical economists were talking about were sectional price levels. To look at the matter from the standpoint of the United States, export prices were expected to rise along with domestic prices. But import prices, determined in Britain, would fall. And the reverse would be true in England. After a purely formal correction for the law of one price, the classical mechanism was unaffected by this criticism.

The third and most fundamental objection in theory was to the reliance on the quantity theory of money. This explanation might have had operational validity in the seventeenth and eighteenth centuries, when the economy was more or less in continuous full employment. It might still serve as a reliable guide for prediction in periods of inflation, such as war. But in the short run the quantity of money was little indication of the level of prices. To put the matter succinctly in modern terms, changes in money occurred without bringing about changes in spending, and changes in spending sometimes affected employment without producing changes in price.

But these theoretical objections were less significant than the facts. What distressed Professor Taussig about the classical theory, which he had helped to perfect and which his students had sought to verify, was that the transfer process in the real world worked far more smoothly than one could have imagined from the classical explanation. Time was presumably required for changes in money supply and prices and then in exports and imports. In actuality, the balance of payments adjusted itself to changes in borrowing (or vice versa?) with remarkable speed and precision and without marked pressures leading to gold flows or exchange-rate changes.

Modern Theory

What the classical theory had neglected were changes in spending and income and their effects on the balance of payments through the marginal propensity to import. More was involved than the fact that borrowers sometimes spent part of loans directly in the lending country. On this portion of the loan, the marginal propensity to import (on the change in spending power) may be said to be one. And, to this extent, transfer takes place automatically. But on the portion of the loan spent at home the increase in domestic expenditure raises income which spills over into imports, and this transfers part of the loan. How much of the loan will be transferred in this fashion depends upon a number of factors. These include the marginal propensities to import and save in the borrowing country, the course of money income in the two countries, and the response, if any, of domestic investment.

It has been enunciated as a theorem that if the marginal propensity to save in the borrowing country is positive and if domestic investment in the borrowing country is changed by no more than the amount of the loan, with no induced changes in investment in either country, changes in income in the two countries will not be sufficient to transfer the whole loan through induced changes in imports. This theorem may be illustrated, in a general way, with the multiplier diagram as in Figure 18.1*a,* using one country only, a

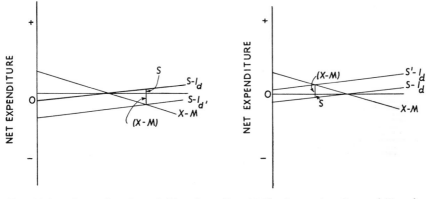

FIG. 18.1*a.* Incomplete Inward Transfer   FIG. 18.1*b.* Incomplete Outward Transfer
with Increased Investment   with Increased Savings

continuous borrowing and investment rather than a single nonrecurring transfer, and eliminating all effect of the foreign repercussion.

Given a marginal propensity to save of 0.1 and to import of 0.3, in the borrowing country, the sum of $MPM + MPS$, which is the reciprocal of the multiplier, will be 0.4, and the multiplier will be $2\frac{1}{2}$. If $10 million of new borrowings from abroad are spent within the borrowing country as additional investment, the increase in income which results is $25 million, the increase in savings $2.5 million, and the increase in imports $7.5 million. The downward displacement of the $S-I_d$ schedule by the $10 million increase in I_d transfers only three fourths of the loan. The remaining $2.5 million, offset by new savings in the borrowing country, will press on the foreign-exchange market, tending to increase the supply of the exchange of the lending country and the demand for that of the borrower. Real transfer of this portion of the loan will require something akin to the price-specie-flow mechanism on the fixed exchange standard or depreciation of the lender's currency under the paper standard.

The same is true if outward transfer is attempted by an increase in savings in the lending country, as shown in Figure 18.1*b.*

Observe, in the first of these simple examples, without foreign repercussion, that if the *MPS* had been 0 (and the multiplier 3.3), the full amount of the loan could have been transferred through income changes. Or with the *MPS* unchanged at 0.1. if there had been a positive slope to the investment schedule of 0.1 or higher, the full amount of the loan, or more, could have been transferred. To summarize, the theorem states that if the marginal propensity to save is positive and if there is no accelerator or other positive slope to the investment schedule, less than the full amount of the loan will be transferred by income changes.

Adding the foreign repercussion does not change matters greatly if that country is also "stable in isolation," i.e., if that country also has a marginal propensity to spend on consumption and investment which is less than one, or if its $S-I_d$ curve is positively sloped. This has been shown in a period analysis in Lloyd Metzler's classic article, reprinted in the American Economic Association, *Readings.* It can readily be demonstrated in other ways.[1] The essence of the argument is that the

[1] It may interest a few readers to compare results with and without the foreign repercussion, using Meade's simultaneous technique, to which we have referred earlier (p. 195).

Without foreign repercussion, and with an MPM_a of 0.3, an MPS_a of 0.1 and an MPC_a of 0.6, a loan of $10 million spent in A increases A's income by $25 and her imports by 0.3 times that amount, or $7.5 million.

If the same values for the propensities exist in lender B, the change in income can be computed from a matrix in which A and B are listed as spenders vertically in columns, and as recipients of spending horizontally in rows. A's marginal propensity to spend at home (MPC_a) is in the upper left-hand box; her marginal propensity to import (i.e., spend in B), immediately below it. B's propensity to spend at home is in the lower right-hand corner, and her propensity to import above it:

Receivers \ Spenders	A	B
A	MPC_a	MPM_b
B	MPM_a	MPC_b

The equilibrium condition for national income in each country is that total spending equals total income. If there is an autonomous increase in spending of $10 million in A, and a similar decrease in B, one can derive two equations:

$$+10 + MPC_a \times dY_a + MPM_b \times dY_b = dY_a$$

and

$$MPM_a \times dY_a - 10 + MPC_b \times dY_b = dY_b ,$$

where dY_a and dY_b (or more simply a and b) are the changes in income in A and B. Filling in the marginal propensities, we have two equations and two unknowns:

$$10 + 0.6a + 0.3b = a$$
$$0.3a - 10 + 0.6b = b$$

If we succeed (after several tries) in solving, we find a and b each equal to a little less than 14.3 million, an increase in A, and a decrease in B. The multiplier is help which comes to Lender B's export surplus from its decline in imports due to its contraction in income is largely offset by the effect of reduced exports in A in dampening A's increase in income and expansion in imports.

This, however, is a much oversimplified model. A variety of its assumptions must be altered in discussion of the real world. These assumptions relate to:

1. The course of spending and income in the lending country
2. The course of spending and income in the borrowing country
3. The marginal propensity of the borrower to import out of borrowings
4. The responses of the banking systems, etc.

The variability which may be experienced within these assumptions is so wide that it is impossible to make any general statement about the extent to which income changes can transfer theoretical international capital movements. It may be fair, however, to conclude from the capital transfers which surprised Professor Taussig that income changes are likely to transfer normal capital movements smoothly, and, from the German reparations experience, that some capital transfers will be very difficult to effect.

The course of spending and income in the lending country will be affected by a variety of factors. These include the way in which the capital to be transferred is raised and the rapidity with which exports increase because of increased spending by the borrower. On the first of these, let us suppose, on the one hand, that the funds are raised through an increase in saving or a decline in investment or an increase in taxes required to collect a reparation payment to be paid abroad. Under any of these circumstances, spending and income will fall in the lending country, and this will help transfer the capital abroad by reducing imports and freeing goods for export. On the other hand, however, the capital may be raised by credit creation or other inflationary means. In this case the process of real transfer will be rendered more difficult, since the increase in exports generated by foreign spending will raise income in the lending country and tend to work against the transfer by increasing imports and limiting exports.

While spending may fall or rise in the lending country, its course

---

evidently much less—nearer $1\frac{1}{2}$ than $2\frac{1}{2}$. B's export surplus is now based on an increase of approximately 4.3 million in exports and a decrease of 4.3 million in imports, for a total improvement of 8.6 million, as compared with the previous 7.5 million. So long as both countries are stable in isolation, then, it adds something, but not very much, to have spending change in both rather than in simply one without repercussion.

is predictable with somewhat more certainty in the borrowing country. Most borrowing is undertaken for capital-formation purposes, and this generally means an increase in spending and in money incomes. But a country receiving reparations from abroad may not respond by lowering taxes or undertaking governmental investment. It may use the receipts merely to pay off government debt. If this fails to lower interest rates and, by this means, to increase other investment, spending and national money income in the receiving country may not be affected. A considerable part of the reparation payment can still be transferred through a reduction in spending in the paying country, but the task of transfer is rendered somewhat easier if both countries alter their spending schedules.

Using the normal marginal propensity to import as a basis for calculating how much of a given capital movement will be transferred in goods through income changes may be misleading because of the existence of a special propensity to import out of borrowed funds which applies to the circumstances of a given loan. Here again there is a wide range of possibilities. It may be that the borrowers are concerned with purchasing power in general, which they intend to spend entirely in the borrowing country, i.e., the propensity to import out of borrowed funds is zero. Or the borrowers may be able to raise at home all the funds they need for expenditure in local currency and may borrow abroad, because of the unavailability of foreign exchange, in order to purchase abroad complementary resources for their capital investment. In this case the propensity to import out of borrowed funds is one. All the loan will be transferred in real terms in the first round of spending, and there will be no transfer left to be accomplished through income changes.

If the banking system in either country permits a multiple expansion or contraction of credit based on the initial changes in savings or investment or upon the movement of short-term credit needed to finance the loan pending real transfer, the normal expectations derivable from the foregoing must be amended still further. This reaction could be subsumed in the remarks about the course of income in the two countries, but it is well to make explicit mention of it.

Most of this wide range of variability can be put into a complex mathematical formula. Rather than do so, however, we may summarize by saying that international capital transfers in money may be transferred in goods through income changes, in part, *in toto,* or in excessive degree (i.e., a larger real transfer than the original money payment), and that real transfer will be fully or excessively effected, the greater the extent to which, other things being equal,

1. Spending and income fall initially in the lending country in the process of raising the money capital
2. The loan is spent by the borrowers in the lending country
3. Money income rises in the borrowing country, due to
   a) A low marginal propensity to save
   b) A positive marginal propensity to invest
   c) In the case of reparations, a readiness to reduce taxation or increase government investment, or of domestic investment to respond upward to a reduction in government debt
4. The foreign repercussion of both countries is low
5. The banking systems of both countries respond to the movements of short-term capital and gold

Conversely, the less that the above conditions are realized, the greater is the likelihood that the capital will not be fully transferred through income changes arising out of the capital transfer itself. Under these circumstances, gold flows will be needed on the gold standard, which may induce income changes of a banking origin; or an exchange-rate adjustment will be needed to accomplish the remaining transfer through price changes.

The Terms of Trade and Transfer

A favorite question asked by the classicists was: What happens to the terms of trade under transfer? If the price mechanism takes the lead in transferring the capital, the terms of trade will evidently turn against the lender and in favor of the borrower. In order to sell more goods abroad to achieve the export surplus, the lending country has to reduce prices either through deflation or through depreciation. To become a more profitable market in which to sell, the borrowing country must raise the prices of its goods either through inflation or through appreciation.

The possibility of transfer through changes in the marginal propensity to import or through income changes, however, alters this. Assume that the investors have a marginal propensity to import out of borrowed funds equal to one and spend the whole loan in the lending country. If they buy the goods that the new savers have foregone, no price will change anywhere in the system, and the terms of trade will remain unaltered. If they buy export goods and the savers economize on import goods, the terms of trade may turn against the borrower. And if the money capital in the lending country is created by bank credit rather than through new saving, there will be an increase in net spending in the lending country, prices are likely to be bid up, and the terms of trade will also turn against the borrowing country and in favor of the lending.

Terms of Trade and Income Changes

When income changes bear the brunt of the transfer, the change in the terms of trade, if any, will depend upon the extent of the income changes in opposite directions in the two countries, the relative propensities to spend for home goods and imports, and the elasticities of supply. The difficulty with analyzing these cases, however, is that they need a combination of two different types of analysis which can be combined only with difficulty. The use of income changes and multipliers assumes linear propensities to save and import, which, in turn, depend upon constant prices based on idle resources. Terms-of-trade analysis, on the other hand, assumes full employment and complete equilibrium. If the terms of trade change, this alters the propensity to import and possibly that to save, which affects the multiplier analysis. While the analysis cannot be made accurate within the scope of this chapter, we may be able to say something of a rough nature about it.

Turn back to Figure 18.1*a.* In this we assumed no foreign repercussion and ignored the lending country. Let us now assume that income remained unchanged in the lending country. Total expenditure increased on the products of the borrowing country by $25 million, representing $10 million of the original loan and $15 million of induced consumption. The increase in expenditure in the lending country amounted to only $7.5 million. If the elasticities of supply in the two countries are anything comparable and not infinite, the terms of trade will turn in favor of the borrowing country.

If income changes occur in both countries, the same general principle holds good and can be put to use. What happens to total spending for the lender's goods as contrasted with the borrower's? If the net change in money income in the two countries is zero, the increase in income in the borrowing country being offset by the decline in the lending, and there are no savings, the criterion is whether the sum of the marginal propensities to import is greater, equal to, or less than one. This can be illustrated with matrixes used in the footnote on page 352.

Suppose the two *MPC*'s and the two *MPM*'s are both alike, and equal, respectively, to 0.6 and 0.4 as illustrated in the accompanying matrix. The sum of the MPM's will be less than one; the increase in spending on A's goods by A will exceed the decrease in spending on A's goods in B; the increase in spending on B's goods in A will be less than the decrease in spending on B's goods in B. Net spending on A's goods will increase; net spending on B's goods will decrease. The terms of trade will clearly turn against B and in favor of A:

Receivers \ Spenders	A	B
A	MPC_a +0.6	MPM_b −0.4
B	MPM_a +0.4	MPC_b −0.6

If, on the other hand, MPC_a and MPC_b are each 0.4 and the two MPM's 0.6, it is evident, or should be after reflection, that the decline in B's spending on A-goods is greater than the increase in A's spending on A's goods; while the increase in A's spending on B's goods exceeds the decrease in B's spending on B's goods. Net spending increases on B's goods, decreases on A's, and the terms of trade favor the lender.

Where the sum of the marginal propensities to import are equal to one, and there are no savings, net spending in each commodity is unchanged, and the terms of trade cannot change. It makes no difference to the terms of trade (though it affects the income changes) whether the marginal propensities to import are smaller or larger than 0.5, as the following matrixes may be used to illustrate:

Receivers \ Spenders	A	B
A	+0.5	−0.5
B	+0.5	−0.5

Receivers \ Spenders	A	B
A	+0.6	−0.6
B	+0.4	−0.4

Receivers \ Spenders	A	B
A	+0.3	−0.3
B	+0.7	−0.7

The example where there is no saving is exactly equivalent to a geometric model with two commodities and two countries, and the transfer effected in kind. Making the transfer in kind takes care of the spending changes. The terms of trade will favor the borrower if the sum of the marginal propensities to import are less than one; or, what amounts to the same thing (again on reflection), if MPC_a is greater than MPM_b, or if MPM_a is less than MPC_b.

If there are savings, if the amount of spending change is different in the two countries, or if the supply elasticities are unequal, the simple criterion of the sum of the marginal propensities to import no longer holds. It is easy to cope with savings. Given equal changes in spending, the terms of trade will favor the lender if the marginal propensity to consume in the borrower exceeds the marginal propensity to import in the lender *and* if the marginal propensity to consume in the lender exceeds the marginal propensity to import in the borrower. The sum of the marginal propensities to import is no longer a valid criterion, as the following matrix suggests. There the sum of the marginal propensities to import is less than one; but it is clear that there will be a net decrease in spending on A's products, and a net increase on B's, producing a change in the terms of trade in favor of lender B.

Receivers	Spenders	
	A	B
A	+0.3	−0.6
B	+0.3	−0.2
Saving	+0.4	−0.2

In the usual case, where spending in the two countries is not identical and of opposite direction, it will be necessary to know the changes in income and the propensities to spend on home goods and imports in the two countries to forecast their terms of trade, given equal supply elasticities. The essential question is how much more (or less) is spent for the goods of the lender and the borrower. To the extent that the rise in income is likely to be greater in the borrower than in the lender and that the propensity to spend on home goods is higher than the propensity to import, the terms of trade will tend to favor the borrower. If the typical case of capital transfer, however, involves a rise in income in the borrower in excess of that in the lender, but a marginal propensity to import in excess of that to spend on home goods and the reverse in the lender, there is no normal outcome. It will be necessary to ascertain the exact amounts of spending on the goods of the two countries.

Terms of Trade and Supply Elasticities

In the real world the assumption of equal supply elasticities is almost certainly invalid. Assume that there are equal increases in spending for the goods of both borrowing and lending countries. Which country is favored by the terms of trade will depend upon the elasticities of supply. If the borrower is a raw-material country and the lender a manufacturing one, the terms of trade of the borrower are likely to improve, since the increase in spending drives up prices, at least in the short run, without expanding output by a great deal. This is in contrast with the position of the lender, assuming the existence of some excess capacity, where the increase in spending tends to expand output but to bring little increase in prices.

Summary on the Terms of Trade

Most readers will mop their brows at this point and conclude that one cannot say much about the terms of trade under capital transfer. Sad but true. The terms of trade depend upon the extent of the income changes, on balance; the relative propensities to import and to spend for home-produced goods, again on balance; and the relative supply elasticities. More accurately, this is the extent to which income changes will affect the terms of trade. If income changes fail to transfer all the capital, additional capital is left to be transferred through price changes. The income impact on the terms of trade may be outweighed by the direct price changes.

But the position is by no means hopeless. We shall attempt below to make a distinction between normal and abnormal long-term capital movements, which may help us. We may anticipate its conclusion enough to suggest that, under normal capital movements, income changes in the borrowing country are more likely than parallel changes in the opposite direction in the lender and that income changes are likely to be sufficiently wide to transfer all the capital—and sometimes even more. This suggests that the net change in income is likely to be an increase. The terms of trade will now favor the country in which the greater part of the increase is spent or the country with the lower elasticity of supply for the sought-after goods, or both, or the net of the two effects if they move in opposite directions.

It is hard to predict which country, in the typical case, will receive the bulk of the spending. The borrowing country will need imported goods if it is underdeveloped, because it probably lacks a capital-goods industry. At the same time, much capital formation consists of construction which must be done in place. Probably, on balance, the borrowing country will spend more for its own output than for the output of the lending country; but the case is not open and shut.

When it comes to supply elasticities, however, there would seem to be a stronger presumption that the supply elasticity of the borrowing country will be less than that of the lending. Lending countries are typically more developed and have greater capacity to expand output in the desired lines. Even if the majority of the net increase in spending is directed to the goods of the lending country, if this majority is not large, it may well be that prices rise further in the borrower than in the lender.

On this showing, which is not conclusive, there is something of a presumption that the terms of trade will favor the borrowing country and be adverse to the lender under "normal" conditions. Borrowing countries typically undertake a considerable amount of capital formation from local resources, and typically have little impact on the prices of the lending in exporting countries, because of their high supply elasticities. It seems probable that the literature overemphasizes the importance of the terms-of-trade effect for normal international lending, and the presumption that the terms of trade favor the borrower is positive, but small.

This presumption does not, however (repeat *not*), extend to a tribute, reparations payment, or other unilateral transfer in which it is impossible to generalize about the likely income changes, propensities, and supply elasticities. The movement of the terms of trade will be dictated by these considerations, and no strong presumption exists in any direction.

Chicken or Egg

Another classical question for debate was whether real transfer typically followed, led, or occurred simultaneously with the money transfer. Under paper-standard conditions without short-term capital movement, the real and money transfers must take place simultaneously, since the borrowers can sell the borrowed foreign exchange for their own currency, if they do not spend it directly, only when an excess supply of the domestic currency is created through an import surplus. But under the gold standard, or under a flexible-exchange rate with stabilizing short-term capital movements which afford an approximation of the gold standard, the question remains open. And the answer—characteristically in economics—is either or both.

Professor Taussig and his students thought of the capital movement as the autonomous factor and of the import surplus of the borrower as induced. This pattern has certainly occurred many times. But it is not a necessary order of things. A country can embark on a program of investment financed locally through credit expansion. The resultant inflation will lead to an import surplus. Foreign borrowing, late in the process, can fill the gap. One reason to borrow abroad may be that the rate of interest locally may have been increased by the central bank as part of its measures to protect the currency in response to the adverse balance.

At the other extreme is the case in which no new expenditure takes place in the borrowing country until the money has been borrowed abroad, or, as in the case of reparations payments, the capital movement is clearly autonomous and the balance-of-payments adjustment, if it takes place at all, is induced.

But there need be no necessary causal leadership in either direction. The money transfer and the balance-of-payments adjustment may both respond equally and simultaneously to deep-seated factors. Such causal factors may be the long-run relationship between the propensity to save and domestic investment opportunities. An excess of investment outlets within a country, relating to the supply of new savings, will tend both to produce inflation and an import surplus, on the one hand, and to induce investors to seek funds abroad, on the other. A clear and intimate connection between the capital movement and the current-account imbalance may, but need not, reflect mutual dependence rather than causality.

Transfer in the Real World

This chapter may conclude with some brief examples of long-term capital transfer, successful and otherwise, to illustrate these principles. There is no reason to depart from the familiar examples with which the literature deals. We shall therefore contrast the Franco-Prussian indemnity with German reparations after World War I. The stabilizing capital movements in central and eastern Europe after World War I will then be compared with the destabilizing movements which succeeded them. Finally, we shall treat the normal capital outflow from the United States in the 1920's and the abnormal inflow in the subsequent decade.

The Franco-Prussian Indemnity. The Franco-Prussian indemnity of 1871 led economics into a great deal of trouble because it created a precedent for German reparations after World War I when the conditions basic to the payment were altogether different. Germany won the brief war of 1870. In addition to the cession of Alsace and Lorraine, it levied an indemnity of approximately 5 billion francs to be transferred in a few large installments. Little more than 500 million francs were paid in gold and silver coin and in German coins spent in France by German troops. The rest was paid in foreign exchange.

France raised the French franc value of the indemnity by two large loans amounting to 5.8 billion francs paid in 1871 and 1872. A considerable part of the subscription to these loans came from abroad, both from foreigners who found the investment attractive and from patriotic Frenchmen who sold foreign investments. Both forms of subscriptions created the foreign exchange which the French government could purchase with the proceeds of the loan. Together they amounted to more than 4 billion francs. The rest of the loans were subscribed out of new savings, partly encouraged by higher rates of interest, partly stimulated by the appeal to patriotic Frenchmen to save and help pay the indemnity to wipe out the blot on French national honor.

The value of gold and silver payments—500 million—and subscriptions to loans in foreign exchange—4,250 million—left little of the indemnity to be paid through the transfer process. In fact, however, the balance of payments transferred more than this, which enabled France to reconstitute part of her portfolio of foreign investments and to repatriate part of the loans originally sold abroad. Exports rose from a level of 2.9 billion francs in 1870 and 1871 by 1 billion in 1872 and remained at 3.9 billion francs through 1875. Imports rose, however, only from 2.9 to 3.6 billion, which produced an export surplus of 300 million, on the average, for the four years from 1872 to 1875. This was the amount of real transfer of the indemnity.

The real transfer was aided by the relative deflation in France, which increased taxes to pay interest on the loans and raised interest rates to help sell them. It was also materially promoted by the German inflation up to 1873. This German inflation was partly the result of the acquisition of gold in part payment of the indemnity. More significantly, perhaps, it occurred simultaneously with the shift of the German monetary standard from bimetallism, in which both gold and silver were included in the German reserves, to gold alone.

The German inflation partly assisted in the transfer by increasing direct imports of goods from France. But, in part, the process was more roundabout. French sales to Britain increased; German sales decreased. Britain consumed the same goods as before but merely shifted her source of supply. The same result could be achieved through British exports. German imports from Britain increased; French imports (relatively) decreased. Britain could sell the same volume of goods as before but helped transfer the capital by shifting exports from France to Germany.

The difficulty for economics posed by the Franco-Prussian indemnity was that it made reparations payments appear transferable between countries, provided that the mechanism were handled properly. In retrospect, however, it appears that this unilateral payment could be effected only because the French were desperately anxious to do so and because Germany acquiesced in permitting an increase in spending. The contrast of the failure to transfer German reparations after World War I made clear that the 1871 episode had been a special, not a general, case.

German Reparations, 1919–31. That France would require reparations from a defeated Germany in 1919 followed automatically from the facts of 1871. But for payment to be effected required a duplication of the position of 1871, or another set of equivalent circumstances. Neither condition was met.

The facts of the 1919 schedule—the breakdown under inflation and the new basis in the Dawes Plan of 1924; the collapse after 1928, producing the ill-fated Young Plan of 1930, closely followed by the Hoover moratorium of June, 1931—none of these will be set out here. For our purposes it is sufficient to observe that Germany did not deflate, nor did the reparations recipients expand expenditure, to produce the required export surplus and import surpluses, respectively. The German government tried to raise the reparations payments in marks through taxation, and this taxation was deflationary. But the increase in the rate of interest and the enthusiasm of the newly established international investment bankers in New York defeated this. Governmental deflation at the national level was offset by provincial and local inflation, as industry and local governments borrowed abroad for spending, on balance.

Nor did Britain and France adjust their spending to fit projected reparations receipts. They regarded reparations receipts not as a new source of income which must be spent to raise national income by a multiple, but as a means of debt reduction. Reparations failed to contract expenditure in the paying country, on balance, or to enlarge expenditure in the recipients. Transfer proved impossible except on the basis of borrowed funds.

The payment produced an important economic controversy. Like so many such debates, no clear winner or loser emerged. In debate with Ohlin, Keynes reached the conclusion that reparations could not be paid (correct, though for the wrong reason). He believed that price elasticities were too low and that Germany could not expand export receipts by lowering export prices. This might have been true, but it was never tested because Germany did not reduce export prices. Ohlin, on the other hand, discounted Keynes's worries about price elasticities of demand as he focused attention for the first time on the possibility that transfer would be effected not through price shifts but through changes in income. He failed, however, to perceive that none of the countries involved were pursuing the internal policies which transfer called for.

With the halt in United States long-term lending to Germany in 1928, this means of paying reparations and enjoying the net import of commodities was no longer available. In 1929 the gap was filled by short-term borrowing, and Germany still experienced a small import surplus on trade account. Beginning in 1930, however, the position changed drastically. Deflation in Germany reduced imports from $3.25 billion in 1929 to $2.53 billion in 1930 and $1.66 billion in 1931. Exports were sustained fairly well, and the balanced trade condition in 1929 was converted to an export surplus of $230 million in 1930 and $715 million in 1931. Real transfer was effected through deflation.

This episode is regarded rather differently by different observers. To some it suggests how effective income changes can be in adjusting the balance of payments. To others it is a reminder that adjustment of the balance of payments at any cost is likely to result in $5\frac{1}{2}$ million unemployed, or 30 per cent of registered workers—hence Hitler and a world war.

Hyperinflation and Capital Movements. The period after World War I in eastern and central Europe illustrates the effects of different kinds of capital movements—long- and short-term—under conditions of freely fluctuating exchanges, and also provides an insight into capital transfer. In most of these countries inflation was inevitable after the war, as households, firms, and governments all simultaneously tried to spend more than their income. Gold and foreign-exchange reserves were quickly dissipated, and foreign-exchange rates were allowed to depreciate.

The currencies of these countries could be said to be valued in two markets: internally in terms of prices; externally in foreign exchange. In the early stages of depreciation, stabilizing speculation took place in both markets. Internally, observing that prices were rising, consumers postponed expenditures in the expectation that they would come down again. At the new level of income and higher prices, consumer saving balanced government deficits and business investment. Externally, foreign speculators, surprised at the low prices for the zloty, mark, shilling, and other currencies, bought them in the expectation of their return to initial or prewar pars.

The foreign stabilizing capital inflow supported the foreign exchange at a rate higher than would otherwise have been the case. In the exchange market the value of speculative purchases plus exports equaled imports, so that the capital inflow was transferred in goods. This import surplus had a braking effect on internal inflation, too, and, together with the consumers' savings, kept the external value of the currency above the internal value. In this phase the currency was overvalued in the foreign market relative to the domestic market.

But expectations of lower commodity prices and higher exchange rates were doomed to disappointment. After a time, the speculators became thoroughly disillusioned and reversed their positions. Consumers spent their income as fast as it was received and, to the extent made possible by past savings and bank credit, faster. The effect on the level of internal prices was explosive. In the external market foreign speculators reversed the field and took their losses, selling the currencies they had bought for the rise. And capital flight began, as domestic holders of currency sold it for foreign exchange.

No net capital movement out of these countries could take place, however, unless exports exceeded imports. With a freely fluctuating exchange and no gold support, depreciation had to proceed far enough to make, say, Poland a cheap place in which to buy before anyone with Polish marks (later the zloty) to sell for pounds could make the exchange. A domestic holder of capital could get pounds if he found a person willing to give up pounds for Polish marks. This would be the case only if the holder of pounds took a speculative view in favor of the Polish mark. After a time this was practically excluded. Or he could buy sterling if the depreciation in the exchange market proceeded faster than the internal depreciation, so that the exchange was undervalued and goods were cheap in Poland despite the rapidly rising price level. In this way an export surplus developed to transfer capital abroad. Some short-circuiting of the process took place after a time. Instead of attempting to buy foreign exchange at ruinous prices, a holder of the hyperinflated currency would buy goods which he would ship abroad for sale in foreign exchange. This method of capital export created its own export surplus and added to the internal inflation. But the explosive character of inflation under destabilizing speculation in both internal and external markets was so marked that it quickly brought about the collapse of currencies and the necessity for their stabilization or replacement by Draconian measures.

After World War II, with the memory of the postwar, hyperinflations of twenty-five years previous fresh in their minds, those countries which failed to maintain adequate controls or to institute monetary reforms reached the stage of explosive hyperinflation much faster. There was no stage of stabilizing speculation internally or externally, since no one believed in a return to normality. All who could took flight into foreign currencies or goods. After World War I the final breakdown of the mark took place in December, 1924, and the depreciation of the zloty was checked in the same year. This was six years after the Armistice. But in 1945–46 the Hungarian pengo lasted only nine months after V-E Day before its value fell to one octillionth.

Normal Capital Movements. Some economists make a distinction between normal and abnormal capital movements. In one sense, all international capital movements are abnormal, if we adopt the classical assumption that factors of production do not move internationally. But if we grant that capital does move, though insufficiently to equate interest rates among countries, a distinction between normal and abnormal movements may be appropriate.

During the nineteenth century, private capital moved from countries where it was plentiful and cheap to those where it was scarce and expensive. London, Paris, and Amsterdam lent. The rest of the world borrowed. Capital flowed from the low-interest-rate countries to the high-interest-rate countries.

It is clear enough that the London capital market will fix a rate of interest on Union Pacific Railroad bonds which will equate the return on capital, after allowance for risk, to the other rates in the London market. We are not talking in terms of this subjective discount, which operates internationally in the same way that it does within a country: a single rate of interest will prevail in a capital market in an abstract sense, even though the market yields on governments and grade B bonds will differ. The theoretical rate of interest is net of subjective risk. The market rate is not.

For present purposes, however, a normal capital movement is one from a country with a lower rate of interest to one with a higher, dealing not in subjective or theoretical rates but in market terms. An abnormal movement is one which runs from a high-interest-rate country to a low.

Some capital movements, abnormal in this restricted sense, are entirely normal insofar as business practice is concerned. Thus, for example, amortization payments or periodic repayments of principal are abnormal to the extent that the original loan was normal, in that the debtor high-interest-rate country is making payment to the low-interest-rate lender. Similarly, investments by a trust anxious to diversify its portfolio may run uphill in "abnormal" fashion, though they may constitute sound disposition of funds. But capital flight from an under-developed country is abnormal in an important respect in the balance of payments, whereas capital movements to such a country are typical and easily handled through the payments mechanism.

Normal Transfer. A normal capital movement is virtually certain to be spent in the borrowing country and to increase national income and imports. Exceptions occur. We have just discussed the German case, in which the bulk of the inflation caused by foreign borrowing—but not all—was offset by governmental deflation to pay reparations. But, as a general rule, borrowing by high-interest-rate countries is borrowing to spend. Deflation may not occur in the lending country. This is relatively unimportant, if income expansion in the borrower is assured.

The nineteenth-century lending was of this normal variety. So was the lending, with the partial exception noted, of the United States in the 1920's. Net long-term lending averaged close to $800 million a year from 1924 to 1928, inclusive, and no difficulty was experienced in its transfer. Gold movements were relatively small, on balance and gross, and can be explained largely in terms of short-term capital movements.

Abnormal Transfer. The capital inflow to the United States in the 1930's, however, was of an entirely different order. Fleeing for safety from taxation, devaluation, and outright confiscation, it failed either to decrease expenditure in the "lending" country or to expand it in the "borrowing." It has been said that the United States did not need foreign capital in the 1930's. This is true; but it fails to make clear why it did not use it. Foreign purchases of American securities raised their prices, relative to what they would otherwise have been; but United States firms did not respond by issuing more securities. Foreign purchases of bonds lowered interest rates, but no significant number of new borrowers chose to borrow. The demand for capital in the United States was inelastic with respect to the price of securities and the rate of interest at this time.

It does not inevitably follow that a normal or downhill movement of capital from a low-interest-rate country to a high will be spent by the borrower or that an uphill movement in the other direction will not be. But the presumption runs in this direction. On this account, transfer takes place fairly readily from the capital-rich to the capital-poor country. It is more difficult to effect from the poor to the rich.

Summary

The transfer process is the means of effecting a real capital movement from one country to another. In the case of autonomous unilateral payment, there is a money or purchasing-power transfer and ultimately a real transfer in goods. Classical economic thought believed that transfer was brought about by the price-specie-flow mechanism. Modern economists, beginning with Ohlin, have looked to income changes.

There is no need, however, for the purchasing-power movement to precede the real movement.

What happens to the terms of trade during transfer will depend upon the net movement in income in the two countries, upon the net marginal propensities to spend on domestic and imported goods, and upon the supply elasticities.

The theory of transfer was built on unilateral payments like the Franco-Prussian indemnity and German reparations after World War I. It has been applied, in a case of fluctuating exchanges, to the currency disorders after World War I. Most important, however, is to sort out normal and abnormal capital movements.

SUGGESTED READING

TREATISES, ETC.

See Haberler, chaps. vii and viii; Viner, chaps. vi, and vii. J. W. Angell summarized the theory in his *The Theory of International Prices* (Cambridge, Mass.: Harvard University Press, 1926). Iversen's monograph concentrated more directly on capital movements and extended the study to 1935. Bloomfield's chapter ix brings the account up to 1950.

The major studies in the verification of the classical views on transfer are:

J. H. Williams, *Argentine International Trade under Inconvertible Paper Money, 1880–1900* (Cambridge, Mass.: Harvard University Press, 1920).

J. Viner, *Canada's Balance of International Indebtedness, 1900–1913* (Cambridge, Mass.: Harvard University Press, 1924).

R. Wilson, *Capital Imports and the Terms of Trade* (Melbourne, Australia: University of Australia Press, 1931).

H. D. White, *The French International Accounts, 1880–1913* (Cambridge, Mass.: Harvard University Press, 1933).

Other monographic literature on the subject consists of:

R. Nurkse, *Internationale Kapitalbewegungen* (Vienna: Springer, 1935).

M. Fanno, *Normal and Abnormal International Capital Transfers* (Minneapolis: University of Minnesota Press, 1939).

E. E. Fleetwood, *Sweden's Capital Imports and Exports* (Stockholm: Natur och Kultur, 1947).

A. I. Bloomfield, *Capital Imports and the American Balance of Payments* (Chicago: University of Chicago Press, 1950).

The Viner monograph has been brought up to date in two articles, one by G. M. Meier who rewrites it in terms of income analysis "Economic Development and the Transfer Mechanism in Canada, 1895–1913," *Canadian Journal of Economics and Political Science,* February, 1953; the other by J. C. Ingram, "Growth and Canada's Balance of Payments," *AER,* March, 1957, who accounts for some of the puzzling phenomena of the actual experience by taking account of a factor missing in the present analysis, the increase in capacity resulting from the foreign borrowing.

The major article on transfer through income changes is L. A. Metzler's, found in the American Economic Association, *Readings,* No. 8. The Keynes-Ohlin controversy is also worthwhile reading for its summary of the state of economic understanding of the problem in the 1920's, and for the origins of the idea of spending changes. It is in the same volume, Nos. 6 and 7.

An excellent treatment of capital movements in the period following World War I is in R. Nurkse's, *The Course and Control of Inflation after World War I* (Princeton: League of Nations, 1946).

The literature on the terms of trade under transfer is rich and varied. See especially two articles by P. A. Samuelson in the *EJ,* June, 1952, and June, 1954; two by H. G. Johnson, *Econ,* May, 1955, and *JPE,* June, 1956; M. C. Kemp, *AER,* March, 1956; J. E. Meade's, *Geometry,* pp. 85 ff.

POINTS

The matrix technique on which the chapter leaned is set out by Meade in *The Balance of Payments,* pp. 36, 88–93, and 125–48.

| Chapter | BONDS, BANK LOANS, |
| 19 | GOVERNMENT LENDING |

Long-Term Debt

This and the following chapter discuss the two principal forms of long-term capital moving between national economies. This chapter deals with debt; the next with equity or ownership capital. The distinction between the two is perhaps too sharp. International trading in bonds already issued and listed on a bond exchange is hardly different from buying and selling by foreigners of New York stock exchange shares. Some points made about one or the other will apply, then, to both. But at the extremes the distinction is real enough.

The traditional form of long-term lending is the bond. For one hundred years, up to 1914, the sterling bond dominated world financial markets. For a period from 1919 to 1930, the New York bond market assumed the role previously played by London. But this interlude was brief. Excessive lending, international disequilibrium, depression, the collapse of export markets, the notoriety given to certain questionable practices by bond promoters, all combined to turn the investor away from foreign bonds, except for those of Canada, which are only quasi-foreign. With few but perhaps gradually increasing exceptions, moreover, borrowers no longer liked fixed obligations in an uncertain world. The foreign bond fell on evil days.

It is nonetheless worth some study. Its behavior differed from that of other forms of long-term debt, such as term bank loans and government lending, because foreign bonds were sold to private investors. The borrower might be governmental, but the lender was not. Investment banks underwrote the sale of bonds which were distributed through the capital market to private institutions and individual investors, whose concern lay with safety of principal and flow of income. The private character of the lenders gave bonds a distinct pattern of behavior affecting both the level of income in the borrowing and lending countries and the balance of payments.

The decline of the bond led to new forms of foreign lending. This chapter formally deals with bank loans and government lending. But banks may be private or governmental. In a world of private bonds, private banks will occasionally make loans for more than a year on the basis of the general credit of the borrower. Since 1930, however, private long-term lending by banks has been limited to advances against gilt-edged security, such as gold, or to loans made with governmental guarantees. Governmental lending has been carried on partly through banking institutions such as the Export-Import Bank in the United States and, since 1946, partly through international agencies like the International Bank for Reconstruction and Development. Other governmental lending has taken place through specially created institutions such as the Lend-Lease Administration, the Economic Cooperation Administration, the Mutual Security Agency, and the International Cooperation Administration, or has been arranged for particular purposes such as ship disposal or disposal of surplus commodities.

We may restrict ourselves, therefore, to private lending through the bond market, and government lending in its many long-term forms. The flow of capital through bank loans can be neglected on the grounds that it conforms largely to the principles of one or the other. To the extent that it has a character of its own, like the international mortgage market, the phenomenon is too small to deserve attention.

Countercyclical Lending

Foreign lending is similar to domestic investment, in that it increases national income and employment. The real transfer of capital abroad through an export surplus gives rise to a multiplier increase in money income, leading to expanded employment. Accordingly, the suggestion has been made that foreign investment should be used as a countercyclical device. Expand it in depression, contract it in boom, and the lending country will make progress toward cyclical stability.

This works out satisfactorily in an economic model. Let us imagine that country A has business cycles due to fluctuations in domestic investment, but that the rest of the world, called B, maintains stability of national income and of interest rates. In depression, the long-term rate of interest is likely to decline in A, making it a more attractive place for B to borrow. In prosperity, on the other hand, the rate of interest increases, making it a less desirable source of investment funds, so that foreign lending declines. Foreign lending expands in depression, contracts in prosperity, and serves as a balancing device to offset all or part of the changes in domestic spending in A.

More is called for than simply the funding of the export surplus which results from the decline in income and the consequent fall in imports relative to exports. This is a task for short-term capital movements; it is needed to sustain the level of exports. Countercyclical foreign lending, however, would produce a positive expansion in exports. In Figure 19.1 national income has decreased from Y to Y' as a

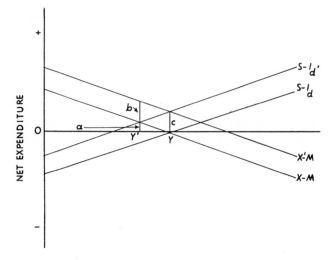

FIG. 19.1.   Countercyclical Foreign Lending

result of a decline in investment which shifted the $S-I_d$ schedule upward to $S-I_d'$; the movement along the $X-M$ schedule produces the export surplus, a. But countercyclical lending calls for an upward shift in the $X-M$ schedule, say to $X'-M$, in which the upward shift by b produces an export surplus of c equal to b, at the new level of income Y. The derived export surplus, a, is wiped out by the reinduced imports.

The Cyclical Pattern of Lending

There is nothing really wrong with this model except that it is not particularly relevant to today's world.

Prior to 1914, international long-term lending, particularly by Britain, tended to be countercyclical except at the turning points. The position was as if there were a given fund of investible resources: when home investment boomed, foreign borrowers went without, but when recession set in at home, loanable funds sought new opportunities for investment abroad. On occasion, home and foreign investment moved together at the turning points, recovering together in the early stages, and declining together in the period of early recession. Cairncross has elaborated this model to suggest the role of the terms of trade as an allocator of these capital resources: when the terms of trade went against Britain in depression, capital moved abroad; in the succeeding boom when prices overseas fell, the terms of trade favored Britain and home investment.

But this pattern, which represented a broad tendency rather than a detailed description, changed after World War I. Private long-term lending tended to be correlated positively with domestic investment, again with the exception of the turning points. The reason is to be found in the familiar acceleration principle.

The decline in domestic investment which leads to a fall in income and imports also affects the prospects for investment abroad. Exports of the foreign country have fallen. In consequence, its national income declines. The country therefore becomes a less attractive place to which to make loans. This is the simple acceleration principle: increases in investment abroad will follow increases in sales, not decreases. In addition, however, the decline in exports in the potential borrower dims the outlook for transfer of interest and amortization on new loans through the foreign exchanges. The higher the level of exports, the more credit a country appears to foreigners to deserve; the lower, the less credit-worthy it seems to be. The acceleration principle makes foreign loans fluctuate positively in the business cycle through variations in the profitability of the export sector in the borrowing country and in its balance of payments.

It is true that the recession phase of the cycle is an excellent time in which to make profitable loans, provided that one can be assured that recovery will ultimately follow. This argument for countercyclical private lending applies as well to domestic loans or purchases of securities. The reason why business is depressed, however, is that not enough people are convinced of the inevitability of recovery.

The positive correlation between domestic and foreign investment is not perfect, however, and may become particularly involved at the turning points. This is due to the behavior of the rate of interest. In late 1928 and early 1929, for example, when the expansion phase of the business cycle in the United States brought about a sharp rise in stock-market speculation and in the rate of interest, foreign lending slumped badly as the call-money market bid for funds for use in brokers' loans. Immediately after the crash, moreover, interest rates declined and led to a short-lived revival in foreign lending. The interest-rate pattern peculiar to a given cycle may cause foreign long-term lending to deviate in some degree from the fluctuations in domestic investment. By and large, however, private lending will be high in prosperity and low in depression, as the over-all force of the accelerator swamps any balancing effects which may be produced through changes in relative interest rates.

The cyclical movement of long-term capital thus accentuates the cyclical problems of countries engaged in the production of primary products. In depression their supply of foreign exchange is reduced on two scores: exports are cut and, with them, foreign borrowing. From the point of view of the lending country, there is a double source of instability—domestic investment, which builds cumulatively up or runs cumulatively down, to produce changes in national income, and foreign investment, which acts in the same way.

We may anticipate our later remarks on government lending to say that a shift from private to government long-term lending does not change this position as much as one would be inclined to think at first blush. The idea of countercyclical spending on domestic public works runs afoul of the fact that much government spending—on roads, schools, post offices, hospitals, etc.—either is not capable of being postponed through a long period of prosperity or is positively geared with the cycle. In prosperity, for example, the expansion of private housing must be accompanied by roads, schools, etc., furnished by public funds. In the same fashion, many of the purposes for which foreign governments are anxious to borrow, and other governments or international institutions are willing to lend, either will be related to the expansion phase of a business cycle based on exports or will not be postponable in time, so that they may be accumulated for depression.

The International Bank for Reconstruction and Development was required by its articles of agreement to do what it could to smooth out business-cycle fluctuations: "The purposes of the bank are: . . . (v) To conduct its operations with due regard to the effect of international investment on business conditions in the territories of its members."

In the event, however, it has stated that its primary task must be economic development, and any major attention to anticyclical timing would come into conflict with this concern.

One can, and below we do, argue that foreign investment is a second-best alternative to domestic investment undertaken simultaneously in a number of countries, or in the case posed in Figure 19.1, investment at home by itself. The international economic position is always most effectively assisted by undertaking home remedies for home difficulties. But even if it were highly desirable to offset home depression by foreign lending in the present pattern of international capital movements, it does not seem very practicable.

Institutional Pattern and Governmental Control

It should be admitted that the international market in capital is far from a perfect one, and the flow of capital between countries is dominated by subjective considerations of risk perhaps as much or more than the quoted return on capital. In addition, the role of investment bankers is important. The result is that lending seems to continue in well-worn channels to a greater extent than can be accounted for by market phenomena or an objective evaluation of the risks. In addition, there has been a considerable degree of government control. The consequence has been that capital movements conform to a rather idiosyncratic institutional pattern, and their understanding calls more for the techniques of the historian than for those of the economic analyst.

Up to 1870, British lending concentrated on the European Continent, and in particular on financing railroad construction, textile mills, steel. In addition, there was some financing, in which German and French investors persisted, of budget deficits, personal extravagance, armaments, and strategic railroads. After 1870, however, with the growing bonds of world trade resulting from the reduction in the cost of ocean shipping, British investors turned attention to the United States, the Dominions, and to a lesser extent the colonies. After World War II, even while capital was tight at home and being obtained from the United States in various ways, a steady flow of capital was maintained to the flourishing Dominions.

French, German, and United States long-term investments were equally channeled into particular grooves. In the interwar period, the United States loaned heavily to Canada, Germany, and Latin America, with but little interest in the rest of the world.

There has been a long history of government interference with and control of private foreign lending which accounts for some of this rigidity of pattern.

In France, during the latter half of the nineteenth century, government control was used to channel French foreign investment into those countries with which the French foreign office was attempting to cement alliances. Much of the French investment, in fact, went to czarist Russia and was repudiated by the successor Soviet government.

In the United States in the 1920's, the State Department asked the financial community to advise it of contemplated loans, so that it might enter an objection to a loan whose purposes were contrary to United States foreign policy. The basis for possible objection was purely political and had nothing to do with the soundness of the loan in question. Later, when the Securities and Exchange Commission was established, foreign borrowers, including foreign governments, were required by law to file a registration statement with the commission, prior to the issuance of new obligations, setting forth a host of financial data by which the soundness of the loan might be judged. It will not surprise systematic readers of this work to learn that these data included balance-of-payments statements, as well as material on the national income, government expenditure and receipts, etc. The SEC passed no judgment on the merits of a particular loan but was concerned solely to ensure that the borrower made full disclosure of information which would enable a purchaser of the bonds to judge these merits for himself.

Diplomatic representations are also made by governments in connection with default on obligations to their nationals by foreign governments. In another day, not long ago, United States Marines were used to protect United States property abroad and to assist foreign countries in the recognition of obligations to American investors. Today, questions of default are regarded as primarily the concern of private groups, such as the Council of Foreign Bondholders in the United States. These groups are entitled to and receive the support of their governments in presenting their cases, to such an extent in Britain that the United Kingdom council is regarded as a quasi-official body. This concern and assistance of government, however, are far from "control."

Government has been associated with international lending in other ways. The Johnson Act of 1934, for example, prohibited borrowing from the public by foreign governments which were in default on obligations to the United States government. This act, passed at the peak of isolationist sentiment in the United States, did not have to be repealed to enable the United States to lend to Britain in the early stages of World War II. It did not apply to the government itself or to its subsidiaries like the Reconstruction Finance Corporation. Even if it had, there might still have been room for the United States to lease or give equipment to other nations, under some such authority as that of the Lend-Lease Act of 1941, so long as it did not lend money.

Governmental controls have, then, been used to interfere in the private process of foreign borrowing and lending for political reasons or for the protection of domestic investors. On occasion, however, these controls have been relied upon as a measure of economic policy. Slowing down foreign borrowing in a country may be sought in order to favor domestic investment to increase employment or in order to relieve pressure on the balance of payments, or both. These were among the purposes of control by the Capital Issues Committee in London after 1931. The student is aware, of course, that, once real transfer outward has taken place, foreign investment gives as much employment as domestic investment, if the same factor proportions are used in the domestic and export sectors of the economy. Restriction on foreign capital issues, however, has been undertaken with the idea of preventing that initial pressure on the balance of payments which occurs in the process of transfer, or perhaps with the view that real transfer is unlikely to take place and that the initial loss of gold or depreciation of the exchange is likely to be permanent.

Recently there have been attempts by government to stimulate foreign lending. Most of these efforts lie in the field of direct investment, discussed in the following chapter, and are concerned with matters of discrimination and taxation. In this area, however, it has been found impossible to push on a string. Government can restrain private foreign investment, but it cannot effectively stimulate it. The collapse of the market for foreign bonds in New York after 1930 has remained complete. Refunding issues are sold from time to time for preferred borrowers like Australia, Denmark, and Norway; and an occasional new loan is made for a Canadian borrower. More than this it has been impossible to achieve. To the extent that foreign lending on long-term capital account has taken place, with lending distinguished from the purchase of equities in direct investment, it has proved necessary for this to be done by governments.

Stabilization Loans

Two general types of governmental (and banking) loans may be distinguished: the stabilization loan and that for financing particular exports of the lender or imports of the borrower. Like others, this distinction cannot be rigidly maintained. The British Loan of $3,750,-000,000 of 1946, for example, was intended primarily as a stabilization loan, to enable the British government to maintain convertibility of sterling into dollars; but it was recognized that a year would have to go by before it would be possible to achieve convertibility and that during this time some of the loan, at least, would have to go to pay for imports needed for British reconstruction.

Purely stabilization loans were made to replenish foreign exchange reserves, especially during the 1920's. Many of these were made by governments, but in some cases, particularly the Dawes and Young loans, the American *tranche*—international finance word for "share" or "portion"—was subscribed by private banks or by the public. In World War I the British government asked J. P. Morgan and Company to act as its agent in stabilizing the pound sterling in the New York market, buying pounds with dollars whenever the rate fell below the rate stipulated by the British authorities. Later, the same banking house loaned the British government funds for this purpose.

Stabilization loans and those to finance imports differ from those for purchasing power in general, in that they are sought in order to get command over foreign purchasing power and present no transfer problem. The fully successful stabilization loan may never be used. Its existence convinces speculators of the strength of the currency, so that speculation becomes stabilizing. In these circumstances the long-term stabilization loan is balanced by short-term borrowing as the funds are held unused on deposit in the lending country. No money changes hands, and no real transfer takes place.

Occasionally, for psychological effect, a stabilization loan is made in gold. It was a frequent suggestion after World War II that $1 billion or some such sum in gold be loaned to the Bank of France and paraded through every town and village in a showcase, to persuade the peasantry of the strength of the currency and induce it to dishoard its louis d'or, napoleons, and eagles (all gold coins). The suggestion was, of course, partly or largely ironical, but it indicates that stabilization loans need not be used.

A more effective example is found in the means taken by the British government to meet the pressure on sterling after the Suez crisis in the fall of 1956. Dollars were purchased from the International Monetary Fund, and a further stand-by IMF credit was arranged; a line of credit backed by dollar securities owned by British nationals was negotiated with the Export-Import Bank. This technique, referred to as "putting the reserves in the front window," was successful. Speculation halted before the necessity to use either credit.

Borrowing to Finance Imports

Prior to 1930, government borrowing took place for stabilization purposes, to finance needed imports, as in the postwar reconstruction loans, or to obtain general purchasing power on reasonable terms. Borrowing at home was expensive in the capital-poor countries; borrowing abroad could take place at much lower interest rates and was cheaper.

The spread of cheap-money principles and practices after 1930, however, eliminated borrowing for general purchasing power. Any government could borrow at home as cheaply as abroad, and generally more cheaply, since it was not necessary to pay a premium to compensate the lender for risks such as that of exchange depreciation. The result was that governmental loans other than for stabilization purposes were limited to those needed to finance imports.

During the depression the initiative for these loans came from the exporting and lending country, anxious to expand income and employment. These might more properly be called loans to finance exports. After World War II, however, the impetus reversed itself. Countries engaged in the process of reconstruction of economic development were bent on financing additional imports.

In the postwar period these changes eliminated the transfer problem of the 1920's. The problem became one of finding finance for an import surplus rather than generating an import surplus to transfer a loan.

But we may spend a moment on the evolution of this type of lending from the depression institution designed to expand exports and discuss the development of the Export-Import Bank.

The Export-Import Bank

The Export-Import Bank was one of the first quasi-banking institutions formed with government funds to finance trade on an intermediate-term basis. Private banking and acceptance houses had been slow in developing capacities in this field. Most of their finance has been short-term in character. Started in 1934, the Export-Import Bank also began slowly.

Although it claimed to be different from the governmental departments established in Europe to guarantee intermediate-term export credits, the Export-Import Bank has never, in fact, financed an import transaction. Its purpose was to expand exports in order to raise prices and to expand income. Some of the early products concerned were agricultural. Some credits were made to finance the export of durable goods for which intermediate credit of more than a year is needed and appropriate. In certain cases, loans were made to firms hampered by exchange control to enable them to receive payment on blocked debts.

At the end of 1938 the Export-Import Bank had disbursed some $61 million in loans and had been repaid to the extent of $35 million, leaving an outstanding net figure of $26 million. Under the act renewing the charter of the bank, passed in 1939, a limit of $100 million was set on credits which could be outstanding at any time. The wartime renewal of the charter in 1941 was the occasion for an increase in this amount to $500 million. This increase in lending was needed to enable the United States to assist Latin-American countries in their adjustment to war conditions. In August, 1945, while the United States was waiting for the International Monetary Fund and the International Bank to get organized and into operation, this sum was further increased to $3.5 billion, largely for purposes of reconstruction loans. The Gray *Report to the President on Foreign Economic Policies,* published in 1950, recommended that the capital of the bank be increased another $1.5 billion to $5 billion to enlarge the capacity of the bank for assisting in the economic development of underdeveloped areas. This last recommendation, however, has not been acted upon by the Congress but was revived in 1958 in modified form.

Tied Loans

The origin of the Export-Import Bank in depression led to an early congressional restriction on the use of its loans to finance United States trade. The proceeds of the bank's loans, for example, could not be used to buy goods in Britain. They were tied to United States exports. In subsequent legislation, a stipulation was included that these goods had to be shipped in American bottoms, where such were available, and, still later, that marine insurance coverage against the risks of transit must be placed with American underwriters.

The restriction of the use of credits to United States goods was of little consequence during the depression, in wartime finance, or during the immediate postwar period. In the first of these the United States wanted to sell goods. The lending was tied to the selling rather than the selling to the lending. However objectionable it might be from the point of view of commercial policy, it is not what we are here discussing. In the second two, the foreign country was anxious to buy goods, and the United States desirous that it should buy them, these goods being obtainable only in the United States. The United States was probably the cheapest place in which to buy the goods, so that the requirement that they be bought from this country was not, in practice, discriminatory. When the borrowing country is concerned with domestic investment rather than with the financing of its imports, however, tied loans can present a considerable obstacle.

Let us assume that a country wants to undertake the construction of a railroad as part of a program of economic development. The total cost of the project amounts to $100 million. Of this total, $50 million, we may say, represent the foreign-exchange value of materials and equipment which must be bought from abroad; the remaining $50 million constitute costs to be incurred in local currency.

Under a system of tied loans, only $50 million could be borrowed in the United States, since the borrower must specify what United States goods are to be purchased with the loan. The United States may or may not be the cheapest place to buy the goods, but the loan is tied to United States goods. The remaining $50 million expended locally are likely to give rise to a foreign-exchange requirement. Whether they will or not will depend upon how the local funds are obtained. If they are acquired through new savings or through taxation which reduces consumption, then the expenditure is not inflationary, i.e., does not increase national money income or imports. If, on the other hand, as is frequently the case, some part or all of the local expenditure is financed through credit creation or deficit spending, the domestic expenditure will spill over into new imports. How large an increase in imports will occur depends, of course, on the marginal propensities to import and save, leaving aside the foreign repercussion. But there is no foreign exchange from the loan available to finance the incremental imports. The transfer process works only for the first round of spending. Any increase from subsequent rounds of spending will have to be paid for out of reserves or, if these are inadequate, will lead to depreciation or foreign-exchange control.

Tied loans have been evoked by some deep-seated mercantilistic instinct in people. In 1949, the Indian government tried to use some dollar aid made available to it by the United States to buy locomotives in Japan. There was a hue and cry against this ungrateful way of dealing with United States generosity, and the United States government felt itself obliged to make additional loans to India so that it could buy some locomotives, much more expensively, in that country. Some years ago Adam Smith excoriated the similar practice of buying only from one's own customers and called it the "sneaking art of underlying tradesmen." But even universities have practiced it in requiring scholarship recipients to live in the dormitories, or to take meals at the Student Union, when these were operating below capacity.

The Project Basis for Loans

The International Bank for Reconstruction and Development started out to make what were essentially tied loans, although the officials of the bank deny that they can properly be called such. Loans were made on a project basis, i.e., a borrowing country had to indicate the purpose for which the loan was sought, and this could not be so vague as "to fill the deficit in the budget." Moreover, the borrower originally was required to specify what new imports were needed for the project, and where these would be bought. If it approved the project and regarded the imports as reasonable, the bank was then prepared to lend the moneys needed to finance the imports.

This procedure, which the bank has now altered, was objectionable on two scores. It was "discriminatory," and it was likely to increase rather than mitigate the foreign-exchange difficulties of the borrowing country. The discriminatory feature is found in the fact that the bank loaned currency which the country expected to spend, rather than loaning purchasing power in general. In a completely nondiscriminatory system, loans would be provided from the cheapest source—that is, the money market with the lowest interest rates—and the proceeds of these loans would be spent where the goods sought were cheapest. Dollars might be borrowed and spent in Britain, or, as during the nineteenth century, pounds might be borrowed and spent on the Continent. To loan only the currencies to be spent is to require the borrower either to borrow in the dearer market for loans or to buy in the dearer market for goods, unless the cheapest markets for goods and loans are the same. This objection was not perhaps important in practice up to 1950, because goods as well as loans were cheaper in the United States. But the principle of tying the currency of the loan to the currency of the projected import is discriminatory.

In the second place, a loan limited to the cost of imports needed for a project is insufficient to balance the international accounts except in the limiting case where all the local expenditure is raised in a deflationary fashion. Any inflationary financing of local expenditures of the project will raise income and imports and unbalance the international accounts. Purchasing power in general is neglected in favor of a limited amount of foreign purchasing power in particular. These loans and projects worsened rather than improved the country's balance of payments.

Capacity to Absorb Capital

The International Bank, which we discuss at greater length below, has argued that the problem it faces is not lack of funds but lack of projects. The capacity to absorb foreign loans, it holds, is limited. What determines the capacity to absorb loans?

If we regard loans as needed primarily to buy foreign capital equipment, the capacity to absorb loans is a function of the number of investment projects, on the one hand, and their foreign-exchange content, on the other. But this, as we have tried to show at some length, is inadmissable. A country borrows not to get command of particular foreign resources but in the usual case to get command over resources in general. If it borrows funds abroad to buy capital equipment and is unable to increase domestic saving, or cut other domestic investment projects, it needs further foreign loans to cover the imports induced by the inflationary investment at home. And if it can increase savings sufficiently, or cut other investment projects *and* shift resources between the domestic and the export and import-competing sectors of the economy, it does not need loans from abroad to buy foreign equipment. It can either reduce imports and shift the resources freed by savings or the cut in investment into the production of substitutes, or expand exports from the same source. If a country has sufficient capacity to reallocate its resources among sectors, the capacity to absorb capital is infinite.

To insist then that foreign loans are needed to buy foreign capital equipment is wrong except in the limiting case where the capacity to transform resources from one sector to another is zero. The corollary of the dictum that loans should not be tied to the foreign-exchange content of particular investment projects is that foreign loans represent resources in general rather than resources in particular—at least to the extent that a country can succeed in reallocating resources among sectors. And if it cannot reallocate resources at all, it is a very risky country to which to lend.

Normal Capital Movements

The notion that the appropriate source of international loans is the capital market with the lowest rate of interest takes us back to the question of normal and abnormal capital movements. This is needed to indicate why government lending may be required as a substitute for private when private lending dries up for one reason or another.

Let us look behind cheap-money rates obtained through vast increases in liquidity in the money market, and consider the marginal efficiency of capital. Assuming no widespread external economies and diseconomies which distort market prices from social values, this will be low in countries with a great deal of capital relative to land and labor, and should be high in countries where capital is scarce unless other resources such as labor cannot effectively use capital through lack of training. If the relationship between savings and investment can differ from one country to another, it follows that savings are likely to be in excess of investment in countries with a lot of capital, and therefore a low marginal efficiency of capital and possibly lower rates of interest than elsewhere; and investment will tend to exceed savings in the country with a high marginal efficiency of capital and high interest rates. If

$$X + Id = S + M$$

and

$$S \text{ tends to be greater than } Id,$$

then it follows that X tends to be greater than M.

This helps to explain why normal capital movements are readily transferred out of low-interest-rate countries and why abnormal capital movements to such countries must be transferred, if at all, in gold movements or through currency depreciation.

Conversely, of course, if Id tends to be greater than S, it follows that M tends to exceed X. This helps to explain why normal capital movements can be transferred readily inward to countries which lack capital, whereas capital exports are difficult to transfer out.

The corollary of all this is that when a country cannot or will not balance domestic savings and investment, it tends to have an export surplus or an import surplus, depending upon whether savings tend to outrun domestic investment or the other way round. This is true whether foreign loans are being made or sought. In the case of a country where savings are high relative to investment opportunities, business will look for foreign sales in an effort to counteract the softness of the domestic market. In opposite circumstances, when investment opportunities tend to outrun savings, business will look abroad for goods to carry out its plans.

One remedy for this situation is to effect balance between domestic investment and savings. That is, if $Id = S$, then $X = M$. But, under certain conditions, savings or investment or both may be inelastic in their response to changes in the rate of interest and may be slow in response to other measures to bring them into equilibrium. In these circumstances, it may be appropriate to lend or borrow abroad. Without the lending, there will be transfer, i.e., an import surplus, but no properly funded loans.

Where private foreign lending is dormant for any reason, governmental loans may be needed to finance the disequilibrium in the balance of payments. The remedy for the export surplus may not be more imports but more loans (and, for the import surplus, not exports but more borrowing). In subsequent chapters we shall try to relate these possibilities more closely to the stages in the development of a country. At the moment, it is enough to make the point that governmental loans may be needed to bring the international accounts into balance, in the absence of private lending and of other measures by which domestic investment and savings can be equalized.

Cumulative Lending

Some observers have raised an objection, however, that foreign loans cannot long offset a deficiency of domestic investment opportunities because of interest and possible amortization. Suppose, it is argued, a country wants to maintain an export surplus on current account of $1 billion annually. The first year it can lend $1 billion abroad. The subsequent year, however, it will have to lend $1 billion more, plus enough to enable the foreign borrowers to pay interest on the first

TABLE 19.1

ANNUAL AMOUNT OF TWENTY-YEAR LOANS REQUIRED, AT VARIOUS
INTEREST RATES, TO MAINTAIN AN ANNUAL EXPORT SURPLUS OF
$1,000,000,000*
(In Billions of Dollars)

YEAR	PER CENT				
	2	3	4	5	6
5th	1.35	1.38	1.43	1.47	1.52
10th	1.81	1.92	2.03	2.16	2.31
15th	2.44	2.65	2.90	3.18	3.50
20th	3.28	3.67	4.14	4.68	5.32
25th	4.41	5.08	5.90	6.88	8.09

* It is assumed that the sum of interest plus amortization on each loan is paid in equal installments.

year's loan and amortization, if the loan contract calls for regular repayments. The higher the rates of interest and amortization, the more rapidly will the rate of lending increase to sustain the stipulated export surplus. Table 19.1, taken from an article by Hinshaw, shows the effect of interest at various rates with amortization. In another table which we do not reproduce, the compound interest arithmetic is carried still further; $46.90 billion would have to be invested as a perpetual loan without amortization if one assumes 8 per cent interest and calculates the requirement for the fiftieth year.

This analysis is applicable to amortization, which is an abnormal capital movement involving difficulties of transfer unless offset by new capital lending. The Export-Import Bank, and increasingly the International Bank for Reconstruction and Development, must undertake each year a substantial amount of new loans if they are to avoid the contractual repayments on old loans producing an inward movement of capital to the dollar area from weaker currencies. To help equalize marginal efficiencies of capital, movement of capital from capital-rich to capital-poor countries should involve perpetual loans, like fixed assets which are kept intact, or British consols. In fact, however, the loans are made for short periods and involve periodic repayments of principal.

The requirement of amortization is a further illustration of the fallacy of composition: useful in the case of an individual loan, it complicates foreign lending as a whole by constituting an uphill movement of capital unless offset by new loans.

Leaving aside amortization, the charging of interest on old loans seems to raise a problem. If lending stops, the payment of contractual interest turns the balance of trade against the lending country. The rate of increase in foreign loans outstanding must equal the rate of interest received on foreign loans to prevent such a shift. If the productivity and income of a country grow at the same rate as the level of the rate of interest at which it lends abroad, and it, on this account, lends abroad at the same rate, the balance of trade, other things equal, will remain constant.

But this analysis is uninteresting. It is partial-equilibrium in character when it should not be, holding other things equal when in the nature of the event they must alter. It makes no sense to cling to the objective of maintaining a constant export surplus as the only way of offsetting an existing excess of savings over investment opportunities, if in fact the receipt of income from abroad raises spending for consumption and gives employment to the resources involved. Nor is the borrowing country condemned to borrow in order to pay interest, if in fact the original loan is invested productively and yields an income out of which interest can be paid. The problem of a geometric growth of lending to stay in the same place would be a real one only if all income from loans were saved, on the one hand, and all loans were consumed rather than invested in capital formation, on the other.

Take first the lending country. It lends and receives an income in the first year. This income has a multiplier effect just like, or almost just like, an increase in exports. The monies from abroad will be partly spent on domestic goods, partly spent on imports, and partly saved. The amount saved in the first round of income creation reduces the multi-

plier below that for normal exports, so that the foreign-interest multiplier may be somewhat smaller than the foreign-trade multiplier. It is
analogous to the balanced-budget theorem known to students with a
knowledge of the finer points of income analysis. That portion spent
at home in the first and respent in subsequent rounds of spending, however, will employ part of the resources previously engaged in foreign
investment. Progressively the need to maintain an export surplus will
diminish.

In the borrowing country, in turn, the notion that a country must
borrow to pay interest on old loans is nonsense. Old loans pay their own
way through increased productivity *and* the transformation of the economy which shifts resources among sectors. It is sometimes held that
investment must take place in the export or in the import-competing
sector to transfer interest on the loans. This is true in the limiting case
when resources cannot be shifted among sectors. If the loans are truly
productive, however, and if the new product releases resources which
can be shifted by the price mechanism or by other means into additional
exports or relieving the necessity to buy existing imports, the old loans
pay their own way. Back of every loan should be capital formation, all
capital should produce more than enough to pay the interest, and any
borrowing economy should be able to induce the marginal shifts in resources thus required.

A significant conclusion regarding interest payments emerges
from this demonstration. When a visible export surplus is financed by
interest-bearing loans, the receipt of interest means that the trade balance is doomed to destruction. Interest income replaces export income
from visible trade.

This can also be reversed. When a merchandise import surplus
is financed by interest-bearing loans, it is necessary to shift to an export
surplus of merchandise trade, but not of the current account as a
whole, to pay interest on accumulated debt. This explains the behavior
of the balance of payments of the United States in the nineteenth century, which we explore more fully in Chapter 21.

By the same token, interest-free loans, or grants which require
no repayment whatsoever, have no effect on the merchandise trade balance of the future. The export surplus of a country carries the seeds of
its own destruction only when it is financed on an interest-bearing basis.

Summary

While proposals have been made to stabilize the balance of payments through the course of the business cycle by countercyclical, long-

term lending, private long-term lending has typically accentuated cyclical balance-of-payments difficulties by being positively correlated with domestic investment. Because of the foreign-trade accelerator, which encourages investments when foreign trade is booming, there is some likelihood that governments, like the International Bank, will have difficulty in achieving a countercyclical pattern of lending. Some gain would be achieved, however, if long-term lending was stabilized.

Stabilization loans are loans of international reserves. These succeed most when the funds do not have to be used.

Loans to finance imports involve the real transfer prior to the transfer of purchasing power. In the depression, these were pushed by the exporting country. After World War II, the importing countries sought goods to enable them to sustain a higher level of consumption and investment.

The tied loans of the Export-Import Bank and the project basis for loans of the International Bank restrict the multilateralization of payments.

Some observers have worried that international, long-term lending will not usefully offset a domestic excess of savings because of the necessity for this lending to rise in geometric fashion in order to take care of the repayment of interest and principal. This view, however, overlooks the effects of the foreign-interest multiplier, and the productivity of capital in the borrowing countries.

SUGGESTED READING

TREATISES, ETC.

For institutional treatments, see the Royal Institute of International Affairs, *The Problem of International Investment* (London: Oxford University Press, 1937); C. Lewis, *America's Stake in International Investments* (Washington, D.C.: Brookings Institution, 1938); and *The United States and Foreign Investment Problems* (Washington, D.C.: Brookings Institution, 1948).

N. Buchanan, *International Investment and Domestic Welfare* (New York: Henry Holt & Co., Inc., 1945), is worthwhile. Section III of the *Staff Papers* presented to the Commission on Foreign Economic Policy (Randall Commission, Washington, G.P.O., February, 1954), discusses modern problems of foreign investment.

POINTS

On the Export-Import Bank, see C. R. Whittlesey, "Five Years of the Export-Import Bank," *AER,* September, 1939; G. Patterson, "The Export-Import Bank," *QJE,* November, 1943.

On the compound-interest problem, see R. Hinshaw, "Foreign Investment and American Employment," *AER*, May, 1946; W. S. Salant, "The Domestic Effects of Capital Export under the Point Four Program," *AER*, May, 1950; and E. D. Domar, "Foreign Investment and the Balance of Payments," *AER*, December, 1950.

A recommendation for anticyclical foreign lending can be found in League of Nations, *Economic Stability in the Postwar World* (Geneva: League of Nations, 1945).

For accounts of nineteenth-century lending by Britain, see L. H. Jenks, *The Migration of British Capital to 1875* (New York: Alfred A. Knopf, Inc., 1927); H. Feis, *Europe: The World's Banker, 1870–1913* (New Haven: Yale University Press, 1931); C. K. Hobson, *The Export of Capital* (London: Constable, 1914); and A. K. Cairncross, *Home and Foreign Investment, 1870–1913* (Cambridge: Cambridge University Press, 1953).

M. F. Millikan and W. W. Rostow discuss the concept of a country's capacity to absorb capital in *A Proposal: Key to United States Foreign Policy* (New York: Harper & Bros., 1957).

Chapter 20

DIRECT INVESTMENT

Nature of Direct Investment

Long-term foreign investment in equity securities and direct investment are divided by a shadowy line. The distinction turns on control. Generally, 51 per cent ownership is sufficient to establish control, except in certain areas where two thirds or three quarters of the owners must vote together to effect certain kinds of changes. But 51 per cent is rarely a necessary condition. If a company has many shareholders, widely scattered and unorganized, a much smaller percentage of ownership will carry with it *de facto*, if not legal, control.

The question of control bristles with legal and practical difficulties. In a wide variety of cases, foreign operations are conducted by corporations specially organized for the purpose. What are the nationalities of the corporation and its assets? In such questions as compensation for nationalization, liability to suffer reparations, necessity to contribute to obligatory war-risk insurance, etc., the question of nationality is important. Most, but not all, countries "pierce the corporate veil," i.e., disregard the nationality of the corporation as such to look at the nationality of the stockholders. A 100 per cent American-owned enterprise in Britain is regarded as American by the Department of State, which pierces the corporate veil; but it is regarded as British by the British Foreign Office, which typically does not. (Both the British and American state departments take the opposite point of view in cases where it is singularly favorable to their position to do so.) But the State Department in the United States has taken the position that any corporation which is 48 per cent American-owned is American.

Practically, the question is where decisions are made and orders come from. Here all sorts of possible shadings are found. A small but cohesive minority of foreigners may operate the corporation, despite a wide majority of national ownership. Or, as in the case of many Canadian corporations with a majority of American stockholders, the local

390

minority may run the company. Or still more complex cases exist where foreign interests are in the minority but sufficiently strong so that the controlling domestic interest must take them into account in the formation of major decisions.

In this chapter we shall be talking about some measure of control. There is considerable investment in equity securities by unorganized individual stockholders from outside the country who want to participate in earnings but not in decisions. Speculation by foreigners in the New York stock market is an interesting subject, but one which will not concern us. Purchase and sale of existing or newly issued equity securities are significant for us only when they affect some element or aspect of control. This is because we shall later be concerned with the practical relevance of direct investment to specific problems, particularly economic development. For the same reason, we shall not take account of small equity investments in houses, farms, estates, or small enterprises, even though these do carry control. The impact of this control is too narrow and small.

Kinds of Direct Investment

It is sometimes useful to make distinctions among direct investments on a legal basis. To restrict ourselves primarily to national examples—foreign assets may be owned directly by an American corporation; by 100 per cent owned foreign affiliates; by American corporations organized to do business abroad; or through partial American ownership in foreign corporations. The Standard Oil Company of New Jersey, Ford International, the General Motors Corporation, the United Fruit Company, and International Business Machines are illustrations of the first. Examples of the second are legion. American Foreign Power, the International Telephone and Telegraph, Silesian American Corporation, and the Caltex Company are American companies organized to operate abroad. International Nickel, Dome Mines, Adam Opel, AG, and the Allgemeine Electrizitäts Gesellschaft are (or were) foreign corporations with a large American interest.

How foreign-controlled assets are held is important for many questions of income taxes, foreign-exchange control, capacity to qualify under laws, etc. These questions need not detain us long. It may be well to recall that an agency is treated like a resident in balance-of-payments reporting, while a foreign branch is treated as a foreigner. In many cases this comes to practically the same thing. But there may be significant differences in the bargaining positions of a foreign company and the exchange-control authorities, depending upon whether the company is fully subject to the local sovereignty or not. If it is, the proceeds of exports will be collected by the foreign-exchange control, and remittance of profits, if any, will take place at the pleasure of the control. If it is not, the foreign corporation may export goods—copper, oil, bananas—and keep the profits in foreign exchange on a given transaction. When the time comes for the next transaction, however, the foreign-exchange control may alter the rate at which it sells local currency for the payment of wages and local materials, or the local government may insist upon a larger share of taxes. If the company is concerned to stay in business over a long period, the short-run difference in practice from the alternative legal bases may not be wide.

But these legal matters are not our concern. There is more interest for us in how these direct investments are related to foreign trade. From the point of view of the investing country, we may distinguish three possibilities: investments which tend to increase imports, investments which substitute for exports, and those which are not directly concerned with foreign trade.

Investments to Increase Imports

British direct investments in the nineteenth century typically were related to the expansion of the supply of commodities for sale to Britain, either through increased production or through cheapened transport. The railroad investments in Europe, the Americas, and Asia performed important services in the local economy. But they were designed—not consciously perhaps so much as by the invisible hand—to gain access to ports for products for shipment to the London market. Investments in plantations, in refrigeration plants, in mines, and in oil wells were of the same general character. American investments in oil, bananas, sugar, rubber, mining, gold, nickel, etc., follow a well-developed British prototype.

For the most part, direct investment for sale to the investing country's market is based on absolute rather than comparative advantage, or upon a uniquely favored natural resource, such as oil or mineral deposits. The expansion of consumption in the United States and the depletion of existing mineral deposits have tended to produce a rapid extension of prospecting for minerals and exploitation of rich strikes. From an exporter of a wide variety of primary materials before World War I, the United States has become a net importer of most metals and minerals. Continued depletion at home and a faster rate of geological discovery abroad than in the United States, which has now been fairly thoroughly explored, are likely to continue to increase American dependence on foreign sources of supply. To the extent that conditions permit, a number of American corporations will want to exploit foreign natural resources directly through wholly owned or controlled corporations abroad.

Most direct investments in enterprises producing for sale in the United States market are located in underdeveloped countries. In Canada these investments are in the underdeveloped parts of the country— the Laurentian shield, stretching from Labrador across Quebec, Ontario, the Yukon, and Northwest Territory to Northern British Columbia, and rich in timber and mineral resources, and the prairie provinces. Whether it is absolute or comparative, the advantage of the country in which the investment is made tends to lie in land which favors supply-oriented industries. Occasionally a foot-loose industry will attract American capital abroad to work for the American market. The case of textile mills which moved to Puerto Rico from New England in quest of cheaper labor comes to mind.

Instances have occurred, moreover, in which an exporting company starting a foreign operation as a substitute for exports, finds it advantageous ultimately to manufacture abroad for sale to the United States because of the growth of foreign skills, or the cheapness of labor, or some unexpected gain in productivity from large-scale manufacture. The Burroughs Adding Machine Company is said to have moved to Scotland to produce for the European market and found it cheaper to manufacture computers for the home market there rather than in the United States. Some particularly labor-intensive processes may be undertaken abroad, such as lenses and shutters for American cameras; or a firm with watch works in Switzerland and the United States may produce its styles calling for long runs in this country, its short runs in Switzerland where labor is cheaper. In general, however, comparative advantages are likely to be narrow in industries where the advantage is based on labor cost—the cheaper wages of foreign countries being offset in whole or in part by the reduced efficiency of labor; and the risk of investment in a foot-loose industry is large because of the possibility of being cut off from the American market by tariff or other protection. For these and other reasons, American industry goes abroad to work for the American market primarily in basic materials.

Direct investment in the underdeveloped country need not be intended for production primarily for the United States. The largest single outlet for American direct investment—oil—is still in limited degree concerned with production for domestic use, at this time. In this industry the United States used to have a large comparative advantage and a flourishing export trade. The growth of domestic consumption gradually cut off the supply available for foreign markets, except in certain specialties such as lubricants. American concerns, particularly the larger companies, undertook to explore abroad for additional supplies to meet foreign requirements. The result is direct investment which both develops foreign sources of supply and substitutes for United States exports. The exports of one foreign country are expanded, and the imports of another.

There can be no doubt, however, that direct investment abroad working for the United States market is of very great importance. The Department of Commerce has shown that 25 per cent of United States imports in 1955 were produced in United States-controlled companies. The major items were crude oil ($580 million, or 87 per cent of total imports in the category), copper ($300 million, or 72 per cent), paper base stocks ($250 million, or 78 per cent), newsprint ($240 million, or 39 per cent), and refined oil products ($230 million, or 62 per cent). In eighteen selected commodities representing more than 40 per cent of United States imports, 58 per cent of imports by value were produced in United States direct-investment companies abroad.

Branch Plants of United States Companies

A large number of United States companies have established foreign subsidiaries to facilitate sales from the parent concern or to take care of a foreign market more economically. Typically, the foreign market is initially covered from the United States. After a time it proves profitable or convenient to undertake one or two processes abroad. With the passage of more time, more of the product is provided from the foreign country itself and less from the United States, until the branch plant substitutes entirely for exports from the United States.

Here, be it observed, is the opposite of the Ohlin theorem discussed in Chapter 6, that trade substitutes for capital movements. In this case, the capital movement substitutes for trade.

A wide variety of reasons may stimulate this sort of foreign investment. The United States company may establish a foreign branch because a product is market-oriented. Originally, assembly is undertaken abroad to save costs of transport through economy of space in packing parts. After a time, certain bulky (supply-oriented) parts are purchased abroad. Gradually other manufacturing may be undertaken locally, possibly as the area develops skills which provide the external economies needed to make the product as inexpensive as that from the United

States plus transport costs. In some cases 100 per cent local manufacture is not reached, and one or more difficult parts continue to be provided from the parent company. Direct investment may then substitute for most, but not all, of the original trade.

The experience of Sears, Roebuck and Company in establishing retail department stores in Mexico City and São Paulo may evolve in a similar way. Initial successes rapidly sold out the American stock with which the stores had been equipped. Exchange restrictions prevented reordering from the United States on an unlimited scale. The company accordingly attempted to buy American-styled merchandise from local manufacturers, furnishing them, where necessary, with technical assistance in the organization of production and with credit. While the direct investment of the company—equity ownership and control—may be limited to the retail stores which furnish services, it may by a roundabout method substitute for exports of goods from the United States.

The impetus to the establishment of the branch need not be transport costs or transport costs alone. Abundant and cheap foreign labor may be a crucial or a contributing factor. Import restrictions or exchange measures by the foreign country may force the company to invest or abandon a profitable market. The vertically integrated nature of some businesses may compel the company to undertake a foreign investment if it wants to gain access to the market for its basic product: in the oil industry, for example, the company which wants to sell crude oil in a foreign market is practically obliged to acquire distributing facilities, storage tanks, and frequently even a refinery. Typically, the industry is vertically integrated so that a share of the market for crude oil requires a company to acquire a share of the separate markets for products at all stages.

In still other cases, the impetus to investment may be a patent and the requirements of local patent law. The impact of patents on international trade is a complex subject. In some countries, however, it is not sufficient, as in the United States, merely to take out a patent. In order to maintain the patent right in good standing on an exclusive basis, it is necessary to exploit it, i.e., to manufacture the patented article. In such an instance it may pay a large company to establish a plant to keep its patent rights alive, since it would lose them if it merely covered the market by exports from abroad.

Patents and technology constitute an important cause of these direct investments which substitute for foreign trade. They may be more significant than differences in factor costs. To this extent, direct investment substitutes for trade which can take place on the basis of decreasing costs between countries with identical factor endowments and identical tastes. In chemicals, pharmaceuticals, optical goods, photographic equipment, soaps, and complex manufactured articles such as sewing machines, vacuum cleaners, etc., not every country produces a full line of all possible varieties of the article. Specialization takes place between countries of the same factor proportions and tastes due to decreasing costs. If capital movements substitute for this trade, they need not run from the richer to the poorer country but may take place among countries of the same stage of development, in either direction or both.

The decreasing-cost case explains why this sort of direct investment occurs especially between developed countries and in all directions. Closely allied to decreasing costs are differences in technology which overwhelm differences in factor proportions, as discussed in Chapter 7. On either of these showings, a variety of United States companies in Britain can be balanced by British companies in similar or closely related lines in the United States. The largest single outlet for American direct investment is in Canada, which has broadly the same factor proportions as the United States, although many of these plants are tariff factories established to circumvent the effects of Empire preference. And, as the whisky companies indicate, Canadian companies maintain direct investments in the United States. Agfa Ansco, American Viscose, Lever Brothers, the Shell Oil Company, Hiram Walker, Seagram, Bausch and Lomb, Sterling Drug, and the Singer Sewing Machine Company in the United States, however, testify to the fact that these direct investments can run "uphill" from countries with a higher to countries with a lower rate of interest, or on a plateau of equal interest rates, without creating difficulties.

An interesting case of this sort of direct investment is furnished by the General Motors–Holden plant in Australia, which was embarrassed by the Midas touch. Profits in 1953–54 ran 14 per cent of sales, 24 per cent of funds employed, 39 per cent of shareholders' equity, and 560 per cent of the General Motors original investment. The dividend paid from these profits amounted to 11 per cent of funds employed, 18 per cent of the shareholders' equity, 260 per cent of the original investment, and 8 per cent of Australian dollar export receipts for 1954–55. Publication of the company accounts made the Australian public gasp and wonder about the dollar cost of automobiles manufactured in Australia. All this occurred despite the fact that the company priced its product below the marginal value, so that it had to ration would-be buyers, and plowed back profits into further expansion.

This experience was explained by a scholar as reflecting that direct investments grow at rapid rates because companies regard profits on these risky enterprises as speculative funds which they are prepared to reinvest as a gamble. In consequence, the original fund can pile up rapidly and produce large dividends to be remitted when compared with the original capital. Possibly. But there is also a large element here of demonstration effect. Australia would have saved in its balance of payments if it had bought the same number of automobiles after the direct investment as before. Each car might have sold at the same price or somewhat more expensively, but the dividends remitted to the United States, plus purchases of parts, would be less than the total costs of the cars. The fact, however, is that Australia was led by the direct investment into buying many more cars than before. It got a bargain, but bargains can drive a family into bankruptcy. Buying a Deepfreeze saves you money if you are able to keep to the old level of living; typically, however, the consumer takes advantage of the purchase of a Deepfreeze to increase his consumption, and the item, in consequence, proves expensive.

Tariff Factories

Direct investment in developed countries frequently has its origin in differential tariffs designed specifically to encourage it. An import duty on finished goods provides a powerful incentive to foreign exporters to establish branches within a country if parts and raw materials remain free of tax. This is primarily true for market-oriented or foot-loose industries. The underlying purpose of the tariff may be self-defense, as in the case of the French tariffs on petroleum products without parallel duty on crude petroleum. This had as its purpose the accumulation of oil stocks in France. In some cases the branch plant may be used to export to other countries which share preferential tariff arrangements: Empire preference, fashioned at Ottawa in 1932, led many American plants, especially in automobiles, to establish branches in Canada to export to the Commonwealth market. The tariff factory may even operate in footloose or supply-oriented industries, provided that we refer to underdeveloped countries and export tariffs: the Indian differential export tax penalizing burlap in comparison with jute, has induced a number of firms in Dundee, which was the center of burlap as well as marmalade manufacture, to establish branches in Calcutta.

It has been argued that there is no net gain from these measures to attract direct investment in branch plants; that the capital inflow would have taken place anyhow because of the difference in interest rates and profit yields; that the tariff forces the factory into areas in which it is basically unprofitable in terms of the law of comparative advantage; and that it would be better to attract capital, through provision of a climate friendly to foreign capital, into the industries in which the country has a comparative advantage. There is much force in these arguments. In a relatively foot-loose industry, however, or in one in which some degree of increasing returns can be expected, a small tariff advantage of a temporary character may provide the marginal incentive to an investment which would not otherwise be made. Like the infant-industry argument for tariffs in general, the technique must be used with great circumspection and restraint.

Domestic Business Abroad

A small portion of direct investment in the world is primarily unconcerned with foreign trade, either in giving rise to it or in substituting for it. For the most part, this involves the straightforward exportation of the techniques of the investing country. Perhaps the most significant outlet is in public-utility systems—in the nineteenth century, railroads; today, electricity, telephones, radio, etc. Other fields are not unrepresented, however. The international insurance companies operating in New York act, for the most part, like domestic underwriters, although their reinsurance with companies abroad is a foreign-trade aspect.

There is something of a tendency in international trade for this sort of direct investment to diminish. The International Telephone and Telegraph Company, for example, is selling its equity participation in a number of foreign telecommunications systems and substituting long-term technical advisory contracts. The company may offer to provide technical assistance to a local telephone system for twenty years, designing its exchanges, long lines, and local equipment for a percentage of gross revenue.

In some cases, patents and manufacturing secrets are contributed to a foreign company in exchange for a minority equitable interest with little or no capital contribution in addition to the "information" and rights. This, of course, differs from a direct investment, in that there is no management control. In other respects, however, it is similar.

Finally, it may be observed that there is a growing invisible trade —difficult to measure and to evaluate because invisible—in patent rights and trade secrets on a straight sale basis, without any continuing interest.

The outright sale of technology or the acquisition of merely a minority interest appears to be developing at the expense of direct investment in purely local concerns unrelated to foreign trade. But the scope of this trend is difficult to establish because of the paucity of data.

The International Combine

In some very large companies which operate in a great number of countries, it is occasionally difficult to tell what the direction of the international flow of capital is. The giant oil companies and the outstandingly large companies in chemicals, certain metals, automobiles, fats and oil, and to a lesser degree other manufactured goods like tires, business machines, and so forth, buy, sell, borrow, invest, remit profits, and withdraw capital among the countries of the world. The net income of some of the largest among them is larger than the national income of many countries. Their actions accordingly have widespread impact.

To the extent that these countries buy and hire in the cheapest market, sell in the dearest, borrow where the marginal efficiency of capital is lowest, and invest where it is high, they provide institutional media of equalizing returns to capital and labor in various parts of the world which are superior to the ordinary workings of the market place. Just as the growth of the national corporation in the United States has equalized the returns to local capital and supervisory labor by determining the location of branch plants in terms of economic efficiency, so could the large international corporation improve on the workings of nineteenth-century capital and labor markets. To do so, they would have to maximize short-run profits. And new firms would have to enter lines where profits were high. This position, however, has probably not been reached. Governmental intervention, or fear of it, makes these corporations undertake some operations which are not fully economic, i.e., buy and hire in dearer rather than cheaper markets; lack of social overhead capital inhibits them from undertaking certain desirable investments; and monopolistic practices, many of them based upon what the Supreme Court calls "conscience parallel action" rather than conspiracy to restrain trade, may on occasion have limited output and held up prices. Not much research has been undertaken into the action of the international combine, and its effects on the allocation of resources and the distribution of income. But there can be little doubt that a considerable amount of economic power is possessed by such companies, and generally used in ways which do not run athwart the public interest.

Advantages of Direct Investment

The major advantage of direct investment over borrowing in the form of debt is that the country in which the investment is made incurs no fixed charges. In a world depression no profits will be made on the direct investment. Hence there is no pressure on the balance of payments. In periods of prosperity, to be sure, profits may be substantial; but foreign exchange is plentiful, so that they can be transferred abroad. This is particularly the case with those foreign investments which produce for sale in a foreign market. When sales and profits are large, the exchange needed to transmit the latter abroad is automatically created. And when the exchange is not available, it usually follows, but not inevitably, that profits are low or negative, so that there is little or nothing to transmit.

This semiautomatic transferability of profits is the major advantage claimed for direct investment. But there are others. Direct investment combines technical capacity with capital in fruitful union. The sale of technical information—patents and trade secrets—without accompanying capital is less productive. There has been a tendency recently to suggest that technology is the important partner in the team and that capital plays a minor role. This is not true. Without singling out one or the other as the more significant member, it is enough to state that, together, they are more productive than either by itself. The control feature of direct investment makes technical assistance more readily forthcoming.

The transfer problem rarely exists for the original investment. There are cases where direct investments are made through the outright purchase of an existing company, or through the creation of a new company in a foreign country, the major assets of which are indigenous. Normally, however, the investor contributes a significant share of the capital in kind rather than in cash. And this contribution is automatically transferred. We have already mentioned investment in technology and trade secrets. Frequently, the equity investment will consist as well of machinery and equipment imported from the investing country, while that portion of the physical capital which can be furnished locally represents either local equity or borrowing from local sources.

To the degree that this is true, in fact, direct investment is comparable to a tied loan and runs the risk of creating a transfer problem in reverse—i.e., the import surplus without the capital to finance it. Suppose a United States corporation forms a subsidiary in a foreign country, creating its equity out of investment in machinery and equipment from the United States but borrowing locally to construct a factory building. The local funds spent for the building may be raised in a non-inflationary way, through new savings. If, however, the financing is done on the basis of credit creation, either through a bank loan or through the sale of bonds which are purchased with the aid of loans, the investment expenditure is inflationary. It will increase national money income and raise imports. The increase in imports will create an import surplus, assuming that the current account had been in balance. Under our assumption, the direct investment provides no financing to meet this deficit. Ultimately the direct investment may improve the balance of payments by expanding exports or making possible a reduction of imports. This must wait until the factory is built and has begun operation. Meanwhile, the capital import may lead to an uncovered import surplus.

This possibility has led at least one country to insist that foreigners who make direct investments within its borders put up the total cost of the investment in foreign exchange. No local financing, whether on equity or on debt, would be permitted under this rule. But this stipulation is likely to cut off direct investment altogether. Business enterprises normally expect a new venture to pay its way on a balanced proportion of equity and debt. To borrow the debt capital in the lending country would be to increase the foreign-exchange risk of the investor in a way which he would regard as undue.

While foreign lending through direct investment is subject to some cyclical variation, it is probably not so variable in its pattern as long-term bonds. The record is complicated by inadequacies of the statistical data. It appears, however, that some lending through direct investment continued throughout the depression of the 1930's, long after the market for foreign bonds had dried up and the capital movement reversed because of repayments. While much direct investment is connected through the accelerator to business conditions in general, some is affected by other stimuli, such as the loss of export markets due to restrictions abroad or new discoveries. Direct investments owned abroad by United States residents declined only slightly from $7.5 to $7.0 billion between 1929 and the end of 1940, despite large markdowns due to losses and exchange depreciation. The Department of Commerce has concluded from this evidence that net outflows of capital of substantial amounts went abroad from the United States, at least after the worst years of the depression.

Not all direct investment is voluntary in character. Restrictions on the remittance of profits may lead to substantial annual increments in direct investment of an involuntary character. Such restrictions are likely to take place primarily in import-replacing and domestic-activity types of investment and constitute an exception to the rule which applies to export-increasing investments that the transfer of profits is semiautomatic. These increases in investment usually take the form of cash assets of the subsidiary company. Occasionally, however, the foreign subsidiary will employ the profits which it is not permitted to transfer in foreign exchange in expanding its activities in existing operations or through vertical integration. The new investment may be made in different lines. A communications company in Germany in the interwar period used some of its blocked profits to buy an interest in an airplane company as an inducement to the company to participate with it in blind-landing experiments. One large British company which was unable to remit earnings from its highly profitable subsidiary in Germany in the 1930's reportedly put its spare cash into real estate, investing most of it in Berlin apartment houses. Unhappily for this venture, if true, the British assets were later reduced to rubble by the RAF and the USAF.

The major advantages of direct investment, however, lie not in their moderate cyclical pattern but in the variability of the burden imposed on the balance of payments of the country in which the investment is made, the combination it provides of capital with technological capacity, and the fact that it is a two-way rather than a unilateral affair.

Disadvantages

But direct investment is not all beer and skittles. It poses a series of problems, partly economic but primarily on the level of politics and international understanding, which have proved increasingly difficult to resolve. Most of these sticky problems apply to the first type of investment—that directed to the exploitation of natural resources abroad to produce goods for export. The difficulty is the same as that encountered in bilateral monopoly. Wide differences will exist in the views of the investor and the country in which the investment takes place, without any objective basis for resolving them. But direct investment requires co-operation between the two partners. In the absence of mutual understanding—which is difficult of attainment—direct investments can function effectively only if one or the other party dictates a solution.

In a world of political dependency, mining concessions—to restrict ourselves to this one example—were usually rather one-sided affairs. The country which owned the real estate would grant a ninety-nine-year concession at a low royalty for mining rights on which the concessionaire would expect to make large profits. There have been occasions when such concessions were signed with a Navy gunboat anchored off the underdeveloped country's capital. If the country was a political dependency, the terms of the concession were apt to be one-sided. In any case, it was probably not clear to the authorities of the underdeveloped country how valuable were the rights which they were signing away. An argument could be offered that the concession was made without full disclosure and was therefore invalid.

Today, this sort of dealing is no longer practiced. This is true for two reasons. In the first place, the underdeveloped countries, now largely possessed of political independence, do not permit it. Secondly, however, companies in the developed countries have learned that one-sided concessions do not last. Whatever the legal validity of a right binding for ninety-nine years, the nascent awareness and power of the underdeveloped countries concerned make it impossible to preserve such rights unimpaired. "Voluntary" adjustments of concessions and agreements in which the balance of benefit is redressed in favor of the country granting the concession are not unusual. The balance may be redressed so violently that the foreign investor is expropriated, with or without the compensation to which he is entitled under international law. In less extreme instances, he may find the conditions so drastically altered that it is impossible for him to continue operating profitably.

Uncertainty about the advantages of direct investment is not limited to underdeveloped countries. India has recently presented the spectacle of two United States oil companies undertaking investments there while two United States automobile companies withdrew. Norway refuses to permit foreigners to develop its resources, and even Canada has wondered whether it is desirable to welcome American investment with such open arms. The Royal Commission On Canada's Economic Prospects (the Gordon Commission) in its *Preliminary Report* has suggested inviting foreign owners of Canadian corporations to offer participation to Canadian interests, hire a significant portion of Canadian personnel, and elect Canadian directors, plus publish accounts of their Canadian operations. Canada chooses to have American capital develop its natural resources at a rapid pace, but it would like to learn what is going on and to have its nationals have a say in the decisions.

Between the extremes of exploitation by the investor or expropriation by the country in which the resources are located, there is a wide area of uncertainty, and no solution which can objectively be said to be fair. The natural resources contributed by the one country, and the capacity to convert these to marketable use, the capital necessary for this purpose, and the marketing facilities, all contributed by the other, are both necessary. Both contributions are necessary; neither is sufficient by itself. In the absence of competitive bidding, among a wide number of dealers on both sides there is no possible basis for evaluating the respective contributions of each.

50–50 Partnership

There has lately developed a 50–50 formula which, however arbitrary, has the advantage of appealing to some people as fair. It is, moreover, the median solution between the limits of one or the other party acquiring the whole gain. It is not, however, the most likely competitively determined solution. Developed by Venezuela in its relations with the oil companies, the formula has spread to the Middle East in this industry and been applied by Venezuela in mining concessions for iron ore granted to the United States Steel and Bethlehem Steel companies. The Venezuelan government receives as royalty and income tax as much as the company and the United States government receive in profits and income tax on profits. The arbitrary character of the formula is underlined by the fact that, in its known applications, no change is made in the formula for tariffs imposed by the importing country or for an increase in wages in the exporting; and both of them reduce profits unilaterally.

While the 50–50 formula helps, it probably does not solve the difficulty created by the differences in interest between the two partners —the investing company and the country controlling the resources. In the first place, there is no single universally agreed-upon concept of what should be divided equally. How much, for example, should properly be allowed for depreciation, given the risks of investment in a foreign country; and what is a fair allowance for depletion? What is the amount of profit when discounts have been given to special customers, including the stockholders, and how should total profit on an enterprise like TAPLINE, which carries oil from Saudi Arabia through Jordan, Syria, and Lebanon be allocated among these countries for purposes of taxation; per mile of length or equally? Secondly, assuming that profits plus certain taxes can be defined in a satisfactory way, there is no certainty that both parties will see eye to eye on whether the level of profits and taxes is satisfactory. In complex cases of vertical integration, the country granting the concession will want profits to be high on operations within its borders and low on subsequent stages carried on abroad, such as smelting, refining, marketing, etc. The company, on the other hand, may have an interest in receiving its profits at later rather than earlier stages. The country and the company may further differ in their views as to the appropriate frame of reference within which profits should be maximized. If the company takes a long view and the country a short, prices and profits will be held below their short-run maximum in order to achieve price stability, to encourage wide consumption, or to discourage entry of competing products. Under imperfectly competitive conditions, the company may be able to control the price of its produce to a degree and set its prices with a view to long-run aims. If the country, however, is unfamiliar with the types of business considerations which guide the company in these decisions, it may think merely that it is receiving too little because profits are too small.

The 50–50 sharing formula, even with its ambiguity eliminated, therefore, still differs from an equal partnership, in that the decision-making power essentially remains with the investing company. The country in which the investment takes place shares in the proceeds but typically has no voice in the determination of their amount. This, of course, is the usual relationship between business and governments which impose corporate taxes in developed countries.

But not all underdeveloped countries view it as satisfactory. Since their resources are being exploited, they want to have a voice in the determination of how this is done—at all levels. A major task in the world of today is to bridge the gap between countries which are acutely conscious of their opportunities for political and economic development, and jealous of any fancied slight to their sovereignty, on the one hand, and, on the other, companies unwilling to face the fact that times have changed and that they have social responsibilities along with duties to their stockholders. Part of this task is to get the underdeveloped countries to accept the obligation to treat foreign enterprise decently, or fairly, or on some other basis difficult to describe objectively which will ensure that the benefits of foreign enterprise are available to it in the long run on a continuous basis. Various national foreign trade councils and international chambers of commerce have drawn up outlines of such requirements which may somewhat overstate the case for private enterprise, but not by much. The other part is for the investing companies to recognize the necessity of taking local peoples into partnership—training them for wider responsibilities in the mine or plant, employing local officers and directors who understand the problems of dealing with the conditions to be found in the country, to the extent that able personnel can be found.

Pride and prejudice play all too powerful roles in these matters. In certain countries, small business cannot undertake direct investment because the services normally provided to business by the state—an educated population, roads, harbors, telecommunications, etc.—are not present. Only a large company operating under conditions of imperfect competition to maximize profits in the long run (but not the short) can afford to undertake the investment in providing the utilities and caring for its employees. A company of this size, however, is likely to loom large in the eyes of a government, if it feels somewhat insecure, and frequently is seen as a threat to its prestige. Unless special effort is made to maintain friendly relations, a vicious cycle of misunderstanding and disregard of the other's real interest may be generated.

Direct Investment and Dual Economy

Direct investment creates a problem and an opportunity in another respect, although whether the problem or the opportunity will loom larger it is hard to say in advance. In a classical world of factor immobility, each country is assumed to have a set of factor prices, which reflects its factor endowments, and a set of factor proportions appropriate to those prices. If capital moves from a capital-rich to a capital-poor country, however, the factor prices at which the foreign investment will operate will differ from those which exist otherwise. In underdeveloped countries the foreign investment is likely to move into the export industries: this will produce one set of factor proportions of domestic land, domestic labor, and foreign capital in the export sector of the economy (or only a part of it) and a separate set in the domestic sector. A two-price system for land and labor is likely to develop alongside that for capital. The foreign plantation can pay higher prices for land and labor than can native operations, which use less capital. The chance for higher rewards in working for foreign enterprise may paralyze local initiative, capital formation, and development.

Some economists, such as the Burmese, Hla Myint, have asserted that direct investment in underdeveloped countries retards economic development by "fossilizing" technological change. There is a once-and-for-all improvement in technology involved in starting a plantation economy, but the process of change then stops. The foreign corporation disrupts the subsistence economy, producing exports and diverting consumption from native to imported products, frequently of lower nutritional quality, and then leaves it at that. Technology becomes frozen; the learning process halts.

The possibility that factor proportions in the foreign investment will resemble those of the investing country rather than those of the country where the investment takes place has led to the characterization of such sectors as foreign enclaves, really part of the economy of the investing country, and separate from the underdeveloped area. What matters for the latter is not net geographical product, which includes the output of the foreign-owned plantations or mines, but national income which excludes that part of the value of output ascribable to, or appropriated by, the foreign factors of production, enterprise, and capital.

We shall discuss this dual-economy case in Chapter 27. Here, however, we shall merely point out that it creates social and political problems as well as economic. The Indonesian producing native rubber has a lower standard of living than those working for foreign planters. The United Fruit Company can produce bananas more efficiently than native small-scale growers and a more marketable standardized product. This creates problems. The sugar industry of Cuba employs workers only six months of the year. For the rest, there is no work for them. In Venezuela a worker for one of the oil companies can earn more than a worker in agriculture. This has stifled the development of agriculture and tended to make people queue up for oil jobs rather than work and save.

Direct Investment as an Outlet for Savings

We have indicated how direct investment may give rise to an import surplus in the borrowing country, for which no foreign exchange is available. A loose parallel may be found in the lending country in an export surplus which provides no offset to existing savings. If savings tend to outrun domestic investment opportunities in this country, capital lending through the purchase of bonds will bring the two back into balance. But direct investment may not. Many companies make a sharp distinction, largely perhaps unconsciously, between borrowed funds and retained profits. The distinction is irrational in considerable degree, but it exists. They are willing to invest retained profits abroad, but not borrowed funds. To the extent that this feeling exists, it follows that direct investment is likely to increase savings as fast as it creates outlets for savings, so that it makes no contribution to an existing surplus of savings over investment opportunities.

In some companies, moreover, direct investment in foreign countries beyond the initial stages is undertaken only to the extent that foreign subsidiaries make profits which can be retained and employed in capital expansion. The corporate income tax on dividends remitted to the head company may play an important role in this separation. The fact that the foreign and the domestic pockets are in the same pair of trousers, however, is disregarded; the foreign operation is taken to be self-sufficient for purposes of expansion. Under these circumstances, direct investment is completely unrelated to national savings and investment opportunities. If the foreign subsidiary's profits had been paid out in dividends, instead of reinvested, of course, consumption, savings, and taxes would all have been higher. As it is, direct investment out of profits, whether foreign or domestic, increases savings as much as it increases investment and provides no offset to any excess of savings which already exists.

The Role of Direct Investment

The United States government from time to time in the postwar period has asserted through its representatives that there was no need to undertake to reorganize the bond market or provide for further intergovernmental lending since the needs of countries seeking foreign capital could be provided by private enterprise through direct investment. When the argument is made by businessmen, it is accompanied by one or both of two qualifications: (1) there is a need for governments to create a climate favorable to foreign investors; and (2) the investing interests may need additional incentives, such as financial guarantees against expropriation, treaties eliminating double taxation, lower taxes on foreign than domestic investment to offset the higher risk, etc.

It is sometimes asserted, in addition, that the role of direct investment is grossly underestimated at present, because of the statistical methods followed in the balance of payments, and that if the appropriate basis of estimation were chosen, direct investment would be seen to be much bigger than indicated in Tables 2.1 to 2.4 given in Chapter 2. In the first place, the quarterly figures for direct investment are given on a net basis, with reinvested earnings subtracted both from the current-account credit, Profits on Overseas Investment, and from new investment. This quarterly netting, which is corrected in the annual figures, is due to the difficulty of getting any but the net figures quarterly, but it may contribute to the view that reinvested profits are somewhat less a new investment than monies invested abroad originating in the United States. In the second place, however, even the annual data which include reinvested profits are net of depreciation and depletion allowances. In this view, these should be added. Direct investment of the United States in 1956 was thus not the $1,633 million of new investment originating in the United States, nor the approximately $2,800 million including reinvested profits, but close to $3,900 million which represents total capital expenditures abroad by United States direct investors.

It is clearly appropriate to include reinvested profits along with new capital originating in the United States, provided that the profits were not blocked by foreign-exchange control, and provided that companies are rational, as it is sometimes asserted they are not, in regarding a dollar earned abroad, and freely transferable, as the equivalent of a dollar earned at home. Whether it is appropriate to gross up the figures to include depreciation and depletion, however, is more debatable. It is true that the provisions for amortization in bond contracts mean that part of gross lending is offset by repayments. But here the individual investor expected to lend only for a specified period of time. Direct investment is usually undertaken for as far ahead into the future as can be seen. If this is the case, an investment should be maintained without regarding this as a new act of investment, and depreciation should not be added to new investment and reinvested profits. Only if a company, as some do, regards all investments as requiring new justification every year, and proceeds to liquidate those which don't measure up, is gross capital expenditure the appropriate measure rather than net acquisition of capital assets.

The issue may seem to be a petty one of mere accounting. But it has attracted considerable attention from business interests in the United States which seek to emphasize the role of direct investment in the international transactions of this country, or, as they would prefer to put it, to ensure that this role is not underemphasized.

Summary

Direct investment is equity ownership of enterprises in a country which are controlled by foreign investors. A variety of legal distinctions among various kinds of direct investment may be made. Important economic distinctions turn on the question of whether the investment is designed to increase imports into the investing country, replace exports, or is unconcerned with foreign trade. Investment to stimulate imports generally takes place in supply-oriented industries in underdeveloped countries. Those to replace exports are for the most part in market-oriented industries and are located in developed countries similar in factor endowment to the investing country.

The advantages of direct investment are (1) that its burden on the balance of payments is variable and (2) that it combines the technological knowledge and entrepreneurial skill of the investing country with the resources (or markets) of the country in which the investment takes place. The disadvantages are, first, that it is difficult to work out satisfactory arrangements between investor and country in which the investment takes place, if the investment is to stimulate imports, and, second, that it may create a dual economy in the country of investment. Direct investment also may fail to solve the problem of oversaving in developed countries—if this problem exists—by encouraging as much new saving as investment, to the extent that direct investment is undertaken out of corporation profits. The importance of direct investment in the balance of payments will vary statistically depending on whether one takes it net of reinvested profits; gross, including reinvested profits; or gross both of reinvested profits and depletion and depreciation allowances.

SUGGESTED READING

TREATISES, ETC.

The literature on direct investment is sparse. F. A. Southard, Jr., *American Industry in Europe* (Boston: Houghton Mifflin Co., 1931); D. M. Phelps, *Migration of Industry to South America* (New York: McGraw-Hill Book Co., Inc., 1936); and H. Marshall, F. A. Southard, Jr., and K. Taylor, *Canadian-American Industry* (New Haven: Yale University Press, 1936), are the only monographs bearing directly upon it, all happily concerned with different parts of the world, but all out of date. Department of Commerce literature on the subject is plentiful but tends to the simple presentation of tabular material. A full statement is contained in "Growth of Foreign Investments in the United States and Abroad," *Survey of Current Business,* August, 1956.

POINTS

The National Planning Association has undertaken a number of case studies such as Casa Grace in Peru; Sears, Roebuck of Mexico; Creole Petroleum in Venezuela; Socony Mobil in Indonesia; etc. They are not highly critical. The Department of Commerce has issued a number of country studies describing the status of investment and investment opportunities in Mexico, Indonesia, etc.

E. T. Penrose's study "Foreign Investment and the Growth of the Firm," *EJ,* June, 1956, deals with the spectacular and embarrassing success of General Motors in Australia. Pyramiding of investment through plowing back profits is also discussed in E. Lundberg and M. Hill in "Australia's Long-Term Balance of Payments Problem," *Economic Record* (Australia), May, 1956.

A wide variety of direct investment problems in materials is discussed in *Resources for Freedom—a Report to the President by the President's Materials Policy Commission* (Washington, D.C.: U.S. Government Printing Office, June, 1952). Especially useful are Volume I, chapter xii, on private investment, and papers on Venezuelan policy and guarantees in Volume V. The opposing Canadian view is indirectly put forward in the Gordon report—Royal Commission on Canada's Economic Prospects, *Preliminary Report,* December, 1956.

The view that direct investment should be recorded gross of depreciation and depletion is set out in a variety of reports and articles. Notable among them are American Enterprise Association, Inc., *American Private Enterprise, Foreign Economic Development and the Aid Programs,* A Study prepared at the request of the Special Committee to Study the Foreign Aid Program, United States Senate (Washington, D.C.: U.S. Government Printing Office, 1957); and E. G. Collado and J. F. Bennett, "Private Investment and Economic Development," *Foreign Affairs,* July, 1957.

The Myint discussion of the impact of direct investment on technological change is given in his "The Gains from International Trade and the Backward Countries," *RES,* 1954–55.

THE INTERNATIONAL

Chapter
21

ASPECTS OF ECONOMIC

DEVELOPMENT

Economic development could be treated in a textbook on international economics under one of a number of separate headings: commercial policy, for many will argue that the commercial policy of a developing country should differ from that of countries which have arrived; under equilibrium, because there is substantial evidence that the process of internal growth in a developing country is disturbing to balance-of-payments stability; or under capital movements, because in the course of development the balance of payments of a country, and its balance of indebtedness, pass through various stages in which the alterations of the capital position figure prominently. An arbitrary element enters into all organizational choices. We have arbitrarily chosen to discuss development in Part IV on The Capital Account. In the course of this chapter, however, we will seize the opportunity to discuss, in highly compressed fashion, some of these other facets of the subject. We treat in order: systems of classification of countries in international economics, including stages of development; the impact of domestic development on foreign trade in undirected economies; commercial policy for developing countries; the need for foreign capital in conscious-development programs; and the impact of economic development abroad on countries already well along. It is recognized that each one of these topics is substantial enough to claim the attention of a separate chapter, but limitations of space forbid.

Systems of Classification

There is a variety of bases for classifying countries from the viewpoint of trade. These include:

Geographical: i.e., North and South America, Europe, Africa, Asia,
Political: Communist, non-Communist; or United States and its possessions, British Commonwealth of Nations; other colonial powers and their colonies, etc.

412

Functional: industrial, nonindustrial; and within the nonindustrial, agricultural, mining, etc.; and within agricultural, foodstuffs and nonfoodstuffs, tropical versus temperate zone, etc.

Monetary: dollar area, sterling area, European Payments Union; Communist bloc, etc.

Stage of
development: level of money income; balance-of-payments position; balance of indebtedness.

Which system of classification is used depends, of course, on the end in view. When it is important to cover the whole world, i.e., to divide world trade as a whole, it may be necessary to make compromises among various systems. Thus the economic research staff of the League of Nations in the interwar period divided the world into

Non-Continental Europe (i.e., United Kingdom, Eire, and Iceland)
Continental Europe
United States
Areas of recent settlement (Canada, Australia, Argentina, etc.)
All other (largely tropical)

This breakdown was partly geographical and partly functional. In postwar discussions, more attention is given to dividing countries by currency areas—separating out, for example, Canada from the Commonwealth because of its currency, and Northern Latin America, which is closely tied to the dollar, from Southern Latin America, which is competitive with the United States in many lines and has traditional complementary trading ties with Europe.

In Europe, a variety of systems of classification overlap. In economic discussions, there are the *three* countries of Benelux (Belgium, Netherlands, and Luxembourg); the *six* countries of the European Coal and Steel Community, the Common Market, and EURATOM (the Benelux countries, plus France, Italy, and Germany); the *uncertain number* of countries involved in the Free Market area currently discussed, which comprises the Six, plus the United Kingdom, and probably the three western Scandinavian countries; the *seventeen* countries of the Organization for European Economic Cooperation which participated in the Marshall Plan and which covered all of free Europe except Spain; and total Europe, participating in the Economic Commission for Europe, including the Soviet Union and its satellites, but excluding for a time, Spain and Germany. If one moves partly out of Europe to the North Atlantic Treaty Organization, which includes the United States and Canada, one gets fourteen countries of western Europe,

414 · INTERNATIONAL ECONOMICS

including Spain, but excluding the neutrals such as Switzerland and Sweden.

Stages of Development

There is equally a wide variety of bases for division from the viewpoint of economic development. One of these is money income. Countries with a money income of less than $100 a year per capita may be regarded as underdeveloped; countries with a per capita income of $100 to $300 form a next category of developing countries; and those with average incomes over $300 per capita constitute the highest category of developed countries. Too much reliance must not be put on these money measures. They are suspect for a variety of reasons and especially the understatement of money income in agriculture and the artificial character of many exchange rates. But as orders of magnitude, they are helpful.

A. G. B. Fisher divided economic activities into primary, secondary, and tertiary classes. Primary employment is in the extractive industries of agriculture and mining; secondary employment is in manufacturing; tertiary in service industries. It happens that the countries with the highest level of income also have the highest proportion of tertiary employment. But this relationship is probably not a simple one. Some rich countries—Denmark, Australia, Canada, and New Zealand—and some rich parts of countries—like Iowa and Nebraska—have a high proportion of income derived from primary occupations; some poor countries have many persons in domestic service—because of the distribution of income; and all these figures have to be corrected for foreign trade.

A rougher but readier guide to the level of income of a country is the proportion of its people engaged in agriculture, corrected for foreign trade. In China 70–75 per cent of the people are tied to the soil; 72 per cent in India; 36 per cent in France; $8\frac{1}{2}$ per cent in the United States. Failure to correct for foreign trade would be misleading, as in the case of Britain's 6 per cent and New Zealand's 24. Britain imports half of its food, so that some portion of its food intake is actually secured by men and women working in factories for export. When the figures are corrected for this, the British figure comes out to $8\frac{1}{2}$ per cent, or the same as that of the United States. This latter need not be corrected for foreign trade, because United States exports of agricultural products are about balanced in value by imports; but some considerable proportion of the energy in agriculture goes into nonfood items.

The New Zealand figure, on the other hand, is far too high on an adjusted basis, since food exports are merely a way of obtaining a considerable portion of the supply of manufactured products. When adjusted for this fact, the New Zealand figure becomes 6.66 per cent, which gives a much clearer view of the comparative income vis-à-vis Britain.

The wise student will be wary of leaning heavily on these comparisons. Particularly dangerous are those which contrast the number of hours or minutes needed to get this or that article of consumption in this and that country. These comparisons are satisfactory if labor is equally abundant or scarce in the two countries and if the articles represent the same degree of comparative advantage in both countries. But one can readily see the danger if it is pointed out that the resident of Buenos Aires can earn a pound of steak in, say, twenty minutes, as compared to forty for an American, while a Parisian stenographer can earn an ounce of Chanel No. 5 in two hours and a half, as compared to seven hours for an American. To use a product in which one country has a comparative advantage and the other a disadvantage is to stack the cards.

Factor Proportions

For purposes of international trade discussion, much interest attaches to the factor proportions of underdeveloped and developed countries. If we take three factors—land, labor, and capital—and only two shadings of each—relatively abundant or cheap, on the one hand, and

TABLE 21.1

RELATIVE FACTOR PRICES

	Labor	Land	Capital
1........................	Cheap	Dear	Dear
2........................	Cheap	Dear	Cheap
3........................	Dear	Cheap	Dear
4........................	Dear	Cheap	Cheap
5........................	Cheap	Cheap	Dear
6........................	Dear	Dear	Cheap
7........................	{ Cheap / Dear	Cheap / Dear	Cheap / Dear

relatively scarce or dear, on the other—we can acquire a system of seven classes. A country may fall into one or another of the categories shown in Table 21.1.

Since these are relative factor prices and not absolute, dear, dear, dear and cheap, cheap, cheap are the same thing.

The seventh category in which land, labor, and capital are equally abundant (and scarce) emphasizes the point that economic development is in large part a process of making capital more abundant and cheaper so as to increase the productivity of labor. A country which is already overpopulated and crowded on the land will find itself, if underdeveloped, in something like category 1. This is the position of India, China, Indonesia, Haiti, and Puerto Rico. It is unlikely that the relative proportions of land and labor can be changed. But it may be possible, if things go well (and the growth in population does not overwhelm the gain in productivity), to increase the abundance of capital, reduce its cost, and increase productivity. This would fit it into category 2. Examples in this class are Japan and possibly Italy.

The standard of living of people will be much higher, to begin with, in a situation the reverse of category 1, with land abundant and population scarce. Brazil, Argentina, Australia, the Canada of twenty-five years ago, and the United States of 1875 illustrate the third category. Here economic development requires an increase in capital intensity. Over time, the population will increase by natural means and immigration. But, until population growth results in crowding on the land, the goal of category 4 is possible of achievement. At the moment, Canada and the United States exemplify this best of all possible conditions.

Category 5 may be illustrated at various standards of living. In the Middle East, land and labor are both cheap relative to capital, but neither is very productive. An example at a higher standard of living is perhaps Cuba, where land and population are both abundant and productive relative to capital. The sixth category, with labor productive, land scarce, and capital abundant, is probably best illustrated by the United Kingdom, the Netherlands, France, and western Germany. The capital abundance is obscured by the loss of capital during the war. Relative to other parts of the world, however, its existence cannot be doubted.

It has been stated that the process of economic development is largely one of widening and deepening the use of capital in the economy to increase the productivity of labor. The exception which proves the rule is furnished by the tiny country of Israel, where the increase in population is taken as given, as the Israeli attempt to provide a home for world Jewry. The task is mostly to acquire capital, but also to reclaim land from the desert. Typically, land can be changed only slowly, if it does not, in fact, shrink through depletion and exhaustion; labor can grow with some speed through immigration and natural increase; but capital is the factor which, most of all, is capable of being raised. And, since almost all men furnish labor for production and only some furnish capital, the objective of increasing material abundance is sought through making capital plentiful relative to land and labor.

This analysis is, of course, vastly oversimplified. In addition to reducing scarcity and abundance to two unique categories, it omits noncompeting groups and other reasons why factor prices fail to achieve equalization. The critical role played by factor proportions in the law of comparative advantage and foreign trade makes it nonetheless worthwhile to stress factor proportions as an essential element in the development process.

The Balance of Payments

Another system of classification focuses attention on the balance of payments at different stages of development. This originally was related to the balance of merchandise or visible trade, and much discussion of policy still runs in these terms. More properly, however, it is the current account as a whole which matters, or, what comes to the same thing with an opposite sign if gold and short-term capital on balance are zero, the movement of long-term capital.

Originally, four stages of development were discerned, based on changes in the balance of indebtedness (Table 21.2).

TABLE 21.2

THE BALANCE OF PAYMENTS BY STAGES OF DEVELOPMENT, 1

Balance of Indebtedness	Balance of Payments on Current Account
Young debtor	Passive
Mature debtor	Active
Young creditor	Active
Mature creditor	Balanced or passive

On this basis, the young debtor is borrowing. The mature debtor is repaying. The young creditor is lending. And the mature creditor has either stopped lending or is consuming capital. The difference between the mature debtor and the young creditor is to be found not in the balance of payments but in the balance of indebtedness. The balance of payments shows a continuous export surplus as the country emerges from the one to the other stage. It is simply that the net excess of liabilities over claims becomes a surplus of claims over liabilities.

While this system is satisfactory for most purposes, the ambiguity about the last stage and the abruptness in the transition between the first and second make it worthwhile to add two more (Table 21.3). Even this scheme may not have enough categories. At a stage before economic development has begun, the current account may have to be in balance because the country lacks credit for borrowing. After stage 6, when the old creditor has used up its foreign assets and lost its credit standing, it, too, must have a balanced position. In a sense, a country may move from stage 6 to stage 1 through a separate con-

TABLE 21.3

THE BALANCE OF PAYMENTS BY STAGES OF DEVELOPMENT, 2

Stage	Balance of Indebtedness	Balance of Payments on Current Account
1.	Young debtor	Passive
2.	Adult debtor	Balanced
3.	Mature debtor	Active
4.	Young creditor	Active
5.	Adult creditor	Balanced
6.	Old creditor	Passive

necting stage. In some cases this stage appears to last from 500 to 1,500 years. Turkey, Iran, Egypt, and India are now young countries able to borrow abroad for economic development. But all of them have old civilizations, once the seats of empire which drew tribute from other parts of the world. From the slough of stagnation, in which foreign capital consumption is complete and borrowing is impossible, they have emerged again into the world economy as countries to be developed.

It used to be thought that the balance of visible trade shifted from stage to stage in the same sequence as the current-account balance. The growth of invisible, and particularly interest, payments, however, results in earlier change in merchandise trade, much along the lines of the discussion of interest in Chapter 19, pp. 387 ff. The United States, for example, did not shift from stage 1 to stage 2 until the first World War. The merchandise trade balance, however, turned favorable after 1874 as the growth of interest payments and ultimately of immigrant remittances required a considerable goods offset, despite the unfavorable character of the current account as a whole. Recent investigation, moreover, has indicated that the British visible account was unfavorable during the whole period of lending which followed the Napoleonic Wars, and not just for the second half of the century. The latter misunderstanding arose from the fact that British foreign-trade statistics had been kept on the basis of "official" values, which understated imports and, in the middle of the century, overstated exports. The merchandise trade balance, which has popularly been thought to have shifted from an export surplus to an import surplus after the repeal of the Corn Laws in 1846, was in reality continuously in import surplus from 1798.

TABLE 21.4

UNITED STATES BALANCE OF TRADE, 1821–1918

(Annual Averages in Millions of Dollars)

Period (Fiscal Years)	Exports	Imports	Balance	Estimated Capital Movement* (+ Outflow; — Inflow)
1821–37	82	93	— 11	— 10
1838–49	116	113	+ 3	Negligible
1850–73	274	338	— 64	— 57
1874–95	783	670	+ 113	— 90
1896–1914	1,691	1,204	+ 487	—111
1915–18	4,908	2,411	+2,497	Large outflow

* These figures are derived from rough approximations of United States investments abroad, and foreign investments in the United States at the turning points, taken from the text of the Bullock, Williams, and Tucker article. The data are as follows:

	United States Claims	United States Liabilities
1821	Negligible	Negligible
1838	Negligible	150–200
1849	Negligible	220
1873	Negligible	1,500
1896	$ 500	2,500
1914	$1,000	4,500
(Dept. of Comm.) 1919	$7,000 (excludes war debts)	3,700

The developmental stages worked out in this scheme do not fit history neatly. The United States was in stage 1 continuously for 100 years. In three years, it passed through stages 2 and 3 and emerged in stage 4. At least two starts were made. Bullock, Williams, and Tucker have prepared estimates of the balance of trade and have given figures for United States assets and liabilities from which a rough approximation of the capital movement can be derived (see Table 21.4). These data show both that the trade balance differed from the balance of payments on current account (i.e., the capital movement with reversed sign) and that the capital inflow, cut off after the panic of 1836, was resumed again in the 1850's. The capital-movement figures, it should be emphasized, are netted and averaged. Capital outflows occurred in the early years of the Civil War and in the panic of the early 1890's. But while the trade balance changed from import surplus to balance, to import surplus again, and to net exports, the country may be said to have remained continuously in stage 1.

Since World War I, moreover, the United States has stayed consistently in stage 4—that of the young creditor.

Foreign Trade and Development

These stages in economic growth can be tied more directly to the development of foreign trade by a stylized scheme, showing the changes which occur in land, labor, and capital as a country develops, and in its capacity for technological change, its capacity for transformation, or reallocating resources among occupations, and the scale of its economic activities. In each case where possible, the nature of the developmental change is accompanied by an indication of its impact on foreign trade. The results are shown in Table 21.5.

The developmental changes in land, labor, capital, technological change, transformation, and scale shown in Table 21.5 compress into a very small compass a great deal of economic-development theory. This is not, unfortunately, the place to expound it. But it may help to explain the table to follow one or two of the parallel changes.

Take land, or resources. In the period of stagnation, land is fixed in quantity. There may be no-rent land which is inaccessible because of lack of transport; or land which cannot be used because of lack of technology, but this is not land in an economic sense at this stage. With the growth of commerce and trade, the quantity of land expands, because of its incorporation in a market, and exports, generally of land-intensive products, expand. With economic development under way, or what Professor Rostow calls the economic "take-off," land expands still faster as exploration adds new land through discovery, as investment in transport facilities links no-rent land to markets and gives it economic value, and as technological change at home and in foreign markets finds new uses for land previously regarded as worthless. This further expands exports. At the next stage of maturity two opposing forces are at work. Discovery and technical change expand the supply of land (and of land-intensive exports); but depletion, i.e., the using up of the most accessible and richest resources, particularly of minerals, tends to reduce exports and increase imports in these lines. In Canada, the first of these factors outweighs the second; in the United States, depletion is more important than discovery. Finally, in economic decline, whether absolute or relative, depletion is clearly

TABLE 21.5

IMPACT ON FOREIGN TRADE OF SEPARATE FACTORS CONDITIONING NATIONAL ECONOMIC DEVELOPMENT

Factors / Stage of Development	Resources (Land) (1)	Social Structure (Labor) (2)	Capital (3)	Technical Change (4)	Transformation (Capacity to Reallocate) (5)	Scale of Production (6)
Stagnation (a)	Fixed	Static	$I_d = S$ (both low) $X = M$ (both low)	Static	None; low supply elasticities; t of matter of luck	Small (village)
Commercial revolution (b)	Expansion (due to incorporation in market) $X\uparrow$	Beginnings of social mobility— money economy	$I_d = S$ (both low) $X = M$ (both $\uparrow$)	Once-for-all change (Myint) $X\uparrow$ (imitation) $M_c\uparrow$ (demonstration effect)	Elasticities expanding but low	Expansion at home; production for world market in enclaves
Economic growth (take-off) (c)	Discovery and technical change expand resources $X\uparrow$	Development entrepreneurial class $S\uparrow$ increased income $M_c\uparrow$	$I_d\uparrow, I_d > S$ $M_p\uparrow M > X$ borrowing abroad	Technical change (imitation) $M_p\uparrow$	Resources mobile $X\uparrow M\downarrow$ income rising $M\uparrow$	Integration of home and world markets $X\uparrow M\uparrow$ growth of M-competing industry $M\downarrow$
Maturity (d)	discovery $X\uparrow$ depletion $X\downarrow M\uparrow$	high income $S\uparrow$	$S > I_d$ $X > M$ lending abroad $X\uparrow$	Innovation new goods $X\uparrow M\downarrow$ new ways of producing old goods $X\uparrow M\downarrow$	Elasticities high income rising demand for services $M\uparrow$ absolutely $M\downarrow$ relatively	Product differentiation $X\uparrow M\uparrow$
Decline (e)	depletion $X\downarrow M\uparrow$	Fair shares $S\downarrow$ Reduced social mobility; demonstration effect $C\uparrow$	$I_d > S$ $M > X$ using up foreign assets	Slowing down of technical change, imitation abroad $X\downarrow$; imitation of foreign innovation $M\uparrow$	Elasticities declining, allocation below optimal t of $t\downarrow$	Declining scale as markets are reduced through protection

C consumption
I investment
I_d domestic investment
S savings
X exports
$\uparrow$ increase
$\downarrow$ decrease

M imports
M_c imports of consumption goods
M_p imports of producers goods
t of terms of trade
> is greater than
< is less than

dominant and tends further to reduce exports and to expand imports.

Take transformation, or the capacity of a country to reallocate resources. In the period of pre-trade stagnation, there is none. Occupations are traditional; technology is frozen; supply elasticities are low. A country's terms of trade may be good, bad, or indifferent, but they do not respond to price changes.

With the beginnings of commerce, all this slowly changes. Markets become linked; elasticities expand. After the take-off, the capacity to respond to price changes grows still further. Exports increase in lines where demand is strong; decline in others where demand is weak. The terms of trade are no longer unaffected by the country's action. In imports, two effects are taking place: one is the growth in real income which spills over into demand for foreign products for consumption (and investment). The other is increasing capacity to produce at home some manufactured products of commonplace technology for which materials are available.

In maturity, transformation capacity is at its height, but foreign trade tends to decline because of the growth of real income and the increased demand for services which are less traded internationally than commodities. Exports and imports both turn down on this score (though not necessarily on others). Finally, in the period of economic decline, capacity to transform weakens; the terms of trade may turn adverse without producing a supply response out of exports into import-competing goods (or they may be favorable without producing an expansion of exports).

Table 21.5 offers in highly stylized form a series of partial glimpses of the impact of economic development on foreign trade, and of what has happened in recent economic growth of an undirected nature. Its application to any one country must be made with care and appropriate (i.e., substantial) allowance for special conditions and, in particular, under modern conditions, for economic planning. It will be noted that the table makes no attempt to aggregate these effects, indicating directions only, and not the quantitative importance of opposing changes. Nonetheless, there is some warrant for believing that, in the typical case, foreign trade first grows and then declines as a proportion of total income. Professor Wallich has suggested that countries in the late stages of development show government expenditure in excess of domestic investment which is in turn larger than exports, while in underdeveloped countries the likelihood is that these magnitudes in declining order of importance are exports, government expenditure, and domestic investment. It will be recalled from our earlier discussion (p. 173) that the percentage of income spent on imports is a function of many things, including size and climatic diversity of the political unit. Nonetheless, there is something in the nature of a law of diminishing (relative) importance of foreign trade in the course of uncontrived economic development.

Professor Wallich has extended the distinction between developed and underdeveloped countries, based on the relative size of exports, investment, and government expenditure, to suggest that there may be a difference as to which of these items of expenditure are autonomous variables and which dependent. In a developed country we tend to think of investment (I), government expenditure (G), and exports (X) all as autonomous, along with an autonomous element in the largely dependent consumption (C), while the dependent variables, along with the dependent portion of C, are taxes (T) and imports (M). In underdeveloped countries, however, only a small part of investment is autonomous; most of it depends on the outlook for exports. A high marginal propensity to import makes it impossible for investment to increase autonomously in the absence of an increase in exports. In addition, the absence of a capital market to finance government deficits, plus the same high marginal propensity to import, means that government spending cannot for long exceed tax revenue (i.e., $G = T$) and government expenditure is equally dependent on exports. The major autonomous variable in open economies, largely underdeveloped, is then exports, and such countries cannot do much to influence the state of their employment or money income.

While Table 21.5 offers only partial insights into the size of exports or imports relative to national income, it does give, in column 3, a general-equilibrium answer as to the condition of the current account of balance of payments at each stage. We return to this subject after a brief excursion, largely by way of recapitulation of the relevant themes of Part III, on commercial policy in underdeveloped countries.

Commercial Policy for Developing Countries

In uncontrived growth, foreign trade may play a stimulating role in economic development as technical change and discovery of new resources provide foreign-trade opportunities. The Industrial Revolution in Britain and the experience of the United States, the Dominions, Sweden, and Switzerland provide examples of this sort. But in the vast majority of underdeveloped countries today, and in particular those which are densely populated, there is felt to be little prospect of new discoveries on a substantial enough scale (except in oil producers) or of substantial innovations, which would lead to development through exports. On the contrary.

Dr. Raul Prebisch, Executive Director of the Economic Commission for Latin America, suggests that developing countries today are unable to expand exports, require imports of producers' goods (see box c.4 of Table 21.5), and run the risk of dissipating their foreign exchange resources through the spilling over into imports of increases in money income (box c.2 of Table 21.5). They need to invest, and should borrow abroad for that purpose. But there are limits on the amount of funds available, and in any event it is undesirable to borrow to finance consumption; accordingly Prebisch envisages as a normal accompaniment of purposeful economic development, programs of import substitution, i.e., the development of domestic industries to produce consumption goods which would otherwise be imported, and protection through import controls while these industries are achieving maturity.

More than mere import substitution is involved, however. Economic planners have limited resources, particularly for investment. Should capital resources be allocated to export industries, or to social overhead projects such as railroads, power production, irrigation which promote exports? Or are the long-run terms of trade likely to run against primary products so that it is important to limit investment in agriculture and mining, even though current prices make such investment look profitable, on the ground that current prices do not adequately discount the future course of supply relative to demand?

In this chapter we can do no more than list the problems and indicate their controversial nature. Prebisch, and others like Myrdal who believe as he does, favor planned economic development in which only limited attention is paid to the law of comparative advantage; while Viner, as a leading exponent of the classical position, suggests that countries should expand wherever the price system indicates there are profitable opportunities, regardless of whether this should prove to be agriculture, mining, manufacturing, or service industries.

In part the underdeveloped-country case against relatively free trade is based on the infant-industry argument; in part, it relies on the existence of external economies in import-competing industry, such as manufacturing, which are not present in primary-producing export areas. One form of this line of reasoning is that advanced by Myint, discussed in the previous chapter, which holds that the advance in training in plantation economies halts after the first step.

But there are many other lines of argument, many of which have been touched upon in Part III: free trade is for the developed country, the innovating country which thus manages to keep down its competition. For countries which get off to a slow start, protection and a chance to catch up are regarded as needed.

Even if the law of comparative advantage in static terms provides a secure basis for specialization in primary products and free trade, two dynamic considerations have given underdeveloped countries pause. One is the possibility of adverse technological change which would displace its product: synthetic rubber, nitrate, silk, wool, quinine, etc. Another is short-run instability. There is very little that can be done about the former, except to continue to improve efficiency and reduce costs in the production of the raw material in question. To meet the instability of raw-material prices, which we have already discussed in Chapter 13, underdeveloped countries consistently advocate primary-product price stabilization.

The Need for Foreign Capital in Development

Column 3 of Table 21.5 indicates the basis of the developing country's need for foreign capital. Savings are small; investment is rising. This means that imports must exceed exports. To finance such a deficit, it is necessary to borrow. Unavailability of foreign capital means cutting investment, and slowing down the rate of growth because it is practically impossible to expand savings. Alone of the various factors represented by the column headings in Table 21.5, column 3, showing the relationship of domestic savings to domestic investment, "explains" what is happening to the balance of payments. All the other columns represent partial-equilibrium tendencies which may or may not be overwhelmed by other factors. But if intended domestic investment is in excess of intended domestic savings at a given level of national income, the balance of payments will indicate imports (current-account debits) in excess of exports (credits) which should be financed by long-term borrowing.

It is sometimes suggested that the need for foreign capital arises from the need for foreign capital equipment. This is evidently in error, as a moment's reflection on the lessons of Chapter 18 will reveal. Foreign capital can be transferred in capital equipment, consumption goods, or even services (see p. 347). If the economy has any capacity to transform resources from one industry to another, foreign capital is needed to add to resources in general rather than resources in particular. If there is a new need for foreign capital equipment, it can be met, provided there are new savings, by transferring the resources represented by the new savings into export industry or into import-competing industry to earn or save the necessary foreign exchange. (This is a long-run proposition, to be sure, and the transitional difficulties may be significant.) It is the lack of savings and/or the inability to shift resources which make foreign borrowing necessary, not the need for specialized foreign equipment.

In addition to the analytical error in this reasoning, it should be emphasized that a very substantial proportion of capital formation in all countries, underdeveloped and developed alike, consists in construction for which primarily domestic resources are needed. If foreigners supply loans in the form of food, surplus, or otherwise, farmers can be shifted from normal production into capital formation and convert foreign consumption goods into domestic capital.

The need for foreign capital, therefore, is the need for resources as a whole. It may arise because a country attempts too rapid a rate of investment, underestimating the cost of various projects, or overestimating the productivity of such projects or the amounts which will be saved out of increments in income. Or a country may plan perfectly but simply be in more of a hurry (for domestic political reasons) than the rate made possible by foreign loans available to it at the market. These are the fundamental factors underlying the complaint of many countries which have embarked on development programs that the supply of foreign loans is insufficient. To limit investment to the supply of domestic and foreign savings available would imply too slow a rate of growth of income.

Impact of Development on the Foreign Trade of Developed Countries

Economic development in a foreign country has two effects on the exports of a country already mature: the trade-creating effect, and the trade-destroying effect. To treat them in inverse order, the trade-destroying effect results from import substitution in the developing country; from the fact that through imitation, the developing country learns to provide for itself many of the wants previously met by imports from abroad (see boxes c.5, c.6, and e.4 in Table 21.5); and because the resources in the developing country previously engaged in exports may be diverted to domestic uses. The developing country quickly learns to provide itself with the simplest kinds of manufactures: salt, matches, cotton textiles, shoes, cheap pottery, with the result that developed-country exports in these lines are difficult to sustain. In addition, however, some rapidly developing countries after

World War II, notably Australia, Argentine, and the Union of South Africa, devoted so much of their total resources to domestic investment that they diverted resources away from production for export and worsened the terms of trade of developed countries by this means.

But the trade-destroying effect need not dominate. Economic development also creates trade. With development income rises and laps over into imports (boxes c.2 and c.5 in Table 21.5). Investment needs create opportunities for selling capital goods (box c.4). It is frequently argued that economic development does not reduce a country's imports but rather changes their character.

Whether a developed country will be more helped or harmed by economic development among its customers turns then in largest part on whether it retains the capacity to transform, i.e., to shift its resources out of old shrinking export lines into new expanding ones; and whether it continues as an innovator, developing itself new goods for its own use and for sale to its previous customers. If a country can transform—and its capacity to do so is based on a number of intangible qualities not yet adequately understood by economists—the trade-creating effect is virtually certain to overwhelm the trade-destroying effect of development abroad.

Summary

Countries can be classified from many points of view—geographical, political, economic. In economic terms it is frequently useful to classify them in terms of their stage of development. Here there are several bases: level of income, factor proportions, the position of the balance of payments, the position of the balance of indebtedness.

In the course of development, a number of aspects of an economy must undergo change: the quantity of land, the quality of labor, the quantity and quality of capital, the state of the arts or technology, the capacity of the society to reallocate resources, and the scale of production and distribution. At every stage, changes in these ingredients and processes of development have impacts on exports and imports. Typically, foreign trade grows with development, but at a less rapid rate than income.

Summary discussions were presented of the appropriate commercial policy for a developing country. In market-led development exports are often a leading sector; in present contrived development, however, exports often lag behind domestic investment. The need for foreign loans is due to an over-all need for resources, not a need for foreign resources in particular. The impact of development on the trade of countries previously developed depends on their capacity to adjust. In this last connection, the trade-creating effects are likely to outweigh the trade-destroying effects provided that developed countries retain the capacity to transform and to foster technical change.

SUGGESTED READING

TEXTS

C. P. Kindleberger, *Economic Development* (New York: McGraw-Hill Book Co., Inc., 1958), has three chapters on international issues of economic development. It also includes separate chapters on the role of resources, social structure, capital, technology, transformation, and scale in economic development. A new and excellent text in the field is G. M. Meier and R. E. Baldwin, *Economic Development* (New York: John Wiley & Sons, Inc., 1957) which, however, somewhat scatters its treatment of international issues in chapters xi, xix, xx, and parts of x, xiv, and xv.

TREATISES

See J. Viner, *International Trade and Economic Development,* which argues for the use of comparative advantage and free trade in developing countries, and a voluminous literature published by the Economic Commission for Latin America and the United Nations, which argues the contrary. See especially, *The Economic Development of Latin America and Its Principal Problems* (Lake Success, 1950).

An impressive item in the literature in favor of import restriction is G. Myrdal, *The International Economy* (New York: Harper & Bros., 1955) chap. xiii.

On the impact of economic development on the trade of developed countries, see the League of Nations, *Industrialization and Foreign Trade,* which is especially useful for its interwar statistics; and E. Staley, *World Economic Development* (Montreal: International Labour Office, 1944).

POINTS

The pathbreaking article by C. J. Bullock, J. H. Williams, and R. S. Tucker on "The Balance of Trade of the United States," *RE & S,* July, 1919, is reprinted in F. W. Taussig, *Selected Readings in International Trade and Tariff Problems* (Boston: Ginn & Co., 1921). These early estimates are in process of revision by D. C. North and M. Simon of the National Bureau of Economic Research.

An elaboration of classification of the balance of payments by stages is given by G. Crowther in *Balances and Imbalances of Payments* (Boston: Graduate School of Business Administration, Harvard University, 1957), Table 1, and pp. 8–12.

A discussion of the impact of economic development on the terms of trade will be found in my *The Terms of Trade* (New York: The Technology Press and John Wiley & Sons, Inc., 1956), chap. x.

PART V

Migration and Transfers

Chapter 22 | THE INTERNATIONAL MOVE-
MENT OF LABOR

The International Labor Market

The classical assumption that goods move internation-
ally while factors do not is invalid for labor as it is for capital. International occupational mobility of labor may not be large, but it is
positive.

Along borders, as in many parts of Europe, between Windsor
and Detroit, between Brownsville, Texas, and Montamoros, Mexico,
there may be daily commuting of an international character. Casual
workers journey seasonally from country to country in search of work,
moving particularly northward with the harvest or in the construction
season—whether Mexicans in North America or Italians in Europe.
Government administrators in colonies, businessmen managing direct
investments, planters, and increasingly professional consultants spend
varying periods of time at work outside the boundaries of the country
of their permanent residence. And for many centuries temporary and
permanent migration has been a familiar phenomenon, as large masses
of people have been attracted overseas by economic opportunity or
driven abroad by one or another kind of trouble at home.

An international market for labor of a sort may be said then to
exist. But the classical economists were right to the extent that this
market is a most imperfect one. The return to labor is not equalized
in identical occupations throughout the world. Indeed this is not true
within a country, except in broad terms; some labor economists make
a lot (too much) of the fact that there is considerable variability for
wages of equal skills even in the same town. Internationally, the
returns to labor differ persistently, despite the fact that labor can move
to a limited extent internationally, and despite the probable tendency
for international trade to bring about some equalization of factor
prices as discussed in Chapter 5.

In a two-factor, two-commodity world in which trade could bring

431

about the equality of goods and factor prices, it is equally true, as observed above, that such equalization could be achieved in the absence of trade by the free movement of capital. With no trade and capital immobility, the movement of labor could evidently achieve the same result. If goods, capital, and labor are all free to move, the outcome is indeterminate. Without further information, there is no indication which in fact of goods, capital, or labor would move and which would not. In the real world, however, this indeterminacy presents no problem. Goods move more freely than capital, and capital more freely than labor. None moves sufficiently to bring about factor-price equalization.

There is even doubt whether the factor-price-equalization model is relevant, except perhaps as a limiting case. We have observed that capital moves to a very considerable extent in well-worn grooves, governed more by institutionalized behavior patterns than by calculations of differences in return. Just as the London capital market lent mainly in areas of recent settlement and the Paris market to eastern Europe, so the international movement of labor follows established patterns, which may have been accidental in origin. The design of many of these flows, of course, has been political in character and related to noneconomic or only quasi-economic considerations.

The Patterns of Labor Movement

We do not propose to discuss in any detail the pattern of movement in border areas, where large numbers of people live on one side of a border and work on the other. Nor can we spend time on the distortions of the international labor pattern introduced by taxes. Professor Meade has pointed out that if one country taxes production and another consumption, it will pay a man to work and invest his capital in the latter but live in the former. A particular incentive to work abroad today is the provision of the income tax laws which exempts a citizen from United States income tax if he is abroad for longer than eighteen months. This encourages movie stars to move on location to the Riveria or the South Seas, and even economists to take on technical-assistance positions exempt from local income tax in underdeveloped countries for an eighteen-month period.

More interesting for our purposes are the waves of immigration to the United States in the period up to 1914, bringing in large numbers of English, German, Scandinavian, Irish, Italian, and eastern European immigrants. Each wave had a pattern of cumulative growth. Small numbers of pioneer emigrants made a successful start, sent for their relatives and friends, and the movement snowballed until the wave died down for one reason or another. Economic historians have debated whether the pull of opportunity was greater than the push of economic difficulty. In any case, however, it seems clear that these forces acted only against the background of a long-run migration cycle, which may or may not have had its origin in economic circumstances. In the burst of emigration from Ireland in the 1840's, the potato famine provided the push. Conversely, given the large-scale movement from Italy and eastern Europe with its beginnings in the collapse of the European wheat price in the early 1880's, the size of the annual flow was affected by conditions in the United States, slowing down as a consequence of the panic of 1907 and picking up with the subsequent revival.

Professor Brinley Thomas has detected a broad pattern in the Atlantic community, in which long cycles, connected with construction, were counterposed in Europe and North America, and produced rhythmical movements in migration. Large numbers of people were left stranded in rural occupations in Europe by the improvement in agricultural productivity in the first half of the nineteenth century and in the second by the technological advance in transport, which made possible grain imports from the rich plains of North and South America, Australia, and the Ukraine. The Industrial Revolution created opportunities for work in European cities. In the upswing of the long construction cycle, the rural exodus was directed internally to the industrial cities. In depression, however, when it was necessary to pause and consolidate the domestic economic position, the rural reserve went abroad. One regulator of the movement, directing the Scandinavian, German, and British peasant now to the city and now to North America and (for the British) the Antipodes, was the terms of trade. When they favored Europe, economic opportunity at home was high in textiles, coal, and steel, and ultimately engineering trades and the chemical industry. In the slump, the terms of trade turned against Europe, and capital and labor went abroad.

This pattern is sketched in broad strokes, of course, and does not fit parts of the picture. In southern Italy, Hungary, Poland, and Russia, there was little industry to attract the rural surplus. For a long time it stayed put. When it moved, it headed almost entirely abroad. It has been said that the South Italian was regarded as an object of derision in the industrial cities of Milan or Turin, and was more at home in New York or San Francisco—once, that is, the movement had gotten under way. It is interesting, too, to note that the migrants upon their arrival in the United States found their way into limited occupations and limited places of residence. Much of this was largely accidental. It is claimed that the Irish settled in Boston in greater numbers than in New York since the transatlantic fare to the former port was five shillings cheaper. German communities in Milwaukee and St. Louis, Swedish groups in Minnesota, Norwegian in the Dakotas, Polish in Baltimore and Buffalo, and Polish and Russian Jews in New York emphasize that the migrants were seeking their own kind, in the beginning, to provide a transition to life in the new world. Construction attracted Irish and Italian labor; Germans and Scandinavians went in for mixed and grain farming; northern Italians for truck gardening; Polish, German, and Russian Jews into the garment industry.

There is evidence to suggest that migration was more significant than capital in the determination of the terms of trade in the second half of the nineteenth century. Capital moved both to areas of recent settlement and to eastern Europe, while migration took place to areas of recent settlement, but from eastern Europe. Eastern Europe did not share in the overseas booms. Its terms of trade with western Europe were steady, and apparently unaffected by the movement of capital from Paris and Berlin to Moscow, Budapest, Bucharest, Sofia, and Warsaw. Borrowing while migrants went abroad was for budget deficits, defense expenditures (including armaments purchased in western Europe), and general extravagance rather than real capital formation. Capital inflow and immigration put a strain on real resources in overseas areas, while in eastern Europe employment opportunities for rural surplus labor were still lacking.

The imposition of immigration quotas by the United States in 1921 and 1924 is explained largely on social grounds. The cumulative flow of migrants from southern and eastern Europe, cut off by the war, showed signs of sharp revival. The check to cumulative emigration provided in Britain, Germany, and Scandinavia in the nineteenth century by industrial development and rising real incomes had never taken hold elsewhere, and the natural rate of increase had shown no signs of diminishing. Potential immigration was accordingly large. Its restriction posed grave social and economic problems for the affected areas, but its continuance would have done so for the United States and other receiving areas as they filled up.

War and its aftermath bring large-scale movements of population, again largely for social reasons. The Turkish expulsion of Greeks, Armenians, Jews in 1921, the eastern European expulsion of German colonists and residents from east of the Oder-Neisse line in 1945, and the displacement of Arabs from the territory made into Israel in 1948, provide examples of strict war origin. The vast movements of Hindus and Moslems between India and Pakistan after independence and partition in 1947, and the westward infiltration from behind the Iron Curtain, culminating in the escape of hundreds of thousands of refugees from Hungary in 1956, reflect social, political, and religious differences. The problem of economic and social settlement of these masses of people is a serious one. Eastern Germans have been absorbed with some difficulty into the life of western Germany. Jewish refugees from all over the world, including eastern Europe and Arab countries, are welcomed in Israel. But few other large groups of refugees have a ready reception. Countries seeking immigrants tend to specify requirements which demand youth, skills, capital, and frequently specialized occupations, including farming. When they do not insist on unmarried men younger than thirty, they prefer families of western European emigrants, and typically the Dutch farmer now in surplus because of the loss of his emigration outlet to the former Netherlands East Indies. The result is an indigestible refugee problem which private, national, and international action, through the International Refugee Organization, is only slowly managing to reduce.

Does Emigration Benefit the Sending Country?

If we leave out the convulsive population movements of the last paragraph, an interesting question which has received some discussion from economists is whether emigration is a good thing. It has been argued against it that sending grown people abroad permanently is a form of capital export: the country of emigration raises them from birth, feeds, clothes, and educates them through an unproductive period; and then loses them as they begin to reach a productive stage. This loss of a productive worker is comparable to the export of productive capital, except that not in all cases does the exporting country get a return on the net marginal productivity of the labor, over and above the maintenance and replacement costs (subsistence).

If the workers were slaves, sent abroad to produce a higher return than at home, and if their net product above subsistence were returned to the capital-exporting country, the capital-exporting analogy would be appropriate, provided that the slaves were raised for the purpose of earning a return. As a rule, however, population growth is independent of the opportunities for emigration, at least in the short run; the choice is not between investing resources in productive workers for migration abroad or investing these resources in more productive domestic lines. It is rather whether labor stays home in unemployment or underemployment, or seeks a job abroad. The resources invested in raising the labor to working age can be regarded as sunk. It is then a question whether a positive return on these resources is possible or, to put it otherwise, whether it is possible to relieve the pressure of unemployed on the domestic labor market through emigration.

If, in fact, emigration means escape from the long-run check to population growth, it may be wasteful in terms of real income per head. The ideal policy would be not to allow emigration until the Malthusian barrier has been broken and family limitation is used to maintain the per capita income.

Even with population growth at a rapid rate, large-scale emigration may produce real income for the remaining population if the rate of remittance to the home country is high. This rate is a function of the ties in the society, partly cultural in character and partly a reflection of the time period that the migrants have been away. In the early stages of migration, where men precede their families, income is remitted home to dependents and relatives, including sums saved to enable these to join the breadwinner. Later, as whole families are united abroad, remittances will decline to the level needed to assist relatives beyond the immediate family. Finally, as a generation passes, remittances dwindle to a trickle. Cultural change has altered the pattern as well as the time profile. In the thirty years before World War I, immigrants into the United States lived in ethnocentric groups in this country and moved only slowly to acquire the standard of living of the second- and third-generation families in the country as a whole. Today, the cultural hold of the immigrant group is virtually non-existent, since numbers are so small, and the pressure is strong on the occasional immigrant, such as the Hungarian refugees, to adjust quickly to the American standard. Even if it were easy and convenient to remit to relatives abroad behind the Iron Curtain—which it is not—social pressures to be assimilated to the new level of consumption reduce the capacity.

One issue in judging whether emigration is harmful or helpful turns on whether the more vigorous and energetic leave or only those who cannot find work at home. Puerto Rico and Mexico in particular are troubled that the pull of New York and southern California to Texas is strongest for those who are the most alert to the opportunity to improve their real income, and hence those who have the most to contribute to economic development at home. Some Europeans today assert, possible largely in jest, that the emigrants from such areas as Sweden were led mainly by the shiftless and ignorant who could not get jobs at decent wages at home. It seems probable that the Thomas thesis above is more nearly correct, that the migrants came from surplus population in agriculture; that the more vigorous went abroad in depression and into domestic industry in periods of industrial boom, with the other persons of average capacities following in their wake in these separate directions under the different circumstances.

The Swedish economist, Wicksell, answering the questions of a Royal Commission as to whether emigration hurt or helped, gave two reasons for thinking the latter. First were remittances, which constituted a useful source of foreign exchange, and second was the indirect effect of their production abroad which improved the long-run terms of trade of Europe. While the process of migration might be linked to adverse movement in the terms of trade in the short run, as capital formation abroad strained available resources and raised prices, the ultimate effect of the output of this capital, when it became productive, was to cheapen the cost of European imports. The analogy with capital exports is close.

Does Immigration Benefit the Receiving Country?

Whether immigration will benefit or hurt a country depends upon the country's resources of capital and land, relative to population, and the dynamic effects of the movements in question. Australia, Canada, Brazil, and similar large, underpopulated countries are interested in immigration of selected types of workers—young, farmers, skilled factory workers, etc.—because their resources are large relative to labor supply, and because the social overhead capital in countries of vast expanse typically produces increasing returns. Broadly, the same investment in interurban roads, railroads, and harbors, for example, is required for a large population as for a small one, and a given population may be well below the optimum.

There is nonetheless likely to be capital expenditure needed as a consequence of immigration. Housing is a particular requirement, where the indivisibilities inherent in a transport network do not exist, and along with housing comes the provision of local overhead capital—schools, intra-urban transport, including streets, hospitals, etc. A considerable volume of investment in Australia today is linked to immigration requirements.

In Israel and western Germany, the large-scale inward movement cannot be said to have hurt these countries, in the long run, despite the fact that they were well above the optimum population at the beginning of the movement in terms of social overhead capital. The reasons lie in the dynamic aspects of the movement. Israel's readiness to receive all Jewish refugees who were able to leave the countries where they constituted minorities contributed substantially to the spirit of dedication which evoked long hours of work and acceptance of low levels of consumption. These were extra-market phenomena which the economist has difficulty in explaining in terms of marginal productivity. In Germany, the dynamism lay partly, but only partly, in the evocation of a national effort. In large measure it operated through short-run pressure on wages, which held profits high, out of which a compulsive and even neurotic drive to work and invest by entrepreneurs rebuilt German capital at a rapid rate.

But immigration does not always bring one's co-religionists or co-nationalists, and even when it does, as in the case of the Palestinian Arab refugees in the Sinai peninsula and Jordan, there is no necessary dynamic result. (In these cases, the receiving countries discouraged efforts of the refugees to improve their economic conditions since this might have implied an acceptance of the view that they were not entitled to return to their land in Israel.)

Apart from external economies in social overhead capital and dynamic forces, immigration has effects on total output and on income distribution. It has been suggested by Lerner that where diminishing returns exist, and where on that account marginal product is below average product, it might be possible for the receiving country to alter the market distribution of income after immigration in order to bribe existing workers to accept an inflow of labor. Immigration lowers the marginal product of labor and hence wage rates; and raises the rent of unchanged factors such as land and capital. Government, however, could pay new workers their marginal product, but old workers their old wages, using part of the increase in rent in the system to make up the difference between the new and old marginal product. Since the marginal product in the new country is higher than in the old, everyone benefits from this operation.

This, of course, is a highly academic proposal. Even if one could start, in a short time the immigrants will want to be assimilated in the receiving country and to end the discrimination against them in wages. And one of the factors encouraging immigration in the first place is its effect on wages in general. The immigrants may be sought because native labor is not available for particular tasks which would be remunerative with cheaper labor available from abroad: the slaves needed to make cotton planting pay in the 1830's and 1840's kept down wage rates in cotton-farming areas. Similarly, the importation of Mexican wetbacks and Puerto Rican truck farm hands lowers wage rates at the margin. The pressure to halt immigration was primarily social but partly economic, the latter stemming from the newly powerful trade-unions which emerged from the war. An authoritative writer on Latin America asserts that support for immigration into these countries comes from employer groups who are anxious to hold down wage rates and maintain rates of profit. As we have had occasion to observe in discussing tariff policy, one policy may recommend itself from an over-all point of view, but another be adopted for distributional reasons where the factor or group which benefits wields political power. In this instance, however, it seems likely, as in the support given for free trade by Manchester liberals in the 1840's and Detroit manufacturers in the 1950's, the distributional argument and the total-efficiency argument overlap. While population is growing rapidly in many of these countries, such as Brazil and Venezuela, they are currently underpopulated relative to resources and already possess an efficient network of social capital.

Cosmopolitan Migration Policy

From a strictly economic point of view, which we are not warranted in taking in this discussion, the optimum policy for the world with respect to migration would be freedom of movement to equalize wages among those countries where the rate of population growth had shown some check. If there were no social and political inhibitions to movement, countries of immigration among them would experience a decline in wages, while wages would rise in countries of emigration. If the overpopulated country has not experienced the Malthusian revolution, however, unlimited migration can only equalize wages by reducing them abroad, as the reduction in the surplus population through emigration is replaced by natural increase.

This position is not fundamentally altered by the demographic counterrevolution in North America and in some countries of western Europe under which the large family is sought, despite its effect on the level of material income per capita, because large families are regarded as good in themselves. The enlarged family should be counted as part of real income. Income increases at a fixed income of $6,000 per family as family numbers rise from four to six, despite the decrease in income per capita from $1,500 to $1,000.

A special problem is posed by migration from a country where family limitation prevails to one where it is not needed, with the consequence of a return to much larger families. Ireland in the last half of the nineteenth century limited the rate of population increase by late marriages. Emigrants from Ireland to the United States were able to obtain incomes and marry at a much earlier age, with the result that the birthrate of the immigrants from Ireland was very much higher than that of the society they left. This case should probably be counted as one in which the Malthusian revolution had not been accomplished.

Increasing Freedom of Movement

Much of the demand for increased international freedom to migrate is humanitarian in character; some of it is political. But in limited instances, there is pressure for increased labor mobility which is partly economic. This is especially the case in connection with the European Coal and Steel Community and the European Common Market.

The Coal and Steel Community which is attempting the rationalization of a major industry in six countries of Europe—France, Germany, Italy, Belgium, the Netherlands, and Luxembourg—evidently has to concern itself with the problem of labor. If one country is short of labor, but possesses the appropriate resources of coal, iron, and capital, while another has surplus workers, the most efficient production requires movement of the workers, if they will go. The most efficient allocation of labor, in fact, is achieved only when men of similar skills earn identical incomes at identical tasks regardless of the country in which they happen to be working. The High Authority has used its supranational powers to eliminate the necessity for national work permits in coal and steel, providing the workers in these industries with papers which enable them to work anywhere in the industry in the six countries.

But it is evident that optimal allocation also requires identical wages for work of identical character for labor in different industries in the separate countries. A skilled mechanic in France should not earn more or less because he is in the steel industry than he would in another industry. Labor mobility restricted to coal and steel in the six countries implies immobility of movement between occupations in the separate countries. It was, on this account, an untenable long-run position. Accordingly, the agreement for the European Common Market provides for increased mobility of workers in all occupations.

There is a fear in some quarters that the mobility of capital may exceed the mobility of labor in the Common Market, and that the result of its adoption may be the stranding of labor in such places as southern Italy and southwestern France, as capital leaves these areas for more profitable occupations. All the steps taken by the ECSC High Authority have not done much to increase labor mobility in coal and steel. A high degree of factor mobility must be preceded by a social basis which makes a man at home anywhere in Europe as an American (or a Canadian) is at home anywhere north of the Rio Grande. Even in Scandinavia, where the first step toward economic integration was the adoption of a common labor market, there was very little movement of labor from Norway or Denmark to the high-wage Sweden.

To meet the possibility that social inhibitions limit labor mobility and that capital may move in the wrong direction, judged by the equalization of wages, the Coal and Steel Community, the European Common Market, and the Scandinavian Economic Union all provide for a common pool of investment funds. This may be used to bring governmental capital to labor if labor will not move to capital and especially if it is deserted by existing capital.

Even where the social basis of integration exists, migration is strongly affected by economic conditions. In the United States, the movement from the farm to the city in the 1920's was reversed in the 1930's in depression, and a net movement to the real-income stability of the farm took place. Similarly in Britain, the net emigration to the Dominions of the 1920's was replaced by net immigration in the 1930's. Noneconomic bases for movement are also subject to variation: A big rise in interest in migration to the Dominions occurred in Britain after the Egyptian seizure of the Suez Canal in July, 1956.

Technical Assistance

Current interest in economic development of underdeveloped areas, with its emphasis on technical assistance, suggests that the international transmission of technology through personal visits is a new phenomenon. It is not so. Flemish weavers taught their secrets to the British woolen industry in the thirteenth and fourteenth centuries. Somewhat later Lombardy merchants and bankers led the commercial revolution in London. After the Industrial Revolution, British engineers built the railroads of the Continent, and British textile and steel workers communicated their skills to French, German, and Italian factories and mills. Up to about 1830 it was illegal in Great Britain to export machinery, for fear of competition; but master workers coming to the United States smuggled it out or reproduced it upon arrival from drawings.

There are, to be sure, differences in the extent and character of international diffusion of technical capacity now as compared, say, to the nineteenth century. International organizations, national governments, and international corporations provide new institutions for this transmission which are evidently more efficient than the single worker or engineer, or the limited colony of workers. The result is that international travel and foreign residence of skilled personnel, professional and manual, have reached new heights each year since World War II. Crews of Texas oil drillers can be encountered anywhere; teams from Morrison-Knudson, Krupp, and similar construction enterprises are found from Afghanistan to Zanzibar; economists from Scandinavia and the British dominions—which produce impressive surpluses for export—are found advising central banks, planning boards and treasuries in Asia, Latin America, and Africa.

Mobility of specialized labor within the United States has been increased by the growth of the national corporation which is prepared to shift executives and professional personnel at all levels from one part of the country to another. Similarly, the increasing number of corporations operating in more than one country is leading to a wider movement of executive and professional personnel internationally, and the diffusion of skills, whether unconsciously or to meet governmental requirements.

Preceding this spread of technical capacity through business may be education abroad. The small countries of Europe have always provided a year abroad in the ideal curriculum. British universities have attracted many students from overseas. Paris, Berlin, and especially Vienna were intellectual centers serving areas well beyond their national frontiers. The role of the United States in this education process has increased, especially since World War II, and large numbers of students move from the United States abroad and from foreign lands to United States universities. Within a country, universal education provides a social basis for increasing mobility. The export and import of education similarly increases the social basis for international mobility, as well as contributing directly to productivity. In some cases the purpose of the educational opportunity is defeated by the expatriation of the student.

Armed Forces

A substantial item in the balance of payments of a number of countries since the beginning of World War II has been the expenditure of armed services in foreign countries, whether of expeditionary forces, occupation troops, or contributed forces. Part of the expenditure is for food, shelter, and local supplies; part is the expenditure of the troops themselves, largely for entertainment. The withdrawal of United States troops from Japan, arranged in 1957, seems certain to produce a serious setback in the credit side of the Japanese current account. The existence of large numbers of troops from the capital-intensive United States in labor-intensive Japan for more than twelve years, however, emphasizes that many considerations other than economic efficiency dictate the direction and size of the movement of armed forces.

Beyond the problems of war and occupation, however, there is the possibility, in making contributions of defense power to a common defense effort, that joint contributions can go a short distance to equalize factor prices. In comparing the defense effort relative to national income in a number of countries, the North Atlantic Treaty Organization has found out that it is difficult to measure the productivity of a soldier. Like the rest of the governmental sector, military output is measured by military expenditure, with the consequence that the higher the level of military pay, the higher the "value" of the military effort. It is, of course, impossible to have some countries contribute capital, some manpower, and some land, since the armed forces of every country are contributed in finished units rather than raw factor inputs. Nonetheless, the likelihood that each country will contribute what it has a comparative advantage in—the densely populated country infantry, and the capital-intensive country complex equipment, leaves some room for raising the price of the abundant factor, and lowering that of the scarce.

Summary

Labor moves across international boundaries in limited amounts, and generally in structured paths. Some movement is daily, seasonal, institutionalized through companies and governmental bodies, and some permanent. The pattern of migration in the nineteenth century tended to be synchronized with alternating long cycles in Europe and abroad. Waves of emigration from Britain, Ireland, Germany, and Scandinavia initially built up in cumulative fashion, and then came to a halt, as the difference in wage rates narrowed between Europe and the areas of settlement. From Italy and eastern Europe, however, the migration built up cumulatively until cut off by war and immigration quotas. Birth rates remained high, and there was no substantial domestic industry to assist in absorbing the rural surplus. Emigration benefits the sending country through remittances, improvement in the terms of trade as a result of expanding production abroad, and relief for structural unemployment. In one sense, however, the raising and education of able-bodied workers constitutes a capital investment when it is not clear that overpopulated countries should export capital. Emigration may also attract the most vigorous elements in a society. Immigration is desirable for a country, provided the process of social assimilation is not serious, if its population is below optimal. In addition, immigration may be undertaken for structural and distributional reasons. Immigration, however, may have dynamic effects in other circumstances which outweigh adverse economic considerations.

Increased freedom of labor movement has been sought in Europe, but the accomplishment thus far is limited. Technical assistance and the co-operative defense efforts provide other means of moving skilled professional and executive labor, on the one hand, and massed manpower, on the other.

SELECTED READING

TEXTS

S. Enke and V. Salera, *International Economics* (3rd ed.; New York: Prentice-Hall, Inc., 1957), chap. xvi.

TREATISES, ETC.

Brinley Thomas, *Migration and Economic Growth* (Cambridge: Cambridge University Press, 1954), studies the experience of the Atlantic migration and contains a detailed bibliography.

H. Jerome, *Migration and. Business Cycles* (New York: National Bureau of Economic Research, 1926), examines whether the push of depression is more significant than the pull of prosperity abroad. Meade, *Trade and Welfare*, chap. xxvii, studies the effects of factor movements.

POINTS

On the relation between migration and the terms of trade, see my *The Terms of Trade*, pp. 130–31.

Among the varied and voluminous literature on the movement of labor in Europe under the various plans for integration, see International Labour Office, *Social Aspects of European Economic Co-operation* (Geneva, 1956). An appendix by M. Byé expresses the fear that foreign corporations will take advantage of the Common Market to take capital out of France and hence strand French labor.

Chapter 23

INTERGOVERNMENTAL ECONOMIC ASSISTANCE

The Growth of Governmental Transactions

Prior to the middle of the twentieth century, government's role in international economic affairs in peacetime was limited largely to the control of private transactions and foreign borrowing. There were exceptions. The Louisiana purchase from France and the Alaska purchase from Russia were significant capital transactions of the United States. The British government granted subsidies to colonies (which might be regarded, however, as internal transactions) and occasional military assistance like that of £10 million annually to support the Arab Legion in Jordan.

In war, the record was different. Allies typically shared treasure as well as blood. President Coolidge's view of the Allied war debts of World War I as a commercial obligation ("They hired the money, didn't they?") sounded strange to many ears even in the 1920's. The British had provided subventions to their continental allies against Napoleon, without the need to justify it.

Disaster also evoked intergovernmental assistance. The Red Cross is semigovernmental only, but the United States took official action in transferring its share of the Boxer indemnity to Chinese relief, and governmental assistance was invoked in the Tokyo earthquake and fire. The largest role internationally in disaster was left to private charities, but governmental action was not totally absent.

In retrospect it seems inevitable that the role of government should expand in international economics, as it has done domestically. The origins of the domestic expansion have been war and depression: in 1929 the governmental budget accounted for less than 5 per cent of national income, as compared with 20 per cent today, and 50 per cent at the peak of the war effort in 1944. Most of the increase in the role of government domestically is due to war—past and prospective. But some substantial amount of today's 20 per cent is attributable to

445

domestic transfers (apart from interest on debt contracted in wartime) such as social security, aid to education, housing, roads, etc. In exact parallel, most of the international governmental transactions in the late 1950's are caused by defense expenditure, but some have their origin in a new principle of international transfers or sharing between countries.

TABLE 23.1

SUMMARY OF UNITED STATES FOREIGN GRANTS AND CREDITS, BY PROGRAMS,
JULY 1, 1940, TO JUNE 30, 1957
(In Millions of Dollars)

	War Period (*July 1, 1940–June 30, 1945*)	*Postwar Period* (*July 1, 1945–June 30, 1957*)
Grants		
Lend-Lease	46,728	1,906
Greek-Turkish aid		653
Mutual Security:		
Military aid		18,050
Contribution to multilateral-construction programs		425
Other aid (economic and technical assistance)		20,251
Civilian supplies (military relief)	813	5,856
UNRRA, post-UNRRA, and Interim Aid	83	3,443
Philippine rehabilitation		635
Surplus agricultural commodities through private welfare agencies		602
Military equipment "loans"		366
Chinese stabilization and military aid	380	261
Inter-American programs		191
Other	124	597
Total Grants	48,128	53,237
Less: Reverse grants, returns on grants, and prior grants converted into credits	7,882	3,981
Net Grants	40,246	49,256
Credits		
Export-Import Bank	329	4,910
British loan		3,750
Mutual security		2,288
Surplus property (including merchant ships)		1,492
Lend-Lease	349	71
Other	417	513
Prior grants converted into credits		2,257
Total Credits	1,096	15,280
Less: Repayments	380	4,539
Net Credits	715	10,742
Net Foreign Aid (net grants plus net credits)	40,961	59,998

Source: U.S. Department of Commerce, Office of Business Economics, *Foreign Aid*, basic data through June, 1953; and *Foreign Grants and Credits by the United States Government*, June, 1957, Quarter.

Table 23.1 sets out the international economic assistance of the United States government from the beginning of Lend-Lease in March, 1941, until June 30, 1945, and from July 1, 1945, to June 30, 1957.

The amounts are impressive. But while we discuss United States economic assistance to foreign countries in this period, it is important to remember that this was not the only country rendering such aid. The United Kingdom dealt with its colonies and allies on liberal terms during World War II, and in turn received economic assistance on a substantial scale from the dominions during the war and post-war period. More recently, discussion of intergovernmental assistance has been complicated by the entrance of the Soviet Union into the field, assisting not only the satellites of eastern Europe and China but also, in a military way, its newly won allies, Egypt and Syria, and providing economic assistance to these and other underdeveloped countries.

Lend-Lease, Mutual Aid, and Military Relief

The principles of Lend-Lease are generally familiar. Goods (not money) were provided to United States allies without payment, on a basis to be settled after the war. A number of these countries in turn provided mutual aid to United States armed forces in their countries. Lend-Lease aid consisted in military equipment and military and civilian supplies. Mutual aid was made up of services rendered to the American forces, including civilian labor, rents, supplies of domestically available produce, and monies distributed as troop pay to American forces for local expenditure. This mutual aid amounted to $7,882 billion, or 16 per cent of Lend-Lease in the opposite direction. In the case of Belgium, the value of mutual aid exceeded that of the Lend-Lease, and ultimate settlement involved a net payment by the United States to Belgium.

Immediately after the end of hostilities against Japan, President Truman and Secretary of State Byrnes halted Lend-Lease, in line with their commitments to the Congress. Goods in transit were delivered, and specialized goods ordered were allowed to be finished and shipped. Lend-Lease procurement facilities were used for prime civilian items such as wheat and gasoline, but only against full cash payment. For past items, settlements were negotiated. A few items in short supply were asked to be returned. Some goods of prime civilian use not yet consumed but in storage or transit were regarded as transferred at full cost on long-term loans. The majority of military equipment and supplies which had been consumed were written off against the contribution of other countries to the war. At the same time, a considerable amount of United States equipment abroad, capable of civilian use, including trucks, tires, tents, military clothing, as well as food, was declared surplus and made available to allied countries under surplus property loans for twenty-eight-year terms at low rates of interest.

Lend-Lease was available to active allies. Liberated countries which did not enter Lend-Lease agreements were recipients of military supplies for civilian use—to maintain order in the zone of military operations—under the so-called Plan A. Bills were later submitted by the Army for these supplies, and these were consolidated into surplus-property settlements. Austria and Italy, which had a status between liberated and defeated countries, received military aid from the United States and Britain before they were transferred to international support from the United Nations Relief and Rehabilitation Agency (UNRRA). United States support for the civilian populations of Germany and Japan was provided under a military budget item entitled Government and Relief in Occupied Areas (GARIOA).

UNRRA and Post-UNRRA Assistance

It was recognized during the course of the war that there would be serious problems afterwards. To this end there was organized UNRRA to provide relief and rehabilitation as its name indicated; the International Bank for Reconstruction and Development, which was to complete the reconstruction and make the transition to the peacetime problem of development; and the International Monetary Fund to organize payments in the reconstructed financial world.

UNRRA was constituted partly with money and procurement machinery, largely in the United States, and partly with surplus United States Army stocks, which enabled it to begin operations rapidly. Its major contributors initially were the United States (72 per cent), the United Kingdom (18 per cent), and Canada (6 per cent). The remaining contributions, including that of the Soviet Union, were small. The first *tranche,* or share, amounting to $1.3 billion, was allocated mainly to countries behind the Iron Curtain, since the countries of western Europe either were contributors, had foreign-exchange reserves, or were occupied. When it came time to vote a second *tranche,* the British wanted to transfer Austria and Italy from military relief, where their share of the cost was greater, to UNRRA. Canada decided to channel its aid direct to Britain. And the Soviet Union, as a price of agreeing to these changes, insisted that the "separate countries" of Byelo-Russia and the Ukraine be entitled to receive rehabilitation supplies. The United States with only one vote in seventeen on the council, despite the fact that it contributed

78 per cent of the second *tranche* (its original share plus the Canadian), resolved to avoid the necessity to bargain about its aid in future. With the allocation of the second *tranche,* UNRRA was wound up. A post-UNRRA relief program was provided by the United States largely for Austria and Italy, as deteriorating relations with Yugoslavia, Poland, and Hungary colored the United States view of their relief requirements.

Export-Import Bank and the Anglo-American Financial Agreement

It was recognized, in the summer of 1945, that the International Bank and Fund would take time to begin operations, and that something was needed to tide over until they did. To this end the capital of the Export-Import Bank was raised by $3 billion. Loans were made for reconstruction purposes to liberated countries like France, and to Latin American allies. For a time $1 billion was earmarked for a loan to the Soviet Union. When it failed to apply, or did not receive an application—but in any event after the deterioration of political relations—the money was made available to other borrowers.

Shortly after the Export-Import Bank capital expansion, it became clear that neither it nor the International Bank would be sufficient to cope with the financial problem facing the United Kingdom. This was especially the case after the abrupt termination of Lend-Lease. In the fall of 1945 a British delegation under Lord Keynes came to Washington to negotiate a very large amount of assistance to put Britain back on her feet and enable her to play a role in the postwar reconstruction of other countries. Aid to Britain was justified under the so-called "key-currency principle" which Professor John H. Williams had enunciated in opposing the Bretton Woods Bank and Fund. He had held that it was a mistake to try to get all countries back on their feet simultaneously but rather that one currency at a time should be restored to strength and relied upon as a pillar of support for others. Lord Keynes had envisaged a substantial loan of $5 billion or more on an interest-free basis, or possibly as a grant. The United States was willing to provide only $3,750 million, however, and on the basis of interest and repayment of principal. It insisted that the British resume currency convertibility within twelve months of the receipt of the loan. When these twelve months were up, in July, 1947, Britain had succeeded in negotiating no agreements for scaling down or blocking the substantial sterling accumulations of its colonies and allies, had permitted substantial export of capital to South Africa and Australia, and had been unable to prevent withdrawals for Belgium and Argentina. Convertibility brought with it a run on sterling which in six weeks had exhausted the bulk of the loan. Foreign-exchange restrictions were then restored.

The Truman Doctrine and the Marshall Plan

By the spring of 1947 it became clear that UNRRA, the International Bank, and the Fund were going to be insufficient to meet the postwar reconstruction needs of Europe, even with the Export-Import Bank capital enlargement and the Anglo-American Financial Agreement. A severe winter and spring had set back agricultural and industrial production, but even before that the reconstruction and restocking of the economy of western Europe were far from complete. Countries like France and the Netherlands were running short of exchange reserves, even after Export-Import Bank, Fund, and Bank loans, and were not in a position to pay their way.

In February, 1947, the British discontinued financial support of Greece. President Truman responded by announcing a program of military and economic assistance for Greece and Turkey, which was similarly threatened by aggression.

In June, 1947, Secretary of State George C. Marshall made an address in which he suggested that if Europe were to devise an over-all plan of recovery to replace the piecemeal, patchwork approach followed thus far the United States would view it favorably. A Committee for European Economic Cooperation drew up such a program. While it was being discussed, an Interim Aid program was put into effect to tide over especially France and the Netherlands. On April 3, 1948, the Marshall Plan went into effect, contemplating an expenditure of some $16 billion over four years. The Soviet Union did not participate, nor did it permit the participation of its satellites. Western Germany, which had carried through a monetary reform in June, 1948, was shifted from GARIOA to Marshall-Plan assistance. The level of aid for seventeen countries from Iceland to Turkey was scheduled at $5.6 billion a year and was expected to decline to zero after June 30, 1952.

It is difficult to evaluate the Marshall Plan in detail because the outbreak of fighting in Korea two years later, in June, 1950, substantially changed the character of the problem. Economic assistance to western Europe declined on, or ahead of, schedule. But military assistance rose substantially. Nonetheless, it is probably safe to say that the aid under the European Recovery Program was on the whole effectively used and that recovery made long strides in every country in the program.

Military Assistance and Defense Support

The Korean hostilities underlined the weakness of the defensive position in Europe and the necessity to take new military measures. The North Atlantic Treaty Organization, covering a somewhat smaller number of countries than the seventeen members of the Organization for European Economic Cooperation, undertook a program of defense expenditure with a number of international aspects. One was the provision of military equipment by the United States to its allies. Another involved the purchase of equipment by the United States from factories in Europe, for ultimate use either by United States or by other European forces. A third was the provision of certain overhead defense installations: airfields, pipelines, storage depots, etc., called by the French the "infrastructure" (in English, not underfoot, but overhead).

In an important sense, buying military assistance in the cheapest market cannot be called military assistance. We are not used today to hiring mercenaries, as George III did Hessians, and there is even something of a loss of prestige involved in using foreign equipment and relying on foreign defense contributions. But if each country ceased to rely on the patriotism of its armed forces, defense might well be an item of international commerce. One could buy defense, as one now buys bananas, coffee, tin, and rubber. To some considerable extent, then, military assistance is not so much assistance to others as a purchase for domestic consumption.

Defense support involves the provision of civilian items to enable a foreign country to devote more of its own resources to defense needs. In the United States, military assistance has been operated by the Department of Defense and defense support by the International Cooperation Administration in the Department of State, which succeeded the Economic Cooperation Administration and its successor, the Foreign Operations Administration. It is given primarily to the Chinese forces on Formosa, the South Korean government, and the Vietnamese.

Technical Co-operation and Development Assistance

Point Four of President Truman's Inaugural Speech in 1949 called for a bold new program of assistance to underdeveloped countries. The content of this program turned out to be mainly technical assistance, largely in the fields of agriculture, public health, and education. This has been carried out partly through the United Nations but primarily through the bilateral International Cooperation Administration. Almost 5,000 United States experts were abroad at one time or another during 1957, and 5,300 foreign participants arrived in the United States in that year for training or visits. Ultimately it became clear that technical assistance was not sufficient to bring about self-perpetuating economic growth in underdeveloped countries, and that, in addition, there was need for capital assistance beyond that available through private enterprise and international agencies. The United States made some such assistance available on the basis of selected projects. Additional amounts consisted in surplus agricultural commodities which could be sold for local currencies which were used for development projects. In the 1958 budget, the Eisenhower Administration requested Congress to establish an Economic Development Fund which could be used over a number of years in contrast with normal expenditures which have to be appropriated annually.

It is important to recognize that these development funds constitute the first intergovernmental economic assistance on a peacetime, semipermanent basis. Wartime, relief, reconstruction, military assistance, and even defense support are each based on programs which some day come to an end, and which have in fact been terminated for the first three. But technical co-operation and development assistance involve outlays which can continue without limit.

Other Forms of Assistance

In addition to military assistance, defense support, technical assistance, and development loans and grants, the United States government has operated a variety of small programs, ranging from assistance to individuals escaping from the Iron Curtain to special programs of such agencies as the World Health Organization or Atoms for Peace or the United Nations expenses for clearing the Suez Canal. Part consists of emergency funds available to meet national disasters—flood, earthquake, famine, Communist subversion. Part is to meet economic emergencies or to assist countries in which the United States is interested, during a period of negotiations involving United States interests.

Intergovernmental Assistance Problems

The foregoing pages do little more than identify the various forms of intergovernmental economic assistance in which the United States has participated in the last fifteen years. In the space that remains in this chapter, not much more can be attempted than to indicate some of the problems and dilemmas to which such assistance gives rise. The astute reader will recognize that some of these dilemmas have had their domestic analogues which time has managed to solve without undue difficulty. It used to be thought, for example, that unemployment insurance ran grave risks of undermining the incentive to work. It may be that time will also be found to settle decisively, in one way or another, certain issues which now appear more delicately balanced. The problems concern the nature of the need for assistance, the principles on which aid should be granted, conditions, etc.

Aid for Limited Purposes versus Provision of Resources in General

During the provision of Lend-Lease to Britain a serious problem related to the size of United States assistance was the extent to which Britain was to continue normal exports. These exports used up resources which would otherwise have been devoted to the war and would therefore have reduced the need for assistance. Whether Britain should be left further in debt to her peacetime trading partners, and with a minimum of normal export trade at the end of the war, is unimportant for the present discussion. The essential point is that any assistance program must consider not only the particular use of the resources made available but the totality of the resources under the jurisdiction of the receiving country.

This principle is not always observed. The project basis for the loans of the International Bank for Reconstruction and Development has been noted. Similarly, the Economic Cooperation Administration was concerned to trace through the use of the steel made available to, say, France under the Marshall Plan, whereas it should have been concerned with the efficient use of all steel, or in fact all resources which might have been used to manufacture steel. It is clear-cut and relatively easy to ensure that appropriate use is made of particular economic assistance. But only total resources are relevant.

This principle raises an important point concerning military assistance and defense support. It has been proposed that both these categories of aid be separated from the question of assistance for economic development and handled through the budget of the Defense Department in the United States. But the distinction between aid to defense and aid for development is a difficult one to keep sharp. Given a fixed military program in a recipient nation, foreign aid for that program releases resources for economic development; and, conversely, given a fixed development program, economic development assistance contributes to military capacity, or consumption, or any other expansible item. The separation between economic and development assistance is only valid if each is determined separately, assuming every other expenditure fixed. If both remain to be determined, they are inseparable.

The same can be said about the project approach to development initiated by the International Bank and followed by the International Cooperation Administration. To allocate assistance for capital projects ensures that it is not wasted only on the untenable assumption that everything else is unchanged. More frequently the project would have been undertaken anyhow; to assist it is to assist consumption, or capital exports, or some other diverse purpose. Economic assistance in particular turns out in the usual case to be economic assistance in general. And it is justified or wasted, depending upon how effectively the country uses its own general resources. This is exactly converse to the principle of economic warfare discussed in Chapter 13. Bombardment (or blockade, etc.) deprive the enemy of resources in particular, rather than resources in general, only when he has no capacity, or is not allowed time, to transfer resources from one occupation to another.

The Appropriate Amount of Aid

In wartime the determination of the appropriate amount of aid is relatively easy. The United States should help Britain rather than use its resources on its own military effort, so long as a dollar of resources in Britain buys more firepower delivered against the enemy than a dollar of resources in the United States. This principle may have to be modified to take account of national pride, the indivisibility of military effort, and similar considerations. But at basis, the calculation is straightforward.

In peacetime, on the contrary, there is no single criterion. It might be argued that aid should be continued until income per capita is equal in the two countries, but this requires a world rather than a national point of view, and few are prepared to urge it.

Under the Marshall Plan, country programs were adopted, and aid was sought to make up the balance-of-payments deficits resulting from these programs. But this was fallacious. As Machlup pointed out, the programs depended upon how much finance could be found for the resulting balance-of-payments deficits, not the deficits on unalterable programs. And when the first approximation of investment programs of the Committee on European Economic Cooperation produced a four-year deficit of $30 billion, the Committee was able to amend the program when Messrs. Clayton and Douglas informed them that this was more than the United States was likely to support.

Not only does the deficit determine the program, rather than the other way about, but to calculate aid on the basis of deficits is to distort incentives and to put a premium on inefficiency. A country which contributes its own resources to capital formation through a rigorous program of austerity will have a smaller deficit than the country which is unable to marshal savings for productive use, and deserves more rather than less aid, according to the principle that the Lord helps those who help themselves. Subsidies, like taxes, can be distortionary in terms of effort. To minimize this distortion, there is something to be said for having the amount of assistance fixed, so that the benefits of its additional efforts accrue to the assisted rather than to the assisting country. Theorists have devised the ingenious (but impractical) scheme of lump-sum progressive taxes, levied on expected earning power. The fixed amount of the tax makes the marginal return from additional effort equal for people of different incomes and minimizes distortion of effort. Similarly, lump-sum subsidies, not necessarily on a progressive basis, would minimize the perverse effects of a subsidy to inefficiency involved in basing economic assistance on the amount of a country's deficit.

The national goal must take into account the available resources, but is likely also to rely on some combination of the historical, the desirable, and the feasible, the last in terms of domestic as well as foreign availabilities. Thus, under the Marshall Plan the goal of Britain involved a standard of living higher than that in Italy, but the projected Italian standard was higher in relation to prewar than the British because of the poverty of prewar Italy.

As noted in Chapter 21, Professors Millikan and Rostow have suggested that underdeveloped countries should be accorded all the capital they can absorb. They have in mind that the limits to capital imports without inflation or capital consumption in most of these countries are set by their capacity to find complementary resources at home and to achieve the appropriate transformation. This criterion presents the difficulty, however, that Canada would be entitled to more economic assistance than India; and to cut off assistance above a certain level of development can be regarded as arbitrary.

A final dilemma is encountered in connection with competitive assistance from the Soviet Union. Should aid from the Soviet Union entitle a country to more, the same, or less aid from the United States?

More is the competitive answer, which the underdeveloped countries would like. On the other hand, if the country can only absorb a limited amount of capital, its requirements are reduced by the availability of other aid. But in any practical situation the response of the United States to Soviet aid to an underdeveloped country could be neither substantially to increase its aid nor to cut it by the amount of Soviet aid, but something in between.

Indirect Assistance

There is no need for assistance to a country to be direct. In some cases, indeed, it is not clear which country is being helped. Under the Hyde Park Agreement of 1941, the United States made available goods on Lend-Lease to Britain which were shipped to Canada and used there in connection with the Canadian war effort on British behalf. This can properly be regarded as aid to Britain if Canada would have been unable to assist Britain in its absence. But if the Canadian assistance would have been forthcoming in any event, and to this extent, the Lend-Lease amounts recorded for Britain in fact aided Canada.

This form of indirect assistance has developed on a much larger scale in the postwar period. The Anglo-American Financial Agreement was recognized as an attempt, through assistance to Britain, to help other countries of the world, including the Dominions and Latin America. By means of this loan, the British were able to buy, and the Dominions and Latin America able to sell, goods which might not otherwise have moved in trade. Later in the European Recovery Program, offshore procurement by the United States in Canada and Latin America financed with convertible currencies the sales of these countries to Europe.

During this stage of the recovery in Europe, it will be remembered from Chapter 15, there was widespread trade discrimination against so-called luxury goods in Europe in the hope of acquiring dollar surpluses for use in buying necessities from North America. Aid to Europe could thus be given by United States purchases of lemons from Italy for delivery to Germany. Italy was helped to sell products for which it could not otherwise hope to receive dollars; Germany received lemons it would not otherwise have been able to enjoy. This system, however, was admittedly stopgap, and required the financing of particular transactions.

The awkwardness of administering offshore purchases led to the development of conditional aid. Suppose France and Britain each have a deficit of $100 with the United States but that France in addition has

$50 in deficit with Britain, which is a British surplus. The United States can now finance the total balance-of-payments deficits of the two countries ($150 for France and $50 for Britain) or their separate deficits with the United States ($100 each). The total of United States aid is the same in either event. In the former case, $50 of the $150 made available to France must be conditional on France's buying its normal imports from Britain and paying $50 in convertible exchange; or if $100 is given to each country, $50 of the amount given to Britain can be made conditional on her financing (by gift or loan) her balance-of-payments surplus with France. It is evident which of the two systems France and Britain will each prefer. And either system will introduce distortion into normal trade patterns. For France, $150 will tend to make her indifferent whether she buys the British goods; and $100 to Britain will make her indifferent whether she supplies the French requirements. Accordingly, the system of conditional aid, which functioned through the Intra-European Payments Scheme, was abandoned in 1950 in favor of the European Payments Union (EPU).

Under EPU, United States contributed $500 million plus to the OEEC to be used to finance multilateral settlements among the countries of Europe. All intra-European trade was multilateralized, i.e., bilateral balances in intra-European trade were converted into balances due from or owed to EPU. Every country had a quota which was divided into five shares or *tranches*. Debtors paid dollars (or gold) and received credit, in varying proportions for each *tranche,* and creditors in turn received dollars and made credit available, according to the following schedule:

TRANCHE OF QUOTA	DEBTORS		CREDITORS	
	Dollars Paid	Credit Received	Dollars Received	Credit Given
	(In Per Cent)		(In Per Cent)	
1.................	10	90	0	100
2.................	30	70	50	50
3.................	40	60	50	50
4.................	50	50	50	50
5.................	70	30	50	50
Average........	40	60	40	60

On the average, debtors on clearing account would pay in enough dollars to requite creditors; but the fund was obliged to have assets to take care of the occasions when more credit was being extended to debtors than was being provided by creditors. Such would be the case, for example, if most debtors were operating at the first or second *tranche* receiving 90 per cent or 70 per cent in credit, while a few persistent creditors were making available only 50 per cent in credit. This was the purpose of the United States provision of capital which was maintained and not used up.

The suggestion has been made that assistance to Asia or Latin America take the form of grants to an Asian or Latin American Payments Union. There is little merit to the idea. The European Payments Union worked effectively until it was modified in favor of more dollar payment and less credit as an approach to convertibility, because the countries involved traded a lot with each other, and because most of them had no particular imbalances in intra-European trade. The deficits of the early persistent debtors—Austria, Greece, Turkey—were financed by the United States as additional aid. A number of the countries changed sides during the course of time: replacing initial deficits with surpluses (Germany), modifying substantial initial surpluses (Belgium), or moving back and forth (Netherlands). None of these conditions obtain outside of Europe. There is little intraregional trade, and what there is is highly skewed rather than balanced, to fit into the pattern of outside trade. Japan needs to earn dollars and sterling in Asia to pay for its imports from overseas. It cannot be expected to have a balanced position in the area in the same fashion as was broadly expected from European countries.

The United States initially made $200 million available for an Asian Development Fund contingent upon Asian proposals at the Simla Conference in India in May, 1955. None were forthcoming. There were suggestions that the money be given to Indonesia or India to buy goods in Japan, but no plan provided for the money to be used more than twice. Some means of indirect assistance for development is possible outside of Europe through the sort of offshore procurement or conditional aid originally worked out in Europe: the provision of wheat to Japan, for example, as aid conditional upon Japanese supply of capital equipment for development in other Asian countries. But the possibilities seem limited to *ad hoc* deals.

Conditions of Aid

There is general agreement among political scientists, if not among politicians, that the major condition of economic assistance should be that the particular country is doing its best to improve its position. This poses the dilemma of incentives discussed above. But it also raises a host of other questions, ranging from the purely political to economic conditions of aid which can be construed as undue interference.

The purely political questions lie outside the scope of an economics text but are nonetheless (or all the more?) real. Does Pakistan get more aid than India, on some comparable basis, because Pakistan has joined the Southeast Asia Treaty Organization, while India is a strict neutralist? Is aid for Yugoslavia a good thing when Tito remains Communist? Is help to Polish reconstruction indirect assistance to the Soviet Union by relieving her of a burden, or does it more significantly increase the independence of Poland from the Soviet Union?

Apart from such larger political questions, however, there is a variety of lesser dilemmas of a quasi-political or political character which involve economic issues. Do the benefits of aid go largely to one class inside a country; and does action by this class block economic development, or recovery, in a significant measure? Does the country oppose private enterprise and drive away foreign capital which could lessen its requirement for foreign assistance? Does foreign aid enable the internal political forces to escape the necessity to face hard decisions, such as how the burdens of recovery or economic development shall be shared, and thus to postpone effective domestic action?

One method devised in the European Recovery Program, and extended in some of the development assistance programs such as those involving surplus agricultural products, has been to require United States agreement to the disposition of the local-currency counterpart of United States aid. Commodities representing United States aid are not given to consumers and firms but sold for local currency. The use of these funds has important consequences. If they are saved, i.e., used to retire public debt, and particularly central-bank loans to the national treasury, the deflationary impact of the assistance is evident. They may, however, be used for capital formation or even for regular expenses, which would maintain or increase the level of national income and give rise to increased imports.

The requirement that the United States approve the disposition of these funds involves this country's representatives in a discussion of the financial aspects of the recovery or the development program. The significance of this involvement may vary widely. At one limit, as in Britain in the European Recovery Program, the deflationary impact of the piling of counterpart funds can be fully offset by other Treasury and central-bank operations. The British went for several years without making any proposals regarding the use of counterpart funds, leaving it obvious that they resented the necessity to obtain United States permission. At the other extreme, however, a country like Greece built much of its financial policy around the use of counterpart funds and sought United States advice on this policy in its total aspects. When inflation in a country has deep political roots, to withhold counterpart funds sought to pay normal governmental expenses may overthrow the government in a financial crisis. The limits of the technique are thus evident. But in other cases, the requirement that the United States approve the disposition of counterpart funds gave useful leverage to a finance minister or central banker fighting a political battle against internal forces of inflation by enabling him to appeal to necessity from without.

There are some who believe that aid should be given without strings of any kind. This may be appropriate in a few cases, such as between Britain and the Dominions, where the aiding country and the aided operate at the same level of political and economic sophistication and understand one another fairly completely. But it is otherwise naïve. At the minimum, the aiding country should know how the country being assisted proposes to use the help and have some idea of whether it is capable of carrying out its intentions. And if it approves of the goals, all other conditions should be directed to their efficient achievement. On the political side, this suggests that short-run objectives should be minimized as irrelevant or even capable of interfering with the long-run political goal of political and economic independence. In economic terms, it means merely that the country use its resources as efficiently as it can.

One condition which the United States attached to most of its assistance programs—Lend-Lease, the postwar settlements, the Anglo-American Financial Agreement, and the Marshall Plan—was that the recipients dedicate themselves with the United States to the construction of a world trade and payments system of a multilateral, nondiscriminatory character. It was relatively easy for the recipients to provide an affirmation of faith which lacked operational significance (except for the disastrous requirement of convertibility in the British loan). They were doubtless, too, sincere in this affirmation at the time it was given. Moreover, the commitments probably served as a restraint on some autarkic or discriminatory action which would otherwise have taken place. But the commitments have failed to produce a world of nondiscriminatory trade and convertible currencies, nor is it likely that they could have done so. Some observers object to the requirement of sub-scribing to long-run principles. Not every country can afford to ignore its short-run for its longer-run interests, and there is a danger, when repeated professions of faith are sought, that they may come to mean little more than the hymns intoned by those about to be fed by the Salvation Army.

Loans versus Grants

The religious objection to interest on loans, in pre-Reformation Europe and in much of the Moslem world today, was based on the ethical injunction not to take advantage of the distress of others. In economic conditions where the harvest was variable, borrowing took place in times of distress, and for consumption. To charge interest was to exploit a brother's bad luck.

When lending became predominantly for capital formation rather than for consumption, the Christian church modified its opposition to interest. Since the borrower was going to benefit from the loan, he could afford to pay for the use of the capital which the lender was temporarily giving up.

Similar ethical considerations seem to dominate the question of whether international economic assistance should take the form of loans or grants. Military assistance and defense support take the form of grants because the *quid pro quo* is the contribution of the recipient to the joint military effort. For the rest, disaster rehabilitation and reconstruction assistance are largely on a grant basis, while economic development or reconstruction assistance which enlarges capacity is regarded as suitable for loans. The failure to recognize the ethical aspect of reconstruction assistance was responsible for evoking the moral outcry against the collection of the war loans after World War I and against the precipitous halting of Lend-Lease after World War II.

Note that these distinctions, which are applied only loosely, turn on the nature of the demand. From the point of view of the suppliers, it might be noted that international economic assistance involves giving up of real resources, that this is painful, and that it therefore ought to be on an interest-bearing loan basis. The fact is that the supply side is considered only in a few cases, such as aid in the form of surplus commodities. These are given away or loaned on a "fuzzy" basis calling for repayment in local currencies (which may then be allocated for economic development) because the cost of the loans can be regarded as sunk. The Commodity Credit Corporation has already acquired the commodities. To lend them abroad involves no pain of parting with scarce resources but rather relief from the embarrassment of redundancy.

Some observers try to make a distinction between assistance for social overhead capital—roads, ports, schools, hospitals, etc.—which it is felt should be given on a grant basis, and that for industrial capital, which is appropriate for loans. Others believe that assistance which increases the capacity of a country to export or to replace existing imports can be appropriately charged on a loan basis, whereas assistance to a mainly internal project which does not directly help the balance-of-payments position should be granted. In the former case, it is implicitly believed that loans are inappropriate where there is no local agency collecting the money proceeds of the sales of the output of the capital; in the latter, the distinction rests upon the assumed impossibility of transferring interest and capital repayment unless the assistance modifies the balance of payments.

Neither of these points of view is valid. If the social overhead capital is productive, that productivity shows up somewhere in the economy and a portion of it can be captured by the government and used for repayment. There may be occasions when improved housing, health, education, and travel go into consumption rather than into increased productivity, and it might be argued that assistance to consumption, like distress loans, should not be expected to furnish repayment. If a country chooses to increase its consumption in these lines, however, it should be willing to reduce it in some small part in others for the purpose of debt service, provided that its total real income has increased. And the fallacy of insisting that each project provide its own balance-of-payments basis for repayment was analyzed earlier (p. 387).

The social ethic need not limit grants to cases of distress, or for maintaining consumption, while loans are exacted for increased productivity capacity or increased consumption. An international social welfare function could call for grants to countries with per capita incomes less than a given level, whether they used the assistance for consumption or capital formation, and loans to countries above that level. It makes a curious kind of logic to give billions to the United Kingdom to maintain its consumption above $750 per capita (say) while insisting on lending capital to India to get her income per capita up from $60.

The point to be emphasized is that the issue of loans or grants is not an economic one but moral, ethical, and social. One shares within the circle of family and friends, and deals on a business basis outside it. And some relationships change between friendship and business in complex and unpredictable ways. We recur to this question in Chapter 29.

Bilateral versus Regional versus International Administration

An additional political issue to which we give only slight attention is the question of administering aid programs. The difficulty faced by the United States in UNRRA has been mentioned earlier. With 78 per cent of the cost and only one vote in seventeen on the disposition of the funds, the United States might have been able to continue with UNRRA if there had been an objectively determined set of principles on which aid was to be divided. But when the division of aid is settled politically, it behooves the provider to safeguard his interests.

The division of aid is a political matter. Within the European Recovery Program, the United States asked for a recommendation by the seventeen countries as to how aid should be divided, while it retained the right, through bilateral agreements, to approve the level of aid to any individual country. The multilateral recommendation was important in deflecting dissatisfaction about the level of the assistance for any country from the United States to the Organization for European Economic Cooperation. The retention of the right to veto aid for any one country was important to ensure that the objectives would be met in every case.

The task of arriving at a multilateral recommendation to the United States was a difficult one, and required an underlying basis of political cohesion. It is not clear whether this basis is present in other areas of the world; whether, that is, the Arab countries could agree on a basis of sharing a given amount of assistance made available to them as a group, or the Far Eastern countries, a given amount for them. In the Colombo Plan, like the Marshall Plan, all aid is bilateral, as all development plans are unilateral rather than co-ordinated. The Colombo Plan has in fact no permanent secretariat, like the OEEC, but one which meets only a few weeks each year to draft a report.

Voting power in the International Bank for Reconstruction and Development and in the International Monetary Fund and the proposal for SUNFED recognize these dilemmas by which the providers of assistance must have the right to refuse it, unless there is an agreed and unambiguous set of principles for its use. Lacking this right, assistance develops into taxation. When one pools sovereignty with other countries, one agrees in advance to abide by the outcome of the total decision, made according to agreed procedures. Taxation is appropriate in this circumstance. But when sovereignty is retained, intergovernmental assistance means that the ultimate decision to give or withhold aid must rest with the donor. It is nonetheless desirable to widen the basis for agreement as far as possible and achieve international and regional recommendations for the character, scope, and division of aid. In Chapter 29 we give some reasons for thinking that intergovernmental economic assistance is here to stay.

Summary

With the rise of government transactions in general, there has been an increase in the volume of international governmental business and nonbusiness transactions. These were large during the war, and continued at an impressive scale through relief, rehabilitation, reconstruction, and, more recently, in technical and capital assistance for economic development. The resurgence of interest in national and international defense arrangements has led to an increase of intergovernmental business and assistance in this area.

It is difficult to distinguish aid for particular purposes from aid in general unless the particular purposes are served in partial equilibrium with everything else equal. There are problems and dilemmas to be faced in determining the appropriate amount of aid in a given case: financing deficits is clearly wrong; capacity to absorb capital is ambiguous; there is no objective basis for determining whether a given goal aims too high or too low. There are also interesting issues concerning which countries receive aid; and some means are available for using the same funds to assist two or more countries in different ways. The European Payments Union is an example of a particular form of indirect assistance which is not extendable to other areas. Intergovernmental economic assistance involves an almost inevitable watering down of the lines of division of national sovereignty, and interference by one nation in the affairs of others. Counterpart funds are one means for doing so, with widely varying degrees of effectiveness. The decision whether aid should be on the basis of loans or grants cannot be made on economic grounds but involves ethical and moral considerations. Similarly, the decision whether to administer aid on international or bilateral grounds is a political one. There are reasons for encouraging international bodies to propose, while national donors dispose.

SUGGESTED READING

TEXTS

Behrman and Schmidt, chaps. xvii, xviii, xix, xx; T. C. Schelling, *International Economics* (Boston; Allyn and Bacon, Inc., 1958) chaps. xxvi, xxvii, and xxviii.

TREATISES

For an early discussion, see W. A. Brown, Jr., and R. Opie, *American Foreign Assistance* (Washington, D.C.: Brookings Institution, 1953). The European Recovery Program is analyzed in H. S. Ellis, *The Economics of Freedom* (New York: Harper & Bros., 1950). The intra-European trade and payments aspects are treated in W. Diebold, Jr., *Trade and Payments in Western Europe* (New York: Harper & Bros., 1952). An evaluation of the United Nations' work in the area is given in R. E. Asher, W. M. Kotschnig, W. A. Brown, Jr., and Associates, *The United Nations and Economic and Social Cooperation* (Washington, D.C.: Brookings Institution, 1957).

For a proposal emphasizing the regional approach to United States programs of intergovernmental economic assistance, see W. Y. Elliott (ed.), *Foreign Economic Policy for the United States* (New York: Henry Holt & Co., Inc., 1955).

Useful discussion of the issues involved in intergovernmental aid is contained in T. C. Schelling, "American Foreign Assistance," *World Politics,* July, 1955, which is a review of the Brown and Opie book; and his "American Aid and Economic Development," in The American Assembly, *International Stability and Progress* (New York: Columbia University Graduate School of Business, June, 1957).

POINTS

For historical, as well as analytical, accounts of the postwar planning and operations, see R. S. Gardner, *Sterling-Dollar Diplomacy* (New York: Oxford University Press, 1956); and E. F. Penrose, *Economic Planning for the Peace* (Princeton: Princeton University Press, 1953).

The latter is limited to the viewpoint available to an American official in London.

PART VI

Balance-of-Payments Disequilibrium

and Adjustment

BALANCE-OF-PAYMENTS
EQUILIBRIUM

Equilibrium, Disequilibrium, and Adjustment

Thus far we have discussed the various elements in the balance of payments, more or less separately. The time has come to interrelate them more thoroughly. To be sure, we have not altogether neglected the interconnections among the various items in the current account, or between the current and the capital account. The chapter on transfer, for example, was directed specifically to these interrelations, and early chapters in Parts I and II dealt with the adjustment mechanism in the balance of payments, including the roles of price and income in producing adjustment.

This final part of the book therefore constitutes partly a review (or repetition) of what has gone before. But it is important to focus our attention completely on the establishment and maintenance of balance-of-payments equilibrium. This is the central problem in international economics today. In the course of this discussion, moreover, we shall have an opportunity to describe and analyze most of the postwar organizations for achieving or maintaining equilibrium.

Before we can proceed with the analysis of disequilibrium, however, it will be necessary to state with as much precision as possible what we mean by "equilibrium." Such is the purpose of the present chapter.

Definition

Equilibrium is that state of the balance of payments over the relevant time period which makes it possible to sustain an open economy without severe unemployment on a continuing basis. This definition raises more questions than it answers. To answer them we must analyze separately: (1) the relevant time period; (2) the nature of the openness of the economy; (3) the question of unemployment; and (4) the continuing basis of the equilibrium.

Equilibrium through Time

Balance-of-payments equilibrium may relate to an hour, day, week, month, season, or year; to the business cycle or part thereof, and, within the general class, the short cycle, the nine-year cycle, and one or more longer cycles; or to a phase of long-run growth. One period's equilibrium, moreover, may be another period's disequilibrium. Whether the balance of payments is in equilibrium or not in a given period depends upon the length of time for which the judgment is being made.

This proposition may be illustrated with reference to the seasonal pattern. Australia sells her wool-clip at auctions held from November to March. Sheep are shorn in the spring, but the seasons are reversed in the antipodes as compared with the Northern Hemisphere. During and after the clip, exports exceed imports by a large amount, and sterling balances pile up. Later, as these balances are drawn down, imports exceed exports. The seasonal inequality between exports and imports, however, is not a sign of disequilibrium as it might be over a whole year, since the season is not the relevant time period.

Static Equilibrium

In this connection we may make a distinction between static equilibrium and several more dynamic kinds. In static equilibrium, exports equal imports. These, of course, include exports of services as well as of goods, and the same for imports. To the extent that exports equal imports, the other items on the balance of payments—short-term capital, long-term capital, and monetary gold—are, on balance, zero. If any net movement of short-term capital takes place, it must be balanced by an opposite movement in long-term capital or gold or both.

From one point of view, it is wise to make it a condition of static equilibrium that there be no movement of any kind among gold, short-term capital, and long-term capital. A movement of gold sets in motion monetary changes which will involve a subsequent change in spending or interest rates, either of which would disturb the equality of exports and imports. A change in interest rates, too, may produce a short-term capital reaction. Short-term capital movements, as we have seen, may bring about monetary changes with repercussions in spending or interest rates; in addition, they will ultimately be reversed, since in the long run no one wants to take a speculative position in a foreign currency. A movement of short-term capital, financed by gold, may be allowed unless, however, the condition is one of destabilizing speculation, in which case the capital movement may increase until monetary changes take place. A movement of long-term capital, balanced by gold or short-term capital, is almost certain to involve a change in spending or in money supply or possibly even in interest rates. A truly timeless static equilibrium then requires that exports be equal to imports and that long-term, short-term capital and gold are zero on balance and separately. We may relax this last requirement somewhat and say that static equilibrium requires long- and short-term capital movements and gold flows to be small separately and together algebraically zero.

In this sort of static equilibrium, with $X = M$, $S = I_d$ because $X + I_d = S + M$. There is no change in national income being brought about by changes in exports and imports and, conversely, no change in the balance of payments arising from domestic expenditure. Not only is the balance of payments in equilibrium; national money income is in equilibrium vis-à-vis money incomes abroad.

The foreign-exchange rate must also be in equilibrium. There are several ways of saying this. On one basis, the foreign-exchange rate is such that, given (1) factor endowments, (2) prices at home and abroad, (3) production functions in both places, (4) consumers' indifference maps, and (5) stable national money incomes at home and abroad, consumers and investors at home tend to buy from foreigners the same value of goods which foreign consumers and investors buy from domestic producers. At a higher or overvalued rate, given these production possibilities, tastes, and incomes, imports would be in excess of exports; at a lower or undervalued rate, exports would exceed imports.

Another way of putting the foreign-exchange equilibrium condition involves the purchasing-power-parity doctrine. It will be recalled that purchasing power parity is a comparative concept designed to measure departures from an equilibrium exchange rate by subsequent price comparisons. This is valid to the extent that production possibilities, tastes, etc., have not changed and that changes in prices reflect changes in money income with no real income implications. The heroic character of this assumption is evident: the movement of the price level is assumed to induce no change in relative prices and the change in money income carries with it no change in the composition of real income. This implies the complete absence of money illusion, i.e., that tendency which most of us have to think that our income has changed when income and prices both change in the same direction by the same percentage.

A third way of looking at the foreign-exchange aspect of static equilibrium is what some writers have called the positive formulation of the purchasing-power-parity doctrine, i.e., that the foreign-exchange rate is in equilibrium when a given sum of money can buy the same amounts of the same goods in two countries. This is wrong. There is a limit to the equalization of prices which can be brought about by trade —a limit set by transportation costs. Some goods and services do not move in trade at all because transport costs are wider than price differences. These may be completely unrelated through the exchange rate. Rent is cheap in Vienna compared with New York. But transport costs make it impossible to get equality of purchasing power internationally, even of traded goods. Export goods will be relatively cheap, and import goods relatively dear. The positive formulation of purchasing power parity is wrong and cannot be used to assist in determining foreign-exchange equilibrium.

We can pursue some of these equilibrium conditions further. The foreign-exchange rate is in equilibrium. So are goods prices. It is quickly evident why the prices of foreign-trade goods must be settled in relation to prices abroad, the foreign-exchange rate, production functions, and tastes. But so must the prices of domestic goods, since a change in their average will change the propensity to import or the propensity to consume and, in either event, produce a change in the balance of payments. Back of goods prices, moreover, lie factor prices, which must fit into the general equilibrium.

Back of the equilibrium of national income, too, lies a host of other variables: money supply, rate of interest, distribution of income, state of fiscal policy, including both government taxation and government expenditure. Some of these variables play several roles. A change in the distribution of income will produce a direct change in the propensity to import, if one class of income recipients has a different set of tastes regarding imports than another. A shift of income from East Coast manufacturing communities to Middle West farmers, for example, brought about through the shift in farm prices relative to parity or, in our language, a shift in agricultural terms of trade, may result in a lower level of imports at the same value for national money income. But redistribution will also directly affect consumption and hence the level of national income. There will be both a shift of the import schedule and a movement along the schedule. Or, an example we have used before, an increase in savings and investment in a developing country, which left national money income unchanged, might disturb the international equilibrium position because the import content of investment expenditure was much higher than that of consumption. This entails a movement of the import schedule.

A fundamental question arises as to whether there is one equilibrium position or many and, if many, whether a particular one is an optimum. We shall have to address this question again in connection with unemployment and import restrictions. Here it may be said, however, that there are many equilibria and that, for most purposes, the balance of payments, the foreign-exchange rate, and other aspects of the international economy are different among them. Let us assume that the economy can adjust either to money supply *a* or money supply *b*. A shift from *a* to *b* will produce a change in interest rates, in spending, investment, the propensity to save, the locus of employment, the factor proportions appropriate to the economy, the allocation of resources, the comparative advantage and disadvantage of the economy, etc. Admittedly these responses may be small. But, assuming that they are noticeable and that the difference between the balance of payments with money supply *a* and that with money supply *b* can be detected, each has a separate balance-of-payments equilibrium. Unless we know more about the rest of the economy, we can only say that the international economic order is indifferent between the two equilibria.

Dynamic Equilibrium

The balance of payments need not and cannot rest in static equilibrium. Regular fluctuations of a seasonal, monthly, weekly, and daily character occur. Long-run departures from this equilibrium have also been a feature of the international economy. Short- and long-term capital and gold movements have significant roles to play in these deviations from static equilibrium which are fully consonant with equilibrium in a dynamic sense.

The seasonal illustration of the pre–World War I balance of payments of the United States which we have used before in this book can help us again. Each autumn and spring there is a departure from static equilibrium. In the autumn, exports exceed imports and are balanced by short-term capital outflow and gold inflow. The result is production in excess of consumption and investment; increase in the supply of money; growth in national money income; appreciation of the dollar, within the gold points; decline in export and import prices in local currency, etc. The list could be extended indefinitely. All these changes ruled out in static equilibrium are required to maintain equilibrium in another time dimension. Only if the movement in the desired direction is excessive, or if a given change takes place in the direction contrary to the requirements of the dynamic equilibrium, is it apparent that change means disequilibrium.

In long-run secular equilibrium, we return to our stages of development. Here long-term capital movements of a normal character are required. The young debtor borrows; imports more than it exports; maintains a foreign-exchange rate overvalued in terms of static equilibrium; and has too high a level of national money income, too large a money supply, too much investment in relation to domestic savings, too high prices, too low a rate of interest.

Balance-of-payments equilibrium requires that the capital movement take the form as well as the direction which is appropriate to the time period. There may be national income, foreign-exchange rate, and every kind of equilibrium except balance of payments if a young debtor country is borrowing at short term and adjusting to the inflow as if it were a long-term capital movement. Imports exceed exports, and domestic investment is larger than savings by this amount. But, institutionally, short-term capital is expected to amount to zero in the long run, and short-term capital movements must reverse themselves before the development of national income will have reached a point appropriate to them. If long-term capital movements are called for but only short-term capital is available, dynamic equilibrium is not achieved.

The condition of static equilibrium is that exports equal imports, that long-term capital movement is zero, and that gold movement and short-term capital movements are small and net out to zero.

The condition of dynamic equilibrium for short periods of time is that exports and imports differ by the amount of short-term capital movements and gold (net) and that there are no large destabilizing short-term capital movements.

The condition for dynamic equilibrium in the long run is that exports and imports differ by the amount of long-term autonomous capital movements made in a normal direction, i.e., from the low-interest-rate country to those with high rates.

Import Restrictions

A requirement of equilibrium which applies in all time periods is that there be no undue restrictions on imports. Most writers try to be precise about this and get into difficulties. The problem can be solved only by being purposely vague. What we mean by the requirement of an open economy, or no undue restrictions in imports, is not that there can be no tariffs or quantitative restrictions, but none for the primary purpose of limiting imports to the level of exports. Protective tariffs are concerned with the price of a given article or series of articles and not with the level of imports as a whole or with broad classes of imports. The same may be said for limited quota restrictions. The fact that the United States has quotas on feeder cattle imports from Canada—range steers bought by corn farmers for fattening—on butter, cheese, potatoes, and other commodities does not mean that the dollar is fundamentally in disequilibrium. If exports equaled imports in static terms and national money income, the money supply, interest rates, etc., were stable, an equilibrium would be reached compatible with quota restrictions. This equilibrium, to be sure, would not be the only equilibrium and would not be an optimum from the viewpoint of efficiency.

There will be other circumstances, however, in which, after all tariffs and quota restrictions desired for specific protective purposes have been in operation, the foreign-exchange rate is overvalued, national income is too high in relation to incomes abroad, and imports exceed exports. If imports are reduced to the level of exports by an adjustment of the foreign-exchange rate or by a deflation of national income, the new position would be regarded as one of equilibrium. But if imports are reduced by quota restrictions on all imports or broad classes of them, such as luxuries, or by prohibitive tariffs, the result is a disequilibrium position. Purchasing power is being rationed by direct controls rather than by price.

The distinction is one of degree rather than of kind. Broad quotas and tariffs have protective as well as balance-of-payments effects. Similarly, selective quotas and tariffs have an impact on the balance of payments, on national money income, price levels, the exchange rate, and so on. The distinction also turns on intent. But here the confusion in the minds of the mercantilist-protectionist makes it frequently impossible to divine the true purpose of a measure. Tariffs may be imposed partly for raising domestic prices in certain lines and partly for acquiring a favorable balance of trade and gold.

Some writers have suggested that tariffs are compatible with equilibrium, while quotas are not. This view is inadmissible. Tariffs and quotas are virtually the same thing when there is adequate knowledge of the shape of the demand and supply curves. And the belief that tariffs have no balance-of-payments effect is in error (see p. 230). Accordingly, it is the purpose and the extent of the import restrictions which count. Equality of exports and imports brought about by import restrictions to achieve balance represents a disequilibrium situation. Equality of exports and imports, however, under conditions where imports are less than a maximum or an optimum, may still be regarded as equilibrium in static terms, provided that the import restrictions primarily serve other purposes.

This discussion makes clear that there are equilibria and equilibria. The United States may be in equilibrium with a protective tariff. It is possible for it to remove the tariff and achieve disequilibrium if the result is an excess of imports over exports. It is also possible, however, for it to remove tariffs and, by increasing savings and reducing investment or some other means of restraining national income, achieve a new and superior equilibrium in comparison with the original. The free-trade equilibrium is an optimum in terms of efficiency. But the student should remember both that the free-trade position does not automatically produce equilibrium and that equilibrium is no guarantee of a welfare optimum.

The openness of the economy evidently implies the absence of foreign-exchange restrictions as well as those on imports, i.e., foreign-exchange restrictions on current account. These are exactly comparable to quotas, but they are evidently undertaken for the purpose of protecting the foreign-exchange position. It is possible to construct a model in which a country's exports and imports are in balance not only over-all but with each trading partner. In the absence of clearing arrangements, this might be an equilibrium position. Even if the imposition of clearing requirements involved no alteration in exports or imports, the change would be regarded as one to disequilibrium, since the capacity of the system for adjustment and modification would be gone. Any clearing, payments, or foreign-exchange restrictions on current payments which divert trade from channels which they would take without restriction are clearly incompatible with a foreign-exchange equilibrium in this sense.

Unemployment

One way to achieve equality between exports and imports under certain conditions is to reduce national income by an amount which will produce a movement along the propensity-to-import schedule sufficient to bring imports into line. This may result in unemployment. Some writers have stated that this is not an equilibrium position and that equilibrium requires a level of national income which will yield "full" or "high-level" employment.

A balance-of-payments position maintained by large unemployment is less desirable than one in which unemployment is of the normal frictional amount. Whether it should be called a position of equilibrium or disequilibrium, however, is purely definitional. To the extent that students of national income refer to "underemployment equilibrium" in national income, it is appropriate to regard equality of imports and exports achieved through unemployment as equilibrium, but far from optimum. To the extent, however, that governments in the postwar world do not long tolerate unemployment, it should be regarded as a disequilibrium position. This is to call attention to the likelihood that steps will be taken to eliminate the unemployment and the fact that such steps will disturb the balance of payments.

If all the countries of the world have substantial unemployment and all balances of payments on current account are algebraically zero, the position may be described as an equilibrium one or a disequilibrium, depending upon one's predilections and one's forecast of what is likely to happen. If no country is going to do anything about it, or if every country is going to move in harmony to correct unemployment, the balance-of-payments positions are secure. But if some countries will react to unemployment by expanding expenditure, while others will not, the temporary balance-of-payments stability is doomed. This example shows, among other things, that balance-of-payments equilibrium may or may not be less significant than removal of unemployment as an aim of economic policy, and that different countries will put different valuations on the two.

The nature of the unemployment disequilibrium involves a complication. We shall distinguish between unemployment of all three factors—land, labor, and capital—on the one hand, and unemployment of a single factor, on the other. Within the first of these categories, we may separate two general cases—one in which the unemployment is located for the most part in the export industries; the other in which it is spread through domestic industry as a whole.

We shall postpone discussion of a structural unemployment which applies to one factor. This will occupy us for a considerable part of a chapter later on. It is sufficient here to say that this may be represented by the case of Italy today: two million unemployed workers; each year large additions to the labor force and few job opportunities. Here the point is not lack of effective demand. Factors are used throughout industry in the wrong proportions.

Both cases where resources in general are unemployed may be illustrated by the same diagram as set forth in Figure 24.1. $X = M$ (i.e., $X-M = 0$) and $S = I_d$ (i.e., $S-I_d = 0$) at an equilibrium level of national income (Y) below the full-employment level (Y_{fe}). An increase in domestic investment sufficient to bring the intersection of

$S–I_d'$ and $X–M$ to the full-employment level (that is, an increase in investment of a which will *lower* the $S–I_d$ schedule to $S–I_d'$) will leave an import surplus of b. Exports are unchanged, but imports increase along the $X–M$ schedule and produce a deficit.

An increase of d' in exports (equal to a), however, would result in an export surplus of b' (equal to b). This is a disequilibrium position, too.

The appropriate measures to achieve full-employment equilibrium consist in a combination: an increase in domestic investment of b, and an increase in exports by the difference between this and a, or in other words by b'.

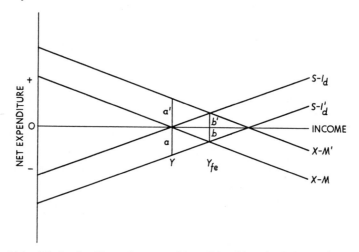

FIG. 24.1. Eliminating Unemployment without Disturbing the Balance of Payments

These two sorts of unemployment can be illustrated by Germany in 1928–32 and Britain in 1925. The German case was one of domestic unemployment brought about by deflation, which caused the balance of payments to change from import to export surplus. In the British case unemployment brought about by the revaluation of the pound sterling to the prewar level was located in the export industries, i.e., in coal, shipbuilding, and textiles.

The German experience, to which we have already referred in connection with reparations in the chapter on transfer, fails to conform to our model in one respect. Considerable structural unemployment appears to have existed as early as 1927, when 1.4 million, or 9 per cent of the working force, were already unemployed. With the decline in investment, when the flow of private long-term capital into Germany shut down at the end of 1928 and short-term borrowing came to a halt a year later, national income began to fall. In part, the cause was the decline in investment; in part, the deflationary impact of the taxes needed to raise the mark equivalent of reparations. Reparations were transferred, and even some repayment of long- and short-term borrowing. But this required a sharp decline in national income, which fell from RM 75.0 billion in 1929 to 45.3 billion in 1932 and gave rise to a large increase in unemployment. From 1.4 million in 1927, unemployment rose to 1.9 million in 1929, 3.1 million in 1930, and 4.6 million in 1931. Employment in the export trades was fairly well sustained, since the dollar value of exports in 1931 was less than 15 per cent below that of 1928. Unemployment was concentrated in the domestic sector of the economy, as deflationary pressure needed to transfer reparations in the absence of capital imports pushed the economy to even lower levels.

The British case is the one which made economists conscious of the role of unemployment in balance-of-payments equilibrium. The pound sterling depreciated after World War I and costs and prices had adjusted to the depreciated level. British governments, however, were anxious to restore the pound to its prewar value. Their reasons included partly the conviction that the step was necessary to re-establish confidence in the pound sterling—confidence on which London's banking, insurance, and commission business depended and which earned the United Kingdom an important segment of its invisible income—and partly the desire to avoid a decline in prestige.

The opportunity to raise the pound sterling to par came in 1924 with the difficulties experienced by the French franc, which we shall have occasion to discuss presently. A large outflow of capital was taking place from France. The announced intention of the British authorities to restore the pound to par invited this capital to come to Britain and to speculate for a rise in the pound as well as for a fall in the French franc. This was destabilizing speculation, which produced the result it was hoping for. The pound appreciated to par.

This overvaluation of the pound produced pressure on costs and prices, starting in the export industries. Unless wages and prices were reduced, export prices would be too high to enable exports to be sold. The value of exports, in fact, fell from £801 million in 1924 to £773 million in 1925 and to £653 million in 1926, in spite of world-wide prosperity. An attempted wage cut led to the disastrous coal and general strikes of 1926.

The critical unemployment was located in the export industries. There were unemployed in other lines, but the multiplier effects of an increase in exports would have eliminated this. Nonetheless, if the pound had been devalued to the point where all the unemployed attached to the export industries had found work in these industries (assuming that this result could have been achieved), the position would still have been one of disequilibrium. Under these circumstances, the full-employment level would show an export surplus, equal to b' in Figure 24.1. To have achieved equilibrium of the balance of payments with optimal employment would have required an increase of some substantial proportions in exports, followed by an increase in home investment and the transfer into domestic employment of the remaining unemployed workers previously attached to export industries.

The devaluation of the pound in 1931 unhappily cannot be fitted neatly into this analysis. Too many other factors entered the picture. Devaluation failed to produce the expected expansion in exports and a worsening of the terms of trade (as export prices in local currency increased less than import prices). Instead of import prices rising in local currency, they fell in foreign exchange, and the deflation became cumulative. Devaluation produced, or at least was accompanied by, a fall in import prices in local currency and an improvement in the terms of trade. With an inelastic demand for imports with respect both to price and income, substantial improvements in the balance of payments and in real income came from this fall in import prices. The result was analogous to the income effect of a tariff discussed earlier (pp. 227 ff.) and illustrated in Figures 12.6a and 12.6b. It was different, however, in that it was produced by a decline in price with inelastic demand rather than an increase in price with elastic demand. With its food bill cheaper, the British public had income left over which it used to finance a housing boom. The improvement in the terms of trade was perhaps neither necessary nor sufficient to produce this result. An important contributing part was played by cheap money, resulting from the refunding of the British War Loan from a 5 per cent to a 3 per cent basis.

It should be noted that the housing boom in Britain raised imports from certain areas, notably Sweden, which supplied timber for housing construction, and spread the effects of prosperity through Scandinavia in the familiar multiplier way. Under the pressure of the boom, moreover, the depressed areas in export coal, export steel, and textiles began to lose workers to the prosperous manufacturing areas of southern England.

On a Continuing Basis

This is a catchall expression to round up exceptions to the general rules expressed in the rest of the definition. The essence of a meaningful equilibrium is that it is capable of being sustained. The dead center of a tornado is not calm in an equilibrium sense. In the same way, equality of exports and imports, national income, goods prices, factor prices, money supply, interest rates, etc., which contains the seeds of change, does not constitute an equilibrium situation.

One exception of this sort must be made for inventories. Suppose that national income is steady but that domestic investment includes a significant element of inventory accumulation or decumulation. In one way of looking at the matter, the steadiness of income is an equilibrium condition; in another, the inventory change will inevitably come to a halt, and national income will then change. If national income depends on inventory accumulation far above normal levels, it is too high on a continuing basis; if it covers up inventory consumption which must soon stop, it is too low. Balance-of-payments equilibrium based on the equality of exports and imports which contains much inventory change is equally transitory.

This qualification is of considerable importance. The revised Department of Commerce figures for the United States balance of payments of the 1930's show current-account deficits of $156 million, $218 million, and $31 million for 1935, 1936, and 1937 calendar years. These data include silver as a merchandise import rather than as money. If they are revised to shift silver—purchased on the world market at the insistence of the silver senators and ruinous to the silver currencies of China and Mexico—to the specie account, the current account shows a surplus of $240 million in 1935, a deficit of $104 million in 1936, and a surplus of $57 million in 1937. This deficit of $104 million in 1936 has led some observers to conclude that the current account was in appropriate long-run balance during this period. If the export surplus of the last four months of 1937 were eliminated, the same could be said of that year.

But this cannot be regarded as the true position. Part of the increase in imports (and decline in exports) was due to the drought of 1936. This was a random structural change in the terminology adopted later. But from 1935 through August, 1937, businessmen were engaged in the rapid expansion of inventories in fear of John L. Lewis, the CIO, and the rising level of commodity prices. Inventory profits were easily made, and inventories grew. The rush to acquire working stocks had two effects on imports—one direct, one indirect. The direct effect was that it altered the propensity to import. The schedule shifted upward and to the left. This increased imports (and lowered national income). At the same time, the increase in domestic investment and in inventories had the effect of increasing national income, through an upward shift of the investment schedule, which increased imports through a movement along the schedule. The result was a small import surplus. But this level of imports could not be sustained. An inventory boom is transparently short-lived. As expectations change, when entrepreneurs become conscious of the burden of unused stocks and with them the vain character of hoped-for inventory profits, accumulation is replaced by decumulation. This shifts back both the propensity-to-import schedule and the schedule of domestic investment. Imports dropped from an annual rate (uncorrected for seasonal, but this is small) of $3.8 billion at the peak in March, 1937, to $1.7 billion in July, 1938.

A similar illusory recovery in imports occurred in 1948, again on the basis of inventory accumulation. Imports rose spectacularly from an annual rate of $5.1 billion in August, 1947, to $8.6 billion in December, 1948. Inventories in the hands of manufacturing concerns, reported by the Department of Commerce, had recovered from a postwar low of $17.9 billion in December, 1945, to $23.0 billion in August, 1947, and continued to rise thereafter to a peak of $34.4 billion in January, 1949. The inventory peak followed the import peak by a month. Since inventories cannot climb forever, the late 1947 and 1948 figures borrowed imports from the future.

Action was followed by reaction. In the mild recession of the spring of 1949, imports plummeted to $5.5 billion (annual rate) in July, 1949, from $8.6 billion seven months previously. The sharp fall in sterling-area exports caused by the necessity to pay back exports borrowed in 1947 and 1948 put great pressure on the pound and contributed importantly to the devaluation of September, 1949.

The United States experience of 1936–37 and 1948–49 was repeated in that country and in Germany in 1950–51. After the outbreak of the Korean War, both these countries tumbled over themselves to buy raw materials for inventory purposes, and their balances of payments on current account appeared to be much more adverse than in fact they were in the relevant long-run sense. The position was particularly striking in the case of Germany which was financing its inventory imports through the newly established European Payments Union, and which appeared to be headed to be a deficit country—a posture later belied by the facts. But attention should also be paid to the obverse. During 1950 and the first part of 1951, the British balance of payments appeared to be very favorable. This was partly due to the prosperity of her sterling-area banking clients who were depositing in London large sums of money accumulated as a result of the raw-material boom. But in part it was due to the fact that Britain let her inventories run down, while those of Germany and the United States were rising. Aside from the speculative profits or losses, it may make little difference from the point of view of balance-of-payments equilibrium whether a country's foreign-exchange reserves are being converted into raw-material inventories, or vice versa. To worry unduly about such losses of reserves when inventories build up or take too much comfort in rising reserves when inventories are falling is to fall into error.

As one aspect of equilibrium then, the equation $X + I_d = S + M$ must have I_d broken down into long-term domestic investment (I_{dlt}) and domestic investment in inventories (I_{dinv}). The static condition of equilibrium then requires that

$$X + I_{dlt} + I_{dinv} = S + M$$

and $X = M$ when I_{dinv} is zero, or of either sign but not large and not rapidly becoming large.

Another aspect of the continuing basis is found in the money supply and its relation to the demand for liquidity. In the absence of restrictions on capital movements, an important condition of equilibrium is that the quantity of money and the rate of interest are appropriate to the liquidity-preference schedule, i.e., the desire of people with capital to hold it in the form of money and near-money. This applies nationally and, in those countries where some portion of capital is typically held abroad, internationally. The balance of payments is in disequilibrium, whatever the state of the current account and the national income on which it depends, if rentiers or owners of capital are fearful of national monetary policy and capable of demanding domestic money for conversion into foreign. This was the position in France in 1926 before Poincaré re-established confidence in the franc. The earlier inflationary government expenditures of the postwar period had been gradually pruned away, as the realization bore in on French governments that reparations from Germany would not pay for reconstruction. Exports recovered, and imports were coming down. But the national debt was held largely in the form of floating debt, or short-term bills, and the government was unable to refund this into long-term obligations because of lack of confidence. The equality of exports and imports could not long endure, in the absence of capital controls, because the stability of the currency was not on a continuing basis.

Even with capital controls, it is not clear that this situation should be regarded as one of equilibrium. A high state of liquidity in the money market and lack of confidence in government are not likely to leave the balance of payments unaffected for long, despite the facts that the liquidity represents capital assets and that controls inhibit their flight abroad. Flight may take place into real assets within the country, which will increase national income and imports and disturb balance-of-payments equality in one direction. Or the liquid assets may be used to acquire goods domestically which are shipped abroad. This produces an income effect and a resultant increase in imports but an offsetting impact on exports.

It is impossible to enumerate all the other conditions of the economy which may be varied to give the impression of stability but contain within them the seeds of drastic change. Inventory change and lack of confidence plus liquidity, however, may be sufficient to illustrate the principle.

Balance-of-Payments Equilibrium and Political Equilibrium

It may be well merely to mention a noneconomic set of conditions which may produce change in balance-of-payments equilibrium as narrowly expressed in market terms. This is the political situation. It is, of course, impossible to let the connection get remote or roundabout. In history, in the longer run, all events are interrelated, just as all human beings are cousins. But the connection between balance-of-payments equilibrium and political stability has been made clear in such legislation as the Marshall Plan and Point Four. A redistribution of income in favor of the well-to-do may increase saving, reduce national income, and restore balance of payments in a narrow sense. If it sows the seed of political revolution, which cuts the country off from the world trading area almost entirely, however, or even if it leads to a change of political party and a redistribution of national income in the opposite direction, the balance-of-payments equilibrium is not continuing.

Much will depend on the capacity of political institutions to bring about adjustment to international economic circumstances. The decline in the price of wheat in the world market, for example, led to the liquidation of British agriculture and the migration of 1,000,000 agricultural workers to the city in the years after 1879. In the British case, it produced change—a working class herded into slums, a labor party, and a different attitude toward the free-enterprise economy. Given different political attitudes and institutions, an unstable political situation would have resulted. An attempt to adapt to changed world conditions in this way in France or Germany would probably have produced a violent political response, reacting, in turn, on the international economic position.

Too little is known about the way large communities behave politically. Here we can simply call attention to the interaction between the balance of payments and the political position. One day it may be possible to incorporate political variables into equations dealing with balance-of-payments stability, but not yet.

Summary

Equilibrium is that state of the balance of payments over the relevant time period which makes it possible to sustain an open economy on a continuing basis without severe unemployment. The chapter is devoted to the exposition of this definition. Equilibrium may be static or dynamic, depending upon the time period involved. In static terms, it means $X = M$. Dynamically, $X \gtreqless M$, provided that the inequality is a transitional one.

The openness of the economy is concerned with import restrictions and tariffs. These are compatible with equilibrium if their purpose is protection, but not if they are intended to limit imports to the level of exports. Large-scale unemployment, either of a single factor or of all three factors and, in the latter case, either in domestic or in export industry, is compatible with a market equilibrium, which is far from the optimum equilibrium. On one definition, unemployment means disequilibrium, since government action to remove it is likely and will disturb the balance-of-payments position.

The requirement that the equality of X and M be continuing is a catchall phrase to take care of seeds of change which lie in other aspects of the various factors which must adjust to one another. Two sources of such change are indicated—inventories and excess liquidity.

It is suggested that, on a wider view of the social sciences, equilibrium in the balance of payments should be combined with political stability into a more generalized equilibrium. This is not yet possible.

SUGGESTED READING

TREATISES

The best statement of the theory is by Nurkse, American Economic Association, *Readings*, No. 1. See also his "Domestic and International Equilibrium," in S. E. Harris (ed.), *The New Economics* (New York: Alfred A. Knopf, Inc., 1947). See also the 1936 Paish essay, American Economic Association, *Readings*, No. 2.

Other useful statements are: A. H. Hansen, "A Brief Note on Fundamental Disequilibrium," and a comment by Haberler in S. E. Harris (ed.),

Foreign Economic Policy for the United States (Cambridge, Mass.: Harvard University Press, 1948); and the statements by Triffin and Haberler in *International Monetary Studies.* See also H. S. Ellis, "The Equilibrium Rate of Exchange" in *Explorations in Economics* (New York: McGraw-Hill Book Co., Inc., 1936). R. F. Mikesell has an article on "International Disequilibrium" in the *AER* for June, 1949.

For a demonstration of the importance of inventories to short-run equilibrium, see the Bank for International Settlements, *Twenty-Seventh Annual Report* (Basle, June, 1957), p. 55, which shows how the British and Dutch economies frequently switch from foreign exchange into stocks and back.

POINTS

For accounts of the British, German, and French experience discussed in the text, see Nurkse's *International Currency Experience* and *The Course and Control of Inflation;* W. A. Lewis, *Economic Survey, 1919–39* (Philadelphia: Blakiston Co., 1950); A. E. Kahn, *Great Britain in the World Economy* (New York: Columbia University Press, 1946); and A. C. Pigou, *Aspects of British Economic History, 1918–1925* (London: Macmillan & Co., Ltd., 1948); and W. F. Stolper, "Purchasing Power Parity and the Pound Sterling from 1919–1925," *Kyklos,* Bern, 1948.

A crude attempt to combine economic and political considerations into a general social equilibrium is made in the Appendix to my *Dollar Shortage* (New York: John Wiley & Sons, Inc., and Technology Press, 1950).

Chapter	CYCLICAL DISTURBANCE
25	TO EQUILIBRIUM

Kinds of Disequilibrium

Many variables are interrelated to constitute equilibrium in the international economic position of a country; national incomes at home and abroad, the prices of goods and factors, the supply of money, the rate of interest. Back of these are still further variables and parameters, or values which can be taken as unaltered for the problem to be considered. To list a few: the supply of factors, production functions, the state of technology, tastes, the distribution of income, the state of anticipations, etc.

It follows that there must be many kinds of disequilibrium—at least one for each variable which can get out of adjustment. A change in any variable or parameter which fails to bring about the appropriate changes in other variables will produce a disequilibrium position.

But this is a highly academic way of looking at it. In the first place, it is unrealistic to vary one item at a time and keep all other values constant by assumption. Some pairs of variables are linked, and not by any unique relationship. If we double the money supply, for example, it is wrong to assume the price level and the level of money income constant; but it does not necessarily follow that both will be exactly doubled.

Secondly, and more important, even when we make explicit the partial nature of our reasoning, we must be careful not to hide significant relationships. Assume a change in taste against a country's exports. Correct this by lowering the exchange rate. It will be recognized that depreciation may exert pressure for expansion on national money income, but let us assume that the national monetary and fiscal authorities successfully carry out a policy of holding national money income constant. Is the exchange-rate change responsible for correcting the balance of payments? To say yes is to give only a partial-equilibrium answer. In a broader and more realistic sense, balance-of-payments equilibrium was restored by the change in the exchange rate *and* the action of the authorities in maintaining the level of national money income in the face of depreciation.

Despite these difficulties, we must organize the discussion along partial lines. For present purposes, all disequilibria are regarded as those of price, of income, or—an intermediate category which should include the totality—those of price and/or income. Within each of these broad categories we can distinguish two subdivisions (see Table 25.1). Income disequilibria are those in which income changes in relation to national incomes abroad (or vice versa) without significant changes in relative prices; structural changes are those which occur primarily in relative prices, without necessarily significant changes in the level of national income. The intermediate category includes the case of over- and undervaluation of the exchange rate produced by changes in the exchange rate, or by domestic inflation. These are cases of income *and* price. It also covers systematic technological changes which may produce increases in money income, reductions in prices,

TABLE 25.1

KINDS OF INTERNATIONAL ECONOMIC DISEQUILIBRIUM

	Income	*Income and/or Price*	*Price*
Short-term	Cyclical disequilibrium	Inflation; inappropriate exchange-rate change	Structural disequilibrium at the goods level
Long-term or deep-seated	Secular disequilibrium	Systematic technological change	Structural disequilibrium at the factor level

or both. It must be emphasized again that this breakdown is highly arbitrary. Whatever the convenience of the Keynesian model, in the real world no income change can take place without producing changes in relative prices; the cyclical behavior of the terms of trade between the agricultural and manufacturing sectors of the economy provides one proof of this. Income elasticities for all goods would have to be identical, and supply curves similar, to make possible changes in price level which take place without change in relative prices.

Conversely, there is little chance of change in relative prices without some change in the total level of income. Any change in export or import prices which produces a change in exports or imports, for example, will result in a change in income. Y will be affected by any change in X or in $M(Y)$.

This schema produces six types of disequilibrium, which we propose to discuss in three chapters. The present chapter treats of cyclical disequilibrium and of the mixed type of the short-term variety. The next chapter on secular disequilibrium deals with the long-term income disturbance to equilibrium and systematic technological change. Finally both types of structural disequilibrium are dealt with in Chapter 27 which carries that title.

Inflation

There are many economists who regard the great bulk of balance-of-payments difficulties as the result of domestic inflation. It follows as a corollary that most balance-of-payments troubles can be cured by disinflation (eliminating the inflationary gap and reducing effective demand to the level of full employment), or at least by halting the inflation and adjusting the exchange rate.

There is a large element of truth in this position. In many situations, disinflation can produce substantial improvements in the balance of payments. Partly, the decline in income reduces imports directly and releases goods previously bought in the home market for sale abroad. Partly, a reduction in prices makes the market a better one for foreigners in which to buy and a worse one in which to sell, thus assisting exports and reducing imports. Partly, in these days of administered prices, disinflation results in the cancellation of domestic orders and thus reduces delays in filling orders for export. And, finally, the halting of the inflation and the correction of the exchange rate tend to reverse the destabilizing speculation which added to the loss of foreign-exchange reserves produced directly by inflation, and tend to produce, if the operation is well handled, a return flow of domestic capital and a reconstitution of foreign working balances.

Where inflation is demand-led, through excessive consumption, investment, or government expenditure, the disequilibrium is primarily of the income variety, although, as just mentioned, there will be price distortion. Where inflation is the result of a wage-price push—administered wage increases being followed by rises in administered prices—one can point primarily to price relationships. If the country sells in highly competitive markets, export prices are given and the inflationary pressure will squeeze profits of exporters. Where the exporters themselves administer their prices, profit margins may remain intact, but goods will gradually be priced out of world markets.

It will be appreciated that we refer to relative and not to absolute inflation. If all countries inflate at the same rate, and there is no money illusion, so that no one will change his spending habits in the mistaken notion that his real income has increased because his money income has risen, there can be no balance-of-payments disequilibrium.

The difficulty arises because the tendency to overspend, or the price-cost push, is faster in one country than another. The possibility that this will occur systematically is discussed in the next chapter.

How much deflation will improve the balance of payments by how much? In the immediate postwar period, R. F. Harrod suggested that there was a dollar-for-dollar relationship (or rather, since he was talking about Britain, pound-for-pound). But the answer turns on the nature of analysis. In multiplier terms, with no foreign repercussion, the change in imports is given by the change in investment, the multiplier, and the marginal propensity to import. A cut of £100 in spending will cut national income by £300, if the multiplier is 3, and imports by £75, if the marginal propensity to import is 0.25. Only if the marginal propensity to save is zero will a cut in spending produce an equal reduction in imports. Or the analysis may run in terms of foreign markets: a cut in investment may improve the balance of payments more than a cut in consumption because there is a strong foreign demand for the released capital equipment but not for consumers' goods.

Overvaluation after an Interruption in Trade

War and postwar reconstruction bring inflation. During the interruption of trade caused by high domestic demand and shortages, plus in many instances the blockage of trade routes, inflation can proceed at different rates in different countries. With the resumption of trade, exchange rates are out of line. Because of the difficulty in reducing wages and money incomes—wages being asymmetrical in that they rise faster and more easily than they fall—it becomes necessary as a rule to adjust exchange rates to the disparate rates of inflation. This case has already been discussed in Chapter 3 in connection with the purchasing-power-parity doctrine of Gustav Cassel.

The foregoing discussion of the mixed income-price case of inflation or of inappropriate exchange rate has been kept brief and even terse. Much of the subtlety which could be put into the argument is saved for the discussions of the cyclical disequilibrium (pure income disequilibrium, or as pure as it is possible to be) and of structural disequilibrium at the goods level (pure price). Much of what is said below about cycles can apply to temporary inflations which are not regular in pattern.

The Cyclical Path of Income

Cyclical disequilibrium occurs either because the patterns of business cycles in different countries follow different paths or because income elasticities of demand for imports in different countries are different. We may illustrate this with some simple diagrams for two countries. In Figure 25.1, national money income is stable in B and fluctuates cyclically in A. Income elasticities of demand for imports may or may not be the same. The income elasticity of demand for imports

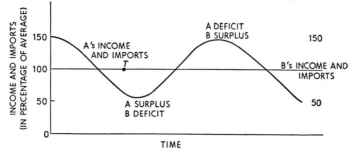

FIG. 25.1. Cyclical Disequilibrium: Different Income Patterns and Identical Income Elasticities for Imports

in B is not involved, since income is stable. In this situation, A's imports (and B's exports) will decline in depression and rise in prosperity. B's imports (and A's exports) will continue steady. The result is that A will have an export surplus in depression and an import surplus in prosperity. And B will have a deficit when A is depressed, and a surplus when A is prosperous.

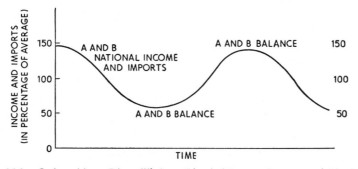

FIG. 25.2. Cycles without Disequilibrium: Identical Income Patterns and Elasticities

If the national incomes of A and B both follow the cyclical path of A and income elasticities of imports in both countries are unity, and hence identical, there will be no disequilibrium. This is illustrated in Figure 25.2. Exports and imports rise and fall with national income, but by the same amount. Cycles are a necessary condition of pure cyclical disequilibrium, but not a sufficient one.

The Role of Income Elasticities

Figure 25.3 suggests the position where national incomes vary in the same cyclical paths but income elasticities for imports differ. In this case, A may have an income elasticity greater than unity; B, an elasticity less than unity. A's imports are luxuries—tourist travel, perfumes, and whisky, let us say. B's imports, on the other hand, are necessities—

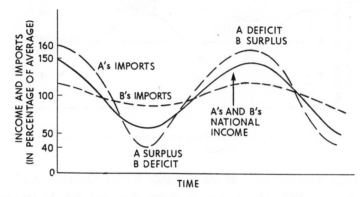

FIG. 25.3. Cyclical Disequilibrium: Identical Income Patterns, Different Income Elasticities for Imports

wheat, coal for space-heating, and newsprint. With these assumptions, too, A will have an export surplus in depression, when its imports (B's exports) have sunk lower than its exports (B's imports); and A will have an import surplus in prosperity. B's balance of payments will show the simple obverse.

Price Elasticities

The analysis can be still further complicated by adding price changes and price elasticities. If prices rise in prosperity and decline in depression, a country with a price elasticity for imports greater than unity will experience a tendency for a decline in the value of imports in prosperity, while those for which import price elasticity is less than one will experience a tendency for increase. These tendencies may be overshadowed by the effects of income changes, of course. Conversely, as prices decline in depression, the elastic demand will bring about an increase in imports, the inelastic a decrease.

An attempt has been made in discussing the effects of business cycles on the balances of payments of primary-producing countries to combine price and income demand elasticities into a single pattern. Four classes of primary products are distinguished by S. G. Triantis, each dominated by a characteristic demand elasticity. These classes, with illustrations of the commodities concerned, are:

Class A—low price elasticity: grains, coffee, tea, sugar, tobacco
Class B—high price elasticity: fruits, vegetables, dairy products
Class C—low income elasticity: petroleum and products, coal, coke
Class D—high income elasticity: metals and ores, rubber, fibers, vegetable
   oils

The writer finds that countries which are major exporters of A and D products tend to lose in depression, but countries exporting B and C products do not fare so badly and may even improve their balance of trade. This follows because exporters of A products suffer major price declines in depression and exporters of D products suffer significant reductions in volume. Whether P or Q declines sharply, PQ, or the value of exports, falls. On the other hand, B and C products hold up relatively well in depression in price and quantity, respectively. A complete statement of the position would require knowledge of the composition of imports, the supply schedules for exports and imports respectively, and the magnitudes of the income changes involved; but the combination of price and income elasticities into a single framework is suggestive.

In all probability, one could make comparable distinctions of industrial products. Countries manufacturing older staple commodities, such as textiles, shoes, simple iron and steel manufactures, etc., probably experience a demand which is income-inelastic in the long cycles, though it may have great variability in inventory cycles. Countries producing luxury goods are likely to have wide cycles. Other countries, exercising technological leadership and innovating in the production and sale of new goods in international trade, probably experience a still different pattern. This is an area which requires investigation.

Similarly, as we have mentioned in Chapter 11, there are some economists who have combined income and price movements in a single cyclical analysis in asymmetrical form. Speaking of underdeveloped countries, one or two of them have asserted that such countries suffer in terms of the balance of payments both from low prices in depression which hurt exports and from high incomes in prosperity which give rise to soaring imports. Others, referring to European countries, have suggested that these countries are hurt consistently by high import prices during periods of world prosperity, and by low incomes abroad during periods of depression. It is clear, however, that these two statements are contradictory and that the conclusion that underdeveloped and developed countries are both hurt in terms of balance-of-payments equilibrium by prosperity and depression alike cannot be accepted. True, the balances of payments of underdeveloped countries are adversely affected by the income effect in prosperity and the terms-of-trade (price) effect in depression. But before one can draw any general conclusions about the net impact on such countries of cycles, one must study the income effect in depression and the terms-of-trade effect in prosperity; and the converse for developed countries.

Deflation as a Remedy for Cyclical Disequilibrium

Most discussions of business-cycle disequilibrium and its therapy have been conducted on the assumption that the problem followed the model set out in Figure 25.1. The analysis has been directed particularly to the question: What should country B do at point T in this diagram? Its import surplus is due to no fault of its own. Exports have declined, leaving it with a considerable loss of real income, whether output has fallen and prices remain stable or output held steady and prices fallen. In the former case, there are unemployed factors attached to the export industries; in the latter, resources engaged in exports are receiving a rate of return much below those of other industries.

If nothing is done beyond paying for the import surplus through gold, short-term assets, or short-term borrowing, the multiplier effects of the loss of exports will bring about a reduction in domestic income and employment. The stability maintained by country B in Figure 25.1 is conceivable only under the circumstance that anticyclical measures of some sort are consistently taken to offset the depression and subsequent boom in the export industries generated by A.

The gold-standard remedy was deflation and the spread of unemployment from exports to the domestic industries. If this were followed smoothly and without lags, something like the pattern of Figure 25.2 would result. All balance-of-payments disequilibrium would have been eliminated, but at the cost of as serious a business cycle as in A. If income elasticities for imports differed in the two countries, of course, the cyclical patterns of income would also have to differ to eliminate balance-of-payments imbalance. If B's income elasticity for imports was greater than A's, for example, the amplitude of its income fluctuations could be more moderate. If, on the other hand, the position were that set forth in Figure 25.3, balance-of-payments equilibrium will be produced only by wider income movements in B than in A. It is not worth drawing a new figure to represent this. Turn back to Figure 25.3 and change the designations of the curves. "A's imports" becomes "B's income"; "B's imports," "A's income"; and "National Income A and B" is relabeled "Imports A and B." Under these circumstances, B must experience greater deflation than A in order to correct the balance-of-payments position.

On this showing, the gold-standard remedy of deflation for balance-of-payments disequilibrium was discarded as worse than the disease. To some degree, as we have seen, the foreign-trade multiplier transmitted business cycles automatically. Income fell in the export industries, and this decline was spread throughout the economy by the multiplier. In a few cases, it is possible that the foreign-trade accelerator would exercise an effect. Exports would fall and, with them, new investment in the export industry. Net investment in the export sector might even become negative in a severe depression if gross investment declined below the level of depreciation. National income would then fall from the impact of two multipliers. And a domestic accelerator might be touched off. The situation was likely to be ripe for deflation without conscious monetary and fiscal policy to accentuate it, as the gold-standard "rules of the game" required. But the development of the view in the 1930's that unemployment was the most wasteful possible economic course for a country to pursue disposed countries to attempt to eliminate not only secondary unemployment but even primary. Given these attitudes, the use of monetary deflation and fiscal contraction as a remedy for cyclical disequilibrium was excluded.

Cyclical Depreciation

The next possibility was exchange depreciation. This was abhorred at the end of the 1930's because it was thought to lead to retaliation. Competitive currency depreciation benefited no one. The depreciation of the pound sterling in September, 1931, was followed by that of the Japanese yen in December of the same year; the dollar, after a struggle, in March, 1933; and the gold bloc, consisting of the French, Swiss, and Belgian francs and the Netherlands guilder, from 1934 to September, 1936. The result of the competitive exchange depreciation was to leave the world's major currencies in approximately the same relationship with one another but in a different one from gold. This effect has monetary implications of its own—raising the value of central-bank reserves in local currencies and increasing the value of the stream of new gold injected into the world monetary system annually. But to change the relationship of all currencies to gold as a measure of world price stability—as some economists have suggested—

was quite a different matter from competitive depreciation, one currency at a time, with consistent speculative pressure against the weakest currency until it cracked.

A distinction can be made between depreciation to the point of equilibrium in the balance of payments and depreciation to an undervalued level which will positively expand exports, depress the propensity to import, and give a positive lift to income. While interest has revived after World War II in currency depreciation to the point of equilibrium, in the atmosphere of the 1930's it was regarded almost exclusively as going beyond that point to a "beggar-thy-neighbor" policy, i.e., achieving one's own ends at the expense of making things worse for others. Hence the universal distrust of exchange-rate manipulation at the end of the 1930's. This distrust has moderated with the passage of time, which will require us to reconsider depreciation once more in this chapter.

Cyclical Import Cuts

While restraint should be exercised in applying deflation or exchange depreciation, a course to be avoided in correcting a balance-of-payments disequilibrium is restrictive commercial policy. The balance-of-payments impact of tariffs is, as we have seen, uncertain. Quota restrictions are more effective in limiting imports in the short run. But the latter are highly inappropriate. The loss of exports by the depressed country pushes it deeper into depression. The allocation of factors is distorted, involving expensive shifts of resources which may later have to be returned to their previous occupations. Discontinuous changes in the quantities of goods permitted in international trade increase uncertainty, limit the willingness of producers to work for foreign markets, and are destructive of world specialization. Import restrictions may be unavoidable, if depreciation and deflation are ruled out, unless the country concerned has an adequate supply of foreign-exchange reserves. In this case it can ride out the depression abroad, and help to cure it, by buying its normal imports, permitting its current account to go into deficit, and allowing the depressed country to be buoyed by an export surplus. But if reserves are inadequate, this will not be possible.

Adequacy of Foreign-Exchange Reserves

Some considerable attention has been paid in the postwar period to the adequacy of foreign-exchange reserves. The basis for this concern has been widespread, but the question has arisen particularly in connection with the question: When do a country's reserves suffice to enable it to restore full convertibility of its currency for current-account, if not for capital transactions? Statistics on reserves are closely watched in countries which publish them, and changes in reserves from week to week or month to month are an important factor taken into account in decisions on international economic policy.

First, what are reserves? Evidently definitions vary. Reserves can be interpreted narrowly in a legal sense, and consist in those assets denominated in gold or foreign exchange which the central bank or the treasury is required to hold against its liabilities. These assets may be counted gross, or net of liabilities to foreigners. In the United States, for example, the question has been raised by some as to whether we should subtract from our $22 billion of gold, the $8 billion of assets held in this country by foreigners which could be withdrawn.

Among assets, moreover, there are a number of choices. Should one count the clearing balances of the authorities in inconvertible currencies? The assets of the private market such as the dollar securities held by British private investors? Evidently, decision must be made largely on a practical basis, and in terms of the problem to be considered. The private assets of the market are reserves in reckoning up the country's assets to support a long war, but they are hardly reserves for financing a cyclical imbalance. For this purpose, the reserves are those convertible or usable assets available to the authorities which may be expended in time of balance-of-payments difficulty. We can take these reserves on a gross basis, since their adequacy can be measured partly in terms of the likelihood that some portion of them will be needed to pay off creditors.

The adequacy of a country's reserves evidently depends upon the nature of the difficulty it faces and the standard of conduct it proposes to follow during it. The size of reserves needed will vary positively with the amplitude of the cycle abroad, the income elasticities of demand for imports, the variability in the prices of exports and imports, the size of the related price elasticities, and with the amount of destabilizing speculation in exchange and inventories or the smallness of stabilizing activity; all these, on the one hand; and, on the other, and of equal importance to the foregoing, the extent to which the monetary authorities insist on avoiding foreign-exchange control. Reserves adequate for a country which occasionally resorts to foreign-exchange control will not suffice for a country which absolutely refuses to restrict exchange transactions as a matter of principle.

The possibility of stabilizing or destabilizing speculation raises a vital and paradoxical point. If all speculation is stabilizing and there is a great deal of it, a country needs no reserves of any kind for cyclical disequilibria. Speculators will buy its currency when it is weak, sell it when it is strong, and thus finance the deficit and surplus respectively. A number of economists believe that this process would be assisted by fluctuating exchange rates. On the other hand, if there is only desta-bilizing speculation, and a great deal of it, no amount of reserves may suffice to meet a balance-of-payments deficit. This point can be under-lined by contrasting the position of Britain in the nineteenth and twentieth centuries. In the last quarter of the nineteenth century, largely characterized by stabilizing speculation, for example, no one raised the question of the adequacy of the Bank of England's gold reserves when the total stock for this world currency amounted to between £20 and £40 million, or $100 to $200 million. Today, in a world of destabiliz-ing speculation, it is clear that $2 billion of reserves are inadequate, and likely that $3 billion are still short of the appropriate level.

It should in any case be clear that the question of the adequacy of reserves arises only in connection with temporary imbalances on in-ternational payments, such as those occasioned by cycles, or by short-term disturbances, randomly distributed, whether monetary or struc-tural. If a country has a persistent deficit in its balance of payments, no amount of reserves is adequate.

At the end of the interwar period, international monetary reserves throughout the world may have been, or possibly were not, adequate *in toto* to meet world needs, but they were badly distributed. The United States owned 68 per cent of the world's monetary gold at the end of 1939. Accordingly, the monetary experts of the United Na-tions, who met at Bretton Woods in 1944 to design a postwar interna-tional monetary mechanism, foreswore deflation, limited devaluation, and tried to avoid trade discrimination by providing additional inter-national monetary reserves. Country B was supposed to borrow when A was in depression and pay back the loan when A recovered, thereby being enabled to pursue a policy of stable national money income and stable imports. Stabilized income in B would help A, which would be aided by the export surplus in maintaining its income. The device created for this purpose was the International Monetary Fund.

International Monetary Fund

The International Monetary Fund is a pool of central-bank re-serves and national currencies which are available to its members under certain conditions. The pool can be regarded as an extension of the central-bank reserves of the member countries. Limits and rules are necessary if the pool is to be a revolving one and not simply a fund which is frozen in a single series of lending operations which cannot be repaid.

The rules require all currencies to be more or less tied to gold, and hence to one another, under a system of stable exchange rates which are altered only on occasion. The occasion must be a disequilibrium, and the Fund must be notified of the proposed exchange rate. If the change is less than 10 per cent, the Fund shall raise no objection. If the change is more than 10 per cent, the Fund is required to approve or disapprove, using the criterion that exchange depreciation is appropriate only in case of "fundamental disequilibrium." Disapproval of an exchange-rate change requires its abandonment; or, if the country proposing the change goes through with it, the Fund may refuse to make its resources available to the country or even to expel it from the Fund.

Fundamental disequilibrium is nowhere defined in the articles of agreement of the Fund. The concept was left to be given life by the course of events. Some have argued that "fundamental disequilibria" are those of deep depressions abroad, with prolonged unemployment. Others are convinced that exchange depreciation is most appropriate in structural disequilibria and that this must therefore be what the experts at Bretton Woods had in mind. A good case can be made for the view that no particular character of disequilibrium was meant so much as a serious and prolonged one, which did not appear to be correcting itself.

In the second place, among the purposes of the Fund, after the promotion of exchange stability, was the elimination of hampering foreign-exchange restrictions. Restrictions on capital movements were permitted; and the Fund could even require a country to impose controls over outward movements of capital. The attempt is made to distinguish between current and capital transactions. Current transactions may continue to be restricted after the war during a transitional period of five years. Since the Fund actually commenced operations in March, 1947, the transitional period expired in March, 1952. This expiration was the signal for the Fund to examine exchange restrictions in effect among its members and to consult with member countries as to their further retention.

The elimination of restrictions on current-account transactions is the goal of the Fund. Once this has been achieved, however, the articles of the Fund permit exchange restrictions under one condition: if the demand for a particular currency becomes so great in relation to the supply of it that the Fund's capacity to meet this demand is threatened, the Fund may declare that currency "scarce," and members may with impunity impose exchange controls over it. The fact that one or two countries which use a currency widely in their foreign transactions have run into balance-of-payments difficulties is not sufficient to render a currency scarce. The scarcity must arise from the disequilibrium of the country whose currency it is—country A, in Figure 25.1, in deep depression. And the currency must be scarce in the fund. If the Fund should choose not to make a currency available to countries which wanted to purchase it with their own currency, that currency would not be scarce. It is a remarkable fact that the dollar has not been declared scarce by the Fund in the period since 1947.

With devaluation and exchange restrictions limited, the Fund was expected to help by making available international reserves. Each country was given a quota. This determined both what it could obtain in the way of help if it ran into difficulties and the amount of its own currency to which other countries might gain access if the shoe were on the other foot. A country paid to the Fund 25 per cent of its quota in gold or dollars, and the remaining 75 per cent in its own currency. This was the limit of the resources which the Fund could put at the disposal of other countries. The country itself, however, might do better than this. It could purchase foreign exchange from the Fund against delivery of its own currency until the Fund's holdings of its currency amounted to 200 per cent of its quota. Since the Fund originally held its currency to the extent of 75 per cent of its quota, this means that the member can purchase foreign exchange up to 125 per cent of its quota. The first 25 per cent of this represents the original subscription in gold and foreign exchange. The Fund has tended to permit this to be bought back for local currency rather automatically. Successive 25 per cents, however, no more than one of which could be drawn upon in any one year, are purchasable only with the permission of the Fund's board.

The Fund originally represented on the whole the conception of H. D. White of the United States treasury rather than that of Lord Keynes who headed the British delegation at Bretton Woods and who had prepared a Keynes Plan in opposition to the White Plan. One of the differences between the plans lay in whether drawings would be automatic or permissive. The White insistence on permission to draw won. Another difference lay in the extent to which the surplus countries were penalized. The Keynes Plan would have required creditors to accept deposits on an international clearing fund which were automatically issued to debtors and would have charged them interest on credit balances as well as charging debtors interest on debit balances. This automatic expansion of the Fund, up to a limit, involved the creation of international reserves through new credit under the Keynes Plan, in contrast with the White Plan where the reserves were limited to the 75 per cent quota contributions of the creditors. This made for a difference in total international reserves, on the one hand, and in the ability of the Fund to meet a given disequilibrium. As constituted, the Fund had a total quota of $8 billion. This of course does not represent what can be loaned at any one time, since for every deficit, which permits borrowing against one quota, there is a counterpart surplus on the part of another country, which because of its surplus does not need to borrow. As a rule, therefore, only half of the quotas can be in use at any one time. Half of $8 billion is $4 billion; 25 per cent of this— which is all that could be loaned in a year—would be $1 billion.

A way of judging the adequacy of the size of the Fund is to compare the British quota of $1.3 billion, one quarter of which is $325 million with the reduction in British reserves in 1949, from $2.1 billion at the end of March to $1.3 billion on September 18, 1949, or the similar decline of $1.1 billion between March, 1951, and March, 1952. To be sure, these reserves belong to the sterling area as a whole, so that the quotas of Australia ($200 million), India ($400 million), and the Union of South Africa ($100 million) should perhaps be added (New Zealand is not a member of the Fund). These amount to $700 million and bring the sterling-area quota to $2 billion, with an annual possible borrowing of $500 million. This is still inadequate as compared with a scale of possible need. In 1955 the gold and dollars of the United Kingdom fell by $642 million, and at the height of the crisis over Suez, they fell by $363 million in the two months of October and November, 1956. Again in 1957 when speculation turned against the pound and in favor of the Deutsche mark, British reserves dropped by $520 million in August and the first three weeks of September until the Bank of England raised the discount rate to 7 per cent.

A number of proposals have been made for increase in the size of the Fund. A group of experts appointed by the secretary-general of the United Nations to study international measures for combatting unemployment, recommended, for example, that countries with surpluses in their current account arising from a decline in imports be required to furnish their own currency to the Fund in the amount of the decline in imports, and that this currency be then loaned out to those countries with deficits. Safeguards were devised to ensure that no country could use the Fund's resources to expand its imports free, and it was provided that interest be paid on debit balances and that loans be repaid. Some earlier proposals recommended that exchange be furnished to deficit countries to enable them to finance their deficits without the necessity for repayments.

The inadequate size of the Fund has been attacked in two ways. In 1956, in addition to using the Fund, the British government arranged to waive payment of interest on its United States and Canadian loans, amounting to some $181 million, sold $60 million of United States government bonds, and arranged for a line of credit from the Export-Import Bank against the security of $750 million of United States shares. In addition, the Fund itself permitted the British to draw $561,470,000, or almost 43 per cent of its quota, and arranged a stand-by credit of the remainder of its quota, or $738,530,000, which could be drawn upon any time at the request of the United Kingdom within twelve months of its opening. Thus there was the possibility that the whole quota would be drawn in less than one week, as against the original intention of limiting drawing to 25 per cent of a quota in any twelve months.

Operation of the Fund

The Fund came into operation in the spring of 1947—a year of crisis in Europe when a number of countries had run out of wartime accumulated reserves, used up immediate postwar aid, but not yet gained access to United States aid under the European Recovery Program in 1948. France, the Netherlands, and the United Kingdom borrowed as much as they could at the time, to sustain imports and consumption. Similarly Mexico and India used their 25 per cent of their quotas to borrow for imports rather than to meet any temporary balance-of-payments disequilibrium.

In the field of foreign exchange, the Fund also played a passive role. It accepted the par values notified to it by member countries, despite the fact that deficits created a presumption that many of them were overvalued. It confined its interest in exchange rates through 1948 largely to technical questions, urging the elimination of multiple cross-rates, discussed above in Chapter 15, and advising countries with multiple exchange rates to simplify them.

In 1949, however, it helped to precipitate the devaluation of sterling by raising the question. This is one of the major difficulties with international organizations for the settlement of international monetary questions. To discuss the financial position of a country is to question it, and this encourages the speculators to attack the currency. When the

British did devalue, they told the Fund, rather than ask it, and they went through a drastic short-term crisis without using the resources available in the Fund.

British exchange crises of 1947, 1949, 1951, and 1955 were in fact all handled without recourse to the Fund. The two-year periodicity of the earlier crises is worth some attention. Two theories have been erected to explain it: one, that the underlying element in the crises was inventory speculation, and that this reversed itself and was ready to start over again in a space of two years; the other, that the two years represented the period of time in the sterling area for decisions in behalf of sterling to get made, communicated to the dominions, put into effect, and finally to lose their potency. The two-year cycle was, therefore, either an inventory cycle or a planning cycle, or some combination of the two.

Further evidence of the passivity of the Fund is that it failed to take a leading role in the building of the European Payments Union. Gradually, however, as postwar reconstruction became completed, the Fund's articles were modified in practice to enable it to meet emerging

TABLE 25.2
IMF OPERATIONS
(In Millions of Dollars)

	Total Member Drawings	Total Repayments	Cumulated Net	Stand-by Arrangements Available
1947	467.7	6.0	461.7	——
1948	208.0	11.4	658.3	——
1949	101.5	2.3	757.5	——
1950	——	24.3	733.2	——
1951	34.6	73.8	694.0	——
1952	85.1	101.5	677.6	55.0
1953	229.5	320.4	586.7	50.0
1954	62.5	210.0	439.2	90.0
1955	27.5	32.4	234.3	62.5
1956	692.6	113.3	813.5	1,117.4
1957*	625.3	23.4	1,415.2	814.5

* Through June 30.
Source: IMF, *International Financial Statistics*, September, 1957, p. 5.

problems and conditions. Since a country could not count drawing rights from the Fund as reserves if it was uncertain whether they would be granted or not, the Fund arranged for stand-by credits, i.e., arrangements in advance that credit would be available over a period. The British credit of this kind has been referred to. France, which was suffering acute balance-of-payments difficulties from inflation, arranged for a similar credit a few weeks before the attack on Suez. Second, the Fund has attempted to encourage borrowing for short periods, lowering rates on short-term loans and raising them for periods longer than a year. Third, as already mentioned, the Fund made loans in excess of 25 per cent of the British quota. These more active policies brought it about that the fund's net drawings and stand-by credits, shown in Table 25.2 (p. 503), rose substantially in late 1956 and early 1957 after having fallen to less than one third of the original reconstruction drawings.

But the ultimate role of the Fund is subject to limitations. Secondary reserves are like primary reserves: no amount is adequate if a country has a persistent deficit in its balance of payments. The question is whether the world conforms to the model of Figure 25.1.

Cyclical Patterns

The Fund was constructed on the principles that cyclical disequilibria for a given country would balance out over a complete cycle and that cyclical disequilibria would be randomly distributed among countries. On the first of these principles, a country which had a deficit in depression should turn around and have a surplus in prosperity. This would enable it to repay the borrowing and to finance the deficit. Conversely, a country which ran a surplus in its current account in depression would pile up a deficit in prosperity. This would allow its currency, drawn by the Fund in depression, to be paid back. With respect to the second principle, every country contributed its currency to the common pool on the assumption that it was equally likely that the currency of any country, making due allowance for differences in size, would be needed. If country A has a surplus and country B a deficit in this depression, this is because it happens to be that way; and it is as likely as not that the positions will be reversed in the next depression.

Based on these two principles, a common pool of national currencies, provided it were large enough, could be used as a revolving fund to finance cyclical disequilibria. If certain countries consistently behave in certain ways in particular phases of the business cycle, however, and if surplus and deficits do not cancel each other over the cycle, the fund may get itself into difficulties. The currencies of certain countries will become scarcer; those of others more abundant.

Let us suppose that A is prone to deflation and B to inflation. A's national money income may appear, in relation to the full-employment level of income, something akin to that in Figure 25.4a. B's, on the other hand, will resemble more the pattern of 25.4b. Since the area above the full-employment line cannot represent much more in the way of employment, it must indicate price inflation. It is assumed, perhaps rashly, that this is eliminated in the early stages of the depression before unemployment begins.

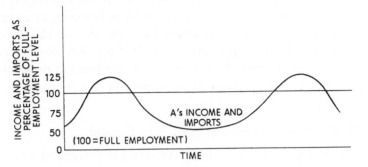

FIG. 25.4*a*. Cyclical Pattern of Country Prone to Depression

FIG. 25.4*b*. Cyclical Pattern of Country Prone to Inflation

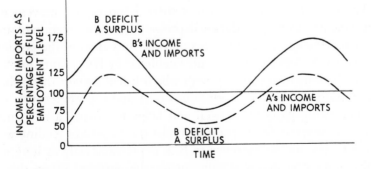

FIG. 25.5. Cyclical Disequilibrium: Different Income Patterns—Inflation-Prone and Deflation-Prone; Identical Import Elasticities

On the assumptions of income elasticities of imports equal to one, and hence identical, and, furthermore, of an exchange rate which would give balance-of-payments equilibrium when both countries were at full employment, these two curves may be put together as shown in Figure 25.5. A polished treatment of the example would require assumptions about the price elasticity of imports on the part of A and B as well as income elasticities, because prices change above the full-employment level. We may ignore this aspect of the problem, however, by assuming price elasticities equal to unity, which leave the income elasticities in charge. Country B will experience deficit in depression and prosperity alike. If B were to borrow A's currency from the Fund in prosperity, it would be unable to pay it back in depression. In fact, it would need to borrow more.

The Cyclical Movement of Long-Term Capital

This is a good place to recall the cyclical pattern of long-term capital movements which we discussed earlier (p. 372). It will be remembered that, historically, long-term lending tends to be correlated positively with the cycle rather than inversely. Lending expands in prosperity and contracts in depression.

This pattern fits into Figure 25.5. A is the lending country, which has a tendency to deflation relative to B, while B has a relative tendency to inflation, as compared with A. This aspect of the question will be examined at greater length in the next chapter. For the moment let us assume that there is something appropriate about the lending countries with more savings having wider cyclical fluctuations in employment, and borrowing countries with less savings having wider fluctuations in prices.

The long-term lending from A to B finances B's import surplus during prosperity. This import surplus represents real transfer of capital. The difficulty, however, is that there is no capital movement to finance the import surplus during depression. And the creation of an International Monetary Fund for this purpose runs afoul of the possibility that, with this pattern, there is no likelihood of B's earning exchange to repurchase its own currency with which it had bought the exchange in depression. When the depression is over and exports recover, long-term borrowing picks up as well and helps to finance a new import surplus. A monetary fund operating under this pattern of lending would be able to pay out A's currency to B in depressions only as long as its supply of A's currency was sufficient for the purpose. When this was exhausted, the fund would be obliged to stop.

To B, this appears to be a most unhappy world. The supply of A's currency loaned to it declines. This may start first if interest rates in A rise at the peak of prosperity. And just as it gets adjusted to this blow, the depression in A deprives it of exchange earned by exports. The peak of this instability was probably reached in the 1928–32 depression in the United States (see Table 25.3).

TABLE 25.3

THE DECLINE IN DOLLAR SUPPLY, 1928–32
(In Billions of Dollars)

	1928	1929	1932
United States imports......................	4.1	4.4	1.3
Other current payments.....................	1.8	2.0	1.0
Total current payments..................	5.9	6.4	2.3
Total long-term capital outflow..............	1.6	1.0	0.1
Total dollars supplied on current account and long-term capital outflow.................	7.5	7.4	2.4

Elasticities of Demand

There is one more way in which we can plague and torment the unhappy B. Let us alter the assumption of identical income elasticities equal to unity and instead, leaving A's alone, assume that B's income elasticity for imports is greater than unity in the expansion phases of the cycle and smaller than unity in periods of contraction. The effect of this can be illustrated in part in Figure 25.6, which assumes that na-

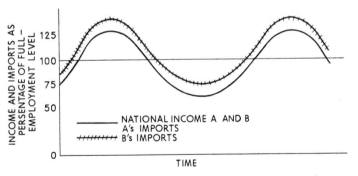

FIG. 25.6. Cyclical Disequilibrium: Identical Income Patterns. B's Imports: Income Elastic in Expansion; Income Inelastic in Contraction

tional income is identical in the two countries, following a cyclical pattern similar to that in Figure 25.2. If national income were to follow different patterns, say those in Figure 25.5, imports of B would soar high above national income, relative to the full-employment level in prosperity, but decline less than national income in the depression phase of the cycle.

The student will think that an ace has been dealt off the bottom of the deck against B in the assumption of asymmetry in the income elasticity of demand for B's imports. What possible reality can there be to this sort of import demand? There is much to be said for indignation on this point, and yet the possibility cannot be excluded. Professor Duesenberry has made clear that people increase their consumption more readily than they reduce it and holds that this asymmetry has important consequences for consumption theory and the determination of national income. Most of us are familiar with the phenomenon of a good which was once regarded as a luxury but which has become a necessity. This is perhaps a short-range response; given more time, we can get used to doing without automobiles, deep freezers, mechanized lawnmowers, and the like. But the business cycle is a short-run phenomenon, and at any time in the growth of the real income of a person, and possibly of a country, there may be some objects of expenditure, imported from abroad, which may be luxuries before they have been bought but become necessities when the standard of living gets adjusted to them.

Alternatives to Discrimination

What, then, may be advocated as an alternative to trade discrimination in depression? Deflation is excluded; depreciation may fail to work; a pool of international reserves fails to meet the need to the extent that depressions do not occur in random fashion and disequilibria do not balance out over the entire cycle.

One possibility which remains to be discussed is international commodity reserve schemes. These can apply only in a limited number of primary commodities which are standardized and storable. They fail to meet the need of the industrial countries which may have a deficit in depression. They also involve difficult problems of finance. Who undertakes the countercyclical purchases of commodities, and at what price? We shall return briefly to this question in Chapter 29, but at this juncture it may be appropriate to foreshadow that our conclusions are largely pessimistic.

There may be no means of avoiding trade discrimination. We have seen in Chapter 15 that trade discrimination has its advocates, particularly in a situation in which it is impossible, or very difficult, for the deficit country to increase exports; where resources are relatively immobile; and where the difficulty is transitory. These requirements fit the cyclical pattern. If international lending cannot be made to work and if depreciation and deflation must be avoided, there may be no alternative but to impose exchange control and hold down imports to the level of exports. When A is depressed, B tightens up on import restrictions. When A's national income and imports pick up, B can ease up. This is very close to the position to which most of the world has come.

But there may be some sense in trying to re-establish the conditions in the world where the mechanism of short-term lending represented by the Fund will work. In the world of today it cannot function. That this is recognized by the Fund itself is attested by its inactivity in operations. If the underlying position could be altered so that depressions occur in more nearly random fashion, if a given disequilibrium tended to balance itself out over the whole cycle, short-term lending would be an appropriate method of financing cyclical balance-of-payments disequilibria. This provides a useful introduction for the study of secular disturbances to equilibrium in the next chapter.

Summary

An arbitrary classification of disequilibria is adopted. Included in this chapter are along with short-term income disequilibria those due to inflation, which are likely to involve distortion of income and price levels, relative to the exchange rate.

Cyclical disequilibria are caused by countries having different cyclical patterns of income, or the same income pattern with different income elasticities, or identical income patterns and income elasticities but different price elasticities.

Remedies for disequilibrium are discussed; depreciation is excluded on the grounds that it shifts resources which may be difficult to move and should not be changed in response to a short-run change, or that it will accentuate deflation abroad and fail to correct the balance of payments. Deflation is to be avoided, since this extends depressions in space. If world trade is to be sustained, import restrictions and tariffs are likewise undesirable. This leaves the use of foreign-exchange reserves and short-term lending.

The adequacy of reserves, however defined, is a function of the anticipated nature of the disequilibria as well as the characteristics of the economy. Of great importance is the presence or absence of destabilizing speculation.

The International Monetary Fund was created during the war to assist in financing cyclical deficits. Until recently it has not operated effectively in this regard. In part, this has been due to structural and other disequilibria. In part, the difficulty appears to be that cyclical disequilibria are not randomly distributed by countries, nor do they balance algebraically over the full cycle. On this account, the solution for cyclical disequilibria and the way to make the International Fund function effectively is to eliminate secular disturbances.

SUGGESTED READING

TREATISES, ETC.

The classical discussions of cyclical movements in balances of payments are by the League of Nations, *The Course and Phases of the World Economic Depression* (Geneva, 1931); and G. Haberler, *Prosperity and Depression* (3rd ed.; Geneva: League of Nations, 1941), chap. xi.

H. Neisser's monograph, *Some International Aspects of the Business Cycle* (Philadelphia: University of Pennsylvania Press, 1936), is dated. H. C. Wallich, *Monetary Problems of an Export Economy* (Cambridge, Mass.: Harvard University Press, 1951), has some useful remarks on dependent economies.

Econometric studies of world business cycles using multipliers and international "reflection ratios" have been undertaken by Hans Neisser and Franco Modigliani in *National Incomes and International Trade* (Urbana: University of Illinois Press, 1953); and J. J. Polak in *An International Economic System* (London: Allen & Unwin, 1954).

A voluminous literature has accumulated on the International Monetary Fund. Outstanding is J. H. Williams, *Postwar Monetary Plans* (3d ed.; New York: Alfred A. Knopf, Inc., 1947). See also R. F. Mikesell, *U.S. Economic Policy and International Relations* (New York: McGraw-Hill Book Co., Inc., 1951); B. Tew, *International Monetary Cooperation, 1945–52* (New York: Longmans, Green & Co., 1952); Robert Triffin, *Europe and the Money Muddle* (New Haven: Yale University Press, 1957), chap. iii.

The myriad publications of the Fund should also be consulted, especially annual reports, reports on exchange restrictions, and *Staff Papers*.

POINTS

T. C. Chang, *Cyclical Movements in the Balance of Payments* (Cambridge: Cambridge University Press, 1951), and S. G. Triantis, "Cyclical Changes in the Balance of Trade," *AER*, March, 1952, discuss income and price elasticities. The latter is referred to in the text.

For proposals to amend the articles of the Fund, see United Nations experts, *National and International Measures for Full Employment* (New York: United Nations, December, 1949); and T. Balogh, *The Dollar Crisis* (Oxford: Basil Blackwell, 1949).

The discussion on the adequacy of monetary reserves is based on an important paper with that title prepared by the International Monetary Fund for presentation to the Economic and Social Council of the United Nations and published in *SP*, October, 1953.

For a discussion of the impact of changes in investment on foreign balance, see the article by R. Nurkse, "The Relation between Home Investment and External Balance in the Light of British Experience," *RE & S*, May, 1956. The book to which it was addressed, and to which reference was made above, was R. F. Harrod's, *Are These Hardships Necessary?* (London: Hart-Davis, 1947).

An interesting literature has accumulated on the question why the 1953–54 recession in the United States did not have more of an impact on the British balance of payments when this impact was so strong in 1937–38 and 1948–49. See especially: H. K. Zassenhaus, "Direct Effects of a U.S. Recession on Imports," *RE & S,* August, 1955; J. J. Polak, "The Repercussion of Economic Fluctuations in the U.S. on Other Parts of the World," *SP,* August, 1956; G. Lovasy, "Prices of Raw Materials in the 1953–54 U.S. Recession," *SP,* February, 1957; and Donald MacDougall, *The World Dollar Problem* (London: Macmillan & Co., Ltd., 1957), chap. ii.

Chapter 26 | **SECULAR DISTURBANCE TO EQUILIBRIUM**

Secular Disequilibrium

The discussion of economic development in Chapter 21 has provided almost all the theoretical strands needed to deal with secular disturbance to balance-of-payments equilibrium. The word "secular" does not mean "worldly," in contrast to "ecclesiastical," but refers to long periods of time in which change takes place slowly. Secular disturbances to equilibrium are those which occur because of long-run and deep-seated changes in an economy as it moves from one stage of growth to another.

It has already been demonstrated that the current account tends to follow a varying pattern from one period of growth to another. In the early stages of development, domestic investment tends to exceed domestic savings, and imports to exceed exports. Disequilibrium, under these circumstances, may arise because insufficient capital is available to finance the import surplus, or, stated the other way round, the import surplus is too large in relation to the availability of capital from abroad.

At a further stage of development—that of the young creditor—domestic savings tend to exceed domestic opportunities for investment, and exports outrun imports. Disequilibrium may result because the long-term capital outflow falls short of the surplus savings or because surplus savings exceed the amount of investment opportunities abroad.

At a still later stage, when savings are equal to domestic investment and long-term capital movements are, on balance, zero, it may be considered a sign of disequilibrium to permit any change at all. The balanced stage, it will be remembered, was called that of the adult creditor. To move to the stage of the mature creditor, which consumes capital because consumption and investment outrun production, is perhaps a sign of disequilibrium by itself, even if the resultant import surplus can be readily financed.

512

Leaving aside this last possible exception, however, we can summarize by saying that in secular equilibrium the movement of long-term capital and the deep-seated forces affecting the equilibrium positions of savings and investment are adjusted to each other. Secular disturbance to this equilibrium occurs when either the long-term capital movement gets out of adjustment with the deep-seated factors affecting savings and investment or scheduled savings and investment change without an offsetting change in the movement of long-term capital.

This statement putting balance-of-payments equilibrium in terms of the relationship between domestic savings and domestic investment (more properly, intended domestic savings and intended domestic investment) is formally correct. It does not, however, explore the factors which underlie these quantities. Investment may exceed savings in a young country, for example, because of an increase in investment in advance of savings, or because of an increase in consumption at the expense of savings, while investment remained unchanged. Either change in investment or consumption, moreover, may occur in a given state of the arts, i.e., with unchanged technology in the world, or in response to an innovation at home or abroad. Secular disequilibrium should perhaps properly be discussed in relation to the whole range of factors affecting economic growth discussed in Chapter 21—resources, capital formation, social capacity of the labor force, growth of markets, transformation, and technological change. Our treatment is limited to but two of these factors in which the analysis usually runs: capital formation (in relation to savings) and technological change.

Capital Formation and Domestic Savings

If investment adjusted itself readily to the amount of domestic savings plus foreign capital, there can be no tendency for secular disequilibrium. Or if the international capital flow for its part fell neatly into line with the requirements of domestic investment minus domestic savings, the balance-of-payments position would always be in order. Any tendency to secular disequilibrium that exists must arise from the fact that the difference between domestic investment and domestic savings leads an independent existence from the foreign capital flow, and vice versa, and for these differences to be systematic.

In the nineteenth century, when no tendency to secular disequilibrium was observable, was this because the capital flow adjusted to the investment position, or because the investment position fell into line as the dependent variable? Taussig and his students, it will be recalled from Chapter 18 on transfer, assumed that the balance of payments on current account, and with it domestic investment and savings, followed the lead of the capital movement. In his discussion of the German reparations, Keynes demurred and stated:

> Those who see no difficulty in [fixing the volume of foreign remittance and compelling the balance of trade to adjust itself thereto] are applying the theory of liquids to what is, if not a solid, at least a sticky mass with strong internal resistances.

This is almost the equivalent of suggesting that the foreign capital movement should be adjusted to "sticky" domestic investment and savings. A tendency to secular disequilibrium in the twentieth century, however, must mean that the excess of domestic investment over domestic savings, or vice versa, and the foreign capital flow are independent of each other and of different magnitudes.

The reasons why domestic investment may exceed domestic savings are evident enough. Some underdeveloped countries offer substantial investment opportunities. In still others, it is believed that social overhead investment in roads, railroads, ports, electric power, land reclamation, and education will create opportunities for profitable investments. Along with these analytically separate cases comes another type which is also conceptually different but indistinguishable in the concrete situation: the excess of domestic investment over domestic savings which arises because of increases in consumption. These are often due to what is characterized as "demonstration effect," discussed on page 119—an attempt to pattern behavior after that of developed countries. One form of demonstration effect involves direct imitation of consumption patterns: the incorporation in the domestic standard of living of new items of consumption. Another may be demonstration effect in production and involve an increase in investment to employ a laborsaving device (though labor is abundant), or a device which improves output efficiency in general. And consumption may rise, and savings be reduced, through a still more subtle form of demonstration effect: an increase in governmental expenditure, whether for social investment or social consumption, which is paid for by progressive taxation. To the extent that the taxes reduce savings rather than consumption, the net effect of the new government expenditure is inflationary despite a balanced budget.

The detailed path is unimportant. The tendency for underdeveloped countries to overinvest and/or undersave can hardly be doubted. The leaders of these countries, and in good part the followers, are conscious both of the gap between their economic level and those of developed countries, and of the fact that it may be possible to narrow that gap and to increase the level of living in absolute terms. Following the pattern of the Soviet Union, though differing widely in application, most of them have adopted development plans which call for as much investment as possible. In making such plans, they tend today to overestimate the contribution of domestic saving, overestimate the availability of capital from abroad, overestimate the increase in productivity at home, underestimate the possibility of a bad harvest which would cut exports and increase the need for imports for consumption. The tendency to overspend follows fairly automatically from the character of the economic effort: a balance-of-payments surplus indicates missed opportunities for capital formation; a balance-of-payments deficit in excess of foreign investment, preferably a very small one, suggests that a country is making the maximum use of its resources. For an underdeveloped country to invest in foreign-exchange resources which are unproductive, or at best earn a modest rate of return in the money market of a developed country, makes little sense when it has vast need for real productive capital.

Trouble ensues, however, if this under- and overestimation goes far. When sizable uncovered deficits appear, speculation turns adverse; foreign investors avoid the country in favor of others; domestic capitalists seek safety for their funds abroad; and the inflationary process becomes cumulative, distorts the pattern of domestic investment, wastes resources. Occasional surpluses to rebuild reserves and limiting deficits to those which can be met out of foreign loans and reserves push development faster than any other course. While there may be a *tendency* to secular disequilibrium, it should be resisted.

The tendency for investment to outrun savings in developed countries of the mature-creditor type is again likely to be related to demonstration effect and the technological change which will be considered presently. Innovations elsewhere increase investment opportunities; new goods available abroad raise opportunities for spending without increasing productivity in parallel or greater fashion. Some foreign investment may be available in new lines for branch plants, and these may impose a substantial strain on the balance of payments through the remittance of profits, if the consumption item is popular. But for the most part foreign investment runs the other way, as private investment opportunities in many industries are more attractive at home than abroad. The secular disequilibrium may take the form of a balance-of-payments surplus smaller than positive foreign investment, or, in an extreme form, a balance-of-payments deficit accompanied by net positive foreign investment.

This case will be developed more during the discussion of technological change. It is important to remember, however, that a technological change which produces secular disequilibrium must be accompanied by a difference between domestic investment and domestic savings not covered by autonomous foreign investment. The disequilibrium may take place in a given state of the arts, i.e., with fixed technology, and from an equilibrium position, and involve an upward shift in domestic investment, a downward change in the savings schedule, or a decrease in the inward flow of autonomous capital—each individual change unaccompanied by offsetting changes. Or it may result from a change in the state of the arts, i.e., a technological innovation. But in this case the innovation must produce its balance-of-payments disequilibrium by increasing domestic investment or reducing savings.

Technological Change

Chapter 7 introduced the subject of changes in technology, showing how they might alter the flow of trade from that dictated by factor endowments. Chapter 11 used technological changes to illustrate one among a number of relations between the income and price mechanisms in producing balance-of-payments adjustment. The discussion in Chapter 7 was largely concerned with the introduction of new goods in international trade; the simple model used in Chapter 11 restricted the discussion to new ways of producing a single good, or export-biased innovation.

If new goods and improvements in productivity for old goods could occur anywhere in the world, they would not lead to secular disequilibrium. Any disturbance produced by a given innovation would be structural and of random character. Innovations would be as likely to lead to dollar surfeit as to dollar shortage. The difficulty arises from the fact that innovation tends to be concentrated. In the underdeveloped stages, a country becomes aware of the existence of more efficient techniques for producing standard goods. Its imitative phase leads to increased investment. In the mature stage of growth, a country loses its position as a technological leader and must imitate to stay up with the new leaders. If it consumes the new goods while getting ready to produce them, consumption rises and savings decrease. The adult country which enjoys a leadership in technological change does not long suffer balance-of-payments deficit from the creation of new investment opportunities. In time these new opportunities exist and raise the investment schedule simultaneously everywhere in the world. The initial increase in productivity in the innovating country quickly raises income and savings, tending to develop or add to balance-of-payments surplus.

If technological change is skewed in this way, and favors a given group of developed countries, note that the secular disequilibrium may occur for one of two reasons. A given change or a series of changes which comes to a halt may lead to a chronic tendency abroad for investment to exceed savings, and at home for savings to exceed investment. Or the secular disequilibrium may represent only the accumulation of a series of transitional disequilibria, always in the same direction, which will come to an end with the last change. Each change implies a new comparative advantage, which the other country adjusts to; but the adjustment process itself produces a balance-of-payments deficit. Starting from equilibrium, the innovation leads to increased exports if it is a new good or an export-biased innovation in an old good; or to a decline in imports if the innovation is import-biased in an old good. A new equilibrium then requires either increased imports or reduced exports, and the law of comparative advantage can bring this about with a transitional deficit. But just as the new equilibrium emerges, another innovation occurs, and a new transitional deficit is added to the first.

Professor Williams and Sir Dennis Robertson emphasize these transitional difficulties, which, cumulated through time, may lead to secular disequilibrium of the dollar-shortage type. Sir Donald Mac-Dougall is skeptical of the view that United States productivity increases faster in general than that of other countries, but believes that there may be something to the technological argument otherwise. Sir Geoffrey Crowther emphasizes the importance of new goods, particularly the most modern equipment in highly competitive lines, such as printing machinery, road-building equipment, etc. His analysis implies that innovation in new goods produces a long-run tendency outside the United States for investment to exceed savings, relative to the level of foreign lending, rather than a series of short-run transitional deficits.

Something turns on whether the higher rate of technological progress is absolute or relative. If the United States is undertaking technical innovations and the rest of the world's productivity is static, import-biased changes in technology and export-biased changes in commodities of high income-elasticity will lower real income abroad. But if the rest of the world is also progressing technically, though not as fast as the United States, it can be argued that its real income may not actually decline, and that it should not therefore be expected to have a balance-of-payments deficit. Any such deficit in these circumstances is the consequence of consuming too much, even though the skewness and rate of technological change in the United States mean that the rest of the world loses the benefits of its own increased efficiency. This is a harsh doctrine, perhaps, which says that increases in efficiency cannot result in increased real income if external changes result in a reduction in terms of trade. The real question, however, is not the moral one of whether to attribute deficits to increased consumption, or to something less "reprehensible." The question to the social scientist is whether, in these circumstances, deficits occur.

Technological change has an impact on secular disequilibrium in still another way. In a given state of the arts, or in one which changes only slowly, the marginal efficiency of capital would tend to be higher in less developed countries of the world than in the more developed. This is evident in those countries with extensive natural resources. In others it follows from the smaller supply of capital relative to labor. With a lower marginal efficiency of capital, the developed country is readier to export capital to balance its tendency to an export surplus.

But if innovation is rapid in the developed country, capital tends to be used at home. An increase in investment might be expected to correct the balance-of-payments surplus; the difficulty, however, is that the innovation increases investment opportunities elsewhere as well. The technological change increases investment opportunities and absorbs the previously surplus savings at the same time that it increases the disparity between investment and savings abroad. It may help to account for the smoothness with which British lending obviated any tendency to secular imbalance in the nineteenth century that it grew in size mainly after the rate of technological advance at home had slowed down and had been superseded by more rapid technical progress in Germany and the United States.

Exchange-Rate Adjustment and Secular Disequilibrium

If secular disequilibrium is due mainly to the incongruence of foreign lending or borrowing, with excess domestic savings over investment or of investment over savings, the evident remedies lie in changing foreign lending or borrowing, on the one hand, or domestic savings or investment, on the other, or both. Thus the two major therapies to explore are foreign lending and borrowing and monetary and fiscal policy. Before we proceed with these, however, we must examine the bearing on secular disequilibrium of exchange-rate adjustment and trade policy.

The history of economic development is full of exchange depreciation. Eight hundred years ago the pound sterling used to represent the
value of a pound of silver, as did the lire. Continuous inflation, clipping,
and exchange depreciation through the course of history have increased
the currency prices of gold and silver and reduced the gold and silver
value of money. In more recent history, the nineteenth-century stability
of the pound and the dollar is the exception; exchange-rate change, the
rule. The outstanding example of the rule is perhaps the currency of
Brazil. This is now the cruzeiro, formerly the milrei, which replaced the
rei. The relationship between the latter two currencies is evident to the
student of high-school Latin. One milrei = 1,000 reis. The milrei was
substituted for the rei when that became so small in value that it was
inconvenient to transact everyday business in it. The Brazilian unit of
account, therefore, has been depreciated to roughly one thousandth of
its original worth in 100 years.

The cause of this depreciation is to be found in excessive expansion in income arising from domestic investment or even from an original increase in exports. In Brazil the successive booms in sugar, rubber,
coffee, and cotton have been overdone. The increase in exports leads to
an export surplus. The foreign-trade multiplier raises income; the accelerator raises it still more. Foreign borrowing stimulates still further
increases in investment. The increase in income goes to the point where
the increase in imports outdoes the original increase in exports. The
accumulation of foreign balances at the start of the boom is used up.
Credit is exhausted. Depreciation is used in an attempt to balance the
international accounts.

In the absence of monetary and fiscal restraint and new injections
of foreign capital, the alternatives open to a country are depreciation
and trade restrictions. The difficulty with depreciation is that unless
income and prices can be held relatively constant, it is a mere dimen-
sional change: an alteration of the ruler to make the board fit. Depreciation requires elastic demand schedules. In underdeveloped countries the demand for exports is apt to be inelastic, except in the case of
competitive products in which the depreciating country plays so small
a role in the world market that its competitors do not retaliate. For
Brazil, successively in sugar, rubber, coffee, and cotton, this condition was not met.

The world supply of goods for import into countries like Brazil
is elastic enough. The question of the elasticity of demand for imports,
however, is a different matter. Such imports as enter into the standard
of living have an inelastic demand, since the standard is close to the

subsistence level. Luxury imports, consumed by a relatively small income group, are elastic with respect to income but probably fairly inelastic in price. And capital goods, needed for development, are evidently also price-inelastic. On this showing, depreciation will not work smoothly and easily to adjust the balance of payments. The depreciation which will balance exports and imports must be substantial and will involve a substantial loss in the terms of trade.

Depreciation plays an important role in redistributing income within a developing country. In Brazil this may have been its main significance. When the export sector has overexpanded and reduced its world price, it can shift the burden of the loss to the urban consumer by depreciation, which raises the price of exports, the profits of the export sector, and the cost of living of the masses of the people. The country as a whole may lose, if the cost to the consumer is greater than the gain to the export sector. But if the export sector has power, its gain may be more important a political consideration than the greater national loss.

One special formula for secular disequilibrium can be found into which exchange depreciation fits not too badly. Suppose that in the developed country A, technological progress is taking place faster in all commodities than in country B, which is less developed, and that this is reflected in a progressive reduction of prices in A as compared with B. It is assumed that money incomes in A and B are unchanged as a result of the faster progress in A and that relative prices within each country are undisturbed.

The decline in A's prices relative to B's tends to produce an export surplus in A and an import surplus in B. If the elasticities of demand and supply are high enough, the way to restore balance-of-payments equilibrium due to this secular cause may be exchange depreciation in B and appreciation in A. Provided that money incomes remain unchanged, this will produce a new equilibrium position, in which some of the increase in real income in A is represented by increased consumption of B-goods, and some of the increased efficiency in the production of A-goods brings about their substitution for local goods in B's expenditure.

Tariffs and Trade Restrictions

Some economists have argued that a program of economic development requires either foreign investment or trade restrictions to keep out consumption goods, since it is clear that development requires imports of capital goods from abroad. This analysis is faulty.

Foreign capital is needed not because new foreign goods are bought but because total resources are inadequate. If production could be increased, or consumption reduced, foreign equipment could be bought without borrowing abroad or limitation of imports. The new output, or the output produced by the resources released from working for consumption, can be sold abroad or used to replace imports for consumption previously bought from abroad. Only if the country has no capacity to reallocate resources does the need for foreign equipment imply a need for foreign capital, or for trade restrictions to cut down on imports for consumption.

There are other defenses for tariffs in underdeveloped countries: the infant-industry argument; the GATT exception to the rule of nondiscrimination which permits customs unions among developing countries in a single commodity or series of commodities; or the tariff for revenue. None of these apply here. The question is rather whether tariffs or quotas are justified on balance-of-payments grounds.

Tariffs improve the balance of payments, it will be remembered, only to the extent that there is an increase in savings. In underdeveloped countries where the marginal propensity to save is low, diverting expenditure from foreign to domestic goods is not likely to produce more savings. If the demand for imports is price-inelastic, however, and if the revenue received by government is saved rather than spent, there may be a balance-of-payments improvement.

Quotas, on the other hand, correct the balance of payments more surely, but at the cost of generalizing disequilibrium throughout the system. This disequilibrium extends to income, prices, consumer preferences, and, ultimately, under most circumstances, the allocation of resources. The increase in income may increase the consumption of goods normally exported; if these are staples of income-inelastic demand within the exporting country, however, the spreading disequilibrium will finally pull resources out of the export industries into income-elastic home industries.

The use of quotas in cyclical disequilibria is much more justified than in developmental situations, since the particular phase of the cycle which requires them is expected to be fleeting. The quota will be removed and the price system restored to operation before much harm has been done. In secular disequilibrium, however, the causes at work are deeper seated and slower moving. If consumers' choice is permitted to dictate consumption and if producers are encouraged to maximize their return, the use of quotas to balance the international accounts is likely to lead to progressive distortion of the economy.

The price system may not be intended to serve as a guide to what to produce and with what resources, having been displaced by planning. In this case, the argument against quotas has less force or, alternatively, is shifted to the larger issue of prices versus planning. If the collective judgment of planners is followed in domestic matters, it may equally well be used to determine how much of what shall be imported. The recent history of foreign trade planning—especially in Argentina, but also in Europe—however, gives little reason to believe that this method is clearly preferable to the use of prices.

A compromise between exchange depreciation and quotas is possible in the form of multiple exchange rates, involving selective depreciation, which may limit both the loss in the terms of trade from depreciation and the diversion of purchasing power involved in quota restrictions.

The latter will be true only if luxuries can be imported at some free rate of exchange. These two advantages have recommended multiple exchange rates to many countries engaged in the developmental process, particularly in Latin America. The distortion of the price system produced by quotas is still present, however. Resources are diverted from the production of staple exports in which the country has an advantage to sidelines and to luxuries. Consumption may be favored at the expense of capital formation by encouragement given to imports of necessities. The multiple exchange-rate system is further open to retaliation. The essential commodities which the developing countries want to have purchased at the highest rate of exchange may be subjected abroad to an export tax. The multiple exchange-rate system, in which the developing countries exercise their maximum of monopoly power, increases their real income in the absence of retaliation. What is likely to happen if all the monopoly power in world trade is exerted at once is indeterminate, like the whole problem of bilateral monopoly when a monopolist and a monopsonist face each other.

Long-Term Lending

With economic development really under way, there is much to be said for international long-term capital movements—at least in stages 1, 3, and 4. The young debtor should borrow; the mature debtor should repay; the young creditor should lend. The prescription of capital movements does not extend to stage 6; the mature creditor should not consume capital or borrow. Put in other terms, no country should allow itself to reach stage 6, and those which do should back up into stage 5. But, for stages 1, 3, and 4, capital movements are eminently desirable.

This is not to say how much capital movements. It is impossible to make abstract statements on this point. Equilibrium is possible with no movement at all; the classical economists thought that factors of production did not move internationally. Equilibrium is also possible with the return to capital and interest equalized all over the world. This would require complete and costless mobility of all factors. Everything depends on how much play there is in the system and where. This will concern us shortly. At the moment, however, the point may be made that capital movements do not take place by themselves.

The difficulties in creating adequate institutions for international lending have been indicated in Chapter 19. The breakdown of the market for private lending appears to have been well-nigh complete. Revival can come only slowly. In consequence, governmental lending has been needed to fill the gap. Initially, the Export-Import Bank, on a small scale, attempted to operate on the lender side of the equation. In the postwar world, however, the institution in which high hopes were placed for the fulfillment of this role was the International Bank for Reconstruction and Development, created along with the International Monetary Fund at the Bretton Woods conference in 1944.

The International Bank

Like the International Monetary Fund, the International Bank was established with a capital contributed by many countries. The total nominal amount was originally to be more than $9 billion. The non-adherence of the Soviet Union with a quota of $1.2 billion left the figure close to $8 billion. The subsequent joining of the countries defeated in World War II and newly independent nations brought the total as of June 30, 1957, up to $9,268 million. Each country contributed 2 per cent of its subscription in gold or dollars, and another 18 per cent in local currency. The remaining 80 per cent remains subject to call if needed to meet obligations sold or guaranteed by the bank. The bank can borrow or guarantee the loans of others with the latent support of this 80 per cent only if the government concerned permits it to do so. This is almost, but not quite, the same thing as a government guarantee of the bank's bonds and guarantees.

The 2 per cent of the subscriptions of members provided the bank, as of June, 1957, with $183 million. Roughly $1 billion of $1,670 million, representing the 18 per cent portion of the member quotas, has been made available for lending, and most of this, particularly the United States, Canadian, British, and German portions, is in convertible or usable currencies.

In addition to these capital sums, amounting to $1.2 billion, the Bank has acquired lendable funds from borrowings, operations, the sale of loans to private borrowers, and capital repayments. By far the mosr important of these sources is borrowing. On June 30, 1957, the Bank had outstanding debts amounting to $1,034 million; $833 million of this amount represent bonds sold in the United States. The next largest sum was raised in Switzerland, although Switzerland is not a member of the Bank, and included a special government loan, which the Bank was asked to disburse outside of Switzerland (the opposite of a tied loan). In July, 1957, the Bank borrowed $100 million from the German central bank, which was also embarrassed by excessive supplies of dollars; and in October of the same year another $75 million of bonds was sold in the New York market to bring the debt total to $1,252 billion.

Funds available from operations, i.e., profits and reserves, and principal repayments amounted each to something less than $200 million, while funds available from sale of loans were something more than $300 million. The bank's gross total funds at the end of June, 1957, amounted to $2,950 million (rounded), of which $2,300 million had been disbursed on loans, leaving a balance available for disbursement of $650 million.

By 1957, the Bank reached a level of $390 million of annual loans and $332 million of disbursements. This latter figure represented the highest level of operations, with the exception of the initial year, 1947, when $500 million was loaned to European countries to tide them over for the emergency period between the exhaustion of the Anglo-American Financial Agreement (the British loan) and the beginnings of the European Recovery Program (Marshall Plan). Once the Marshall Plan got under way, the Bank turned its attention from the "reconstruction" in its title to "development."

Beginnings were slow. In 1948, loans amounted to only $28 million. In 1949, the rate picked up sharply to $213. In the middle 1950's, the rate of loans has reached $400 million, although disbursements are generally lower with a peak of $332 million, as shown in Table 26.1.

The Bank has acted experimentally. Initial loans were made on a strict project basis and were limited to the foreign-exchange content of the particular steel mill, irrigation ditch, electrical installation, or port facilities. We have discussed already (p. 519) how this approach is likely to increase the import surplus by failing to provide foreign exchange for the additional imports generated by domestic expenditure associated with the project. When these shortcomings were pointed out, the Bank responded in some degree and made some loans which were not "tied" to particular projects or particular imports. Loans have been made to industrial banks—in Turkey and Mexico—in the hope of devising local institutions which will broaden the numbers and capacity of local business leaders. The Bank's desire to get wider participation of countries among the lenders has perhaps operated to inhibit it from moving toward nondiscriminatory lending, that is, lending currency from the cheapest source and permitting the countries to spend where goods are cheapest.

TABLE 26.1

INTERNATIONAL BANK FOR RECONSTRUCTION AND
DEVELOPMENT LOANS AND DISBURSEMENTS
BY FISCAL YEARS
(In Millions of Dollars)

Year Ended June 30	Loans Committed	Disbursements
1951	297	78
1952	299	185
1953	179	227
1954	324	302
1955	410	274
1956	396	284
1957	388	332

The Bank has spurred economic development in many ways. It has sent missions to make studies of the economic potential of a long list of countries and has published their reports in book form. It operates an Economic Development Institute for training high-level economic civil servants in development problems and in the loan techniques used by the Bank. Restricted to making loans to governments, it supported the establishment of an International Finance Corporation which began operations in 1956 lending equity capital to new enterprises in underdeveloped countries.

The Bank has been in operation now long enough to acquire considerable experience. It has learned, for one thing, that it can enter into loans beyond its cash resources, since the lag of disbursements behind commitments is regular. Repayments have increased to a substantial level, so that disbursements on new loans can make a contribution to the balance-of-payments problems of underdeveloped countries as a whole only if they exceed repayments which continue rising. The Bank has applied strict lending standards in order to maintain its credit standing in international capital markets. The Bank, moreover, has indicated to the United Nations that it is unable to try to regulate its lending so as to contribute to cyclical stability in world markets, as it finds it difficult enough to define and maintain the appropriate standards of lending for development purposes.

Two criticisms may be leveled at the Bank, along with praise for its ingenuity in seeking to get ahead with its job, on the one hand, while it maintains the approval of rather conservative financial opinion, on the other. One is that the level of its lending is too small to meet the requirements of the world for development; the second is that its existence has increased the appetite for development more than it has contributed means of satisfying it. The amount of $300–400 million a year contributed by the Bank does not help when the creation of this and other institutions, plus the general attention given to development throughout the world, have built up a demand for international lending which could use $2½ to $3 billion.

SUNFED

The limited capacity of the International Bank, which has operated along commercial lines, emphasizing bankable loans, has led to widespread interest among underdeveloped countries in the establishment of new institutions for funneling capital from developed to underdeveloped countries. It is continuously being urged upon the United Nations Economic and Social Council, for example, that more funds should be made available for this purpose, and in particular for capital investments of a social overhead variety, like harbors, roads, education, public health schemes, which do not earn back in sales the value of their productivity and hence are not bankable. A group of experts devised a plan for a *Special United Nations Fund for Economic Development*, whose initials were abbreviated to SUNFED, to which the developed nations would contribute the largest share of the original capital, and from which underdeveloped countries would receive grants. The major contributors, the United States and the United Kingdom, however, have continuously voted against the plan. In part the opposition of this country has been based upon the strain on its resources imposed by defense expenditure. On April 13, 1953, President Eisenhower asserted that we would assist underdeveloped countries to realize their economic aspirations when disarmament has made progress. In part, however, it has been stated by the United States that development should rely on private sources of capital and the International Bank.

National Support for Development

Capital loans and grants have been made in support of economic development through a variety of national rather than international channels. The United States Point Four, while it relies primarily on technical assistance, does make some provision of economic aid. The greater part of United States aid, to be sure, has been for military assistance to such countries as Formosa, South Korea, and Vietnam and offshore military procurement in Japan and western Europe. President Eisenhower tried in 1957 to increase the amounts available for purely economic assistance but was voted down by the Congress.

The United Kingdom has made some funds available to its colonies through the Colonial Office. Various members of the British Commonwealth have collaborated in technical assistance and economic aid to spur economic development in southeast Asia through the Colombo Plan. Under this plan, however, all aid is given bilaterally.

The Soviet Union entered into competition with the western nations in giving economic assistance. Some special barter arrangements were made: in some of these, credits were given to the receiving country which could delay shipments to the Soviet Union. In still other cases, the Soviet Union has undertaken to make loans for special capital projects, such as a steel mill in India, providing technical assistance and charging a rate of interest upon the loans of 2 per cent. This is well below the rate required of the International Bank (1 per cent above the rate at which it borrows money in the capital markets of developed countries, plus a special assessment for building a sinking fund—the whole often amounts to as much as $5\frac{1}{2}$ per cent).

The Egyptian project to build the High Dam at Aswan initially was to be financed by the United States and Britain, plus the International Bank for Reconstruction and Development, insofar as the foreign-exchange content of the project was concerned. When the United States and Britain pulled out, there was the possibility for a short time that the Soviet Union would undertake to assist Egypt in the venture. Like many developmental projects, however, the High Dam was more interesting politically than in terms of economic analysis. The demands it would put upon the Egyptian economy would have clearly been inflationary, produced large uncovered balance-of-payments deficits, and exacerbated political relations among the lending nations, the International Bank, and the borrower.

Direct Investment

Part of the capital needed to develop productive capacity in underdeveloped countries has traditionally come from direct investment. Particularly has this been true of investment in raw materials for extraction and sale in the country of the investor. The United States, for example, grew to economic strength with the help of British and other foreign investments in American railroads.

The difficulty with this prescription for the world of today, however, is several fold. In the first place, many countries are eager to undertake responsibility for their own economic development, and regard foreign corporations as inhibiting their growth of capacity to manage their own industry, in the same way that the domination of retail trade and banking by foreign populations will stall the development of indigenous market institutions. This and national pride are the reasons for many requirements that enterprises must be owned by a majority of natives, with more than half of its directors and more than half of its supervisory employees of native citizenship.

Secondly, direct investment in raw materials is appropriate to an early stage of development when the economy first emerges from the subsistence level to join with the world market and become an export economy. Many countries wish to speed through this stage, if they are not already in it, and push forward to the stage of development where emphasis has shifted to import-competing industries, in which foreign capital is far less interested. Direct investment in these industries will take place, as well as in market-oriented industries in underdeveloped countries. For the most part, however, direct investment which displaces the exports of the investing country will be located in more developed countries. As such, it does little to assist in economic development beyond the stage of the export economy.

Finally, the point was made in Chapter 20 that direct investment tends to increase corporate savings in the lending country rather than to provide an offset to existing savings. This is because of the predilection of many corporations to invest corporate profits abroad, but not money newly borrowed or raised from the sale of new stock. To the extent that secular disequilibrium exists because of oversaving in the developed countries rather than overinvesting in underdeveloped, direct investment does not go far to assist it. This criticism, however, would apply much more strongly to the secular disequilibrium of the 1930's than to the present postwar position.

The Appropriate Rate of Foreign Lending

Whether lending be undertaken in debt or equities, by private or governmental lenders, by national or international institutions, will have only a slight effect on its impact on the disequilibrium. More important than the institutions which handle the capital movements are the amounts involved and the institutions which determine the appropriate rate of lending in both developed and underdeveloped countries. The difficulty is in deciding which are to be the variables and which the autonomous factors. Who adjusts to what, and how much? The rate of overinvestment in young countries, of oversaving in developed countries, and of foreign lending must be neatly balanced in equilibrium. If two are variable, it may be difficult to get them both to adjust to the third. Examples are the oversaving of the old countries in the 1930's and the difficulty of getting both investment going in underdeveloped countries and foreign lending to finance it. In the 1950's, overinvestment in underdeveloped countries seems to have been determined separately, while savings in developed countries—mainly the United States—and foreign lending are both asked, in effect, to adjust to that.

If two are fixed and only one can vary, it may be that there is no equilibrium position possible. If foreign lending is fixed at $1 billion annually, while oversaving amounts to $3 billion, no rate of overinvestment in underdeveloped countries will restore equilibrium.

It follows that one can speak of an appropriate rate of foreign lending only on the assumption that foreign lending is variable, through institutions designed for this purpose which are more effective than the International Bank, Point Four, and direct investment and that oversavings in the developed countries and overinvestment in the young countries are so fixed in relation to one another that a single rate of foreign lending will be appropriate. We have already suggested that in the 1930's and again in the 1950's there was no optimum rate of foreign lending. The rate appropriate to restore equilibrium of national income in one group of countries would have produced both balance-of-payments and national-income disturbance in the other. In addition to this, and perhaps as important, the world as a whole has been unable to create institutions which would give the appropriate rate of foreign lending, even if that could be determined.

Capacity to Absorb Capital

Professors Millikan and Rostow have proposed that the United States undertake to make up the level of world lending to that amount which the underdeveloped countries can absorb. Capacity to absorb is not represented by the biggest balance-of-payments deficit a country can run. For all practical purposes there is no limit here. It is rather the amount of positive capital which can be created domestically, without raising the level of living, with no limitations imposed by the balance of payments. The limitations on capital formation, if not lack of foreign exchange, take the form of lack of complementary factors and facilities. A country can build its secondary industry only at the rate made possible by the existence of social overhead capital. Lacking engineers, steel, construction equipment, etc., there are limits to how fast it can build this. If an underdeveloped society were able smoothly and without friction to reallocate its resources among sectors, capacity to absorb capital would be virtually unlimited. But in the nature of being underdeveloped, capacity to transform the economy is small; capital formation must proceed slowly. The balance-of-payments deficit which an underdeveloped country can run without inflation is small.

The International Bank has asserted that the limits to its lending activities have been imposed not by lack of funds but by an inadequate number of suitable projects.

Professors Millikan and Rostow think that if the underdeveloped countries were loaned all the capital funds they could effectively use, the total would amount to no more than $3 billion a year. If $3 billion were available, would the underdeveloped countries still have deficits? Would appetite grow with eating, or is it possible to adjust the economy as to use this much, and no more? This requires us to take a new look at monetary and fiscal policy.

Monetary and Fiscal Policy

The gold standard required that countries adjust their rate of interest and monetary policy to the availability of long-term foreign capital for young countries or to the rate of outflow of long-term capital for lending countries. Monetary policy, to which fiscal policy is added today, adjusted to the level of lending rather than vice versa. If the level of long-term lending were independently given and adjustment to it took place both in the lending and in the borrowing countries, equilibrium was possible of achievement.

This assumes, of course, that long-term lending acts in a fairly stable way. The positive cyclical pattern of lending evidently places far too great a load of deflationary policy on young countries during depression and on inflationary action in developed countries during prosperity. It makes little or no sense to plan for a countercyclical pattern of lending (p. 372). But if foreign lending could be stabilized, at a constant or only gently fluctuating rate throughout the cycle, then would it be possible to correct balance-of-payments disequilibrium by the use of monetary and fiscal policy?

This means, in effect, the elimination of business cycles and particularly of cumulative waves of deflation and inflation. Cumulative deflations are likely to be a particular problem for the developed countries; cumulative inflations for the young. Complete constancy of national income is not called for. Changes in national money income would be needed as changes occurred in the rate of foreign lending, on a modest scale. Even a considerable deviation beyond this could be allowed and be taken up by short-term capital lending, provided that it was randomly distributed and averaged out over time.

This book is not the place to discuss what monetary and fiscal tools are available for increasing stability. Courses in money and banking, national income, and business cycles are replete with their discussion. Whether the emphasis be put mainly upon money and banking measures or mainly on governmental expenditure and taxation is again a matter of indifference in this limited connection, though important in itself and worthy of much study and discussion in other classrooms.

A general and theoretical point can be made, however, about the inevitability of inflation in young countries. It is fine to urge restraint on young countries, suggesting the maintenance of high taxation, constant supplies of money, high interest rates, and low capital expenditure. But the course of economic development is by no means solely a matter for artificial manipulation. It lies deep in the social and political, as well as in the economic, fabric. If social and political change is moving rapidly, economic development—i.e., capital formation and technological innovation—must also move rapidly. It may be impossible to restrain them to the availability of foreign lending, if this is low, in view of the pace of social change. If this is the case and foreign lending cannot be adjusted, secular imbalance is inevitable.

In general, however, the remedy for secular imbalance may be said to be stability of foreign lending at a reasonable level—whatever this may be in the light of the social forces leading to overinvestment in the young countries and oversavings in the old—and then monetary and fiscal adjustment to that stable rate. This may be regarded as the gold-standard prescription and be abhorred on that account by some countries which believe it involves large-scale unemployment, or others which think it would slow down economic development at the insistence of countries already well developed. If foreign lending can be stabilized and if the mature countries can avoid serious depressions—two big if's, to be sure—it is worthwhile for the young countries to try to avoid inflation and a disequilibrium position in international payments maintained by trade restrictions with or without multiple exchange rates. The cost is higher in the short run. In the long run, if social development keeps pace, economic development is more nearly certain.

Stabilizing Foreign Lending

Devising institutions to stabilize foreign lending does lie within the scope of this book, but the writer must confess that the problem remains unsolved. Compensatory lending by governments, expanded when private lending falls and contracted when private lending increases again, may be regarded as a parallel in international lending to countercyclical fiscal policy. Suggestions along this line have been put forward by experts asked by the secretary-general of the United Nations to advise him on eliminating unemployment. But there seems little likelihood that such institutions will prove acceptable to the nations which would have to provide the funds or that they could be operated effectively. The most that can be hoped for realistically is that the International Bank and any new institutions designed to expand the flow of capital internationally can stabilize their rate of lending throughout the cycle and not get carried away by investment opportunities in periods of boom or discouraged by subsequent depression.

Summary

Secular disequilibrium occurs when the rate of foreign lending falls short of the excess of intended savings over intended investment or the rate of foreign borrowing falls short of the excess of intended investment over intended savings. The remedies evidently lie in changing the relationship between savings and investment, by monetary and fiscal action, or in changing the rate of foreign lending. Only in the limiting case where technological progress at a faster rate in one country than in another takes the form of more rapid reductions in prices would exchange depreciation be appropriate. Exchange depreciation occurs as a result of secular imbalance, and recently import restrictions have been used. A fair case can be made for multiple exchange practices in the absence of retaliation. But the major remedies are deflation and borrowing in the young countries; maintenance of income and lending in the developed. Countries past the peak of their development are likely to face the same sort of problem as young countries.

The International Bank for Reconstruction and Development was organized at Bretton Woods to create an institution capable of replacing the private flow of capital which dried up after 1929, except for abnormal movements (capital flight). It has made a start in this lending, but the scale of its operations is limited. A number of proposals for new institutions have been made. A stable as well as a high level of lending is desired. Monetary and fiscal policy in both developed and underdeveloped countries alike should adjust to the stabilized level.

The International Bank and Point Four may have increased, rather than financed, the secular disequilibrium by encouraging greater boldness in expenditure in young countries than in the financing of the ensuing deficits.

SUGGESTED READING

TEXTBOOKS

S. E. Harris, *Interregional and International Trade* (New York: McGraw-Hill Book Co., Inc., 1957), deals at length with dollar shortage.

TREATISES

Books on the dollar shortage seem to have a cyclical periodicity. In addition to T. Balogh, *The Dollar Crisis* (Oxford: Basil Blackwell, 1949); and the writer's *The Dollar Shortage* (New York: The Technology Press and John Wiley & Sons, Inc., 1950); the year 1957 has brought forth the Harris volume above; Sir Donald MacDougall, *The World's Dollar Problem* (London: Macmillan & Co., Ltd., 1957); Sir G. Crowther, *Balances and Imbalances of Payments* (Boston: Harvard University Graduate School of Business Administration, 1957); E. Zupnick, *Britain's Postwar Dollar Problem* (New York: Columbia University Press, 1957); R. Triffin, *Europe and the Money Muddle* (New Haven: Yale University Press, 1957). Of all of these, only the last disbelieves in the existence of a tendency to long-run imbalance.

The International Bank has published a useful account of its activities for the first seven years of its existence. It is called *The International Bank for Reconstruction and Development, 1946–1953* (Baltimore: Johns Hopkins University Press, 1954).

A particularly interesting case study of a rapidly developing country is posed in E. Lundberg and M. Hill, "Australia's Long-Term Balance of Payments Problem," *Economic Record,* May, 1956.

POINTS

The underdeveloped countries' case for special development funds is set out sympathetically in United Nations, *Report on a Special United Nations Fund for Economic Development* (New York, 1953).

The proposals for expanding and stabilizing the level of long-term lending were made by the experts in United Nations, *National and International Measures for Full Employment* (New York, December, 1949).

Chapter 27 : STRUCTURAL DISEQUILIBRIUM

At the Goods Level

Structural disequilibrium at the goods level occurs when a change in demand or supply of exports or imports alters a previously existing equilibrium or when a change occurs in the basic circumstances under which income is earned or spent abroad, in both cases without the requisite parallel changes elsewhere in the economy. The simplest illustration is furnished by a change in demand. Suppose there is a decline in the world demand for Swiss embroidery due to a change in taste. The resources previously engaged in embroidery production must shift into other lines of activity or adjust their expenditures downward. So far as the country as a whole is concerned, the displaced resources or some others must shift into another export line, or the country must restrict imports. If the called-for changes fail to take place or occur in inadequate degree, the country will experience a structural disequilibrium. The resources which continue in embroidery will be earning less than they could earn in another industry, on the assumption that they had been in equilibrium before the decline in demand. Though imports will decline to some extent, owing to the operations of the multiplier and the marginal propensity to import, imports will exceed exports.

History is full of these changes in demand. The rise of synthetic competition with Japanese silk and Chilean nitrates, the substitution of oil for coal, and of detergents for natural fats and oils, the loss of their world markets by British coal and textiles, the competition of overseas grain production experienced on a large scale for the first time in Europe in the 1870's and 1880's—all furnish examples of more or less significance. Structural disequilibrium may be caused by a nonsystematic change in taste or in technology or in anything which alters the price of an export upward or downward. (A systematic series of structural changes, e.g., in technology, merges into secular disequilibrium.)

An increase in the foreign demand for a country's output is structural disequilibrium of a sort, but one with which it is not difficult to deal. The remedy is an increase in output of the product and an increase in consumption and imports by the country. We shall accordingly confine the analysis to the disequilibrium which results in a deficit.

The cause of the disturbance may be a change in supply. The classical illustration was crop failure, which cut off the supply of a country's exports and produced a short fall of exports below imports. A bumper crop abroad which lowered world prices would have much the same effect. Others are the exhaustion of the soil or of mines.

The domestic demand and the foreign supply of imports can change adversely to cause a structural disequilibrium, as well as the domestic supply and the foreign demand for exports. A crop failure or a strike in a major industry may give rise to an increase in imports, as well as to a decline in exports. Illustrations are furnished by the drought of 1936, which required the United States to import corn from Argentina; the 1952 drought (on top of earlier ones), which caused Argentina to import wheat from the United States; and the British coal strike of 1926, which brought United States coal, if not to Newcastle, which is the export port in northeastern England for Scandinavian shipments, at least to London and Liverpool. A commodity which shifts from an export to an import basis in this way must, of course, rise in price by more than twice the cost of transport.

Crop failure is underrated today as a cause of balance-of-payments change. In dry countries, great variability in the harvest is likely to lead to wide changes in the quantity of agricultural products available for export and demanded from abroad as imports. The first five-year plan in India succeeded as well as it did because of a favorable monsoon. In 1947, the bad winter and worse spring together with the summer drought in Europe greatly accentuated the balance-of-payments difficulties of western Europe, while the bumper crops of 1948 exaggerated the efficacy of the Marshall Plan in producing recovery.

More than merchandise trade may be involved. The loss of service income may be a serious blow to the balance of payments on current account. This may arise through bankruptcy of direct investments abroad or their confiscation or nationalization. The loss of income to Britain through the nationalization of the Anglo-Iranian Oil Company by Iran is an outstanding modern instance of this sort. The 1952 riots in Cairo which destroyed Shepheard's and the other tourist hotels cost Egypt some millions of pounds annually in tourist services. But perhaps the most far-reaching and complex case is that furnished by the impact of the last two world wars on the position of various areas, and particularly on Europe.

War, it has been suggested, speeds up economic change and development at all stages, including the penultimate stage of decline. It might be appropriate, therefore, to regard the effects of war as secular and its disturbances to balance-of-payments equilibrium as long-run in character. War produces structural changes which go deeper than goods, down to the level of factor proportions. The European Recovery Program might therefore be regarded as an attempt to correct structural disequilibrium at the factor level. There can be little doubt that the far-reaching effects of war were compounded of every possible kind of disturbance and disequilibrium. For our purposes, however, because the effects were concentrated in such a short space of time and involved so many changes in demand, supply, technology, and institutional arrangements, we may regard the disequilibrium of the postwar period as reflecting in important degree structural disequilibrium at the goods level.

Remedy in Outline

A deficit arising from a structural change can be filled by increased production or decreased expenditure, which have their reflection in international transactions in increased exports or decreased imports. The general change may be in production, with expenditure held constant, or, if production remains unchanged, in decreased expenditure on consumption, investment, or government purchases. We shall exclude the simple case wherein the marginal propensity to import is one and the reduction in exports produces a decline in imports of the same amount, which restores equilibrium immediately.

There is no simple connection between increased production and increased exports or between decreased expenditure and decreased imports. The expansion of production may be in import-competing goods, which will make decreased imports possible. Or decreased expenditure on domestic output may lead to increased exports if it frees goods from domestic consumption for sale abroad.

While it is theoretically possible that a deficit arising from a structural change can be made up entirely from an increase in production, this is the limiting case; the likelihood is that more or less of the correction must come through reduced domestic expenditure. Increased production, equal in value to that which was lost, could come about through an increase in employment, through an increase in productivity, or through a shift of resources into new lines where they were fully as productive as they had been in the old, prior to the structural change. But the first two possibilities do not give us a pure structural change: if there are unemployed resources, the difficulty may be a cyclical disequilibrium or a deeper structural disequilibrium at the factor level; if an increase in productivity is possible, it undoubtedly requires more capital, which involves change in factor proportions and implies structural disequilibrium at the factor level. Only under the extreme circumstances that all the factors—land, labor, and capital—can effectively shift into the new occupation and that their productivity is as high in the new occupation as in the old before the disturbance would it be possible to maintain the levels of consumption, investment, and government expenditure after a structural change under static assumptions. This amounts to saying that it was a matter of indifference prior to the disturbance whether the resources were in one industry or the other.

This leads to the conclusion that in the pure case of structural disequilibrium the remedy is not shift of resources *or* reduction in expenditure but shift of resources *and* reduction in expenditure. How large a reduction in expenditure will be required will depend upon the nature and extent of the disequilibrium and upon the elasticities of demand and supply in the alternative lines of endeavor.

Suppose the disequilibrium has its origin in a change in taste abroad which produces a decline in demand for a country's exports. The price of the goods concerned will fall. The value of exports will fall. Imports will exceed exports. The resources engaged in the affected exports will be required to shift. Assuming that equilibrium existed prior to the change in demand, these resources are necessarily less efficient in any other industry. If they can shift into other export industries, because the demand is elastic, they will reduce the standard of living and the level of investment less than if they are obliged, by the inelasticity of demand for other exports, to shift into an import-competing industry where they have a comparative disadvantage.

Suppose, on the other hand, that the disequilibrium arose from a loss of income earned from past investments overseas. This loss frees no resources into other lines. Reallocation of resources is nonetheless needed. Resources from purely domestic industry must shift into export or import-competing lines.

The shift of resources, moreover, is likely to require some net over-all expansion of expenditure, or inflation, which will produce at least a trace of disequilibrium of what we have called the cyclical type. In theory it would be possible to effect a smooth shift of resources from one use to another by raising wages in the areas to be expanded only in the degree and as rapidly as wages were lowered in the area to be contracted. In practice, however, it has been found that the negative inducement of reduced wages is not so effective in getting resources to change occupations as is the positive pull of increased wages. This asymmetry is the familiar one we have encountered before in the Duesenberry effect. A decline in wages may be regarded as temporary; and the overhead costs of moving to a new job where physical movement is required may be high. Two moves are the equivalent of a fire, as the New England saying goes. The result is that the redirection of resources necessary to correct structural disequilibrium rarely occurs without some increase in money income and a resultant cyclical disequilibrium. It is evidently important to keep this to a minimum.

Entirely apart from the wage level, income changes will take place as a consequence of the disequilibrium. The import surplus caused by the fall in demand will reduce national income. This will tend to assist in the correction of the structural equilibrium. The correction of the structural disequilibrium, on the other hand, will eliminate the import surplus, and this will tend to increase money income, working in the opposite direction against the result produced by the structural correction.

The monetary and fiscal authorities evidently have a range of choices as to policy. They may act neutrally, allowing the income changes produced by the current-account balance but ensuring that these do not become cumulative in one direction or the other; they may attempt to stabilize national income by offsetting the income fluctuations produced by the structural change; or they may try to accommodate monetary and fiscal policy to the most expeditious solution of the structural problem. This would require perhaps a little more deflation than that brought about directly by the current-account deficit in the first instance—but not a cumulative deflation—followed by a little less reflation than that set in train by the removal of the deficit itself.

The Price System and Resource Allocation

What produces the required shift of resources? This is a question which has elicited sharp debate. The "liberal," who believes in the efficacy of the price system, insists that the price system can produce the necessary adjustment. The decline in demand which gave rise to the disequilibrium will lower the price of the export good no longer capable of producing equilibrium and encourage resources to shift into other occupations. Wrong choices or shifts into industries for which the demand is inelastic will result in new declines in price. The fall in income from the original loss in exports will assist in preventing some wrong choices by reducing demand for certain domestic and imported goods and services. A new equilibrium will have been reached when identical factors of production can earn the same return in all industries, making appropriate allowance for noncompeting groups; when the value of exports equals the value of imports, using static equilibrium as a guide, and when all factors are fully employed.

It may be useful to assist the price system by depreciation of the exchange rate. This will tend to raise the prices of internationally traded goods, relative to domestic goods. Resources will then be encouraged to shift into other exports or into import-competing lines and will be less likely to move into domestic production. Whatever the income, if the price elasticities are high enough, the loss of income will tend to be offset by reduced expenditure on export goods and imports. Depreciation will expedite the required shift and reduce the risk of time-consuming and reserve-losing errors. In all this, of course, it is important that the depreciation should not give rise to a new expansion of expenditure, due to spending of cash balances, credit creation, or any other cause. The remedy of the liberal economist for structural disequilibrium at the goods level is thus to halt the inflation and adjust the exchange rate.

Planned Adjustment

The "planners" among economists object to this prescription. They emphasize that resources are relatively immobile and standards of living not readily compressible. This implies that a certain amount of inflation is inevitable during the process of shifting resources and during the period of adjustment to the new and lower standard of living and level of investment. The inflation compounds the balance-of-payments difficulties and distorts the directional signals given by prices to resources. It also implies that price elasticities are low in the operational short run, which means that depreciation will not help the balance of payments—at least, not by much.

The concern of planners with immobility of capital leads them to think that a temporary expansion of expenditure on capital formation is required in the new industries. This adds to the inflation from other causes and suggests that the balance-of-payments deficit must get worse before it gets better, unless special measures are taken to prevent this result.

The planners at the same time are skeptical that the price system will adequately discount the impact on demand of anticipated changes in supply. They are inclined to view planning as superior to price, partly because of the prescience of planners and partly because of the superiority of social standards of choice over those implicit in the private values of the market.

The planner regards depreciation with something of a jaundiced eye. He takes the view that the elasticities are lower rather than higher, that depreciation increases the secondary burden of the adjustment represented by the loss in the terms of trade, and that depreciation gives a fillip to inflation which makes it hard to resist.

The result is that the planners would direct resources into new export-increasing and import-decreasing endeavors and limit the increase in imports which this entails through quantitative restrictions and exchange controls during the period of adjustment. They tend to recognize that import controls do little or nothing to move resources in the desired directions. By increasing the prices of imported luxuries, they may even encourage import-competing production in these lines and pull resources out of export as well as domestic industries. Independent measures to redirect resources must therefore be taken to achieve the long-run correction, while the balance of payments is protected by import restrictions.

The extent to which it is necessary to limit imports will depend upon the availability of capital or assistance from abroad. A country with assets will spend them, at least in the early stages of recovery, if it cannot borrow. The rate of substitution between borrowing and import restriction will vary from country to country, depending upon the nature of the imports concerned (whether vital to the basic standard of living and to the capital expenditure program, or dispensable), and upon the philosophical disposition of the country's authorities.

Disinflation is not excluded as a remedy and, indeed, will be used to assist the import restrictions in relieving pressure on the balance of payments. The planners are perhaps more likely to use taxation and government surpluses to siphon purchasing power out of the system—and progressive taxation, which runs the risk of reducing savings—rather than regressive taxes. The liberal economist, on the other hand, will be more inclined to reduce government expenditure and permit a rise in interest rates to accomplish the same ends. In the final analysis, however, the difference between the two positions probably lies in the fact that the planner regards disinflationary measures as supporting rather than operational, relying on import restrictions (and orders to divert goods to export) for the main effect on the balance of payments and believing that some measure of inflation is inevitable. The liberal economist, on the contrary, is disposed to consider disinflation as the driving force, along with depreciation, in correcting the disequilibrium.

Synthesis

It is possible to reconcile these views to a considerable degree, although not completely. For everyday and small disequilibria, the price system can be relied upon to shift resources without depreciation. This sort of change is going on continuously, albeit in the face of resistance, which takes the form of requests for tariff protection and export subsidy.

If the disequilibrium is more serious, the full liberal treatment may be called for: disinflation and depreciation. This assumes that the decline in expenditure and the shift in resources called for are not too drastic and that elasticities of demand are relatively high.

A still more serious disequilibrium may require the use of some of the planners' therapy, especially if resources are particularly immobile or the standard of living and the level of investment incompressible. Here it may be necessary to begin with the paraphernalia of rationing, allocations, borrowing, and import restrictions; it is important, however, to emerge with an equilibrium rate of exchange which can balance the international accounts after the removal of restrictions. In other words, the planners' medicine may work in the early and acute stages of the disequilibrium; the health of the world economy calls for a gradual shift, as the relocation of resources gets under way and the acute phase of the investment program is passed, to the remedies prescribed by liberals.

The danger with continuing planning methods throughout the disequilibrium is that it may never be possible to get away from the disequilibrium system of overvalued rate of exchange and inflated level of income balanced by import restrictions. The skill of planners is not so great that they can confidently predict what shift of resources into what industries is necessary to correct the structural disequilibrium. An optimistic bias will result in too little correction. The result will be a completed investment program, but import restrictions will still have to be retained. To avoid this, it is necessary to commit the country to a shift to the liberal system of disinflation and depreciation in the gradual removal of import restrictions during the course of the corrective process.

Structural Disequilibrium at the Factor Level

Structural disequilibrium at the factor level results from factor prices which fail to reflect accurately factor endowments. The disequilibrium may not appear directly in the balance of payments. The economy may, for example, adjust to the factor prices as they are, choosing lines of comparative advantage and disadvantage, or exports and imports level of income and exchange rate so that the balance of payments is in equilibrium at those factor prices. The result, however, will be that one or more factors have structural unemployment.

Typically, the price of labor is too high and that of capital too low. The reasons for this may lie in the collective bargaining strength of labor or in the nature of our social interest in economics. The proximate cause, however, may be something like the cessation of emigration from Italy due to World War I and the immigration laws of 1919 and 1921 in the United States, so far as labor is concerned; or the Keynesian doctrine that interest rates are too high and hold back investment, wrongly applied, so far as capital is concerned.

If the price of labor is too high, the country will choose lines of comparative advantage in which labor is used more sparingly than it should be, and will import goods with a higher labor content than is appropriate. The country's comparative advantage in labor-intensive commodities and services will be understated, and its comparative disadvantage in these lines will be overstated. Balance in the balance of payments may still be possible, but only at the cost of unemployed labor. If an attempt is made to employ this labor, it will have to be done at factor proportions which differ from those utilized throughout the economy. There is no spare capital, which is already overemployed because it is underpriced; and we may assume that there is no spare land. Accordingly, the generation of additional employment for labor must be, like WPA, on a leaf-raking or domestic construction basis which uses a maximum of labor and a minimum of capital.

In a broader sense, the balance of payments is in disequilibrium when factor prices, out of line with factor endowments, distort the structure of production from the allocation of resources which appropriate factor prices would have indicated. This is true, whatever the relationship of exports to imports. The same can be said for balance-of-payments equilibria in the narrow sense which are below optimum efficient equilibrium owing to the effects of tariffs, subsidies, or other distorting interferences. But the structural disequilibrium resulting from inappropriate factor prices is more nearly disequilibrium in a narrow sense than would be the case of a tariff; the existence of structural unemployment cries for governmental action, and the action is likely to result in inflation, which gives a narrow static disequilibrium represented by an imbalance between exports and imports.

In the Italian case, post–World War II, the deflationary policy pursued by the government under the European Recovery Program has gone far to balance the international accounts, with a residue of dollar hard-core deficit, and has left the structural unemployment. The influence of the ECA mission in Rome was frequently exerted, it appears, in the direction of expanding employment, particularly in building construction, at the cost of the balance of payments. There is little evidence to suggest that a more thoroughgoing remedy was contemplated.

The German Case

Structural disequilibrium may arise because of a change in factor proportions. In postwar western Germany, for example, capital destruction and consumption had reduced the capital available to western Germany by 25 per cent; the increase in population due primarily to refugees had expanded the total population by 24 per cent. Within the latter over-all increase, however, there was a shift among non-competing groups: a decline in the numbers of able-bodied men between the ages of eighteen and forty-five, and an increase in the ranks of the young, the aged, and women.

This change in factor proportions called for a change in factor prices, in the lines of comparative advantage and disadvantage, and therefore in export and import industry. Wages should have declined, the rate of interest risen, and, within the existing technology, labor should have been substituted for capital throughout industry. The shifts within the composition of labor should have produced changes in export products toward those embodying less skilled labor.

Not all of these changes took place. Wages were held low by westward migration from East Germany, and through 1955 or thereabouts, by a large though declining percentage of unemployment. Capital was scarce, and rates of interest high. But German industry did not substitute labor for machinery on a wide scale, except perhaps in some highly generalized functions like moving materials around a plant; and the character of comparative advantage did not shift from capital-intensive to labor-intensive products. In part this was the consequence of the strong world demand for the types of products typically made by Germany, with demand conditions swamping supply. But in part as well it was due to inertia. Germany traditionally made this sort of thing; Germany would make this sort of thing again despite the fact that factor proportions had changed. For a time, in these circumstances, and due also to monetary disturbance, the German balance of payments was seriously adverse.

The Dual Economy

In some cases, there will be two sets of factor proportions and two sets of factor prices existing side by side in the same country. If Italian unemployed are put to work with shovels to drain marshes, whereas regularly employed workers are typically provided with more elaborate tools, there may be said to be a dual economy involved here. Factor proportions and factor prices may differ between northern and southern Italy, as they have done since 1870. And side by side with the highly mechanized industry of the Ruhr, there may be labor-intensive methods employed in agriculture, housing construction, and clearing of rubble from bombed-out buildings. But the concept has a wider application. It can be used in underdeveloped areas. It has relevance even to the United States.

In underdeveloped areas, there are likely to be two sets of factor proportions—one in the export sector of the economy, where foreign capital is combined with local labor and land of unique quality which gives the country its comparative advantage in the industry; and quite another in the subsistence sector. In the latter area, domestic capital is combined with local labor and land. The result is that the marginal value product of labor and land may be widely different in the two sectors of the economy. The land in the two areas will be noncompeting. It is accordingly quite appropriate that it earn different rates of return. But the difference in wages in the two sectors, where labor is competitive, gives rise to problems.

On occasion, there will be two sets of factor proportions even within the export sector of the economy, one based on the combination of foreign capital with native land and labor, the other with only native factors. This may involve two different industries, as in the case of Cuban sugar, which is highly capitalized, and Cuban tobacco, which is not. Or the two different sets of factor proportions may work side by side in the same industry, as in plantation and native rubber in Indonesia and Malaya, or plantation and native bananas in Central America. In these latter cases the native product is generally sold at a discount because of lack of standardization of quality.

In the United States, two agricultures exist, or used to exist prior to World War II, side by side. One is the commercial agriculture of Iowa and Nebraska corn and hogs, Wisconsin and New York dairy products, California and Texas cotton and vegetables. The other is the subsistence agriculture of the Kentucky and Tennessee hills, of Mississippi sharecroppers, and northern New England general farms. The former uses land and capital intensively and is sparing of the expensive factor, labor, employing the same factor proportions that apply throughout the bulk of industry in the United States; the latter uses labor intensively as if it were abundant and is economical of the abundant factor, capital, to which it lacks access. This subsistence agriculture is not unemployed; on the contrary, it is condemned to unremitting toil. But it may properly be regarded as underemployed, since it works at less than average efficiency in the country. Each unit of labor works with less land and capital than the labor in commercial agriculture.

The dual economy case may or may not represent structural disequilibrium in the balance of payments. In one sense, it is the logical extension of the noncompeting group notion of Cairnes, with which an equilibrium, though not an optimum, is compatible. Again, however, there is a possibility, if not a likelihood, that governmental or other action will be taken which will lead to disequilibrium in the balance of payments.

The greatest source of danger is likely to be a confusion as to what the appropriate factor proportions are. The influence of the export sector of the economy may lead a country interested in economic development to attempt to employ too highly capitalistic and laborsaving technology, without access to foreign capital. This will mean that the capital available to the economy will not be used in the most efficient way. It also is likely to lead to overinvestment, inflation, and disequilibrium of the secular, young-country variety, as the government or the domestic business interests attempt to create capital without savings in order to give labor the advantages of the technology in use in the export sector.

Correcting Disequilibrium at the Factor Level

The alternate solutions for structural disequilibrium at the factor level of the simple variety—where factor prices are out of line with factor endowments—may be stated theoretically with the greatest of ease. Change factor prices to accord with factor endowments, or change factor endowments to accord with factor prices. A compromise is evidently possible at some halfway house. But, while the solution can be simply put in words, in the real world the problem is likely to prove obdurate and unyielding. And, as we shall see presently, the more complex types of structural disequilibrium at the factor level, like the dual economy case, are more difficult to deal with, even in theoretical terms.

Let us take the Italian case. The solution which would adjust factor prices to factor proportions would call for higher interest rates and profits and lower wages. Perhaps some change in the level of rents should also be added, but out of ignorance we may omit this from the account. Higher interest and lower wages constitute a deflationary policy, which is half of the liberal prescription for structural disequilibrium at the goods level.

The difficulty with this line of action is likely to be that it will not work. Factors are, by and large and certainly in the short run, inelastic with respect to price. The Italian worker will prefer unemployment to wages below the customary level, and Italian and foreign social attitudes will support him in this response. Moreover, it is by no means clear that Italian business enterprise will substitute labor for capital at lower wages and higher interest rates. It would be profitable to do so, at least at the rate at which capital can be taken out of existing equipment with fixed input coefficients through depreciation allowances; but Italian, like other entrepreneurs, are likely to favor technology in use in other countries, with perhaps quite different factor proportions and relative prices.

In Italy itself there may be a great deal to be said for changing the regulations requiring firms to hire labor on a long-term basis and forbidding layoffs, on the grounds that they are self-defeating. Italian industry may, in fact, be encouraged to substitute capital for labor through laborsaving machinery, in order to limit the number of workers for which the law makes it responsible. But even without the perverse effects of this legislation, there are few grounds for thinking that Italian or any other industry is likely to change factor proportions in the short run in response to factor prices.

German recovery after 1948 was characterized by low wages and high interest rates and profits, with high levels of unemployment. There is little indication, however, that manufacturing techniques were adjusted to take advantage of the relative change in factor prices.

The alternative of adjusting factor proportions to fit factor price and existing technology recommends itself to governmental authorities, but it has its own difficulties. This solution, it should be noted, goes beyond the scope of the classical theory of international trade, which excludes international factor movements. In the Italian case the remedy consists of encouragement to emigration of workers and to domestic capital formation and the import of capital. If wages are too high and interest rates too low, they can be justified by fewer workers and more capital. The question is how to accomplish these ends.

The question of emigration takes us into a political field. In economic terms, migration should take place until the marginal value product of labor is the same in all parts of the world, or more accurately, until differences between the marginal value products of labor in different parts of the world are less than the cost of moving labor. In the Italian case the incentive to emigration might be increased by the alternative solution, reduction of wages. The unemployed worker would perhaps prefer employment at the new low wages to emigration. Probably, however, the attraction of relatively high wages has very little to do with limiting emigration. This is already held in check by high costs of movement; barriers to immigration in those countries, like the United States, which are favored by potential migrants; lack of capital in some countries like Brazil or Libya which want or could use immigrants; and by social and political inertia, which tends to make Icelanders stay in Iceland and Patagonians in Patagonia, whatever the differential which they could earn by migration.

The inward movement of capital is evidently discouraged by too low a rate of interest and would be favored by the solution of changing factor prices by raising interest rates. But the level of return is not the major barrier to capital inflow. Governmental capital formation from abroad is independent of the rate of return. The major source of foreign capital for Italy has been military assistance, UNRRA, and the European Recovery Program; and the bulk of the import surplus was financed by the United States as a gift rather than a loan. As far as private capital is concerned, moreover, while rates of interest are important, the foremost considerations lie in the attitude of the country toward foreign investment and the success with which it maintains its balance of payments in equilibrium so that it can transfer interest and dividends in foreign exchange. This leaves us with the paradox that the cure for disequilibrium is a movement of capital which can take place only if equilibrium has been maintained for a while—just as the only way for an actress to get a job on Broadway is to have had Broadway experience.

Balance-of-payments disequilibrium resulting from the attempt to employ the unemployed factor, at whatever factor proportions, is likely to reflect implicitly the solution of accommodating factor proportions to factor prices. The inflation causing the disequilibrium results from excessive expenditure. The deficit in the balance of payments is thus the real transfer of the capital. All that is needed in the situation is a source of savings abroad to make the investment.

Perhaps the answer to the question of whether factor prices should be adjusted to factor endowments or vice versa is the one that we have given to many similar questions: a little of both—some disinflation and some capital inflow plus labor outflow. This appears, in fact, to be the policy followed by the Italian government. In the German case, too, disinflation and balance-of-payments deficits representing mostly capital formation, with perhaps some consumption, have been the course followed, though continued immigration of refugees from eastern Germany has taken place and large-scale emigration has been impossible. In Israel, too, the ground gained for existing factor prices by capital imports has been lost by immigration. And the Israeli case illustrates, perhaps as well as any other, the difficulty of establishing a real level of wages which will accord with the resources of land, capital, and labor in the country, given the background, habits, and hopes of the people who make up the country.

Remedy for Dual Economy

It would be fatuous to suggest that the dual economy problem could be solved either by changing factor proportions in the subsistence sector of the economy to the level in the export sector using foreign capital or by encouraging foreign entrepreneurs to lower wages in export industries to the rates existing in the rest of the country. It is clearly necessary to give them both barrels. The critical operational question, however, is the one we have already touched upon. In the intensification of capital development in the subsistence sector, should one cut corners and use the most modern laborsaving machinery or faithfully adjust production at all stages to the progressively changing factor endowments? It is all very well for foreign capital to argue that labor is inefficient because of inexperience, and therefore expensive, so that it is necessary to use technology appropriate to factor endowments in the country from which the capital came. In the subsistence sector of the economy, labor is still cheap relative to domestic savings. At the same time, some of the latest machinery requires the least skill on the part of the vast majority of the labor force, provided that one is able to obtain the critical number of trained workers—from the ranks of native labor or from foreign immigrants—necessary to keep the machinery in good working order.

Which of these solutions is adopted or the weighting of the compromise between them will depend upon the particular circumstances of the country.

A further critical decision turns on the degree to which the efficient export industry should be loaded with responsibility for capital formation in the subsistence economy. This is a case of the goose and the golden eggs in modern dress. How rapidly can one increase the production of golden eggs without killing the goose, or even reducing the present value of her lifetime production discounted at the appropriate rate of interest? Opinions will evidently differ as between the goose and her owner. From either point of view, however, it is clear that there are several alternatives: the export industry operated with foreign capital can be taxed lightly, to encourage more foreign investment, provided that complementary resources of land are available; or it can be taxed out of business; or it can be taxed at a maximum to maintain it in business without encouraging new foreign capital. Maximum speed in total capital formation regardless of the national origins of capital would call for the first of these courses; maximum capital formation with emphasis on, but not exclusive use of, domestic capital would call for the last. Little progress can be achieved through the second process, which seems, however, to be the one most widely pursued in developing countries.

The oil industry is inclined to stress the contrast furnished by its treatment in Mexico and Venezuela. Mexico nationalized British- and American-owned oil companies within its borders; Venezuela encouraged foreign investment in the industry. The Mexican oil industry collapsed; lost its export market; shifted the country to an import basis; and has only recently, with the help of foreign technology, begun to make a comeback in exploration, drilling, and refining. Venezuela, on the other hand, has begun a boom on the basis of expanded oil operations which it taxes heavily but not mortally. Profits from oil are being invested in transportation facilities, to spread the development process wider and deeper in the country.

There has been considerable debate among economists over one important implication of dual economy when labor is employed at two different rates of return in industry and agriculture and is mobile between them. The debate has turned upon the question of whether it is appropriate to regard the cost of labor, for the purposes of calculating comparative costs, as its marginal return in industry or in agriculture. A Rumanian economist named Manoilescu used the case as an argument for a tariff on manufactures, claiming that low wages did not argue for the use of more labor in labor-intensive agriculture and less in capital-intensive manufacturing, but the reverse. Much of the labor in agriculture, he contended, was marginally unproductive, even though it was paid a return, and anything which it could produce in manufacturing would be a net gain. A tariff which stimulated manufactures and shifted labor from agriculture to industry would increase, not reduce, total net product by taking underemployed labor up into efficient employment. This view is in opposition to the classical opinion that increased production in agriculture and exchange of the output abroad for manufactured goods of a capital-intensive country will yield a higher over-all return.

It may be granted that Manoilescu is right. When resources are unemployed or underemployed in one sector of the economy at lower marginal efficiency than in another, the country can achieve a higher yield by shifting labor from the area of underemployment to that where it is combined with more capital or land. This requires more capital and land, however, and these may not be forthcoming.

What emerges from the debate, however, is the desirability of equalization of incomes to factors within a country, to the extent that this is possible. The necessary spatial and occupational mobility are hard to achieve. Caste, racial, religious, and other discriminations must be broken down; the ties that bind the peasant or worker to the place of his birth must be loosened. Institutions permitting aggregation of capital into large amounts must be devised; and this capital must seek a maximum of income by combining with the cheapest possible labor. This may even argue in the long run for the elimination of foreign capital, which is likely to be happy only in particular occupations, although it can better be interpreted as an argument for a true internationalization of capital.

The dual economy within the United States is breaking down. Labor moves north and west; capital moves south and southwest. Regional disparities are being diminished and, along with them, the occupational barriers which exclude Jews, Negroes, immigrants, and first-generation Americans from particular types of jobs. The forces which are producing this equalization of factor prices may be seen in this example to have their roots deep in the social and political fabrics.

There may then be no purely economic solution to the dual economy case, to the Manoilescu version of it, or even to structural disequilibrium at the factor level. These problems lie along the boundaries of the various social sciences and challenge concerted attack.

Summary

Structural disequilibrium is a maladjustment of the price system. At the goods level, it is a malallocation of resources relative to prices, generally arising from a change in demand or supply for internationally traded goods. It calls for a reduction in expenditure and a shift in resources. This is likely to be assisted by exchange depreciation, supported by monetary and fiscal policy, at least in the long run. A policy of borrowing to achieve increased productivity presupposes some other type of disequilibrium in addition. Planned resource shifts, with import restrictions to limit balance-of-payments deficit, are appropriate only in very severe dislocations; and restrictions should be gradually relaxed as correction takes place.

Structural disequilibrium at the factor level involves factor prices inappropriate to factor endowments. Its remedy may be a correction of factor prices—generally deflation—or a correction of factor endowments—generally emigration of labor and capital imports. Dual economy is a special case of factor disequilibrium wherein two sets of factor prices exist side by side. This is a frequent concomitant of economic development and foreign investment. With more development and the conversion of the subsistence into a market economy, a single set of factor prices and endowments is possible. Social as well as economic change is required to effect this.

SUGGESTED READING

TREATISES, ETC.

One of the first articles to make the distinction between structural disequilibrium and income disequilibria, though incidentally, was J. J. Polak, "Exchange Depreciation and International Monetary Stability," *RE & S,* August, 1947. The distinction between the goods and the factor levels of equilibrium is advanced in E. Despres and C. P. Kindleberger, "The Mechanism of Adjustment in International Payments—the Lessons of Postwar Experience," *AER,* May, 1952. An interesting geometric discussion of dual economies is given in R. S. Eckaus, "Factor Proportions in Underdeveloped Areas," *AER,* September, 1955.

POINTS

On the postwar recoveries of Germany and Italy, see H. C. Wallich, *Mainsprings of German Revival* (New Haven: Yale University Press, 1955); H. Mendershausen, *Two Postwar Recoveries of the German Economy* (Amsterdam: North Holland Printing Co., 1955); F. A. and V. C. Lutz, *Monetary and Foreign Exchange Policy in Italy* (Princeton: Princeton University Press, 1950).

The argument that tariffs can improve total income in a dual economy is given in M. Manoilescu, *The Theory of Protection* (London: King, 1931). This was unfavorably reviewed by Viner in the *JPE* (February, 1932); Ohlin in *Weltwirtschaftliches Archiv* (January, 1931); and discussed in Haberler, pp. 196 ff. The strength of the argument is revealed, however, by the fact that Viner and Haberler return to it twenty years after they had originally disposed of it, and this time less unfavorably. See Haberler, "Real Cost, Money Cost, and Comparative Advantage," *International Social Science Bulletin,* Spring, 1951, and "Some Problems in the Pure Theory of International Trade," *EJ,* June, 1950; and Viner, *International Trade and Economic Development,* pp. 64 ff.

For a discussion of dual economy in the United States, see T. W. Schultz, "Reflections on Poverty within Agriculture," *JPE,* February, 1950. For a case history in Cuba, see F. Ortiz, *Cuban Counterpoint: Tobacco and Sugar* (New York: Alfred A. Knopf, Inc., 1947), Part I.

The recommendation of exchange depreciation for structural disequilibrium at the goods level is given by the UN experts, in *National and International Measures for Full Employment.*

Chapter
28

THE MEANS
TO EQUILIBRIUM

Four Remedies, Four Disequilibria

This chapter is almost entirely by way of review and summary. In the course of discussing four particular disequilibria—cyclical, secular, and two kinds of structural—we have indicated that this and that condition call for the judicious combination of four methods of adjustment—monetary and fiscal change, exchange-rate alteration, tariff or quota action, and capital movement. The time has come to sort out these alternative means to equilibrium and to deal with one or two other proposals, or variations of these, which have recently been added to the discussion.

Our purpose in this examination is to see the extent to which equilibrium can be gained and maintained without the use of restrictions on trade. Equilibrium is not lack of change, or stagnation, or that long-run state of affairs, death. It is a condition which is capable of being sustained in a world of change. This makes it a desirable end. The predilection in favor of freer trade, absence of quota restrictions, and nondiscrimination was defended in Chapter 16. Here it may be regarded as a prejudice in favor of specialization on the broadest possible basis, related both to an economic optimum and to international political well-being.

The Classical Assumptions

It is well to remind the student, however, that disequilibria arise and are difficult to correct because the assumptions which classical economists thought underlay foreign trade are not fully met. If these classical assumptions were to obtain today, disequilibrium would be rare, and it would make little difference which road was followed back to equilibrium. There is value in examining the classical assumptions once more as part of this review, to see whether the real effort should be, not the correction of symptoms of disequilibrium, but attack on underlying conditions.

In Part II we referred to the three classical assumptions of competition, mobility, and full employment. Competition and mobility of resources within countries imply, respectively, elasticity of demand and elasticity of supply. These are doubtless the most important. But there are others which cannot be neglected. Of particular importance are those of high income elasticities for imports, the stabilizing character of speculation, and a given state of technology. It may be useful to indicate in summary fashion what is implied by these assumptions.

Equilibrium is disturbed with difficulty and readily restored without the use of trade restrictions in a world where:

1. Demand is elastic:
   a) Consumers are independent of each other.
   b) Consumers are prepared to substitute cheaper for more expensive goods and to give up goods when their prices rise or when incomes fall. This amounts to saying that exit is easy for consumers.
   c) There are many firms in the foreign market, and no single firm can have an effect on the price. Each firm can sell as much as it can produce at the existing price without affecting it.
2. Supply is elastic:
   a) Firms are numerous. Entry is easy into various industries, because the amount of capital needed to enter is small. Exit is frequent through bankruptcy or voluntary liquidation.
   b) Labor, capital, and land will readily shift out of industries in which the return is less than can be earned elsewhere. This means that the amount of capital per firm is low and that firms are numerous. It further means that overhead costs of shifting occupations are low for labor.
3. Full employment is maintained:
   a) On the Keynesian analysis—the consumption function is stable, and investment and savings are equated to each other, at a level which will give full employment, by the rate of interest controlled by the amount of money created.
   b) On the quantity-theory-of-money analysis—the money supply is stable at an appropriate level, without cumulative credit creation or contraction.
   c) In terms of general-equilibrium theory—the supply of factors responds elastically to changes in factor prices which are flexible and adjusted to the level of full employment of each factor. This is made possible by high elasticities of substitution among the factors in existing production functions.
4. High income elasticities for imports:
   This requires either growing real income and full employment so that income spills over into imports continuously, or production at home of necessities and importation of luxuries.

5. Stabilizing speculation:

Speculators' opinions differ on the prospects for change, with a net view in favor of a return to the level from which departure took place. What this requires is primarily a long period of stability.

6. A given state of the arts:

This means unchanged technology. If inventions or discoveries occur, however, these can be permitted as perfectly random changes, which means that they affect demand or supply in random rather than systematic fashion.

The Causes of Disequilibrium and Difficulty of Their Correction

This list can easily be turned inside out. On this showing, disequilibrium may occur, and in serious cases is difficult to correct where:

1. Demands are inelastic:

   a) Consumers refuse to give up many items of consumption even with high taxes—tobacco, American movies, tea and salt in the American colonies, etc.—and attempt to resist declines in income through extra-market action—strikes, union agreements for escalator clauses, farm parity, etc.

   b) Consumer demands are linked through "bandwagon" effects ("Keeping up with the Joneses").

2. Supply is inelastic:

   a) Firms in many industries are few in number. Large amounts of capital are needed to get a start in the industry—witness Kaiser in automobiles and Reynolds in aluminum. Exit is resisted—companies hang on in the hope of tariff protection, RFC loans, new community finance, or other support.

   b) Labor, capital, and land are not readily moved out of existing industries but cling to depressed areas and industries. In part, the difficulty arises from the increased level of skills in all industry, which makes training necessary. In part, it is social attachment to a way of life. In part, costs of transfer are high and institutions are lacking to bear them socially.

3. Inflation or deflation persist or alternate with one another, in secular and cyclical movements of income:

   a) On the Keynesian analysis: investment is responsive to growth of population, discoveries of land, and changes in technology, while savings depend upon socially determined consumption levels and levels of income above them. Both are unresponsive to the rate of interest. Under these circumstances, secular inflation or secular deflation are possible. Excessive spending at any time by firms, households, or government may lead to inflation; insufficient spending to deflation. The interaction of the multiplier and the accelerator gives rise to business cycles.

   b) On the quantity-theory-of-money analysis—the adoption of inappropriate banking institutions permits alternating cumulative credit creation and contraction, leading to business cycles. Gold discoveries or failures of gold mining to keep abreast of economic growth may lead to secular inflation or deflation.

c) General-equilibrium theory—if factors respond inelastically to changes in factor prices, then structural unemployment is possible. This may be due to a failure of entrepreneurs to take advantage of opportunities to substitute factors for one another or to the insistence by factors, particularly labor, for a given standard of living as the price of contributing its services.

4. Low or asymmetrical income elasticities for imports:

a) A country may have a low income elasticity of demand for imports because it depends on foreign countries for its food, as Britain, or because it contains many types of resources within its borders. If the country is a technological leader, it is likely that the demand will be elastic for increases in income abroad for the few products it exports and inelastic for imports.

b) Countries with rising standards of living and increasing productivity are likely to have low income elasticities with respect to declines in income, for imports which contribute to a high standard of living, but may have high income elasticities when income rises.

5. Destabilizing speculation:

In a world of war, revolution, and inflation, the stability needed for inelastic expectations and stabilizing speculation is for the most part missing. On occasion, confidence can be established overnight —as in the Poincaré stabilization of the franc in 1926. But the pattern is difficult to follow.

6. Changing technology:

If technology is changing, not in a random fashion, but with a single technological leader among countries, the static conditions postulated in the classical analysis are replaced with dynamic change. The new position may be reflected in prices, income elasticities, effects on investment and savings. Of perhaps the greatest significance is that the technological leader calls the tune, while the others dance.

The Time Dimension

In this, as in economics in general, important questions turn on the time element. The classical assumption may be fulfilled in the long run, but not in the short, or vice versa. Such is not the case with the full-employment assumption or that dealing with speculation, although time has a relationship to each. The major departure from the classical assumption of full employment in the short run is the business cycle, the existence of which Say's law of markets in effect denies; in the long run, departures from the assumption entail secular stagnation or exhilaration. The relation of time to stabilizing speculation is merely that, in the general case, time is needed to achieve it—time in which stability prevails.

Demand and supply are much more elastic in the long run than in the short, as we have pointed out before. Time gives opportunity for effecting substitutions and cutting losses. It also emphasizes the necessity for adjustment. A reduction in price which is expected to be temporary will elicit no shift of resources, if the movement of resources involves cost. In the long run, it is necessary to face the inevitability of a permanently reduced price and liquidate the industry.

But time does not always favor the classical assumptions. Insofar as technology is concerned, the state of the arts may be taken as given in the short run, though change is certain in the long run. Like the hour hand of the clock or the growth of the small boy, change is imperceptible but relentless. This is perhaps less true today than it was, with the pace of change speeded up out of all recognition by our grandfathers.

Elimination or Correction?

There can be little doubt in most minds that the real world resembles less the classical assumptions than their obverse and that disequilibrium on this account is pervasive and unyielding. Nor will many believe that the road to equilibrium with relatively free trade lies through an attempt to reverse the trend of the last half-century and to effect a return to the classical world. Few have the faith to believe that the antitrust movement or the antiunion movement or some other panacea will succeed and restore an equilibrating world. None is likely to think that sufficient progress can be made on all these fronts.

This is not to condone the abuses of monopolies, cartels, tradeunions, or any other present-day institution, including government, or to abandon the effort to achieve their maximum restriction for flexibility and competition, within the limits of the political compact of present-day society. This sort of gain is desirable. What is intolerable, however, is the attempt on the part of any significant group in society to attack a major institution in another group for the purpose of destroying it. We cannot hope to turn the clock back for others but not for ourselves. Nor can we, in all candor, expect to turn back the clock significantly, even if we can slow the hands a trifle.

Balance-of-Payments Panaceas

Even if it were possible to restore the conditions under which the classical rules of thumb are believed to have worked—the annual balanced budget, free trade, and the gold standard, if they in fact did —no rule of thumb can be set in motion like an automatic pilot and relied upon to steer our economic course today. Rules of thumb have potency only in a world of irrationality where things are done primarily because it is the way they have always been done, and the system worked. In a scientific age, cause and effect must be understood before a mechanism is adopted. A rule gains sanction from its current effectiveness, not from its antiquity.

Moreover, it is now clear, from a study of the past, that the gold standard was a highly managed mechanism; that trade at the peak of free trade was never completely free; and that the rule calling for the balancing of the budget every 365 days instead of every month, business cycle, or growth cycle is arbitrary. Even if one could restore an approximation of the classical conditions—which one cannot—it is unlikely that the world would accept the ancient rules.

In these circumstances, it is natural that a wide number of people will seek new panaceas and gimmicks. Formulas make for peace of mind. It is uncomfortable to be reminded that the world is a highly complex place, in which different combinations of problems will call for different combinations of medicine. "Down with the gold standard; long live flexible exchange rates, or regional payments arrangements, or multiple-exchange rates, or raising the price of gold, or some such cure-all." Frequently the economists identified with simple therapies of these sorts are fully aware of the subtle qualifications with which any measures should be put forward, but strip these away in their public writing for the sake of emphasis.

The list given in the previous paragraph should be expanded. "Trade not aid" is another sovereign remedy which calls for reductions in United States tariffs as a means of correcting secular disequilibrium. International commodity price stabilization is another. A group of economists who object to the "universal" approach embodied in GATT, the International Monetary Fund, and the International Bank have advocated the "regional approach" everywhere, without specifying in detail how much of regional freer trade, regional payments unions, regional investment planning, they have in mind.

Most of these panaceas involve valid partial-equilibrium statements. "If we had some ham, we could have some ham and eggs, if we had the eggs." If we adopt flexible exchange rates, there will be no balance-of-payments disequilibrium, provided that we cut absorption in the depreciating country by the amount of the balance-of-payments deficit to be removed, expand absorption in the surplus country, and eliminate destabilizing speculation. A few of them involve invalid partial-equilibrium dicta. "If my aunt wore trousers, she would be my uncle." If we raise the price of gold, international liquidity will be increased and eliminate future balance-of-payments difficulties.

Study by a recent group of economists produced a book written by their chairman entitled *Trade, Aid, or What?* which was addressed to the cure-all put forward by the then British Chancellor of the Exchequer, "Trade, not Aid." The book's answer was "Trade, Aid and Everything." There is no single prescription for balance-of-payments disequilibrium. Some steps are worth taking for their improvement in world specialization and real income, and to increase resource flexibility, even though they do not bear directly on disequilibrium. Others can be addressed to the disequilibria themselves, usually in combination. In particular any price mechanism like exchange-rate adjustment implies action in the field of monetary and fiscal policy to control absorption.

The Income Disequilibria

But to return to our four disequilibria and four means of adjustment: Trade restrictions are to be avoided. In a limited sense capital movements can be regarded as a way of buying time. This leaves one income formula—monetary and fiscal measures—and one price formula—exchange-rate adjustment. Why can we not fit the income formula to the two income disequilibria—cyclical and secular—and the price formula to the two price disequilibria—structural disquilibrium at the goods and factor levels? This would be convenient for the student to remember. The trouble is that it is not quite so simple.

In the first place, we must recall from Chapters 4 and 11 that exchange-rate adjustments which succeed in producing balance-of-payments effects themselves give rise to income changes which work in the opposite direction. Unless these are offset by positive measures of monetary and fiscal policy in support of the exchange action, the net effect of the latter will be small or nil. Conversely, monetary and fiscal measures have effects on relative prices, at least to the extent that monetary expansion occurs in a full-employment economy. Domestic prices and costs rise; international prices are tied to prices abroad by the law of one price. This produces a price disequilibrium which may call for exchange-rate adjustment. But, even if we allow for the appropriate supporting monetary and fiscal policy when we are talking of exchange action (and vice versa), it is still too simple to say that income disequilibria need an income remedy, and price disequilibria a price one.

Cyclical and secular disequilibria should be attacked by monetary and fiscal measures as far as possible. This means that the country with a cyclical depression should use monetary and fiscal measures to eliminate it and that countries experiencing secular disequilibrium should adjust expenditure for consumption, investment, and government purchases to the level of production and capital lending or borrowing if they cannot adjust capital lending or borrowing. The first of these statements on cyclical disequilibrium does not contribute much, however. The country in depression will want, of its own accord, to eliminate the depression. The question is whether it can do more than mitigate it. And monetary and fiscal policies are not appropriate for the country which has the deficit because of depression abroad.

Even in secular disequilibrium, moreover, it is not enough for one country to use fiscal and monetary measures to bring spending up or down to the level of production minus or plus foreign lending. If one country reaches full employment, the other, in a two-country analysis, may still be depressed or inflated and leave a disequilibrium. It takes at least two to keep secular equilibrium.

The difficulty with these income disequilibria comes when one combines them. Separately, the remedy is simply stated: fiscal and monetary measures to eliminate cyclical depression and to reduce to manageable proportions secular stagnation and exhilaration. Beyond this, long-term capital lending and borrowing adjusted to oversavings and overinvestment, respectively, and short-term borrowing to finance the residual imbalance which cannot be eliminated. The short-term borrowing can be private if speculation is stabilizing, or it may require special institutions like the International Monetary Fund, with exchange control of destabilizing speculation, if it is not.

In combination, however, the cyclical remedy will not work unless the secular disequilibrium has been corrected. If long-term lending is not stable but fluctuates, short-term lending cannot balance out over time. This means that it would be short-term lending in name only. Some experts have proposed, thus far without striking any warm response, that the countries with depression should contribute, not lend, enough to other countries to enable them to maintain the level of their purchases. The analogy is with domestic anticyclical government spending. The time may come when the world is ready for this sort of device, but not yet.

If long-term capital movements are not stabilized and if short-term capital cannot therefore function in a balanced way over the full-length cycle or even several cycles, countries without reserves to spend must be permitted to impose quota restrictions on a temporary basis. The inflationary impact of the quotas in these circumstances will not be unwelcome, since the loss of exports will tend to produce a multiplied decline in income.

Exchange depreciation is not an appropriate remedy for cyclical depression abroad which leaves a country with a deficit. Typically, exchange depreciation is designed to alter the relationship of international and domestic goods and to shift resources into export- and import-competing lines. To the extent that resources are immobile, however, there is little point in moving them one way in depression and the other way in prosperity, beyond the minimum extent necessary anyway.

We must not concentrate so exclusively on the balance-of-payments impact of depreciation that we neglect price effects. Depreciation gives a lift to prices (or a downward push to prices abroad). If no balance-of-payments improvement is sought, devaluation of the exchange rate may nonetheless be undertaken for its anticyclical effects. It is a beggar-thy-neighbor policy unless, perhaps, the depreciation is undertaken to offset the effects of earlier depreciation abroad which is exerting deflationary pressure on prices and incomes. This, it can be argued, was the case in the depreciation of the dollar in 1933, though this is reasoning after the fact.

Fiscal and monetary policy should be applied in the depressed country with a surplus, but not in the deficit country seeking to ward off the depression of others. The latter course would be appropriate only if there were a very high income elasticity for imports, so that the major effect of the decline would be to cut down on imports and balance the international accounts. But if the marginal propensity to import is of normal proportions, monetary and fiscal policy must be excluded in the deficit country.

For growth and decline the appropriate remedy is long-term capital movements. Here the pace of capital investment should be linked to the rate at which the economy as a whole is developing in a social sense, on the one hand, and to the availability of capital, on the other. There is considerable likelihood of inadequate fit. If social capacity for development gets ahead of available capital, as seems to be the case at present, the remedy lies in creating the climate of opinion in which private capital movements can be resumed or in devising the international institutions capable of handling capital movements in the amounts needed, or a little of both.

Trade restrictions and exchange depreciation cannot be recommended. Some tariff for revenue only will undoubtedly be required in a developing country before it reaches the level of sophistication where it can depend on internal taxes, and particularly those on income. The application of these to luxuries has evident advantages. Some tariffs may be needed to encourage industries which offer increasing returns, though these will be but a small fraction of those that regard themselves as eligible.

What is most undesirable is inflation balanced by quota restrictions. This will compound the inflation, distort the price system, divert resources from the areas of greatest productivity, and thwart the development process.

Almost equally undesirable, but perhaps the lesser of the two evils if inflation cannot be avoided and capital is not available, is exchange depreciation. Much depends here on the character of the countries' imports and exports—their elasticities. If the elasticities are high, well and good. If low, the gain in the maintenance of relative prices, scored over the disequilibrium system of quota restrictions, is pretty much dissipated through the loss in the terms of trade.

So long as no retaliation takes place, the combination of the two into a multiple exchange system prevents the loss in the terms of trade, and some, but not all, of the disadvantage of price distortion.

Expanding International Reserves

A number of writers are anxious to cope with short-term income disequilibrium by expanding international reserves. One method is to enlarge the quotas of the International Monetary Fund, which, in the fall of 1957, was fairly fully loaned up, if one counts stand-by credits. Another possibility is to raise the price of gold, which would increase the value of national gold reserves and expand the rate at which gold mining adds to reserves annually. A third technique would be to convert the International Monetary Fund into a mechanism like the European Payments Union, which provides for automatic, though limited, loans from surplus to deficit countries or international overdraft facilities. This would carry the Fund part way back to the Keynes Plan, rejected at the time of Bretton Woods, which would have led to a large injection of international credit.

Two things are wrong with these proposals. They are unnecessary, and they would not work. They are unnecessary because international reserves can be created at will by the mutual central-bank deposits. The Bank of England can buy dollars from the Federal Reserve Bank of New York, and the Federal Reserve Bank of New York can buy sterling from the Bank of England (if it would), and international reserves of both would be increased. The rise of international funds in New York by close to $8 billion since 1949 suggests that the total volume of reserves is adequate, even though its distribution may not be.

These proposals would not produce the desired result because they would lead to increased spending. If reserves of every country were expanded, and at the same time they took all other steps needed to correct the disequilibria in their balances of payments, the expansion of reserves would provide needed insurance against random and cyclical disturbances. But there is no guarantee that in fact all these other steps would be taken. And it is highly likely that some countries, regarding the increase in their reserves, would expand domestic capital formation and attempt to convert the reserves into real capital. The increase in reserves would thus magnify the distortions in expenditure responsible for the disequilibrium. No fundamental attack on the reserve problem for short-run income disequilibria can be made until secular disequilibrium is under control. Given the intensity of the interest in growth in underdeveloped countries and the relatively meager flow of long-term capital, this will not be soon.

Stimulating the Flow of Long-Term Capital and Aid

Much ingenuity has gone into proposals for stimulating direct investment: mainly by government guarantees and tax reductions. The flow of debt capital, on the other hand, has been stimulated through government debt, by the Export-Import Bank, and the International Bank for Reconstruction and Development, but still falls short of the amounts at which underdeveloped countries are interested in creating capital. No attention has been given to the restoration of the bond market, except for the work of Councils of Foreign Bondholders in arranging to clear up old defaults and arrears.

Earlier chapters have given reasons for thinking that direct investment by itself or even with a flow of debt capital through the International Bank, amounting to $400 million a year, will not be sufficient to meet the disequilibrium. It provides little social overhead capital; it remits substantial profits; it frequently creates its own savings in the surplus country so that it is not available for offsetting existing savings; it frequently stimulates new investment in the borrowing country so that it is not available to absorb the demand for imports created by past investment.

Lacking a means of reviving the international bond market, countries have turned to governmental means of enlarging the flow of capital, including intergovernmental aid or transfers.

In this area, too, as in direct investment, help in meeting an existing disequilibrium can only be achieved if new loans or transfers take place without expanding new investment projects, or new savings. The possibility that the International Bank and Point Four have expanded investment as fast or faster than they provided foreign exchange to meet the ensuing deficits has been mentioned. To the extent that this is the case, they have made no contribution to the pre-existing secular disequilibrium.

In short, loans, too, are a partial-equilibrium solution. They require everything else equal. International lending is needed to fund old investment expenditure. If it generates new, the world will keep running but stay in the same place.

The Structural Disequilibria

It can be argued that the price system will work to correct structural disequilibrium at the goods level without the need for interference with any sort of remedy. Assuming that price and supply elasticities are relatively high, we can start from a decline in demand for a particular export and see how this would work. The first reaction is that the returns to factors engaged in the unwanted export line decline. These resources seek other employment. The difficulty, however, is that they may take employment in domestic industries rather than in those which replace the missing exports or assist in the contraction of imports. If this were to happen, the deficit would persist. Exchange depreciation, by raising the prices of export- and import-competing goods relative to domestically traded goods, has a role to play.

If exchange depreciation is not allowed, what then? The alternative is monetary and fiscal change, through the operation of the gold standard, an interdistrict settlement fund, or some other automatic or calculated mechanism. The initial change in income due to the loss of income from exports is enlarged by the multiplier. This leads directly to a reduction in imports. The continued deficit after the unemployed resources have shifted into domestic areas leads to a further contraction of money and credit, which puts pressure on domestic industry, imports, and import-competing industry, but not on exports. The resources displaced out of the contracting line of exports will be shunted into other exports, after sufficient time has elapsed for the several changes in income to have worked through.

Monetary and fiscal deflation are thus less likely to attract resources into import-competing industries than is exchange depreciation. The efficiency of the country's resources is lower in import-competing than in export lines.

If supply elasticities are low, resources will be harder to move. This means that higher prices in export- and import-competing lines must attract them or that more deflation in the contracting line and in domestic industry is necessary to drive them into other export industries.

If demand elasticities are low, moreover, increased output will be hard to sell, except at unfavorable terms.

If the value of the elasticities is not known, a country may choose to abandon exchange depreciation or monetary or fiscal deflation in favor of quantitative trade restrictions or borrowing. These latter methods by themselves do nothing to restore equilibrium. If the quantitative trade restrictions are sufficiently strenuous, they may balance the international accounts, but at the price of distortion in prices and in resource allocation. Borrowing to fill the gap in exports, without reallocation of resources, is capital consumption. These methods are stopgaps, and quotas are a stopgap with declining force over time. In some cases, direction of resource allocation to redress the long-run balance will be taking place behind the stopgap measures. These allocations, which may be inevitable if resources are particularly immobile and demands inelastic, are not likely to be made with a foresight superior to that of the price system.

For structural disequilibrium at the factor level, depreciation and quantitative restrictions are palliatives which fail to come to grips with fundamentals. Needed are measures to alter prices to accord with factor endowments or factor endowments to fit existing factor prices. Assuming that the price of labor is too high and that of capital too low, while the system can be adjusted to the price of land, a monetary policy of deflation with high interest rates will work in the right direction for the first of these. This is the typical disequilibrium of this kind. If, however, the disequilibrium consisted of too high a price of land, too low a price of labor, and a price of capital which was satisfactory, the price changes implied could not be achieved by any single formula of economic policy.

Migration of labor, capital movements, and land reclamation may assist in making factor endowments fit with factor prices in a given situation to restore equilibrium.

A combination of deflation and migration, plus capital imports, may be the best policy in instances of simple structural disequilibrium.

Where there exists a dual economy with noncompeting groups of capital, combined with a competing supply of labor employed at two different wage levels, the difficulty lies deeper in the social and political structure. Here it is desirable to achieve equalization of factor prices and factor proportions, which should be in harmony with one another. But the best methods of so doing have not been analyzed fully. One ingredient of a solution would be widely recognized as capital imports directed into the subsistence, and not the export, sector of the economy. But these capital imports are difficult to provide on commercial terms and, even if made intergovernmentally, may increase exports or reduce imports only in the most roundabout and therefore ineffective way.

Action by the Surplus Country

Thus far we have been discussing mainly measures by the deficit country to get rid of its deficit, and lending by the surplus country to finance it. Some suggestions have been heard that the country which experiences a surplus should take measures to eliminate its own disequilibrium, even though it be of a positive character. These measures, too, fall into the familiar categories—monetary and fiscal, exchange-rate adjustment, and trade policy. A word may be useful on each.

The surplus country has a duty to maintain full employment with monetary and fiscal policy. This was agreed by the United States in the charter of the United Nations, the draft charter of the International Trade Organization. It is stated in the Employment Act of 1946. The intention of the United States to do so has been made clear in other speeches, documents, and statements. What is meant by these intentions? Certainly, it is not meant that the United States must pursue an expansionary monetary and fiscal policy so long as it has an export surplus in the balance of payments or that it promises to avoid any and all increases in unemployment or fluctuations in national income. The most that can be read into it is the resolve of the country to take steps to meet depression which results from a prolonged decline in long-term domestic investment. To eliminate inventory cycles would require new techniques not yet devised. Action to attack a particular business depression can be taken only after adequate time has elapsed for the seriousness of the depression to be recognized and for its cure to be planned and put into action. While the commitment cannot be quantified, it may be taken to mean that declines in national income will be limited to something on the order of 10 or 15 per cent as contrasted with 50 per cent between 1929 and 1932.

Whether the surplus country has a duty to appreciate in order to rid itself of its balance-of-payments surplus is debatable. The most successful appreciations—of Sweden in 1917 and New Zealand in 1946 —are those by small countries concerned not so much to correct a surplus in the balance of payments as to cut off inflationary pressure coming from abroad. The appreciation of the dollar in 1931 and 1932 failed to eliminate the balance-of-payments surplus because it effectively speeded up the process of deflation in the United States. On the other hand, the experience of Germany in the mid-1950's at a time when the Bank Deutscher Laender was unwilling to permit monetary expansion to eliminate the large balance-of-payments surplus created a presumption in favor of exchange appreciation, which the German monetary authorities did not undertake. Export interests were opposed to action to cut down the profitability of their operations. The same was true in some import-competing lines like agriculture. And the German officials held that the difficulty was not of their doing but could be laid to inflation abroad, and hence should not be corrected by them.

A large country may perhaps be expected not to retaliate to depreciation abroad if it has a surplus, and should meet the deflationary pressure by internal measures, but there can hardly be an obligation on it to use appreciation to restore international balance. There is no assurance that such a policy will succeed if the country is important. The depreciation abroad may be offset by inflation—touched off by depreciation and not held in check by monetary and fiscal measures, which will render the effort vain.

In trade measures, however, the surplus country can properly be expected to act, up to the point of freeing imports of all quotas and tariffs, except in those few areas where national defense or vital social values are being preserved. The United States is far from this point in its concern for small but vocal labor-intensive industries in hat bodies, porcelain, cheese, clothes-pins, watches, etc. The expansion of exports in the foreign country may, like depreciation, touch off more inflation and defeat the attempt. But the blame for the disequilibrium is then squarely located.

Freely Fluctuating Exchange Rate

A more widely recommended remedy for most international disequilibria is the freely fluctuating, or at least a flexible, exchange rate with relatively free trade but with support from monetary and fiscal policy and stabilizing capital movements. This device received more and more support from economists after World War II, in an interesting reversal of the prevailing opinion which went into the construction of the Bretton Woods code, which was in favor of par values and opposed to fluctuating rates. At the end of September, 1950, the Canadian government announced that it would free the Canadian dollar from any par value and allow it to find its own level. Reluctant permission of the International Monetary Fund was obtained. The question is how successful this experiment has been, and to what extent is it applicable more widely?

The Canadian experiment has been an unqualified success. The value of the Canadian dollar appreciated from 90 cents United States in October, 1950, to $1.04 by the end of August, 1952. After returning nearer to par in the interval, it later reached 1.06^{11}\!/_{64}$ in August, 1957. Import controls re-imposed in 1949 were quickly removed. Remaining exchange restrictions were limited to commodity protection.

But the Canadian case has been a curious one in some respects, and may be more a tribute to the Canadian economy than to the concept of a flexible rate. An English economist has suggested that it proves only that any country can successfully adopt a floating rate if it simultaneously discovers oil. For the strength of the Canadian dollar has been due to a heavy capital inflow, largely from the United States, to take advantage of discoveries in oil, to push back the mining frontier in northern Canada, and to construct large investment projects such as the Aluminium Company of Canada's hydroelectric installation at Kitimat. The demand for Canadian metal and wood products has been strong in the United States, but less strong than the investment demand for Canadian dollars. The Bank of Canada has accumulated gold and United States dollar reserves, despite a large deficit on current account, because the inward private capital movement has been incompletely transferred to Canada, and has exceeded the deficit. The rise in the Canadian dollar has been permitted by the Bank of Canada in an effort to discourage some of this inward capital movement, which has, however, failed to be impressed by it. Not only equities but also fixed debt obligations have been bought by United States investors, which regard Canadian securities as only semiforeign in any case, and have functioned in a curious destabilizing fashion by continuing to buy as the rate went up.

While this continued inflow of capital to Canada in the face of the appreciation of the Canadian dollar may be regarded as destabilizing in the short run, in the long run there is more or less implicit in the economic relations between the United States and Canada the understanding that the two currencies should exchange for each other fairly close to par. The Canadian government would not let the Canadian dollar go to a premium or discount of, say, 15 per cent. In consequence, it is possible to take a position in Canadian dollars for the long run with some degree of equanimity, if the dollar is below par or not far above it. This means stabilizing speculation.

A floating currency will work well under the favorable circumstances to which it has been subject in the Canadian case. How would it work in more adverse circumstances? Much depends on expectations in answer to this question, and particularly whether the market is able to establish any norm around which stable expectations could be built. We have indicated earlier that the provision of a futures market has nothing to do with this. The futures market is really only a part of the spot market, and net positions cannot be taken in foreign currencies without a movement of short-term capital which puts pressures on the exchanges. A foreign-exchange rate which fluctuates widely in the relatively short run would create such uncertainty in foreign trade as to dry it up. Some stability of expectation is needed not alone for a given transaction but to encourage entry into foreign trade on a sustained basis and covering the overhead costs of staying in the business. A freely fluctuating exchange rate which moves slowly within a relatively narrow range has much to commend it; but in these circumstances in which at least some of the classical assumptions are realized, other measures would probably work almost equally as well. A widely gyrating exchange rate, on the other hand, would achieve a formal balance of imports and exports at the cost of eliminating a large proportion of total desirable trade.

The Regional Approach

The European Payments Union was a spectacular success in permitting the emergence from a contracting deflationary spiral of intra-European trade. When dollars were in short supply, it paid for any one country to discriminate against European imports to acquire dollars. When all countries tried it, however, it could only eliminate intra-European trade, without expanding the European dollar supply, so long as the resources engaged in European trade could not be diverted to working for dollar markets. In these circumstances, a concerted effort to eliminate discrimination against European exports was highly desirable.

This system worked, however, primarily because the countries of Europe conducted a large amount of trade among one another. In Asia and Latin America, similar payments arrangements have little utility. It would be useful for outside countries like the United States to lend dollars to India, say, to buy goods in Japan. Some multilateral arrangements of this sort of lending (with untied dollars) may be fruitful, but they can hardly be said to constitute a regional payments arrangement. For the most part, the Asian and the Latin American countries have only limited trade among themselves, trading mainly with the countries of Europe or with the United States. Their trade structure, therefore, does not lend itself to an automatic payments arrangement.

Trade discrimination against outsiders, or against a particular outsider like the United States, has been frequently recommended for various reasons, including improvement of the balance of payments. It has already been indicated that these arrangements—customs unions, free-trade areas, or even discriminatory preferences—may be said to expand world welfare when their trade creation outweighs their trade diversion. But what is the probable impact on the balance of payments of the relevant countries?

Much depends here on the effect on spending. If a customs union such as that embarked on by the Six, or contemplated by the Scandinavian bloc, the Arab League, the Central American Republics, and the South American members of the Economic Commission for Latin America, expands investment, it worsens the balance-of-payments position in the short run; if its consequence is deflationary, on the other hand, it may improve it. In a world of buoyant spending, with many plants at full capacity, lowering trade barriers mutually is likely to expand investment opportunities and lead to increased deficits vis-à-vis the outside world. Under depressed circumstances, however, where some plants are liquidated and others can expand by taking excess capacity into production, the impact of customs union is likely to be to improve the balance.

These are, of course, very short-run considerations. In the longer period, when the output of new investment is taken into account, the balance-of-payments impact of the customs union or preference area will turn on its effects on output, on the one hand, and on absorption, on the other. If the marginal propensity to save is positive, there is a presumption that enlarged output will improve the balance. It certainly provides an opportunity to do so. But the economies must be stable in isolation, to use Metzler's phrase, and this is not inevitably the case.

Regional planning for economic development can likewise be analyzed in terms of its effect on the balance of payments through its impact on expenditure. There is no way of knowing what this would be, but it seems likely that countries in concert will egg each other on to larger rather than smaller investment plans, and hence tip the scales against equilibrium. This is highly speculative. They may stimulate lending more than they do investment, which would help.

But this is enough to suggest that regional arrangements can in no way serve as an assured remedy for balance-of-payments ills and must be judged on other grounds. They may help, they may hurt, so far as the balance is concerned, but their major effect is on international specialization and real output, and these are the bases on which the separate plans must be judged.

The causation runs as a rule, in fact, the other way. Customs unions run into difficulty because of balance-of-payments disequilibria. For a long time the barrier to consummation of the economic union between the Belgian-Luxembourg Economic Union, on the one hand, and the Netherlands, on the other, was the persistent Dutch deficit. Today the German surplus and the French deficit both create difficulties for the European Common Market.

Regionalism, therefore, like flexible exchange rates, a $50 price of gold, bimetallism, the commodity dollar, the resumption of gold coinage, and a hundred other proposals which approach crackpotism, is no answer to balance-of-payments disequilibrium.

No Single Tool

We emerge with the conclusion that reliance can be put in no single rule of thumb nor simple nostrum. "Everything is more complicated than most people think." The management of a country's international position is an art, not a science, because it takes an intuitive insight to sort out the main causes of trouble and to link them up with the appropriate remedies. In the armory of the Compleat International Monetary Economist, there is room for more than one approach, and more than one device.

Summary

The present chapter is itself in the way of a summary of the relevance of the four remedies—monetary and fiscal policy, exchange-rate adjustment, lending and borrowing, and trade restrictions—to the four disequilibria, two in income (cyclical and secular) and two in price or structural (at the goods and the factor levels). It is pointed out that to the extent that the classical assumptions of competition, mobility, full employment, high income elasticities, stabilizing speculation, and fixed technology are realized, all remedies work more readily; to the extent that the obverse of these conditions obtains disequilibrium is more obdurate.

Trade restrictions are to be avoided; capital movements buy time in short-run disturbances and are needed to offset deep-seated forces in secular disequilibrium. The main methods of desirable adjustment, therefore, are monetary and fiscal policy, which directly affects income, and exchange depreciation, which affects prices in the first instance. Exchange depreciation, however, has income effects, if it succeeds in changing the balance of payments; it is also used to achieve results on income through price effects. And monetary and fiscal policies have effects on relative prices.

A review of the remedies and disequilibria shows that there is no single statement or two which expresses the matter simply. No sovereign remedy for balance-of-payments disequilibria is found among them.

SUGGESTED READING

TREATISES, ETC.

The relevant material has already been cited in connection with earlier chapters which are summarized here. Perhaps the work which most closely relates to this chapter is Meade's, *The Balance of Payments*. However, it supports monetary and fiscal policy for internal stability, and fluctuating exchange rate for external stability, as if they could be separated, as they cannot. Also bearing on the chapter are the several studies by United Nations experts, particularly *National and International Measures for Full Employment, Measures for International Stability, and Commodity Trade and Development*. A rounded and eclectic approach to balance-of-payments disequilibrium is in W. L. Thorp, *Trade, Aid, or What?* (Baltimore: Johns Hopkins University Press, 1954).

POINTS

The regional approach to international economic problems is emphasized in W. Y. Elliott (ed.), *Foreign Economic Policy for the United States* (New York: Henry Holt & Co., Inc., 1955). R. Triffin, *Europe and the Money Muddle* (New Haven: Yale University Press, 1957), and W. M. Scammell, *International Monetary Policy* (London: Macmillan & Co., Ltd., 1957), emphasize an approach which would permit countries in deficit to overdraw on a central fund which created international credit. Milton Friedman's, "The Case for Flexible Exchange Rates," in *Essays in Positive Economics* (Chicago: University of Chicago Press, 1953), is the most definitive statement of this position. The Canadian experience is analyzed by S. I. Katz in *RE & S* for August, 1953, and later in an article (in French) in the National Bank of Belgium's *Bulletin d'Information et de Documentation* for May, 1955. R. F. Harrod's proposal for raising the price of gold is contained in *The Dollar* (London: Macmillan & Co., Ltd., 1953), and in his "Imbalance of International Payments," *SP,* 1953–54. For proposals to stimulate the international movement of capital see the Randall Commission on Foreign Economic Policy, *Staff Papers* (Washington, D.C.: U.S. Government Printing Office, February, 1954).

Chapter 29

INTERNATIONAL ECONOMIC EQUILIBRIUM AND INTERNATIONAL SOCIETY

The Conflict of Goals

This book has been written largely in terms of economic equilibrium. This is at best a limited objective. If international economic equilibrium can be obtained only at the cost of other social goals, such as national political and social equilibrium or international peace, it is not worthwhile. Social scientists are only beginning to explore this subject. The economist thinks in the limited terms of economic equilibrium because he, and every other social scientist, is incapable of handling wider concepts.

The economist is tempted to think that the achievement of economic equilibrium will be compatible with political and social well-being, nationally and internationally. But it is easy to cite examples where the path to economic equilibrium led to severe hardship for one group in society or where equilibrium was rejected because of the unwillingness of one segment of the society, or more than one, to make the adjustment required by its exigencies.

In the 1870's the world price of wheat declined as a consequence of the cheapening of ocean and railroad transport and the opening up of the then Northwest, especially Minnesota and the Dakotas. Europe was inundated by wheat from the United States, Australia, Argentina, and the Ukraine. The European price of wheat fell.

Economic equilibrium called for the shift of resources out of wheat. In Britain, this involved great hardship on agricultural workers, who were crowded into city slums, and losses for the landed gentry deprived of the protection of the Corn Laws in 1846. But the adjustment took place in any event. In France and Germany, on the other hand, the flood of wheat from abroad was resisted by tariffs designed to protect the place in society of the French peasant and the Prussian Junker. British agriculture was liquidated in the interests of economic efficiency. On the Continent, economic equilibrium was thwarted in order to preserve the political position of a class in Germany, or the economic basis for a social institution, as in France.

But we do not have to go back eighty years for our examples. During the depression the price of wheat fell to 40 cents a bushel. No country is going to permit adjustment to economic equilibrium at this level. Tariffs, quotas, export price supports, subsidies, and every other possible interference with the price system may be justified at 40 cents when none would be at, say, 80 cents. In international society some are more justified than others. Export subsidies and other forms of dumping are a beggar-thy-neighbor device more subversive of the international economy than tariffs combined with domestic price supports. But the dictates of the price system cannot rule on all occasions.

A still more modern contrast of economic and political goals was afforded by Germany in the early years after the monetary reform. International economic equilibrium required low wages and high interest rates and profits to encourage substitution of labor for capital, to maximize the rate of capital formation, and to prevent inflation. But low wages and high profits were a poor formula for political stability, at least in the short run. For a time they accentuated the division between economic classes, embittered relations between political parties, and strained national unity. Gradually as the long-run benefits of expanded capital formation became evident, however, the political gap between worker and employer narrowed.

The same dilemma exists in developing countries. If development is to proceed with a maximum of freedom of choice and a maximum rate of capital formation, there must be a maximum of personal savings usefully invested. This means low wages and high profits, rents, and interest, provided that the latter accrue to individuals who are investing their savings productively. In a typical case, this may require first a revolution, to replace the old elite with a new one concerned with increasing production, and then high returns for the new elite and low for everyone else. The requirement for economic equilibrium with growth is thus short-run political overturn followed by a policy of repression or unusual self-restraint.

Equity versus Efficiency

In its rigorous formulations economics has no room for the notion of fair play. Fair trade, fair profit, fair shares, a fair price, a fair deal—these are all concepts which the economist cannot define. He knows what competitive price is, but what is a fair price?

Concepts of equity cannot be eliminated from national economic life, however. When life is highly individualistic and each person is regarded as a single person rather than as a member of a class, economic misfortune may fall on a large number of people without evoking a response. This is in part the explanation of the failure of the British to take action to assist the million or more agricultural workers pauperized by the fall in the price of wheat in the 1870's and 1880's.

But in most national life there is a need to consider equity and to modify the economic goal of efficiency for this purpose. Other goals may intervene and distract attention from equity and efficiency. Stability, freedom for the individual, and security must also be taken into account. The emphasis among these objectives will shift from time to time, as values are revised in the society. But no society can be all out for efficiency, nor can any economist adopt it as the only objective of social policy.

The importance of equity as modifying efficiency can be seen in the field of taxes. To encourage maximum output, producers are urged to maximize their incomes: to buy cheap and sell dear, and to transform goods and labor into goods and services which will sell for a higher return. But this incentive to production and to sale is opposed by the imposition of taxes, which take a higher proportion of income as income rises. This is the equitable principle of contribution to the common good, represented by government expenditure, according to ability to pay.

The equitable principle is stretched to its maximum in the production and consumption habits of the family. Here, in the typical social unit in the United States, the father earns an income, the mother produces services in kind, and the children are merely consumers. No one stipulates that the children should not obtain food and shelter unless they work. Everyone is entitled to share in consumption as a member of the family. The principle of equity may be modified in slight degree by considerations of efficiency: the children may be assigned chores when they get to a certain age. But the father's bonus for extra work is not reserved for his consumption: it is a bonus for the family as a whole and is shared.

As families share, so do nations, whether consciously or not. When nations lose the capacity to share, moreover, they disintegrate. When this happens, it becomes necessary for representatives of one or another class to seize power and impose a division of income by force. Or, in less extreme cases, inflation results from inability to agree on the sharing of specific burdens, inflation which arbitrarily imposes the burden of reduced consumption on certain income groups. It is also usually accompanied by an external deficit in the balance of payments, which assigns part of the burden to past capital or defers it for the future, depending upon whether the deficit is financed by sale of old assets or borrowing.

Let us look for a moment at a country like France. Here the problem is not one of total production and consumption. France is a relatively fertile and productive country, and the French people are not so materialistic that they insist on an impossible standard of living. But the French have difficulty dividing their burdens and sharing among themselves. Chronic inflation is the result of willingness to agree on what needs to be done but inability to decide how it will be paid for. The working classes and poorer groups want to assign the burdens of war devastation and the economic reconstruction according to ability to pay. Through their political representatives, they levy income and other progressive taxes. But the wealthier groups in the community— the industrialists, the large commercial interests, and the professional classes—evade income taxes. The meaning of this French failing is that they do not feel sufficient cohesion with the rest of society to be willing to bear what has been politically determined as their share. The result is budget imbalance, which is inflationary in periods of full employment, or, if the budget is balanced, additional indirect taxes on consumption and employment. Workers try to evade these latter taxes, for the same reasons as other groups, by demands for increased wages. These lead in turn to higher industrial prices. To the extent that it is possible, the peasants experiencing an increased cost of living hold back on agricultural produce and obtain an increase in farm product prices. This in turn affects the urban cost of living. The only ways this inflation can be stopped are to place the burden on some group in the society which is incapable of throwing it off, such as the pensioner and civil servant—which is almost certain to be subversive of political equilibrium—or to evade the issue by running a large foreign-trade deficit.

When the cement of political cohesion with its capacity to adjust shares equitably breaks down, a country is in difficulties. Sometimes the country divides on class lines, as the tendency has been in the French case cited. Repressive political power may be asserted. If this is from the extreme left, communism; if from the extreme right, monarchy or some sort of feudalism; if from the middle classes, fascism. (This is an oversimplification, of course, but perhaps a pardonable one.) Sometimes, however, the country divides on regional lines: the North and the South in the United States in 1860; the Austro-Hungarian Empire after World War I; Spain with its class/regional struggle between industrial Catalonia and the Basque country against military Castile. The emphasis in much of the regional economic literature in New England about "unfair" competition of the South with New England carries with it a hint of the weakening of the geographical cohesion even of the United States and of separatism.

Inability to share is one horn of the dilemma. But there is another. The British have agreed on "fair shares." As early as 1932, the economic mobilization plans of the general staff emphasized that all classes would share equitably. But if fair shares are carried too far, the incentive to produce and to innovate for increased efficiency is weakened. The consumer is entitled to his "share" whether he contributes effectively to production or not. If other motives to produce are strong enough—the patriotic fervor felt in a country at war or the instinct of workmanship developed on an extraordinarily wide scale—it may be possible to produce efficiently and maintain fair shares. The danger, however, is that all will agree on sharing consumption, and each will wait to let the other take the lead in production.

International Equity and Efficiency

This is one difference between international and interregional trade which was not developed in Chapter 1. In domestic trade, the principle of efficiency is highly diluted by equity. In international trade, efficiency has stood by itself, and there has been no room for considerations of equity.

At least this was the case. There is reason to think that the situation may be changing. Henry Wallace was ridiculed with derisive slogans of "Globaloney" and "A quart of milk for every Hottentot." This was twenty years ago. Today one cannot be so sure that milk for Hottentots is much more absurd than milk for Okies.

In the past, the principle of equity has applied internationally in times of war. Alliances attempt to equate blood and treasure, which in the nature of the process means a modification of the principle of minimizing expenditure of treasure alone. The Lend-Lease principle of 1941 carried equitable relations further than they had been developed in earlier alliances. The sharing of the costs of capital defense expenditures in western Europe among the North Atlantic Treaty Organization (NATO) members carried this sharing of defense expenditure still further.

The question may now be raised as to whether this principle of equity is not being extended to the international sphere in peacetime. The Marshall Plan and Point Four are perhaps the most striking evidence for this conclusion. Up to now, however, this experience has been relatively limited. The Marshall Plan, like the Hoover moratorium, which belatedly scaled down European war debts after World War I, was related to war and to the concept of equalizing expenditure of blood plus treasure. Point Four presents perhaps a wider concession in principle to equity internationally but has thus far kept within modest financial bounds.

There are difficult questions of incentives and rewards bound up here, but these are no worse than the same questions within a country. Hercules was advised that the Lord helps those who help themselves. And this is the principle which people have sought to apply, though not always successfully. If a country recovering from war is resolute, cohesive, hardworking, and politically capable of sharing its burdens, its balance-of-payments deficits will be held within modest proportions. This is the sort of country which can follow the classical medicine of "halt the inflation and depreciate the exchange rate." Help may be needed if the structural disequilibrium is sufficiently severe. But recovery will be speedy. Sober, industrious Netherlands provides an example of what is meant.

In other countries, however, the fault may lie not so much in the economic plight as in political malaise. The over-all burden may be slight, but the difficulties of sharing it serious. Should the United States share its income with, say, France because of difficulties which the French have, not in producing an income but in deciding how to share a relatively small burden of adjustment?

As we have said, this question is similar to those faced in equitable decisions within a country. How does one prevent unemployment insurance from discouraging the search for work or encouraging idleness? Can RFC loans be restricted to growing enterprises and be kept from going to bail out the bad judgment or business incapacity of existing enterprises?

A number of proposals have been made in the United States—by Dean Acheson when he was Secretary of State, by Paul Hoffman as the ECA Administrator, by John MacDonald of the Steelworkers in a submission to the Randall Commission, and others—that provision be made to assist those people, both businessmen and labor, who are adversely affected by foreign competition after a reduction in an American tariff. But what, Professor Wilcox asks, if one company in the industry is able to continue after the tariff reduction without shrinking in volume. The other companies are simply inefficient. Equitable treatment is not meant to substitute for the spur to efficiency.

Equilibrium under Communism

It may be well to discuss the international and domestic policies of communism very briefly in these terms. Communism is able to achieve international economic equilibrium, but generally at the expense of certain groups in the society or at the expense of the international economy. This need not always be the case. In 1946 and 1947, for example, Poland was able to provide for its minimum consumption needs and large-scale capital formation without borrowing from abroad and without serious repression. This was because of the surge of national dedication, comparable to that with which the French repaid the German indemnity of 1871, which sprang from regaining national independence. An important contribution was doubtless also made by the German territory east of the Oder and the Neisse rivers, in which large stocks of goods had been abandoned by Germans fleeing before the Russian army.

But, normally, communism simply restricts imports to the level of exports, and that is that. The burden of reduced consumption, if there is one, is allocated among consumer groups, along with rationing in general. On occasion, as in the Soviet Union in 1932, exports will be made at the cost of the domestic consumer, who was starved to death in numbers of more than a million. Forced capital formation or armament accumulation has taken place under the Soviet system, but they may not be necessary ingredients of it. What is necessary, apparently, is that the international economic solution is dictated and that consumers' preferences, political disorder, or anything else which might disturb this adjustment are rigorously suppressed.

In Western society, on the other hand, the international economic order has been one based on certain rules dictated by efficiency, but these rules are being modified by the exigencies of social adjustment and political democracy.

A Return to Efficiency

There is some, but not much, sentiment in the world for a return to the rules which govern international trade and finance in the nineteenth century. Many would like to return to the results, or at least the results as they are now nostalgically viewed. But few people actually believe that the application of the rules would achieve these results.

The rules may be said, briefly, to consist of *laissez faire,* the gold standard, and annually balanced budgets. Where the role of government is not eliminated, as in interference with trade, it is circumscribed by adherence to prescribed modes of behavior. It may be true that the rules of the gold-standard game are not as explicit as is believed by some of those who advocate a return to it. By and large, however, those who would widen the area of private initiative in the pursuit of profit and narrow the scope for government interference have made pretty clear what they have in mind. Some go so far as to say that the return to the nineteenth century requires a reduction in the size and power of large corporations and a renewal of competition of the sort under which no producer or consumer is large enough to affect the price at which he sells or buys.

The difficulties with this prescription are evident enough. Few people and no political party is willing to trust the price system *in toto*. The rate of change is so rapid, rigidities are so great, the possibilities of cumulative inflation and deflation so obvious, that one cannot reproduce a facsimile of the national and international institutions of the nineteenth century and turn them loose with a promise not to interfere with the results. Only a few mystics, cranks, or fanatics would agree to abide by such a policy. Many more who believe in the medicine would like to take it on an experimental basis, prepared to give it up if it failed to produce the required results. But most people, and most parties, would adhere to the view that the clock cannot be turned back, as a whole. It may be possible to achieve freer trade and to improve the mechanism of international payments, to increase national and international competition. But it is out of the question to contemplate governments not responsible for the welfare of their citizens and not ready to intervene in some fashion or other under conditions of rapid change or cumulative income disturbance. These governments will increasingly take into account the repercussions of their actions on other peoples for whom they have no direct responsibility. At this stage of political development, however, it is impossible to return to a world in which the individual is governed best who is governed least.

A Developing World of Equity

One or two writers are beginning to assume that principles of equity should apply internationally, as well as within a country. This is reflected, for example, not only in the view that more equality of incomes internationally is desirable, on which many people might agree, but that it is the duty of the richer countries to take action toward this end.

It is not clear that these people would recommend operations along the lines of perpetual Marshall Plans, Lend-Lease, Point Four, offshore purchases, stockpiling commodity agreements, Hyde Park arrangements, and so forth, or whether these are inadequate because they are voluntary. In the opinion of some underdeveloped countries which are particularly vocal in the Economic and Social Council of the United Nations, it seems almost as if what is needed is a built-in, automatic mechanism for redistributing income, as contrasted with these voluntary arrangements. Perhaps the contrast between charity and the progressive income tax plus social security in domestic life could be extended internationally. The Marshall Plan might be said to be a form of charity, unstable because voluntary, and therefore capable of being withheld and, in some views, carrying a stigma against recipients. What is needed in international economic life, on this showing, is a scheme which regularly redistributes incomes as a matter of right for the recipients. On this showing, the family of nations would share, the way a family of individuals does, as a matter of course.

The suggestion has been made, for example, that the world should enter into a compact to provide that every country whose terms of trade improved by more than 10 per cent above a certain base should contribute to those countries whose terms of trade fell by more than 10 per cent below a certain level. This is the international equivalent to an escalator clause in a wage contract, and the pay-in and the pay-out would be governed by the degree to which the terms of trade had improved or deteriorated beyond the stipulated minima. The proposal has evidently considerable technical difficulties: What if the terms of trade of 60 per cent of the countries of the world went from 100 to 109, while the terms of trade of the other 40 per cent went from 100 to 86? Where would the funds come from to pay off the latter? But the suggestion reveals the interest in an automatic sharing device.

An intervening step between the voluntary and charitable Marshall Plan and an automatic sharing mechanism akin to progressive taxation is represented by partial sharing devices. One such was the projected European Defense Community which was defeated at the last moment by French rejection. This would have provided for the general defense with the expenses shared among those countries able to pay. The national contributions to NATO fall short of this because the decision to contribute is made each year by each nation rather than by the community as a whole. But on an *ad hoc* basis, the so-called infrastructure (or overhead capital) expenses of NATO were divided under this sort of arrangement, and for many particular objects—the sharing of the expenses of the League of Nations, the United Nations, or the special United Nations troops patrolling the Israel-Egypt frontier, the United Nations Relief and Rehabilitation Agency, and a host of similar particular projects.

It is interesting to observe that the recent ventures in returning to the market—the European Coal and Steel Community, the European Common Market, and the Scandinavian customs union—each calls for an investment fund to assist in redressing any social inequities produced by the market mechanism. If, for example, the effect of the common market is to induce capital to leave southern Italy, and thus to strand workers there, the European Investment Fund, made up of contributions from the participating Six members, would be in a position to offset it. A mechanism which operates on nonmarket or modified-market principles is thought to be needed to make the market approach acceptable and workable.

These projected bases for internationalizing common expenditures or investment in development or in conjunction with a common market differ from a wholly automatic system of the intranational type. They are paid for nationally, not by individuals regardless of nationality. And in many of them, but not the common market investment funds, the benefits accrue to nations as a whole, and not to particular localities. If the United States is assisting in the economic development of Turkey, it would make no difference if Mississippi were poorer than Istanbul. A system of internationalizing expenditures on a national basis would still be some distance from using expenditures and taxes levied on individuals to equalize incomes internationally. This would require a world budget covering a considerable number of objects of expenditure, operating with power to tax individuals.

To suggest the requirements of a system of income sharing comparable to those which now exist in most countries is to outline a form of world government going well beyond anything now proposed and to emphasize how far away the world is from readiness to accept such a proposal. Yet there is this much to be said for it, or at least about it: The development of a system of equity requires as its basis a feeling of political and social cohesion in which the various sections or segments are conscious of the well-being of the others and in sympathy one with another. A country adopts progressive income taxes and raises them when the objects of national expenditure require a significant percentage of national income, because the country fundamentally agrees that the welfare of the various members of the society is comparable and that the marginal utility of decremental units of income is smaller for higher-income recipients than for lower.

This sense of political and social cohesion, however, has further important results. It makes competition possible, at the same time that it moderates the Darwinian conclusions of that competition—that the weak fail to survive. It increases factor mobility—the cohesion of the United States makes young people almost equally at home in New England and the Middle West, in the border states or California. It makes possible a uniform system of law, which none will defy except in extreme emergency. It increases the acceptability of the everyday decisions of the market, since it is understood in advance that their most flagrant miscarriages of justice will be modified or prevented.

Economic and Political Integration

There are many who advocate achieving this sense of political and economic cohesion, which they call "integration," through developing "economic integration." Customs union, co-ordination of investment programs, functional programs to integrate the economy of iron and steel (like the Schuman Plan) or agriculture, or some other segment of economic life are to become vehicles for growing political understanding and unity.

There can be no doubt that political and economic integration are interdependent and that one cannot be achieved without the other. Yet it is important to make clear that the more difficult and the more necessary aspect of the intimately related conditions is political integration. Without the feeling of political cohesion, the institutions constructed to achieve economic integration will fail in practice, no matter how clever the experts who have devised them. The failure will not be in plans but in lack of the conditions necessary for their implementation. At the same time, going through the motions of carrying out economic integration will not produce political integration, although it may speed the process if it has been initiated and is being pushed along by other forces.

It may be objected to this statement that Zollverein in the 1830's preceded the unification of Germany in 1870. The facts are true, but the political cohesion among the German states had been a reality since the Napoleonic Wars and before. Zollverein did not create this unity. Economic integration in Europe today cannot create political cohesion, though it may assist in the process.

Halfway House

In the nineteenth-century world, a competitive mobile world could exist to the extent that it actually did, because individuals were powerless, and many states, especially Britain, subscribed to *laissez faire*. Today the requirement for a competitive world is acceptance of the verdict of the market not only by states but also by other combinations capable of affecting trade—cartels, firms, unions, farm groups, professional associations, etc. A return to *laissez faire* will not increase international efficiency if it results in merely the redistribution of income in favor of existing monopolies and oligopolies. Only when all market forces accept the verdict of a competitive market because of a sense of worldwide political and social cohesion will a return to efficiency as a system be possible.

At the present time, the world is in a halfway house, between the two extreme positions in which the market system can operate effectively. A return to *laissez faire* and market impotence is out of the question. An advance to a system of world equity, in which the economic and political integration now existing, say, within the United States can be duplicated globally, must await the development of the political and social basis. Some assistance in this direction may be afforded by such efforts as enlarging the scope of the common defense expenditures under NATO or broadening the efforts of the United Nations in economic development. But the political and social gap is too vast to be bridged in any single step or series of steps which can now be envisaged. We are required to spend some time in a position halfway between the extremes and to work out ways and means for international economic survival thus suspended.

One useful step would be for the United States to abandon the notion of reciprocity in its movement for freer trade and to undertake gradually to achieve freedom of importation into the United States, without *quid pro quo's*. The writer doubts that this would solve the world disequilibrium or even drastically reduce the export surplus of the United States. Additional dollars earned from additional exports would undoubtedly be spent on additional imports from the United States, and possibly even more. The United States should foreswear the escape clause and use different methods of taking care of the problems produced by enlarged imports, whether special subsidies to induce new industries to move to distressed areas or payments to move resources out. In a world where the United States professes to be concerned about the economic well-being of other countries, however, it is no longer sensible to give foreign countries the excuse that the responsibility for international disequilibrium belongs to the United States by trying to care for a limited volume of stranded resources at the expense of foreigners.

Another problem for policy decisions lies in export fields. Here one question is when to protest against foreign measures to exclude United States goods. Another is whether to subsidize foreign consumption or a shift in domestic production. In the latter case much will depend on the nature of the goods. Subsidization of foreign consumption of acceptable but not eagerly desired goods—the prunes, apples, tobacco, dried eggs, flour (instead of wheat), shipping, etc.—makes little sense. It might be desirable to subsidize the production of things the United States and the rest of the world wants and to shift resources out of abandoned export lines into other export and domestic industries.

What this means in both cases is the abandonment of the pretense that reciprocity is meaningful when disequilibrium is persistent. Neither reciprocal expansion of trade nor retaliatory narrowing of it makes sense, particularly if the United States believes in its own claim that it is sensible of the problems of foreign countries and national groups.

In the capital account, the task is to work to expand the level of international long-term lending, while cutting capital investment in developing countries to realistic levels. Lending, such as direct investment, which expands capital expenditure along with providing the funds to balance deficits, may be desirable in itself but does not help relieve existing stress.

There is need for a new institution of long-term lending. But institutions only develop where there is a meeting of minds. The International Bank cannot be reorganized because there are too many different views of the new directions in which it should go. The Special United Nations Fund for Economic Development represents an idea of the recipient countries unaccepted by the countries who would be chosen as providers of the wherewithal. A return to an institution like the bond sold by governments to private investors is prevented by the reluctance of some governments to honor old obligations and the fear of investors in capital markets that governments either do not want to pay their obligations or may not succeed in so doing.

Meanwhile the world has come a long way since the dark days of 1947. UNRRA, the Bank, and Fund, created amid the ties of war, have helped. The Marshall Plan helped further. A rather hesitant approach to development problems has perhaps gained a bit more. It is ironic to note that some of the greatest progress has come about through the threat or the actuality of foreign aggression. Defense efforts in Korea and western Europe and international defense spending have gone a long way to close the dollar gap. For a time there appeared a possibility that while the United States had a tendency to excessive saving compared to domestic investment, relative to the mature countries of western Europe and the underdeveloped countries of Africa, Asia, and Latin America, this was more than offset by its tendency to spend for defense at home and abroad more than these countries. (The balance-of-payments strength of Germany was that it both oversaved relative to investment and underspent in defense.) The widening balance-of-payments difficulties of the rest of the world in 1956 and 1957 are associated in part with the cutback of defense expenditures in the United States and abroad.

The world faces substantial problems—particularly the resolve of the underdeveloped countries to raise their real income by one means or another. In this circumstance, there may not be enough political and social cohesion between the developed and the underdeveloped countries to make it possible to evolve an international trade and payments system which recommends itself to every country. Gunnar Myrdal has suggested that the world integration needed for world cohesion may need to wait until economic development has narrowed the still widening gap between average national per capita incomes in the world. Until this gap begins to close, the underdeveloped countries will have no interest in an international system which imposes restraints on them.

But there may be some room for agreement. It is by no means clear that inflation and balance-of-payments deficits controlled by import restrictions are the fastest means of developing economically. If enough capital is forthcoming to enable them to achieve positive forward motion, the underdeveloped countries of the world may slowly come to appreciate that they benefit from a functioning international economy, and be prepared to accept some restraints on their conduct, in exchange for those on developed countries, and for the international lending.

SUGGESTED READING

TEXTS

Marsh's chapter xxii, which introduces his Book III, is entitled "Choosing the Ends of International Policy" and covers some of this subject.

TREATISES, ETC.

See G. Myrdal, *An International Economy* (New York: Harper & Bros., 1956), who discusses the significance of international integration in terms of factor-price equalization. For further discussion of the relations between economics and politics, see the appendix on "The Distribution of Income, Political Equilibrium and Equilibrium in the Balance of Payments," in my *The Dollar*

Shortage; and my "Group Behavior and International Trade," *JPE*, February, 1951.

POINTS

Balogh's references to international equity are scattered through *The Dollar Crisis*. See especially pages 137, 139, 150, 179–80, etc.

Wilcox's article referred to in the text is "Relief for Victims of Tariff Cuts," *AER*, December, 1950.

For a discussion of fair and equitable prices, see the United Nations experts' *Commodity Trade and Economic Development*. The proposal for international transfers when the terms of trade depart from a range is contained in this same publication at Appendix D.

See also Q. Wright, "The Mode of Financing Unions of States as a Measure of Their Degree of Integration," *International Organization,* Winter, 1957.

Appendixes

(to Chapter 3)

THE FORWARD EXCHANGE

MARKET

The Forward Exchange Market

The forward market for exchange is not normally a separate market, and it is inaccurate to speak of it as such. It is more properly regarded as a segment of the foreign-exchange market as a whole. The link between the forward and the spot rates of exchange is the rate of interest in the two markets involved, and what is known as "interest arbitrage." In the absence of anticipated movements of the foreign-exchange rate, the future rate will be the same as the spot rate if rates of interest are the same in the two money markets concerned. If the three months' interest rate is 3 per cent per annum in London and 1 per cent in New York, however, three months' sterling should sell at a discount equivalent to 2 per cent per annum. This rate, by the way, is \$2.786, given a spot rate of \$2.80 and a discount of \$0.014 (2 per cent × \$2.80 ÷ 4 = \$0.014). But a usual way to express the discount or premium is in terms of per cent per year.

If forward sterling sold at any higher figure, it would be profitable for banks in New York to put more spot funds in London and sell these forward, because they could earn more than 1 per cent. If the discount on the pound were greater or the premium on the dollar more, it would pay London banks to put more money in New York, where it could earn 1 per cent per annum plus a premium on forward dollars of more than 2 per cent. This would be better than the 3 per cent obtainable at home. Interest arbitrage, i.e., the lending of funds at interest in a foreign money market covered by forward sales of the foreign exchange, is the link between the spot and the forward market.

Interest rates may differ between national markets for a number of reasons. The monetary and banking authorities may be trying to expand or contact lending by the banks, and the rate, therefore, will be low or high, respectively. The rate may be dominated by considerations affecting the government bond market. Or, as we shall see presently, the rate may be changed upward or downward in order to attract or repel foreign funds.

When interest arbitrage is prohibited by the exchange authorities in charge of a currency, in order to limit the outflow of capital, the forward market and the spot market become separate. Discounts or premiums on a currency can now rise to as high as 30, 40, or 50 per cent per annum. Rates of this magnitude will mean that the forward market is thin; those people anxious to sell the currency forward must offer a large discount to entice buyers. Any forward sale consummated must find a forward purchaser, since swaps of spot for forward exchange are not permitted. When the forward market is cut adrift from the spot market in this way, it fails to perform its hedging function and provides only a limited outlet for a balanced number of speculative buyers and sellers.

When it is functioning as an integral portion of the foreign-exchange market as a whole, through swaps which carry out interest arbitrage, the forward market performs a credit as well as a hedging function. Suppose that a prospective importer in the United States anticipates a need for sterling. Assume that the forward dollar is at a discount and sterling at a premium, because the interest rate is higher in New York than in London. If the importer buys forward sterling, he drives the premium on forward sterling still higher. This encourages a New York bank, let us say, to buy spot sterling and sell it forward at a premium (to the importer). The spot funds transferred to London and held by a New York bank against its forward contract with the United States importer may be regarded as those which the importer will ultimately use to make his purchase. Exactly the same result would have been achieved if he had borrowed the amount from a bank in New York, bought spot sterling, and invested it at 1 per cent per annum in London until he ultimately needed it in three months. The net cost of covering the exchange risk in this case is the cost of funds in New York less the possible return in London. This is the same as the premium on sterling in the forward market. For the New York banks and for the importer it makes little difference which way the transaction is carried through, except that the importer is less well equipped than the New York banks to handle the London transaction. On this account, the forward market provides him with an alternative way to eliminate the exchange risk to that achievable through borrowing, and the hedging facility has an element of credit connected to it. By the same token, the forward market is either a device which translates the net position taken by nonbank speculators into a short-term capital movement in the spot market, or, if it is cut off from the spot market by fiat and forced to clear itself, a limited device for hedging.

Covered Working Balances

The question may be asked how the New York banks can have a covered position—i.e., assets in foreign currency equal to liabilities —and still have supplies of foreign currency on hand to sell to customers who need it. A covered position means no excess of claims or liabilities; and yet there must be a working balance of sterling to cover the requirements of customers who want to buy telegraphic transfers. The banks cannot expect to be offered each day in telegraphic transfers the foreign currency they sell each day in the same way. Like any business, they must have some inventory.

The answer lies in the forward market and in the fact that the foreign-exchange market embraces London as well as New York. All the banks in New York have a minimum need for working balances of, say, £50,000,000. It would be possible to hedge these in the forward market in New York if the banks' customers were willing to buy forward £50,000,000 more than they sold forward. But there is no reason to expect these customers to go long in the forward market by this amount. They, too, may be expected, as a rule, to have a balanced position, with spot and forward claims balanced by net spot and forward liabilities. Under these circumstances, they will not be able to buy £50,-000,000 forward from the banks, except in the unlikely situation in which they have in prospect an import surplus of £50,000,000 for which importers require more sterling than exporters are able to provide.

The solution for the banks is found by selling £50,000,000 forward in London. In order to buy this much forward sterling (sell this many dollars forward), the London banks must buy the equivalent number of dollars ($140,000,000 at $2.80) in the spot market. In this fashion, the London and New York foreign-exchange markets can be provided with working balances in each other's currencies without undertaking an exchange position, each market contracting to sell the spot exchange forward in the other. New York will then hold £50,-000,000 spot and sell the same amount forward in London. London will hold $140,000,000 in New York, which it has sold forward to New York banks. Neither country has an open exchange position. Each has an inventory of exchange for sale to customers desiring it.[1]

---

[1] It should perhaps be pointed out that the forward contract does not count as a current asset or liability in calculating capital movements. New York owns £50,000,000

If New York banks on balance want to open an exchange position, let us say £2,000,000 short, they can now sell this amount spot or forward. The spot sale will simply eliminate £2,000,000 of their £50,-000,000 of working balances (a capital inflow into the United States, it may be observed). If they choose to make a forward sale, however, this must be done in London unless the nonbanking public in the United States fortuitously undertakes an equal exchange position of opposite sign, i.e., is willing to go £2,000,000 long. The forward sale of sterling in London by New York banks will require London banks to sell dollars and buy sterling forward. In order to keep their position covered, the latter will be obliged to buy more dollars spot. In this way the sale of forward sterling by New York banks would result in an increase in London deposits in New York (a capital inflow into the United States) in the amount of $5,600,000.

SUGGESTED READINGS

A small literature exists on the forward exchanges, notable among which are J. M. Keynes, *Monetary Reform* (New York: Harcourt, Brace & Co., Inc., 1924), chap. III, sec. 4; and P. Einzig, *The Theory of the Forward Exchange* (London: Macmillan & Co., Ltd., 1937). For other references, see A. I. Bloomfield, *Capital Imports and the American Balance of Payments, 1934–39* (Chicago: University of Chicago Press, 1950), p. 21 note.

---

and owes $140,000,000 spot. It is therefore on balance neither a borrower nor a lender. Conversely, London has a balance of assets and liabilities. So far as the capital movement is concerned, the currencies in which claims and debts are denominated make no difference. The forward contract is neither an asset nor a liability except in a contingent sense, in which it is both, so that it does not count in reckoning the balance of indebtedness.

(to Chapter 5)

PRODUCTION, FACTOR

SUPPLY, AND TRADE

The Derivation of the Transformation Curve
from the Production Function

A production function is a statement of the relationships between physical quantities of inputs of factors and the physical output of a given commodity. Geometrically it can be shown by plotting the various combinations of two factors needed to produce given amounts of the commodity in question. In Figure B.1a, T–T is an *isoquant* representing equal quantities of a single commodity, cloth. T'–T' is a higher isoquant, i.e., a greater amount of cloth such as 200 yards, in comparison with the 100 yards represented by T–T. At any given point such as W, the ratio of marginal physical products of labor and land is equal to the ratio of the prices of the two factors. A line tangent to an insoquant therefore represents the relative price of land and labor. Given the production point W one can deduce the relative price of the factors, equal to the slope S–S, or given the quantity to be produced, T–T and the price of the factors, S–S, one can find the least-cost combination, W. OR is an expansion path for the relative price S–S (to which S'–S' is parallel). By adding inputs of land and capital, with the relative prices equal to the slope of S–S, one proceeds to higher isoquants by the path OR. If there are constant returns to scale, the expansion path at constant factor price will be a straight line. This simplest form of production function is called *linear homogeneous*. The isoquant T–T in Figure B.1a shows that labor can fairly easily be substituted physically for land, in the production of cloth, and vice versa.

The foregoing is by way of review. In Figure B.1b we show two production functions, for wheat and cloth, in which factor proportions are rigidly fixed but different in each commodity. The expansion paths, OX for cloth and OY for wheat, are straight lines for any positive set of factor prices. Any different set of factor proportions, such as OR instead of OW on the isoquant T–T will reduce the marginal physical product of one factor (in this case land) to zero. Its price will also fall to zero.

In Figure B.1*b* cloth is unambiguously labor-intensive and wheat unambiguously land-intensive. At any positive relative price of land and labor, cloth will use more labor relative to land than wheat.

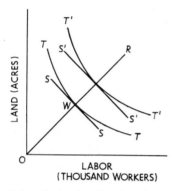
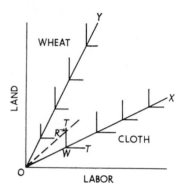

FIG. B.1*a*. Production Function for Cloth

FIG. B.1*b*. Production Functions with Fixed Factor Proportions

In Figure B.2 we construct a so-called Edgeworth box diagram, in which the dimensions of the box represent the amounts of capital and labor in a country, which we shall call Britain. The production

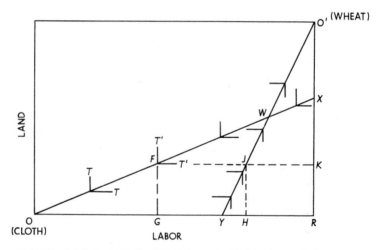

FIG. B.2. Edgeworth-Bowley Box Diagram with Fixed Factor Proportions

function for cloth is drawn with its origin in the lower left-hand corner of the box at *O*, and with its isoquants, *T–T*, *T'–T'*, etc., moving out and up to the right. Its expansion path is *OX*. If all the labor in

Britain (*OR*) were used to make cloth, only *RX* of land would be required, and *O'X* of land would be left unemployed. At *X*, the marginal physical product of land would be zero.

The production function for wheat is drawn reversed and upside down, with its origin at *O'* and extending downward and to the left. Its expansion path is *OY*. At *Y*, all the land would be employed, and *YR* of labor, but *OY* of labor would be unemployed. *OX* and *O'Y* intersect at *W* which is the only production point in the box diagram where there can be full employment and positive prices for both factors. At any other point on either expansion path, say *F*, on *OX*, land and labor will be able to produce at *J* on the expansion path for wheat; *OG* of labor will be engaged in cloth, and *HR* in wheat. *KR* of land will be employed in cloth, and *KO'* in wheat. But *GH* of labor will be unemployed.

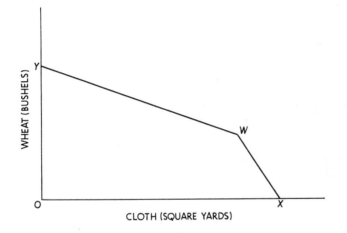

FIG. B.3. Transformation Curve Derived from Edgeworth-Bowley Box Diagram with Fixed Factor Proportions

The curve *OWO'* is a transformation curve, showing the various combinations of wheat and cloth which can be produced in Britain, given the factor endowments of the country. The only point providing full employment of the two factors and positive factor prices is *W*. *OWO'* does not look like a transformation curve, because it is given in terms of physical units of land and labor, rather than physical units of production. If we express the graph in terms of units of wheat and cloth, and turn it right side up, it appears to be a normal production-possibilities curve, though kinked at *W*, as in Figure B.3.

If cloth and wheat were produced with fixed-factor coefficients, and these were identical, the two expansion paths would coincide, as in

B.4*a*, and the transformation curve becomes a straight line as in B.4*b*. But this means that land and labor are always used in the same combination so that they might well be regarded as a single factor. This is equivalent to the labor theory of value and its resultant straight-line transformation curve. A similar straight-line transformation curve would be produced by constant costs and identical production functions in the two commodities. But note the difference between constant costs and constant opportunity costs. The straight-line transformation curve represents constant opportunity costs. If the production functions for the two commodities differ, the transformation curve will exhibit curvature even though there be constant returns to scale in each commodity taken separately.

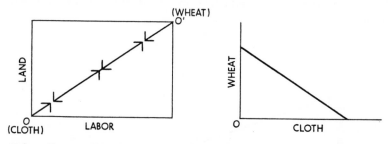

FIG. B.4*a*. Constant Opportunity Costs: Identical Fixed Factor Proportions

FIG. B.4*b*. Transformation Curve Derived from Figure B.4*a*

Where there is the possibility of substitution between the factors in the production of both commodities, there are no unique expansion paths of the separate production functions. Instead, we draw the locus of successive points of tangency between the two sets of isoquants. This locus represents the maximum efficiency path and is shown in B.5*a*. Suppose that production were to take place at *W*, off the maximum efficiency locus. *W* is on cloth isoquant 7, and on wheat isoquant 5. But there is a point *T*, also on cloth isoquant 7, which is on a higher isoquant (6) of wheat. It would be possible, therefore, to produce more wheat without giving up any cloth. The point *W*, off the efficiency locus, is not optimal.

The maximum efficiency locus, which is called the "contract curve," when the Edgeworth-Bowley box is used in the theory of consumption, is further instructive because it shows factor combinations and factor prices. Unlike the transformation curve (B.5*b*), however, it cannot show the relative price of wheat and cloth. If we assume that production is at *T*, however, the factor proportions in cloth are represented by the slope of *OT*, and the factor proportions in wheat by *O'T*.

It will be obvious that these proportions employ all the land and all the labor. The relative price of land and labor with these outputs is represented by the slope of the tangency to the maximum efficiency locus at *T*.

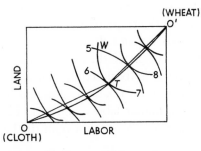

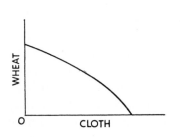

Fig. B.5*a*. Maximum Efficiency Locus under Variable Factor Proportions

Fig. B.5*b*. Transformation Curve Derived from Figure B.5*a*

Factor Price Equalization

In Figure B.6 we construct two Edgeworth-Bowley boxes representing the different factor endowments and linear-homogeneous production functions of Britain and America in wheat and cloth assumed to be identical. They are given a common origin in cloth at *O*. The dif-

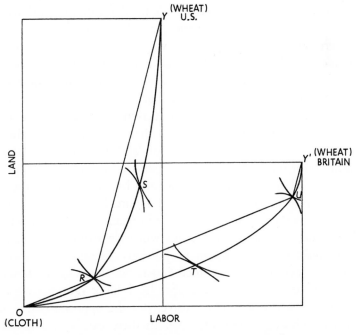

Fig. B.6. Factor-Price Equalization after Trade

ferent factor proportions result in two separate origins for wheat, Y in the United States and Y' for Britain. The maximum efficiency loci are OY for the United States and OY' for Britain. Before trade, both countries are assumed to be producing and consuming at S and T, respectively, determined separately by demand conditions. The land/labor ratio is higher in wheat and cloth, respectively, in the United States than in Britain. (The diagonals are not drawn in, to simplify the diagram, but OS is steeper than OT in cloth, and SY than TY' in wheat.) With more land employed in both commodities in the United States than in Britain, land will be relatively less expensive, compared to labor. Conversely, with a higher labor/land ratio in both commodities, Britain will have a lower return to labor than the United States.

When trade becomes possible, it is assumed that prices are fully equalized in the two countries because of the absence of transport costs and other barriers to trade. With identical production functions showing constant returns, and equal prices of goods produced, the returns to factors must be identical if the factor proportions in the production of each commodity are identical between countries—if, that is, trade results in production at such points as R and U. At R and U, the equality of factor proportions is demonstrated by the fact that R lies on the straight-line OU (there are identical factor proportions in the production of cloth in both countries) and YR and $Y'U$ are parallel.

There are a variety of reasons why two such points as R and U may not exist. After trade, one or both countries may be completely specialized, Britain producing cloth at Y' or the United States wheat at O. Demand conditions may be so sharply different in the two countries that trade results in shifting production in the United States from S toward Y, rather than toward O so that it would export the labor-intensive good despite its abundance of land. Or land and labor may so substitute for one another in the production of either cloth or wheat that wheat is labor-intensive in Britain and land-intensive in the United States. This possibility is illustrated in Figure B.7 where each production function is represented by a single isoquant. Here the definition of which product is land-intensive and which labor-intensive cannot be settled without specifying factor proportions. These are represented by rays from the origin. In the United States, the slopes of the tangents to the respective isoquants show a higher land/labor ratio for wheat than that for cloth; wheat is land-intensive. But the opposite is true in Britain, where wheat is labor-intensive. In these conditions, it has been shown that the contract curves in a diagram such as Figure B.6 move on opposite sides of the diagonals to the boxes and factor-price equalization is impossible. And it is evident that if both countries export the

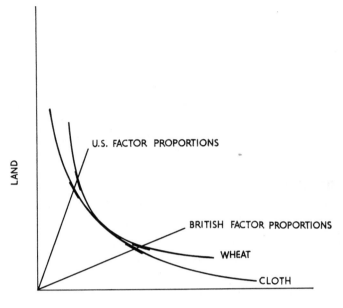

FIG. B.7. Factor Intensity of Commodities Where Production Functions Permit Wide Range of Substitution

labor-intensive or the land-intensive good (although each exports a different good), factor prices will be widened, not equalized.

Opportunity Costs versus Real Costs

The original theorists who developed the law of comparative costs using the labor theory of value thought of labor as disutility and of the cost of goods as a real cost. With the substitution of the law of variable proportions for the labor theory of value, there was seen to be a difficulty. Land and capital may not involve real costs. One can think not of real costs, but only of the opportunity cost, i.e., the cost of giving up something else.

Real-cost theorists, however, have not been willing to abandon their position. In particular, Professor Viner has continued to adhere to a real-cost position, claiming that in many respects one can regard labor as the main cost, or capital as past labor, and adhere to something very close to the labor theory of value. Less time is spent in defense, however, than in attack. The opportunity-cost doctrine is strongly criticized for its assumption that men are indifferent among occupations and willing to work no matter what the price of labor. This assumption of inelastic supplies of factors is evidently unrealistic. If the transformation schedule is built up out of production functions which are statements of physical possibilities, there is no necessary reason, in Viner's view, why a country should be on the frontier of its transformation curve rather than somewhere inside it. The implicit assumption of the transformation curve that the supply of factors is completely inelastic vitiates its validity. The opportunity-cost doctrine has no room for the possibility that trade enables a country to work less for the same real income rather than work the same amount and earn a higher return in commodities.

But difficulties are not absent from the real-cost side. It is impermissible to gloss over the question of the absence of real costs in land, and the sunk character of real costs in capital. More, the doctrine fails to take account of the possibility that different people have different responses to different kinds of work, so that a given volume of output will represent a different real cost depending upon who is engaged in it.

This dispute between the real and the opportunity cost view is largely unresolved. Opportunity-cost theorists emphasize the differences among outputs; real-cost theorists the differences among inputs. Both have part of the truth; neither a monopoly.

SUGGESTED READING

The literature on the relations of factors to trade has grown enormously since Professor Leontief's pathbreaking "Domestic Production and Foreign Trade; the American Capital Position Re-examined," *Proceedings of the American Philosophical Society,* September, 1953, reprinted in *Economia Internazionale,* February, 1954. Of especial importance are R. Robinson, "Factor Proportions and Comparative Advantage," *QJE,* May and November, 1956; R. W. Jones, "Factor Proportions and the Heckscher-Ohlin Theorem," *RES,* November, 1956. See also T. Rybcynski, "Factor Endowment and Relative Commodity Prices," *Econ,* November, 1955, and K. Lancaster, "The Heckscher-Ohlin Trade Model: A Geometric Treatment," *Econ,* February, 1957.

The literature on factor-price equalization is very extensive, and cannot be mentioned in its entirety. The articles of P. A. Samuelson in the *EJ* for June, 1948, and June, 1949, deserve mention, along with A. P. Lerner, "Factor Prices and International Trade," *Econ,* February, 1952; S. F. James and I. F. Pearce, "The Factor-Price Equalization Myth," *RES,* 1951–52; L. MacKenzie, "Equality of Factor Prices in World Trade," *Econ,* July, 1955. See also the excellent presentation of J. E. Meade in *Trade and Welfare,* pp. 331–92.

On the controversy between real and opportunity costs, see Viner, pp. 489–

93, and Haberler, pp. 126, 175. See also G. Haberler, "Real Costs and Opportunity Costs," in *International Social Science Bulletin,* Spring, 1951. J. Vanek has in preparation an article distinguishing the *technical* transformation curve derived from production functions which does not allow for unemployment, and an *economic* transformation curve which takes into account the responses of factors to changes in factor prices, disutility in different occupations, etc. It will be too bad in a way to resolve this interesting controversy.

(to Chapter 6)

THE RELATION OF THE OFFER CURVE TO THE PRODUCTION-POSSIBILITIES CURVE AND THE CONSUMPTION-INDIFFERENCE MAP

In the first edition, the statement was made that the offer curve assumed fixed supplies of the two goods. This is not necessarily the case. Recently Professor Meade has set out a neat geometric device, building the offer curve out of the production-possibilities curve and the consumption-indifference map. The beauty of the technique rests partly in its bridging this gap, but also in that it enables one to demonstrate neatly and simply, the impact of trade on production, consumption, the gains from trade, etc. While many students may remain terrified at the prospect of learning still another geometric technique, the braver among you are encouraged to plunge ahead and acquire a highly useful analytical tool.

The first step is to draw the production block and consumption-indifference curve for country A without trade, in the usual way, except for the fact that they are in the northwest rather than the usual northeast quadrant of the system of co-ordinates. This is done in Figure C.1. Following Meade's notation, the horizontal axis measures A's exportables, which are B's importables; the vertical axis, B's exportables.

Now, holding it level and upright, slide the A production block up and down the no-trade consumption-indifference curve, keeping it tangent to the same consumption-indifference curve, *I*. The origin of the block, *O*, will trace out a trade-indifference curve *i*. At every point on this curve, A will be indifferent whether it trades or not. It can remain at O and produce and consume at *F*. Or it can move along the curve to the point where the origin of its production-possibilities block is at *T*. It will then produce at *G*, and trade *HT* of A-exportables for

604

HO of B-exportables. The reason that it is indifferent between *O* and *T* is that it can produce at either *F* or *G* along its production-possibilities schedule (transformation along the schedule is assumed to be costless); and *G* is on the same consumption-indifference curve as *F*. At *G*, of course, it consumes *GS + HO* of B-exportables, and only *SH* of A-exportables.

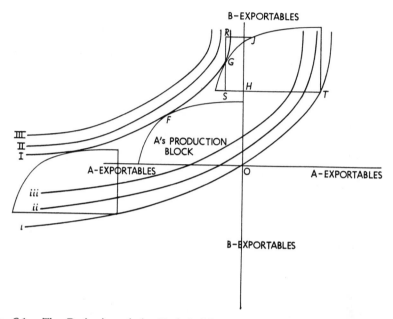

Fig. C.1. The Derivation of the Trade-Indifference Map from the Consumption-Indifference Map

Note that the trade-indifference curve has a different shape than the consumption-indifference curve. This is because production has shifted as well as the proportion of goods consumed. If *J* in the upper right-hand position of the A-block corresponds to *F* in the no-trade position, it is clear that in shifting from *O* to *T*, production of A-exportables has increased by *RJ*, and production of B-exportables decreased by *RG*. A trade-indifference curve is flatter to take account of these production changes. When production is fixed and no movement of resources is possible, the trade-indifference curve will parallel the consumption one.

There is a trade-indifference curve corresponding to every consumption-indifference curve, and hence a trade-indifference map. A country is better off, the higher a trade-indifference curve it is able to reach. Along any single curve, it is indifferent between one position and another. But in Figure C.1 country A is better off the higher the trade-indifference curve it can reach (moving from SE to NW).

A's offer curve will now be constructed. It represents the locus of a series of tangencies of various price lines to the trade-indifference curves. This is shown in Figure C.2. The initial slope of the offer curve

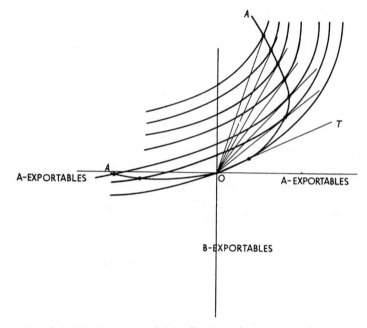

Fig. C.2. The Derivation of the Offer Curve for Country A from Its Trade-Indifference Map

through the origin represents the price which would prevail without trade. As higher and higher prices for A-exportables are offered in terms of B-exportables, A will be enabled to move to higher and higher trade-indifference curves, and will be disposed to offer, as the figure is drawn, more and more A-goods for B-goods. Note that if the price for B-goods gets higher than *OT,* A will export B-exportables in exchange for A-goods. The offer curve moves into the SW quadrant, but only for very high prices for B-exportables, which have their name belied by being imported by B.

Country B's offer curve can similarly be traced out from a series of trade-indifference curves imposed on the same set of co-ordinates, but developed from sliding B's production-possibilities block along its consumption-indifference curves in the SE quadrant. Figure C.3 shows the A and B offer curves intersecting at the balanced trade position where the terms-of-trade line, *OT,* is tangent to trade-indifference curves of A and B and go to the origin. There are other tangencies of trade-indifference curves, and a contract-curve, *K–K,* may be drawn along them. Only at the intersection of *OA* and *OB,* however, do the terms of trade balance A's exports and B's imports under free trade.

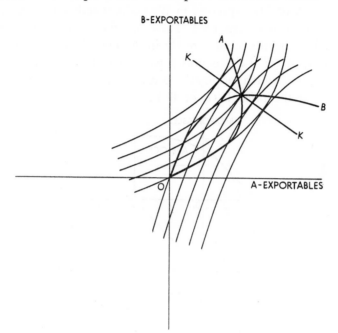

Fɪɢ. C.3.   The Contract Curve and Trade Equilibrium

These three figures neatly show the relationship of the offer curve to consumption-indifference curves and to production. The technique can be used in its simple manifestation, however, to show the gains from trade. This is done by leaving the A and B production-possibilities blocks at the trading position, as in Figure C.4. Trade- and consumption-indifference curves and the offer curves are omitted to eliminate clutter.

In Figure C.4, production is measured from the intersection of the origins, *T,* of the production blocks. In A, production consists of *QG* of B-exportables and *GM* of A-exportables. B produces *NH* of B-exportables and *FH* of A-exportables. These outputs can readily be added to give production of *GJ* of A-exportables in the two countries and *JH* of B-exportables.

Consumption is measured from the original co-ordinates, intersecting at *O*. A consumes only *GR* of A-exportables, but *GL* of B-exportables; in its turn, B consumes only *SH* of its B-good, and *KH* of the A-exportable. This is made possible by trade, in which A exchanges

DT of the A-good against *TE* of the B-good, at the terms of trade *OT*.

This is a free-trade position, without transport costs. Thus the terms of trade are equal to the internal prices (*WP* and *ZH* are parallel to *OT* and to each other). National income in A is *WO* expressed in A-exportables, or *PO* expressed in B's good, whether we take income produced, or income consumed. These are the same because trade is balanced. Income produced directly in A-goods is *YO*, which is the same as *GM* or *QT* (*YQ* is drawn parallel to *OT*). That part of income produced which originally consisted of B-goods, *GQ*, is the equivalent, at the price *WG*, of *WY*.

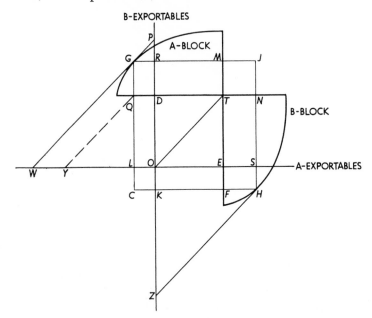

FIG. C.4. Production and Consumption under Trading

Taking income consumed, *GR* of A-exportables is equal to *LO*, and *GL* of B-exportables, at the price *WG* is the equivalent in A-exportables of *WL*. *WL + LO = WO*. Similar exercises can be carried through for national income in A measured in B-goods and for income produced and consumed in B in either good.

The gains from trade are more elusive and present an index-number problem. We can measure the gain in terms either of A's prices before trade, or A's prices after trade. In Figure C.5, *a* and *b* are the before-trade terms of trade drawn to the A production block after and before trade, respectively. On the other hand, *c* and *d* represent the post-trade prices drawn to the same block positions; *a*, *b*, *c*, and *d* intersect the horizontal axis at A,B,C, and D. The gains from trade in A, expressed in A-exportables, may then be regarded *AB,* using the terms of trade before trade, or *CD,* representing it in after-trade prices. But one should not make the mistake of regarding the gains from

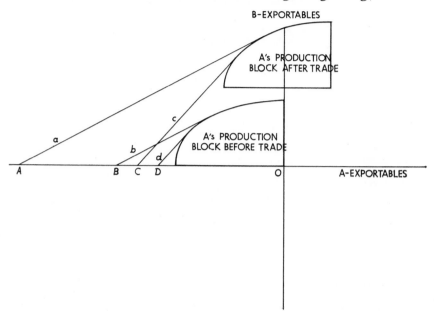

FIG. C.5. The Gains from Trade Measured in Terms of A-exportables

trade as measured from the national income in the no-trade position at no-trade prices (*BO*) to national income with trade at the with-trade price (*CO*). In that event, the gain from trade would be negative, or a loss (*BC*).

SUGGESTED READING

This appendix is based on J. E. Meade, *A Geometry of International Trade,* chap. i–iv.

We seek to establish the condition under which a depreciation of the exchange rate will improve a country's balance of trade. In this derivation, the balance of trade will be measured in foreign currency; a derivation in terms of domestic currency follows the same general principles but would result in a slightly different condition whenever the value of exports differed from the value of imports. It seems more natural, however, to express the balance of trade in terms of foreign currency.

The usual treatment proceeds as if exports and imports each consisted of a single homogeneous commodity. This procedure is, of course, contrary to the facts, but it illustrates the conditions involved well enough.

The following notation will be used:

X = physical quantity of exports
M = physical quantity of imports
p_x, p_m = foreign prices of exports and imports, respectively
q_x, q_m = domestic prices of exports and imports
r = exchange rate, expressed as units of domestic currency paid per unit of foreign currency
ϵ_x = (foreign) elasticity of demand for exports
ϵ_m = (domestic) elasticity of demand for imports

By definition, $p_x = \dfrac{q_x}{r}$ and $q_m = p_m \cdot r$.

Functional dependence will be denoted by round brackets following the dependent variable. The demand for exports is a function of their foreign price, or $X = X\ (p_x) = X\left(\dfrac{q_x}{r}\right)$. Total revenue from exports (in foreign currency) will then be $X\left(\dfrac{q_x}{r}\right) \cdot \dfrac{q_x}{r}$. Demand for

[1] By Egon Sohmen.

610

imports is a function of their domestic price, or $M = M\ (q_m) = M\ (p_m \cdot r)$, and total expenditure on imports in terms of foreign currency becomes $M\ (p_m \cdot r) \cdot p_m$.

As a consequence, the balance of trade in terms of foreign currency is:

$$B = X\left(\frac{q_x}{r}\right) \cdot \frac{q_x}{r} - M\ (p_m \cdot r) \cdot p_m . \qquad (1)$$

A simplifying assumption, usually made to render the derivation more easily manageable, is that the supply elasticities in both countries are infinite, so that the domestic prices of each country's exports when expressed in its own currency (q_x and p_m in our notation), are constants. The assumption does, of course, some violence to the facts. A general formula for the case in which this restriction is removed will be given at the end of this appendix.

With q_x and p_m assumed constant, the balance of trade becomes a function of the exchange rate alone, and the effect of a change in the exchange rate is found by differentiating $B(r)$ with respect to the exchange rate:

$$\frac{dB}{dr} = \frac{dX}{d\left(\frac{q_x}{r}\right)} \cdot \left\{-\frac{q_x}{r^2}\right\}\frac{q_x}{r} + X \cdot \left\{-\frac{q_x}{r^2}\right\} - \frac{dM}{d(p_m \cdot r)} \cdot p_m{}^2 . \qquad (2)^2$$

This can be rewritten:

$$\frac{dB}{dr} = X \cdot \frac{q_x}{r^2}\left\{\frac{dX}{d\left(\frac{q_x}{r}\right)}\left[-\frac{\frac{q_x}{r}}{X}\right] - 1\right\} + \frac{M \cdot p_m}{r}\left\{-\frac{dM}{d(p_m \cdot r)}\frac{p_m \cdot r}{M}\right\} . \qquad (3)$$

In the first bracket, we recognize the foreign demand elasticity for exports, ϵ_x, in the second, the domestic elasticity of import demand, ϵ_m. The minus signs make the expressions for the elasticities positive

[2] Mathematical note: The reader will recognize that use has been made of the rules for the differentiation of a product,

$$\frac{d(u \cdot v)}{dx} = \frac{du}{dx} \cdot v + u\frac{dv}{dx},$$

and of a fraction

$$\frac{d\left(\frac{c}{x}\right)}{dx} = -\frac{c}{x^2},$$

where c is a constant.

(in the absence of Giffen's paradox). We can therefore take their absolute value and write

$$\frac{dB}{dr} = X\frac{q_x}{r^2}\left\{|\epsilon_x| - 1\right\} + \frac{M \cdot p_m}{r}|\epsilon_m| . \tag{4}$$

With our definition of the exchange rate, a depreciation is indicated by an increase of r. To improve the balance of trade, it will have to result in a rise of B, the balance of trade. The condition for a successful depreciation is therefore

$$\frac{dB}{dr} > 0,$$

or, after some reshuffling,

$$\frac{M \cdot p_m}{X \cdot \frac{q_x}{r}}|\epsilon_m| + |\epsilon_x| > 1 . \tag{5}$$

$X \cdot \dfrac{q_x}{r}$ is the value of exports,

$M \cdot p_m$ the value of imports, both expressed in terms of foreign currency. If trade was balanced to begin with, the above condition says that the sum of the demand elasticities has to exceed unity if a small depreciation should be successful. This is the Marshall-Lerner condition in its original form.

If there is an import surplus $\left(M \cdot p_m > X \cdot \dfrac{q_x}{r}\right)$, a (small) devaluation will still result in an improvement even if the sum of the demand elasticities falls below unity. The permissible deficiency depends on the size of the trade deficit, as indicated in the condition above.

Relaxing the assumption that both supply elasticities are infinite, the general condition becomes[3]

$$\left[\frac{M \cdot p_m}{X \cdot \frac{q_x}{r}}\right]\frac{|\epsilon_m|(1 + \eta_m)}{|\epsilon_m| + \eta_m} - \frac{\eta_x(1 - |\epsilon_x|)}{\eta_x + \epsilon_x} > 0, \tag{6}$$

where η_x and η_m are the supply elasticities of exports and imports, respectively.

[3] See Joan Robinson, *AEA Readings,* p. 90, n. 8 for a method of derivation. Mrs. Robinson, however, works with the balance of trade in terms of domestic currency, rather than in foreign currency as above.

(to Chapter 10)

THE FOREIGN-TRADE

MULTIPLIER[1]

Notation and Assumptions

Y_a = national income in country A
C_a = private domestic consumption in country A
G_a = governmental expenditure in country A
I_a = domestic private investment in country A
M_a = imports in country A
X_a = exports of country A
S_a = savings in country A
α = a parameter expressing a parallel shift in any one of the expenditure schedules
λ = an arbitrary constant relating a shift in spending in B to a shift in A.

A similar notation with the subscript b applies to country B.

C_a, M_a, I_a, G_a, and S_a are assumed to be continuous differentiable functions of Y_a; and similarly for country B. Consumption is a function of income rather than disposal income, i.e., taxes and subsidies are not precluded but are assumed for simplicity to be independent of the level of income.

We write "primes" for first partial derivatives of the functions. Thus, for example, $M_a' = \dfrac{\partial M_a}{\partial Y_a}$.

The latter will be recognized as the marginal propensity to import in country A, discussed in the text, and similarly for other expenditure and saving functions of Y_a. This is merely to simplify the notation.

Derivation of the General Formula for the Multiplier, $\dfrac{dY_a}{d\alpha}$

Since one country's exports must be another country's imports (i.e., $X_a = M_b$ and $X_b = M_a$), we can write the basic income identities in the two countries as

[1] By Jaroslav Vanek.

613

$$Y_a = C_a + G_a + I_a + M_b + \alpha \, , \qquad (1)$$

and

$$Y_b = C_b + G_b + I_b + M_a - \lambda\alpha \, . \qquad (2)$$

In the initial equilibrium, α is assumed equal to zero; a parallel shift of any component of income may be expressed as a small change in α away from its equilibrium value.

Differentiating relations (1) and (2) totally with respect to α and rearranging, we obtain

$$[1 - C_a' - G_a' - I_a']\frac{dY_a}{d\alpha} - M_b'\frac{dY_b}{d\alpha} = 1 \, , \qquad (3)$$

and

$$[1 - C_b' - G_b' - I_b']\frac{dY_b}{d\alpha} - M_a'\frac{dY_a}{d\alpha} = -\lambda \, . \qquad (4)$$

Or, in matrix notation,

$$\begin{bmatrix} (1 - C_a' - G_a' - I_a') & -M_b' \\ -M_a' & (1 - C_b' - G_b' - I_b') \end{bmatrix} \begin{bmatrix} \dfrac{dY_a}{d\alpha} \\ \dfrac{dY_b}{d\alpha} \end{bmatrix} = \begin{bmatrix} 1 \\ -\lambda \end{bmatrix}. \qquad (5)$$

Solving for $\dfrac{dY_a}{d\alpha}$, we obtain[2]

$$\frac{dY_a}{d\alpha} = \frac{1}{\Delta}[(1 - C_b' - G_b' - I_b') - \lambda M_b'] \, , \qquad (6)$$

where Δ is the determinant of the coefficient matrix, i.e.,

$$\Delta = (1 - C_a' - G_a' - I_a')(1 - C_b' - G_b' - I_b') - M_a'M_b' \, . \qquad (7)$$

Relation (6) is the most general form of the foreign trade multiplier.

Particular Multipliers

1. Foreign-trade multiplier without foreign repercussion.

In this case we assume income of country B to be independent of changes in α, i.e., $\dfrac{dY_b}{d\alpha} = 0$. Equation (3) then suffices to determine

[2] Readers unfamiliar with matrix algebra may check the result (relation (6)) by solving (3) for $\dfrac{dY_b}{d\alpha}$, substituting the result in (4) and solving for $\dfrac{dY_a}{d\alpha}$.

the multiplier. Solving (3) for $\dfrac{dY_a}{d\alpha}$, we get

$$\frac{dY_a}{d\alpha} = \frac{1}{1 - C_a' - G_a' - I_a'} . \tag{8}$$

Assuming, as in the text, that government spending and domestic private investment are independent of the level of income, i.e., $G_a' = 0$, and $I'_a = 0$, we get

$$\frac{dY_a}{d\alpha} = \frac{1}{1 - C_a'} . \tag{8'}$$

We know that under our assumptions $1 - C_a' = S_a' + M_a'$. Consequently (8') can be written as

$$\frac{dY_a}{d\alpha} = \frac{1}{M_a' + S_a'} . \tag{8''}$$

2. Multipliers with foreign repercussion.
i. $\lambda = 1$

We observe from relation (2) that when $\lambda = 1$, an initial increase in income of country A will be matched by an equal initial decline in income of country B. This will occur any time an initial increase of imports of country B (exports of country A) is accompanied by an equal decline in domestic spending in B, or when, as in capital transfers, new savings in B are matched by new spending in A.

In this case, relation (6) reduces to

$$\frac{dY_a}{d\alpha} = \frac{1}{\triangle} \left[(1 - C_b' - G_b' - I_b') - M_b' \right] . \tag{9}$$

Assuming again $I' = 0$ and $G' = 0$, with $1 - C' = S' + M'$, we obtain from (9)

$$\frac{dY_a}{d\alpha} = \frac{S_b'}{(M_a' + S_a')(M_b' + S_b') - M_a' M_b'} , \tag{9'}$$

and after some simplification,

$$\frac{dY_a}{d\alpha} = \frac{1}{M_a' + S_a' + M_b' \dfrac{S_a'}{S_b'}} , \tag{9''}$$

which is the formula on page 192.
ii. $\lambda = 0$

When $\lambda = 0$, it follows from relations (1) and (2) that the initial change in spending in country A is not matched by an initial change in B, even though all subsequent changes in income are inter-related. This may be the case for any one of a number of reasons:

a) There may be an autonomous increase in consumption, investment, or government spending in country A or a reduction in taxes;
b) Country B may increase its imports from A without a reduction in domestic expenditure.

In any of these circumstances, relation (6) reduces to

$$\frac{dY_a}{d\alpha} = \frac{1}{\triangle} [1 - C_b' - G_b' - I_b'] . \tag{10}$$

With $I' = G' = 0$, and $1 - C' = S' + M'$ in both countries, we obtain the formulation of the foreign-trade multiplier on page 192:

$$\frac{dY_a}{d\alpha} = \frac{1 + \dfrac{M_b'}{S_b'}}{M_a' + S_a' + M_b' \dfrac{S_a'}{S_b'}} . \tag{10'}$$

iii. $0 < \lambda < 1$

An infinity of intermediate cases can be envisaged where a change in spending in A is matched in part, but not wholly by an opposite change in spending in B. Thus, for example, if country B increases its imports from A half out of savings and half as a substitute for domestic goods, $\lambda = \frac{1}{2}$. In all these cases, one must use the most general expression of the foreign-trade multiplier with foreign repercussion, set out in (6).

SUGGESTED READING

See the articles by R. Robinson and L. A. Metzler in the reading recommendations to Chapter 10. See also F. D. Holzman and A. Zellner, "The Foreign Trade Multiplier and the Balanced-Budget Multiplier," *AER,* March, 1958. Holzman and Zellner make allowance for the fact that some exports out of previously produced goods such as stocks may not increase income, and some imports may not be consumed or invested. This requires the use of coefficients on M_a and M_b to relate exports to income-increasing, and imports to income-decreasing, expenditures.

Appendix F | (to Chapter 12)
THE OPTIMUM TARIFF

A tariff improves the terms of trade when there is elasticity to the foreign offer curve. But a country must be careful not to raise the tariff too high, or the loss in the quantity of trade will outweigh the improvement in the terms of trade. What is the tariff which

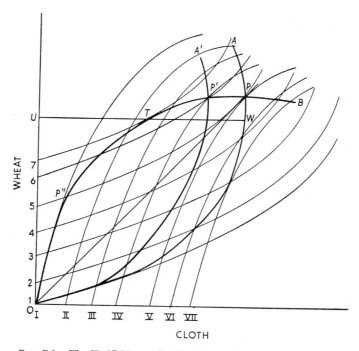

FIG. F.1. The Tariff-Distorted Offer Curve and the Optimum Tariff

will maximize a country's gain, improving the terms of trade to the highest point before this gain is offset by excessive reductions in trade volume?

Figure F.1 shows the offers curves of Britain (*A*) and the United

States (*B*) in terms of cloth and wheat, together with the relevant trade-indifference curves of the two countries, 1, 2, 3, 4, 5, 6, and 7 for Britain and *i, ii, iii, iv, v, vi,* and *vii* for the United States. The two offer curves intersect at *P,* which makes *OP* the free-trade terms of trade. Britain is on trade-indifference curve 5; the United States on number *v.*

The imposition of a tariff by Britain will distort its offer curve by moving it to the left to *A'* while holding the origin at *0.* A 20 per cent import tariff on wheat will shift the curve upwards, if the tariff is to be collected in wheat, or, what amounts to the same thing, leftward, if it is to take the form of giving less cloth for the same amount of wheat. The new British offer curve will intersect the United States offer curve at *P'* and produce new terms of trade *OP'* (not drawn). They will also land Britain on a higher indifference curve (6), while setting the United States back to a lower indifference curve (*iv*). A still higher tariff which shifts A's offer curve so that it intersects the *B* offer curve at *P''*, would keep Britain on the same trade indifference curve as under free trade (number 5). Between these is the point (*T*), where the United States offer curve is tangent to the highest possible British trade-indifference curve (7). This calls for a larger tariff than our first, in this case a tariff close to 100 per cent $\left(\dfrac{TW}{UT}\right)$. But it is much smaller than the limiting tariff at *P''* of something like 600 per cent, which would make the United States virtually indifferent whether it trades or not.

Figure F.2 presents another method of measuring a tariff. Point *T* is on the United States offer curve (*B*). At *T,* the United States is willing to trade *TQ* of wheat for *OQ* of cloth. But the price line *OT* (not drawn) is not tangent to a British trade-indifference curve, and Britain will not be in equilibrium trading *OQ* of cloth. Britain will trade at *T* only at a price tangent to its trade-indifference curve at *T*. Draw such a tangency and extend it through the vertical axis at *R* to the horizontal axis at *S*. This is the equilibrium price in Britain. Britain will trade at *ST* and the United States at *OT* if exports of cloth *OQ* are subject to an export tax of $\dfrac{SO}{OQ}$ in Britain, or if imports of wheat *UR* are subject to an import tax of $\dfrac{RO}{UR}$. For comparability with the discussion of Figure F.1 take the former.

What is the elasticity of the *B* offer curve at *T?* To measure the elasticity of a point on an offer curve we must draw a tangent at the given point and extend it to the relevant axis (the vertical axis for the

B offer curve, the horizontal axis for *OA*). We must also drop a straight line, *UT*, to the relevant axis. The elasticity of the offer curve at the given point is represented by the distance from the point of intersection of the straight line on the vertical axis to the origin (*UO*) divided by the distance from the intercept of the tangent to the origin (*RO*). If *R* lies halfway between *U* and *O*, the elasticity of the *B* offer curve at *T* is 2. If the offer curve is a straight line from *O* to *L*, the elasticity at *L* is infinity, since the vertical distance to *L* divided by 0 (where the

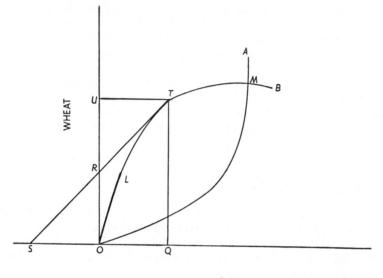

CLOTH

Fɪɢ. F.2. Calculating the Optimum Tariff

tangent to the trade-indifference line intersects the vertical axis) is infinity. The elasticity of the offer curve at *M*, where the tangent and the straight line are assumed identical, is 1. If the *B* offer curve slopes downward after *M*, its elasticity is less than 1 since the tangent intersects the vertical axis further from the origin than the straight line to the axis.

We are now in a position to derive the formula for the optimum tariff. If *T* is a point on *B*'s offer curve which touches the highest possible trade-indifference curve of *A*, the optimum tariff at point *T* is $\dfrac{SO}{OQ}$. *OQ* = *UT*. By similar triangles,

$$\frac{SO}{UT} = \frac{RO}{UR} = \frac{1}{\dfrac{UR}{RO}} = \frac{1}{\dfrac{UO - RO}{RO}} = \frac{1}{\dfrac{UO}{RO} - 1}.$$

Since $\dfrac{UO}{RO}$ is the elasticity of the offer curve at point T, the optimum tariff

$$\left(\frac{SO}{OQ}\right) = \frac{1}{\dfrac{UO}{RO} - 1} = \frac{1}{e - 1} \Bigg].$$

If at point L the elasticity of the offer curve is infinity, the optimum tariff is evidently zero $\left(\dfrac{1}{\infty - 1} = 0\right)$. Where the offer curve is a straight line, no tariff can improve the terms of trade. At M, where the elasticity of the foreign offer curve is one, the optimum tariff is infinity $\left(\dfrac{1}{1 - 1} = \infty\right)$, which is to say that the optimum tariff has to be at a point where the elasticity of the opposing offer curve is greater than 1. At any lower elasticity it is evident that a higher indifference curve can be reached by a tariff.

SUGGESTED READING

Meade, *A Geometry of International Trade,* pp. 76, 87–90; Marsh, chap. xxi, and esp. pp. 316–21. See also a series of articles in *RES* by J. de Graff (1949-50); H. G. Johnson (1950-51 and 1953-54); J. J. Polak (1950-51); T. Scitovsky, "A Reconsideration of the Theory of Tariffs" in AEA, *Readings in the Theory of International Trade.*

Appendix G	(to Chapter 13) THE MONOPOLY EFFECT OF A QUOTA

A significant difference between a tariff and a quota is that the conversion of a tariff into a quota which admits exactly the same volume of imports may convert a potential into an actual monopoly. Figures G.1 and G.2 provide a demonstration.

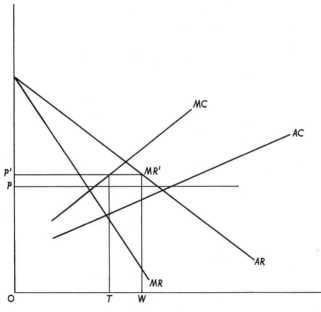

FIG. G.1.   Potential Monopoly in Partial Equilibrium with Tariff

In Figure G.1, *AR* is the average-revenue or demand curve for a commodity in the domestic market. In the absence of international trade, *MR* is the marginal-revenue curve facing the domestic industry. *AC* and *MC* are the relevant average- and marginal cost curves of the domestic import-competing industry. The world price, assumed to be unchanged by anything which might transpire in the importing country, is *OP*. A tariff *P–P'* raises the price at which imports can be sold to *OP'*.

With international trade, and the tariff *P–P'*, *O–P'* is not only the domestic price at which foreigners will supply goods. It is also the marginal-revenue curve facing the domestic industry (*MR'*). No consumer will be willing to pay more than *O–P'* for a domestic product when he can get the same thing from abroad for that price. The domestic industry will produce where marginal cost equals marginal revenue, i.e., the amount *OT*. The remaining demand at this price will be supplied by imports, *TW*.

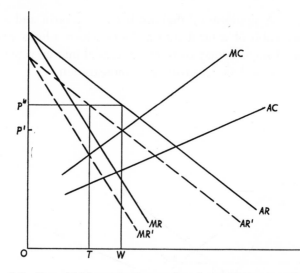

FIG. G.2. Potential Monopoly Converted to Actual Monopoly under Quota

Let us now suppose that the tariff is converted to a quota, and that the licenses are auctioned off. The revenue, terms-of-trade, and the initial balance-of-payments effects are the same as under the tariff. But the protective, consumption, redistribution, and ultimate balance-of-payments effects are altered because the potential domestic monopoly has been converted to an actual one.

In Figure G.2, the *AR* curve is displaced to the left by the amount of the quota, *TW*, and a new marginal-revenue curve, *MR'*, drawn to the displaced curve, *AR'*. The marginal-revenue curve facing the domestic industry is this new curve *MR'*, not the world price. Domestic production will settle where this curve intersects the marginal-cost curve. This volume of domestic production plus the import quota, *TW*, will produce a price of *OP''*, which is well above the old world price plus tariff, *OP'*.

Conversely, to be sure, the conversion of quota restrictions into tariffs which admit an equal volume of imports will eliminate domestic monopolies by threating them with potential competition from increased imports. This is a strong argument for customs unions, and for trade liberalization, i.e., removal of *QR*'s and their conversion to tariffs.

SUGGESTED READING

See H. Heuser, *The Control of International Trade* (London: George Routledge & Sons, Ltd., 1939), chap. xi, and especially diagrams 8 and 9.

INDEXES

INDEX OF NAMES

INDEX OF SUBJECTS

*This book has been set on the Linotype in 12
and 10 point Garamond No. 3, leaded 1 point.
Chapter numbers and chapter titles are in 18
point Spartan Medium. The size of the type
page is 27 by 46½ picas.*